S0-BUB-833

MAP OF JAPAN

THE WHOLE JAPAN BOOK
By
Boye De Mente

ACKNOWLEDGEMENTS

I am grateful to the following companies, organizations and individuals for helping me in the preparation of this book:

Japan Air Lines
Japan National Tourist Organization
Japan Travel Bureau
Foreign Press Center
Keizai Koho Center
Japan External Trade Organization
Nippon Steel Corporation

Morris Simoncelli
Geoffrey Tudor
Yoshio Kimura
Toshi Ikubo
Kiyoshi Hirayama
Yasuyuki Yabuki
Takashi Nagaoka
Tsutomu "Tommy" Sugiura
Shiro Hazue
Hiroshi Mitsukawa
Joel Friedman
Earle Okumura
Paul Maruoka
Frank Kawahara
Haruo Shinoda
George Pokrovsky
Masaharu Hirukawa

COVER DESIGN: Ultra Graphix/Mary Hancock
PHOTOGRAPHS: Japan National Tourist Organization & Japan Air Lines
LINE DRAWINGS: Keiko Yokoyama
MON (CRESTS): Kiyoshi Kawamoto (from "The Elements of Japanese Design"), used with the permission of the publisher, John Weatherhill Inc.

PUBLISHER'S NOTE: This book was written on an IBM Personal Computer, using a WordStar processing program. The text was printed on an NEC Spinwriter 3500Q, in Times Roman, then photo-offset from the printed pages.

THE WHOLE JAPAN BOOK

Boye De Mente

A PHOENIX BOOKS ORIGINAL

OTHER BOOKS ON JAPAN BY THE AUTHOR

Japanese Manners & Ethics in Business
Bachelor's Japan
How to Do Business in Japan
Japanese Secrets of Graceful Living
The Tourist & the Real Japan
The Japanese As Consumers (with Fred Perry)
Businessman's Language Guide to Japan
Businessman's After Hours Guide to Japan
Some Prefer Geisha
Exotic Japan—The Land, The People, The Places, The Pleasures
Reading Your Way Around Japan

Copyright © 1983 by Boye De Mente
All rights reserved.
Not to be reproduced by any means without written permission from the publisher.

Published by Phoenix Books/Publishers
P.O. Box 32008
Phoenix, Arizona 85064 USA

Library of Congress Catalog Card Number
83-61461

International Standard Book Number
0-914778-52-8

First Edition

PREFACE

Most Westerners will readily accept the proposition that they and the Japanese are different. Others, however, persist in the belief that while there may be surface differences, Japanese and Westerners are very much alike.

Having been intimately involved with Japan since the late 1940s, I can attest to one difference that goes beyond any facade, and is a vital factor in Japan's transformation from an isolated feudal society to a major economic power in just a few decades.

Immediately after Japan's doors were opened to the West in the mid-1850s, the Japanese began to stream abroad in official government-sponsored study-missions as well as privately, seeking to absorb and synthesize everything the West had to offer.

This phenomenon was to continue for generation after generation, reaching a peak in the 1950s and 60s, when unending droves of note-and-picture-taking Japanese were a common sight in the laboratories, factories and stores of the West.

Japanese interest in what is going on in the outside world, in discovering, recording and studying every attitude, every action—including changes in the weather—is as strong as ever, and has been refined to where it is probably the most comprehensive and sophisticated information gathering network ever seen.

In contrast, most Westerns not only remain almost totally ignorant of Japan and things Japanese, they show little if any interest in learning.

This disinterest in Japan is a handicap of enormous proportions. It has had and will continue to have serious economic and political implications...and must be overcome if we and the Japanese are to maintain friendly, mutually beneficial relations.

This book is designed to serve as an introduction to Japan—in a novel and provocative way—and to encourage further study in the hope that this will lead to a better understanding and appreciation of both our differences and similarities.

Just as the Japanese have learned a great deal from us since the 1850s, there are many things we can learn from them—things that have to do with personal relations, social responsibility, aesthetics and philosophy.

Hopefully, THE WHOLE JAPAN BOOK will serve as a beginning.

Boye De Mente
Tokyo, Japan

INDEX

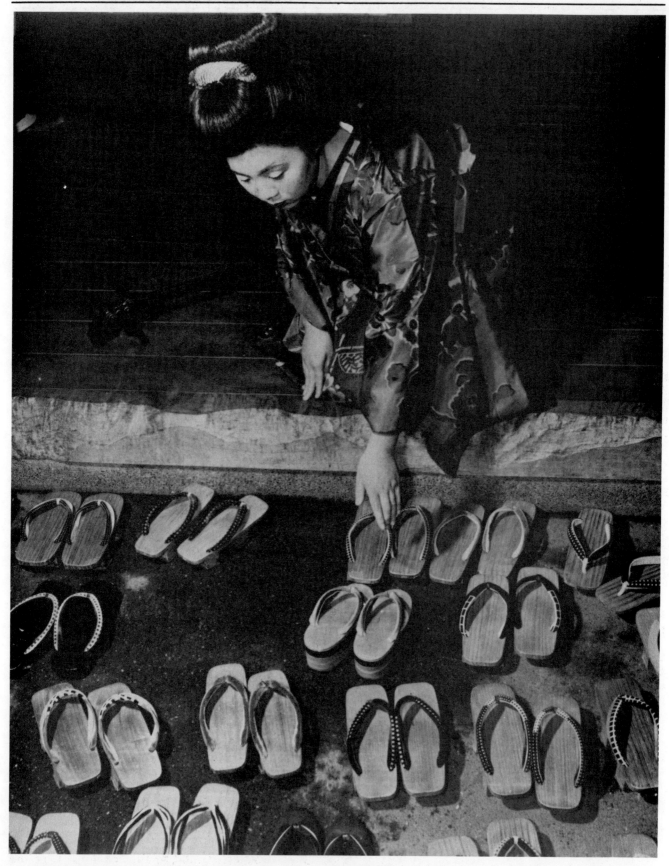

A geisha arranges her geta in the genkan (vestibule) of an inn. P。 108

ABACUS / SOROBAN (Soe-roe-bahn)

The soroban or abacus was developed in China well over one thousand years ago and brought to Japan in the 1500s. Just as it had in China, this marvelous calculating device was to become a vital part of Japanese life, influencing not only the conduct of business, but the manual and mental dexterity of the people.

Often described as the world's first computer, the soroban differs from the computer, in particular the electronic calculator, in that it requires both physical and mental skill to use properly. The user actually does all of the calculating mentally and merely records the results on the soroban.

When the electronic pocket calculator became popular in the mid-1970s it was feared that the use of the soroban would die out, and along with it, the special skills that it developed. But this was not to be the case. There was a sudden drop-off in the number of young people signing up for soroban classes, but a few years later it began to make a surprising comeback.

Now, between three and four million people a year take the Japan Chamber of Commerce and Industry's annual abacus proficiency test, according to records kept by the National Abacus Education Federation (NAEF).

Interestingly enough, almost half of the people who take the test each year are children, some of them as young as 12.

The Federation says the main reason so many young people are interested in the soroban is that is simple to learn and operate, and introduces an element of fun and personal achievement into mathematics.

Japanese teachers and educational leaders are delighted with the continuing popularity of the soroban because using electronic calculators requires neither manual skill nor mental agility, and as a result has a detrimental effect on students and others who use them regularly.

For those who might believe the soroban is too inefficient and/or to slow to compete with computers, consider this: at a number of contests between computer and soroban users held in Tokyo, the soroban users not only held they own,

they won several of the contests!

In another surprising development, it was learned that people who use electronic calculators are much more prone to make mistakes than people who use the soroban. In the early 1980s, many Japanese companies, concerned about problems caused by operator errors, began to restrict the use of calculators in favor of the abacus.

Perhaps even more surprising, there is a Soroban Institue in the United States, at the University of Southern California in Los Angeles, founded by Dr. Leo Richards.

Dr. Richards believes that the abacus has value in the psychological processes of learning. He says it provides youngsters with a hands-on experience of mathematical processes, and that any concept can be taught with the abacus-- in fact, that users create mathematics.

Richards added that the soroban instills discipline and confidence, while the calculator, which performs all of the operations itself, is alienating. Japan's NAEF agrees. It says that the soroban can turn a mathematical duffer into a whiz kid, removing a lot of the intimadating mystery from math.

Many Japanese companies still require proficiency with the soroban as a necessary qualification for employment. In 1883 the Nakano Abacus Institute in Tokyo began a program to increase the popularity of the soroban in Western countries.

Recommended reading: THE JAPANESE ABACUS--Its Use β Theory, by Takashi Kojima (Tuttle).

A-BOMB / GENSUI BAKUDAN (Gain-sooey Bah-kuu-dahn)

Japan is the only country ever to have been atom bombed. The cities of Hiroshima and Nagasaki were destroyed by atomic bombs dropped by American Air Force planes on August 6 and August 9 in 1945. The rationale used by the American government in making the decision to drop the bombs was that without such a demonstration of awesome power and destructive capability, Japan would not surrender, an invasion of Japan's homeland islands would be necessary to end the war, and many more lives would be lost in the process.

Besides almost totally leveling the two large cities, the bombs killed over 200,000 people, injured several hundred thousand others and left dozens of thousands suffering from radiation ailments that did not show up until years later.

In the years following the end of

hostilities between the U.S. and Japan, both Nagasaki and Hiroshima were rebuilt. Now the only physical evidence of the bombs and man's inhumanity to man are memorials erected to commemorate the events and serve as a reminder in the hope that atom bombs will never again be used.

See HIROSHIMA and NAGASAKI.

ABORTION / SOHA (Soe-hah)

Article 14 of Japan's Eugenic Protection Law specifies that abortions may be performed for economic reasons. All a pregnant girl or woman has to do to qualify for an abortion is sign a form attesting that giving birth would result in an economic hardship. In effect, this means that abortions are virtually uncontrolled in Japan, and there is currently a movement underway to get the law changed.

Other attempts to eliminate or weaken Article 14 have failed, however, and this new movment is strongly opposed by many groups.

Abortions have been common in Japan for several decades, and in the mid-1950s were estimated to be as many as 4 million or so a year. With economic growth and a significant improvement in the standard of living, abortions fell off drastically, and are currently running between 500,000 and 600,000 a year.

Women's groups charge that the proposed change in the law does not reflect the views of most Japanese women, who generally insist that it is the woman's right to decide on whether or not she should have an abortion.

ACUPUNCTURE / HARIKYU (Hah-ree-que)

The earliest known text on acupuncture is believed to have been written by China's legendary Yellow Emperor, Huang Ti, who supposedly lived from 2,697 B.C. to 2,596 B.C.

In any event, acupuncture has been practiced in China for well over 3,000 years. Ancient Chinese doctors learned that there are many points on the surface of the body that have a direct relationship with the various internal organs and their functions.

It was learned that these points were well-defined and constant, and that they could be used to diagnose ailments as well as to relieve or cure many bodily malfunctins. It was also learned that the best way to effect such cures was to stimulate these focal points with needles.

The Chinese reasoned that people live and function as the result of a life-force or body energy that flows through the body in a prescribed manner, from organ to organ. When this body energy is diminished or disturbed, one or more organs can no longer function properly, and the body becomes ill.

Acupuncture, the inserting of needles into the body's energy focal points, was developed as a method of re-directing and re-charging the energy levels of the different organs.

The practice of acupuncture was introduced into Japan from China in the 6th century, and gradually spread throughout the medical community. When Western medicine was officially introduced into Japan in 1884, acupuncture and other Chinese treatments were officially abandoned. But acupuncture did not disappear from the scene, and is now more popular than ever.

Acupuncture was first introduced to the West in the 17th century by Jesuit priests who had been dispatched to Peking. The art/science made practically no headway in the West, however, until French Sinologist and diplomat Soulie de Morant published a definitive study on the subject in the 1940s. Western doctors simply could not believe there was anything at all to the practice.

Beginning in the late 1950s, Western interest in acupuncture began to pick up, and it is now both an accepted and growing form of medical treatment in most countries around the world.

In Japan there are numerous clinics offering acupuncture treatments, and it is the subject of serious research in many medical centers, hospitals and universities. According to Dr. Yoshio Manaka, a leading authority on acupuncture, the liver, spleen and gall bladder are especially susceptible to treatment by acupuncture, as are most of the other major organs.

Recommended reading: THE LAYMAN'S GUIDE TO ACUPUNCTURE, by Dr. Yoshio Manaka and Dr. Ian A. Urquhart (Weatherhill, Tokyo/New York).

ADAMS, WILLIAM / ANJIN MIURA (Ahn-jeen Mee-uu-rah)

William Adams was the role model for the famous Anjin (Ahn-jeen) or Pilot of Robert Clavell's novel and TV extravaganza SHOGUN (Show-goon). Born in Gillingham, England in 1554, Adams was a shipwright, a ship's captain and the operator of his own trading company. In June 1598 he joined a Netherlands trading fleet of five vessels to search for a new and faster route to the East Indies.

While crossing the Atlantic Ocean the fleet encountered a great storm. The De Liefde, on which Adams served as the pilot major, was the only ship to reach the Pacific and continue the voyage. On April 19, 1600, with most of the crew dead and the survivors near death from starvation, the De Liefde drifted into a cove on the coast of Bungo near Oita, Kyushu, the southernmost of Japan's four major islands.   Only 25 of the Leifde's original crew of over 100 were still alive. The ship was towed to the harbor of Funai in Kyushu, and was almost immediately thereafter visited by Portuguese Jesuits.

At first, Adams and the surviving crew members were treated kindly by the Japanese authorities.   Then the Portuguese, who were in Japan as traders and missionaries, accused Adams and the sailors of being pirates, and they were immediately imprisoned by the local authorities.

Adams, apparently the ranking survivor and spokesman for the crew, and Jan Justen, a Dutch crew member, were escorted to Osaka where they were taken before Ieyasu Tokugawa, then the leading contender for political and military power in Japan. Tokugawa was so impressed with Adams that he ordered the rest of the crew freed, and for Adams to be taken to Edo (Tokyo), his fief headquarters.

Adams' shipmates were allowed to leave Japan, but Tokugawa decided to keep Adams to oversee the construction of ocean-going vessels and to instruct him and his retainers in navigation and other Western sciences. After Tokugawa became Shogun in 1603, Adams negotiated a trade agreement between the Shogunate and the Dutch East Indies Company.

Tokugawa gave Adams the rank of Samurai and a fief on Miura Peninsula, near presentday Yokosuka just south of Yokohama. Adams realized the Shogun had no intention of letting him leave Japan, and although he had a wife and children in Kent, he adopted the Japanese name Anjin Miura (after the Miura district where his fief was located), married the daughter of Magome, an official in charge of Tokugawa Shogun's horses, and had a son and daughter.

Adams lived for a while in Ito, where he built the first ships for the Shogun's fleet, then established a shipyard at Uraga and moved to Hemi, nearby. In addition to supervising the construction of at least two ocean-going vessels, Adams also gave the Shogun lessons in gunnery, mathematics and navigation.

Adams wrote to England, urging the East India Company to set up a trading post in Japan. In 1613 the company sent Richard Cocks and five other merchants to Japan, where they set up a company on Hirado Island just off of Nagasaki. The post was doomed to failure, however. The English were not able to deal in the popular Chinese silk. The woolen goods they did offer were not that much in demand. Cocks turned out to be a weak manager, and sailors off the English ships that called at Hirado caused numerous problems.

Adams was given permission to make several voyages on the ships he built—going as far as China and Siam. He was on one of these trips in 1616 when Ieyasu Tokugawa died. Ieyasu's son and successor, Hidetada, was not the man his father had been.

The Jesuits continued to stir up trouble. Hidetada frequently sent for Adams to ask his advice but there was no friendship between the two. Hidetada eventually restricted the English to trading only through Hirado, hastening the failure of the company.

By this time the Shogunate was convinced that the Portuguese priests were a serious threat to Japan and ordered them banished from the country. The Shogun allowed the Dutch to maintain one tiny post on a man-made island called Dejima in Nagasaki harbor.

Anjin Miura died on May 16, 1620, while on a visit to the British trading company in Hirado, where he was staying with a Japanese friend, Utaemon Kidayaji. He was 66 years old, and as the only foreigner ever to have become a Samurai, and a close advisor and friend of the founder of the great Tokugawa Shogunate, had become something of a legend in Japan.

Just before his death, Adams told Richard Cocks, the manager of the trading house they had established at Hirado:

Ever since drifting into this country I have enjoyed a comfortable life until now, due the kindness of the Tokugawa Shogun. So bury me atop Hemi Hill, and face the tomb to the East so that I may face toward Edo and my spirit guard the capital forever.

Later Adams' ashes were buried on Tsuka Hill, part of the estate given to him by Ieyasu Tokugawa.

The Shogunate continued to curtail the rights of the English trading post after Tokugawa Ieyasu died in 1616, and in 1623, three years after Adams died, the post was closed down. The East India Company ordered Cocks to return home and stand trial for mismanaging the affairs of the company, but he died at sea before reaching home.

In 1947 a monument was erected to Adams' memory two kilometers south of Ito Station at the mouth of the Okawa River. Adjoining the monument is a stone tablet with a poetic epigram written in 1948 by the famous English poet Edmund Blunden, commemorating his visit to the monument.

The memory of the famous foreign Samurai/pilot is celebrated on the 14th of April each year at Hemi, at the site of The Pilot Mound, which was rediscovered by an Englishman named Walters in 1872. The ceremony is attended by Japanese, Dutch and English dignataries. A memorial observance is also held at the Adams Monument in Ito in mid-summer each year. See HISTORY, TOKUGAWA.

ADDRESSES / JUSHO (Juu-show)

The addressing system in Japan is altogether different from the systems used in most other countries. Rather than being related to whatever street or lane they may be on, the addresses of houses and buildings are determined on a area basis--areas that vary in shape and size.

At first, all of the buildings in any one area had exactly the same address. As the areas became more crowded, houses or buildings were numbered in the order in which they were built. Until the late 1950s and 60s, there were still many areas that had dozens of homes and buildings with exactly the same address.

An attempt was then made to rationalize the system by giving individual homes and buildings their own private numbers. This helped considerably, but it still causes problems because the numbers of the houses and buildings do not always follow in sequence along a given street or lane.

The problem is further complicated by the fact that most streets and lanes in Japan are not named. It was not until the 1950s and afterward that even major thoroughfares were named--although there were a few historical exceptions.

Still today it is not common to refer to places by whatever street they might be on, again with the exception of a few main streets in the leading cities, and then only as an additional means of locating places.

Japanese addresses are backwards as far as most Westerners are concerned, but they are certainly forward from the viewpoint of commonsense. Addresses begin with the country. Then comes the prefecture, and next the city, town or village. If the address is in a city of any size, the next step down is the ku (kuu) or ward (into which cities are divided). This is followed by a smaller division that often has an area name, like Ginza, Roppongi, or Minami-Aoyama (South Aoyama).

Next comes a still smaller area called cho-me (choe-may), which might be equated with a block--although it may be much larger than a typical block, and is not likely to be square, since most streets are not diagonal to each other. The next division is the ban (bahn) or lot number and finally, the go (goh) or building number.

Thus we have the following typical address (in case of mail from overseas): Japan, Tokyo, Shibuya-ku (Shibuya Ward), Harajuku (area name), 4-chome (the 4th of several chome), 3-12 (the 12th house on the 3rd lot). Person's name.

Out in the countryside, the sequence would be: Japan, prefecture, area name and lot or house number, and resident's name. There are slight variations of these, in various areas, depending on the system of naming areas.

Mail addressed in English Western style is, of course, accepted by the Japanese postal system. There is also a growing tendency for people and businesses to put the house and lot number before the area name and chome, as a result of Western influence.

ADVERTISING AGENCIES / KOKOKU GAISHA (Koe-koe-kuu Guy-shah)

From a dead standstill in 1945, advertising agencies in Japan grew at such a phenomenal rate that by the 1960s they were among the top economic forces in the country. Shortly thereafter, Dentsu (Dane-t'sue), the largest agency in the country, went on to become the largest advertising agency in the world.

One of the outstanding features of Japanese advertising is the incredibly high quality of their production work, noted Peter L. Cove, president of Cove-Ito Advertising Ltd., in Tokyo. Just as the Japanese are fastidious about product design and appearance, agency people are fanatical about attention to detail, he added.

Other leading advertising agencies in Japan include Chuo Senko, Cosmo, Dai-Ichi, Daiko, Grey-Daiko, Hakuhodo, McCann Erickson-Hakuhodo and Young β Rubicam.

Advertising rates for major daily newspapers in Japan tend to startle foreign businessmen who are not used to publications having such large circulations. See NEWSPAPERS.

Japanese advertising agencies typically handle competing accounts without apparent friction. They manage this by keeping the accounts in separate, vertically arranged, exclusive divisions.

Advertising agencies are of special importance to foreign companies operating in Japan because they are called upon to provide much more than just the creating and placing of ads. They act as both advertising and marketing advisors, and often get involved in product development and packaging as well.

Among Japan's top advertisers are Nissan Motor Company, Kao Soap, Toyota Motor Sales, Lion Dentifrice Co., Toshiba, Matsushita, Daiei (supermarket chain), Shiseido, Hitachi, Honda Motor Co., Toyo Kogyo (Mazda), Sharp, Ajinomoto and Sony.

Dentsu, Japan and the world's largest advertising agency, is so large and engages in so many aspects and areas of product marketing that it has far more influence than the typical advertising agency in other countries.

One of Dentsu's many publications is the English language DENTSU JAPAN MARKETING/ADVERTISING, which is published twice a year, in January and July. It carries special articles on Japanese management, on marketing in Japan, on communications, and on newspapers, magazines, television, radio and other subjects of interest to foreign businessmen.

The publication is available from Dentsu offices around the world (New York, Los Angeles, Honolulu, Chicago, Washington D.C., San Francisco, London, Paris, Hong Kong, Taipei, Singapore, Bangkok, Beijing, Shanghai).

AESTHETICS / BIGAKU (Bee-gah-kuu)

In the Western world the study and appreciation of beauty has traditionally been relegated to a few categories of people, generally professional. As a result, Western definitions and standards of beauty tend to be loose and variable, and there are no commonly known foundations for recognizing and appreciating beauty.

In Japan, on the other hand, some of the primary threads of the cultural fabric are pure asethetics. By 700 A.D., members of Japan's nobility and priesthood were already making the study and appreciation of beauty a part of their daily lives.

Over the centuries their cultural descendants created and institutionalized a number of ways to develop asethetic ability and to exercise it. The epitome of this aesthetic impulse was the tea ceremony, which was practiced by a small minority of the population, but as time passed, the principles taught by the tea masters became an integral part of the culture, and were reflected in all the arts and crafts of the country.

After centuries of exposure to the principles and practices of a refined kind of beauty and elegance, the Japanese developed the ability to recognize and produce this quality almost instinctively.

While considerably weakened by the imperatives of an industrialized society, the aesthetic impulse is still strong in Japan. It is still a primary theme--often the dominant one--in many areas of their lives.

Recommended Reading: JAPANESE SECRETS OF GRACEFUL LIVING, by Boye De Mente (Phoenix Books/Publishers). See TEA CEREMONY, IKE-BANA, MOONVIEWING, etc.

AGRICULTURE / NOGYO (No-g'yoe)

Japan was almost totally an agricultural society until the controlled advent of industrialization in the 1860s, 70s and 80s.

Today, fewer than one percent of the total population engages in farming as their primary activity, and less than three percent of the gross domestic product is made up of agricultural goods.

Less than 15 percent of the total land area of the country is under cultivation--the official figure is approximately 5,400,000 hectares, or about 13,500,000 acres. There are some four and a half million farm families in Japan, but only 12 percent of them engage in only farming. The average cultivated area per farming household is only a little over one hectare, or slightly under three acres.

Japan is self-sufficient in the production of rice, still the staple of the Japanese diet, and raises large quantities of vegetables and fruits. But over 90 percent of its wheat and soy bean needs are imported. To be more specific, some 99 percent of Japan's bread wheat is imported, 87 percent of its cheese, 76 percent of its shrimp, 72 percent of its sugar and 66 percent of its seaweed.

Land reforms enacted in 1945 (after World War II) were a boon to Japanese farmers, who previously had mostly been tenant farmers. By the mid-1960s, the living standard of Japan's farmers had made them the envy of less affluent nations in Asia and the rest of the world.

Recognizing the importance of the agricultural sector, the Japanese government provides its farming population with very generous protection against price fluctuations and international competition.

In the early 1980s, the government announced a three-point growth program designed to improve the efficiency of its farming industry and keep it competitive with agriculture in other advanced nations. This program is based on improved marketing procedures, continuing technical innovation and improving its competitive position internationally.

Farmland accounts for a little less than 15 percent of Japan's total land area, and is shrinking as urbanization and industrialization grows. Approximately 55 percent of the cultivated land is devoted to rice-growing. Orchards take up about 23 percent, meadows and pastures about 11 percent. Rice, livestock products and vegetables are the main agricultural products, but overall, Japan is only about 72 percent self-sufficient in its food needs.

There are approximately four and one half million farms in Japan, with the average land holdings being 1.2 hectares or 2.8 acres. As a result of this small size and low labor productivity, only some 32 percent of Japan's farming families derive all of their livelihood from farming. In the majority of farm families, one or more of the members works part-time or full-time in some other industry.

The productivity of Japan's farmlands is very high, however, and as mechanization increases, labor productivity is also rising.

AIKIDO (Aye-kee-doe)

One of the leading member's of Japan's famous Minamoto family, Yoshimitsu, who lived from 1045 to 1127, is credited with founding the first school of aiki jujutsu, as aikido was then known. The secrets of the art were handed down within the Minamoto family for several generations, and then was taken over by the Takeda family of Kai Province, eventually becoming the exclusive skill of the branch of the Takeda family that lived in the Aizu district.

Morihei Ueshiba (1883-1970) learned the art from Sokaku Takeda, the 7th generation of the Aizu Takeda's, and developed it into the form of aikido that is practiced today.

Aikido was originally practiced only for learning form, and it was strictly a martial art designed to be used without a weapon. Kenji Tomiki, a disciple of Ueshiba, developed it into the freestyle method that resulted in in being reorganized as a sport.

The aim of aikido is to alllow the practitioner to throw an opponent or disable him by attacking a weak point or applying a pain-hold to pin him down. The practice of sports aikido develops both mental and physical control, along with physical health since it helps keep the muscles and joints flexible.

Recommended reading: AIKIDO AND THE DYNAMIC SPHERE, by Adele Westbrook and Oscar Ratti (Tuttle). DYNAMIC KARATE, by Gozo Shioda, translated by Geoffrey Hamilton (Kodansha Int'l).

AINU (Aye-nuu)

When the ancestors of the present-day Japanese first began pushing into central and northern Honshu from the south, they encountered a race of people already inhabiting the region, as well as the island of Hokkaido. These aboriginal inhabitants of Japan were a Caucasoid race, larger than the Japanese in stature and with imposing features, who called themselves Ainu.

The Ainu were light-skinned and had large, light brown to golden eyes. The men were exceptionally hairy, and had thick black beards. Despite their formidable appearance, the Ainu were gentle in nature. The women, who were often exceptionally beautiful, customarily wore decorative tattoos around their mouths and on their hands.

As the Japanese population grew and more pressure was brought against the Ainu, skirmishes became common and the Ainu were gradually pushed further and

Serving sake the traditional way. P. 23

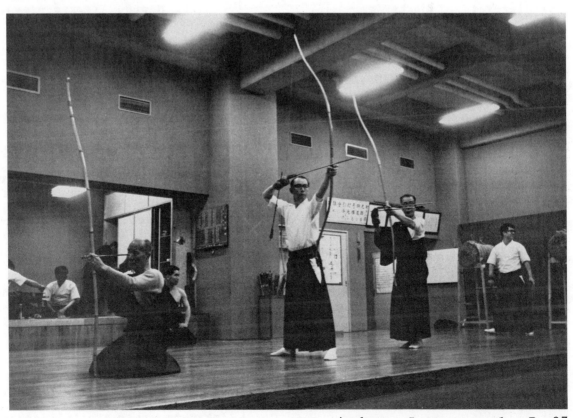

Archery, Japanese style. P. 27

further northward. As the Japanese expanded and increased their control of the northern regions of Honshu, rebellions among the Ainu became frequent.

On a number of occasions during the first centuries A.D., the Emperor appointed a Sei-i-tai-Shogun or Barbarian Subduing Generalissimo to carry out military campaigns against the Ainu.

The bear was the chief religious totem of the Ainu, and a number of their ceremonies and festivals centered around bears. They were primarily hunters and fishermen.

By the middle ages, there were only a few pockets of Ainu left on the island of Honshu. They had been driven to Hokkaido or assimilated into the main Japanese population. One of the last major campaigns against the Ainu was in 1457, when an Ainu chief named Koshamain rebelled against the local Japanese overlord.

From this period on, the Ainu were prominent only on the northernmost island of Hokkaido--and both they and the island were called Ezo (Eh-zoe).

By 1900 there were only about 40,000 pure Ainu left in Hokkaido. Their numbers have continued to decrease and there are now only about 17,000 throughout the island in some 100 villages. Most of these villages are in the Abashiri, Hidaka, Iburi, Kushiro and Tokachi districts of Hokkaido.

The life-styles of most of the Ainu have been Japanized except for those in a few villages, and the residents of Shiraoi and Chikabumi. Here, the old ways are still followed--as commercial tourist ventures much like the Polynesian Village of Hawaii.

Biratori Village, southeast of Tomakomai in the valley of the Saru River, is one of the oldest and largest Ainu communities in Hokkaido. The Ainu of this village have retained most of their traditional culture. The racial mingling of the Japanese and Ainu is particularly noticeable in many towns and villages of the Tohoku district of northeastern Honshu. The mixtures are conspicuous because of their decidely Caucasian appearance, and especially because of their eyes, which are often exceptionlly large and luminous.

When Tohoku women who are part Ainu inherit the Ainu eyes, they are often so beautiful, so entrancing, it is unreal. A number of them became popular movie stars and models in the 1950s and 60s.

Besides visiting one or more of the Ainu villages, it is worthwhile to see the Ainu Memorial Hall in Chikabumi, northeast of Sapporo. Various articles relating to the daily lives of the early Ainu are on display in the hall, and ceremonial dances are performed there on a scheduled basis. Several Ainu houses are on display in Arashima park, a few minutes west of Chikabumi Station.

The Ainu traditionally believed in a life-after-death. In earlier years when a married woman died her house and all of its contents were burned in the belief that she would need them in the other world. Now a small replica of the house is burned in a symbolic gesture.

AIRLINES / KOKUKAISHA (Koe-kuu-kie-shah)

Japan has several air lines, including Japan Air Lines, All Nippon Airways, Japan Asia Airways (the latter a subsidiary of Japan Airlines), Toda Domestic Airlines, Southwest Airlines (which services the Okinawan islands), and Nihon Kinkyori Airways.

Japan Airlines (JAL), the country's flagship line, was founded in 1953, and inaugurated its first international service in 1954, between Tokyo and San Francisco.

JAL now provides service to over 30 countries and some 50 major cities around the world, and is one of the top four airlines in the world.

All Nippon Airways provides domestic service to cities throughout Japan, while Japan Asia Airways provides service to Taiwan. See JAPAN AIR LINES and ALL NIPPON AIRWAYS.

The largest general aviation airport in the country is the Yao Airport, located eight nautical miles southeast of Osaka. It handles some 80,000 flights a year, making it the fifth or sixth busiest airport in the country.

There are some two dozen Japanese-language trade publications on the airline industry in Japan, and seven in English. These latter include the JPE Aviation Report, the Japan Air Transport Handbook, Japan Aviation Directory, and Travel Journal International.

Nearly 40 foreign airlines serve Japan, and an additional 30 countries (from Afghanistan to Zaire) have requested air treaties with Japan. See AIRPORTS.

AIRMILES

In its position off the northeastern coast of the Asian continent, Japan is distant from most of the capitals of the world. The following air miles from Tokyo to other capitals around the world reveal just how distant. From Tokyo to Seoul it is 869 miles, to Hong Kong 1,933 miles, to Manila 1,916 miles, to Beijing 2,092 miles, to Bangkok 3,121 miles, and to Singapore 3,448 miles.

Also, to Anchorage it is 3,527, to Moscow 4,986, to London 8,041, to Paris 8,280, to Hamburg 7,967, to Sidney 4,934, to Vancouver 4,788, to San Francisco 5,247, to Honolulu 3,870, and to New York 7,037.

AIRPORTS / HIKOJO (He-koe-joe)

Japan has 78 airports, of which eleven provide international service. The three major international airports are Tokyo International Airport at Narita, some 40 miles northeast of Tokyo. Nagoya International Airport and Osaka International Airport.

Haneda Airport in Tokyo was the country's primary international gateway until the opening of Narita. At this writing the only international flights in and out of Haneda are those by China Airlines of Taiwan—a political gesture toward The People's Republic of China.

AJINOMOTO (Ah-jee-no-moe-toe)

A powdered seasoning made of monosodium glutamate, Ajinomoto has long been popular in Japan for its food enhancing qualities. It is now known and used around the world. Mono-sodium glutamate was originally extracted from seaweed, but is now processed from sugar cane molasses.

AKASAKA (Ah-kah-sah-kah)

Part of the northwestern portion of Minato Ward in Tokyo, Akasaka is noted for its concentration of cabarets, night clubs, bars, restaurants, geisha district, hotels and shops.

Among the major hotels in Akasaka, or the immediate vicinity, are the New Otani, Akasaka Tokyu, the original Hilton, the luxurious Okura, and the gorgeous Akasaka Prince.

Japan's government center is on a low rise overlooking Akasaka from the north, and the American Embassy adjoins it on the southeast. Akasaka Mitsuke (Akasaka Intersection) is one of the major subway terminals in the city.

AKASAKA DETACHED PLACE / GEIHINKAN (Gay-e-heen-khan)

This is the magnificient structure near Yotsuya Station in Tokyo, within sight of the New Otani Hotel, that so impresses visitors to Japan. Completed in 1909 as the residence of the Crown Prince, the Palace was patterned after 18th century French architectual styles, and was later used as an Imperial chamber and for other purposes.

Granite and marble imported from France, Italy, Greece and Norway were used in the construction of the palace, and oil paintings by European as well as Japanese masters were used to decorate its walls.

Many of its great rooms are famous for their gorgeous decorations, including ceiling motifs said to have been inspired by a noh play.

The palace is now Japan's official State Guest House.

ALCOHOLIC BEVERAGES / NOMI MONO (No-me Moe-no)

On a national average, the Japanese are not big drinkers when compared to the French, West Germans, Italians, Australians, Canadians, British and Russians (in that order). With the French at the top, consuming an average of well over 15 liters of pure alcohol equivalent a year, the Japanese average is only a little over five liters.

This is certainly contrary to the popular conception, because there are so many drinking establishements in Japan (over 225,000, plus dozens of thousands of other places where drinks are served), and most of them are jammed with drinkers most evenings. The reason for the disparity is that most alcoholic drinks in Japan are consumed by men between the ages of 22 and 52, in all social and work categories.

The most popular alcoholic drink in Japan is beer, followed by sake, whisky and brandy, shochu (a much stronger version of sake, favored by laborers), wine, mirin (a sweet sake) and liqueurs.

Japanese-made beer is popular in many places around the world for its mellow and refreshing taste. The top brands are Kirin (Kee-reen), Asahi (Ah-sah-he) and Sapporo (Sop-poe-roe). Japan is also famous for its Scotch whiskey.

ALIEN REGISTRATION / GAIJIN TOROKU (Guy-jeen Toe-roe-kuu)

All foreigners intending to stay in Japan for more than 90 days must register within 60 days with the local ward or district office where they live. Upon registration, they receive a Gaijin Toroku Shomeisho (show-may-e-show), or Alien Registration Certificate, a small identification booklet which must be carried at all times.

ALL NIPPON AIRWAYS (Neep-Pone)

Founded in 1952 as the Japan Helicopter β Aeroplane Transport Company, ANA changed its name in 1957, and in 1958 merged with Kyokuto Airlines. Other mergers followed in the 1960s and by the 1980s, ANA was Japan's biggest airline in terms of fleet-size and passengers carried.

ANA presently operates over 70 routes throughout Japan, with around 500 daily flights. The airline has several wholly owned and partly owned subsidiary and affiliated companies, including a trading company, a restaurant chain and a tour wholesaler.

ALLOWANCES (EMPLOYMENT) / TEATE (Tay-ah-tay)

Japanese companies generally pay their employees allowances of one kind or another, in addition to their regular base wages. These allowances cover such things as housing, children, dangerous work, trips, transportation, weddings, funerals, etc.

The most important of these allowances is often the housing allowance, which is not taxable. Larger Japanese companies also often provide housing for their executives, and dormitories for their single factory workers. They also may guarantee low-cost loans for the construction of housing.

Allowances, like bonuses, are an important part of the overall income of Japanese employees--and are a significant factor in the cost of labor in Japan.

AMERICAN/ALLIED OCCUPATION OF JAPAN

Within a few days after World War II ended on August 15, 1945, American troops began arriving in Japan to begin a 7-year military Occupation that was to be one of the most extraordinary experiments and experiences in history.

The Occupation of Japan was officially an Allied affair, but for all practical purposes it was American. All Occupation forces were under the command of General Douglas MacArthur, who, with his aides, was to be the primary architect and enforcer of Occupation policies.

Japan officially surrendered to the Allied powers on September 2, 1945. The signing of the surrender documents took place aboard the battleship USS Missouri in Tokyo Bay.

The decision had been made to maintain Japan's Emperor Hirohito, as the symbolic head of the nation, and to govern the country through its elected and appointed officials.

Over the next several months, Japan's social and political structures were reorganized according to democratic principles, setting the stage for the dramatic recovery Japan was to make in the next decade. The Allied military Occupation of Japan ended in May 1952.

The story of the American Occupation of Japan, to my knowledge at least, has never been fully told. It was a drama of such scope and depth that it virtually defies telling in more than a cursory manner.

It was made up of the interaction of literally millions of Japanese with hundreds of thousands of Americans, on every level of human activity. That it was almost totally a peaceful experience, following a protracted war of extraordinary intensity and violence, serves as a monument to both the Americans and Japanese who survived the fighting and went on to work together for peace and a new order of things that would remake Japan.

The Occupation certainly ended the old belief that East and West could never meet on common ground--at least in a romantic sense. Much of the real story, in fact, is the story of hundreds of thousands of romantic liaisons between American men and Japanese women--a phenomenon that played a fundamental role in both the character and quality of the Occupation's role in eliminating feudalism from Japanese society, and introducing Western social concepts.

One American writer who succeeded in giving a glimpse of what life was like for many people in Occupied Japan is Donald Richie. His book THIS SCORCHING EARTH (Tuttle) is recommended.

AMERICAN CHAMBER OF COMMERCE IN JAPAN

Established in Tokyo in the early 1950s, immediately following the end of the military occupation of Japan by the Allied Powers, the American Chamber of Commerce in Japan (ACCJ) was little more than a social club during the first several years of its existence.

It was not until the early 1960s--by which time Japan was well on its way to becoming a world economic power and much of the Occupation Mentality had dissapated--that new directors and new members of the Chamber began to see it as something other than a club.

Another decade was to pass, however, before the combination of Japan's growing economic power and a new generation of American businessmen in Tokyo were to really turn the Chamber around and develope it into a useful and influential organization.

Today the ACCJ plays a vital role in the conduct of business in Japan by American companies, and in ongoing economic and political relations between Japan and the U.S.

The specific role of the ACCJ is to promote measures calculated to benefit and protect the interests in Japan of companies and citizens of the U.S. To represent, express and give effect to the opinions of the business community regarding trade, investment, commerce, finance, industry and related questions, and to collect, evaluate and disseminate among its members, statistical and other information concerning commerce or other undertakings of interest to the members.

The ACCJ sponsors briefing breakfasts for newcomers and visitors, has an active speakers program that brings in leading American and Japanese business, government and academic leadersµ holds regular seminars on a wide variety of trade topicsµ and publishes a monthly journal, a newsletter, position papers and a number of books of special interest to its members and the foreign business community in Japan.

All American businessmen interested in doing business in Japan are strongly urged to contact the ACCJ, and to become members. It is one of the best investments any company could possibly make to help ensure its success in the highly competitive Japanese market.

The ACCJ has two offices in Japan-- one in Tokyo and one in Osaka. The Tokyo office, very near the American Embassy, is in the Fukide Building No. 2 (7th floor), at 1-21, 4-chome, Minato-Ku, Tokyo 105 Japan.   The Kansai (Osaka) office is in the Nihon Seimei Imabashi Bldg., 4th floor, 3-12-1 Imabashi, Higashi-ku, Osaka 541, Japan.

AMERICAN CONTACT

The first American of record to have contact with Japan was a Captain Kenrick, whose ship, the Lady Washington, took shelter in the Kii Channel of Japan's Inland Sea in 1817. Five years before this, however, another American ship captain, David Porter, wrote a letter to President Madison urging him to begin trade and diplomatic negotiations with Japan.

In his letter, Porter said: The time may be favorable and it would be a glory beyond that accomplished by any other nation for us, a nation of only forty years standing, to beat down their rooted prejudices, secure to ourselves a valuable trade, and make that people known to the world.

President Jackson in 1835 tried to send a letter to the Emperor of Japan (in which he said the U.S. was probably the only nation that could bring about the opening of all of Japan's ports to foreign trade), but the envoy carrying the letter, Edmund Roberts, died suddenly in Macau before he could make arrangements for the letter to be delivered.

In 1837, W. C. King, an American businessman with a company in Canton, tried to return seven shipwrecked Japanese fishermen who had been picked up by American vessels. His vessel, the Morrison, was fired upon by shore batteries when he anchored off of Uraga, a port near the tip of Miura Peninsula which was the official inspection station for barges entering Tokyo Bay. King then sailed to Kagoshima, where an official came aboard, provided him with a pilot and told him a senior government official would arrive to discuss the matter with him the following day.

Warned by a friendly Japanese boatman that all aboard the vessel were to be arrested, King began making preparations to sail out of the harbor. The ship immediately came under cannon fire from the shore, but was able to escape unharmed and return to China with the Japese fishermen still aboard.

When the news of this incident reached the U.S. there was a great deal of indignation, but the situation in Japan was even worse. A number of Japanese who criticized the actions of the government were imprisoned, forced to commit suicide or ostracized.

In 1845 another American vessel, the Manhattan, under the command of Captain Mercator Cooper, arrived at Uraga with some Japanese fishermen who had been picked up adrift in the Pacific. This time the Japanese were allowed to disembark because they had not been aboard the ship when it left port, and Cooper sailed away without incident.

The following year, the U.S.'s President Polk, acting in accordance with a resolution passed by Congress, sent Commodore James Biddle and two ships to Japan with a letter addressed to the Emperor, requesting that diplomatic and trade relations be established. Biddle's ships arrived at Uraga, the entrance to Tokyo Bay, in the summer of 1846.

His ships were immediately boarded by Samurai who treated him and his men with arrogance, finally demanding that he leave his vessel and wait on a Japanese ship for an answer to his letter. Mistaking the ship he was to board, Biddle was struck by a Samurai and knocked backward into his own boat.

The Japanese authorities apologized to Biddle and offered to punish the Samurai, but Biddle declined. Shortly thereafter he received an unofficial message saying his request had been denied and that he and his ships were to leave Japan immediately and not return.

News of this incident aroused some anger in the U.S., and in 1849 when Commander Glynn of the USS Preble sailed into Nagasaki to demand the release of American castaways being held by the Japanese, he went prepared to fight. After making his initial demand, he waited for three days, then delivered what amounted to an ultimatum if the men were not released within the following three days.

Before the deadline expired, the Japanese delivered 13 American castaways to the Preble, and Glynn sailed away. In 1851 Glynn met President Fillmore as the representative of several groups interested in Japan being opened to foreign trade, warning him that if the U.S. did not act soon, Russia, England or some other nation might be the first to establish relations with Japan. The American consul in Singapore had already suggested that the U.S., Great Britain and France send a joint expedition to Japan to force its doors open.

In the meantime, the ferment within Japan was increasing, as those who opposed the Shogunate and favored the opening of Japan became more active and gained support. A few Japanese were already studying English (some of them taught by a man named MacDonald who had been turned over to Commander Glynn in 1849), and the Japanese were feverishly trying to learn as much as they could about the U.S.

Besides the Dutch traders in Nagasaki (see HISTORY, DEJIMA, TOKUGAWA, PORTU-GUESE, ADAMS), their primary source of information about the the United States was a man named Manjiro Nakahama, whose fishing boat had gone down in the Pacific when he was a boy and who had been rescued by an American whaling ship which took him to Fairhaven, Massachusetts. There he learned English, was converted to Christianity, and returned to Japan nine years later aboard the whaler Sarah Boyd. See NAKAHAMA. MANJIRO.

In June 1851 an expedition under the command of Commodore Aulick set sail for Japan, intending to stop over in Hong Kong to pick up 17 Japanese castaways and return them to their homeland. But Commodore Aulick was recalled to Washington from China because of some other matters, and Commodore Matthew C. Perry was picked to replace him.

Perry left Norfolk, Virginia in November 1852, sailed to Shanghai on the frigate Mississippi, and took command of the squadron Commodore Aulick had left there. Leaving Shanghai, he first went to the Ryukyu Islands south of Kyushu, Japan's southernmost main island, and arrived in Tokyo Bay on July 8, 1853.

The Japanese had been warned of Perry's expedition, and the preparations being made by other nations to force Japan to open their doors to the outside world. Still, the Shogunate was not prepared to take this bold step. After some very stiff formalities, the Japanese agreed to talk to Perry at Kurihama, south of Edo (Tokyo).

After delivering his letters to the representatives of the Shogunate (the Americans still did not know that the Shogun was not the Emperor), Perry sailed back to China, telling the Bakufu (Bah-kuu-fuu) or Shogunate government officials he would return the following July for their answer.

Thus it was in July 1854 that the stage was set for the beginning of diplomatic and trade relations between Japan and the United States, and for the United States to play the leading role in bringing Japan into the community of nations.

See HISTORY, PERRY, HARRIS, ADAMS (ANJIN-SAN).

ANDO, HIROSHIGE (Ahn-doe He-roe-she-gay)

Probably the best-known of Japan's great ukiyoe (ou-key-yoe-eh) woodblock print artists, Hiroshige was born at Yaesu in Edo (Tokyo) in 1797, the son of an official of the Tokugawa Shogunate fire department. After failing to become a student of Hokusai, the most famous ukiyoe artist of his day, Hiroshige studied under Toyohiro Utagawa, another popular artist.

Hiroshige is best known for his landscape paintings, especially the Fifty-Three Post Stations of the Tokaido, which made him famous at the age of 30. Among his other popular series of prints were Noted Places of Edo, Eight Landscapes of Edo Suburbs, One Hundred Scenic Spots of Edo, and Eight Scenes of Omi.

Hiroshige inherited his father's position as a fire department official, but soon handed the position over to his young son so he could devote all of his time to painting. He died in 1859 during a great cholera epidemic that struck Japan, and was buried at the Tokaku Temple in the Asakusa district of Tokyo.

ANIMALS (WILD) / YASEI NO DOBUTSU (Yah-say-e no doe-boot-sue)

Because most of Japan is mountainous, covered with forests, and basically uninhabited, there are still many animals in the wild, despite the dense population.

There are three distinct types of wild animals in Japan, depending on the region. Hokkaido, at the northern end of the island chain, is known for its brown bears, sables and northern foxes.

The other three major islands of Honshu, Kyushu and Shikoku are home to wild boars, deer, raccoon dogs, monkeys, bears, weasels, mandarin ducks and pheasants.

The southern islands of Okinawa and Amami have fauna similar to that found in Taiwan and India, along with an indigenous snake (habu), and the Amami hare.

AOYAMA PALACE (Ah-oh-yah-mah)

In the northern section of Tokyo's huge Minato Ward, the Aoyama Palace, which adjoins the Akasaka Detached Palace, is where the late Empress Dowager Teimei lived, and the home of the late Prince Chichibu. Before the fall of the Tokugawa Shogunate in 1868, the grounds were part of the mansion estate of the Kii branch of the Tokugawa family.

ANTI-MONOPOLY LAW / KOKUSEN KINSHI HO (Koe-kuu-sin Keen-she Hoe)

Following the end of the Pacific war in 1945, the American forces occupying Japan fostered the passage of laws prohibiting private monopolies, to prevent the concentration of excessive economic power such as had been yielded by the notorious Zaibatsu combines (see ZAIBATSU).

With the deterioration of relations between the U.S. and Russia, the American attitude toward Japan changed rather rapidly, however, and in 1949 the anti-monopoly laws were altered to permit intercorporate stockholding and interlocking multiple directorates.

When the Occupation of Japan ended in 1952, the Japanese government further changed the law, allowing the formation of depression and rationalization cartels, and further relaxing the controls on stock ownership, multiple directorates and mergers.

The revision of these laws made it possible for the reappearance of huge industrial combines reminiscent of the prewar Zaibatsu, but primarily owned by stockholders instead of a few privileged families.

Among the mergers that took place as a result of these new laws was the one that combined the Yawata and Fuji steel companies into the Nippon Steel Corporation, now the world's largest producer of steel.

Mid-1980 trends have been to strengthen the anti-monoploy laws somewhat in a effort to protect weaker companies from take-over bids, and to guarantee the interests of the public. See MITSUI, MITSUBISHI, ZAIBATSU.

ARCHERY / KYUDO (Que-doe)

It is not known if archery developed on its own in Japan or if it was introduced from the Asian mainland. It was widely used for hunting and fighting by the early centuries, and was promoted as a martial art as early as the 8th century.

Over the centuries, the Japanese developed a bow that was much longer and much more powerful than those generally seen in Asia and Europe. It is recorded that a warrior who happened to catch the enemy in ranks was able to kill three of them with the same arrow, so great was its penetrating power.

In the middle ages, Japanese pirates foraging along the coasts and islands of Southeast Asia were especially feared because of their extraordinary prowess with swords and bows.

As with other martial arts, kyudo, or the way of the bow, became imbued with Zen Buddhist and Confucian principles, and Zen concepts were used in its practice. Japanese history is replete with the exploits of archers who achieved incredible skill.

With the advent of prolonged peace in 1603, archery became more of a mental and spiritual exercise, but was kept alive by the Samurai emphasis on such training, and with annual contests held in many places around the country.

Kyudo contests are still popular in Japan, generally sponsored by a particular temple, and staged during festivals. The most popular of these contests are those that take place from horseback, and are known as yabusame (yah-buu-sah-may).

Originally a Shinto rite that began in the 6th century to ensure good harvests, and later a ceremony performed by courtiers at the Butokuden Palace in Kyoto, Yabusame is now performed as part of Culture Day (Bunka-no Hi) at Meiji Shrine in Tokyo and at several other shrines around the country in the fall.

Basically, Yabusame consists of archers on horseback, racing down a prescribed path and firing their arrows at special targets while at full gallop. It was originally a form of divination—with the horses' hoof-prints and where the arrows struck having different meanings.

Today the ceremony in Tokyo is presided over by the Great Japan Traditional Horsemanship and Great Japan Archery and Horsemanship Associations. A dozen or more horsemen, dressed in colorful period costumes, race down a 217-meter long track, shooting at targets erected on both sides.

ARCHITECTURE / KENCHIKU (Kane-chee-kuu)

Traditional Japanese architecture is distinctive in that the only building material used was wood, regardless of the purpose, size or ornateness of the structure. This resulted in most buildings being simple in design with regular lines, but often with a subtlety that made them the epitome of refinement and elegance.

The best examples of pure Japanese architecture can be seen in Shinto shrines, the form of which dates back to the dawn of Japan's history. These buildings have crossed rafters at the end to hold the ridgepoles, cross-pieces to hold the roof-thatch in place and gabled ends.

The temples that were built after the introduction of Buddhism into Japan in the 6th and 7th centuries, incorporated many Chinese concepts, including the use of huge pillars placed on granite foundation stones, tile roofs, hipped roofs, projecting eaves, and red paint on the exteriors. The pagoda style building was another import from China.

As the decades passed, more and more mansions and palaces were built, the mansions following the form and pattern established by Shinto shrines, and the palaces patterned after the splendid buildings popular in China at that time.

One of the temples built in Nara in the 7th century, the Horyu, still stands and is regarded as the oldest wooden building in the world. The Todai Temple in Nara, built during the 8th century, is the world's largest wooden building.

Most ordinary buildings in Japan that came after the Nara Period were refined combinations of shrine and temple architecture.

Japan's golden age of castle-building occurred in the 15th and 16th centuries. Before 1576 the castles in Japan were built in mountainous areas that were difficult to approach and easier to defend, and were little more than forts. In this year, Nobunaga Oda built a castle out in the open at Azuchi adjoining Lake Biwa. It had a central tower seven stories high, a soaring copper-rust roof and white walls, and was designed and furnished to be both a castle and a villa.

Hideyoshi Toyotomi, who followed Oda as the most powerful military leader in Japan, also followed his example and built similar castles at Fushimi and Osaka. Thereafter, it became customary for the Daimyo (Dime-yoe) provincial lords to build their castles on the plains and to emphasize architectural beauty as well as luxurious interior decorations.

The best existing example of these great castles is the one at Himeji on the Inland Sea, southwest of Kyoto and Osaka.

Up to this time the mansions of the nobles of Japan were based on Zen Buddhist temple arichtecture, but when the feudal lords began building luxurious residential castles that in effect were palaces, the nobles also begin to build splendid palaces for themselves.

These great mansions had dozens of rooms separated by sliding screen doors. The walls and ceilings were profusely decorated with rich paintings in white and black on gold backgrounds. The transomes were embellished with ornate

Kumamoto Castle. P. 183

The Bridge of Heaven. P. 41

carvings, and metal fittings were everywhere.

The greatest sobering force during these decades was Zen Buddhism, which still maintained a strict simplicity that was epitomized in the structures built especially for the tea ceremony.

The practice of building elaborate mansions continued in the Edo Period (1603-1868) when the Tokugawa Shogun made it mandatory that all the feudal lords in the country build mansions in Edo (Tokyo) and leave their families there. There was a strong competitive element among the lordly Daimyo, and those who could afford the expense outdid themselves in building palatial mansions in the environs of Edo Castle.

Much of the architecture of early Japan still exists in hundreds of temples and shrines around the country, as well as in private residences, palaces and castles. Kyoto, the Imperial capital of Japan from 794 to 1868, is a treasure trove of outstanding architectural examples, and is a must on the itinerary of most visitors to Japan.

Following the opening of Japan to the West in the 1850s and 60s, the government commissioned foreign architects to design and build government and public offices. Among the first of these buildings were the Osaka Mint in 1871, Shimbashi Station in 1872 and Yokohama Station, also in 1872.

The British architect J. Condor was engaged to teach architecture at the Tokyo Imperial University, which graduated its first four Western-trained Japanese architects in 1879. The first steel-frame building was erected in Tokyo in 1909 by Toshitaka Sano, for the Maruzen Co. Ltd.

From 1914 on, the construction of ferro-concrete buildings became common—although their height was limited to eight stories because of the danger from earthquakes.

The famous American architect Frank Lloyd Wright was commissioned in 1916 to design and build a new Imperial Hotel, construction of which was completed in 1921. (When the Great Kanto Earthquake struck in 1923, leveling much of Tokyo and Yokohama, the Imperial Hotel was one of the few buildings to survive virtually undamaged—not only proving the durability of Western style architecture, but also making both Wright and the Imperial Hotel world-famous.)

Contemporary Japanese architecture is a blend of Western and traditional concepts, and came of age in the 1960s when rapid economic growth resulted in a building boom that was to continue for several decades. The development of earthquake-resistant building techniques in the 1960s resulted in the 31-meter height limitation being abolished, and the construction of Japan's first super highrise in 1968--the 36-story Kasumigaseki Building near the government center in Tokyo.

Japan now has almost as many highrise buildings as it does towering volcano mountains, with some of the largest and most spectacular being in the Shinjuku section of Tokyo.

Probably the best-known of Japan's architects during the immediate postwar decades was Kenzo Tange, whose buildings include the National Indoor Athletic Hall and the adjoining gymnasium built for the 1964 Tokyo Olympics.

Tange was born in 1913 in Imabari, Shikoku. He attended Tokyo University, worked for a few years and then returned to the unversity for graduate study and the academic life of a professor of architecture.

His design of the Hiroshima Peace Center in 1949 brought him international attention, and during the next decade he became recognized as one of the world's leading architects.

Recommended reading: THE CLASSIC TRADITION IN JAPANESE ARCHITECTURE--Modern Versions of the Sukiya Style, by Teiji Ito (Weatherhill). Also, EARLY BUDDHIST ARCHITECTURE IN JAPAN, by Kokichi Suzuki (Kodansha International).

AREA CODES

Japan has nine telephone area codes. 01 is for Hokkaido, Aomori, Iwate and Akita Prefectures. 02 gets you Miyagi, Yamagata, Fukushima, Niigata, Nagano, Ibaragi, Tochigi and Gunma Prefectures. 03 is the code for Metropolitan Tokyo, and 04 covers the suburban areas and Saitama, Chiba and Kangawa Prefectures.

The code for Yamanashi, Gifu, Shizuoka, and Mie Prefectures is 05. For Metro Osaka it is 06. For Osaka's suburbs, Toyama, Fukui, Shiga, Kyoto, Hyogo, Nara and Wakayama Prefectures it is 07. Tottori, Shimane, Okayama, Hiroshima, Yamaguchi, Tokushima, Kagawa, Ehime and Kochi Prefectures are 08. Fukuoka, Saga, Nagasaki, Kumamoto, Oita, Miyazaki, Kagoshima and Okinawa Prefectures are 09.

The international code number for Japan is 81.

ARITA (Ah-ree-tah)

The small town of Arita, some 96 kilometers from Fukuoka on the Sasebo Line, is noted as the place where white porcelain was first produced in Japan. A Korean potter with the Chinese name of Li-sang P'ing brought the art to Arita in 1616. Porcelain made in Arita is now an important export industry.

ARMED FORCES

At the end of World War II in 1945, Japan's armed forces were demobilized. All arms were confiscated, and the new constitution, promulgated in 1947, renounced the nation's right to use war as a means of settling international disputes.

This did not mean that Japan had renounced the right to defend itself, and in 1950 a National Police Reserve was established. In 1952, when soverignity was returned to Japan, the NPR was reorganized as the Peace Preservation Corps.

The present-day Self-Defense Force grew out of the Peace Preservation Corps, and consists of three branches: the Ground Self-Defense Force (army), the Maritime Self-Defense Force (navy), and the Air Self-Defense Force (air force).

The Prime Minister is the chief commanding officer of the SDF, but the armed forces are administered by the Directory of the Defense Agency, who has the rank of a minister of state.

Service in the three branches of the armed forces is on a volunteer basis. At present, there are less than 300,000 members in the combined forces.

ARRANGED MARRIAGES / MIAI KEKKON (Me-aye Keck-kone)

Until the end of World War II in 1945, nearly all marriages in Japan were arranged--either by a friend or employer of the bride or groom, or by professional marriage go-betweens called nakodo (nah-koe-doe).

With the elimination of the feudal family system at the end of the war, young Japanese men and women were free to make their own choices. Still today, however, some 20 to 30 percent of the marriages in Japan are arranged.

In the miai system, eligible young men and women are introduced to any number of prospects, usually at a restaurant or coffee shop, until they both agree to the match.

Love plays no part in these matches, but the individuals concerned are almost never forced to marry anyone whose looks or personalities are disagreeable to them.

Once the marriage is agreed to, the couple normally has several days or weeks to get acquainted with each other before the wedding takes place.

The success of arranged marriages is as good if not better than love matches, at least in part becuase the couples concerned are not that emotionally involved, and are therefore less susceptible to disappointment. See MARRIAGE.

ASAKUSA (Ah-sock-sah)

In the northeastern part of Tokyo's Taito Ward, Asakusa is a major railway terminal for northern and eastern cities (including Nikko), and a nationally famous entertainment, shopping and wholesaler district.

For several generations, Asakusa was the location of one of Japan's most famous gay quarters, the Yoshiwara (Yoe-she-wah-rah), which closed in 1956.

Among the major attractions in Asakusa today are the Asakusa Hongan (Hone-gone) Temple, the famous Asakusa Kannon (Khan-noan) Temple, and a covered shopping street known as Nakamise (Nah-kah-me-say), which leads to the temple.

The Kannon Temple dates from the 7th century, and is one of the most popular in the country, drawing huge crowds on New Years's Day. There is a major festival in the area on May 17-18.

While Asakusa's hundreds of restaurants, theaters, bars and night spots attract people from all over Tokyo, it is best known as a mecca for people who live in the prefectures adjoining Tokyo on the north and east.

ASHIYA (Ashiyah)

The Beverly Hills of the Hanshin (Osaka-Kobe) district, Ashiya is one of the most prestigious residential areas in Japan. A picturesque community on the foot of Mt. Rokko between Osaka and Kobe, Ashiya offers a commanding view of the surrounding countryside, and is equally famed for its mild climate. It is 19 kilometers from Osaka, and 10 kilometers from Kobe.

ASSOCIATIONS OF FOREIGN WIVES

Foreign women who marry Japanese men are still unusual enough that they have formed an association in Tokyo, and hold regular meetings. Notice of such meetings appears in local English-language newspapers. There is also an organization in Tokyo called Kokusai Kekkon wo Kangaeru Kai, which translates more or less as Association of Those Thinking About a Foreign Marriage (but which is referred to in public notices as Group of Japanese Women Married to Non-Japanese).

The Allied military Occupation of Japan from 1945 to 1952, and subsequent contacts on a major scale, resulted in dozens of thousands of marriages between Western men and Japanese women. During these early years, marriages between Western women and Japanese men were rare, however.

As time went by, the number of Western women marrying Japanese men increased, and in a surprising turnabout, surpassed the number of Western men-Japanese women marriages in 1975--a trend that has continued.

This development was surprising because of the traditional customs in Japan that separate men and women, not only in the home but in the worldplace and in the huge world of entertainment as well.

The problems facing most such marriages, generally including an inability to communicate well with each other, are formidable, and require extraordinary adjustments on the part of most of the foreign wives. (In the case of Western men marrying Japanese women, most of the adjustments are left to the Japanese wife.)
See INTERNATIONAL MARRIAGES.

ATAMI (Ah-tah-me)

One of the most popular hotspring resorts in Japan, Atami is situated on the northeast neck of Izu Peninsula, which juts out into the Pacific Ocean about 100 kilometers south of Tokyo (55 minutes by Kodama Express Train).

The name of the city means Hot Sea, and is derived from an old legend that says a hot geyser suddenly appeared in the sea just offshore, killing the fish in the area. A Buddhist priest, famed for having conquered the nine-headed dragon of Lake Ashi (Hakone), came to the area in 749 and prayed for the geyser to move, which it did--onto the beach.

Also one of the most spectacular resorts in Japan, Atami is perched on the steep wall of a great volcanic crater, half of which collapsed and fell into the sea ages ago. The volcanic nature of the surrounding hills accounts for the large number of hotsprings in the area, many of which have proven medicinal value.

The hotspring inns of Atami begin on the waterfront, and spiral upward, offering scenic views of the oceanfront and offshore islands. The area abounds in equally scenic drives. One climbs the crater wall to Jukkoku (Juke-koe-kuu) or Ten Province Pass, enroute to Lake Ha-

kone. Another, the Izu (Ee-zoo) Skyline Parkway, runs along the ridge of mountains that form the backbone of Izu Peninsula.

Views from the Izu Skyline Parkway include snowcapped Mt. Fuji and Suruga Bay, celebrated in woodblock prints for their extraordinary beauty. A sea-road, cut in the cliffs, runs along the coast from Atami toward Ito (Ee-toe), another seaside hotspring resort to the south.

There are numerous historical sites and attractions in Atami, including the famous Atami Plum-Tree Garden and Atami Art Museum (which is in the hall of the headquarters building of the Church of World Messianity), on a hill overlooking Atami Station.

Further up along the slopes of the collapsed crater is a golf course, one of the most spectacular and rugged in the country (where I played my first game of golf in 1950).

ATOMIC BOMB DOME

On the morning of August 6, 1945, one of the most beautiful buildings in Hiroshima was the Industrial Promotion Hall, whose majestic dome framed the skyline of the former castle town.

At precisely 8:15 a.m. that morning an atom bomb exploded over the hall, completely devastating everything within a three-kilometer radius. Only the gutted steel frame of the dome was left etched against the smouldering sky.

After World War II ended and reconstruction began, it was decided to leave the atomic bomb-ravaged dome as a grim reminder of the bombing. It was later consecrated as the Atomic Bomb Dome, and is now a special memorial that is visited by hundreds of thousands each year.

ATSUGI (Aht-sue-ghee)

Famous since 1945 as the site of an American air force base, and the place where the first American Occupation troops and General Douglas MacArthur first set foot on the Japanese mainland, Atsugi, near Yokohama, is now a major industrial center.

ATSUTA SHRINE / ATSUTA JINJA (Aht-sue-tah Jeen-jah)

Near Atsuta Station in Nagoya, the Atsuta (Hot-Field) Shrine is the second most important Shinto shrine in Japan because it is the repository of the Sacred Sword that, together with the Mirror at Ise Jingu and the Jewels at the Imperial Palace, make up the Three Regalia of the Emperor.

Founded in the third century, the

shrine was totally rennovated in 1955. Its annual festival is on June 5.

According to legend, the Sacred Sword, called Kusanagi-no Tsurugi or Grass-Mowing Sword, was presented to Prince Takeru Yamato, the son of Emperor Keiko, by Princess Yamato when he visited the Ise Jingu Shrines before starting out on an expedition against rebels in the east.

During the expedition, the enemy set fire to the grass surrounding the Prince, whereupon he used the sword to mow the grass down. The prince then left the sword hanging in a mulberry tree, and it was later carried away by Princess Miyazu.

The Princess placed the sword in a cedar tree but it shone so brightly that it set the tree on fire, which fell and set the field around it ablaze--thus the name Hot Field.

AUTOMOBILES / JIDOSHA (Jee-doe-shah)

In 1980 Japan bypassed the United States as the world's leading producer of automobiles, in what has to have been one of the big industrial upsets of the century.

At the turn of the 20th century, Japan was only a few decades away from a feudal society made up of peasants, artisans, shop-keepers and sword-carrying warriors. It was thus several decades behind the U.S. and Europe in starting an automobile manufacturing industry. Then Japan's auto makers had to virtually start over from scratch at the end of WWII in 1945.

Japan's largest automobile manufacturers are Toyota Motor Company, Nissan Motor Company, Mitsubishi Motor Company, Toyo Kogyo Company and Honda Motor Company. (By the way, Honda is pronounced Hone-dah, not Hahn-dah--and Datsun is not a real Japanese word. It was made up from the initials of the three men who developed it--D.A.T.--plus son. In other words, the son of... But son was spelled sun. See NISSAN, HONDA, TOYOTA.

AVERAGE LIFE EXPECTANCY

In 1901 the average life expectancy of Japanese males was 39.4 years. The average for women was 49.5 years.

By the 1980s Japan had one of the longest life-expectancies in the world-- 78.8 years for women and 73.3 years for men.

This extraordinary increase in the average life-span is attributed to advances in medicine and better diet, both of which have brought about a drastic reduction in infant mortality and the incidence of pulmonary tuberculosis among the young.

Currently the major causes of premature deaths in Japan are adult diseases, primarily apoplexy, cerebral hemmorrage, cancer and heart disease.

AWA DANCE / AWA ODORI (Ah-wah Oh-doe-ree)

One of the most picturesque and popular of Japan's folk dances, the Awa Odori is also one of the major attractions of the city of Tokushima on Shikoku Island, the smallest of the four main islands of Japan.

The dance was originated in the mid 1600s, and is performed in the streets of the city from August 15 through the 18 every year. The dancers wear colorful yukata (yuu-kah-tah) robes and distinctive hats, and dance through the streets to the accompaniment of flutes, drums and shamisen (sha-me-sane) music.

The festival attracts large number of visitors from the other islands of Japan, as well as from abroad. It is also highlighted on national television.

BAMBOO / TAKE (Tah-kay)

It has often been said, seriously, that the Japanese might not have developed the high form of civilization they did without bamboo. A partial listing of just some of its more important uses just begins to suggest its importance in the past. These include water pipes, fan ribs, chopsticks, lantern frames, food, flower vases, baskets, scoops, rulers, wind and sun screens, eating bowls, serving trays, furniture, fencing swords, garden fences, insect cages, flutes, wind chimes, doors and handbags.

Bamboo is said to have been introduced into China and Japan from India. There are more than 600 varieties of the plant, but only about a dozen of these are used regularly for utilitarian and art purposes. These types are selected because of their form, size and natural beauty. They include a long-jointed type that has amazing plasticity, a type that has unusually beautiful patterns on its bark, a type that is multi-colored, and one that is almost black.

Over the centuries, the Japanese developed something of a cult surrounding the use of bamboo. Certain types were always used to make certain items, but never others. One type of bamboo was appropriate for one purpose while another was not. Bamboo generally was regarded as a symbol of virtue, fidelity and constancy, but only certain types of bamboo were used to represent this symbolism.

The most conspicuous use of bamboo in Japan today is for decorative purposes, both by itself and in the form of functional objects such as lattice-work, sun blinds, corner posts, planters, vases and in the interiors of homes and inns.

It has a distinctive texture and charm that adds significantly to Japanese life.

Recommended reading: BAMBOO, by Robert Austin and Koichiro Ueda (Weatherhill).

BANKING SERVICES

Japan is still largely a cash economy. People ordinarily pay for their purchases with cash. Companies are required by law to pay their employees in cash if the employees so desired--and most do. Some bills may be paid by bank transfer. Telephone, gas, electric and water bills may be paid by bank transfers by filling out a form authorizing your bank to debit your account.

Services in Japanese banks are comparable to banking services in the U.S. One interesting difference: customers generally have to go to a teller's window twice--once to initiate their business and the second time when it is finished. Most banks using this system have places for customers to sit and wait.

Foreign banks in Japan are strictly controlled, and can have only one branch in a city. This limits their ability to serve individuals, but many foreign residents in Japan prefer to bank with foreign banks because of other special advantages.

See BANKS.

BANKS / GINKO (Geen-koe)

There are eight categories of financial institutions in Japan--government banks, commercial banks (which include city banks, regional banks and foreign banks), long-term credit banks, trust banks, mutual savings banks, credit associations, credit cooperatives and insurance companies.

In the commercial bank category, there are 13 city banks--Dai-Ichi Kangyo, Fuji, Sumitomo, Mitsubishi, Sanwa, Tokai, Taiyo Kobe, Mitsui, Kyowa, Daiwa, Saitama, Hokkaido Takushoku, and the Bank of Tokyo (which is primarily a foreign exchange bank).

These city banks have an average of over 205 branches each, and besides their services to individuals, play a leading role in enterprise financing. All of them are closely identified with one or more of Japan's major industrial groups, and hold equity positions in many of the firms they help finance.

There are a total of 63 regional banks in Japan, with nearly 6,000 branches. There are some 65 foreign banks in Japan--the latter with few if any branches.

Long-term credit banks, of which there are only three (Industrial Bank of

Japan, Long-Term Credit Bank of Japan, and Nippon Credit Bank), primarily engage in long-term financing using funds obtained by issuing debentures.

The two government banks are the Export-Import Bank of Japan, and the Japan Development Bank. Their primary purpose is to supplement and encourage financing by private financial institutions.

The first American bank to open a branch office in Japan was National City Bank of New York (Citibank) in 1902, in Yokohama.

BANZUIIN, CHOBEI (Bahn-zoo-een, Choe-baye)

Japan had its Robin Hoods--or as such individuals were known in Japan, its Kyokaku (K'yoe-kah-kuu), which translates as Hosts of Heroism.

The Kyokaku were common men (not Samurai) of extraordinary courage and martial skills who became famous during the early decades of the Tokugawa Period (1603-1868) for championing the rights of the ordinary people against corrupt officials of the military Bakufu government, and arrogant--often murderous--Samurai who were legally permitted to kill anyone who broke the law or insulted them.

The Kyokaku were generally members of Japan's traditional underworld of gamblers and gangs who operated outside the Establishment, but were often considered heroes by the lower classes who had no rights other than those given to them by their feudal lords.

The most famous of these Kyokaku was a stalwart man named Chobei Banzuiin, born in 1640. Among the many celebrated exploits of Chobei, none caught the popular imagination more than his saving the life of a swordsmith named Gonpachi Shirai, who later became a notorious criminal in order to get money to redeem the girl he loved from a life of servitude in a brothel.

Gonpachi was caught and crucified, and his lover committed suicide on his grave.

In 1657, when he was 37, Chobei became the victim of a trick arranged by Jurozaemon Mizuno, a senior retainer of the Shogun, and was killed. He was buried at Genku Temple in Higashi Ueno, in Tokyo's Taito Ward. His life and exploits have since been immortalized in songs, plays and films.

BARBER SHOPS / TOKO YA (Toe-koe Yah)

Japan is rightly famous for its barber shops, which dispense far more than a haircut and shave. The typical Japanese barber shop carries on the traditions of special service that have been an integral part of life in Japan since ancient times.

The normal barber shop session lasts for anywhere from 30 minutes to an hour, and includes a meticulous haircut, and shave if desired, along with a head and shoulder massage. It is a thoroughly relaxing experience that makes a visit to a barber shop something more than just getting a haircut.

BARRIER GATES / SEKI SHO (Say-kee Show)

During much of Japan's early history, and in particular during the Tokugawa Shogunate from 1603 to 1868, the Daimyo (Dime-yoe) feudal lords and Shogun maintained barrier gates on the roads leading into their fiefs. The barriers were in effect border inspection stations where travelers had to present identification papers to guards and give their reason for traveling.

One of the most famous of these barriers was in Hakone on the shore of Lake Ashi, which controlled traffic on the Tokai Do, the great road that connected Kyoto and Edo (Tokyo). This barrier was erected in 1618, and manned until 1868. An exact replica of the Barrier Guardhouse was built across the road from the old site in 1965, and is now a popular tourist attraction.

Near the present Barrier Guardhouse is the Hakone Historical Materials Museum (Hakone Shiryo-Kan), which houses weapons, documents and other things mainly connected with the Barrier.

The Hakone Museum, across the street from the Hakone Hotel, also has numerous artifacts relating to the Barrier and to the life-style of the times.

Many of Japan's most popular plays and folk songs make references to these barriers because they played such a vital role in the lives of people over many centuries.

BAR (LEGAL) SYSTEM

Japan's first regulation concerning lawyers was passed in 1876, and a Lawyer Law went into effect in 1895. But the bar association was under the direct supervision of chief prosecutors attached to district courts.

The present Lawyer Law was passed in 1949, and Nichibenren (Nee-chee-bane-rane) the Japan Federation of Bar Associations, was founded on the same day. The law guarantees the independence of the association, and sets standards for lawyers.

Persons who pass the national bar examination or have taught law as a university professor for at least five years, as well as foreign lawyers who have been screened by Nichibenren, are eligible to practice law in Japan.

Nichibenren, headquartered in Kasumigaseki, the government center in Tokyo, has 52 local branch offices, including one in each prefecture. All lawyers are required to register with their local branch office and the main office of Nichibenren. Lawyers are required to have offices, and must follow guidelines set by the bar association in charging fees.

Most of Japan's 12,000-plus lawyers are in Tokyo and Osaka. Fewer than 300 of Japan's lawyers are women.

BASEBALL / YAKYU (Yah-que)

It is often said that baseball is more popular in Japan than in the United States, where it was invented. In any event, it is one of Japan's most popular sports.

Baseball was introduced into Japan in 1873, and quickly became popular among university students and nonprofessional company teams. Professional baseball made its debut in Japan in 1934, but did not really flourish until after World War II.

There are two leagues, the Central League and the Pacific League, each with six teams. Just as in the U.S., the two league winners compete in a playoff--the Japan Series--at the end of the season.

The teams in the Central League are the Yomiuri Giants (Tokyo), the Hiroshima Carps (Hiroshima), the Hanshin Tigers (Osaka), the Yakult Swallows (Tokyo), the Chunichi Dragons (Nagoya), and the Taiyo Whales (Yokohama).

In the Pacific League are the Hankyu Braves (Osaka), the Kintetsu Buffaloes (Osaka), the Lotte Orions (Tokorozawa), the Nankai Hawks (Osaka), and the Nippon Ham Fighters (Tokyo).

Each team plays 130 games per season, which runs from April through October.

There are over 10,000 baseball and softball fields in Japan, including 4,203 owned by companies, 3,181 that are public, and 1,759 that belong to elementary, junior and senior high schools.

The leading homerun hitter of all-time is a Japanese--Sadaharu Oh, who had 868 homeruns to his credit when he retired in 1980. Other top Japanese batters are Isao Harimoto (504 homeruns), Masahiro Doi (465 home-runs), Katsuya Nomura (657 home-runs), along with Katsuo Osugi, Shigeo Nagashima and Koichi Tabuchi, who all hit over 400 home-runs in their careers.

Still today competition between Tokyo's Big Six university baseball teams (Waseda, Keio, Meiji, Hosei, Rikkyo and Tokyo) is fierce, as is that between Japan's high school teams.

Japan also has a nonprofessional inter-city baseball tournamemnt, representing teams from various commercial companies. One of the most successful of these teams is the Japan Steel Corporation team, which has won four All-Japan championships in recent years.

Each of Japan's professional baseball teams is allowed to have two foreign players on the parent team, and one on their farm team. Over the years, many of the American baseball players picked up by Japanese teams have become national heroes.

BASHO, MATSUO (Mot-sue-oh Bah-show)

Regarded as the father of modern haiku poetry, Matsuo Basho (1644-1694), and his disciples, elevated the previously low-class haikai (Hie-kie) to the level enjoyed by Japan's ancient renga (rane-gah) style poetry and to Chinese poetry.

Basho infused his haiku with an elegance and freshness that made them eternal and as new as each day's morning dew. His work and that of his 10 most famous disciples, known as the Juttetsu (Jute-tate-sue) or Ten Great Disciples, was collected in a book called Shichi Bushu (She-chee Buu-shuu), which is prized as the sacred book of haiku.

See HAIKU.

BATHHOUSES, PUBLIC / SENTO (Sin-toe)

Not only has nude communal bathing suffered a setback in image-conscious Japan since the mid-1950s, public bathhouses as well are losing ground.

A traditional and vital part of rural and urban life in Japan since ancient times, Japan's hot public bathhouses are losing out to growing affluence, different lifestyles and rising costs--at least in the major cities.

In Tokyo where over six million people a day went to the public baths in the early 1970s, only about three million people now use the city's some 2,300 public bathhouses.

The head of the Tokyo Public Bath Owners' Union blames the steady disappearance of the sento on the fact that approximately two-thirds of the households in Tokyo now have their own baths.

To bolster their income, Tokyo's sento operators are now offering such things as coin-operated laundry machines, saunas and adjoining coffee shops and supermarkets. Another approach is to add game rooms, reading rooms and facilities for practicing such traditional arts as flower-arranging and the tea ceremony.

In earlier years, there were yuna (you-nah) or water-women bathhouses as well as regular sento. In the yuna, attractive young women scrubbed the backs of patrons, served drinks, and were available for various sensual pleasures as well--an area now served by Turkish baths.

The normal water temperature in Japan's sento is between 105 and 108 degrees F., and is guaranteed to take the kinks and strains out of tired bodies.

BATHHOUSES, TURKISH / TORUKO BURO (Toe-rue-koe Buu-roe)

Turkish-style bathhouses have been popular in Japan for centuries, and in a manner of speaking, are the successors to the country's great gay quarters which flourished until the mid-1950s.

Today's Turkish baths are not the elegant inns of the gay world, which for many generations were both the inspiration and center for much of the literature and theater for which Japan is now famous.

Some of the Turkish bathhouses are very large and ornate, but they are esentially massage parlors that cater primarily to a male clientele out looking for more than a bath and massage. A number of those catering to foreign clientele have lounges stocked with copies of the Wall Street Journal, Fortune Magazine and other amenities.

One of the largest Turkish baths in Osaka has a floor reserved exclusively for women.

BATHING / MIZU WO ABIRU (Me-zoo oh ah-bee-rue)

Very early in their history as a people, the Japanese developed the custom of bathing regularly in hot water as part of their religious life. Unlike Westerners who ordinarily wash themselves while they are in the bathtub (a very unsanitary habit, if one stops to contemplate it), the Japanese thoroughly scrub themselves before entering the bath, and are therefore able to enjoy soaking in clean, hot water--at the same time, making it possible for several people to use the same water.

It was also customary for the Japanese to bathe together in larger private and public baths, without there being the slightest sexual connotations to the practice. This custom continued in public bathhouses until the 1950s, when, as a result of pressure from female members of the Diet (Japan's Parliament), a few Christian religious leaders, and some Westernized wives of prominent men, a law was passed requiring that all public baths be sexually segregated.

This required that walls be built, separating the large common baths into two sections. Until such walls were built, many bath operators strung a rope across the bath to distinguish the sections.

After the walls were built, the attendants, sometimes male and other times female, sat between the two sections on a rise that provided them with an unobstructed view of bathers in both male and female areas. When paying their fees, taller bathers could also peer into the other sections if they so desired.

In their homes and in hotspring spa baths, the Japanee still enjoy the healthy practice of mixed-bathing. While not overtly sexual, bathing is still a very sensual activity in Japan. They have recognized since ancient times the lustration effect of water--that bathing not only washes away dirt, but spiritual and emotional grime as well. A good scrubbing followed by a relaxing soak in a hot tub has the effect of returning one to a virginal state of mind.

Recommended reading: BACHELOR'S JAPAN, by Boye De Mente (Tuttle).

BEACHES / BICHI (Be-chee)

With one of the longest coastlines in the world, Japan has literally thousands of sand-covered beaches, large and small, in easily accessible areas, as well as in tiny coves and inlets that can be reached only on foot or by boat.

Until the 1950s, the Japanese were not great beach-goers. The young did not date, and did not engage in the kind of individualized free-for-all fun that is typical of beach behavior today. Married couples did not go out together for such public forms of recreation. Most men preferred the more traditional forms of entertainment at hotspring spas and in the great entertainment districts--and sunbathing was not the custom.

With the personal freedoms and improved standard of living that followed the ending of the Pacific War in 1945, and the example set by huge number of young American members of the Occupation forces, the Japanese began flocking to the beaches by the millions.

Today there are hundreds of beaches around the country that are crowded from late spring to early fall. Those in the vicinity of Tokyo and Yokohama, on Chiba, Miura and Izu Peninsulas, are especially crowded during the summer months.

They include Kujukuri and Byobugaura Beaches on Chiba Peninsula, Enoshima, Fujisawa, Chigasaki and Oiso along Sagami Bay (formed by Miura and Izu Peninsulas).

BEAUTY / UTSUKUSHISA (Uut-sue-kuu-she-sah)

The Japanese are the only people I know who developed specific standards of beauty that were taught and practiced and became an integral part of the culture.

The principles of beauty in Japan evolved from Shintoist concepts of purity and simplicity, and were refined and codified by Zen Buddhists. This standard of beauty, described by the words shibui (she-buu-e) and shibumi (she-buu-me), is based on naturalness and a highly refined elegance that is found in the epitome of simplicity. Both shibui and shibumi mean astringent, simple, natural--the opposite of gaudy or extravagant.

The principles of shibui beauty are exmplified in traditional Japanese architecture, in their handicarfts, in the tea ceremony, flower arranging and other aesthetic arts.

Recommended reading: JAPANESE SECRETS OF GRACEFUL LIVING, by Boye De Mente (Phoenix Books/Publishers).

BEEFSTEAKS / BIFU SUTEKI (Bee-fuu Sutay-kee)

It is somewhat surprising, at least to the cattlemen and beefsteak eaters of Western America, that many beefsteak gourmets say the best steaks they have ever eaten were served up by steakhouses in Japan.

This reputation derives from the fact that beef raised in the Matsutaka area of Kobe, for the country's leading steakhouses, gets very special treatment that results in the meat being both incredibly tender and very tasty.

This special treatment consists of a special diet that includes beer, and--according to the popular story--being massaged by the farmers (and of course the farmers' daughters), who first spray the pampered cattle with high-grade sake from their own mouths.

Having witnessed this latter treatment a number of times in years past, there might be something to it.

Among Japan's most famous steakhouses are those in the Suehiro (Sway-he-roe) chain. The beef served in these restaurants is called Kobe beef or Matsutaka beef.

BEER / BIRU (Be-rue)

The brewing of beer was among the technologies imported into Japan from the West when its doors were open to foreign trade in the 1850s and 60s. Since that time, the Japanese have become world-reknowned masters of the art.

Beer is now the leading alcoholic beverage consumed in the country, having outstripped the traditional O'sake (Oh-sah-kay) many times over. Among the popular brands are Kirin (Kee-reen), Asahi (Ah-sah-he) and Sapporo (Sop-poe-roe).

Japanese beer is noted for its mellow taste--and for coming in both small (ko-bin) and large-sized (O-bin) bottles. See ALCOHOLIC BEVERAGES.

BEER HALLS AND GARDENS

Beer halls and gardens, many of them European-styled, are popular in Japan. Those that are European in style generally feature some kind of entertainment, ranging from singing to elaborate floor shows.

During the summer months, the rooftops of several buildings in Tokyo and other cities suddenly blossom into beer gardens--some of them with elaborate entertainment that is imported.

For names and locations, see current editions of TOUR COMPANION (a visitors' guide) and the TOKYO WEEKENDER.

BENEDICT, RUTH

Ruth Benedict was the author of THE CHRYSANTHEMUM AND THE SWORD, one of the most famous books ever written about Japan.

An American anthropologist who had never been to Japan, Benedict was asked in the early 1940s by the U.S. government to research and write a cultural-/psychological profile of the Japanese that could be used as guidelines during the expected military occupation of the country following the end of World War II.

Most of Benedict's research consisted of interviews with Japanese-Americans living in the U.S. The study played an important role in the manner in which Gen. Douglas MacArthur set up and conducted the occupation of Japan.

The book also greatly influenced many of the post-war studies and books that have been done on Japan, and continues today to be a popular title on the country. (Tuttle).

BEPPU (Bape-puu)

One of the most unusual of Japan's hundreds of hotspring resorts, the Beppu district on the northeastern shore of Kyushu has eight spa resort areas, with dozens of Ji Goku (Jee Go-kuu) or Hell Springs, which are boiling mud ponds that detonate loudly, burping hot mud several inches into the air.

The mud ponds come in different colors and at different temperatures. Many of them have been developed into mudbaths. The entire Ji Goku circuit is some 20 kilometers long, and is a two-and-one-half hour bus trip.

There are some 3,795 hotsprings in the Beppu area, with nine different types of water. Dozens of them have been developed as spas since the dawn of Japan's history. One of the most popular spas among foreign visitors is the Takegawa (Tah-kay-gah-wah), which includes hot-sand baths on the beach.

Excusions ships from Osaka and Kobe call at Beppu daily.

BIWA (Bee-wah)

The biwa is a four or five-stringed pear-shaped lute that was originally introduced into Japan from China in the 7th and 8th centuries--the first version (muso-biwa) was primarily used by blind priests, and the second version (gaku-biwa) used for court music.

The earliest version was used by Buddhist priests when chanting sutras, the latter by court musicians when performing for Court functions.

In the 13th century, narrative storytellers began using the biwa as accompaniment, and in the 16th century ballad singers took up the instrument. These traditional epic-like ballads were known as jouri (joe-uu-ree), and were later to be accompanied by the shamisen. Modern forms of music for the biwa were developed during the late 1800s and early 190s.

BLACK MIST / KUROI KIRI (Kuu-roy Kee-ree)

The Japanese love euphemisms, and black mist is one that is popularly used in reference to scandals, usually those involving business or government figures.

BLYTH, REGINALD H.

A Briton who went to Japan in the 1930s to teach English, Reginald H. Blyth married there and remained in Japan for the rest of his life. He became a noted scholar on Japanese poetry and Zen, and authored many books that are now classics.

BON FESTIVAL / BON MATSURI (Bone Mot-sue-ree)

Held in Japan in mid-July since the 7th century, this Buddhist celebration is one of the country's most important annual events. It is often called The Festival of the Dead or The Festival of Lanterns, and is similar to All Souls' Day observed in Catholic countries.

The purpose of O'Bon is to perpetuate the memory of ancestors, and to inspire filial piety by reminding everyone of the debt we owe our forebearers.

While the occasion is solemn, the festival is primarily a joyful one. People clean their homes and family graves, and prepare offerings for the spirits, which are believed to return to their former homes at this time.

On the eve of July 13 in the more traditional families, the pious go to the family graves, burn incense, and then invite the spirits to return home, lighting the way for them by carrying lanterns (or in some mountainous districts, torches).

At home, the spirits are treated as if they were still alive. On the 15th, the last day of O'Bon, special farewell rice dumplings (okuri-dango) are presented to the spirits. On the following day, the traditionalists still light bonfires in front of their homes, to help guide the spirits back to the world of the dead.

Many communities celebrate O'Bon with dances--Bon Odori (Bone Oh-doe-ree)--usually held on the precincts of the local shrine or temple. The dances, to the tune of drums and flutes, often last until near dawn.

Bon Odori that are national attractions include those in Kiso, Nagano Prefecture, Sado Island off the coast of Niigata, Tokushima City on Shikoku, and Shiraishi Island in the Inland Sea.

BONKEI (Bone-kay-e)

Bonkei is a miniaturized landscape on a dish or a tray that may be made of just about any natural material--stones, pebbles, moss, plants, etc., combined with something man-made--a house, gate, or bridge, etc. Bonkei are sometimes called hako niwa (hah-koe nee-wah) or garden boxes.

Recommended reading: BONKEI Tray Landscapes, by Jozan Hirota (Kodansha International).

BONSAI (Bone-sigh)

The art of cultivating dwarf trees, or bonsai, was originated in Japan in ancient times, and is now a popular past-time around the world.

The primary attractions of bonsai are the art itself, and the fact that one's handiwork, if properly tended, may have a lifetime and bring pleasure for several centuries.

Basically, the art of bonsai consists of planting a tree in a ceramic pot, then controlling its growth and shape through periodic transplanting, root-trimming, regulating the water and fertilizer, and other techniques.

Bonsai may be sculptored into any number of shapes, depending on the desires of the bonsai artist. Pine trees are probably the most popular subjects for bonsai, but other ones also commonly used include fruit trees and various evergreens.

Recommended reading: BONSAI WITH AMERICAN TREES, by Masakuni Kawasumi (Kodansha International).

BONSEKI (Bone-say-kee)

Bonseki is a dry, miniature landscape that consists of rocks and white sand arranged on a black lacquer tray, representing mountains, rivers or the ocean. Bonseki developed as an art in the Muromachi Period (1392-1573)--the same period that saw the development of the tea ceremony and flower arranging.

It is a popular traditional handicraft, and is sold in department stores as a decorative item.

BONUSES / BONASU (Boe-nah-sue)

In addition to regular monthly wages, Japanese companies generally pay their employees seasonal bonuses, in June and December, that are regarded as a basic, integral part of their income.

The amount of the bonuses is usually based on the equivalent of one or more month's pay, and varies considerably from company to company, and industry to industry. Companies that are very profitable may pay the equivalent of three or four months' wages on each of the two bonus-paying occasions.

When companies suffer financial reverses, they will often borrow money to pay bonuses rather than let their employees go without.

Most Japanese families save a signi-

ficant percentage of their bonuses. The two annual bonus-paying periods also coincide with major gift-giving and shopping periods during the year.

BOOK PUBLISHING / HON NO SHUPPAN (Hone no Shupe-pahn)

Book publishing in Japan grew more slowly than magazine publishing. In the mid-1920s, low-priced editions of collected works of four or five volumes each became very popular. This was followed in 1926 by the One Yen books, of which some 200 titles were published. The next year Iwanami Bunko (E-wah-nah-me Boon-koe) introduced its series of inexpensive pocket books featuring classics from all over the world.

The first successful postwar book was Nichi-Bei Kaiwa Techo (Nee-chee-bay-e Kie-way Tay-choe), or Handbook of English Conversation. It came out in September 1945, one month after the war ended, and sold 3.6 million copies.

Another significant early postwar success was the People's Encyclopedia, published by Heibonsha (Hay-e-bone-shah) in 1961.

Today there are over 4,000 book publishers in Japan, but fewer than 100 of them are of any size. Some 1,300 of them have less than 10 employees, and some 4,000 of them publish less than two titles a year.

The three biggest book publishers in Japan--Kodansha (Koe-dahn-shah), Shogakkan (Show-gock-khan) and Shuei-Sha (Shuu-a-shah)--account for around 20 percent of the industry's total sales of both books and magazines.

Most books in Japan are distributed through commissioned agents. The two largest distributors are Tohan (Toe-hahn) and Nippan (Neep-pahn), which together handle some 70 percent of the industry's sales of books and magazines. Two well-known publishers who who do use commission agents are Iwanami (Ee-wah-nah-me) and Miraisha (Me-rye-shah). They distribute directly.

Just as in the U.S., Japan's book industry is facing serious problems, including rising costs and complaints that the distribution and retailing of books is grossly inefficient.

Japanese book publishers now average printing only about 6,000 copies of a first edition--not nearly enough to go around to all bookstores. One advantage that authors have in Japan--most publishers pay royalties on the basis of print-runs, not sales, and they pay soon after the printing.

An early 1980 development in Japan was the appearance of super bookstores carrying as many as one million books.

Each year between 2,500 and 3,000 foreign books (not counting children's book and reference books) are translated and published in Japanese. Altogether, about 28,000 titles are published annually.

The 10 leading book publishers in Japan are Kodansha, Shogakkan, Shuei Sha, Kadokawa Shoten, Iwanami Shoten, Chuo Koron Sha, Shincho Sha, Hayakawa Shobo, Bungei Shunju and Meiji Tosho Shuppan.

BOSO PENINSULA (Boe-soe)

This is the large peninsula that juts out into the Pacific in a southeasternly direction from Tokyo, and incorporates Chiba Prefecture, with Tokyo Bay on the west and the Pacific Ocean on the east.

Like virtually every other region of Japan, Chiba is dotted with historical places--temples, shrines, etc. It is also the location of the New Tokyo International Airport, which is on the outskirts of the city of Narita, some 68 kilometers from central Tokyo. It also boasts two quasi-national parks (Suigo-Tsukuba and Minami Boso).

The peninsula is part of the Keiyo (Tokyo-Chiba) Industrial Zone, and is also a major agricultural area, frequently called the Kitchen of Tokyo because of its peanuts, soy beans, vegetables, fish, dairy products and natural gas.

There are several popular beaches along the peninsula, but its most famous attraction is Tokyo's Disneyland, which see.

BOSS / OYABUN (Oh-yah-boon)

In feudal Japan, the operators of certain kinds of businesses as well as gang leaders were called Oyabun, and their employees or followers were called kobun (koe-boon). Oya means parent and ko means child, which is an indication of the relationship that existed between the two.

In many such businesses, the kobun lived on the premises in their own rooms or in dormitories, depending on their status. They were expected to be totally loyal to their master, and to obey him as would a dutiful son.

In return for such loyalty, the boss was expected to accept complete responsibility for the welfare and interests of his kobun and their families. This same attitude and a similar relationship still exists today, although in diluted form, between employers and workers.

The word is still very much a part of the vocabulary (and psychology) of modernday Japanese.

BOWING / OJIGI (Oh-jee-ghee)

Bowing is the traditional Japanese way of greeting people and saying farewell, as well as to show respect, and is one of the most important aspects of Japanese culture--far more meaningful and important to the Japanese than the handshake or wave in Western cultures.

The bow, done at the right time and in the right way, is more important to the Japanese because their social etiquette is much stricter and more demanding than the etiquette of most other countries.

In feudal times, failing to bow or bowing incorrectly was a very serious offense that in the case of a commoner could and often did mean immediate death at the hands of a haughty Samurai.

Generally speaking, the lower the bow and the longer it is held, the stronger its implications. The higher the rank of the person receiving the bow, the lower the bow tends to be. When the bow is in the form of a supplication or apology, the trunk of the body may be bowed as low as a 90-degree angle.

The best way to learn how to bow properly is to observe the Japanese in different situations.

BRIDGE OF HEAVEN / AMA-NO HASHIDATE (Ah-mah-no Hah-she-dah-tay)

On the Japan Sea coast west of Kyoto, a short distance from Nishi Maizuru, Amanohashidate, or Bridge of Heaven, is so beautiful that it has been reknowned since ancient times as one of the three most scenic spots in Japan (the other two are Matsushima near Sendai and Miyajima in the Inland Sea).

The spot consists of a pine-tree covered sandbar which projects out into the Bay of Miyazu forming a lagoon, and a slender island, all connected to the coast by bridges. There are a number of viewing spots in the area, plus the Nariai Temple (28th in the string of 33 holy Kannon temples that make up a popular pilgrimage in Western Japan), in the vicinity.

The area around Amanohashidate is a fashionable summer vacation resort for people from Kyoto, Osaka and Kobe.

BUDDHISM / BUKKYO (Buke-yoe)

Buddhism was founded by Sakyamuni Gautama in India in the 5th century B.C., and is a religion in which the ultimate goal is to attain enlightenment in which one is sprirtually free and has an understanding of the relationship between man and the cosmos.

Bukkyo teaches that the way to reach nirvana--the divine state of release from physical pain and sorrow--is through correct living and self-denial. Over the centuries various techniques for speeding up this process have been developed and taught by innovative priests. One such method is asceticism (aragyo), in which practitioners fast for several days and splash cold water on themselves in winter--or stand under waterfalls--while chanting sutras.

It has been found that such shock-treatments will sometimes result in a separation of the mind and body, and the attainment of a holy state.

Buddhism was introduced into Japan from Korea and China in the 6th century A.D. but it made very little impression until the beginning of the 7th century when Crown Prince Shotoku, one of the most famous persons in Japan's history, became a patron of the new religion and worked diligently to spread the belief among the aristocracy.

When Buddhism was introduced into Japan in the middle of the 6th century, the government was controlled by two powerful clans, the Soga family and the Mononobe family. The Soga clan advocated the acceptance of Buddhism, while the Mononobe's opposed it.

The Mononobe held that Buddha was a foreign god and was incompatible with the native Shinto beliefs of the Japanese.

Buddhism was inextricably bound up with China's highly advanced culture, and the acceptance of one meant at least the partial acceptance of the other. But as both the tenets and physical aspects of Buddhism flowed into Japan, both were repeatedly modified to fit the unique Japanese environment.

Despite the opposition from the Shinto traditionalists, Buddhism and its highly sophisticated culture gradually permeated the Imperial Court and ruling families. With strong Court backing, the new religion eventually developed into a national cult, alongside of Shintoism.

By the mid-700s, the foreign origins of Buddhism were virtually forgotten, and it was held up as the guardian faith of the nation. Many of the emperors and princes of 6th, 7th and 8th centuries were dedicated scholars of Buddhism, along with such reknowned priests as Saicho (767-822), also known as Dengyo Daishi, and Kukai (774-835), known as Kobo Daishi.

The great priests-teachers Dengyo and Kukai introduced the doctrine that the native Shinto gods were manifestations of the various Buddhas, thus making it possible for the two religions to exist side-by-side. They differed in other doctrinal matters, however, and the two sects they founded became great rivals--the Tendai sect headquartered on Mt. Hiei northeast of Kyoto, and the Shingon sect on Mt. Koya, south of Osaka.

These two famous monasteries became the twin fountains of Buddhist learning in Japan, but the more powerful they became the more secular and corrupt they became, giving rise in the 13th century to four new sects--Zen, Jodo, Jodo-Shinsu and Hokke (also known as Nichiren)--all reformist in their aims.

Prince Shotoku (537-621) set up schools to teach Buddhism and began a program of constructing temples around the country that was to continue for several centuries. Emperor Kotoku, who reigned from 645 to 655 decreed that Buddhism was a legitimate religion.

Thus between the 6th and 12th centuries, Buddhism, along with the architecture, arts and crafts of China, were totally Japanized and became an integral part of the mainstream of Japanese culture.

With the founding of the first Shogunate in Kamakura in 1192, Japanese religious leaders began changing Buddhism even more, formulating their own doctrines that were closer to the hearts of the Japanese and better fitted the times. Four of the leading Buddhist sects made their appearance at this time--Jodo, founded by Honen. Jodo-Shinshu, founded by Shiran. Zen, taught by Eisai and Dogen, and Hokke, founded by the irrepressible Nichiren.

The internal strife that characterized this period in Japanese history, along with the attempted invasions by the Mongols of China, made the Japanese ripe for the propagation of new religions that offered salvation to the common people as well as the elite, with no more effort than a profession of belief and prayer.

Zen, which taught a very strict system of mental and physical discipline aimed at total self-control and will-power, became the religion of the new class of Samurai warriors, and was to play a leading role in the country for the next 600 years.

Soon after Buddhism became a religion of the masses, corruption set in. As in other mass religions around the world, formalities and ceremonies became more important than keeping or teaching the faith.

The abuse of power became rife among most of the Buddhist sects, and the faith of the common people weakened. Thus when Christianity first appeared in Japan in the mid-1500s, there were many who listened to this new message.

But the political and financial machinations of the Portuguese priests who brought Catholicism to Japan resulted in them being expelled, and shortly after the beginning of the Tokugawa Shogunate in 1603, it was decreed that all common Japanese would register as Buddhists at their neighborhood temple and thereafter become regular donors to the temple.

The degeneration of Buddhism had gone too far, however, and for most Japanese, membership in a local temple was little more than a kind of taxation. As the hedonistic decades of the Tokugawa period went by, more and more people began to question the legitimacy of Buddhism as a state religion.

Scholars went back to the early history of Japan and discovered that Buddhism had usurped the native religion of Shintoism. These same scholars also found that the Shogunate was also illegitimate, having usurped the power of the Emperor.

Public sentiment began to swing in favor of Shintoism and the Emperor in Kyoto, and helped to bring the downfall of the Shogunate in 1868. Almost immediately thereafter, Buddhism was officially declared a heresy, and banned. Shintoism was elevated to the status of a state religion.

Buddhism was too much a part of Japanese culture to be wiped out by a ban, however, and it survived the nationalistic fever of the next 78 years, and remains today an important influence in the lives of the Japanese.

There is no God in the Buddhist faith. Adherents believe that the ultimate state is self-enlightenment which is achieved by a total recognition of the true essence of life and reality. A primary goal of Buddhists is to rid themselves of the idea that everything is everlasting, and to eliminate feelings of jealousy and hate through infinite love. Tolerance and equality are the hallmarks of the Buddhist faith.

Even though most Japanese are not religious in the general sense of the term, Buddhism exercises an important influence in their lives. They go to temples on special occasions, and are buried according to Buddhist rites.

Over the centuries, Buddhism has permeated every part of Japan's culture, moulding their way of thinking, their architecture, art, literature and morals.(Buddha means The Awakened One.)

Recommended reading: INTRODUCING BUDDHISM, by Kodo Matsunami (Tuttle). RELIGIONS IN JAPAN, edited by William K. Bunce (Tuttle). BUDDHISM: JAPAN'S CULTURAL IDENTITY, by Stuart D.B. Picken (Kodansha Int'l).

BUDDHIST TEMPLES / BUKKYO NO OTERA (Buke-yoe No Oh-tay-rah)

Soon after the introduction of Buddhism into Japan in the early centuries, Buddhist priests began traveling all over the country, seeking out places that were sublime in their scenic beauty as sites to build temples.

As a result of this religious compulsion, which lasted for many centuries, thousands of temples were built—some of them on a scale so large and grand that they are startling even today.

Still today there are over 100,000 Buddhist temples in Japan. See KYOTO, NARA, etc.

BUDGET TRAVELING

It is possible to travel in Japan for extended periods of time, and be comfortable, well-fed and thoroughly enjoy yourself, without spending the kind of money one hears about in relation to luxury hotels and exclusive restaurants.

In fact, the Japan National Tourist Organization has prepared special guides and other literature for people interested in budget traveling. These guides include places to stay (hotels, inns, lodges, youth hostels, etc.), plus tips on less expensive bus and train travel, and eating in non-tourist restaurants.

Japan has a large number of Western style hotels below the luxury class that are comfortable as well as interesting. Many are first-class, but about half or one-third the cost of the name luxury hotels. Even those that would be considered second-class are comfortable and perfectly safe, for someone who is really economizing.

Food, always a major concern of travelers, presents no such problems in Japan. There are thousands upon thousands of restaurants serving Western-style dishes or Japanese and Chinese dishes that may sound different and look different but still consist of meat, vegetables and seafoods. Small convenience markets where you can buy fruit, lunch meats, cookies, crackers, candies, nuts, breads, canned goods and other familiar items abound, and they welcome touring visitors.

You can buy enough food in such shops to make three full meals for as little as what you would pay for a snack in a popular tourist-type restaurant.

To take advantage of budget travel opportunities in Japan, check with the nearest JNTO office (see individual listing), and once you are in Japan, buy a copy of EATING CHEAP IN JAPAN (Shufunotomo).

Another important point: you do not have to be concerned about the sanitary conditions in small, inexpensive looking neighborhood type restaurants that cater to local residents. Their standards of cleanliness are among the highest in the world.

You can categorize budget-priced Japanese restaurants by their location as well as type: department store dining rooms, office building restaurants, special lunch menus at first-class hotels and restaurants, shopping center restaurants, back-street restaurants, fast-food and franchised places, and coffee shops with so-called morning service.

Japan's department stores have large dining rooms that are primarily operated for the convenience of their customers, rather than profit. They usually have several choices of Japanese, Chinese and Western dishes, along with soft drinks and beer--and are good. Hours are generally 10:30 a.m. to 5:30 p.m.

Restaurants in office buildings--the general type, not the sushi or tempura, etc. specialty shops--are also moderately priced, and served various rice, noodle and meat dishes.

Many first-class restaurants and hotel dining rooms have daily businessmen's lunches or quick lunches during the week that are priced well below their regular menu choices.

Restaurants in underground shopping centers and clustered around railway stations cater primarily to younger people and ordinary workers, and are budget-priced--especially for continental type breakfasts, and lunch.

Backstreet restaurants is a broader category, but basically these are small restaurants in the basements or on the first and second floors of small buildings--that do not advertise in foreign-language media.

Foreign fast-food chains, all low-priced, that abound in larger cities in Japan include Dairy Queen, Denny's, Dom Dom, Doughnut Art, Kentucky Fried Chicken, Lottelia, McDonald's, Mosburger, Mr. Doughnut, Peter Pan, Sant Ole and Wimpy.

Popular Japanese chains--that have extensive menus but are still moderately priced--include Fujiya, Morinaga, Lion, Coc d'Or and Benihana (which is not a specialty teppan-yaki steak house as it is in the U.S., but a general menu restaurant).

Many coffee shops offer a special morning service that consists of a light breakfast for the price that one often pays in similar establishments for just a cup of coffee. There are also stand-up counters at train terminals where you can get coffee or tea, toast and a boiled egg for a very moderate price.

All of the above categories of restaurants are in central down-town locations. They do not have service charges. Tipping is not customary. Virtually all have menus in English as well as Japanese, most of them have wax models of their choices on display, and in many of them some of the staff speak enough English to get by.

If you are adventurous to any degree, you won't have any problem finding a clean, modestly priced restaurant wherever you might be in Japan. In Tokyo, for example, there are some 90,000 of them!

BUILDINGS/ BIRUDINGU (Bee-rue-ding-goo)

Except for castles, storage towers and a few other special structures, all buildings in Japan were constructed of wood up until the 19th century. Wood was plentiful and inexpensive. Japanese carpenters were masters at using it in aesthetically pleasing ways. It was practical in the humid climate of the country, and the Japanese long ago devised construction methods that made wooden buildings fairly earthquake resistant.

Both the world's oldest wooden building and the world's largest wooden building are in Japan. The former is the

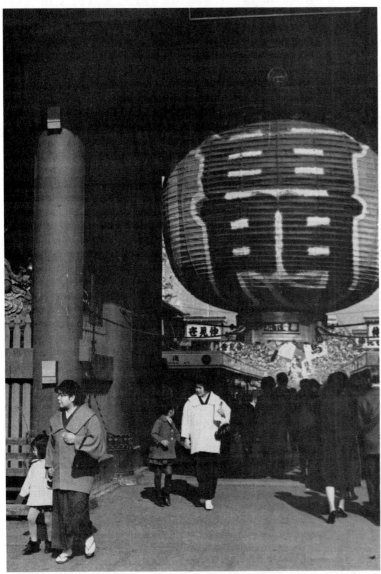

Chochin (Asakusa Kaminari Gate) Tokyo. P. 31

The Great Todai Temple of Nara. P. 43

Horyu Temple in Nara, which was built in the latter half of the 7th century. The world's largest wooden structure, the Todai Temple, is also in Nara. It is 159.45 feet high, 188 feet wide and 165 feet in depth. Inside the huge Todai Temple is one of the world's largest statues of Buddha.

Because of the constant threat of earthquakes, Western style brick and concrete buildings were limited to 31 meters in height until 1960, when new technology was introduced. Now there are highrise buildings in most major Japanese cities. Several buildings in Tokyo are over 50 stories high, and are a prominent feature of the skyline.

Since the appearance of highrise buildings in Japan there have been no major earthquakes to test their durability.

BUNRAKU (Boon-rah-kuu)

One of the three classical forms of theater in Japan, bunraku or puppetry has been popular since the 17th century. Each of the puppets is manipulated by three puppeteers, who wear black robes with flaps covering their faces, even though they are generally not visible to the audience.

One puppeteer works the puppet's head and right hand. Another one manipulates the left hand, and the third one works the feet—on male puppets. Female puppets have no feet and the third puppeteer manipulates the skirts of female puppets to simulate walking and other leg movements.

Bunraku puppets perform stories that are told in special chants called jouri (joe-oou-ree), to the accompaniment of shamisen (shah-me-sane) music.

Puppet dolls consist of a head, trunk, hands, feet (on male dolls) and costume. They range in size from about one meter to a meter and a half.

Altogether there are about 60 different puppet heads or characters, of which some 40 may play more than one role. Some bunraku puppets have eyes, eyebrows, mouths and fingers that move.

Experienced puppeteers become masters at expressing emotions by subtle movements that make the dolls appear to be alive.

Osaka is considered the bunraku capital of Japan, and the bunraku theater there (the Bunraku Za) is regarded as its headquarters.

Developed at the same time as Japan's more famous kabuki (kah-buu-kee), bunraku deals with the same themes and was a more popular medium for playwrights than kabuki. Many of kabuki's most famous plays were originally written for the puppet theater.

Chikamatsu Monzaemon (1653-1724), often described as the Shakespeare of Japan, wrote many bunraku plays that were later adapted for kabuki.

Recommended reading: BUNRAKU--The Art of the Japanese Puppet Theater, by Donald Keene (Kodansha Int'l).

BUNYA PUPPETRY

This is a style of puppetry originated in feudal Japan by a wandering minstrel named Bunya Okamoto. Later another minstrel introduced the art to the island of Sado in the Japan Sea, some 35 miles off the coast of Niigata in northwest Honshu.

The art took root there and the island came to be regarded as its center. After World War II bunya almost disappeared, but in 1971 it was designated an Important Intangible Cultural Property by the government, and has since undergone a revival.

There are now 10 bunya troupes on the island of Sado. They stage performances for local residents as well as visitors, and tour the rest of the country.

BURIAL / MAISO (My-soe)

It is the law in Japan that the bodies of the deceased be cremated. The ashes may then be placed in a tomb or buried or kept wherever the survivors wish. Burial services are usually Buddhist in nature, but may be Shintoist. It was traditional for someone to stay up all night with the deceased on the first night after death. See DYING IN JAPAN.

BUSINESS JAPAN

A monthly magazine published by the Japan Industrial Newspaper (Nihon Kogyo Shimbun), Business Japan carries articles on Japanese management, technological developments and relevant economic and political subjects. Contributors are both foreign and Japanese, and it is one of the more interesting and useful English-language magazines on Japan.

BUSINESS PUBLICATIONS

Among the top weekly and monthly Japanese-language business publications in Japan are the weekly Economist, which is published by the giant Mainichi Newspaper Company. Industrial Japan (published by a company by the same name). Nikkei Business (a management-oriented by-weekly published by Nikkei-McGraw Hill). Nikkei Mechanical (a bi-weekly aimed at mechanical engineers also published by Nikkei-McGraw Hill).

Also, President, a monthly that is affiliated with Fortune magazine of the U.S. and carries some 20 percent of its content. Shukan Diamond, a weekly that goes after the businessman who is concerned about both domestic and international problems. The Oriental Economist Weekly, and Zaikai, a biweekly that caters to the top-level financial community in the country. See ZAIKAI.

BUSHIDO (Boo-she-doe)

During Japan's Kamakura Period (1185-1333), the Samurai warrior class who came into power based their personal and professional codes on Confucian concepts that eventually came to be identified as Bushido, or the Way of the Warrior.

Bushido put loyalty to one's superior as the paramount morality, followed by an overwhelming sense of self-sacrifice, martial spirit, honor, justice, refined manners, frugality, purity and modesty.

Death was the ultimate test of the Samurai's adherence to Bushido, and the Samurai and their families were taught that it was their duty to make this final sacrifice for their clan lord. Death in battle and self-destruction on other occasions thus came to be glorified.

But a willingness to die for the sake of their lord and honor was not the only traits that distinguished the Bushido-steeped Samurai. The code demanded that its followers pursue both physical and spiritual training of the highest order, and thus resulted in the development of a class of people who were extraordinarily disciplined and accomplished.

After the beginning of the Edo Period in 1603 and over two centuries of peace, much of this rigorous training in the precepts of Bushido was gradually channeled into more constructive pursuits, such as art, architecture, literature and various aspects of graceful living.

Recommended reading: BUSHIDO: The Soul of Japan, by Inazo Nitobe (Tuttle).

BUSH, LEWIS

An Englishman who went to Japan to lecture on literature at the Hirosaki and Yamagata High Schools in 1934, Lewis Bush became an avid student of things Japanese, and published his first book, called JAPANALIA, in 1938.

Bush was still in Japan when war broke out between Britain and Germany in 1940. He joined the Royal Naval Volun-teer Reserve and was serving as a sub-lieutenant with an MTB flotilla in Hong Kong when he was captured by Japanese forces on Christmas day in 1941.

Bush spent the remainder of the war years as a prisoner, first in Hong Kong, and then in Omori, Tokyo and Yokohama. From 1947 to 1954 he represented British film interests in Japan, and then worked for the Japan Broadcasting Corporation (NHK) for several years. He was also a columnist for The Japan Times.

His postwar books include CLUTCH OF CIRCUMSTANCES, which details the years he spent as a prisoner of war, revisions of the original JAPANALIA and NEW JAPANALIA, published in 1977.

In 1964 Bush was awarded the Order of the Rising Sun Third Class for his contributions to British-Japanese relations.

CABARETS / KYABARE (K'yah-bah-ray)

To most Westerners, a cabaret and a night club are more or less synonymous, and the words are used interchangeably in a generic sense. But in Japan that is not the case. They are two quite different types of establishments.

The Japanese-style cabaret is a club or lounge or bar that features hostesses who are automatically assigned to all customers who come in. If the customer has a choice, he may request a specific hostess. Otherwise, he takes whoever is sent to his table.

The hostesses in cabarets may wear either Western style dress or kimono. There are some cabarets where kimono is the prescribed costume for all of the hostesses, and others where dresses or gowns are the uniform of the day.

In cabarets it is also automatic that when any individual or group comes in, they are served a plate or tray of peanuts, tiny sembei rice crackers or some other kind of snack food—called tsumami (t'sue-mah-me)—that goes with drinking. And there is a charge for the tsumami.

Another characteristic of Japanese cabarets is that when business is slack, the hostesses—usually with the understanding and permission of customers—will rotate, so one group of customers ends up being entertained by two or three groups of hostessess—all of whom are charged for at separate, set prices.

Not knowning anything about these established practices, foreign visitors who wander into cabarets often get very upset when they find themselves billed for snacks and hostesses they didn't order.

Another distinguishing feature of cabarets in Japan is that they are primarily used by company managers or executives entertaining customers or customer-prospects at company expense. Bills are sent to their companies for payment.

Since most cabaret entertainment is charged, it is necessary for would-be patrons to first establish credit with the cabarets they want to patronize—another factor that foreign customers must also take into consideration.

Some of the more exclusive cabaret-/lounges do not have menus or posted prices. Regular customers know approximately what their bill is going to be from the number of guests they have, how many hostesses are assigned to them and how long they stay at the cabaret.

For this system to function effectively and smoothly, a great deal of goodwill and faith are necessary.

Every city and town of any size in Japan has its cabarets, varying in size from small lounges with three or four hostesess to huge theater-like places with 500 to a 1,000 hostesses. The Mikado in Tokyo is an example of the latter.

The larger the cabaret the more likely it is to have live entertainment (and to serve full meals). The Mikado, for example, features elaborate Las Vegas-type shows, with imported as well as local talent.

Another characteristic of Japanese cabaret patrons is that they like to visit more than one place during an evening, so it is common to see customers, already having fun, going from one place to another.

Japanese cabarets are usually concentrated in well-known entertainment districts, and there may be a dozen or more in one district in the larger cities—with dozens of such districts in the major cities.

The legal definition of a cabaret in Japan is a club or bar that employes hostesses. See NIGHT CLUBS and MIZU SHOBAI.

CALLIGRAPHY / SHODO (Show-doe)

Calligraphy is the art of beautiful handwriting, and has been practiced in the West for many centuries. But because of the nature of the ideograms with which the Japanese (and Chinese) write their languages, calligraphy there is a far more demanding art and has achieved far greater heights of artistic expression.

Skill in calligraphy has been a highly prized art in Japan for well over a thousand years, and for one long period in the history of the country, a person's character was equated with his or her ability with the writing brush.

Drawing the complicated kanji (khan-jee) characters with which Japanese is written forces all Japanese to spend a great deal of time practicing the art during their early school years. The aim of those who go on to develop skill as a calligrapher is to imbue the strokes with a living personality of their own, expressing beauty, refinement, discipline and appreciation for the metaphysical and spiritual side of life.

It is customary for devotees of calligraphy to write auspicious words and poems on January 2 each year in an observance that is called First Writing of the Year, or Hatsu Sho (Hot-sue sho).

Calligraphy has been a major art in Japan since the 7th and 8th centuries—or shortly after the kanji style of writing was introduced into Japan from China. Shodo is written—or drawn, rather—with a brush, using a dark, Japanese-style India ink (sumi), which is made from soot and glue.

The beauty of the drawing is an integral part of the message and is inseparable from it. The key to shodo, masters say, is that it must be done with the whole body and mind working in perfect unison—not just the hand.

In days gone by, the beauty of one's writing was equated with cultural achievement and morality. Many of Japan's great figures of the past are known for their calligraphy as well as their achievements in religion, education, statesmanship, and other fields.

Examples of calligraphy, printed on silk and paper scrolls, are traditionally displayed in the tokonoma (toe-koe-no-mah) of Japanese homes. See TOKONOMA.

CAPSULE HOTELS

Leave it to the Japanese to miniaturize hotels. Going after businessmen and travelers who couldn't afford or didn't want to bother with regular hotels, entrepreneurs in the early 1980s introduced the capsule hotel to Tokyo and Osaka.

The capsule hotels offer sleeping berths and the use of a shower room, and have been compared to railroad sleeping cars. The berths are lined up along aisles, and guests have to climb ladders to reach those above the floor level.

Each capsule room is six feet long, three feet wide and three feet high (just high enough for a small person to sit up in), and contains a bunk, a television set, a radio, clock and reading light. The rooms are made of heat-resistant moulded plastic.

Some of the capsule hotels have sauna baths available, and some of them set aside some of their rooms for women. The rooms are also rented by the hour to people who want to take short naps. The capsule hotels have from 70 to 240 rooms. Rates are from one-fourth to one-third of what regular hotels charge.

Addresses and price lists for the capsule hotels are available from Japan National Tourist Organization offices around the world.

Indications are that the capsule hotel concept will become another successful Japanese export—for airports, recreational camps and possibly even prisons.

CARPENTERS / DAIKU (Die-kuu)

Since the civilization of Japan was virtually built on wood, carpentry has traditionally been one of the country's leading professions. From earliest times, the profession was based on a master-apprentice system, in which young, pre-teenaged boys were assigned to master carpenters for many years before they could become journeymen.

Another characteristic of the trade was that most carpenters belonged to gumi (guu-me) or groups, headed by an oyabun or boss. Some of these gumi were quite large, and controlled all carpentry work in designated areas.

The daiku of Old Japan, and still today in many respects, were a distinctive breed of men who took pride in their work. They dressed in sandals, leggings and short happi jackets that were a mark of their trade, and had a code of their own that set them apart from other tradesmen.

Throughout much of Japan's early history, the building of great temples, villas, castles and palaces was on ongoing event—now in this part of the country, and then in another. It was thus common for crews of daiku to travel about the country, often being away from their homes for years when engaged in huge projects like the shrines of Nikko.

One of the very special but tragic reasons for the importance of carpenters in early Japan was the incidence of fires. With fatal regularity, Japan's cities of wood and paper were swept by conflagrations that reduced great areas of them to ashes.

Such fires were so common in Edo (Tokyo) during the Tokugawa Shogunate (1603-1868) that people would gather at night on the low hills of the city to watch them—a practice that came to be known as viewing the Flowers of Edo.

CASTLES / SHIRO (She-roe)

The first castles in Japan were simple forts known as ki (kee), and were in use by the 1st century B.C. As the centuries passed, these forts became more elaborate and more permanent.

These earliest castles were entirely for defense purposes, and were built in places that were the easiest to defend—in rugged passes and so on.

It was not until near the end of the 14th century that castles began to take the form that is known today—large edifices of stone and wood, but still primarily in mountain passes and other places difficult for enemies to approach.

With the appearance of Nobunaga Oda and Hideyoshi Toyotomi on the scene in the mid-1500s, when they began to consolidate the feudal fiefs under their military rule, the nature of warfare changed from basically single combat or combat in small groups, to battles between large armies.

This led to the construction of larger and more formidable castles on plains and low hills surrounded by plains, which afforded the defenders a wide view of the countryside. These new castles, which were built to function as places of residence as well as forts, were usually surrounded by one or more moats, with high stone ramparts along the inner bank.

There were high wooden or stone walls along the ramparts, with spaced holes through which the defenders could fire upon attackers. The center of each castle was called the Hon Maru or Center Circle, and featured a high tower.

When the Tokugawa Shogunate came under attack by Imperialists in 1867, there were 182 such castles throughout Japan. Among the most famous were the ones in Hikone, Inuyama, Kokura, Himeji, Iwakuni, Komabi, Hiroshima, Kanazawa, Kumamoto, Inaba, Kochi, Matsumae, Maruoka, Matsue, Matsuyama, Niji, Okezaki, Osaka, Sendai, Wakayama and Uwajima.

The Nagoya Castle, built in 1611 by Kiyomasa Kata, was regarded as one of the finest castles in the country. Its walls were 15 to 18 feet thick. Its five-story donjon (tower) was 144 feet high. The roof was made of copper, and the scales of decorative dolphins at the ends of the roof were made of pure gold. (One of these dolphins was loaned to an exhibit in Vienna in 1863. The ship returning it to Japan sank off the coast of Izu Peninsula, and it was six months before it was recovered and returned to the roof of the castle.)

Some 150 of these castles were destroyed in the fighting that surrounded the fall of the Shogunate and the restoration of the emperor to power in the late 1860s. Others, including the Nagoya Castle, were destroyed during the bombing raids of World War II.

After WWII several of the greater castles were completely or partially restored, and now serve as impressive reminders of Japan's feudal age. These include the Hikone Castle and the castles in Himeji, Hiroshima, Inaba, Inuyama, Iwakuni, Kanazawa, Kochi, Kokura, Komaki, Kumamoto, Matsumae, Maruoka, Matsue, Matsuyama, Niji , Okazaki, Osaka, Sendai, Wakayama and Uwajima. See individual listings. Recommended reading: FEUDAL ARCHITECTURE OF JAPAN (CASTLES β MANSIONS), by Kiyoshi Hirai (Weatherhill).

CATS / NEKO (Nay-koe)

Cats have a long history in Japan and are interwoven into the culture, usually been depicted as having magical powers and being both ungrateful and evil. At the same time, they were highly prized at the Imperial Court in ancient times—a practice also imported from China.

Cats with long tails were generally regarded as more likely to possess supernatural powers, and this is the primary reason why short-tailed cats were preferred (and those born with tails often had them snipped off).

The best-known cats in Japan include the Nemuro Neko (Nay-muu-roe Nay-koe) or Sleeping Cat at the entrance of Ieyasu Tokugawa's mausoleum in Nikko, carved by one of Japan's greatest sculptors, Hidari Jingoro (Left-Handed Jingoro). And statues of Maneki-Neko (Mah-nay-kee Nay-koe) or Beckoning Cats, often found in front of shops in geisha-house districts, where they are used to entice customers.

CERAMIC WARE / SETO MONO (Say-toe moe-no)

The Japanese word for ceramic ware literally means Seto things or things from Seto, because the area around Seto City in the Chubu district near Nagoya has been a ceramic ware center since the 13th century.

The manufacture of ceramic ware has been important in Japan since prehistoric times—two of the country's major prehistoric periods are named after earthenware associated with these ages (jomon and yayoi).

But it was in the 5th and 6th centuries, following the importation of new techniques from Korea and China, that Japanese potters began turning out beautiful, high-quality artistic ceramics.

As the generations passed, they developed their own unique techniques and styles.

Among the best-known name categories of ceramics today are Oribe-yaki (Oh-ree-bay-yah-kee), Kyo-yaki (K'yoe-yah-kee), Shino-yaki (She-no-yah-kee), and Raku-yaki (Rah-kuu-yah-kee). Famous Japanese porcelain styles include Kutani-yaki (Kuu-tah-nee-yah-kee), Arita-yaki (Ah-ree-tah-yah-kee), and Kiyomizu-yaki (K'yoe-me-zoo-yah-kee).

Recommended reading: THE WORLD OF JAPANESE CERAMICS, by Herbert H. Sanders with Kenkichi Tomimoto (Kodansha Int'l).

CHAMBERLAIN, PROF. BASIL HALL

One of the best-known of the foreign scholars who went to Japan shortly after the fall of the Tokugawa Shogunate in 1868, Prof. Basil Hall Chamberlain taught for many years at the Imperial University of Tokyo, but is primarily remembered because of two popular-styled books he wrote about Japan--THINGS JAPANESE and A HANDBOOK FOR TRAVELLERS IN JAPAN--the latter borrowing heavily from a book called HANDBOOK FOR CENTRAL AND NORTHERN JAPAN, written by Sir Ernest Satow and Lt. A.G.S. Hawes which was published in 1881.

CHANBARA MOVIES (Chan-bah-rah)

These are historical movies depicting events that took place during Japan's early days and later feudal periods, especially during the period from 1192 until 1868, when the country was ruled by Daimyo lords and sword-carrying Samurai.

Chanbara refers specifically to action movies, in which the heroes and villains battle it out with swords. The word refers to the sound swords make when lots of them are being clanged together.

This genre of movies has its popular stars (Toshiro Mifune was one during his early years), and is one of the most popular movie forms in Japan. The movies are often based on the lives of real individuals and on true historical events.

The chanbara are an excellent medium for getting a feel of what Japan was like in its pre-feudal and feudal ages, as the settings and manners of the times are very accurately portrayed.

CHERRY BLOSSOMS / SAKURA NO HANA (Sah-

Cherry blossoms have been the national flower of Japan since ancient times-- apparently because of the extraordinary beauty of the blossoms, as well as their fragility and short life-time.

The custom of cherry blossom-viewing is also an old one, and still today is an aesthetic pursuit that each year attracts millions of people to well-known groves of cherry trees.

The Samurai of fedual Japan were especially attracted to cherry blossoms, seeing a close similarity in the tenous short life of the beautiful blossoms and their own obligation to die for their lord at a moment's notice.

There are over 100 varieties of cherry trees in Japan, and they bloom at different times in the spring, depending on their location and type. Some trees in southern Kyushu begin blooming in late March. The season then gradually spreads northward, reaching Hokkaido in the middle of May.

Virtually every area in Japan has its well-known spots for cherry blossom-viewing. Among those that have been nationally famous for centuries are Mt. Yoshino near Kyoto and Naraμ Ueno in Tokyo and Hirosaki in Aomori Prefecture. See YOSHINO.

CHESTNUTS / KURI (Kuu-ree)

Roasted chestnuts have been a popular snack item in Japan for centuries, and there have traditionally been two kinds of vendors--one in a regular shop, and the other selling the tasty nuts from a wheeled pushcart.

Both types of vendors take advantage of the same advertising technque--they let the distinctive aroma of the roasting nuts herald their presence.

Chestnut stores can be found on busy shopping streets and in centers around commutor terminals. The pushcart vendors prowl the streets of entertainment and shopping districts, especially in the winter-time when the hot nuts are particularly delicious.

CHIBA (Chee-bah)

Chiba is both a prefecture and a city of nearly 600,000 that serves as its capital. The prefecture encompasses Boso Peninsula, which adjoins Tokyo on the east and forms the northeastern shore of Tokyo Bay.

Chiba has been settled since very early times, first as an agricultural area, and since the 1960s and 70s, as a major industrial zone--with most of the industrial development along the coast of Tokyo Bay on reclaimed land.

The prefecture has numerous historical sites and contemporary recreational areas, including swimming beaches, the Funabashi Health Center (one of the largest recreational centers in Japan) and the Tokyo Disneyland or Magic Kingdom.

The prefecture has several famous temples, including the Chiba Temple, founded in 709 by Priest Gyoki. See DISNEYLAND.

CHIKAMATSU, MONZAEMON (Chee-kah-mot-sue, Moan-zie-moan)

Japan's greatest playwright, who is often compared with Shakespeare, Monzaemon Chikatmatsu was born in 1653 to a Samurai family in the service of the Lord of Mori.

Rather than take up the arts of fighting, Monzaemon entered a Buddhist temple and later went to Kyoto, where he went to work for a high court noble named Ichijo.

Monzaemon later left the service of Lord Ichijo to devote himself to writing kabuki and bunraku puppet plays and joruri dramatic poetry full time.

Besides the volume of his output, Monzaemon's writings are said to reflect the great insights into human nature that are typical of Shakespeare's works. He died in 1724.

Some of Monzaemon's most popular plays have been translated into English by Prof. Asataro Miyamori.

CHILDREN'S SONGS / KODOMO-NO UTA (Koe-doe-moe-no Uu-tah)

Children's songs, most of them passed down for generations, are especially popular in Japan and are a distinctive part of the lives of all children.

One of the most popular of the numerous songs is about the legend of the Badgers of Shojo Temple, who listened to the chief priest teaching songs to the local children and learned how to keep time with the music by beating on their protruding bellies. Only trouble is they became so enthusiastic some of them beat themselves to death. They were buried by the kindly priest who later won a rich lottery and was able to refurbish the temple.

The badgers song, composed by Ujo Noguchi in honor of the legend, is known by virtually everyone in Japan. It goes like this:

Sho, sho, Shojoji
Shojo no niwa wa,
Tsun, tsun, tsukiyo da
Mina dete koi, koi, koi.
Oira no tomodachi
Pon, poko, pon no pon

In the garden of Shojoji
Under the harvest moon,
Come, everyone,
For our friends
Are beating their drums
Pon, poko, pon!

CHINA TOWN

Internationally known for its 70-some Chinese restaurants, numerous bars, cabarets, tea houses, and shops selling Chinese foodstuffs and souvenirs, China Town is one of the most popular districts in Yokohama. It is located some 500 meters south of Yamashita Park, near where one of the first foreign communities in Japan was situated (behind a great barrier fence).

The attractions of China Town draw people from Tokyo and neighboring cities throughout the week.

CHINDON-YA (Cheen-doan-yah)

Chindon-ya are street musicians who are hired by businesses and others to promote openings and public events. They wear period costumes, and usually have a drum-beater, along with flute and shamisen players.

They carry banners and other signs, and make a colorful procession as they parade through the streets, playing their instruments and engaging in comic routines.

The sound of the chindon-ya (from whence the name comes) is very distinctive, and is bound to attract the children of a neighborhood and bring a smile to the faces of adults.

CHINESE / CHUGOKU-JIN (Chuu-go-kuu-jeen)

There are some 55,000 Chinese who are permanent residents of Japan, primarily in the Tokyo and Yokohama areas. Virtually all of the Chinese who work are engaged in one kind of business or another, or work for foreign companies, since Japanese companies do not hire them. See FOREIGN WORKERS IN JAPAN.

Most self-employed Chinese are in the restaurant business or operate import-export companies.

CHINESE FOOD / CHUGOKU RYORI (Chuu-go-kuu rio-ree)

There are an estimated 55,000 Chinese restaurants in Japan, including several nationally known chains. Most of these are the small neighborhood type restaurant that the average Westerner would not recognize as Chinese.

Regular Chinese restaurants, or those that offer menus similar to Chinese restauants in China, Hong Kong, Taipei and other Asian centers, number in the several hundred and cater to the more affluent.

While the neighborhood Chugoku ryori-ya mainly offer noodle and rice dishes that have been somewhat Japanized over the decades, the international-class restaurants boast the same dishes one expects to see in a first-class Chinese restaurant regardless of its location.

All of the first-class Chinese restaurants are ran by Chinese, and a number of them import their chefs from Hong Kong or Taiwan. Some of the better-known and best Chinese restaurants in Tokyo are the Jade Garden, Tokyo Dai Hanten, Akasaka Hanten, Mandarin Palace, and the Nan-Goku in Harajuku.

Highly recommended: HOW TO ORDER CHINESE FOOD, by Boye De Mente (Phoenix Books/Publishers).

CHOCHIN (Choe-cheen)

The beautiful paper lanterns that accompany many Japanese festivals, and announce the presence of bars and traditional styled restaurants, are called chochin, and are made of thick, oiled paper stretched over bamboo frames.

Chochin are most often red, but also come in other colors such as white, black and yellow. They are a distinctive and nostalgic reminder of traditional Japan, adding a special ambience to the contemporary scene.

CHOPSTICKS / O'HASHI (Oh-Hah-she)

Chopsticks, as primary eating utensils, were already in use in China around 2,000 B.C., and made their first appearance in Japan sometime in early A.D. The ease in making them and their utter simplicity appealed to the Japanese, and they were soon adopted as the only eating utensil—soups were sipped from the bowl, and larger pieces of meat, seafood and vegetables were chopped up in the process of preparation.

There are several kinds of O'hashi, including metal ones for cooking. In homes, they are usually made of ivory, bamboo or plastic. In less expensive restaurants, they are usually made of soft wood and are still attached together at the top, so diners will known they have never been used.

These restaurant chopsticks are called wari-bashi (wah-ree bah-she) or half-split chopsticks.

It takes only a short while to become adept at using O'hashi, if you start out holding them the right way—the bottom one in the crook of your thumb and hand, and held with a slight amount of pressure against your ring finger, and the top one held between the thumb and the first two fingers. The bottom stick is kept stationary. You move only the top one, in a grasping motion.

A set of ivory chopsticks makes a much appreciated gift. (In exclusive Chinese restaurants, the chopsticks are almost always long and heavy, and made of plastic or ivory. They are more difficult to handle than the lightweight wari-bashi or Japanese-sized plastic versions.)

CHRISTIANITY IN JAPAN

Francis Xavier, a Catholic missionary belonging to the Society of Jesus, is credited with introducing Chrisianity to Japan in 1549, upon his arrival in Kagoshima, Kyushu, from Macau.

Used to dealing with overlords, Xavier soon made friends with members of Japan's ruling class, who were primarily interested in Western technology and culture and gave him permission to teach the Catholic faith in exchange for some of his knowledge of the outside world.

With the blessings of a number of clan lords and other high personages, Christianity spread rather rapidly in Southern Japan, and by the early 1600s there were an estimated 750,000 converts. The peasants liked the human rights ideals of the Catholic religion.

By this time, missionaries from other Christian sects had arrived in Japan, and as were their wont, soon became involved in political intrigue and machinations against each other.

Fearing that the growing influence of the foreign missionaries might endanger the feudal government, Shogun Hidetada Tokugawa banned Christianity in 1613. Most of the foreign missionaries in Japan were banished from the country, and for several decades thereafter, Japanese Christians were vigorously persecuted.

The feudal government's campaign to completely rid Japan of Christians of whatever nationality resulted in most Japanese converts renouncing the faith, but a few thousand of them continued to practice their beliefs in secret, and eventually came to be known as the Kakure (Kah-kuu-ray), or Hidden, Christians. In their final stand against the Shogun's forces, several thousand converts took refuge in a castle on Shimabara Peninsula, and were besieged and slaughtered. See SHIMABARA.

In 1859, just before Japan's feudal government began to break up and the country began to establish diplomatic relations with the U.S. and Europe, missionaries once again began flocking to the islands.

At present, there are an estimated 490,000 Protestants and 370,000 Catholics in Japan--a very significant sign that given a free choice, the Japanese are not particularly attracted to Christianity.

There are several Christian-run universities in Japan, the best known being International Christian University (ICU) and Sophia University or Jochi Daigaku (Joe-chee-Die-gah-kuu), both in Tokyo.

Japan's first Catholic cardinal, Tatsuo Doi, was elected in 1960.

CINEMAS / EIGAKAN (Aa-e-gah-khan)

There are presently some 550 movie theaters in Japan, most of them owned by the country's two largest entertainment conglomerates, Toho (Toe-hoe) and Shochiku (Sho-chee-kuu). The theaters show Japanese as well as foreign films. The latter usually have subtitles appearing on the films for the benefit of viewers who do not understand the language of the films.

CITIES / SHI (She)

Despite its small size, Japan is second only to the U.S. in number of large cities. The reason for this exceptional number of populous cities is the clan-feudal system that existed for several centuries. There were altogether some 270 clans around the country prior to 1868, each with its own boundaries, and to a considerable extent self-sufficient.

Each of the clans had its own headquarters, usually centered around the castle of the Daimyo (Die-m'yoe) or Lord. As the long decades of the Muromachi (1392-1573) and Tokugawa Eras (1603-1867) passed, these headquarters grew into cities.

Most of the earliest of these castles were built in mountainous areas for strategic purposes. With the coming of peace, many of the lords abandoned their old castles and had new ones built in plains areas where most of the people lived, requiring that their warrior retainers and the leading merchants also move into the vicinity of their new castles, resulting in the rapid development of new communities.

Some of the best known of these Joka Machi (Joe-kah Mah-chee) or Castle Towns, are Odarwara, built around the Hojos clan's Odawara Castle. Kai-Fuchu, built around the Takeda clan castle.

Suruga-Fuchi, built around the Imagawa clan castle. and Yamaguchi, around the Ouchi clan castle. Osaka, Fushimi and Sendai are pure castle towns. Tokyo and Nagoya are also joka machi.

More than half of every castle town was reserved for the homes of Samurai families, which were built in circles around the castle. Outside of this circular area were the commercial districts where the merchants lived and worked. Immediately beyond the merchant district were the homes and shops of craftsmen and artists. Furthest out was the temple area, which was intended to be the first line of defense in case of an attack.

Each castle town was surrounded by a moat or a high dirt embankment. All the streets were built in a labyrinthine layout so that none of them led directly to the castle.

The main castle towns (all of which are cities today) were: Ueno, Tsu and Matsusaka in Mie Prefecture. Hikone and Nagahama in Shiga Prefecture. Maizuru, Miyazu, Kameoka and Fukuchiyama in Kyoto Prefecture. Osaka, Kishiwada, Ibaraki and Ikeda in Osaka Prefecture. Miki, Himeji, Tatsuno, Ako, Sumoto, Toyo-oka, Itami and Amagasaki in Hyogo Prefecture, and Yamato-Koriyama in Nara.

Also, Wakayama, Tanabe and Shingu in Wakayama. Tottori in Tottori Prefecture. Matsue and Hamada in Shimane. Okayama, Tsuyama and Takahashi in Okayama. Hiroshima, Miyoshi and Mihara in Hiroshima. Hagi, Iwakuni and Tokuyama in Yamaguchi. Tokushima in Tokushima. Takamatsu in Kagawaμ Saijo, Imabari, Matsuyama and Ozu in Ehime. And Kochi and Sukumo in Kochi.

Along with Fukuoka, Kurume and Yanagawa in Fukuoka. Saga, Kashima and Karatsu in Saga. Fukue and Omura in Nagasaki. Kikuchi, Uto, Hitoyoshi and Yatsushiro in Kumamoto. Oita, Nakatsu, Hita, Kitsuki and Usuki in Oita. Nobeoka and Saito in Miyazaki. And Kagoshima in Kagoshima Prefecture.

In addition to Japan's castle towns, there were five other types of towns, many of which grew up to be cities. These include Shukuba Machi (Shuu-kuu-bah Mah-chee) or Inn Towns, Monzen Machi (Moan-zen Mah-chee) or In Front of Temple Gate Towns, Jinai Machi (Jee-nie Mah-chee) or Towns Within Temples, Ichiba Machi (Ee-chee-bah Mah-chee) or Market Towns, and Minato Machi (Me-nah-toe Mah-chee) or Port Towns.

Inn-Towns were towns that developed as way stations for travelers along feudal-age roads. They became especially important during the Tokugawa period

A "Bullet Train" zips by Mt. Fuji. P. 313

Osaka Castle still stands guard. P. 245

when all the Daimyo Lords were required to spend every other year in Edo (Tokyo), making it necessary for them to march to and from their fiefs, with large numbers of retainers, in alternate years. See PROCESSIONS OF THE FEUDAL LORDS.

To accommodate these privileged travelers, these stop-over towns developed elaborate inns for the Lords and their closest retainers called Honjin (Honejeen) or Headquarters. Less ostentatious inns called Waki Honjin (Wah-kee Honejeen) or back-up headquarters were built for the other members of the Lords' entourage. Chaya (chah-yah) or restaurant-entertainment houses grew up around these two types of inns.

Among the more famous of these Inn towns that are now cities: Nabari, Otsu, Moriyama, Moriguchi, Himeji, Gojo, Ibara, Otake and Takeo.

In-Front-of-the-Gate-Temple-Towns are towns that grew from restaurants and shops that lined the approaches to famous temples. Those that became cities include Ise, Yawata, Osaka, Yao, Nishinomiya, Gobo, Shingu, Soja, Kasaoka, Tokushima, Zentsuji, Kanonji and Okinawa.

Towns-Within-Temples began in the compounds of temples--mostly Shinshu Sect temples, because this sect built huge compounds to ward off attacks by other sects, and had its followers establish their homes and businesses inside the compounds. The biggest of these compounds was around the Ishiyama Hongan Temple, which enclosed six towns that finally merged to form Osaka, one of the great cities of the world.

Beginning on the southernmost island of Kyushu, Japan's major cities include Kagoshima, Fukuoka, Hiroshima, Kita-Kyushu, Kobe, Osaka, Kyoto, Nagoya, Yokohama, Kawasaki, Tokyo, Sendai and Sapporo. In addition, there are literally dozens of smaller cities that have been and still are of special importance in Japan. These include Nara, Kamakura and Nikko. See individual listings.

Japan has 19 cities with populations over half a million, 10 of which are well above the million mark: Kawasaki, Kita-Kyushu, Fukuoka, Kobe, Sapporo, Kyoto, Nagoya, Osaka, Yokohama and Tokyo.

CLARK, DR. WILLIAM S.

A chemist and botanist who was born in Massachusetts in 1826, studied in Germany, taught at Amherst University and then became the president of Massachusetts Agricultural College, Dr. Clark was invited by the Japanese government in 1876 to establish an agricultural college in Sapporo, Hokkaido and serve as its first dean.

Although Clark taught at the new college for only one year, he left an extraordinary legacy and his memory is still honored by the Japanese. When he left Sapporo his students rode with him on horseback to Shimamatsu, 24 kilometers south of Sapporo. His parting words to them was: Boys, be ambitious! and this has since been accepted as the motto of millions of young Japanese boys. Several of Clark's students went on to become celebrated scholars.

In 1960, the city of Sapporo built the Clark Memorial Hall to honor his memory.

CLASS DISTINCTIONS

Prior to the end of World War II in 1945, Japanese society had a privileged upperclass aristocracy, and a number of immensely wealthy families, mostly Zaibatsu families, whose wealth gave them aristocratic standing. At the end of the war, all class distinctions were legally abolished, except for those pertaining to the Imperial family.

With two more conspicuous exceptions, Japan is now virtually classless. Even great wealth does not grant or guarantee special privileges. The two exceptions are the the Imperial family, and a fairly large group of people formerly known as Eta (Eh-tah) and not counted in the general population, who are the descendants of a caste that was associated with the slaughter of animals and working with animal byprodcuts.

Over the centuries these people were segregated from the rest of the population and became hereditary outcasts.

There are occasional public indications that not all of the prejudice against this group has disappeared.

The Japanese, in fact, have been conditioned during centuries of isolation and insularism to immediately and completely distinguish between anyone who is not racially Japanese. Being a Japanese is not just a matter of nationality--it is racial first, ethnic second and political third, with the last two not counting except in the legal sense.

Generally speaking, social status in Japan is determined by one's own ability, ambitions and success in any professional field.

CLIMATE / KIKO (Ke-kooh)

One of the best ways to understand and appreciate Japan's climate is to equate it with the climate on the east coast of the United States, from Bangor, Maine down to Jacksonville, Florida.

Japan's four main islands stretch some 3,000 kilometers (1,860 miles) in a north-southwest direction. The northernmost island of Hokkaido is in the sub-frigid zone and the southern end of the southernmost main island of Kyushu is in the sub-tropic zone.

The next most important factor in Japan's climate is ranges of high, rugged mountains that run nearly the full length of the country, effectively dividing it into two conspicuously different climatic zones.

The Japan Sea or Asian continent side of Japan is buffeted by cold winter winds from Siberia, Korea and Northern China, bringing regular heavy winter snows that have resulted in the Niigata Prefecture area often being referred to as Yuki Guni (You-key Goony) or Snow Country.

At the same time, the famous Kuroiso (Kuu-roy-soh) or Black Current that comes up from the South Pacific bathes the Pacific side of Japan, keeping the temperatures moderate.

All of Japan except for Hokkaido has hot, humid summers, and a pronounced rainy season called baiu (by-you), which usually begins in early June and lasts until mid-July. Some inland regions of Honshu and Shikoku tend to be very dry except during the annual rainy season and when typhoons hit the islands.

On the Pacific side of Honshu, the largest and most heavily populated of the four main islands, winters range from mild to relatively cold. Dry clear days, sometimes with wind, are common in the winter months.

On the Japan Sea side, there is very little rain in the summer, and the winters are marked by an abundance of snow. The mountainous areas of the islands are cool in the summer and cold in the winter, with varying amounts of snow. The further north and west you go, the more snow.

Hokkaido, the northernmost island, is cool in the summer and very cold in the winter. It has a great deal of snow in the winter but gets very little rain in comparison with the islands to the south.

Japan's famous Inland Sea area--the sea separating Shikoku, Honshu and Kyushu--is noted for its relatively mild winters.

Japan's typhoon season usually begins in late summer and may last as late as November. While very important to Japan's rice crop and to its other water needs, the annual typhoons are responsible for considerable wind and flood damage almost every year.

The four seasons are distinct in Japan, and have played fundamental roles in the development of Japanese culture, influencing virtually every aspect of life, from housing, wearing apparel, food, arts and crafts to the appreciation of nature in general and to aesthetics in particular.

See individual cities for local weather information.

CLINICS / KURINIKU (Kuu-ree-nee-kuu)

Because of the closed nature of Japan's hospitals, which generally do not allow outside doctors to bring their patients in for any purpose--which also prevents hospital doctors from earning higher incomes--there are a very large number of clinics in the country that for all practical purposes are small private hospitals.

These thousands of clinics are owned and operated by doctors who are in private practice, often without any kind of relationship with university and public hospitals. Doctors who are on the staffs of various hospitals also sometimes own or are in partnership with private clinics.

Some clinics and hospitals do not have emergency rooms, and may refuse to accept patients brought in on an emergency basis. In such cases, it is necessary to call ahead and make advance arrangements.

CLOISONNE / SHIPPOYAKI (Sheep-poe-yah-key)

First introduced into Japan from Persia and Europe through China in the 8th century, the art of making cloisonne flourished for a while and then died out. It was reintroduced from Korea in the 17th century, and has been very popular since the 19th century following numerous improvements in the technology.

Cloisonne refers to a style of decorating ceramic, glass or various metals by baking onto them designs created from vitreous enamels.

Japan is especially known for high-quality personal ornaments and craft-works decorated in this style. The Japanese word shippoyaki means something like Seven Precious Stones Baked Ceramic.

Some cloisonne artists use wire to outline their designs.

COFFEE SHOPS / KISSA TEN (Kees-sah Tane)

Coffee shops have played a special and important role in Japanese life since their first appearance in the 1920s--a role that became even more important following World War II.

The first coffee shops in Japan were founded by Japanese who had spent several years abroad, usually in France, and wanted to recreate some of the ambience of Paris' famous cafes.

These first shops eventually run into trouble with the prewar militaristic government and at one time were closed down. Following the Pacific War and the revolutionary changes that were introduced into the lives of the Japanese, the coffe shops came back in a new form and were an immediate success.

These new postwar coffee shops were short-order restaurants that also served coffee, tea and eventually carbonated drinks. Their patrons were businessmen who needed a place to meet and talk to customers, and the millions of young Japanese men and women, now with a modest amount of discretionary money to spend, who found the coffee shops ideal places to meet their friends and dates. See COURTING.

As time went by, several different kinds of coffee shops developed--usually classified by the kind of recorded music they offered. There were jazz coffee shops, chamber music coffee shops, folk-song coffee shops, etc. There were also Bijin (Bee-jeen) or Beautiful Girl coffee shops--so-called because their waitresse were picked for their beauty.

Tokyo also usually has a number of coffee shops that cater especially to single foreign patrons--as an attraction for Japanese who want to meet foreigners.

There are at least 10 different categories of coffee shops in Japan today, and while they are now less used by businessmen as extensions of their offices, they are as popular as ever as meeting places and for light snacks.

COMICS / MANGA (Mahn-gah)

Comics apparently have a universal appeal, but it is difficult to imagine a country where they are more popular than they are in Japan. Having been a highly

sophisticated people for many centuries, the Japanese have long had an intense interest in oral narratives with a humorous slant, with humorous writing and with comic entertainment.

Woodblock prints with humorous and often ribald themes were popular during the middle and later years of the long Tokugawa Shogunate period (1603-1868). This impulse was generally stifled during the early nationalistic decades of the 1900s, but with the coming of an open society and affluence after the Pacific War ended in 1945, cartoons and cartoon books proliferated.

By the mid-1960s there was a flood of comic magazines and books on the market, some of them achieving circulations of well over a million copies a month in very short periods.

They are now a major part of the publishing industry, and range from super heroes and space adventures to historical themes featuring Samurai or ninja (neen-jah) characters. Many of the manga are overtly sensual, often with strong macho and masochistic themes. See NINJA, PUBLISHIHNG, LITERATURE.

COMIC STORYTELLERS / RAKUGU (Rah-kuu-go)

One of the special categories of traditional entertainment in Japan is that of the rakugo or comic storyteller. Dating back to feudal times, the rakugo specialize in long anecdotal monologues that are characterized by many twists and turns, by numerous puns and by surprise or witty endings.

These professional raconteurs appear regularly on nationwide television shows, and are among the most celebrated artists in Japan. There have been two foreign rakugo artists in Japan--one of them an American named Robert Strickland who was also known as the operator of a steakhouse in Kyoto that employed orphaned mixed-blood youngsters. The other man was an Englishman named Black.

The language skills and cultural knowledge necessary to become a recognized rakugo artist are formidable even for a Japanese. That Strickland and Black were able to achieve such an accomplishment is testimony to their fluency and knowledge.

COMMUTING

With over 80 percent of its limited land-space mountainous, and inadequate housing in the central portions of its major cities, commuting from 30 minutes to two hours or more is a way of life for millions of Japanese. It is not uncommon for people to commute two hours each way going to and from work.

Most people commute by public transportation--trains, subways and buses--since existing roadways and streets would not accommodate more than 10 or 15 percent of the commuting public, and parking space is not available for more than 5 to 10 percent.

As a result, Japan's commutor transportation system is among the most crowded in the world. Its trains and subways are so jammed during rush-hours that extra platform attendants are hired to help push people into coaches so the doors will close.

In the wintertime, when people wear heavy coats, the crowding is even worse because the extra bulk from the coats means less room for people. Train and subway coaches carrying four times their rated capacity are commonplace.

Despite this extraordinary strain on the commutor systems in Japan, they are incredibly efficient, keeping split-second schedules that are the envy of much of the world.

COMPANIES / KAISHA (Kie-shah)

There are some six million recorded enterprises or business establishments in Japan--not including farmers, fishermen or proprietary forestry workers. Of this huge number, approximately 70 percent are unincorporated.

In manufacturing industries, over half of the companies involved have fewer than five employees. Only about one-half of one percent have 300 employees or more, or some 4,000 companies.

Continuing this breakdown in just two categories of business--manufacturing and wholesaling/retailing: of some categories of business--manufacturing and wholesaling/retailing--among some 840,000 manufacturing companies, some 434,000 have 1-4 employees, 190,000 have from 5-9 employees, 149,000 have from 10-29 employees, 31,000 have from 30-49 employees, 21,000 have from 50-99 employees, 12,000 have from 100-299 employees, and 4,000 have 300 or more employees.

In the wholesale/retail trades in Japan there are some 2,868,000 enterprises. Of them, some 2,176,000 have from 1-4 employees, 434,000 have from 5-9 employees, 192,000 have from 10-29 employees, 26,000 have from 30-49 employees, 13,000 have from 50-99 employees, 5,000 have from 100-299 employees, and 1,000 have 300 or more employees.

There is a very large gap between the fringe benefits, pensions and wages paid by the smaller enterprises (those with fewer than 300 employees) and the larger firms. Wages at smaller enterprises are anywhere from 30 to 40 percent less than what they are in large companies.

This disparity accounts for the overwhelming ambition Japanese youths have to get an education and go to work for a major enterprise.

COMPANY HOUSING

Many of Japan's larger companies provide or subsidize housing for their employees. Before industrialization it was common for employees of restaurants, shops and other types of businesses to live-in. After industrialization in the latter part of the 19th century, when many factories and mines were in distant locations, it was necessary for employers to provide housing in order to attract workers.

As time went by, it became customary for Japanese companies to regularly transfer employees from one location to another as part of their on-the-job training. Company-provided housing became an important part of this program.

Larger factories almost always provide dormitory-type housing for unmarried employees. Executives in companies are often provided housing at low rents or at no cost as part of their compensation.

The giant Nippon Steel Corpration, for example, owns close to 30,000 housing units, and provides housing for some 35 percent of its married employees. Dormitories are available for single employees who do not live near their place of work.

COMPETITION / KYOSO (K'yoe-so)

The Japanese did not have a word for competition until the latter part of the 1800s, when the term kyoso was coined by famed educator Yukichi Fukuzawa.

The reason there was no such word is because the concept of competition as it is used in the West did not exist in Japan prior to the modern era--although there was competition in certain sports, and certainly there was competition between clans and groups and even individuals.

In all group efforts, however, the primary Japanese principle has always been cooperation--try to get along, by compromising, so that no one loses and all gain.

During feudal days, travelers on the road were expected to apologize and ask permission to pass slower walkers to avoid giving the suggestion of aggressive impropriety.

In Japan today competition in business is still primarily a group thing as opposed to individual effort. In fact, in the Japanese context of things, the individualist is the oddball and has no place in most companies.

COMPUTERS / KOMPYUTA (Kome-pyu-tah)

In the 1960s the Japanese government, in concert with various research institutions and electronics companies, made the decision that the rapid development of the computer industry in Japan would be a primary goal.

The joint program of research and development has made Japan a leader in the computer field, further advanced in some areas than the United States Until 1980, IBM (Japan) was the top computer company there in terms of sales. Since that year, Fujitsu has been number one.

Other leading Japanese computer manufactuers are Hitachi, NEC, Oki, Mitsubishi and Toshiba.

Until the early 1980s, all Japanese computer software was written in English. Now much of it is written in the Japanese language in a mixture of kana (kah-nah) and hiragana (he-rah-gah-nah). See JAPANESE LANGUAGE for an explanation of these terms.

If current trends continue (and there is every reason to believe that they will), Japan will be the first country to achieve virtually complete computerization of its industry and life-style.

CONSTITUTION DAY / KEMPO KINENBI (Kimpoe Kee-name-bee)

This May 3rd national holiday commemorates the promulgation of Japan's constitution on May 3, 1946 (it went into effect one year later).

CONSTRUCTION INDUSTRY

There are some half million construction companies in Japan, but only a few of these are major enterprises operating on a national and international basis. The Big Five are Kajima Corporation, Ohbayashi Gumi, Shimizu Construction Co., Taisei Corporation and Takenaka Komuten Co.

Japan ranks second only to the U.S. in the scale of its construction industry, and since the 1960s has become increasingly active abroad.

One of the special reasons for the success of Japan's con-struction industry is the fact that so many of the building sites in Japan are on reclaimed land and in earthquake-prone areas that it was necessary to develop special technology and skills to overcome these handicaps.

The industry has also benefited from a high degree of automation.

CONTRACTS / KEIYAKU (Kay-e-yah-kuu)

Traditionally in Japan, most contracts were based on verbal agreements, and among the Samurai in matters of consequence the commitment was total—a matter of life and death.

The conclusion of agreements in Japan was generally marked by toasts and by the formalized clapping of the hands three times in rapid unison, a practice known as Te-uchi (Tay-uu-chee). This same practice was also common to mark the end of a special party.

Written contracts, particularly between foreign interests and Japanese, are common today, but the Japanese still feel that if there is enough mutual trust and confidence in each other to make an agreement in the first place, a signed contract is superfluous.

The Japanese are also uncomfortable with written contracts that are based on hard, specific absolutes, pointing out that circumstances change and that arrangements between two parties should be flexible enough to allow for periodic adjustments arrived at by mutual agreement.

Western businessmen who are used to formal, binding contracts that have little or nothing to do with personal feelings, often find it difficult to negotiate deals with Japanese companies—and once such contracts are signed, more problems in working effectively with their Japanese counterparts.

Recommended reading: JAPANESE MANNERS β ETHICS IN BUSINESS, by Boye De Mente (Phoenix Books/Publishers). Also, HOW TO DO BUSINESS IN JAPAN by the same author.

CONVENIENCE AGENCIES / BENRI-YA (Banee Yah)

A type of agency that developed in the late 1970s, the benri-ya are odd-job services that do such things as housework, shopping, yard clean-up, moving heavy things—and spying on students suspected of not studying and spouses suspected of playing around.

Women often use the benri-ya to help them win divorce cases, and when they need help around the house.

The first benri-ya was the Ukon Service Company, founded by Katsuyoshi Ukon in 1979. Some two dozen of the companies that cropped up soon thereafter were founded by ex-Ukon employees who went out on their own as soon as they learned the business.

CORMORANT FISHING / UKAI (Uu-kie)

One of Japan's most popular tourist attractions is fishing with trained cormorants, primarily on the Nagara River near Gifu, southwest of Nagoya.

The large, pelican-like birds are controlled by a cormorant fishing master who has them on individual leashes. A cord ring is placed around their necks to keep them from swallowing fish above a certain size.

Coromant fishing takes place at night. Fires are lighted and held out over the water from boats to attract the fish. The huge birds are then sent splashing into the river. When their pouches are full, they are pulled into the boat and relieved of their catch.

A cormorant fishing master can handle up to a dozen of the large seabirds. From July 1 to August 31 cormorant fishing is demonstrated on the Uji River in Kyoto's Arashiyama Park.

Cormorant fishing is mentioned in the KOJIKI (Koe-jee-kee), a record of Japan's early history that was compiled in 712. The birds used for this kind of fishing are caught in winter off the coast of Ibaraki Prefecture and on Shino Island in Mikawa Bay.

The birds stand about 60 centimeters high when grown, and weigh two to three kilograms. The first bird is caught by placing bird lime on the rocks where they ordinarily land, and this bird is then used as a decoy to attract others.

The cormorants are kept in large bamboo lattice baskets. When being used they are controlled by thin 3.6 meter leashes attached to the cords around their necks.

The birds are given about two weeks of individual training and then are put into the water with cormorants that are already trained. Each cormorant boat is manned by four men, a steersman, the fishing master and two assistants.

The fishing master stands in the bow of the boat, controlling 12 birds at the same time. His two assistants, amidship, each manage two birds. The steersman is in charge of the decoy fire which is kept burning in an iron grate at the bow.

Boats, gaily lighted with lanterns,

usually go out in groups of five or seven, either before the moon rises or after it sets, because fish are not attracted to the fires on bright nights.

Each time a cormorant is put into the water it catches from two to four fish, and on a good night will catch from 40 to 50. Individual boats will accommodate from 8 to 30 sightseeing passengers.

The fish the cormorants go after are called ayu (ah-you), a trout-like fish with very sweet meat that is found all over Japan.

Emperor Daigo (885-930) was especially fond of ayu caught by cormorants, as was Yoritomo Minamoto, who established Japan's first Shogunate in Kamakura in 1192. In fact, Yoritomo like the fish so much he had them delivered to him regularly.

The presentation of cormorant-caught ayu to the Shogun became a formal custom that was continued into the Tokugawa period that began in 1603.

Ayu from Gifu's Nagara River also remained a favorite of Japan's Emperors. In 1890 three sections of the river were set aside as the private ayu preserves of the Imperial Court, and placed under the charge of special cormorant masters.

COURTING-DATING / DETO (Day-toe)

Until the 1950s Western style courting or dating was not part of Japan's social scene. Virtually all marriages were arranged, and with few exceptions unmarried men and women did not date in the usual sense of the word.

Following an arranged meeting between a prospective bride and groom, the two were often allowed to meet a few times before the wedding took place, but these were get-acquainted dates, not courting dates.

In the prewar feudal family system, unmarried daughters especially were subject to the wills and preferences of their fathers. The old family system was abolished in 1945, but it was to be well up in the 1950s before young Japanese men and women began to date and choose their own spouses.

The Allied military Occupation of Japan from 1945 to 1952 by several hundred thousand young American and other Western men had a lot to do with the rapid assimilation of dating and courting customs in Japan. Within months after the end of the war in 1945, a significant percentage of the younger GIs had Japanese girl friends.

It wasn't too long before young Japanese men picked up on the custom, beginning a revolution in Japanese society that was to change traditions that had endured for nearly 2,000 years.

COURTS / SAIBAN (Sie-bahn)

There are five categories of courts in Japan: the Supreme Court, high courts, district courts, family courts, and summary courts. In addition, there is a court of impeachment in the Diet to try judges whose dismissal is sought.

The Supreme Court nominates judges for all of the lower courts, and the Cabinet makes the final appointments.

There are 15 justices on the Supreme Court. They are subject to review by popular vote at the first House of Representatives election following their appointment. A majority of votes against a particular justice results in his dismissal.

High courts are located in eight cities--Tokyo, Nagoya, Osaka, Hiroshima, Takamatsu, Fukuoka, Sendai and Sapporo. There are 50 district courts and 50 family courts--four each in Hokkaido and one each in the 46 other prefectural capitals.

Family courts handle civil cases involving domestic matters, such as divorce, inheritance and juvenile delinquency. (In Japan, anyone under 20 is considered a juvenile.)

Summary courts handle initial trials involving monetary claims of 300,000 yen or less, and minor offenses such as gambling or organizing a gambling establishment. Other cases, civil as well as criminal, are initially tried in district courts.

Trial procedures are similar to those in the U.S., but a larger number of suspended sentences are handed down-- around 60 percent of all short-term sentences.

CRESTS / MON (Moan)

Japan's famous Fujiwara clan, whose lords were the de facto rulers of Japan from the 8th to the 11th centuries, are credited with popularizing the practice of using emblems to identify high ranking courtiers. From there the custom spread to lords of clans and their retainers.

At first, the mon were used only on costumes worn for official occasions-- one in the center of the back, and one on each sleeve.

These first family crests were elegantly designed and featured such popular symbols as the crane, wisteria, peony and other flowers.

The Samurai warrior clans that came into power at the end of the 12th century used mon on their banners, flags, weapons and other paraphanalia, as well as their clothing. Only the immediate members of the Samurai lord's family were allowed to wear his crest, but their retainers were allowed to use a variation.

During the age of wars in the 15th century, when it was very important that the warring clans be able to identify their own soldiers, especially during combat, the crests of the clans were simplified and made easier to recognize.

Following the establishment of the Tokugawa Shogunate in 1603 and the beginning of a long period of peace, the mon became more refined and elegant, and it became the custom to enclose them in a circle.

Up to this time, only the privileged Samurai had their own crests, but from this period on, merchants and other successful common people began to create and wear their own family mon.

In 1868, when the Emperor was restored to power, the use of any form of chrysanthemum was reserved exclusively for the Imperial family. By this time, there were some 500 basic mon designs in Japan, with several thousand variations. See FAMILY CRESTS.

CRIME / HANZAI (Hahn-zie)

Japan is rightfully noted for being one of the safest countries in the world. The incidence of violent crimes against people--assault, armed robberies, rape, murder and so on--is one of the lowest, if not the lowest, in the world.

That is not to say that all Japanese are totally law-abiding. At present, some one and a half million criminal cases are reported to the police each year.

But the overwhelming majority of these cases concern nonviolent crimes-- thefts (approximately 86 percent), fraud and embezzlement (about seven percent). Well under four percent of these cases involve intimadation and/or assault, and vicious crimes (murder, armed robbery, and arson) account for only one half of one percent. See JUVENILE DELINQUENCY.

CULTURAL AFFAIRS / BUNKA (Boon-kah)

With its long history and powerful traditions, the Japanese are very cognizant of the importance of culture to the quality and continuity of a society. Since 1968 the country has had an Agency for Cultural Affairs (ACA).

The ACA is in charge of administrative affairs relating to the preservation and utilization of cultural properties, and the promotion and dissemination of culture, including matters concerning religions.

The country's national museums, the national museums of modern art, the National Museum of Western Art, the National Language Research Institute, the National Research Institutes of Cultural Properties, and the Japan Art Academy come under the jurisdiction of the Agency for Cultural Affairs.

One of the most laudable things the ACA does each year is to select outstanding men and women to receive the Order of Cultural Merit, and to designate Persons of Cultural Merit (who are regarded as national treasures). The Agency holds special ceremonies for the presentation of these awards on Culture Day (Bunka no Hi), November 3.

In addition, the Agency sponsors an annual Japan Art Festival and awards prizes in such fields as theater, broadcasting and the cinema, every fall.

The ACA regularly adds to its list of designated cultural properties, and in the early 1980s began a program to preserve rows of old homes, and portions of the country's old pedestrian highways. See TOKKAIDO.

Recommended reading: APPRECIATION OF JAPANESE CULTURE, by Donald Keene (Kodansha Int'l).

CULTURAL MEDALS

In 1937, the Japanese government instituted the practice of honoring men and women who made extraordinary contributions in the fields of arts and sciences by awarding them Cultural Medals.

Since 1973 recipients of the annual awards also receive annuities.

Only a few people are deemed worthy of the Cultural Medal each year, as the standards are very high.

Recommended reading: THE LIVING TREASURES OF JAPAN, by Barbara Adachi (Kodansha Int'l).

CUSTOMERS / O'KYAKU-SAN (Oh-K'yack-sahn)

The Japanese have long been famous for the extra special respect and care with which they treat customers. That this practice is an integral part of their culture is revealed by the fact that the word O'kyaku is used for both customer and guest.

The tradition of not distinguishing between guest and customer is bound up in their custom of personalizing every relationship, of putting everything in a human perspective, including business. This basic impulse is just the oppo-

site of what most Americans and many other Westerners are taught, particularly where business is concerned. We say that business is business, meaning personal concerns should not be allowed to play any role in business dealings.

Since these two concepts are diametrically opposed, it is not surprising that the Japanese and American way of doing business is quite different.

See JAPANESE MANNERS β ETHICS IN BUSINESS, by Boye De Mente (Phoenix Books/Publishers).

DAIMON TEMPLE FIRE FESTIVAL / DAIMON JI YAKI MATSURI (Die-moan Jee Yah-kee Mot-sue-ree)

A major annual spectactor event in Hakone, the Daimon Temple Fire Festival is held on August 16 on the slopes of Mt. Myojo. Torches arranged in the outline of a huge Chinese kanji character Dai, meaning Great, are set afire to mark O'Bon, the Festival of the Dead.

The purpose of the bonfires is to light the way for the spirits of the dead to return to Buddhist paradise after a few days of visiting with their living relatives.

The crossbar of the Dai ideogram is 108 meters in length, giving an idea of the overall dimensions of the figure.

DAIMYO (Dime-yoe)

During the long Tokugawa Shogunate, Japan was divided into fiefs presided over by feudal Lords known as Daimyo, literally Great Name. The Daimyo were divided into two groups based on their relationship with Ieyasu Tokugawa, the founder of Japan's last great feudal house. The first group were those who had been allied with Ieyasu before the Battle of Sekigahara in 1603. The second group was made up of those who had opposed him or were neutral.

There were also three ranks of Daimyo, depending on the revenues of their fiefs and whether or not they owned a castle. These three classes were Kokushu (Koe-kuu-shu)--provincial lords whose fiefs produced at lease 300,000 koku (koku=4.96 bushels) of rice, Joshu (Joe-shu) or castle-owning lords whose annual income was 100,000-300,000 koku of rice, and Ryoshu (Rio-shu), or lords without castles, with incomes from 10,000 to 100,000 koku of rice.

The Daimyo were responsible to the Tokugawa Shogunate for upholding the policies of the central government and were restricted in matters having to do with the security of the Shogunate, but within their domains their power was absolute. See SOGORO'S SACRIFICE. PROCESSIONS OF THE LORDS. DATE, MASAMUNE.

DANCING / ODORI (Oh-doe-ree)

There are three types of traditional Japanese dancing--one associated with kabuki (odori), one associated with noh (mai), and folk dancing.

Mai is described as a more static dance form, in keeping with noh. While odori is more dynamic. Both are very stylized forms of dancing generally seen today in the kabuki and noh theaters, among small groups of devotees, and among geisha entertainers.

Folk dancing is very common in Japan and is also stylized but can be very robust and lively. It is common at festivals (of which there are thousands around the country every year), and on television, etc.

There are a number of different schools of dancing in Japan today, each teaching some variation of mai, odori or folk dancing. Among the better known of these schools are Nishikawa, Hanayagi, Fujima and Wakayagi.

All forms of popular Western-style dancing are just as popular in Japan, and all have their heydays.

DATE, MASAMUNE (Mah-sah-muu-nay Dah-tay)

Masamune Date, one of the most important feudal lords in Japan during the wars that marked the end of the Ashikaga Shogunate (1336-1598) and the founding of the Tokugawa Shogunate in 1603, played a key role in the history of Sendai in northeastern Japan, and in the introduction of Christianity into the country.

Born in 1566, Date was a minor provincial Daimyo until he allied himself with Hideyoshi Toyotomi who became the military ruler of Japan in the 1580s, and then joined forces with Ieyasu Tokugawa who succeeded Hideyoshi and went on to establish the Tokugawa Shogunate.

When the second Tokugawa Shogun began persecuting Christians in 1613, Date had Franciscan Father F. Luis Sotelo released from prison and brought to his fief headquarters. There he had Sotelo tutor him on the outside world, and gave him permission to preach in the province.

Later Date sent one of his retainers, Tsunenaga Hasekura, and Sotelo on a mission to Spain and Rome. When Date died in 1636, his fief was the largest one north of Edo (Tokyo).

Cormorant fishing near Gifu. P. 61

A young student practicing her kanji. P. 48

DATING (See COURTING)

DEATH / SHI (She)
Cancer, cerebral hemorrhage and heart disease are the three major causes of death in Japan. Other significant causes of death are pneumonia, bronchitis, disasters and accidents. Cancer is the leading cause of death, accounting for around 23 percent of the total.

DECISION-MAKING
Generally speaking, the Japanese way of making decisions is to arrive at a concensus among all of those concerned. When two opposing groups cannot reach a decision, it is traditional to bring in an outside advisor or consultant to help resolve the issue.

The outsider then attempts to help the two sides work out a compromise to where both can agree. If a compromise cannot be reached, which is rare, then the advisor tries to persuade the minority view to accept the majority opinion. This outside consultant/advisor is often referred to as Ten-no Koe (Tane-no Koe-eh) or The Voice of Heaven.

The golden rule of any confrontation in Japan is compromise, since they regard rule by the major as tyranny of the majority.

Many of Japan's larger companies use a system called ringi seido (reen-ghee say-e-doe) in making management decisions. In this system, proposals for management action are written up, usually by lower management, and then circulated up and down the managerial ladder for comments and approval.

If the proposal is not approved but comes back with suggestions for changes, it may be revised and circulated again. If the reaction is conspicuously negative, it is usually dropped. To avoid having a proposal turned down, it is customary for it to be unofficially circulated first, to pretty much pin down what the response is going to be.

Recommended reading: JAPANESE MANNERS β ETHICS IN BUSINESS, by Boye De Mente (Phoenix Books/Publishers).

DEJIMA (Day-jee-mah)
In 1639 when Iemitsu, the third Tokugawa Shogun, decreed that all foreign missionaries would be expelled from Japan, he also expelled the Portuguese traders who had been the first to open the country up to trade with the Western world. This left only a few Dutch traders in the country, since the English and Spanish had already been squeezed out. See PORTUGUES, HISTORY, ADAMS.

At the same time, Shogun Iemitsu banned all travel to and from Japan, with the exception of the Dutch. But to minimize the influence the Dutch could have, he ordered that a small islet be constructed in Nagasaki harbor and that the Dutch trading company be confined to that one tiny isolated and guarded spot.

When the island was completed in 1641 it was named Dejima, which literally means Exit Island. Holland maintained a small company of traders on Dejima for the next 213 years, providing the only window Japan had to the outside world.

Diaries and notes left by some of these Dutch traders over the generations make fascinating reading--especially accounts of the few times when one or more of their party were allowed to go ashore on the mainland for some special purpose.

One Dutch doctor who was allowed to travel as far as the Shogunate headquarters in Edo expressed shock at the lascivious life-style he witnessed in the hundreds of inns and restaurants along the way.

DEMING, DR. W. EDWARDS
Dr. W. Edward Deming, an American who most Americans never heard of, is something of a legend in Japan. In 1950 he was invited by the Union of Japanese Scientists and Engineers (JUSE) to give a series of lectures in Japan on quality control.

The lectures were so popular that Dr. Deming was invited back to Japan several times. To commemorate Dr. Deming's contribution to quality control in Japan, and to further its development, the JUSE shortly thereafter established the Deming Prizes to be presented each year to the Japanese firms that demonstrated the most outstanding advances in quality control.

As Sumitomo Metals once announced in a large advertisment ran in Asian Wall Street Journal: The Most Famous Name in Japanese Quality Control is American.

Too bad somebody didn't invite Dr. Deming to give his lectures in the U.S. See QUALITY.

DEMOCRACY / MINSHUSHUGI (Meen-shu-shu-ghee)
The modern political concept of democracy was introduced into Japan, in part, in 1989 when the first constitution was promulgated. It was not until 1945, however, following the end of World War II, that representative government became a significant reality.

But the Japanese concept of democracy

differs from the typical Western concept. Very broadly speaking, the Western view of democracy is that it provides for rule by the majority. The Japanese, on the other hand, feel that it is undemocratic for a simple majority to rule over the minority.

Their approach, in principle at least, is that government by compromise, which takes into consideration all viewpoints, is the most democratic form of government.

To the average Japanese, the most important thing that democracy has brought to Japan is individual freedom and the protection of their personal rights.

DEPARTMENT STORES / DEPATO (Day-pah-toe)

The department store concept was invented in Japan during the feudal Tokugawa Shogun era, and they have remained leaders in the field ever since. To say that leading Japanese department stores are large and carry a wide range of merchandise does not do justice to them.

Besides being just very large department stores, the typical Japanese depato offers dozens of other services to customers, from restaurants and financial services to miniature zoos and recreational parks on their rooftops. All of them sponsor several different kinds of cultural and art shows each year that are free to the public.

One of the most extraordinary departments in a Japanese department store is its food floor (or floors), which are usually below ground level. Besides dry goods, fresh produce, seafood, breads, pastries and the like, the departments also offer various cooked and ready-to-eat items.

Any visitor to Japan who fails to visit a name department store is missing one of the experiences of a life-time. There are 20 leading department store chains in the country. In the order of their sales, they are:

Mitsukoshi, Daimaru, Takashimaya, Seibu, Matsuzakaya, Tokyu, Marui, Hankyu, Isetan, Sogo, Yokohama Takashimaya, Kintetsu, Odakyu, Marui Imai, Tenmaya, Hanshin, Tobu, Matsuya, Keio and Meitetsu Hyakkaten.

The main categories of merchandise sold in depato are clothing, foodstuffs, household utensils, sundries, personal effects, and services.

Several Japanese department stores have overseas branches. Mitsukoshi, one of the most active, operates branches in Paris, Rome, London, Dusseldorf, Frankfurt, New York, Honolulu, Singapore and Hong Kong.

DESCENDING FROM HEAVEN / AMA KUDARI (Ah-mah Kuu-dah-ree)

Ama Kudari refers to the well-established practice of high-ranking bureaucrats in Japan's government ministries joining major companies (as high-ranking executives) after they step down from their lofty positions--retire from government service.

Given the nature of the personal relationships and obligations that develop between ministry officials and those they groom to succeed themselves, such life-long ties became a very valuable asset to commercial firms.

DESIGNER CLOTHING

On the whole, the Japanese are probably more interested in what they wear, and more concerned about their appearance, than any other people. The reason for this is that during the country's very long feudal period, wearing apparel was closely related to one's social class and occupation.

During the last great Shogunate dynasty (1603-1868), the Shogunate went to the extreme of designating what type of clothing each class should wear--even specifying by law when people would change from summer to winter attire and back again in the spring (regardless of how hot or cold it might be on the date specified).

Wearing the right apparel therefore went beyond just being important. It was vital to the personal security of the individual, and in extreme causes was a matter of life and death. Any commoner, for example, who might have been tempted to dress up as a Samurai, put his life and the security of his family in jeopardy.

This concern for appearance has carried over into modern times, and helps make the Japanese not only especially conscious of styles but of name-brands as well.

All these factors combined have resulted in the developement of a thriving apparel industry made up of a large number of designers, thousands of boutiques that specialize in designer clothing, and a market for designer apparel that is second to none.

In the late 1950s when I was editor of The IMPORTER Magazine in Tokyo (at that time the leading English-laguange journal covering Japanese-made consumer products for export), I began predicting that within a decade Japanese fashion designers would be on a par with those in Paris, Rome and New York.

I was about one decade early, but I firmly believe that the cultural traditions of Japanese fashion designers give them a significant advantage that will eventually take them to the top of the world of fashion.

DESSERTS / DEZATO (Day-zah-toe)

Sugar was not known in Japan until the 16th century, and prior to this period the only desserts available were fruits and other things that were naturally sweet. With the introduction of sugar, cakes and buns stuffed with sweetened bean paste became popular, and by the early years of the 18th century, close to 400 different varieties of cakes and confections were being made.

Today there are thousands of different confections available in Japan, including dozens of varieties of cakes and pastries that are baked in single-serving sizes and sold in bakeries and coffee shops in virtually every neighborhood.

Traditional Japanese meals are generally followed by a fruit in season instead of a prepared dessert--or nothing sweet at all.

Ice-creams, sherberts and yogurts are big sellers in Japan as snack items.

DICTIONARIES / JIBIKI (Jee-bee-kee)

Language dictionaries are very important in the study of Japanese, and there are some very good ones available-- including ones in which the Japanese is in Roman letters (Roma-ji) for those who cannot read the kanji (kahn-jee) ideogram characters.

One of the best series is published by the Sanseido Press in Tokyo. For English-speaking students of the language, I recommend SANSEIDO'S NEW CONCISE ENGLISH-JAPANESE DICTIONARY and the Japanese-English edition of the same series.

My favorite over the years has been the ENGLISH-JAPANESE CONVERSATION DICTIONARY, by Mr. and Mrs. O. Vaccari, which gives sample sentences with each word entry. See VACCARI, ORESTE.

DIET BUILDING / KOKKAI GIJIDO (Koke-kie Ghee-jee-doe-my)

The National Diet Building of Japan is on a hill near the Imperial Palace, in the Nagato-cho area of Tokyo, overlooking Japan's other primary government buildings (clustered around it) and the downtown area only a short distance away.

The building was completed in 1936 after 17 years of frequently interrupted construction. It has one basement and three floors above ground, plus a central tower that is nine stories high. There are 449 rooms in the central block of the Diet Building.

The Kokkai Gijido is built of white granite and marble, with ornately carved fine woods used in the interior.

When facing the building, the left wing is the House of Representatives, and the right wing is the House of Councillors. The central hall is used only when the Emperor visits the Diet on the day the newly elected legislators report for their first session. This is the only occasion when the central gate is opened.

There is a special chamber on the third floor, called the Gokyusho (Goque-show), or Place of Rest, that is reserved for the exclusive use of the Emperor and his family. It is a magnificent room, with lacquered cedar and pure gold fittings.

In the spring and summer tourist seasons, visitors line up in the hallway outside the chamber to peer through a glass panel at the redolent decorations on the inside.

The Diet Building is located in the Nagato-cho area of Kasumigaseki district. The Prime Minister's official residence, a low yellowish brick building, is behind the Diet Building. Other buildings in the immediate area are the Diet members' office buildings, the Diet Press Club, Diet Library, headquarters of the Liberal Democratic Party and the Japan Socialist Party, and the official residences of the speaker of the House of Representative and the president of the House of Councillors.

The term Nagata-cho is often used to mean the government or the prime minister, or government policies.

For security reasons, members of the Diet wear special lapel pins to identify themselves. It became mandatory for members of the House of Representatives to wear pins in 1903. The same law was applied to House of Councillor members in 1953.

The pins for the two Houses differ, and have been changed several times. Today both pins depict an 11-petaled chrysanthemum. The Lower House with a maroon border and the Upper House with a deep blue border.

Numerous other government officials

who are in and out of the Diet Building regularly also wear pins to identify themselves.

DINING OUT

There are probably more restaurants in Japan than in any other country in the world. In fact, there are more restaurants in Tokyo alone than in most countries. This, of course, indicates that the Japanese dine out a great deal, which they do.

Dining out in Japan is an old custom that apparently derived from several factors--houses constructed of wood, with paper interiors, the use of charcoal braziers for cooking, making it impractical to cook very much or very many complicated dishes, and also dangerous to cook inside the house because of smoke and the threat of fire.

Not being able to cook more than basic dishes at home, and yet being lovers of food in both variety and volume, the appearance of a large number of restaurants was a natural development.

Today, on a nationwide basis, the Japanese spend approximately 15 percent of their food budget in restaurants. Families in which the head of the household is 24 years old or under, spend some 24 percent of their food budget dining out. Those between 25 and 29 spend close to 16 percent of their food money in restaurants, and those between 30 and 49 spend between 14 and 15 percent.

DIPLOMATIC HISTORY
1853-1981

1853, JULY 8....America's Commodore Matthew C. Perry and his fleet of Black Ships arrived at Uraga--the opening wedge in convincing Japan to reopen its doors to the outside world.

1854, MARCH 31...The first Japan-U.S. treaty of friendship signed.

1855, FEB. 7....Japan-Russia treaty signed at Shimoda, setting the northern boundary between the two countries at midway between the Kurile islands of Etorofu and Urup.

1875, MAY 7....Japan-Russia treaty signed, giving Sakhalin to Russia and the Kurile Islands to Japan.

1894, JULY 25....Beginning of the Sino-Japanese war.

1895, APRIL 17....Sino-Japanese peace treaty signed at Shimono-seki.

1902, JAN. 30....Anglo-Japanese Alliance signed.

1904, FEB. 10....Russo-Japanese War begins.

1905, SEP. 5....Russo-Japanese Peace Treaty signed at Portsmouth in the U.S., with U.S. acting as mediator.

1910, AUG. 22....Japan annexes Korea.

1914, JUL. 28....World War I begins (Germany declares war on Russia August 1).

1914, AUG. 23....Japan enters WW1 on the side of the Allies.

1915, JAN. 18....Japan issues 21 Demands to China.

1919, JUN. 28....Treaty of Versailles and League of Nations Covenant signed.

1920, JAN. 10....Japan joins the League of Nations.

1922. FEB. 6....Five-Power Naval Disarmament Treaty signed in Washington, D.C., setting parity at U.S. 5, Britain 5, Japan 3.

1925, JAN. 20....Japan-USSR Treaty signed, restoring diplomatic relations.

1931, SEP. 18....Manchurian Incident occurs, marking the start of Japan's expansion into China.

1932, MAR. 1....Japan takes over Manchuria and establishes the state of Manchukuo.

1933, MAR. 27....Japan withdraws from the League of Nations.

1934, DEC. 29....Japan cancels Washington naval treaty.

1936, NOV. 25....Japan signs Anti-Comintern Pact with Germany.

1937, JUL. 7....Clash at Marco Polo

Bridge between Japanese and Chinese troops marks the beginning of full-scale war between Japan and China.

1940, SEP. 27....Japan, Germany and Italy sign the Tripartite Pact.

1941, APR. 13....Japan and USSR sign a neutrality agreement.

1941, DEC. 8....Japan attacks Pearl Harbor, and declares war on the U.S.

1945, AUG. 6....U.S. drops atom bomb on the city of Hiroshima.

1945, AUG. 8....Russia declares war on Japan.

1945, AUG. 9....U.S. drops atom bomb on the city of Nagasaki.

1945, AUG. 14...Japan surrenders unconditionally.

1945, AUG. 15....Emperor Hirohito makes his first radio broadcast to the nation, announcing that Japan has surrendered to the Allied Powers.

1945, SEP. 2....Japan signs the documents of surrender aboard the U.S. battleship Missouri in Tokyo Bay.

1951, SEP. 8....Peace treaty between Japan and the Allies, and a Japan-U.S. Security Treaty is signed in San Francisco.

1952, APR. 28....San Francisco peace treaty goes into effect. Japan-Taiwan peace treaty signed.

1954, NOV. 5....Japan-Burma peace treaty and other agreements signed.

1955, SEP. 10....Japan joins General Agreement on Tariffs and Trade (GATT).

1956, MAY 9....Japan-Philippines reparations agreement signed.

1956, OCT. 19....Diplomatic relations restored with Russia.

1956, DEC. 18....Japan admitted to the United Nations.

1960, JAN 19....New Japan-U.S. security signed in Washington goes into effect on June 23.

1963, AUG. 14....Japan signs partial neuclear test ban treaty.

1964, APR. 1....Japan accepts International Monetary Fund (IMF) Article 8, regarding currency regulations.

1964, APR. 28....Japan joins the Organization for Economic Cooperation and Development (OECD).

1965, JUN. 22....Japan establishes diplomatic relations with the Republic of Korea, signs other agreements.

1966, APR. 6....First Southeast Asia Development Ministerial Conference opens in Tokyo.

1968, APR. 5....Agreement with U.S. for the return of the Ogasawara Islands to Japan, effective June 26.

1969, NOV. 21....Japan signs joint statement with the U.S. on return of Okinawa to Japanese soverignty.

1970, JUN. 22....Japan announces the automatic renewal of the Japan-U.S. Security Treaty.

1971, JUN. 17....Treaty signed with the U.S. for the return of Okinawa, effective May 15, 1972.

1971, AUG. 27....Japan floats the yen, following August 15 dollar defense measures announced by the U.S.

1971, OCT. 15....Japan-U.S. textile negotations concluded.

1972, SEP. 29....Japan, China renew diplomatic ties.

1973, OCT.20....Oil crisis leads Cabinet to change Middle East policy, demand that Isreal withdraw troops from occupied territories.

1974, NOV. 18....U.S. President Gerald Ford makes the first visit to Japan by an incumbent president.

1975, JAN. 16....USSR proposes good-neighbor, cooperation treaty.

1975, SEP. 30-OCT. 14....Emperor Hirohito pays state visit to the U.S.

1975, NOV. 15....Prime Minister Takeo Miki attends the first summit conference of advanced industrial nations at Rambouillet, near Paris.

1976, JUN. 8....Japan ratifies the Nuclear Non-Proliferation Treaty.

1976, JUN. 16....Japan-Australia treaty of friendship and cooperation signed.

1976, JUN. 27....Prime Minister Miki attends the second summit conference of advanced industrial nations, in San Juan, Puerto Rico.

1976, SEP. 6....Soviet MiG-25 plane lands at Hakodate Airport in Hokkaido, and the pilot defects.

1977, MAY 7....Prime Minister Takeo Fukuda attends the third summit conference of advanced industrial nations, in London.

1977, MAY 27....Japan-USSR provisional fishery treaty signed subsequent to Soviet declaration of a 200-mile economic zone.

1977, JUL. 1....Japan begins enforcing 12-mile territorial waters and 200-mile economic zone.

1977, AUG. 6....Prime Minister Fukuda announces a new Southeast Asian policy.

1978, JUN. 22....Instruments of ratification of the Japan-Republic of Korea continental shelf agreement exchanged.

1978, JUL 16....Prime Minister attends the fourth summit of advanced industrial nations, in Bonn.

1978, AUG. 12...Japan-China Treaty of Peace and Friendship signed in Beijing.

1979, MAY 9....Prime Minister Masayoshi Ohira attends the Fifth United Nations Conference on Trade and Development, in Manila.

1979, JUN. 28....The 5th summit of advanced industrial nations is held in Tokyo.

1979, OCT. 2....Foreign Affairs Vice Minister Masuo Takashima lodges a protest with the Soviet Ambassador to Japan over Soviet military build-up on Kunashiri and Etorofu, and its new deployment of military forces on Shikotan.

1980, FEB. 1....Japan protests the Soviet invasion of Afghanistan, and boycotts the Moscow Olympic Games in July-August.

1980, FEB. 1....Foreign Minister Saburo Okita represents Japan at the 6th summit conference of advanced industrial nations in Venice, following the death of Prime Minister Masayoshi Ohira.

1981, JAN. 8-20....Prime Minister Zenko Suzuki visits the five member countries of the Association of Southeast Asian Countries.

1981, MAY 7....Prime Minister Suzuki meets U.S. President Ronald Reagan in Washington. Foreign Minister Masayoshi Ito resigns after disagreement with Suzuki over the joint communique issued after the summit meeting.

1981, JUN. 9-21....Prime Minister Suzuki visits West Germany, France, Britain, Italy, Belgium and the Netherlands.

1981, JUL. 20-21....Prime Minister Suzuki attends the 7th summit of advanced industrial nations, in Ottawa.

1981, OCT. 12....Prime Minister Suzuki meets with PLO leader Yasser Arafat in Tokyo.

1981, OCT. 21-23....Prime Minister Suzuki attends the International Meeting on Coorporation and Development--the so-called North-South Summit--at Cancun, Mexico.

***

DISNEYLAND OF TOKYO

Japan's own Disneyland, also known as the Magic Kingdom, opened in April 1983 in the town of Urayasu on Chiba Peninsula, about half an hour from downtown Tokyo.

The Japanese Disneyland, owned and operated by Oriental Land Company (which is a subsidiary of Mitsui Real Estate Development Company and the Keisei Railway Electric Company) was the first Disneyland park to be built outside the U.S.

With 115 acres, the Tokyo Disneyland is slightly larger than the original California and Florida versions, but the park is a faithful reproduction of the many attractions of the American originals.

Because it rains a lot in the area, however, many of the Magic Kingdom attractions are covered. And because the winters are colder, the jungle is provided with heaters.

The entrance to the park is Main Street, modeled after old Americana. It is covered with a skylight roof, and is lined with shops and restaurants. The street leads to a plaza in front of

Cinderella's Castle, from which Tomor-rowland, Adventureland, Westernland and Fantasyland are accessible via bridges.

The park has the same kind of live and animated entertainment that proved so successful in California and Florida. Many of the familiar characters and cartoon figures are played by young foreign boys and girls, hired locally for the parts.

The Japanese Disneyland cost over 650 million dollars to build--all of it financed by the Japanese partners, who bought the rights to use the name and the technology from Disneyland Product-ions of the U.S.

Among the special features and ser-vices of Tokyo Disneyland are a Lost Children Center, Baby Center, Coin Lock-er, Pet Club, Picnic Rest Area and guided tours. There are 95 public tele-phones.

The park has a staff of 2,000 full-time employees and some 4,500 part-time workers, including 300 professional act-ors, musicians and dancers. Several dozen foreigners, mostly Americans work at the park. See TOKYO DISNEYLAND.

DISTRICTS OF JAPAN

Japan is divided into eight districts according to geographical location, to-popgraphy and historical precedent. These regions (from the north) are Hok-kaido, Tohoku, Kanto, Chubu, Kinki, Chugoku, Shikoku and Kyushu. These divi-sions are used in reference to many things, from climate and industrial development to population and regional dialects.

HOKKAIDO (Hoke-kie-doe)--Japan's nor-thernmost main island, Hokkaido makes up 22.1 percent of the country's land area but has less than five percent of the population. The island has several spec-tacular mountain ranges and high peaks and two large plains. Its distance from the center of Japan's cultural and eco-nomic activity over the centuries, plus the rigorous climate, kept in isolated and undeveloped until the 1960s and 70s.

Dry-field farming and dairy farming are major industries in Hokkaido, as are fishing, pulp, paper, beer, sake, sugar and cement.

TOHOKU (Toe-hoe-kuu)--On the northern end of Honshu, the Tohoku region in-cludes six of Japan's 47 prefectures: Aomori, Akita, Iwate, Yamagata, Miyagi and Fukushima.

Another area that has been in the backwash of economic development, the Tohoku region has 17.7 percent of Ja-pan's land, and just over eight percent of the population. It is broken up by three mountain ranges that run parallel north and south, with plains and basins in between.

The Kurile Current coming down from the north on the Pacific side of Tohoku keeps it cool in summer and cold in winter. The Japan Sea side is warmed by the Tsushima Current coming up from the south. Both sides have heavy winter snowfalls, particularly in the moun-tains.

Tohoku produces some 25 percent of Japan's rice, and 70 percent of its apples. Fishing is also important, as the meeting of warm and cold currents of the Pacific, plus many coastal bays, give the region rich fishing grounds.

Large-scale industry is limited in Tohoku, but the region is noted for its handicrafts, such as ironware and koke-shi dolls, along with dairy farming and horse-raising.

Tohoku was once a stronghold of the Ainu (Aye-nuu), Japan's indigenous race of Caucasoid people, many of whose descendants--mostly mixed with Japan-ese--still live in the region.

The Tohoku area is famous for its beautiful women (Tohoku Bijin), and for the Texas-type attitudes and behavior of its horse-loving men.

KANTO (Kahn-toe)--The primary cultu-ral and economic hub of Japan, the Kanto region includes the prefectures of Iba-raki, Tochigi, Gunma, Saitama, Chiba, Kanagawa and Tokyo. While it has only 8.6 percent of the land area, it has approximately 30 percent of the popula-tion.

The northwestern portion of Kanto is characterized by numerous mountain ran-ges. The Kanto Plain, Japan's largest plain, makes up most of the southeastern portion of the region.

Farming is a major activity in the Kanto region, as is fishing (one-fifth of the nation's total). Choshi, in Chiba Prefecture, is famous as a deepsea fish-ing port.

The Kanto region is also Japan's largest industrial center. With the exception of textiles, all of Japan's major industries are represented in the sprawl that incorporates and surrounds Tokyo, Tokyo Bay, Yokohama and Chiba Prefecture.

CHUBU (Chuu-buu)--The historical crossroads between Kyoto and Tokyo, Chubu is made up of nine prefectures: Shizuoka, Yamanashi, Nagano, Niigata, Toyama, Ishikawa, Fukui, Gifu and Aichi. It has 17.7 percent of the land area, and approximately 17 percent of the population--the only region where these two figures are well matched.

Because it sprawls across the waist of Honshu from east to west, Chubu is subdivided into the Tokai district on the Pacific side and the Hokuriku district on the Japan Sea side. The two districts are separated by central highlands with several peaks above 3,000 meters. The Tokai area owes much of its viability to the Nobi Plain.

The Japan Sea side of Chubu experiences heavy winter snowfalls, as do the central mountains. The eastern or Tokai area climate, influenced by the warmer waters of the Pacific, has mild winters.

Farming, primarily rice, is a major industry on the west side of Chubu. Shizuoka Prefecture is famous for mandarin oranges and tea, and Yamanashi is noted for its grape industry. Lumbering is big in the central highlands (one of the forests in this area, Kiso, is regarded as being one of the three most beautiful forests in Japan.

Shizuoka, on the eastern coast, is a major deepsea fishing port, and its Hamana Lagoon is famous for its artificial breeding of eels.

Nagoya is the largest city in Chubu, and is the hub of a major industrial area (called Chukyo for economic, marketing and other purposes), where heavy industries and textile spinning are prominent. There is a huge oil-refinery complex in nearby Yokkaichi. Hamamatsu is noted for its output of musical instruments (Yamaha, etc.). Toyota is an automobile manufacturing center. Fuji is big in paper, and Suwa is a center for the production of precision machinery.

KINKI (Keen-kee)--The great cities of Kyoto, Osaka and Kobe are in the Kinki region, which is the cradle of Japanese civilization. It consists of the prefectures of Mie, Shiga, Kyoto, Nara, Osaka, Wakayama and Hyogo. Encompassing 8.7 percent of Japan's land area, it has over 18 percent of the population.

The northern portions of Kinki are mostly mountainous. The central portion has numerous hills and some mountains, but also the large Osaka Plain and numerous small basins. Lake Biwa, the country's largest lake is in Kinki. See LAKES.

The weather in Kinki is similar to that in the rest of Honshu--lots of winter snow in the north and on the west side, lighter snows in the lower central regions, and milder winters along the Pacific coast.

Fruit and vegetable farming are important industries in Kinki. The Uji district of Kyoto is famous for its tea. Wakayama is noted for its oranges. Fishing is also important, with ports on both the east and west coasts, as well as in Lake Biwa.

The combined areas of Osaka and Kobe (called Hanshin), are Japan's second largest industrial area, with both heavy and light industries, including textiles, highly developed.

CHUGOKU (Chuu-go-kuu)--With 8.4 percent of Japan's land space and only a little over 6 percent of its population, Chugoku is lightly populated when compared with Kinki, Chubu and Kanto, primarily because there are few plains and basins in the area.

The west side of Chugoku fronts on the Inland Sea (Seto Naikai), which separates Honshu, Shikoku and Kyushu, and has been a traditional waterway between Kyushu and central Japan.

The massive Chugoku Mountain Range runs east-west through this district, again creating two vastly different climatic regions. The Japan Sea side (called San'in) has very few basins or plains of any significant size, and is noted for its huge sand dunes. The east or Inland Sea side (called san'yo) is also characterized by hilly and broken terrain that prevents large-scale farming.

While the San'in area has the usual heavy wintertime snows, the Inland Sea district has mild winters with many sunny days.

Western Chugoku, which has numerous terraced fields and irrigation ponds, is popular for its pears, peaches and rice. Okayama Prefecture is especially noted for its peaches.

Fishing is still an important industry on both of Chugoku's coasts, but the volume of fish caught in the Inland Sea has dwindled with the increase in pollution from coastal industrial plants and huge land reclamation projects.

The major industries strung out along the Inland Sea coast include petrochemicals, textile spinning, and cement. The area is also noted for its cottage industries, producing traditional as well as contemporary items.

SHIKOKU (She-koe-kuu)--The smallest of Japan's four major islands, Shikoku was out of the mainstream of economic development in Japan until the 1960s and 70s. With five percent of the nation's land, Shikoku has less than four percent of the population, which puts it well below the average in population density.

Central Shikoku is mountainous, and there are small plains scattered along the coastlines. The mountains and the plains provide a natural division of the island into four sections, which from early times developed culturally, politically and economically independent of each other. The island was under the control of four feudal lords. Each clan had its own castle, around which a town and then a city developed.

Northern Skikoku has a mild climate that is typical of the Inland Sea area. The southern portion of the island, exposed to the Pacific Ocean, has the typical oceanic climate of this region-- muggy hot summers, mild winters, spring rains and fall typhoons.

Shikoku's southern plains, once a popular rice-growing area, are now primarily devoted to providing vegetables for the population centers of Osaka, Kobe and Kyoto. A number of fishing fleets are stationed in Shikoku, some of them concentrating on bonito in the nearby Japan Current. Others are primarily tuna fleets that fish in distant waters.

The island's major industrial activity includes petrochemical plants along the Inland Sea, and paper and pulp plants in the southern area where forests and electrical power are plentiful.

KYUSHU (Que-shuu)--This is the south-westernmost of Japan's four main islands, and during much of the early history of the country was the gateway between Japan and the Asian mainland. The port of Fukuoka is only some 120 miles from Korea's port city of Pusan.

Kyushu is about half the size of Hokkaido, with 11.8 percent of the total land area, but has over 12 percent of the country's population.

Like all the other islands, Kyushu is very mountainous (Mt. Aso, a huge volcanic cone with an impressive crater, is its most famous mountain), but is blessed with a number of fairly large plains, with Tsukushi (T'sue-kuu-shee) and Kumamoto (Kuu-mah-moe-toe) being the largest.

Kyushu is hot in the summer (the southern portion of the island is far enough south to be semi-tropical), and has very mild winters. Rainfall is abundant, and typhoons (which bring even more rain) are an annual fall event.

The island is famous for its sweet potatoes and other vegetables, oranges, wheat, rice, tobacco and dairy farming. Fishing is a major industry in Kyushu, with Nagasaki noted as a center for trawling operations.

Industry in Kyushu is headed by coal-mining, the manufacture of iron and steel, and shipbuilding. Cottage industries of many kinds have also been highly developed since the early centuries.

DIVORCE / RIKON (Ree-kone)

Still low by international standards, Japan's divorce rate has been climbing steadily since 1963. It is now approximately 1.32 percent of all marriages, as compared to 0.73 percent in 1963.

Most divorces in Japan occur during the first few years of marriage, when the women are in their mid to late 20s, and the men are in their early to mid-30s.

In early feudal days, women did not have the right of divorce, and were totally subject to their husbands' wills. As a result, it eventually became accepted that if a wife could escape from her home and make her way to special temples, she would be given sanctuary.

A man could divorce a wife, however, simply by having her name removed from his family register at the local district office.

In Japan today, divorces are handled by special family courts, and generally do not involve lawyers or any substantial expense.

DOLLS / NINGYO (Neen-g'yoe)

Dolls have played an important role in Japanese life since long before any known contacts with Korea or China. As in China, however, clay figurines, called haniwa (hah-nee-wah) have been unearthed from ancient burial mounds.

Throughout the history of Japan, clay and wooden dolls have been an integral part of religious observances, festivals, the theater and home-life.

Warrior dolls are a central theme during Boy's Day. Hina (he-nah) or Imperial Court dolls are traditinally displayed during Girl's Day.

So-called hakata (hah-kah-tah) dolls, made of fired clay and then painted, from the Hakata area of Fukuoka Prefecture in Kyushu, are sold throughout Japan as traditional handicraft items, and are known world-wide by doll lovers and

Dancing in the streets of Tokushima. P.33

Mickey Mouse-San and friends. P. 71 & 308

collectors.

The dolls are made in the form of kabuki actors, beautiful women from around the world, fishermen, old men and women, etc. and are noted for their finely detailed realism.

The manufacturer of female wooden dolls called kokeshi (koe-kay-she) has been a traditional winter industry in northeast Japan for centuries. The kokeshi have cylindrical bodies and round heads turned out on lathes. Two or three colors are used to draw girls' faces on the dolls and decorate them with various abstract and pictorial designs.

Recommended reading: HANIWA: Arts of Japan 8, by Fujio Miki (Weatherhill).

DRIVER'S LICENSE / JIDOSHA-UNTEN MENJO (Jee-doe-shah-uun-tane Mane-joe)

For a Japanese, getting a driver's license is an expensive and formidable undertaking. The driving test is strict, and the written test includes not only the rules and regulations of driving, it is also necessary for applicants to have a rather extensive knowledge of the engine and other mechanics of cars and how to repair them.

Before taking the tests for a license, most Japanese attend special--and expensive--driving schools. It is common for both male and female applicants to fail the test from one to three or four times before they are able to achieve a passing score.

Foreigners in Japan who do not have an International Driver's License or a regular driver's license issued in their own country, must take the same test. With a regular license all the foreign visitor or resident has to do is fill out the various forms and show the valid foreign license.

It is advisable for the foreign applicant to have an official translation of the foreign license if the application is being made in any city other than Tokyo. Such translations are available from the Japan Automobile Federation.

The booklet to study before approaching the license office is Rules of the Road, published by the auto federation and available at license offices.

Another important point about driving in Japan: you must present proof that you have an off-street parking place for a car before you can be issued license plates.

DRIVING IN JAPAN

In Japan, driving is on the left side of the road, and requires considerably

more expertise than is generally seen in the U.S. Most streets in Japan are narrow and apt to contain numerous obstacles (besides pedestrians), since they were originally designed as foot-paths and walking lanes, and do not have sidewalks.

Despite rigid requirements for obtaining a driver's license, once the license is obtained, driving is more of a free-for-all insofar as turning corners, switching lanes and pulling out of parking areas and alleys. It is up to the individual driver to avoid collisions, regardless of what the other driver may do.

Another factor is the number of new, inexperienced drivers on the roads at any one time (not to mention trucks, bicycles and scooters, etc.). The authorities recognize this problem by requiring all drivers with less than a year's experience to identify their vehicles with a green and yellow decal.

Japan uses the uniform International Traffic Signs on its roads and highways, and they are outstanding, since their meaning is generally clear regardless of the language. But most other road and highway signs are in Japanese only, and unless you can read them or really know your way around, driving from one place to another can be a matter of luck.

Recommended: READING YOUR WAY AROUND JAPAN--A Sign for Every Occasion, by Boye De Mente (Phoenix Books/Publishers).

DRUG ABUSE / MAYAKU JOSHU (May-yah-kuu Joe-shuu)

Japan's laws against the manufacture, import, possession, sale and use of unprescribed drugs are strict and harshly enforced. Despite this, drug abuse has been increasing in recent years. Narcotics arrests have been going up as much nine percent a year, exceeding 20,000 cases in 1982.

DYING IN JAPAN

Dying anywhere is often a drag, but dying when you are overseas can cause special problems if you are not familiar with local laws. In Japan, it is against the law to move a dead body for any reason (unless a doctor is present) until it has been examined by a medical examiner and a release issued.

If a doctor is not present, the first step is to call a doctor, then the police, then your embassy.

Another point to keep in mind: an ambulance may not be used to transport a body. It has to be an authorized undertaker's vehicle.

In the event of a death of an American in Japan, someone should call 583-7151 and asked for the American Citizen Services Branch of the Consular Section.

EARTHQUAKES / JISHIN (Jee-sheen)

Earthquakes are so common in Japan that hardly a day goes by without one occurring somewhere in the islands. Fortunately, most of these quakes are very minor and detectable only by a seismograph. But every year there are usually a few that are strong enough to make themselves known to everyone in the area.

Japan lies on top of one of the earth's largest and most active faults, which accounts for its earthquakes and its large number of active and dormant volcanoes.

Since the beginning of recorded history, Japan has been struck by many earthquakes that left death and destruction in their wake, primarily from fires and tidal waves that followed the quakes.

The fact that homes and other buildings in Japan were traditionally built very close together and made of wood and paper, and that open fires were used for cooking, heating and lighting, made them especially susceptible to fires caused by earthquakes.

The most destructive earthquake of modern times struck the Tokyo and Yokohama areas just before noon on September 1st, 1923. The force of the quake caved in and topple several hundred thousand homes and buildings, but it was the fires that followed that caused the most damage.

The heat of the fires was so fierce that it caused freak tornado-like winds that fanned the fires even more. One large group of people who took refuge in a shallow lake in the Asakusa area of Tokyo died when these winds and the fires sucked all the oxygen out of the air around them.

Over 100,000 people died in the conflagrations that followed this great quake. See IMPERIAL HOTEL, NEWSPAPERS.

EASTERN JAPAN

References to Eastern and Western Japan are often confusing to foreigners who visulize the Japanese islands as being in a more or less straight north-south line, and think of Kyoto, Osaka and other major cities of western Honshu as being south of Tokyo.

The island chain actually is curved like a crescent. The curve in Honshu, the longest and largest of the islands, is especially pronounced--going from latitude 142 to 131--with the result that the lower half of the island angles almost due west from the Tokyo area.

When viewed from Kyoto, Japan's Imperial capital for over a thousand years, Tokyo and all the prefectures north of it are in the east--thus the name Tokyo (Eastern Capital).

EAST MAGAZINE

Founded in 1963, THE EAST magazine is intended for people interested in both historical and contemporary Japan. Its articles cover history, traditional culture, geography, industry, society, celebrities and the arts.

It often runs excerpts from classical Japanese literature, and pieces on the Japanese language--generally all from a sociological point of view. Well-done and recommended. Available in the U.S. form The East, P.O. Box 2640, Grand Central Station, New York, NY, 10164. Or directly from The East Publications, 3-19-7 Minami-Azabu, Minato-ku, Tokyo 106, Japan.

EATING / MESHIAGARU (May-she-ah-gah-rue)

Over the centuries, eating in Japan became imbued with religious and aesthetic practices, and was stylized to a meticulous degree. Great significance was attached to the appearance and arrangement of food, as well as to the utensils used.

Beauty and harmony were the hallmarks of a well-prepared and served meal, and it was important to observe a carefully prescribed dining etiquette. Learning how to eat properly was therefore an important part of the education of every Japanese child.

Eating etiquette is considerably less demanding in modern-day Japan, but it is still a distinctive feature of Japanese life, and in formal situations, the traditional ways are still followed. The biggest difficulty foreigners have in adapting to the Japanese way of eating is in manipulating chopsticks and sitting on the floor for long periods of time.

The only solution for this challenge is practice.

When eating a Japanese style meal in a Japanese setting it is better all around for you to at least try to follow Japanese etiquette and custom in sitting, handling your chopsticks and the various small saucers and bowls.

It is customary to pick up bowls and small dishes and bring them up near and under the mouth when eating, especially in the case of small soup or noodle bowls and rice bowls, to help avoid spilling or dropping anything. Both rice and small bowls are frequently brought right up to the mouth--with the soup sipped and the rice more or less shoveled into your mouth.

Before beginning to eat, whether a snack or full meal, it is important to say, Itadakimasu (Ee-tah-dah-kee-mahss), which is a form of thanks and appreciation for the food you are about to eat. When you finish eating with someone else who is the host, it is equally important to say, Gochisosama (Go-chee-so-sah-mah), the institutionalized expression for thanking them for feeding or treating you.

ECONOMIC INFORMATION CENTER / KEIZAI KOHO CENTER (Kay-e-zie Koe-hoe)

Established in 1978 by the Japan Federation of Economic Organizations, the country's most powerful and prestigious business group, the Economic Information Center is charged with developing and disseminating information about Japan's ecomony.

In 1982 the KKC undertook a new program--a direct-mail promotional campaign, aimed at the U.S. and Europe, to help explain the position and trade policies of Japan's major corporations.

The KKC's mailing list, consisting of high-level businessmen, academics and political leaders, originally was made up of some 10,000 names. In 1983 an additional 2,000 leaders in Southeast Asia were added to the list. See OTHER SOURCES for KKC's address.

ECONOMIC PROGRESS AFTER 1868

Following the resignation of the last Tokugawa Shogun and restoration of Imperial power in 1868, Japan began a systematic program to totally remake the industrial base of the country.

The first industrialization project launched by the new Meiji government was the export of raw silk and use of the foreign currency earned to start a small-scale cotton-spinning and weaving industry. This pattern of development was quickly expanded to include a wide range of light and heavy industries--including shipbuilding and military arms. The government subsidized many of these industries, and later turned them over to private interests, contributing to the appearance and growth of huge industrial conglomerates known as Zaiba-tsu (Zie-bot-sue). See ZAIBATSU.

Annual growth was only about three percent until the advent of World War I. At a safe distance from the main action of the war, Japanese industry became a large-scale supplier to the warring nations. Its machinery industry in particular made great progress.

The economic benefits of WWI encouraged a strong expansionist element in Japan's armed forces, however, eventually resulting in its invasion of China, Southeast Asia, the South Pacific, and finally an attack on Pearl Harbor in 1941--which ended in 1945 with utter defeat for the Japanese empire.

With its foreign colonies gone, its home economic base virtually wiped out by massive bombing raids, and over six million demobilized soldiers and civilians suddenly returned to a starving Japan in 1945, the country was at the lowest point ever in its long history.

With generous support from the United States, and demonstrating an almost unbelievable degree of cooperation, hard work and sacrifice, the Japanese began the task of rebuilding their devastated economy.

Domestic purchases by the American occupying forces made a significant contribution during the first five years of Japan's struggle to overcome its gravest crisis. An even more important factor was the outbreak of the war in Korea. The U.S. began to use Japan not only as a staging area for carrying on the war in Korea, but also as a major supply source.

Primarily as a result of the economic impetus provided by the Korean War and the new American policy of helping Japan become an economic bastion in Asia, the Japanese regained their prewar economic level by 1955--only 10 years after suffering total defeat.

For the next 18 year, the Japanese economy, fueled by massive infusions of new technology and a world-wide demand for Japanese-made consumer merchandise, Japan's economy grew at the incredible rate of 9.9 percent to 11.8 percent. Its GNP passed the 100 billion dollar mark in 1966.

The international monetary crisis that developed in 1971--triggered to a considerable extent by American reactions--followed by the first Oil Crisis in 1973, slowed the mighty Japanese industrial engine down to more modest growth rates, but it continued to expand.

In 1978, when the second Oil Shock came, the Japanese were prepared, and weathered the storm better than most of the other advanced nations. In that same year, its GNP surpassed the one trillion dollar mark.

Despite the fragility of an economy based almost entirely on importing massive amounts of raw materials from around the world, and then exporting in turn huge amounts of finished products, the Japanese have managed to balance the economic and political factors involved, going from a virtual stand-still to one of the three major powers in the world in 25 fast years.

Recommended reading: MIRACLE BY DESIGN: The Real Reasons Behind Japan's Economic Success, by Frank Gibney (Times Books).

EDO / (Eh-doe)

Edo, which means Estuary, is the old name of Tokyo. It began as a tiny fishing-farming village at the head of Edo (Tokyo) Bay, and was first mentioned in history at the end of the 12th century when Taro Shigenaga Edo, a member of the famous Taira clan, was appointed political agent in charge of the province of Musashi (where the village was located) by Shogun Yoritomo Minamoto, head of the Taira clan.

But Edo was to remain in the backwaters of history until 1457 when warrior/poet Dokan Ota, a high-ranking retainer of the Uesugi clan which then controlled the area, chose the site for a castle fortress.

One hundred and forty-three years later (1590), the soon-to-be famous Ieyasu Tokugawa was given the eight provinces on the Musashino Plain (Kanto) by Hideyoshi Toyotomi, whom he had helped become the military leader of the country.

Ieyasu made Edo his fief capital, and its population immediately began rising. When he replaced Hideyoshi and became Shogun in 1603, Edo became the headquarters of the Shogunate government. All of Ieyasu's 80,000 retainers and soldiers and their families moved to Edo.

The small town was turned into a sprawling city in just a few weeks time. One can just image the great hustle and bustle as these new residents built homes and businesses, and went about providing for themselves and the needs of the Shogunate Court.

In 1635 Edo received another great boost in population when the third Tokugawa Shogun, Iemitsu, decreed that all the 270 Daimyo (feudal lords) in Japan would build mansions in Edo, leave their families there (well attended by servants and retainers) at all times, and themselves spend every other year in Edo in attendance at the Shogun's Court.

This Shogunate order resulted in another great burst of building in Edo. Large areas of the shallow bay were reclaimed and a number of lagoons and marshes were filled in so the mansions of the Daimyo could be built in the vicinity of the Shogun's castle (known as the Edo or Chiyoda Castle).

Despite moves to widen the city's major thoroughfares--usually after major fires, such as an unusually destructive one in 1657--Edo remained a city made up of hundreds of communities grouped around the different Daimyo estates with little rhyme or reason to its overall layout--a legacy present-day Tokyoites must still contend with.

The heyday of the Edo Period was from 1688 to 1704, and was known as the Genroku (Gane-roe-kuu) era. There was a general relaxation of political control, economic conditions were good, and the arts and other endeavors flourished.

Many businessmen amassed wealth and those who could afford it lived extravagantly, dressing in beautiful silk kimono, attending popular playhouses and treating themselves to sumptuous feasts.

The quality of the Shogunate leadership fluctuated. The fortunes of the Samurai class declined as the financial power of the merchant class grew and money began to replace rice as the primary medium of exchange.

Scholars studying Japanese history began to question the right of the Shogunate to govern Japan. News of the growing power and activities of foreign nations continued to seep into Japan, raising the question of national defense.

In 1792 and again in 1804 Russia sent envoys to Japan, demanding that the country open its doors to trade. In 1808, an English warship pursued a Dutch vessel right into Nagasaki Bay, and left only after members of the crew had caused a furor. Many Japanese expected the country to be invaded at any time, and the Shogunate went to special lengths to fortify Hokkaido against possible Russian intrusions.

Several of the largest clans, particularly those in Kyushu, set up strong coastal defenses.

By 1731 Edo had a population of 562,000, not counting the Shogun's thousands of retainers and the families of all the feudal lords. Just 56 years later (1787) Edo had a population of 1,368,000, making it one of the largest cities in the world.

When the Tokugawa Shogunate fell in 1868, the Imperial Court was moved from Kyoto to Edo, which was then renamed Tokyo or Eastern Capital. See HISTORY, TOKUGAWA, MEIJI, TOKYO.

EDUCATION / KYOIKU (K'yoe-e-kuu)

Japan's educational system is based on six years of elementary school, three years of junior high school, three years of senior high school, and four years of university.

Some children are enrolled in private kindergartens as early as the age of three, but elementary school starts at six. In elementary schools, one teacher generally teaches all subjects in each class. Primary emphasis is given to teaching the young students how to first read and write the relatively simple hiragana (he-rah-gah-nah) and katakana (kah-tah-kah-nah) characters, which are phonetic representations of the syllables making up the Japanese language. Then the students go on to the much more complicated kanji (kahn-jee) characters, borrowed from China over a thousand years ago.

The first nine years of school in Japan are compulsory, and the rate of attendance is normally 100 percent. From junior high school on, individual subjects are taught by different teachers, and students are introduced to the study of English.

In order to get into senior high school, junior high school students must pass rigorous entrance examinations. In addition to general academic subjects, senior high students usually also take such vocational subjects as engineering, agriculture, commerce and fishing.

The entrance examinations for universities in Japan are tougher still. The competition to get into name universities is surely the toughest in the world. See EXAMINATION HELL.

Degrees in medicine and denistry require six years. A masters degree requires two years, and a Ph.D. requires an additional three years. A doctoral program lasts for four years.

Japan has both private and national universities, with private universities being the most common. There are also junior colleges with two-year curriculums, and specialized vocational high schools with five-year terms.

Prior to 1872 and during most of the long Tokugawa Shogunate period (1603-1868), the children of Samurai families were taught in Han (Hahn) or clan schools operated by the ruling Samurai authorities. In these schools, the emphasis was on moral, martial and cultural subjects designed to prepare the young privileged students to eventually assume the duties of their class.

In addition to these han schools, there were some 20,000 tera koya (tay-rah koe-yah) or temple schools for the children of farmers and townspeople. Attendance at these temple-run schools was not compulsory, and there were no age limits. It is estimated that some 40 percent of the common people studied at these schools. One of the most popular subjects was how to use the soroban or abacus.

The lecture format is the usual method of instruction in Japanese universities, and because of limited facilities and a shortage of professors, up to 500 or more students may attend individual lectures.

Ambitious students wanting direct, personal guidance by their professors may attend seminars conducted by professors on an on-going basis.

The academic year in Japan is from April to March, and is divided into two semesters--from April to September and from October to March.

During the 1960s and 70s, many Japanese students became involved in political movements, and were able to effect national events and policies. The number of students participating in such activity has declined significantly in recent years.

Since 1970, Japan has had the highest literacy rate of any country in the world--well over 99 percent. Interestingly enough, only Korean students spend more time studying after school than the Japanese. Almost 20 percent of Japanese students study more than three hours a day at home, 30.9 percent study from two to three hours, and 32.9 percent study from one to two hours.

More and more Japanese parents are enrolling their children in kindergarten to give them a headstart on the uphill struggle to get into more desirable universities. Some parents engage private tutors for their children before they are old enough for kindergarten.

The percentage of children going to kindergarten jumped from 28.7 percent in 1960 to 64.4 percent in 1980, and is still climbing.

There are over 15,000 kindergartens, over 25,000 elementary schools, close to 11,000 junior high schools and well over 5,000 senior high schools in Japan.

Besides these regular schools, there are 72 schools for the blind, 110 schools for the deaf and 695 schools for the handicapped in Japan.

For those who like statistics, Japan has over 18,000 public and private research institutions, 16,452 public halls, 1,200 libraries, 493 museums, 709 national and public children's and youth centers, 89 women's halls, and 690 audiovisual centers and libraries.

In addition, there are some 50,000 social educational classes and lectures set up by boards of education, with nearly three million people enrolled. There are also close to 200,000 Boy Scout troops, 218,631 facilities for physical education and sports, including 1,915 athletic fields, 10,297 baseball and softball fields, 30,911 swimming pools, 4,946 outdoor basketball courts, 1,911 golf course, 850 ice skating rinks, and 769 ski areas. Public cultural facilities include 548 cultural halls, 11 archaeological activities centers, and 264 historical and ethnological museums.

EIGHTY-EIGHT SACRED PLACES OF SHIKOKU

During the peaceful centuries of the Tokugawa Shogunate era (1603-1868), various religious pilgrimages around Japan became very popular. Written accounts of some of these trips indicate they were as much for pleasure as for pious reasons, and sometimes lasted for several months.

One of the most popular and longest of these pilgrimages was a visit to each of the Eighty-Eight Sacred Places of Shikoku--88 temples of special reknown, along a circuitous route around the island. Among the temples on the route that are still noted: Hotsumi Saki, Kokubun Ji, Kongofuku Ji, Kakurin Ji, Shido Ji, and Tatsu Ji.

A full list of the 88 temples is available from the Japan National Tourist Organization (see listing)

Recommended reading: JAPANESE PILGRIMAGE, by Oliver Statler (Morrow). Using his own temple pilgrimage as a starting point, Statler weaves the history of Japan into this fascinating book.

ELECTRICITY / DENKI (Dane-kee)

A difference in electrical voltage between East and West Japan makes it neccesary to be careful about buying household appliances or recreational equipment in one part of the country and using it in another.

The electricity in Eastern Japan (The Tokyo-Yokohama area and everything north) is 50 cycles and 100 volts. In Western Japan (Kyoto-Osaka-Kobe and everything west and south), it is 60 cycles and 100 volts. U.S.-made appliances will work in the Tokyo area but at reduced efficiency. Voltage regulators are available.

ELDER STATESMEN / GENRO (Gane-roe)

Japan has a long history of regents, retired emperors, shoguns and influential politicans advising and sometimes directing the government from the background. In the modern era, the most famous of these advisors were the Genro, appointed to the position by the young Emperor Taisho when he ascended the throne in 1912 at the death of his ilustrious father, Emperor Meiji.

Those appointed to the position of genro were Princes Yamagata, Oyama, Katsura and Matsukata, and Marquis Inoue. The sixth and best-known of the genro, was Prince Kimmochi Saionji, appointed to the position in 1921 when he was 70, to replace Field Marshal Yamagata who had died.

Prince Saionji is one of the most interesting figures in Japan's modern history. Raised at the Imperial Court in Kyoto, he was a favorite of Emperor Komei and a playmate to Prince Mutsuhito who was to become the Emperor Meiji.

At 19, Saionji was made a commander in the Imperial army and took part in an important battle. He was later appointed governor of Echigo, then studied French in Nagasaki and in 1871 sailed abroad with a large entourage, some still wearing their full Samurai regalia.

In Washington D.C. Saionji was introduced to society by President Grant. From there he went to New York, London and Paris, where he studied law. Returning to Japan nine years later, Saionji wrote a book about his travels, founded a liberal newspaper and lectured at Meiji Law School. A very controversial figure who continuously criticized corruption in the Satsuma and Choshu clans--the ones responsible for the Restoration of Emperor Meiji--and scandalized his family and friends by appearing in public with geisha, Saionji was appointed Minister to Austria in 1885, and to Germany and Belgium in 1887.

Back in Japan in 1889, Saionji became a member of the Privy Council, leader of the Seiyukai political party in 1903, and president of the Privy Council and prime minister in 1906. He again served as prime minster in 1911.

As a former prime minister, Sionji continued to serve the government in various ways, including representing Japan at the Peace Conference at Versailles following the conclusion of World War I.

Between 1921--when he became a member of the Genro--and 1925, all the other Elder Statesmen died, leaving only Saionji. From that time on until his own death in 1940 at the age of 91, he was one of the most revered and influential men in Japan.

Saionji was a direct descendant of Emperor Seiwa (859-876), whose son Shinno Sadazumi took the name Minamoto and founded one of Japan's greatest families. The story of the family was told in the famous novel, GENJI MONOGATARI (Gane-jee Moe-no-gah-tah-ree) or Tale of Genji, written in the 11th century by Lady Murasaki Shikibu.

ELECTIONS / SENKYO (Sen-k'yoe)

Japan's election campaigns are apt to be noisy affairs, with candidates riding around in vehicles equipped with public address systems, broadcasting their views to all within a several block distance--or with their staff playing recordings of their appeals over and over.

Since 1945 both women and men who have reached the age of 20 have the right to vote. Voters write the name or names of the candidates of their choice on ballots. House-to-house canvassing is prohibited by law, as is especially noisy methods of getting the public's attention, but the latter, it seems, is not strictly enforced.

Members of Japan's Diet (Parliament), prefectural governors and assemblymen, along with city, town and village mayors and assemblymen, are chosen by direct election. The assemblymen who run Tokyo's 21 wards are also elected by direct vote.

EMPEROR / TENNO (Tane-no)

Although there is some doubt about the date of Japan's first emperor, the tendency is to unoffically accept the year 660 B.C. as accurate. On this basis, Emperor Hirohito (He-row-ssh-toe), who ascended the throne in 1926, is the 124th emperor of Japan, and his son, Crown Prince Akihito (Ah-kee-ssh-toe)

will be the 125th.

Except for the earliest years, for which records are questionable, plus brief periods in later centuries, Japan's emperors have not actually been the rulers of their country. Until 1868 when the Meiji Restoration placed power in the hands of a constitutional monarachy, real control was exercised by various members of the nobility, and from the 12th century on, their successors, the Samurai warrior class and several Shogun dynasties.

Despite the fact that for over 1,000 years real power was in the hands of the nobility and various military dictators, the Imperial system was continued, and each of these governments in turn based its authority on the soverign right conferred upon it by the reigning emperor.

Living emperors are generally not referred to by their given names, and are given a posthumous name upon their death. Emperor Hirohito was born on April 29, 1901, and at this writing has reigned longer than any of his ancestors. He is an accomplished biologist, and has written 14 books on the subject.

Crown Prince Akihito was born in 1933, and attended Gakushuin University in Tokyo, where he studied politics and economics. The first member of the Imperial family to be raised more or less as an ordinary child, the Crown Prince is known to have gone out drinking with friends, and in 1959 married a commoner, Michiko Shoda, the daughter of an old and successful business family.

Prior to 1945, the Emperor was treated as divine, and to a degree was treated as a living god. When he left the Imperial Palace and traveled about the city or country, people were not permitted to gaze upon him drectly, especially from a position above the ground level. Those who were out in the open had to prostrate themselves on the ground as his entourage passed.

Today the Emperor has no governmental power. He is treated as the head of state in diplomatic and ceremonial functions. The constitution declares that he is the symbol of the State, and that he derives his position from the will of the people.

The Japanese have ambivalent feelings toward the Imperial family. In a recent survey, 44 percent said they felt affection toward the Emperor, Empress and their family, but 45 percent said they felt nothing at all. Only six percent of those surveyed said they thought the Emperor's status should be elevated, while 82 percent said it should remain the same. Eight percent said the system should be abolished.

The second son of Emperor Hirohito and Empress Nagako is His Imperial Highness, Prince Hitachi. They also have a daughter who is married to the scion of the famous Shimadzu family.

ENERGY RESEARCH

The almost complete lack of domestic oil resources, making it necessary for Japan to import a significant percentage of its energy needs, is a primary factor in Japan's energy-related research and development programs.

The Organization for General Development of New Energy is charged with the responsibility of carrying out research in nuclear power, coal, coal gas, solar heat, geothermal heat, and alcohol.

Research is also being conducted in the use of biomass, wind power, wave power, ocean temperature differentials, and in small and medium-sized hydroelectric systems.

ENVIRONMENTAL POLLUTION

By the early 1960s, Japan was suffering from serious pollution problems as a result of rapid industrial development. Laws intended to prevent and control pollution were passed as early as 1949, but it was 1970 before Japan had a comprehensive legal system for protecting the environment, and began a crash effort to do something about its problems.

The situation was so bad in the early and mid-1960s that traffic policemen at major intersections had to work in short shifts, alternately breathing oxygen from special tanks provided for that purpose. Tokyo was almost permanently shrouded in smog that was so thick it was said that children four and five years old had never seen the stars at night.

There were also incidents of poisonings from industrial wastes, resulting in a national outcry that something be done. Something was done, and Japan is now noted for its stringent pollution controls, and for the progress it has made in cleaning up its environment.

ENCYCLOPEDIA OF JAPAN / NIHON NO HYAKKA-JITEN (Nee-hone no H'yack-kah-jee-tane)

Published in the fall of 1983 by Kodan-sha Ltd., the Kodansha Encyclopedia of Japan is a nine-volume English-language encyclopedia that covers over 10,000 topics, and is the most comprehensive source on things Japanese ever compiled.

The compilation of the work was under the direction of Professor Gen Itasaka of Harvard University and the Reference Department of Kodansha. Some 1,400 scholars, specialists and writers--half of them Japanese and half foreign--contributed to the project.

Produced in an 8 1/2 x 11-inch format, with some 1,000 illustrations, eight volumes of the handsome set have 352 pages each, and the ninth volume, and index to the other eight, is 288 pages. The set is priced at 130,000 yen.

ENGLISH LANGUAGE STUDY

The military Occupation of Japan by the U.S. from 1945 to the spring of 1952, along with the subseqent emergence of Japan as an international economic and political power, set the stage for English to become Japan's second language.

This might suggest that most Japanese speak very good English. That is not true. The overwhelming majority of Japanese speak very little or no English, but the number who are studying English, and the time and energy they devote to it, may dramatically change this situation in the years ahead.

Most Japanese study English in high school, and literally millions make an effort to learn it on their own or in special language schools or from private tutors. But there are not enough good teachers to go around, especially with conversational fluency. The language is hard for the Japanese to learn, and the majority have very little opportunity to practice it on English-speaking foreigners.

On the other hand, virtually every major company in Japan has or has had some kind of English teaching program in which native-born teachers are hired to conduct classes for interested employees. It is common for senior Japanese executives, including those who are in their 60s and 70s, to attend such privately held classes. (The author conducted such classes for the Japan Travel Bureau in 1953-54.)

The head office of Nippon Steel in Tokyo regularly offers some 30 courses in English and other foreign languages to its employees.

ENO ISLAND / ENO SHIMA (Eh-no She-mah)

A tiny islet connected to Katase Beach by a long bridge, Eno Shima is one of several seaside resorts on Miura Peninsula about an hour's train ride south of Tokyo that is famous for its shrines, temples, and recreational facilities. Actually, when people say Eno Shima they generally mean the Katase beach area, with its mile-after-mile of beach-front hotels and restaurants.

In the summer months, the Katase/Eno Shima area is jammed with beach-goers, with as many as a million people littering the sands from the island causeway to the adjoining Kugenuma Beach.

During the Kamakura Period (1192-1333), Katase Beach was the Shogunate's official execution grounds. It is the spot where Kublai Khan's envoys were beheaded in 1275 when they demanded that Japan pay tribute to China. The great priest Nichiren, founder of the sect bearing his name, would have been executed there but the executioner's sword broke when he tested it. The incident was taken as an omen that the priest should not be killed, and his execution was cancelled.

ENTERTAINMENT EXPENSE / SHAYO (Shah-yoe)

Japan is famous for its nightlife (see WATER BUSINESS), which centers around a larger number of bars, cabarets, and night clubs per capita than in any other country in the world--not to mention Turkish baths, hotspring spas, Geisha inns and other types of entertainment that are unique to Japan.

Much of the several billion dollars a year that is spent on night-time entertainment in Japan comes from the expense accounts of company executives, managers and salesmen, entertaining themselves, their colleagues and customers at company expense.

Such expense accounts vary from a few hundred dollars to several thousand dollars a month. In a few cases the expense account is paid directly to the company employee. In most cases, the clubs, restaurants, inns and other establishments bill the company directly.

The more the individual member of the Shayo Zoku or Expense Account Tribe is authorized to spend, the more and better service he and his guests get.

This system makes it very difficult for foreign businessmen living in Japan or visiting there to keep up with their Japanese colleagues on the entertainment front. See NIGHT CLUBS, CABARETS.

ENTRANCE EXAMINATIONS / NYUGAKU SHIKEN (Nyu-gah-kuu She-kane)

In Japan getting a white-collar job with a large company or in the more desirable agencies, bureaus and ministries of the government, depends almost entirely on one's education--and the particular schools attended to get this education.

Since there are not enough openings in the more desirable schools (from kindergarten on up!), entrance into these schools is based on competitive examinations.

While the kindergarten, grade school and high school one attends is important, the critical jump is from high school into college, as many of the most desirable employers in Japan hire only from or primarily from certain schools (usually the ones their top executives graduated from).

As a result, the entrance examinations for Tokyo University, Keio, Waseda and the other top universities are extremely difficult. Well over half of the students who take them each year fail-- because the exams are hard and because there are not enough openings to go around.

The trial of preparing for these examinations is a serious strain on the mental and physical health of many students, and is often referred to as the Examination Hell.

EPIC SONGS / NANIWABUSHI (Nah-nee-wah-buu-she)

A very popular genre of epic folk songs, naniwabushi tell stories of the rise and fall of Japan's great feudal families, of the triumphs of the weak over the powerful, and the inevitability of justice. The songs are rendered in a high-pitched, formalized style of recitation to the accompaniment of shamisen music.

ERAS / JIDAI (Jee-die)

From ancient times in Asia it was the practice to count years according to the reign of an emperor or an imperial line. This custom of reckoning years by eras was adopted in Japan in the 7th century. From that time until the 19th century, the reigning Emperor decided when one era would end and another one would begin.

Under the current system, adopted following the ascension of Emperor Meiji in 1868, the era begins the day an Emperor ascends the throne and continues until his death. Thus the Meiji Era began in 1868 and lasted until 1912. The present era, Showa, began in 1926 when Emperor Hirohito ascended the throne. 1983 was therefore Showa 58.

Presently, official documents are dated according to the Era, and many older people still reckon years by the system for both personal and business affairs, but the Western calendar is by far the most common system for recording and keeping track of dates.

ESCALATOR SYSTEM

The Escalator System refers to the system of promotion in Japanese companies and other organizations. Japanese companies and organizations generally hire only on the entry level, selecting the new employees they want each year from classes graduating from high schools and colleges.

Thereafter, promotion up the ladder of success is primarily based on seniority, and occurs only after the individuls concerned have spent a certain number of years in grade--just as in the military.

People who joined the company the same year, tend to be promoted at the same time, at least until they reach the managerial or executive level, at which time the most able are singled out for further advancement.

The concept of the escalator comes from the fact that unless a person commits some kind of serious offense, he will not be fired, his income will gradually go up and he will be automatically advanced in rank.

Those who prove to be inept are still carried along by the system, and often end up in the position of manager. This is not as serious as the Westerner might think, because the Japanese hiring system precludes the employment of complete klutzes in white collar jobs, and once hired, the system of continuing job-rotation assures that they will learn a great deal about how the company operates and what its needs are.

Futhermore, the higher a Japanese businessman rises in his company, the less specialized expertize he is expected to have. Generalized knowledge, a broad and long view, the ability to get along with people and a knack for keeping everything working smoothly are the traits the manager must have to succeed in Japan.

ETIQUETTE / SAHO (Sah-hoe)

In Japanese society all things, including people, are ranked in a superior / inferior system. Because of the importance of maintaining the relation-ships this system entails in accordance with standards that were developed by the exacting demands of first the Imperial nobility and then the feudal Samurai class, the Japanese developed an etiquette system that was the most comprehensive, the most specific and the most demanding the world has ever seen.

Until the end of the Tokugawa Shogunate in 1868, virtually every move or action a Japanese might make or take was prescribed in minute detail. This included sleeping, sitting, walking, eating, dressing and working. How well one learned and followed this etiquette was equated with both one's education and morality.

In feudal days, failure to follow the prescribed manner in many actions was a serious and sometimes fatal offense. The role models and guardians of the system were the sword-carrying Samurai, and they were very strict disciplinarians indeed.

The legal sanctions and Samurai standards that made etiquette a matter of life or death during Japan's long feudal period have long since gone, but a very carefully prescribed and detailed etiquette is still an important part of life in Japan.

Much of the etiquette is bound up in the language, and requires different levels and styles for different occasions, making it difficult or impossible for Westerners to do as the Japanese do, unless they speak the language very, very fluently.

The most that the average non-Japanese can do is learn the physial aspects of traditional Japanese etiquette--in greetings, partings, dining, drinking and so forth--and just be polite in his or her native tongue.

EXAMINATION HELL / JIGOKU SHIKEN (Jee-go-kuu She-kane)

The entrance examinations of Japan's ranking universities are so difficult and so competitive, that the process of preparing for and taking them is known as Examination Hell. Only a small percentage of the high school graduates who take the examinations each year get passing marks.

It is not uncommon for students to suffer physical and mental breakdowns as a result of their efforts to get into the more desirable universities. See ENTRANCE EXAMINATIONS, RONIN.

EXPO Memorial Park

At Suita City between Osaka and Kyoto, the EXPO Memorial Park is the site of a World Exposition held in 1970. After the exposition ended, the grounds and buildings were turned into a huge recreation and amusement center, which opened in 1972.

The park includes a Japanese Garden, the Japan Folk Art Museum, EXPO Memorial Hall, EXPO Land, and numerous other attractions on a 264 ha. (580-acre) site.

EXPORTING / YUSHUTSU (You-shute-sue)

The Japanese are presently among the most successful exporters in the world. They have achieved this extradinary position because of a number of very specific factors. Among them:

The Japanese are a proud and ambitious people. They think of themselves (as do many other nationalities) as among--if not the--best, most talented, and hardest-working people in the world.

They have a very strong desire to be the best in the world and an extraordinarily competitive spirit that drives them unmercifully. They are very nationalistic, and more often than not will put the interests of their country above their personal interests.

The Japanese have an insatiable appetite for learning, and drive themselves to learn all they can about things of importance to them--especially knowledge about foreign affairs, politics and economics.

All Japanese are acutely aware that the great industrial economy they have developed depends entirely on the importation of huge amounts of raw materials, from oil to iron, and they all know that they only way they can pay for these imports is to export a lot.

Japanese manufacturers, no matter how small or insignificant their operation, are likely to be export-minded. The great export boom that began in Japan in the 1950s was not just the doing of large companies. It was also the work of thousands upon thousands of small and medium-sized companies whose employees worked 10 to 12 hours a day six and seven days a week.

Few of these manufacturer/exporters could speak any foreign language. Almost none of them had ever been abroad. But they persevered, and if they were not able to export directly, they went through trading companies. Today, hundreds of these compan-ies are large, internationally known firms.

Another of the major reasons for Japan's success as an exporting nation is the insatiable appetite American and other Western importers, wholesalers and retail chain store operators have for making money--regardless of its economic, political or social implications-- along with the appetite Western consumers have for buying goods at bargain prices.

Then there was American procurement of supplies in Japan during the Korean War. See HISTORY, ECONOMIC PROGRESS AFTER 1868.

FACE / KAO (Kah-oh)

As a tightly knit, group-oriented society in which people are not free to move from one job to another, discard old friends and make new ones or move away and start over when they have problems or fail, the Japanese are very much concerned about their face--their reputation.

The loss of face during feudal times often had fatal consequences, and still today there are people who take their own lives to resolve a sullied reputation.

Maintaining one's face in Japan today is still of vital importance, although the sanctions imposed by society are far less severe than in feudal times. It is especially important in both social and business situations that one be equally careful about not causing someone else to lose face.

In a Japanese company, every employee has a face that goes with his or her person and job. Because of the group orientation and concensus approach to management, the face of each person is inextricably linked to that of his co-workers on all levels, and to the face of the company.

Each person must know and maintain the face that is proper for his position. If he steps out of bounds, he endangers his own face as well as that of his co-workers.

Foreign businessmen dealing with the Japanese should be aware that many of the things they say and do--all perfectly common and acceptable in their own countries--may very likely be seen as a threat to the face of the Japanese and their company.

See JAPANESE MANNERS β ETHICS IN BUSINESS, by Boye De Mente (Phoenix Books/Publishers).

FACE / HAND TOWEL / OSHIBORI (Oh-she-boe-ree)

The oshibori is a small, dampened face/hand towel, cooled in the summer and heated in the winter, given to customers by many businesses in Japan, including Japanese style restaurants, some bars and cabarets, inns and Chinese style restaurants.

Some places of business impregnate their oshibori with jasmin scent or some other delightful aroma that adds a very special touch to the ambience of their place of business.

Whether one is sweaty from the heat of summer or bitten by the cold of winter, the oshibori is one of the most refreshing and relaxing customs every invented--and one that I believe should be adopted by every country.

FAMILY CRESTS / MON (Moan)

In feudal Japan all clan families had their individual family crest, which was put on their formal kimono, their lanterns and their banners. The practice of establishing a family mon then spread to Samurai families who served the clan lords, and finally to merchant families.

A mon may consist of a plant, a stylized bird or Chinese character or some other motif that struck the fancy of its creator. In the days of the Tokugawa Shogun, when clan lords and large numbers of retainers had to march to and from Edo (Tokyo) every other year, the mon were of vital importance in identifying the various processions as they traversed the country's great walking roads. See PROCESSIONS OF THE LORDS.

Formal kimono bearing the family crest are known as mon-tsuki (moan-ski) or bearing a crest.

After the break-up of the Tokugawa Shogunate in 1868 many ordinary Japanese families and businessmen created crests for themselves, but nowadays they are seldom used.

Recommended reading: THE ELEMENTS OF JAPANESE DESIGN--A Handbook of Family Crests, Heraldy β Symbolism, by John W. Dower (Weatherhill). See CRESTS.

FAMILY REGISTER / KOSEKI (Koe-say-kee)

In the 7th century the government of Japan as well as Buddhist temples began keeping registers of the families making up villages, towns and clans. These family registers included records of birth, schooling, marriage, divorce, death and any criminal acts committed by the individual.

The registers were used for tax purposes, recruiting labor for public works, and so on. When a man married and set up his own household, a new register was started in his name.

The koseki system was made into a national law in 1870, making it mandatory that everyone in the country (including foreign residents) be registered with the appropriate village, town or city office. No birth, marriage, divorce or death is officially recognized until it is entered in the official family register.

In Japan a copy of the family register (koseki tohon) is the ultimate identification, and is required on many occasions.

FAMOUS PRODUCTS / MEIBUTSU (May-e-boot-sue)

Over the centuries many areas in Japan have become famous for particular local products that are referred to as meibutsu or famous products, and are much sought after by visitors to these areas. Among the most famous of these areas and their products are:

ARITA--Porcelain ware of the finest quality.

BEPPU- Bamboo and wooden items for kitchen and household use.

KAGOSHIMA--Silk fabrics and Satsumayaki porcelain ware.

KANAZAWA--Porcelain ware known as Kutani-yaki, lacquerware, silk, kaga dolls and toys.

KOBE--Silk and silk goods, bamboo ware, tortoise shell ware.

KYOTO--Brocades (especially silk embroidered Nishijin), woodblock prints, cloissone, damascene, lacquerware, fans, screens, curios, porcelain ware and dolls.

NAGOYA--Lacquerware, porcelain of many types, cloisonne, curios, fans and toy.s. Nagoya is Japan's porcelain ware center.

NAGASAKI--Coral ware, tortoise shell ware, Koga folk dolls.

NAHA--Lacquerware, Tsuboya-yaki porcelain, Bingata cotton, linen and silk cloth dyed in paper patterns, and cloth made of banana fiber (bashofu).

NIKKO--Wooden ware, lacquerware, curios.

OSAKA--Silks, toys, curios, old and new works of art.

SAPPORO--Ainu-made wooden and textile handicraft items.

SENDAI--Folk dolls, bamboo ware, wooden ware, silk fabrics, lacquerware.

TAKAMATSU--Parasols, wooden and bamboo ware, lacquerware, engravings.

TOKYO--Pearls, books, cloissone, sil- ver ware, brocades, ivories, woodblock prints, fans, toys, handmade paper, porcelain, cameras, lacquerware, electronic items of all kinds, curious.

FAMOUS SIGHTS

Japan has more identified and cataloged famous sights than any other country--a circumstance that derives from the existence of so much scenic beauty and a culture in which the recognition and appreciation of natural beauty has traditionally been an important part of the lives of a large segment of the population.

While each area of the country invariably has its famous scenic spots, natural beauty is also ranked on a national level. For hundreds of years, Japan's Scenic Trio have been Amanohashidate on the Japan Sea coast north of Kyoto, Itsuku Island in Hiroshima Bay, and the pine-clad islands of Matsuhima Bay near Sendai on northeastern Honshu. See individual listings.

FANS / SENSU (Sane-sue) also UCHIWA (Uu-chee-wah)

Fans have played an extraordinary role in Japan since their introduction from China in the 6th and 7th centuries. The fans first imported from China were the flat, rigid kind (uchiwa), and were used not only for cooling one's self during the humid summer months, but also became an integral part of court and later formal wear.

The making of fans became a handicraft art, which led to the invention by a Japanese fan-maker of the ribbed folding fan, called sensu.

The folding fan was first used for strictly functional purposes, but under the influence of court dilitantes, became an accessory that was essential in proper etiquette, personal as well as ceremonial. Folding fans made of cypress slats first appeared in Japan's Imperial Court in the 7th century, and by the 8th century were an indispensable part of Court attire. These first sensu were thin sticks held together by ribbons. Paper covering was added later.

As the centuries passed, fans began to play a similar role in religious ceremonies, in dancing and in the theater, particularly in kabuki and noh.

As more time went by, fans became an integral part of the formal dress of the privileged classes, representing not only a symbol of this class, but a symbol of cultural achievement and good manners. They were used as an accessory to speech and became an important part of non-verbal communication in formal as well as informal settings.

The ladies of the Imperial Court in Kyoto became especially adept at carrying on surreptitious communications with their fans.

Fans also became an essential ingredient in the aesthetic ritual of the tea ceremony that developed in the 15th century, and were a highly valued gift.

The making of sensu folding fans is still a major handicraft industry in present-day Japan, and they are still an important part of the ensemble of a man or woman dressed in formal Japanese attire. They are also still popular gifts, especially for someone who is going on a trip or has become engaged to be married.

Flat, rigid uchiwa fans, used for fanning, come in many designs and colors, ranging from simple natural tones of bamboo to colorful landscapes, portraits, and kanji characters with auspicious meanings.

FARMERS / NOFU (No-fuu)

As late as 1960, nearly 17 percent of of all Japanese were farmers. Today that number has dropped to less than six percent--or some seven million people.

Land reforms instituted in Japan in 1945 by Allied Occupation forces, revolutionized the country's farming industry. Most of the arable land in the country was owned by nonfarming landlords. This lands were bought up and given to the tenants who actually worked it.

This step, plus the introduction of more and more technology, resulted in amazing increases in production--despite the rapid loss of land to industrialization. This increase in production, plus government subsidized prices for rice, beef and pork, resulted in the incomes and living standards of farm families keeping pace with industrial workers.

Many Japanese farmers became wealthy by selling off their lands to major industrial companies seeking sites for factories. For several years in a row in the 1960s, Japan's top money earners included one or more farmers.

FARMING / NOGYO (No-g'yoe)

Japan,s main agricultural products are rice (see RICE), vegetables, fruit, wheat, barley, rye, soybeans, beef, pork, chickens, eggs, milk and cheese.

Vegetable production (radishes, tomatoes, cabbage, onions, etc.) just about matches demand, primarily because of the wide-spread use of hot-houses that make year-around cultivation possible.

The most popular fruit in Japan is the mandarin orange (O'mikan), which is now controlled by the government to prevent over-production. Apples, peaches, pears, plums, and persimmons are also raised and consumed in great quantities.

One of the most delicious of all of Japan's fruits is a hybrid pear/apple called 20th Century Pear, or Ni-ju Seki Nashi.

Japan's production of wheat, barley, rye and soybeans meets less than 10 percent of the national demand. The shortfall is made up through massive imports from the U.S., Canada, Australia, etc.

The production of chickens and eggs in Japan just about covers the demand. The production of beef and pork, however, is far below demand, with the result that it is necessary to import huge amounts to even partially satisfy the market.

Japan's beef industry in particular strongly opposes any significant increase in the percentage of imported beef, but consumers are strong advocates of more imports to help lower the prices they now have to pay for beef.

The dairy industry in Japan has advanced remarkably since 1960. There is currently an over-production of milk for drinking, but a shortage of milk to be used for processing into cheese and other dairy products.

Because of Japan's economic vulnerability, the government has an on-going policy of self-sufficiency in food. About the only categories in which the policy has been successful is rice, some lesser vegetables and some fruits.

Of all the 800,000-plus farm households engaged in fruit farming in Japan, 37 percent of them produce mandarin oranges (mikan).

FASHION MODELS

Fashion modeling, now an important industry in Japan, grew apace with the ready-made apparel industry from the mid-1950s on. Apparently in imitation of the world of fashion in Paris and New York, the industry preferred tall, lean models, in this case with a Western look.

In the early years, virtually all of the manikins in Japanese boutiques and department stores were made in the image of Caucasian Westerners--providing both a cosmopolitan and exotic atmosphere.

Because of this predilection for the Western/exotic, a number of Western women living in Tokyo became well-known as fashion models. By the mid-1960s, extraordinarily beautiful young women of Japanese-Caucasian parentage began entering the field.

These young women were especially popular as models because they were both Japanese and foreign at the same time, and in most cases were fluent in English as well as Japanese.

It was also during these early years that a number of mixed Japanese-Ainu girls broke into modeling and became stars. (See AINU). Some of them were even more beautiful and exotic than the Japanese-Western mixtures, particularly those who had what I call Ainu Eyes-- eyes so large, so luminous and so magnetic that they have a hypnotizing effect on viewers.

By the early 1980s, Japan's world of fashion modeling had matured, and as in the U.S. is dominated by a few companies that exercise considerable influence over the industry.

FAST FOODS

Many Westerners were surprised when foreign-style fast-food restaurants caught on in Japan in the 1960s. They shouldn't have been. Fast-food restaurants have been popular in Japan since the middle ages (if not before). Japanese-style, of course.

The biggest-selling fast food item in Japan is not MacDonald hamburgers (which is number two). It is sushi--slices of raw fish and other seafood on little buns of slightly vinegared and sweetened rice.

Sushi restaurants and stands have been going strong in Japan since early times, but what is new is the appearance in the 1970s of take-out sushi chains. The largest sushi chain, Kozozushi Hombu, racks up sales in excess of 65 billion yen a year.

Besides MacDonald hamburgers, other popular fast-food items in Japan include fried chicken, noodles, gyu-don (sukiyaki-style beef on rice), and yaki-tori (barbecued chicken on skewers).

One of the earliest take-out fast-foods in Japan was nigiri (nee-ghee-ree) or nigiri-meshi (may-she), meaning hand-made riceballs. Riceballs were already a popular food among the nobility of 11th century Japan (the common people at that time mostly ate millet), who customarily ate them outside, when traveling and on picnics.

Chances are, nigiri were specifically invented to be eaten outside or while traveling--as they still are. See STATION BOX LUNCHES.

Among the more popular varieties of riceballs are nori-musubi (wrapped in seaweed), umeboshi (pickled plums embedded in balls of rice), sansai (rice mixed with vegetables), sekihan (rice and red beans), and shake-nori (a rice ball with a chunk of salmon in the center, wrapped in seaweed).

FENOLLOSA, ERNEST FRANCISCO

An American art critic, Ernest Francisco Fenollosa went to Japan in 1879 and taught at Tokyo Imperial University. He became a great admirer of Japanese art, and his books and lectures did much to make it known around the world.

Fenollosa also studied Buddhism, converted to that religion, and when he died in London in 1908 left instructions that he was to be buried at the Miidera Temple close to Lake Biwa, near Kyoto.

FESTIVALS / O'MATSURI (Oh-mot-sue-ree)

Having two major religions as an integral part of their culture (Shintoism and Buddhism), with both of these religions emphasizing group ceremonies and celebrations, Japan is blessed with many festivals. Every major shrine and every major temple around the country-- and there are thousands--has an annual festival.

The festivals are street processions of parishioners of particular Buddhist temples and Shinto shrines, held to honor the tutelary diety of the temple or shrine.

Most of them include a mikoshi (me-koe-she), which is a portable shrine in which the spirit of the diety can be moved about. Carrying the mikoshi through the streets was thought to spread the purifying power of the diety and neutralize any evil in the vicinity.

Eight of the largest and most important of these festivals have been institutionalized into national holidays. They are:
GANJITSU (Gahn-jeet-sue), the first day of the New Year, when people visit shrines, relatives and friends, drink sake and eat special New Year dishes. Children play special card games, shuttlecock and battledore, and fly kites.

The homes (of some) are decorated with sacred straw ropes and pine boughs, the latter symbolizing trees by which the gods may descend from heaven.

All businesses are closed down for at least three days during New Year's, a period called sanga-nichi (sahn-gah-nee-chee), and some remain closed for five or more days.

At the stroke of midnight on New Year's eve, the great bells of many nationally known temples are rang 108 times to symbolize the elimination of as many bad things during the year ending, so that all may enter the new year with a clean slate.

The clappers in some of the huge bells consist of immense logs suspended from the ceiling by stout ropes. Young men, usually warmed up by sake, take turns swinging the log against the bell--a ceremony that is televised nationwide from a number of locations.

HINA MATSURI (He-nah Mot-sue-ree), on March 3rd, also called Girls' Day, is to honor young girls and wish them future happiness. Besides displaying dolls dressed in the costumes of ancient court ladies, along with peach blossoms, a sweet drink called shirozake (she-roe-zah-kay) is served.

Nowadays, young girls are also likely to get gifts, and be taken out for dinner.

TANGO NO SEKKU, on May 5th is the annual festival for boys, and symbolizes the hopes of parents that their sons will grow up to be healthy and strong. Warrior dolls are displayed, iris leaves are placed under the eaves of homes to ward off evil, and large banners shaped like carp are flown on poles over homes in which there are young boys. These latter streamers are what most people associate with Boys' Day--the symbolism of the carp being that they persevere in their attempts to swim up-stream against whatever odds.

TANABATA (Tah-nah-bah-tah), the Star Festival, on July 7, celebrates the meeting of two lovers, the star Altair personified by a cowherd, and Vega, as a weaving girl, separated by the Milky Way the rest of the year.

Poems celebrating the story are written on pieces of paper and attached to bamboo poles set up in the garden. Special food offerings are made, and young girls hope that they will be as skillful in their cooking and other home duties as Vega was reputed to be.

OBON (Oh-bone), celebrated in mid-August in the countryside and in July in major cities, is one of Japan's major festivals. This is the time when people visit and clean up the graves of their ancestors, and those who have moved to cities, visit their birthplaces.

Usually translated as Festival of the Souls, Obon includes the preparation of special foods to be offered to the spirits of dead ancestors, hanging up lanterns so the spirits may find their way back to their former homes, and praying for their repose.

This is also the season for the bon-odori (bone-oh-doe-ree) or bon dances, which are staged outdoors, usually in the precincts of shrines, in villages and towns all over the country. People dress in light summer yukata, and dance, watch and stroll around, enjoying the cool of the evening.

Vendors usually set up stalls at such festivals, selling knicknacks and snack items.

TSUKIMI (T'sue-kee-me), held on nights of the full moon in August, literally means Moon-Viewing, and that is what people do, while drinking Osake, eating dango (dahn-go), a dumpling--and if they are moved by the muse, compose poetry celebrating the beauty of the moon.

HIGAN (He-ghan), is celebrated twice a year during the spring and autumn equinox, over a period of seven days on each occasion. During higan, families attend Buddhist rites, recall their ancestors and visit family graves.

SHICHI-GO-SAN, on November 15, is still today one of Japan's most popular festivals. This is the occasion when parents take children who are three, five and seven to shrines to pray for their future. These odd numbers are chosen because they are considered lucky.

The children are dressed up in their most colorful attire--the girls usually in bright kimono--and everybody has a great time. It is naturally one of the most popular picture-taking days of the year.

As mentioned earlier, local festivals abound in Japan. Among the most popular:

The KAMAKURA FESTIVAL, held during the New Year holidays in Akita Prefecture, is for children. Adults help child-

Celebrating Girl's Day. P. 91

Celebrating Boy's Day. P. 91

ren build snow igloos, called kamakura (kah-mah-kuu-rah), into which are put altars dedicated to the God of Water. At night, children gather in the kamakura, eat rice cakes and drink amazake (ah-mah-zah-key), a sweet wine.

The kamakura festival grew out of an ancient custom in which adults in the central and eastern portions of Japan built small huts for use during the New Year period as part of a purification ritul. They would live in the huts for a few days, without eating or drinking, to purify themselves.

Sapporo's annual SNOW FESTIVAL has received international publicity in recent years. It is held from the first Friday in February through the following Sunday, and is part of a popular Winter Carnival.

The snow festival consists of a large number of snow sculptures in the form of animals and figures from legends and mythology. It is held in Odori Park.

The DONTAKU (Doan-tah-kuu) FESTIVAL is held in Hakata, Fukuoka Prefecture, from May 3 to 5. It is marked by spectacular parades of floats and participants made up to represent deities riding on horseback. Children in kimono ride on the floats.

One of Kyoto's most popular events, the GION (Ghee-on) FESTIVAL sponsored by the Yasaka (Yah-sah-kah) Shrine, originated in the 9th century as a supplication to ward off a plague. It begins on July 1 and lasts until the 29th.

The big days of the festival are the 16th and 17th. On the evening of the 16th, lanterns are hung from the eaves of homes in the old section of the city. Special blue curtains are hung in doorways. Flowers are set out on cloth spreads, and decorative wind screens are displayed.

Floats, gaily lighted with lanterns and accompanied by music, make their way through the streets. On the 17th, the highlight of the festival, the brilliantly decorated floats parade through the city streets.

Each year the Gion Festival attracts thousands of foreign tourists who coordinate their trips so they will be in Kyoto on this occasion.

Akita City's KANTO (Kahn-toe) FESTIVAL, August 5-7, is held to drive away the demon of drowsiness that afflicts people at work during the year.

A kanto is a long bamboo pole with numerous cross-bars on which are hung from 46 to 48 lanterns. The highlight of the festival is when groups of young men dance through the streets to the accom-paniment of drums, vieing with one another in balancing the poles on their hands, shoulders and heads.

Tokushima's AWA ODORI DANCING FESTIVAL, from August 15 to 18, also attracts international interest. Residents dance in the streets in a celebration that dates back to the end of the 16th century, when their new lord moved into the city's castle.

Men and women of all ages, dressed in light, colorful yukata and sometimes traditional hats, dance the evening away to music provided by shamisen, flutes and drums.

The OKUNCHI (Oh-kune-chee) FESTIVAL of Nagasaki features Chinese style dragon dances from the 7th to the 9th of October. Staged by the Suwa Shrine, the festival is designed to bring good luck to the participants and viewers. The dragon concept was apparently imported from China when Nagasaki was the only Japanese port open to the outside world.

One of the most spectacular and the most interesting of Kyoto's many festivals as far as history buffs are concerned, is the JIDAI MATSURI (Jee-die Mot-sue-ree) on October 22, sponsored by the equally famous Heian Shrine. It features a unique procession of men and women clad in authentic costumes representing each of the 10 centuries during which Kyoto was Japan's Imperial capital.

The parade, in effect, gives one a glimpse of one of the most fascinating periods in the history of the country, and attracts foreign visitors by the dozens of thousands.

Jidai Matsuri can be translated as Festival of the Ages.

On of the most unusual of Japan's popular local festivals is the NAMAHAGE (Nah-mah-hah-gay) MATSURI on Oga Peninsula in Akita Prefecture. Aimed at frightening the laziness out of laggards, the December 31 event involves young men dressed as demons, and carrying papier-mache knives, clubs and paper bags, going from house to house, warning sluggards to mend their ways.

The term namahage is a corruption of namami-hagi, the treatment used for getting rid of calluses caused by sitting close to a fire for a long time.

While Japan's numerous matsuri began as part magical, part religous rites to attract a particular god or goddess down from heaven to ensure bountiful harvests, and to gain the favor of the spirits in warding off bad luck or natural disasters, they have evolved with the times.

Over the centuries the matsuri retained their religious significance, but also came to be popular just for the fun of them, as a time to eat, drink and be merry. Some of the festivals are pure Shintoist while others are Buddhist. Some are a subtle mixture of both.

Some of the more unusual of Japan's festivals are one for silkworms at the Mie Temple in Gifu on January 31, the seaweed festival at the Mekari Shrine in Moji (founded by the Empress Jingu in the 4th century), and the Laughing Festival of Nagahama in Shiga Prefecture held to celebrate the gift of a large sum of money from Hideyoshi Toyotomi on the birth of his son.

There are dozens of others, among which are those that have to do with phallic worship. One of the most important of these fertility festivals is the Honen Matsuri, held each spring at the Oagata Shrine in Inuyama and the Taagata Shrine in Komaki, both in Aichi Prefecture.

The theme of these ritual celebrations is that the sexual joining of male and female elements is necessary to produce bountiful crops. The festival at Taagata centers around the male symbol, represented by replicas of the male organ in varying sizes, including ones carved out of huge logs.

During this festival, a mikoshi (portable shrine) bearing a large replica of the male organ is carried through the streets while young men shout encouragement and young women vie to get lucky sexual charms.

The Oagata festival centers around symbols of the female organ. A portable shrine bearing a wooden representation of the female vulva is carried through the strees, followed by a procession of decorated horses and men carrying banners. A second mikoshi carries a large clam, and good-luck rice cakes which are thrown to the crowd.

Several of the most fascinating of Japan's festivals are held each year in Kyoto. They include the Gion Matsuri held by the Yasaka Shrine in July, the Jidai Matsuri or Festival of the Ages held by the Heian Shrine in October, and the Aoi Matsuri held in May by the Shimogamo and Kamigamo Shrines.

The Aoi Matsuri or Festival of the Hollyhock dates from the 7th century when rites were held to propritiate the gods after a series of great storms. The festival consists of a procession including an Imperial messenger and his entourage of warriors, pages and others, going from the old Imperial Palace to the Shimogamo Shrine where leaves of the hollyhock are offered to the dieties.

The procession then proceeds to the Kamigamo Shrine where a similar ceremony is held, after which it returns to the palace.

All of the people participarting in this ancient matsuri are dressed in authentic costumes of the period.

One of my favorite festivals is the great Sennin Gyoretsu or One Thousand People Procession in Nikko, held each year on May 17 and 18, to commemorate the day in 1617 when the remains of Ieyasu Tokugawa, founder of Japan's last great Shogunate (and the role model for the television special SHOGUN), were moved from Shizuoka to Nikko, accompanied by 1,000 people.

Now the festival includes mikoshi or portable shrines symbolizing the spririts of Ieyasu along with two other great Japanese heroes--Hideyoshi Toyotomi and Yoritomo Minamoto--which are conveyed to the astoundingly elaborate Futarasan Shrine in Nikko.

The procession re-creates the original, with a thousand men and women dressed in costumes of the early Tokugawa Period, passing along a road lined by 8,000 cedars planted by Masatsune Matsudaira, one of the commissioners responsible for constructing the shrine.

Iemitsu Tokugawa, the grandson of Ieyasu and the third Tokugawa Shogun, had the masuoleum built for his grandfather. The project took 12 years to complete, and was done by 12,000 craftsmen and 7,000 laborors who were sent from all over Japan by their lords.

A similar shrine was built in Nikko for Iemitsu 18 years later, with the various Daimyo (provincial lords), contributing to the project.

FIREWORKS / HANABI (Hah-nah-bee)

Fireworks were introduced into Japan from China in 1543, but as in so many other instances, the Japanese quickly made revolutionary improvements that far exceeded anything ever seen in China.

The manufacture of hanabi became a hereditary craft passed on within families who became famous for their distinctive products. Fireworks displays were staged for the Shogun at Yedo Castle, but were eventually banned because of the danger of fires.

It then became an annual summer event to stage a fireworks display on Sumida River on the outskirts of Yedo to mark the opening of the river for sweet trout fishing--Kawabiraki (Kah-wah-bee-rah-kee). This event gradually took on religious overtones as a Buddhist ceremony to console the victims of a great famine and epidemic.

As more time passed, it became an annual festival at which the fireworks makers competed for prizes and honor. One of the famous stories connected with the hanabi involved a master of the craft who witnessed a murder. Fearing for his life if he publicly revealed the identity of the murderer, he recreated the scene of the murder in fireworks, and during the next hanabi shot them into the sky where the murderer was revealed for all to see.

After 223 years this great annual celebration ended in 1956, because of the congestion from buildings and traffic.

In July 1977 the annual fireworks tradition was revived, and has been going strong ever since. An average of 15,000 fireworks are shot into the sky during each display, and well over a million people are on hand to enjoy the event.

Other fireworks displays are held at other locations in Japan today, and the descendants of the families that began the industry are still in business, shipping their merchandise around the world.

FISHING / GYOGYO (G'yoe-g'yoe)

Fishing has been a primary part of Japanese life since the dawn of the people, and seafood has been and still is one of the Big Three in the Japanese diet.

In the early years, Japan's fishing was confined to coastal waters, but as the population and demand grew, its fleets began expanding their ranges. By the end of the 1960s they were fishing in waters as far away as the Atlantic.

The establishment of a 200-mile coastal economic zone by many nations in the mid-1970s was a serious blow to the Japanese fishing industry. As quickly as possible, Japan negotiated fishing rights with the U.S., Russia, Canada, New Zealand and other countries to allow its fleets to continuing operation within the restricted zones.

But the problem was far from solved. While the demand for seafood in Japan continued to grow, the areas where they could fish were gradually decreasing.

To help compensate for this, the Japanese fishing industry and government began promoting aquaculture, and so far have had significant success in the growing of shrimp, yellowtail fry, scallops and oysters. They are now experimenting with farming other types of seafood as well.

The problem of fulfilling the national demand for seafood may eventually become much less of a challenge, as the diets of younger Japanese are swinging away from such traditional fare and the overall consumption of fish is declining.

In the meantime, fish and shellfish remain very important in Japan's food supply, providing half of the animal protein consumed. Cod, sardines and mackerel make up a large portion of Japan's annual fish catch. Major fishing ports include Wakkanai and Kushiro in Hokkaido, Ishinomaki in Miyagi Prefecture, Choshi in Chiba Prefecture, and Fukuoka in Fukuoka Prefecture.

FLOWER ARRANGING / IKEBANA (E-kay-bah-nah)

The word ikebana literally means living flowers, and refers to the idea of arranging flowers so that they look alive and embody the principles of heaven, earth and man.

Broadly speaking, ikebana is an exercise in aesthetics, in recognizing and achieving harmony with nature, in developing good character, and therefore morality.

The art of ikebana originated in the 15th century, apparently in the tearoom of the Silver Pavilion of the Jisho Temple in Kyoto (which was built for the 8th Shogun of the Ashikaga family, Yoshimasa).

With the beginning of the Tokugawa Shogunate in 1603, the practice of ikebana became widespread and many schools developedμ some advocating the formal (rikka) or standing style, others a natural style known as nage-ire or thrown-in. The formal school gave birth to the heaven-earth-man (ten-chi-jin) principle, which all schools now follow.

Flower arranging was once popular with both men and women, but it is now practiced primarily by women, and is considered a vital part of the upbringing of all young girls, several million of whom take lessons in it each year.

There are over 20 well-known ikebana schools in Japan today, plus numerous offshoots and branches. Among the best-known are Sogetsu-ryu, Misho-ryu, Saga-ryu, Ohara-ryu, Ikenobo, Kyofu-ryu, Ko-ryu, Enshu-ryu, Adachi-shiki and Nakayama Bumpo-kai.

Recommended reading: FUN WITH FLOW-ERS, by Martha and Marvin Neese (Weatherhill). Also, IKEBANA: A New Illustrated Guide to Mastery, by Wafu Teshigahara (Kodansha Int'l).

FOLK ART / MINGEIHIN (Meen-gay-e-heen)

During all of its early history, Japan was divided into literally hundreds of distinct regions and areas by its mountains, rivers, long distances, and political subdivisions.

For most of these centuries, each of these districts had to be pretty much self-sufficient in most things. Thus each area had its own craftsmen who produced the majority of items they needed for their livelihood, as well as specialty folk art items.

These folk arts ranged from dolls and cast-iron kettles to bark work (kaba zaiku), made in Akita Prefecture for use in boxes and other containers.

These traditions of folk art have been continued down to the present time, and are well-known products of these areas. Besides the cast-iron kettles of Iwate Prefecture and the bark-work of Akita, there are the snow boots (yuki gutsu) of Yamagatau lacquered tableware from Aizu-Wakamatsu, wooden horses from Miharu, kokeshi dolls from Akita, Yamagata, Miyagi and Fukushima.

Also, Mashiko pottery from Tochigi, and lacquerware and magemono woodwork from Nagano, copperware from Toyama Prerecture, porcelain from Aichi, tea utensils and other pottery items from Shiga, and scores of other things.

The best way to see and buy folk-craft products from all over Japan is to visit the prefectural trade promotion offices in Tokyo, in the Kokusai Kanko Building on the north side of Tokyo station.

Recommended reading: FOLK TRADITIONS IN JAPANESE ART, by Victor and Takako Hauge (Kodansha Int'l). Also, FOLK ARTS OF JAPAN, by Hugo Munsterberg (Tuttle).

FOLK SONGS / MINYO (Meen-yoe)

Folk songs have been popular in Japan since ancient times, and are usually associated with the districts in which they originated. They include work songs, drinking songs, play songs and sacred songs.

Most of the folk songs popular among the Japanese today are based on work songs that first became popular in the 16th and 17th centuries, and eventually became associated with entertainment or religion.

Following the industrialization of Japan in the late 1800s, many work songs became party and festival songs. In more recent years, several folk songs have become popular hit tunes on various record labels.

The Japanese love to sing, and virtually every party brings on a songfest--including solo performances at cabarets where patrons often carry on despite the noise and other competition.

FOOD / TABEMONO Tah-bay-moe-no)

Like many people around the world, the traditional Japanese diet consists of a mixture of vegetables, grains, fruits, seafood, chicken and, after 1868, small quantities of meat--usually pork until recent times. Prior to 1869 Buddhist religious taboos forbid the consumption of meat from any four-legged animal.

Also like other native diets, what distinguishes Japanese food is the manner of its preparation, plus the various items the Japanese eat that are not common in other countries.

The main characteristics of Japanese dishes include preservation of the natural appearance of the food, the minimal use of gravies, heavy use of soy sauce, pickling, and eating many foods raw.

Secondary characteristics of a typical Japanese meal are that the main dish is boiled rice, and that all the other foods that go along with the main course (of rice) are side-dishes. Or, various vegetables, seafoods and other tidbits are mixed in with rice to make a rice-dish.

About the only category of traditional Japanese food that does not include rice as the main dish are the various soba and udon noodle dishes.

In a traditional Japanese meal, the appearance and manner of serving food is as important as what is served. Like virtually all other areas of life, the Japanese developed the preparation and serving of food into a highly refined art--and art that was designed to nurture the spirit as well as the body.

The various items of food are arranged on the dish or tray in such a way that perfect harmony is obtained in color and size. Slices of a colorful fish, for example, may be served in a deep black lacquered bowl or tray. Roe of seabream with peas in the pod may be served on a curving slab of stoneware.

A clear soup containing two or three white beans, a slice of red ginger cut in the shape of a starfish, two pieces of twisted kelp, and ear-shell and a sliver of pink fish may be served in a lacquered bowl that has a milk-white bottom fading rapidly into a soft russet tinged with brown and cream. The lid, decorated with a pattern of wild grain sprigs, may be a fusion of gold and russet.

An accompanying petal-sized saucer for sauce may be a brilliant vermilion with only a hint of a pattern extending down one side toward the center.

Other dishes follow suit, all artistically placed on pottery, lacquerware, bamboo trays or woven straw. When served by a kimono-clad waitress in a typical Japanese setting--a room with a tatami reed-mat floor with a tokonoma (beauty alcove) and a picture window looking out on a valley scene or a tree-clad mountain--the atmosphere is one of serenity and restfulness that is literally out of this world.

Traditional Japanese food is different enough that a taste for it must be acquired over a period of time. Since food is very much a part of our psychological profile and has a direct bearing on our physical and mental well-being, any introduction to Japanese food should be voluntary and gradual.

The Japanese have the same problem adapting to Western foods. When a Japanese who is not already conditioned to eating Western food goes abroad, he or she must be very careful to avoid becoming quite ill. When they have no choice but to eat unfamiliar dishes, especially heavy meat dishes and dishes with lots of oil or butter, their health suffers.

Recommended reading: JAPANESE SECRETS OF GRACEFUL LIVING, by Boye De Mente (Phoenix Books/Publishers), and EATING CHEAP IN JAPAN, by Kimiko Nagasawa and Camy Condon (Shufunotomo). THE BOOK OF MISO, by William Shurtleff β Akiko Aoyagi (Ten Speed Press).

Rice has traditionally been the main dish of all Japanese meals. Other traditional dishes include soups, boiled vegetables, fish or vegetables cooked in soy sauce, fried foods, broiled foods, fish, shell fish and vegetables served with vinegar, vegetables and seafoods cooked in pots, grilled eel, pieces of raw fish and pickled vegetables.

Special items include rice cakes (mochi), a thick broth containing mochi (zoni), vegetables and seafood cooked tempura-style (covered with batter and deep-fried in oil). Steamed egg custard with chicken and vegetables. Grilled beef and vegetables. And numerous noodle and macaroni-type dishes. See individual listings.

Traditional Japanese dishes are not about to disappear, but the diet of the young urban Japanese has already changed significantly, They eat less than half the amount of fish consumed by their parents and grandparents, and far more meats and breads.

FOOD CARTS / YATAI MISE (Yah-tie Me-say)

One of the most traditional and nostalgic sights in Japan are the yatai mise or wheeled food carts with roofs, that appear around dusk in popular station and entertainment areas.

The carts specialize in a particular kind of traditional food, ranging from bake sweet potatoes and boiled corn (in season) to a style of cooking called oden (oh-dane), which consists of seafood, vegetables, chicken and rice-bread boiled in a special stock.

The yatai mise that specialize in hot foods are particularly popular in the winter months, especially among those who have been out late and are on their way home.

The yaki-imo-ya or baked sweet potato vender, is another of the most popular of these yatai mise. The sound of the potato vender's horn and his cry of Yaki-moohh! echoing through the streets in the evening is one of the special sounds of Japan that is sure to touch the heart of Japanese and foreigners raised there.

FOREIGN COMPANIES IN JAPAN

There are currently some 1,400 foreign companies with their own operations, or with affiliated operations, in Japan. American-owned companies make up approximately half of this total, followed by West Germany, Britain, Switzerland, Hong Kong, France, Netherlands, Sweden and others. West Germany, which is second, has fewer than 100 companies in Japan.

Of the the U.S.'s top 200 companies, over 100 have branch or affiliated operations in Japan.

Among the industrial categories represented by the foreign-owned companies in Japan are foods, chemicals, oil, rubber products, nonferrous metals, general machinery, electrical machinery, and other manufacturing and service companies. The only category in which these foreign firms have a significant percentage of Japan's market is oil (approximately 48 percent).

The secret of success for a foreign company in Japan is being able to adapt to the local environment--a concept that is difficult for many Western businessmen to grasp. A number of the larger American companies that have succeeded in Japan did so only because they were big enough and rich enough to survive their early mistakes.

The smaller foreign companies now thriving in Japan had to work smarter to get where they are. Among these smaller firms are some with extraordinary stories. One example: E-Z Trading Company and E-Z Ware Company, founded by Mike Solomko, a former baseball player who spent six years with the Hanshin Tigers and then set up his own business rather than leave Japan. The E-Z companies sell TV-promoted cook ware at housewives' parties.

Another example is International Business Information (IBI), founded by C. Tait Ratcliffe, which now has 25-30 percent of the English-language annual report business in Japan. Ratcliffe first visited Japan with a glee club.

From the 1950s to the 1970s, one of the main problems facing larger foreign firms in Japan was attrcting qualified job-applicants and managers. The best high school and college graduates preferred to go with Japanese organizations for reasons ranging from trust to concern about getting along in a foreign enterprise.

It was also rare for a competent, experienced manager to quit a Japanese company to go with a foreign firm (something that is still unusual in Japan, although some mobility has developed in the electronics industry among young engineers who are frustrated by the seniority system in Japanese companies).

For the most part, foreign companies recruiting in Japan must depend on the few disenchanted employees of Japanese firms, on women (who often prefer working for foreign companies because they are paid more and treated more equally), and on the pool of Japanese who for one reason or another (often schooling abroad) did not become a part of the corporate Establishment immediately upon graduation from a Japanese high school

or university--and generally cannot get in at a later date.

The Ministry of International Trade and Industry estimates that around 350,000 Japanese work for foreign and foreign-affiliated firms in Japan. Of this number, some 150,000 are women.

FOREIGN CORRESPONDENTS / GAIKOKU SHIMBUN-KISHA (Gie-koe-kuu Shim-boon-kee-shah)

There are a large number of foreign correspondents stationed in Tokyo, representing the various wire services (Associated Press, United Press International, Reuters, Tass, etc.), and many of the world's larger magazines, newspapers and special publications, including newsletters.

In pre-World War II days, foreign reporters in Japan were apt to be regarded as intelligence agents. Following the war, they were officially welcomed but unofficially were not held in very high esteem because it was felt that they would not interpret the Japanese scene in a way that would benefit the country.

Part of this fear was well-founded. Virtually none of the foreign correspondents stationed in Japan during the late 1940s, 50s and 60s could read, write or speak Japanese (the exceptions were a few Japanese-Americans), with the result that the reporters had to depend upon secondary materials and sources for their information.

Most correspondents hired Japanese assistants or used their Japanese girl friends as interpreters and translators, and got most of their news from the Japanese press and English-language handouts.

During these years, the activities of foreign correspondents were a frequent target of the more sensational weekly and monthly vernacular magazines, which gave the public the impression that the Foreign Correspondents' Club in downtown Tokyo was the proverbial den of iniquity. The stories did attract a certain class of women to the club, but that is the only positive effect they had.

In the 1970s, the situation began to change. The quality of the average correspondent--especially those from European countries--went up significantly. Many of the newer, younger correspondents had studied Japanese, and some of them were quite fluent in the language.

This resulted in a gradual improvement in the reputation of foreign correspondents in Japan--and in the Foreign Correspondents' Club. Ranking Japanese politicians and businessmen now appear regularly as speakers at club functions, and the club is one of the most popular luncheon places in Tokyo.

FOREIGNERS IN JAPAN

All residents of Japan who are not racially Japanese are counted as foreign regardless of their citizenship. On this basis, the largest group of foreign residents is Korean (some 670,000), followed by Chinese (approximately 55,000)--most of whom are Japanese citizens or have permanent resident status. Other groups--American, English, French, Australian, etc.--range from a few hundred to a few thousand, and are primarily in Japan as businessmen, diplomats, students, entertainers, and so on. The activities of foreigners in Japan is strictly controlled by immigration measures, and is determined by the individual's visa status. See VISAS.

Most foreigners in Japan live in Tokyo, Yokohama, Osaka and Kobe, but there are little pockets and sprinkles of foreign residents throughout most of the islands. Certain residential areas in the major cities are favored by foreigners (by virtue of the housing in these areas having been designed for Western-style living)

An estimated 150,000 foreigners live in the Tokyo area, making this the largest foreign community in the country by far.

There are English-language newspapers and magazines, clubs, restaurants and other facilities that cater specifically to the foreign communities in Japan.

Recommended reading: LIVING IN JAPAN (American Chamber of Commerce in Japan).

FOREIGN CHILDREN BORN IN JAPAN

A child born in Japan of foreign parents must be registered as a foreigner within 60 days, at the local ward or city office. Prior to this, the parents must obtain a passport for the child from their embassy in Japan.

FOREIGN WORKERS IN JAPAN

Japan's Immigration Control Act prohibits foreigners from entering the country to find work. In order to qualify for a work visa to enter Japan as a temporary resident, it is necessary to have a job contract and a guarantor (an employer may also act as guarantor) beforehand.

The period of stay allowed is determined by the type of work one is engaged to do, and ranges from a few months to three years. Businessmen, educators, missionaries, foreign correspondents, and technical specialists invited to Japan normally receive 3-year visas. Students, artists and others in skilled professions generally get 1-year visas. Sports people and entertainers are normally limited to three to six months.

Temporary residents who are in Japan under any visa category may apply for an extension at least one time, and most--with the exception of tourists and other short-term residents--may extend their periods of stay any number of times as long as they remain in good standing with Japanese authorities.

Until the 1980s, major Japanese companies seldom if ever employed any non-Japanese in Japan. The exceptions were part-time English teachers and other specialists who were brought in for temporary periods--such as copywriters for advertising agencies.

This policy was so strictly adhered to that in 1981 when a major department store chain announced that it would hire several young foreign men and women to work in its Tokyo stores, the event made the national news and was the talk of the town for several weeks.

In the department store announcement it was noted that the reason larger Japanese firms had not hired foreigners in the past was because of the language problem and because they did not believe foreigners could adapt to the Japanese way of doing business.

It was also big news when the Oriental Land Company, the owner and operator of Japan's Disneyland, began advertising for foreign job applicants in 1982.

FORESTS - FORESTRY / SHINRIN (Sheen-rene)

Nearly two-thirds of Japans' total land area is covered by forests, but the demand for lumber products is so great that it is able to produce less than 30 percent of its annual needs. The balance is imported from North America, the USSR, Southeast Asia, the Philippines and New Zealand.

To help overcome this deficiency, the Japanese government has an on-going 20-to-50-year range forestation program in the national forests (which account for a third of the country's forested areas). So far, the program has not been able to keep up with the growing demand.

Although some two-thirds of Japan's land area is covered by dense forests, there are a number of fundamental factors that limit the forestry industry. A significant percentage of the forested areas is on steep slopes. Forest roads are undeveloped, the majority of the trees are young, and many of the forests are in national park areas where lumbering is not permitted.

Japan now depends on imports for over 60 percent of its timber needs, which are mostly used for lumber, plywood and pulp. Japan's largest lumber suppliers are the U.S. (27 percent), Indonesia (21 percent), Malaysia (20 percent), USSR (15 percent), and Canada (10 percent).

FORGET-THE-YEAR-PARTIES / BONENKAI (Boe-nane-kie)

From around mid-December on until near the end of the year, it is customary for the Japanese to hold bonenkai or forget-the-year-parties as a formal way of forgetting all the bad things that happened during the year and getting ready to start the new year off with a clean slate.

The parties may be held at home, in company offices, in restaurants or in carbarets or clubs. The main thing is to let go of old grudges, bad memories and other negative thoughts, and forgive each other of any transgressions.

FORTY SEVEN RONIN / YONJU SHICHI NO SAMURAI (Yoan-juu She-chee no Sah-muu-rie).

The story of the 47 Ronin (masterless Samurai) of the Province of Harima is probably the best-known story of the valor and ideals of Japan's famous Samurai warriors.

In 1701 two young Daimyo (provincial lords), Naganori Asano, the Lord of the Castle of Ako in Harima Province, and Munehara Date, Lord of Sendai, were appointed by the Shogunate to act as hosts during the forthcoming visit of a member of the Imperial Court in Kyoto.

The Lords were inexperienced at that sort of thing, so the Shogun appointed an elderly high official named Yoshinaka Kira to assist them. Kira, whom history describes as greedy and conceited, became very angry at Lord Asano for not presenting him with expensive gifts (to show appreciation, etc.) and became very abusive and insulting toward Asano.

Finally unable to take the insults, Asano drew his sword (itself a capital offense when done inside Edo Castle), and attempted to kill his tormentor. He succeeded only in wounding the arrogant official, and was quickly seized by castle guards.

That very same day the Shogunate ordered Asano to commit harakiri, which he did. The Shogun also ordered that Asano's fief be confiscated.

When Yoshio Oishi, Lord Asano's chief councillor in Ako, heard the tragic news, he immediately called a meeting of Asano's retainers. The decision was made to petition the Shogun to re-establish the House of Asano with Lord Asano's younger brother, Daigaku, as its head. It was also resolved by the key retainers that if the petition was refused, they would refuse to turn the castle over to the Shogun's agents and defend it to the death.

In the next few days, while the Shogun's agents were on the road enroute to Ako, all of the Asano Samurai who had opposed the petition deserted the castle, leaving only 60 loyal men behind. Before the Shogun's men could reach the castle, Daigaku Asano sent a letter to the chief retainer Oishi, asking him to obey the orders of the Shogun, and hand the castle over.

Oishi and the 59 other Samurai accepted Daigaku's request as binding on them as the word of Lord Asano himself, but before they quit the castle they made plans to take revenge against Kira, whose un-Samurai-like character had brought their lord and house to such a tragic end.

The men split up to conceal their plans from Kira, who naturally suspected that Asano's retainers would try to get revenge against him. Oishi went to Yamashina, a suburb of Kyoto, and spent his days in apparent idleness and his evenings sporting with prostitutes in the gay quarters--always under the watchful eyes of spies sent from Edo by Kira.

The Shogunate, also concerned that the affair might not be ended, arrested Daigaku Asano and sentenced him to confinement in the main villa of the Asano family, thus ending any remaining hope that the House of Asano might be re-established.

At a secret meeting, Oishi and his men decided that the time had come to move against Kira. But Oishi would allow only 47 of the men to participate in the attempt. He sent the other men back home to their families.

One-by-one, Oishi and his men infiltrated Edo, and on a snowy night of December 14, 1702, they attacked the mansion of Kira, in Honjo. Kira's Samurai guards fought fiercely, but when Oishi and his men gained access to the mansion, Kira hid himself in a small outhouse on the grounds.

Oishi and his men searched the house, and then came to the place where Kira was hiding. Without knowing for sure he was in the outhouse, they ran a spear through it. The spear pierced Kira, but did not kill him. He quickly wiped the blood from the spear as it was withdrawn from him.

The ruse did not work, however. Oishi dragged Kira out into the open and beheaded him. He then dispatched the youngest member of the band to Ako to inform the wife of Lord Asano that he had been avenged. They then took Kira's head to their lord's grave, and there presented it to his spirit, asking him to again strike the head with his own sword that he might rest in peace.

Oishi then sent word to the Magistrate of Edo, informing him of what had been done and telling the official that he and his men would be at the Sengaku Temple in the Takanawa area of Edo, awaiting orders from the Shogunate.

After many days of deliberation, for the incident immediately became a highly controversial matter, the Shogunate ordered Oishi and 45 of his men to commit suicide. The youngest one--the one who had been sent to Ako with the news of Kira's death--was exempted from the sentence.

The rest of the men were divided into four groups and handed over to four different Daiymo who were ordered to supervise and witness their harakiri. When all had killed themselves in the manner prescribed for Samurai, they were buried on the grounds of the Sengaku Temple in Edo.

Still today, thousands of Japanese visit the grave of the 46 Ronin each year, and the story is mentioned and retold as an example of the spirit of Japan.

FREEDOM OF SPEECH

Japan's Constitution guarantees freedom of speech, including freedom of the press. Consequently, there is no censorship. Individuals and organizations are free to publish newspapers and magazines as they wish, and to publish any article that does not violate the Penal Code or other laws. Even when a publication infringes on a law, it cannot be closed down.

Television and radio broadcasters must obtain a license from the government, and must operate within the range of the wave-lengths assigned to them. But the Broadcast Law leaves all programming and program content to the broadcasters themselves.

Citizens are free to assemble and to express their views without fear of repression or censorship. Japan is thus one of the world's freest societies.

FREEWAYS / KOSOKUDORO (Koe-soe-kuu-doe-roe)

Japan's first freeway (or expressway as they are generally called) was the Meishin Expressway from Nagoya to Kobe, which was completed in 1965. This was soon followed by the Tomei Expressway connecting Tokyo and Nagoya. Then came the Chuo and other Expressways.

The chain of mountainous islands now has over 3,000 kilometers of expressways, including several that disect Tokyo. A government program initiated in 1954 calls for a national network of 24 arterial expresses.

One innovative feature of Japanese freeways that may eventually be adopted by other countries: instead of having motorized police patrolling the highways to catch speeders, the Japanse have installed combination radar and camera devices that clock the speed of passing cars. If they are exceeding the speed limit, the cameras take photographs of their license plates, and a few days later they receive a ticket in the mail.

FRINGE BENEFITS

Fringe benefits make up an important part of the income of most Japanese workers. By law, companies must provide their employees with health insurance, welfare annuity insurance, employment insurance and labor hazard insurance.

Companies with five or more employees must participate in the government's health insurance and welfare annuity insurance programs. Those with one or more employee must join the employment insurance and labor hazard insurance programs.

FRUIT / KUDAMONO (Kuu-dah-moe-no)

Fruit has been an important part of the Japanese diet for a long time. The two most popular fruits are mandarin oranges (mikan) and apples (ringo). Peaches, melons, pears and persimmons are also popular. A special treat is a hybrid apple-pear called 20th Century Pear (Ni-ju Seki Nashi).

Various tropical fruits such as bananas and papaya are imported--bananas in substantial volume.

Children's festival in Snow Country. P. 287

Shrine festival in Tsurugaoka. P. 91

Companies and employees share the cost of health and welfare annuity insurance premiums (with the company paying the larger share). All of the cost of labor hazard insurance is paid by the employer.

Other fringe benefits that are common in larger companies include such things as low-cost or free meals, low-cost dormitory housing, free or low-cost accommodations at resorts, and annual expense-paid company trips to resort areas.

FUCHU (Fuu-chuu)

A satellite city of Tokyo, 20 minutes northwest of Shinjuku Station by the Keio Line, Fuchu played a significant role in the history of the Kanto Plains area. In ancient times it was the capital of the province of Musashi, and is noted for the Okunitama Shrine, believed to have been founded in 111 A.D.

The shrine was a favorite of Ieyasu Tokugawa, founder of the great Tokugawa Shogunate in 1603. In 1614 he had keyaki trees planted along the approach to the shrine. Most of them are still there.

Following World War II, Fuchu became the site of an American airbase. It is now best-known as a residential community, and as the site of the Tokyo Race Track, regarded as one of the finest racing tracks in the country.

The Kurayami Fesvital held by the Okunitama Shrine on May 5-6 each year attracts substantial crowds from the surrounding areas.

FUKUOKA (Fuu-kuu-oh-kah)

The capital of Fukuoka Prefecture and Japan's 10th largest city, Fukuoka is on the Japan Sea side of northwestern Kyushu, facing the Asia mainland.

Fukuoka is divided into two parts--Hakata and Fukuoka proper--by the Naka River. The Hakata side of the city has been an important port since ancient times, and was the focal point of the two attacks against Japan by Kublai Khan's Mongol fleet in 1274 and 1281.

Following the first attack, which was driven off by a typhoon that sank most of the Mongol ships, the feudal lords (Daimyo) of Kyuhsu cooperated in building a 15-foot-high stone wall along Hakata Bay, from Hakozaki to Imazu. When the Mongols arrived the second time, very few of them ever got over this wall, and soon after the attack began another typhoon struck, again devastating the invasion fleet.

The commerical, shopping and enter-taiment centers of Fukuoka are mostly on the Hakata side of the river. Prefectural government and other public offices are mostly in Fukuoka proper.

In addition to serving as a foreign trade port, Fukuoka has several industries of note--electrical appliances, foodstuffs, silk textiles, machines and tools, and Hakata Ningyo or Hakata Dolls, a handicraft speciality of the area that has been famous for centuries. The pottery dolls take their theme from nature, depicting people, places and things with such reality they are regarded as works of art.

Here again, there are dozens of extraordinary places of interest, including the usual ancient temples and shrines (Sumiyoshi Shrine, Shofuku Temple, Kinryu Temple, Dazaifu Shrine and Kanzeon Temple), the entertainment district of Higashi Nakasu, Higashi park (which contains a monument commemorating the Mongol invasions and numerous sports facilities), and the remnants of Fukuoka Castle.

One of the most important shrines in the city is Hakozaki Hachiman, which was established in 923 and includes several parts that have been designated Important Cultural Properties. The shrine sponsors two popular festivals a year.

Within a short distance of Fukuoka are numerous other places and things, including hotspring spas, that attract visitors the year around.

FUNERALS / SOSHIKI (So-she-kee)

Funerals in Japan are mostly conducted according to Buddhist rites. Traditionally, a Buddhist priest is called to read sutras over the body of the deceased, which is then placed in a coffin with the head turned to the north. Twenty-four hours or more later, the body is taken to a crematorium in a hearse. In earlier years, relatives and friends folllowed the hearse. Men carried real flowers, others carried artifical flowers, an incense burner, banners and long-handled silk parasols.

Today such processions are rare, as people follow the coffin to distant crematoriums in cars. The funeral ceremony takes place in a temple or a funeral hall of the cemetery. Priests recite sutras to the accompaniement of bells, gongs and hollow wooden blocks, and pray for the souls of the dead. All present then pay their respects to the dead by burning incense before the coffin.

Most families also erect a butsudan (boot-sue-dahn) or family altar in their homes, and place on it a picture of the deceased, along with a mortuary tablet and other sacred articles. Incense is burned on the altar, and members of the family pray before it.

Shinto funeral rites are similar to the Buddhist, but the head of the deceased is turned to the eastμ offerings of fish, fowl and vegetables are made, and instead of burning incense, strips of white paper and twigs of the sacred sakaki tree are offered.

The Shinto priest offers prayers and reads an account of the life of the deceased. The spirit-tablet used in Shinto funeral ceremonies is plain wood, while Buddhist tablets are lacquered and gilded.

Families traditionally mourn their dead for 49 days, and then mark the first, third, seventh and thirteenth anniversaries by engaging a priest to perform a prayer service for the dead.

FUTAARA-SAN SHRINE (Fuu-tah-ah-rah-sahn)

The Futaara-San, or Three Shrines of Futaara, in Nikko are among the most revered in Japan. The Futaara shrines are dedicated to three Shinto dieties-- Okuninushi, his consort Princess Tagori and their son, Prince Ajisukitakahikone --who were reknowned for their virtues and for bringing prosperity to Japan.

The dieties were closely associated with Mt. Futaara (now Mt. Nantai). The first of the three shrines, Oku-Miya or Inner Shrine was built on the summit of the mountain in 784 by Priest Shodo. Because many people could not ascend the mountain to worship at the shrine, a sceond one, Chugushi (Middle Shrine), was built on the shore of Lake Chuzenji at the foot of the mountain.

The third shrine, Honsha (Head Shrine), was built on the banks of the Daiya River, a short distance from Nikko's famous Toshogu Shrine which memorializes the great Ieyasu Tokugawa, first of the Tokugawa Shoguns.

GAKUSHUIN UNIVERSITY (Gah-kuu-shu-een)

Near Mejiro Station on Tokyo's Yamanote Line, Gakushuin University is the former Peers' School, established after the fall of the Tokugawa Shogunate in 1868 as a private school for the sons of the nobility.

The young Crown Prince Akihito attended this school. His route to school each day took his chauffered limousine by Shinjuku 2-chome, a popular redlight district. A high wooden fence was built along the street to block the Prince's view of the area.

GAMBLING / KAKEGOTO (Kah-kay-go-toe)

Gambling has been a popular past-time and profession in Japan from early times. Nearly two thousand years ago, sumo matches were popular betting events. This was eventually followed by cock fights, dog fights and bull fights, and in more recent years, horse racing, bicycle racing and other types of sporting events.

Various kinds of card games, as well as go and mahjong (see GAMES) have also been popular betting events for a long time. During the long feudal age, and in particular during the Tokugawa era (1603 -1868), professional gamblers abounded.

These gamblers were a conspicuous breed of men who developed their own style of dress and speech, had a well-defined code of honor, and often became heroes to the common people whom they often defended against unscrupulous Samurai.

GAMES / YUGI (You-ghee)

The three most popular indoor adult games in Japan are go (goh), shogi (show-ghee) and mahjong. Go is played on a square board that is divided into 361 squares. Players--limited to two--alternately place small button-like stones on the board in such a way as to surround as much area as possible. The player who encloses the largest area is the winner. There are two sets of stones, one black and the other white.

The player recognized as being the best, gets the white stones. Black always moves first. Various handicaps make it possible for two players with different skills to play a more evenly matched game. Handicaps are achieved by allowing Black to place a certain number of stones on the board before the game begins.

Go originated in China and was first introduced into Japan in the 8th century, where it quickly became popular among the aristocracy. It did not begin to become popular among the common people until the 13th century, and has since become a national past-time, played regularly by hundreds of thousands of people.

Shogi, also imported from China in the 8th century, is also played by two players on a board, but in this case there are only 81 squares. This game is sometimes compared to chess because the object is to immobilize the other player's King and capture him.

Each shogi player has 20 pieces that have eight different ranks. A skillful player may remove one or more pieces from the board at the beginning of the game to give the other person a handicap.

Like judo and karate practitioners, go and shogi players are ranked in grades (dan) from one through nine. There is another grading system for novices, called kyu (que). The less skillful, the higher the kyu number (just the opposite of the dan system).

When go and shogi players win tournaments they are awarded various titles, including meijin (may-e-gene), kisei (key-say-e) and 10th dan.

Both go and shogi are played professionally, and the competition and skill involved is just as intense as it is in chess. Go and shogi are more likely to be played by intellectuals and well-educated people.

Mahjong, more of the average person's game, is also more likely to be played for the fun of it--or as a gambling game. A mahjong set consists of 136 tile-shaped ceramic pieces, each of which is identified by a Chinese kanji (kahn-jee) character on its face--usually in an attractive color.

At the start of a game, each player (there are usually four) gets a hand of 13 pieces, called pai (pie) in Japanese. The remaining 84 pieces are placed, face down, in the middle of a table. Players take turns picking up pai from the pile, discarding unwanted pieces as they try to build up various combinations. The first player to meld wins the hand, and receives a certain number of points determined by the combinations he has built up.

Mahjong is relatively new to Japan, having been introduced in the 1920s by

Japanese returning from visits to China and the U.S. (where it was played by Chinese Americans). The game really became popular after WWII, and there are now mahjong parlors all over Japan.

One of the oldest home games in Japan is a card game based on 100 famous waka (wah-kah) poems, that was developed in the 13th century. Each waka poem consists of 31 syllables arranged in three lines of five, seven and five syllables each.

To begin the game, all cards that have only the second part of a waka are laid down face up, with the players sitting around in a square or circle. As the waka that can be seen are read out loud, the players try to pick up the matching card. The one who picks up the most cards is the winner.

To become an expert at this game you have to memorize all of the 100 waka poems, and be able to quickly link the right parts. Besides being played in the homes by old and young alike, there are factory and regional tournaments, especially during New Year celebrations.

There are a number of similar card games for children, with proverbs and popular sayings on them, that have been played in Japan for centuries.

Recommended reading: THE GAME OF GO, by Arthur Smith (Tuttle). Also, SHOGI: Japan's Game of Strategy.

GANGS / GUMI (Guu-me)

Organized gangs operating outside the law have been a significant aspect of Japanese society since early feudal days. The gangs were not the kind that robbed and killed, but have traditionally engaged in various businesses such as gambling, sporting events, night-time entertainment, prostitution and the like.

During the feudal period, these gangs often acted as protectors of the common people against abuse by Shogunate authorities and unprincipled Samurai.

The gangs and many of their traditions have continued into modern times, and are known today as yakuza (yah-kuu-zah). The gang leaders and their members are known to police authorities, but remain in business by operating behind legitimate fronts.

On occasion, when the activities of a gang in a particular area become conspicuous, authorities will round up as many as two or three hundred gang members in a series of coordinated raids. But most of them are soon back on the streets.

When members of the gangs are involved in violence, it is usually connected with inter-gang rivalry over territorial rights. On some of these occasions, gang members battle it out with swords, knives and guns.

The world of the yakuza is often featured in Japanese movies and television dramas, and has been the theme of a number of American-made movies.

GARDENS / NIWA (Nee-wah)

The art of landscape gardening in Japan goes back to at least the 6th century. During the reign of the Empress-Regent Suiko (554-628), gardens with beautifully designed artifical hills and ornamental ponds were already popular.

The aim of Japanese landscape gardening is to create in miniature a scenic landscape that suggests something on a large scale that looks completely natural.

Such gardens were an integral part of landscaping by the time Japan's Imperial capital moved from Nagaokakyo to Kyoto in 794, where a garden of immense size called Shin Sen En or Sacred Fountain Garden was a centerpiece in the new city.

The introduction of Zen Buddhism into Japan during the Kamakura Period (1185-1336), had a significant influence on garden landscaping. They became less decorative and were designed to impart a sense of tranquility and happiness. The Zuisen Temple in Kamakura is an example of the hundreds of gardens designed during this period.

It was also during the Kamakura era that two of Japan's most famous books on landscape gardening were published-- Emposho (Book of Gardens), written by the priest Zoen, and Sakuteiki (Book of Garden Planning), written by Nagatsune Fujiwara. Both books are still regarded as authoritative.

Kyoto abounds in gardens dating back to this and the following Muromachi (1392-1573) period, including those of the famous Silver Temple Pavilion and the Gold Pavilion Temple. So-called flat gardens (hira niwa), using only stones and trees arranged in a flat area, also became popular during the Muromachi era.

Between 1573 and 1615, during the

wars that culminated in the consolidation of the Tokugawa Shogunate, both landscaping and architecture increased in scale and grandeur, taking on the heroic spirit of the age. Gardens designed during these years tended to be more colorful and vigorous.

At the same time, this was also the age of several of Japan's greatest tea masters, who designed some of the country's most reknowned gardens. Among the most famous of these garden designers were So-ami, Mon-ami, Zen-ami and the great Sen-no Rikyu (1521-1591). Rikyu was the leading tea master of his day, and created many gardens, including that at the noted Chishaku-in Temple in Kyoto. See RIKYU, SEN-NO for the story of this remarkable man's untimely end.

Another of the great tea masters who also gained fame for his garden designs was Enshu Kobori (1579-1647), whose most outstanding work is the celebrated garden of the Katsura Imperial Villa in Kyoto. He also designed the garden of the Kohoan of the famous Daitoku Temple in Kyoto, as well as those at the equally famous Nanzen and Chion-in Temples.

The beautiful gardens of Nijo Castle, the Shugakuin Palace and the Hompo Temple in Kyoto were designed by Koetsu Hon-ami. Altogether there are more than 50 outstanding gardens in Kyoto that have been preserved and are open to the public today.

After Ieyasu Tokugawa established his Shogunate in Edo (Tokyo) in 1603, and his grandson later passed the decree that all the nation's some 270 feudal lords would build mansions there, Edo became the new center of garden landscaping activity, and the designing of such gardens gradually passed out of the hands of the tea masters and priests to profesional gardeners.

The wealthier feudal lords vied to make the gardens of their Edo mansions into works of art, and also constructed gardens of great beauty around their fief estates. Among the more famous ones that may still be enjoyed are the Kenrokuen in Kanazawa, the Ritsuen in Takamatsu and the Korakuen in Okayama.

Only a few of the great gardens constructed in Tokyo by the feudal lords of the Edo era remain today. Among them: Kyosumien at Fukagawa, Rikugien in Komagome, Korakuen in Koishikawa, Chinzanso in Mejiro, Shiba-Rikyu Onshi in Shiba, Tokaiji in Shinagawa and the Akasaka Rikyu Garden in Moto-Akasaka.

Unlike most gardens in the West, which generally create an artificial landscape, Japanese gardes strive to symbolize a large natural landscape in a small, concentrated area. The materials used by Japanese gardeners are all natural--shrubs, rocks, trees and water--with the emphasis on harmonious spatial beauty instead of geometric forms favored by Westerners.

The underlying philosophy of Japanese gardening is a combination of Shintoism, which reveres nature, Buddhism, which reveres life, and Zen, which seeks to perceive the fundamental reality in all things and abide by the laws of nature.

Generally speaking, there are three styles of Japanese gardens, the tsukiyama (t'sue-kee-yah-mah) or pond/sea-hill. The karesansui (kah-ray-sahn-sue-e) or dry water and waterfall. And the shakkei (shock-kay-e), or water-mountain-woods.

The tsukiyama style uses a central pond to symbolize the sea and banks of earth and rocks to represents mountains. The karesansui uses white sand to represent the sea and blue rocks to represent waterfalls. The shakkei uses all of the above plus the views of surrounding natural mountains and woodlands.

The Tenryu (Tane-ree-you) and Saiho (Sie-hoe) Temple gardens in Kyoto are famous examples of tsukiyama style gardens. The Ryoan (Rio-on) and Daisen-In (Die-sin-een) gardens, also in Kyoto are noted examples of the karesansui style. Two of the most famous shakkei gardens in Japan are those surrounding the Katsura (Kot-sue-rah) Imperial Villa and the Shugaku-In (Shuu-gah-kuu-Een) Villa in Kyoto.

Recommended reading: THE GARDEN ART OF JAPAN, by Masao Haya-kawa (Weatherhill). Also, JAPANESE GARDENS FOR TODAY, by David H. Engel (Tuttle). JAPANESE COURTYARD GARDEN LANDSCAPES FOR SMALL SPACES, by Shigamori Kanto (Weatherhill). IMPERIAL GARDENS OF JAPAN, by Teiji Ito (Weatherhill). A JAPANESE TOUCH FOR YOUR GARDEN, by Kyoshi Seike, Masanobu Kudo and David H. Engel (Kodansha Int'l).

GEISHA (Gay-e-shah)

During the 1600s in Edo (Tokyo), women entertainers who were skilled at playing the shamisen and singing gradually came to be known as geisha--gei meaning art and sha meaning person.

In those days especially, such entertainment usually took place in gay quarters or in ryokan inns and ryotei restaurants where prostitution was practiced. Thus geisha came to be regarded by many as courtesans who were also skilled entertainers.

As the decades passed, the profession of geisha grew in stature. The training became more formalized and strict. With the deterioration of the large, elaborate, licensed gay quarters following the downfall of the Tokugawa shogunate in 1868, the social status of professional prostitutes began to drop and that of geisha to rise. Within a few decades their positions were completely reversed --geisha were the most elite of public women and prostitutes were the lowest. Well-to-do businessmen and politicians began to vie with each other to make the most famous geisha their mistresses. Their training included lessons in etiquette, grace, flower-arranging, singing, dancing, the tea ceremony, and how to be a stimulating conversationalist. While lower-class geisha were generally available as prostitutes, those of extraordinary talent and beauty were sought after as entertainers and, before and after the turn of the 20th century, as wives.

Given the social system in which wives did not participate with men in business or politics, and therefore could not act as hostesses for their husbands under any circumstances, geisha came to perform valuable functions not only in dressing up business and political meetings held in inn restaurants, but also in helping these meetings run smoothly.

Apprentice geisha, who often start their training before they are in their teens, are called maiko (my-e-koe), a term that originated in Kyoto. (In pre-1945 days, apprentice geisha in Tokyo were called hangyoku.)

Today, many waitresses and bar-maids who wear kimono and the elabroate wigs of the geisha are often passed off as geisha (Instant Geisha). True geisha are members of very tightly run geisha associations, and for the most part are simply too expensive for the average person to afford.

Most geisha live in or near the districts where they work, and can be seen in the evenings going to and from the various ryokan and ryotei that utilize their services--some still by jinrikisha (man-powered vehicle).

It is these clusters of ryotei which call in geisha that are known as geisha houses and geisha districts. Most of the geisha do not actually live where they work. Three of Tokyo's best known geisha districts are Shimbashi, Akasaka and Yanagibashi.

One of the most celebrated stories of a Meiji era personality buying a geisha had its beginnings in the city of Shimonoseki in the 1860s. The city's leading gay quarter was a favorite playground of several of the country's most daring young revolutionaries, who were then plotting to overthrow the feudal Tokugawa government.

Among these revolutionaries was a man named Ito. His favorite house of recreation was the Hayashiya, which was presided over by a well-known madam named Toku. Like all the young men who frequented the Hayashiya, Ito had his regular courtesan. Then he broke the rules by taking up with a geisha named Ume, who was the mistress of a merchant.

One night Ito's courtesan caught him and Ume in a compromising situation, and immediately reported him to the council of elders responsible for handling such breaches of conduct. A famous gang boss of the period tried to persuade the courtesan to forgive Ito and the geisha, but she was adamant.

According to the code of the gay quarters, the only way Ito could redeem himself was to buy his freedom from the courtesan and also buy Ume from her patron. This involved more money than Ito had.

Finally, Toku, the madam of the Hayashiya, gave Ito the money he needed. Ito then married the geisha, and went on with his revolutionary activities, eventually becoming one of Japan's outstanding prime ministers and the foremost statesman of the Meiji era--known to the world as Prince Hirobumi Ito.

In 1882 Ito was sent to Europe by Emperor Meiji to study the constitutions and codes of laws of various countries. On his return to Japan, he and several others drew up the country's first constitution, which was promulgated February 11, 1889.

After an outstanding career in government, Ito was appointed Resident-General of Korea in 1905, and served in that capacity until 1909. In October of that year, while visiting in Harbin, he was assassinated by a Korean dissident.

GHOSTS β GOBLINS / YUREI β BAKEMONO (You-raye and Bah-kay moe-no)

Ghosts and goblins played a major role in the legends and myths of Japan, and until the mid-1900s were an important aspect of folklore. In ancient times, goblins were said to have originally been dieties who became depraved and were banished from heaven. There were many different kinds of bakemono or goblins, associated with rivers, mountains, valleys and other areas. Ghosts were also plentiful, and came in different forms.

Ghosts and goblins are still popular themes in Japanese movies, TV films, plays, and literature, and there are dozens of such stories that are known by all Japanese.

Recommended reading: KWAIDAN, by Lafcadio Hearn (Tuttle).

GIFT-GIVING

Gift-giving has traditionally been a very important part of life in Japan--more important than in most countries. In earlier times, the practice was so important, and so formalized and institutionalized, that the guidelines for gift-giving would fill a large book.

Not only was the type of gift appropriate for specific occasions prescribed, so was the materials in which it was to be wrapped as well as the manner of wrapping. The act of presentation was also meticulously detailed. In upper-class families, there was often a member who was responsible for making sure these guidelines were followed.

Such formalities are not nearly as strict today, but gift-giving is still important--on the usual festive occasions as well as to establish and or maintain relations with doctors, teachers, employers, benefactors, etc.

The two biggest gift-giving seasons in Japan are Chugen (Chuu-gain) in the summer and Seibo (Say-e-boe) at the end of the year.

Chugen gifts are to express appreciation for daily services and favors received from individuals as well as from professionals (superiors, teachers, good customers, doctors, lawyers, accountants, etc.). These gifts are not necessarily expensive.

O'Seibo gifts at the end of the year serve the same purpose as chugen gifts, and are giving to superiors, good customers and other people to whom one feels a special obligation. Year-end gifts tend to be more costly than mid-year gifts.

The Japanese also customarily give gifts to someone leaving on a trip (usually money), and to people who do them favors while they themselves are travel-

ing. These parting gifts are called senbetsu (sin-bate-sue), and nowadays are usually limited to people leaving on long trips.

Senbetsu gifts carry with them the strong obligation for the receiver to bring back presents or souvenirs of their travels for each person who gave them a parting gift--often requiring the recipient to keep a list of the names of the people involved.

Giving the right gift at the right time can be a very important matter in both personal and business situations, and the foreigner who is not familiar with the intricacies of the ins and outs of gift-giving Japanese style would be well-advised to consult with a Japanese friend or contact.

GIFTS / OMIYAGE (Oh-me-yah-gay)

Since gift-giving has been a very important part of social and business life in Japan for many centuries, the manufacture and sales of gift-items is a major industry.

In addition to art, folk-crafts and various handicrafts, other popular gift items include fruit, cakes, traditional accessories and decorative items, seaweed, sembei rice crackers, mochi rice cake, tea, sake and other alcoholic beverages.

The custom of gift-giving as a vital part of social and business obligations very early led to highly refined packaging that in itself is often a work of art, and ranges from wrapping paper to wooden boxes.

Visitors to Japan are often taken aback by the variety, quality (and price) of gift items in department stores.

GIFU (Ghee-fuu)

Thirty kilometers northwest of Nagoya at the foot of Mt. Inaba on the Nagara River, the city of Gifu came into Japanese history as a castle town on the famous Nakasen Highway.

The castle was occupied by feudal Daimyo Nobunaga Oda in 1564, and was passed on to his son Nobutada and then his grandson Hidenobu. After the Battle of Sekigahara in 1600, Ieyasu Tokugawa's forces captured the castle, and it was given to the Owari Clan.

Gifu grew into a thriving farming and cottage industry center during the Tokugawa Shogunate. In 1891 most of the city was destroyed by an earthquake and great fire, but it was quickly rebuilt.

The city is now noted for the scenic beauty of the surrounding area, cormo-

Kyoto geisha going to work. P. 108

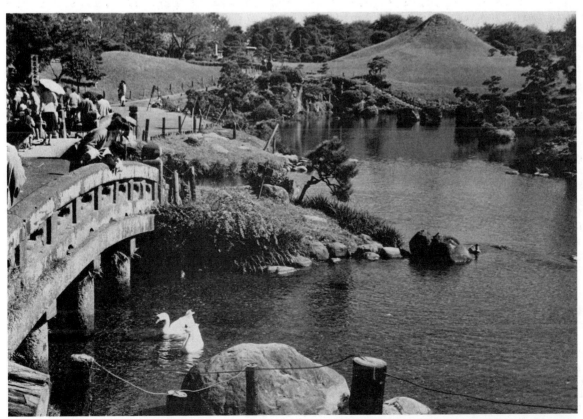

Suizen Garden in Kumamoto。 P. 183

rant fishing (ukai), its paper umbrellas, lanterns and fans, hand-made paper, persimmons, the Zuiryu Temple, and the Shoho Temple with its 13.6 meter image of Buddha.

GINZA (Gheen-zah)

The Ginza in Tokyo is Japan's best-known shopping and entertainment district. Measuring about a mile in length and half a mile in width, the Ginza extends north-south from Kyobashi to Shimbashi and east-west from Tsukiji to Hibiya in downtown Tokyo. The name comes from a silver mint (ginza) established in the area in 1612, shortly after the beginning of the Tokugawa Shogunate (1603-1868).

Shops, restaurants and drinking establishments grew up around the mint, and by the late 1700s, the Ginza was one of the most colorful and liveliest areas in Edo. The interesection at Ginza 4-chome, where Ginza Dori, the main north-south avenue, crosses Hibya Dori, the main east-west thoroughfare, was to become one of the main crossroads of the city.

Ginza Dori was the first street in Japan to be paved and to have sidewalks (of brick), following the construction of brick buildings along the avenue in 1873.

The first electric lights on the Ginza were installed in 1879, quickly replacing the wax candle lanterns that had been in use for generations. Soon thereafter, strolling the Ginza (Gin-bura / gheen-buu-rah) became a fashionable past-time of the city.

There are numerous other huge shopping-entertainment districts in Tokyo today, but the Ginza retains its drawing power. Its hundreds of shops, boutiques, bars, lounges, restaurants and huge department stores give it an ambience that is magnetic to Japanese and foreign visitors alike. On Sundays, Ginza Avenue is closed to traffic and becomes a bazaar of food stalls and stands selling gift and novelty items, attracting thousands of strollers and shoppers.

GIRI (Ghee-ree)

Giri refers to the very strong feelings of obligation and responsibility the Japanese have for doing what is expected of them in all areas of life. What is expected of them is to obey and abide by traditional customs regarding education, marriage, gifts, parties, their job, work, and so on.

Basically, upholding the demands of giri is upholding one's honor and reputation by doing what is expected, even though it may be unpleasant or result in unhappiness. In earlier days, when the demands of giri could not be reconciled with a person's own wishes, suicide was often the way out.

Even today among older Japanese there are many who are giri-gatai--very strict in their observance of giri.

GIONMACHI (Ghee-own-mah-chee)

One of the most famous of Japan's traditional geisha quarters, Gionmachi is a section of Kyoto on the east bank of the Kamo River. In addition to the traditionally styled geisha inns, the area also boasts the country's oldest theater, the Minami Za, founded in the early 1600s, where all-star kabuki performances are staged every year in December.

Also in Gionmachi is the famous Kaburenjo Theater, noted for its spring Miyako Odori (Cherry Dance festival).

GLOVER MANSION

The Glover Mansion, originally called the Glover House, is a large residence built on a prominence overlooking Nagasaki harbor by a British trader before the turn of the 20th century. The mansion is believed to be the original setting for the story on which the famous opera Madame Butterfly is based.

In Japan the word butterfly (cho-cho) has long been used to describe a person --especially a man--who is not content with one woman and flutters like a butterfly from one to another.

GO-BETWEENS / NAKODO (Nah-koe-doe)

The use of go-betweens, in arranging marriages and in handling personal and business matters where there is ill-will or the likelihood of problems, is a tradition in Japan.

The reason for this custom is simple--a third party who is not personally or emotionally involved in a matter is more likely to make rational decisions, and it provides a way for both parties to avoid putting their reputations on the line.

GOD-SHELF / KAMI-DANA (Kah-me-dah-nah)

Until recent times, nearly all homes in Japan had a miniature Shinto shrine that was placed on a special shelf, the kami-dana, along with various religious articles. On special occasions, such as memorial services, offerings of food and consecrated twigs, etc., are placed on the shelf.

Many homes, particularly in rural

areas where religious observances are more common, still have the kami-dana.

GOLDFISH / KINGYO (Keen-g'yoe)

Japan is now synonymous with beautiful goldfish that come in all sizes and color combinations. Goldfish were introduced into Japan from China in the early 1600s, and there were later infusions from the Netherlands and Hawaii.

The Chinese goldfish were quickly adopted as pets by the aristocracy in the Imperial capital of Kyoto. Japanese goldfish breeders both developed and introduced new varieties, and keeping goldfish gradually became a national past-time. Goldfish peddlers, pushing their bowl laden carts, became a familiar sight on the lanes and streets of towns and villages. Their cry of Keeeennnng-yohhhhhh! was one of the most nostalgic sounds of the country.

Kingyo vendors are still seen in Japan, especially around temples and shrines during festival time, and at resort beaches.

GORGES / KYOKOKU (K'yoe-koe-kuu)

With its moutainous terrain and high rainfall, Japan has an exceptionally large number of mountain streams that over the eons have carved out thousands of gorges, many of which have been famous for centuries for their incredible beauty.

Among the best-known gorges in the country are Tachikue near Izumoshi on the west side of Honshu, and Takachiho in the Sobo-Katamuki Quasi-National Park, near Kumamoto in Kyushu.

GOVERNMENT / SEIFU (Say-e-fuu)

Japan's government is composed of a legislative branch called the Diet, an administrative branch, which includes the Prime Minister and his Cabinet, and a judiciary branch.

The Diet, made up of a House of Representatives and a House of Councilors, is the highest organ of state power and the sole law-making body. Members of both Houses are elected by popular vote.

In addition to the power to pass laws, the Diet also designates the Prime Minister (usually the leader of the most powerful party or faction), approves budgets and treaties, and has the power to impeach judges and amend the constitution.

In administering the country, the Prime Minister and his ministers are collectively responsible to the Diet. Altogether there are 12 ministries, each of which is headed by a Cabinet Minister.

The Prime Minister may dismiss the cabinet ministers at his discretion. He also may be removed from office by a vote of non-confidence by the majority of the Diet.

The judiciary consists of the Supreme Court and a number of lesser courts, including high courts, district courts, family courts and summary courts. The Prime Minister and Cabinet appoint all of the judges of the courts, including the Chief Judge of the Supreme Court.

There are a total of 763 Diet members, 511 of them in the House of Representatives, and 252 in the House of Councilors. The House of Representatives outranks the House of Councilors. Business in the Houses can be conducted only if at least one-third of the membership is present. All matters are decided by a simple majority vote, or in special cases, by a two-thirds majority.

Members of the House of Representatives are elected from prefectural electorates for 4-year terms that may be terminated by the Cabinet if it decides to dissolve the House. Members in the House of Councilors are elected from both national and prefectural constituencies. Their term of office is six years. Half of the membership comes up for election every three years, and the House of Councilors is never dissolved.

The 12 ministries are Justice, Foreign Affairs, Finance, Education, Health and Welfare, Agriculture Forestry and Fisheries, International Trade and Industry, Transport, Labor, Construction and Home Affairs.

Besides these ministries, there are nine administrative agencies that are attached to the Office of the Prime Minister--the Administrative Management Agency, Hokkaido Development Agency, Defense Agency, Economic Planning Agency, Science and Technology Agency, Environment Agency, Okinawa Development Agency, National Land Agency and National Public Safety Commission.

Each of Japan's 47 prefectures is administered by a popularly elected governor, as is the metropolis of Tokyo.

The House of Representatives has been totally dominated by the Liberal Democrats since 1955. The next largest number of seats is held by the Komeito Party, followed by the Democratic Socialist Party, the Japan Communist Party, the New Liberal Club and Independents.

In the House of Councillors, the LDP has well over twice as many members as the Japan Socialist Party, which is followed well down the line by the Komeito Party. The Japan Communist Party, the Democratic Socialist Party, Shinsei Club, the Dainin Club, the Ichi no Kai and the Independents bring up the rear with a few members each.

GOVERNMENT, LOCAL

Since 1947 Japan has had a Local Autonomy Law that guarantees the right of local communities to govern themselves, by popular vote. Anyone 30 years of age or older may run for governor of a prefecture. The mayor of a village, town or city must be at least 25 years old. Tenure in all cases is four years.

Each village, town and city in the country has its own unicameral assembly, which is empowered to enact and abolish ordinances, approve budgets, and authorize expenditures. Local residents have the right of a wide range of appeals, including the demand that ordinances be abolished, that the assembly be dissolved or the chief executive officers and assembly members be recalled.

Prefectural and municipal governments share the functions and responsibilities of administration with the national governement. The local governments are responsible for most functions regarding land preservation and development, disaster prevention, pollution control, labor, education, social welfare and health problems.

Local taxes account for about 30 percent of the revenues of municipal and prefectural governments, with the national government making up the balance through tax transfers and allocations plus reimbursement for work done under national programs.

GRAND MASTERS / IEMOTO (E-eh-moe-toe)

One of the most distinctive and important aspects of life in Japan is the so-called iemoto system in such fields as martial arts, the performing arts, asetheticpursuits andsumo.

Iemoto is generally translated as Grand Master, but its root meaning is House Founder.

In the early decades of the Tokugawa Era (1603-1868), different schools developed in all of the above disciplines, each one founded by a man of woman who became its iemoto or grand master, and exercised virtually absolute authority over the activities of the schools and their graduates.

The position of grand master was hereditary or passed to the favorite disciple, who continued the system. The grand master has the exclusive right to issue graduation certificates and grant licenses for former students to teach-- for which the grand master or head school receives what amounts to franchise fees.

Despite criticism of the system, especially in the years following the end of World War II in 1945, the system has not only persisted, it has gained in strength and importance and must be reckoned with in any dealings with these various disciplines.

It is particularly important in flower arranging, the tea ceremony and in sumo.

GRANDMOTHER THROWING-AWAY MOUNTAIN/ OBASUTE YAMA (Oh-bahh-sue-tay Yah-mah)

Some 21 kilometers south of Nagano, on the slopes of Mt. Kamuriki, is an area known as Obasute or Grandmother Throwing-Away.

It is said that in ancient times, nearby poor villages developed the custom of taking old women, who could no longer work or take care of themselves, to the mountainside and leaving them there to die of exposure.

The area is now known as a popular place for viewing the moon when it is reflected in the water of hundreds of rice paddies terraced onto the slopes of the mountain.

GRAND SHRINES OF ISE (E-say)

The most venerated spot in Japan, where the spirits of all past emperors are enshrined, Ise is on the Pacific Ocean side of Shima Peninsula, south of Nagoya in Mie Prefecture.

The city of Ise is actually made up of two towns, Uji and Yamada, that were joined to form one municipality. The area was selected as a site for the Imperial Jingu shrines in part because of the incredible beauty of the area, and also because it was regarded as holy ground by the ancient Shinto leaders who chose it.

The Ise Jingu Shrines are actually made up of two extensive complexes that are 6.2 kilometers apart--the Naiku or

Inner Shrine and the Geku or Outer Shrine.

The Outer Shrines, dedicated to the Goddess of Farms, Harvest, Food and Sericulture, consist of nine major buildings, including an Imperial House of Sojourn where the emperor rests when he visits the shrine, the Place of Assembly where other members of the Imperial family rest, a sacred dance pavilion, the Hall of Worship and the Main Hall.

The grounds of the Outer Shrine, surrounded by a great grove of ancient Japanese cedars, covers and area of 89 ha. (213.6 acres). The shrine was originally located in Manai in what is now Kyoto Prefecture. But it was moved to Ise in 478 by Emperor Yuryaku, following a revelation from Amaterasu O-Mikami, the Sun Goddess.

The Inner Shrine (Naiku) dates from about 288 A.D., and it is here that the Three Sacred Treasures that make up the Three Regalia of Japan's Imperial Throne --a mirror, sword and jewel--are kept.

According to Japanese mythology, the Mirror was given by the Sun Goddess to her grandson Ninigi-no Mikoto when he came down to earth to reign (on the spot now occupied by the Outer Shrines of Jingu). The Mirror was first kept in the Imperial Palace in Yamato, as instructed by the Sun Goddess. But in 92 B.C. it was moved to a shrine in Kasanui near Nara because of fear that being in close contact with too many people might desecrate it.

Apparently this same fear resulted in it being moved again around 288 to what was then distant Ise.

There are eight major structures in the Inner Shrine, similar to the main buildings in the Outer Shrine. The shrines are constructed of Japanese cypress (hinoki), one of the most beautiful of woods, obtained from a national forest in the Kiso Mountains. Their architecture is pure Japanese, dating back to before the introduction of Buddhism and Chinese influences into Japan.

The Grand Shrines of Ise are as fresh today as they were over a thousand years ago because from early times it has been the custom to rebuild them completely every 20 years. The last such rebuilding, called Sen-Gu-Shiki, was done in 1973.

There are several annual festivals held at the Jingu Shrines. The most important are held in May, October and November.

GRAND ISE SWEAT

Ise is also famous for something else: the Ise Training Center, which is a kind of spiritual and physical training camp for employees of Japanese companies. The Center holds two 4-day training sessions each month, putting its recruits through a training program that would cower most would-be commandoes.

Companies do not require their employees to go to Ise, but many of them strongly encourage it, and pay all tuition costs.

The regime includes strenuous physical workouts, intensive lectures on social roles and obligations to children and parents, group singing and dancing, and--in winter--a dip in the icy waters of the Isuzu River.

The purpose of the Center is to teach team spirit and team achievement in the proper social context, and, as the director says, to help the trainees empty out their old selves and become new people. Part of the uniform at the Center is a headband imprinted with the kanji characters for love and sweat, which is a good description of the Japanese approach to business.

There are a number of other such training camps for company employees and managers around Japan. In some of them the training is more strenuous than the regime at Ise. One, on the waist of Mt. Fuji, quite literally aims at breaking the individual's ego shell, and remaking him or her into the perfect team player.

GREAT BRIDGE OF CHOSHI / CHOSHI OHASHI (Choe-she Oh-hah-she)

The Great Bridge of Choshi, spanning the Tone River at its mouth on Boso Peninsula, which adjoins Tokyo on the northeast, is the longest river bridge in Japan. The bridge is 1,450 meters in length and links Choshi City and Hasaki Town in Ibaraki Prefecture.

GREAT BUDDHA OF KAMAKURA / KAMAKURA DAI BUTSU (Kah-mah-kuu-rah Die Boot-sue)

Cast in the year 1252 by either Goroemon Ono or Hisatomo Tanji, both famous casters of the period, the great bronze image of Buddha in Kamakura is one of the world's most impressive sights.

Sitting in the precincts of the Kotoku-in Temple in a narrow valley that is close to a mile from the sea, the Great Buddha is 11.4 meters high, 29.4 meters at the base, and has a face that is 2.3 meters in length. A silver boss on the Buddha's forehead weighs 13.6 kilograms, and the image altogether weighs over 93 tons. A spiral staircase inside the statue leads up to the shoulder level.

The expression on the Great Buddha's face is one of passionless calm, and over the centuries has inspired millions of worshipers and sightseers, including Rudyard Kipling, who made the image known to millions of others in one of his poems.

After the Great Buddha was cast and completed, a great hall was built around it. In 1369 a typhoon severely damaged the large wooden building, and in 1495 a tidal wave entered the valley from the distant ocean and carried the huge hall away. Since that long ago time, the Great Buddha has sat out in the open.

One of the first foreigners to visit the Great Buddha was an Englishman named John Saris, who was a ship's captain. In 1613 he entered the statue and carved his name and the date into its inner wall.

After British poet Rudyard Kipling visited Kamakura in the late 1890s, he wrote a poem entitled Buddha at Kamakura. Three of the most quoted verses in the poem:

O ye who tread the Narrow Way
By Trophet-flare to Judgement Day,
Be gentle when the heathen pray
To Buddha at Kamakura.

Yet spare us still the Western joke
When joss-sticks turn to scented smoke
The little sins of little folk
That worship at Kamakura.

A tourist show, a legend told,
A rusting bulk of bronze and gold,
So much, and scarce so much, ye hold
The meaning of Kamakura.

Recommended reading: SCULPTURE OF THE KAMAKURA PERIOD, by Hisashi Mori (Weatherhill).

GREAT BUDDHA OF NARA

The Great Buddha (Daibutsu) of Nara is the center-piece of Todai Temple, which was erected between 745 and 752 and is still the largest wooden building in the world. The great bronze statue was commissioned by Emperor Shomu, and work on it was first begun in 743 at Shigaraki Palace south of Lake Biwa.

This effort ended in failure, however, and it was started again in Nara in 745, and was completed in 749 after eight attempts.

The seated figure is 16.2 meters in height, and its face is 4.8 meters wide. A total of 437 tons of bronze, 75 kilograms of mercury, 130 milograms of pure gold, seven tons of vegetable wax and an unrecorded amount of charcoal and other materials were used in the casting of the image.

The dedication ceremony for the Great Buddha was held in 752, and was attended by the Empress Regent Koken and her parents, the ex-Emperor and Empress Shomu, all the court dignataries, and over 10,000 priests and nuns.

In 855 an earthquake shook the Great Buddha's head off, but it was replaced in 861. A fire in 1180 melted the head and right hand of the statue, which were replaced. Again in 1567 the head was lost in a fire and it was 1692 before it was completely repaired--and kept in repair since.

The Great Buddha of Nara is one of the most popular visitor attractions in Japan.

GUIDE SERVICES

With tourism and international business so important to the Japanese economy, Japan is one of the few countries that has a Guide-Interpreter Business Law. The law requires anyone who wants to engage in the guide/interpreting business to pass a national examination conducted by the Ministry of Transport, and obtain a license from the governor of the local prefecture.

There are over two thousand such guides in Japan, over half of whom belong to the prestigious Japan Guide Association. The rates charged by the guides are controlled by the JGA. Among the languages spoken by the guides are English, French, German, Russian, Chinese, Italian, Spanish and Portuguese.

Ritsuin Garden in Kagawa. P. 107

The Great Buddha of Kamakura. P. 115

HACHIMAKI (Hah-chee-mah-kee)

This is the headband that the Japanese have traditionally worn when engaged in strenuous physical work, participating in some festival activity or engaging in some kind of labor or political demonstration.

The wearing of the hachimaki is a very old custom in Japan, and is said to have developed in ancient times as part of Shinto religious ceremonies. It is both a practical and picturesque custom that adds to the coloful ambience of life in Japan.

HAIKU (Hie-kuu)

A highly stylized and refined form of poetry that fascinates both Japanese and Westerners alike, haiku was developed in the middle of Japan's Edo Period in the late 17th century by the famous poet Matsuo Basho.

Basho took the opening verse (hokku/hoke-kuu) of the long-established haikai-renga (hie-kie rane-gah), a linked verse form, and made it into an independent form. It was not until the end of the 19th century that Masaoka Shiki made the name haiku the generic term for this form of poetry.

Haiku poetry consists of 17 syllables (the Japanese language is made up of syllable sounds), arranged in three lines of five-seven-five syllables each.

This style of poetry traditionally deals with nature and life in a highly austere, elegant way that distills the essence of a thing, presenting a clear but fleeting glimpse of what the author has seen or felt.

It is also traditional to use a season word in every haiku—referring to a plant, animal, event, or custom in a particular season—thus evoking mental images of spring, the mountains, the brevity of life, and so on.

One of the most famous of Basho's haiku:

Yagate shinu	The cicada's cry
Keshiki wa miezu	Gives no sign
Semi no koe	It is about to die

Recommended reading: A HAIKU JOURNEY, by Matsuo Basho, translated by Dorothy Britton (Kodansha Int'l). Also, THE JA-PANESE HAIKU, by Ken Yasuda (Tuttle).

HAKONE (Hah-koe-nay)

Situated in the mountains southwest of Tokyo, and adjoining Mt. Fuji, Hakone is one of the most beautiful and popular resorts in all of Japan. The heart of the Hakone district is a huge volcanic crater that is 40 kilometers in circumference, and includes a beautiful lake (Ashi-no Ko, popularly known as Lake Hakone), and 12 hotspring spas that have been known and used since ancient times.

These spas, several in picturesque gorges whose beauty is beyond words, are: Yumoto, Tonosawa, Miyanoshita, Dogashima, Sokokura, Kowkidani, Giga, Gora, Ubako, Sengokuhara, Ashinoyu and Yunohanazawa.

The oldest of these spas is Yumoto. The three most famous (especially among foreign visitors to Japan) are Miyanshita, Gora and Kowakidani.

Hakone is served by bus and train lines, and is a popular overnight and weekend trip by car from the Tokyo and Yokohama areas. Besides its superb scenery and dozens of hotspring inns (whose waters are classified according to their mineral content and effects of various ailments), the cool summer weather makes Hakone doubly popular in the summer months.

The most famous tourist attraction in Hakone is the annual re-enactment of one of the great Daimyo Processions of the Tokugawa Period, when all the feudal lords had to march to the capital at Edo every other year to attend the Shogun's court. The event usually takes place on November 3rd, but may vary by a day or so.

The Procession begins at Yumoto, goes to Tonosawa in the morning, and returns to Yumoto in the afternoon.

There are dozens of historical sites in the Hakone area, including a replica of one of the famous Barrier Gates that were erected along the great walking roads that led to Edo. During the long period of the Tokugawa Shogunate, Hakone was one of the largest and most important of the post stations that lined the old Tokaido Highway.

Some of the huge Japanese cedars that lined the Tokaido along the shores of Lake Hakone are still alive, making it easier to visualize the passing of one of the great Daimyo Processions (some of which consisted of over 1,000 warriors and retainers, all in their official regalia. See PROCESSIONS OF THE LORDS. Also BARRIER GATES.

HAKODATE (Hah-koe-dah-tay)

The third largest city on Hokkaido, Japan's northernmost main island, Hakodate (Box Castle) owes its origin and name to the Kono clan, which built a box-shaped castle there in the 15th century.

The gateway to Hokkaido, the port city is located at the neck of Hakodate Peninsula, which extends out into the Straits of Tsugaru and has a spectacular mountain at its tip.

Hakodate first became of special importance in the history of Japan when it was designated as a coaling station for foreign ships in 1855 under the terms of the Kanagawa Treaty, which was negotiated by the American Townsend Harris.

Then on July 1, 1859 Hakodate became one of five ports opened to foreign commerce (the others were Yokohama, Kobe, Nagasaki and Niigata), but it was so far away from the population and industrial centers that it did not enjoy the rapid growth experienced by the other ports.

Hakodate is now a major fishing port and a center for food processing and shipbuilding. There are dozens of points of interest in the Hakodate area, including Hakodate Park, famous for its cherry blossoms in the late spring, the Hakodate Museum which is Japan's oldest local museum, the Goyokaku which was the country's first Western-style military fort (completed in 1864) and the site of one of the last major battles surrounding the downfall of the Shogun in 1868.

Also: the famous Yunokawa Spa, which boasts over 100 inns and restaurants set among hotsprings that have an average temperature of 66 degrees C., plus a Trappist convent.

HAKOZAKI-CHO (Hah-koe-zah-kee-choe)

This is the location of Tokyo International Airport's city terminal. It is the station for limousine buses that arrive from and leave for the airport, in Narita some 60 kilometers away, every few minutes. Several airlines, including Japan Air Lines, have check-in facilities at the City Terminal.

Hakozaki-cho is in Chuo Ward about 15 minutes from central Tokyo.

HALL OF POETS / SHI SENDO (She Sane-doe)

One of the most beautiful examples of Japanese architecture and gardening is the famous Hall of Poets in Kyoto. A short distance north of the noted Temple of the Silver Pavilion, the Shi Sendo

was founded in 1631 as a retreat by Jozan Ishikawa, a famous poet and scholar of that period.

The temple takes its name from the Shi Sen or Poet Room, where the portraits of 36 famous Chinese poets line the walls. The temple is also known for the exceptional beauty of its white-sand garden, lined with azaleas that have been sculptured into numerous shapes, and surrounded by a grove of maple trees.

HAMA DETACHED PALACE (Hah-mah)

Originally a villa of the Tokugawa Shogun's family, the Hama Detached Palace in Tokyo was taken over by the Imperial Household in 1871, and was frequently used as a State Guest House. Former American president U.S. Grant stayed there when he visited Japan after leaving office.

The site was given to the city of Tokyo in 1945, and since 1946 has been open to the public. The 25 ha. (60-acre) grounds include a tidal pool spanned by three bridges that lead to an islet in the heart of the landscaped garden.

The buildings and garden give an impressive insight into the way the feudal lords of Edo lived, and spent their time. The area is especially attractive in the early spring when the cherry trees on the grounds are in bloom.

The garden is only a short walk from Shimbashi Station in downtown Tokyo.

HAND-CLAPPING AT SHRINES/KASHIWADE (Kah-she-wah-day)

Worshippers at Shinto shrines clap their hands to concentrate their own attention on their prayers, and to attract the attention of the diety of the shrine.

HANDICRAFTS / MINGEIHIN (Meen-gay-e-heen)

Japanese historians have traced the country's famous handicraft industries to metal work that was already in evidence in the 7th century. Several thousand items on display in the Shosoin Repository in Nara were first presented to the Todai Temple in 756. They include swords, mirrors, ornaments, musical instruments, and other items.

During the Heian Period from 794 to 1185 great progress was made in both metal and lacquerware handicrafts. With the rise of the warrior class, swordsmiths proliferated, and over 20,000 of their names were recorded. The three best-known of the great swordsmiths of this period were Yoshimitsu, Masamune and Yoshihiro.

Metalware, metal-pot casting, lacquerware, ceramics, glassware, and cloisonne continued to make significant progress during these centuries, and really flowered during the long, peaceful Tokugawa Period (1603-1868) that preceded the reopening of Japan to the outside world.

The secret of the quality and beauty of Japanese-made handicrafts can be found in the master-apprentice system, and in the fundamental concepts of beauty that grew out of Shintoism and Zen Buddhism. This was a classic beauty that emphasized the natural essence of the material. See BEAUTY, QUALITY.

The master-apprentice system was already well-entrenched in Japan by the 7th century. Under this system, boys were apprenticed to tradesmen when they were as young as seven or eight, and would learn a craft from the bottom up over a period of many years. In some of the more demanding crafts, the period of apprenticeship lasted for up to 30 years or even longer--sometimes until the master died.

It was almost always at least 20 years before an apprentice was permitted to go out on his own and set up his own shop, thus the products that came out of Japan's handicraft industries were routinely of a quality that has not been surpassed in any country.

Recommended reading: FAMOUS CERAMICS OF JAPAN SERIES (Kodansha Int'l), THE ARTS OF JAPAN SERIES (Weatherhill), JAPANESE CLOISONNE--History, Technique β Application, by Lawrence A. Cohen and Dorothy Ferster (Weatherhill).

HANEDA AIRPORT / HANEDA KUKO (Hah-nay-dah Kuu-koe)

Tokyo's original international airport, located only a 15 to 20 minute taxi ride from downtown Tokyo, Haneda is now the city's domestic airport--but it still has one international client: China Air Lines.

As a result of a diplomatic arrangement with Taiwan, CAL was allowed to continue using Haneda when all other international operations were moved to the new international airport in Narita. See AIRPORTS.

HANGING SCROLLS / KAKEJIKU (Kah-kay-jee-kuu)

The focal point of the main room or guest room in a Japanese house, inn or mansion is the tokonoma (Toe-koe-no-mah), a recessed alcove designed for the express purpose of displaying a flower arrangement, a hanging scroll or some other work of art.

Kakejiku are long, vertical scrolls of silk or paper bearing a painting or a choice selection of calligraphy, or both. The painting or calligraphy is often seasonal, and is selected for display on the basis of the season it fits.

Kake means hanging, and jiku means axis or roller, and refers to the wooden rollers at the bottom (and sometimes the top) of the scrolls, which allow them to be easily rolled up when not in use.

Kakejiku are also called kakemono or hanging things.

The custom of building tokonoma into Japanese homes and other buildings is an ancient one. It began as a private Buddhist altar where an incense burner, flowers and a Buddhist scroll were hung. It then developed into an integral part of the aesthetic practices that are a distinctive part of Japanese culture-- practices that derive from Shintoism themes that celebrate nature and man's relationship with the cosmos, and from Taoist and Buddhist teachings that the appreciation of nature and beauty is necessary for the whole man.

See IKEBANA, TOKONOMA.

HAPPI COATS (Hop-pee)

The happi is a short, kimono-styled slip-over jacket worn by workmen and Daimyo retainers since early times--and also worn by youths and men as a sort of costume when they participate in many festivals. It is also called hanten (hahn-tane).

While strickly a common workman's jacket as for as the Japanese were concerned, foreign residents and visitors in Japan in the late 1940s and 1950s picked up on the happi coat as casual wear, and it became a popular gift item. The Westeners were probably mislead by the word happi, which they pronounced as happy, and took it to mean that the jacket was for recreational wear.

Regular happi coats traditionally had the name or crest of the wearer's employer on the back.

HARAKIRI (Hah-rah-kee-ree)

The Japanese word harakiri is widely recognized around the world (invariably mispronounced as something like harry-kerry) because of the sensational nature of ritual suicide.

An understanding of the cultural and social role that harakiri played in Japanese life for so many centuries is one of the most fascinating facets of Japanese history, and is a key to understanding that history. See SUICIDE.

HARAMAKI (Hah-rah-mah-kee)

The haramaki or stomach-band is a long band of cloth, usually woolen these days, that was traditionally wrapped around the abdomen by Japanese men--especially working-class men--and especially during winter but often during other seasons as well.

The custom is still followed by many laborers who work outside (and some older men). Its purpose being to prevent the abdomen from getting chilled. The practice goes back to the ancient concept that the solar plexus is the center of one's life-force.

HARMONY / WA (Wah)

One of the primary aspects of any society or social system are the various customs and laws that are designed to maintain harmony all--or at least most--of the time among the members of the society.

In Japan this harmonious state has traditionally been referred to as wa, a term that is simple enough in itself but has very broad implications when used in its Japanese context.

It goes back to one of the primary principles of Shintoism--that peaceful, harmonious relations must exist among human beings and between humans and nature in order for everything and everybody to stay in balance, prosper and fulfill their purpose.

The ultimate goal of wa permeates and colors every facet of Japanese culture and the Japanese social system, from the way the language is constructed and used to the customs and rules that apply to behavior in personal relationships.

Wa does not have anything to do with equality. Its essence is that everything and everybody has a proper place and a proper role, and must conform to this proper role in order to stay right with the world.

All of the many artifices that make up the Japanese social and business system, from the bow, the use of respect language, the use of introductions and go-betweens, the concensus approach to decisions, the role of cabarets and drinking, and so on are aspects of maintaining harmony.

HARRIS, TOWNSEND

Following the success of his trade and diplomatic mission to Japan in 1853-54, Commodore Matthew C. Perry recommended that Townsend Harris, a merchant with extensive experience in the South Pacific and Orient, be appointed the U.S.'s first consul to Japan.

Harris' appointment was made in August 1855, and in July of 1856 he arrived at the small fishing town of Shimoda at the tip of Izu Peninsula south of Edo (Tokyo), which had been designated as the site for the first American consulate and trading post.

Harris was accompanied by an interpreter named Heusken, a Dutchman who had lived in Japan and could speak fairly good Japanese. Harris soon recognized that Shimoda was useless as a trading port. His primary goals were thus to conclude a treaty with Japan providing for freedom of trade, the opening of additional ports, and moving the American consulate from Shimoda to the Shogunate capital of Edo.

The Gyokusen Temple, located in Kakisaki Village about two kilometers east of Shimoda on the harbor road, was assigned to Harris as his residence. According to his descriptions, it was a dilapidated and uncomfortable place.

Harris immediately requested permission to travel to Edo to present his credentials to the Shogun, but was told he would have to hand them over to the local governor who would forward them to Edo. Harris recognized this as a delaying tactic, and refused. In November 1857, after more than a year of frustrating negotiations, Harris was permitted to travel from Shimoda to Edo to officially announce his presence and begin his work.

The majority of Japan's feudal lords were bitterly opposed to opening the country to foreign trade and diplomatic relations, no doubt recognizing the threat to their positions.

During Harris' trip to Edo, which he made in a palanquin, a form of travel reserved for the ruling class, an attempt was made to assassinate him, but the would-be killers were caught

Harris was courteously received by Shogun Iemochi Tokugawa. A tentative agreement was reached, and he returned to Shimoda in March 1858. The following month he returned to Edo for the Shogun's reply.

The reply was not ready. Harris returned to Shimoda in June and in July was summoned to Kanagawa (now part of Yokohama), where the treaty was signed. Shogun Iemochi had consulted with his strongest supporters among the feudal lords before agreeing to sign the new treaty, which opened the ports of Yokohama, Kobe and Nagasaki to trade, allowed religious freedom in Japan, for Japan to build ships in the U.S., and for the U.S. to act as mediator in the event of disputes between Japan and European countries. The treaty was signed on July 20, 1858, but did not go into effect until July 4, 1859.

This new treaty divided the country into two factions--those who agreed with the Shogun that the country should be opened to the outside world, and the traditionalists who believed that the Shogun and his allies had betrayed the country into the hands of barbarians.

Soon after the new treaty was signed Shogun Iemochi became ill, and Lord Kamon Ii of Hikone was appointed prime minister (Tairo). Lord Ii was in favor of the treaty, and thus became the leader of the forces working toward elimination of the exclusion policy. The opposition group was headed by the Lord of Mito, who was a member of the Tokugawa family, but a strong traditionalist.

While enroute to the Shogun's castle in Edo on March 23, 1860, Lord Ii was attacked by Mito Samurai. His head was cut off and taken to Mito where it was exhibited in public. The Samurai than surrendered to the Shogunate authorities, saying they had killed Ii because he had gone against the wishes of the Emperor in signing the treaty with Harris.

The following year, Harris' secretary, the Dutchman, was murdered, and in July of the same year a group of foreigners from the British Legation were set upon by ronin Samurai. Two of the Englishmen were wounded and several of their guards were killed.

The Shogunate was alarmed by these attacks, fearing that they would provoke the foreign powers into declaring war on Japan. All foreign residents of Edo were escorted to Yokohama, where they would be safer in the foreign compound.

The U.S. Senate approved Harris' appointment as Minister to Japan in January 1859, and on July 7 he established the American Legation in Edo in the Zempuku Temple, said to have been founded by the famous Kobo Daishi in the 9th century. Harris continued as the American minister in Japan until 1861, when he retired from government service. He died in 1878 and was buried in Brooklyn, New York.

The Zempuku Temple was to continue to serve as the American Legation in Edo until 1869, by which time the Shogun had stepped down and a new government formed by Emperor Meiji. In 1936 the American-Japan Society erected a stone monument at the temple to commemorate its history in Japan-U.S. relations.

The monument was inlaid with a bronze disk bearing Harris' likeness, and an inscription that reads: On this spot Townsend Harris opened the first American Legation in Japan, July 7, 1859.

On the back of the monument, in Japanese, is a handwritten note by Baron T. Matsuda that says: The site of the residence of early American envoys.

During the three years he stayed in Shimoda, Harris was kept under close watch by local and Shogunate authorities, and was not allowed to leave the town except on his two official trips to Edo. He greatly resented being isolated in this manner, and lodged numerous protests with the Japanese authorities.

Hoping to both mollify and distract Harris, the authorities assigned an ex-prostitute to him as a woman servant. While it has been intimated that Harris carried on an affair with the maid, he records in his diary that he was too ill from an unsatisfactory diet and various ailments to notice her.

In the 1920s, Edgar A. Bancroft, the American Ambassador to Japan, Viscount E. Shibusawa and Prince Iesato Tokugawa (then president of the American-Japan Society), had the Gyokusen Temple, Harris' first place of residence in Japan, renovated and a granite tablet erected commemorating the event. The tablet bears an inscription from Harris' dairy in which he recounts the raising of the first American flag in Japan, his problems with huge mosquitoes and lack of sleep, and grave reflections about the omnious changes he foresees for Japan.

Underneath this note is the inscription: In memory of Townsend Harris, American Consul-General, who by the Treaty of Yedo, July 29, 1858, opened Japan to the world, and on this spot, September

4, 1856, raised the first Consular flag in this Empire and here resided until November 23, 1857. Erected by Viscount E. Shibusawa, Edgar A. Bancroft and Henry M. Wolf of Chicago, September 4, 1927.

On the back of the granite slab is a glowing tribute to Harris in Japanese, written by Viscount Shibusawa.

Inside the temple is a framed portrait of Harris and a glass case containing a number of momentoes from his days there. The most valuable artifact in the temple is an eight-volume dairy in Japanese detailing Harris' life in the village, written by the elder of the village on orders from the authorities.

In 1862 the Shogunate sent a mission to the U.S., requesting that the dates for opening the ports be postponed. That same year an Englishman named Richardson and some friends went out riding from Yokohama, and while on the road met the procession of the Lord of Satsuma.

When the procession of a Daimyo was passing, common people were required by law to clear the road and bow down to the ground. Claiming that the English party did not pay proper respect to their Lord, the Samurai guards attacked the party, killing Richardson.

The British demanded that the guilty Samurai be punished and that the Lord of Satsuma and the Shogunate pay indemnities for Richardson's death. When their demands were ignored, British warships were dispatched to Kagoshima, capital of the Satsuma fief, and destroyed much of the city by cannon fire.

The turmoil in the country continued. In 1864, the Daimyo of Choshu, who had set up cannon overlooking the Straits of Shimonoseki, began firing on foreign freighters. In September, an allied fleet of 17 warships sailed into Shimonoseki, forcing the Lord of Choshu to come to terms, and to pay an indemnity of three million dollars.

The foreign powers began insisting that the Emperor, as the head of state, ratify the treaties the Shogunate had signed, and this he did in 1865--greatly strengthening the position of those who favored the Emperor over the Shogun.

A short while later, Shogun Iemochi died and was succeeded by Yoshinobu Tokugawa. The reigning Emperor (Komei) also died. Yoshinobu recognized that the Shogunate was no longer able to rule the country, and on the advice of the Prince of Tosa, resigned, leaving the running of the government to the Emperor.

The new Emperor Meiji was only 16 years old when he ascended the throne,

so Yoshinobu was ordered to continue the Shogunate until preparations could be made for the full restoration of Imperial power (which had been lost to the Imperial throne in 1185).

The supporters of the Shogunate were not willing to give up so easily, however, and persuaded Yoshinobu to go to war against the backers of the Emperor. The Shogunate loyalists met the Imperial forces at Fushimi, near Kyoto, and were defeated. Yoshinobu fled to Osaka Castle and then to Edo Castle, where he surrendered and went into retirement.

Other groups of Tokugawa loyalists still refused to give up, and in the next several years battles were fought at Wakamatsu, at Ueno in Edo, and in Hokkaido, but the Imperial forces emerged the victor, and the new Emperor and his advisors were in firm command of the country.

One of the most celebrated of these incidents involved 19 young Samurai boys from the Aizu clan in Iwashiro. These youths were assigned to protect the castle of the Lord of Aizu, and stationed themselves on the summit of Mt. Iimori, near Wakamatsu.

Seeing a large fire they thought was coming from the castle, the youths believed that the castle had been captured and put to the torch. Rather than face capture and death at the hands of their enemies, the young Samurai committed suicide.

See HISTORY, MEIJI RESTORATION, PERRY.

HATSU-MAIRI (Hot-sue My-ree)

Literally First-Visit, this refers to the traditional custom of visiting a Shinto shrine or Buddhist temple immediately after the beginning of the the new year. For millions of people, this means staying up late New Year's Eve, and visiting the temple or shrine of their choice just after midnight.

Some people travel long distances to keep this popular tradition at a nationally famous shrine or temple. At the latter there are often nationally televised ceremonies of ringing out the old year and ringing in the new--with huge bells that have giant logs for clappers.

Young men take turns swinging the logs (suspended on stout ropes) against the temple bells.

The most popular Hatsu-Mairi place in Tokyo is the great Meiji Shrine near Harajuku Station just outside the city's inner loop.

HATSU SHIMA (Hot-sue She-mah)

This is an island that can be seen

from the famous hotpsrings resort of Atami on Izu Peninsula. It is 10 kilometers off the coast, about three kilometers in circumference, and a popular campsite for young people during the summer months. It is 40 minutes by boat from either Atami or Ito (the next seaside resort below Atami).

HEARN, LAFCADIO

Lafcadio Hearn, probably the best-known of the earlier writers on Japan, was born in the Ionian Islands in 1850, the son of a British army surgeon and a Greek mother. He was educated in England and France and migrated to the U.S. when he was 19, following the death of this father, which reduced the family to poverty.

In the U.S., Hearn held many jobs, ranging from dish-washing to hack-writing. He then moved to the French West Indies, and later wrote a book, TWO HEARS IN THE FRENCH WEST INDIES, that was quite popular. In 1890 Harper β Row, his publisher, commissioned him to go to Japan and write a series of articles on the Japanese islands.

Once in Japan, Hearn was so delighted with the country, he accepted a position teaching English at the Matsue Middle School, and severed his relationship with Harper β Row.

Hearn later said the next two years were the happiest of his life. He married a Japanese woman named Koizumi, and began studying and writing about things Japanese. He was then invited to teach at the Kumamoto Higher School, and began writing for the Japan Chronicle Newspaper in Kobe.

In 1896 he was invited to become a lecturer in English literature at Tokyo Imperial University, the most prestigious university in the country. He was to stay there until two years before his death in 1904.

In the intervening years, Hearn published many books about Japan, became a naturalized citizen and adopted the name Yakumo Koizumi, after his wife. He also translated the works of several famous French writers, and wrote a number of literary critiques that are still highly regarded.

Hearn achieved some notice before he died, but he was not to become world-famous as an interpreter of things Japanese until well after his death. Among his best-known books--which are still in print--are GLIMPSES OF UNFAMILIAR JAPAN, JAPAN: AN ATTEMPT AT INTERPRETATION, KOKORO (Heart), GLEANINGS FROM BUDDHA FIELDS and KWAIDAN.

HECHIMA (Hay-chee-mah)

The hechima is a washing sponge made from a long cucumber-shaped gourd. It has been in use in Japan for centuries, and not only gets one clean but also provides a stimulating massage.

HEIAN SHRINE (Hay-e-on)

One of the most famous of Kyoto's Shinto treasures, the Heian Shrine, in Okazaki Park, is dedicated to Emperor Kammu, who founded Kyoto (Heian) in 794, and to Emperor Komei, the emperor who last reigned in Kyoto before the capital was moved to Tokyo following the Meiji Restoration in 1968.

The Heian Shrine, built in 1895 to commemorate the 1,100 anniversary of Kyoto, consists of two main halls, a Great Hall of State, two pagodas, a huge Main Gate and a torii. All of the buildings are exact replicas, except on a reduced scale, of the palace of the founder, Emperor Kammu, built in 794.

The shrine sponsors two of Kyoto's most popular festivals. One on April 15 and the other on October 22. The latter one, the fam-ous Jidai Matsuri or Festival of the Ages, attracts spectators from around the world. See FESTIVALS.

HEIKE (Hay-e-kay)

Heike is another name for the famous Taira clan, which began its rise to power in the 1100s when Kiyomori Taira, a leading member of the new Samurai warrior caste that had appeared in the previous two centuries, became the paramount military force in the land and usurped most of the power from the reigning emperor. See TAIRA, KIYOMORI.

HEIKE MONOGATARI (Hay-e-kay Moe-no-gah-tah-ree)

The Heike Monogatari or Tale of Heike is a famous war narrative that recounts the rise and fall of the Taira clan in the 12th century. The long story, like other chronicles written during this period, is characterized by strong Buddhist concepts that the lives and fortunes of men are in the hands of fate, and that the mighty will fall. See TAIRA, KIYOMORI.

HELLO KITTY

Hello Kitty is a cartoon character created by the Sanrio Company as a trade name that has become one of the most successful in the history of mass-market merchandising.

The trade mark now appears on dozens of different lines of merchandise, from leisure wear to stationery. It was first used in the U.S. by the publisher Random House on a line of children's books, and was subsequently franchised to manufacturers of toys, T-shirts and other products in the U.S.

HEPBURN, REV. JAMES C.

The Portuguese traders who arrived in Japan in the mid-1500s were the first to attempt to establish a uniform system of writing the Japanese language in Roman letters. The Dutch and other nationalities as well each devised their own system.

But there were so many ways of spelling individual words that none of the systems became established, and as each new nationality arrived and began its own system, the Romanization of Japanese became even more complicated, and was often virtually unintelligible to all except its creators.

It was to be an American missionary and doctor named James C. Hepburn who brought order out of the chaos, and thus made a profound and lasting contribution to the entry of Japan into the community of nations.

Hepburn spent many years studying the Japanese language and translating the bible into Japanese. In the process he developed a system of spelling Japanese that came to be known as the Hepburn System (and is the one used in this book).

Hepburn also founded Meiji Gakuin, one of Tokyo's best-known schools today, as well as the predecessor of Ferris' Girl School in Yokohama. In 1905 Emperor Meiji conferred the Order of the Rising Sun. Japan's highest award, upon Dr. Hepburn, who was then 90 years old, in recognition of his contributions to the country. He died in 1911 at age 96, one of the most honored of the many foreigners who devoted their lives to Japan.

During the subsequent periods of strong nationalism, there was a concentrated attempt by militaristic government leaders to substitute a made-in-Japan system for the Hepburn System. But was incomprehensible to most foreigners, and following the end of the Pacific War in 1945 was dropped.

Probably the most famous story about the use of the government-approved system involved the passenger ship Chichibu Maru, which became Titibu Maru when spelled according to government edict. Besides foreign passengers missing the ship because they didn't recognize the name, Titibu became the subject of salacious jokes.

HIBACHI (He-bah-chee)

A brazier or fire-box in which charcoal is burned, the hibachi was traditionally the Japanese cook stove and source of heat in the winter.

Foods were boiled, broiled and fried by most Japanese over open hibachi--in kitchens that were open to the outside--until after World War II, when natural-gas plates, stoves and electric ranges were introduced on an increasingly mass scale.

The hibachi used for heating were either in a room at floor level, or were placed inside a pit (kotatsu) in the floor, then covered by a table over which a large cloth was spread to keep the heat in. To take advantage of the heat, you sat with your legs extending into the pit and the cloth draped over your lap.

These traditional kotatsu were a marvelous way to keep your feet and legs warm, and were great for bringing people close together, but it was necessary to wear several layers of clothing to keep the upper part of your body from freezing. There was also the added danger of carbon monoxide poisoning from the burning charcoal.

The kitchen hibachi and the kotatsu--both open flames inside homes made of paper, wood and straw--were the cause of so many disasterous fires in Japan that fires were equated with earthquakes and typhoons, both of which have struck Japan with unfailing regularity since the birth of the islands.

Kotatsu are still popular in Japan because they are so much a part of the social interaction of the people, but instead of open charcoal flames they are warmed by especially designed electrical heaters.

Hibachi are also still in common use--but for outside barbecue purposes and by many restaurants that specialize in such charcoal broiled delicacies as yaki-tori (barbecued chicken).

HIDDEN CHRISTIANS / KAKURE KIRISHITAN (Kah-kuu-ray Kee-ree-she-tahn)

When the practice of Christianity was forbidden by the Tokugawa Shogunate in the early 1600s, a group of Japanese

converts to the Christian faith continued to practice Christian rituals in
secret, although behaving as regular
Japanese in public.

The group passed their beliefs and
rituals on to their descendants for the
next 200 and some years--until freedom
of religious choice was again granted in
1873. When their presence was discovered
in the 1870s, they were given the name
Hidden Christians.

HIDDEN TALENT / KAKUSHI GEI (Kah-kuu-she Gay-e)

Japanese have traditionally developed
a partcular skill, such as singing,
dancing solo, doing imitations, and so
on, that they keep quiet about--thus the
sobriquet hidden talent--knowing it is
going to come in handy.

At parties, dinners and other social
gatherings, it is common for the participants to be called on to perform some
kind of entertainment act. Having a
kakushi gei prevents them from being
embarrassed and allows them to demonstrate their skill.

Many foreign residents of Japan, and
others just visiting there, have been
put on the spot at such gatherings, and
not having a hidden talent were unable
to come through. Their hosts and friends
were not trying to embarrass them, however, as they have been conditioned to
take it for granted that everybody has
at least a little kakushi gei.

HIGH-RISE BUILDINGS

The first high-rise building in Japan
was the 36-story Kasumigaseki Building
in Tokyo, which was completed in 1968.
The building, based on new earthquake
resistant technology, was designed by
Toshiro Yamashita and the Mitsui Real
Estate Development Company, and was put
up by the Kajima Corporation and Mitsui
Construction Co.

Prior to this, the highest building
in Japan was 18 stories. Now there are
dozens of highrises in Japan's major
cities, particularly in Tokyo.

HIKONE (He-koe-nay)

The headquarters city of the famous
Ii clan, Hikone is noted today for the
Ii (Hikone) Castle, the Villa and garden
of the Ii family, the Taga Shrine, a
popular beach and its textile industries.

Hikone Castle was constructed in 1603
by Naokatsu Ii immediately after he
returned home from the Battle of Sekiga-
ara--which resulted in Ieyasu Tokugawa
becoming the new Shogun. In the mid-
1800s, Naosuke Ii was the chief minister
of the Tokugawa Shogunate, and was active in helping open Japan to the Western
world.

The Ii clan castle is an Important
Cultural Property, and is one of the
Eight Views of Lake Biwa.

HIMEJI (He-may-jee)

An hour from Kobe by train, on the
coast of the beautiful Inland Sea, Himeji is one of the best-known of Japan's
many castle towns.

Now the leading industrial and commercial center of the surrounding Harima
Plain, Himeji became important in Japan's history in 1581 when Hideyoshi
Toyotomi had a castle built there to
control the area. In 1600 the castle was
taken over by Terumasa Ikeda, one of
Hideyoshi's generals, who remodeled its
main tower. The castle was enlarged to
its present grand size during the Genna
era (1615-1624).

The castle, registered as a National
Treasure, is regarded as the best, in
design and architectual technique, ever
built in Japan. It is called the Hakuro
Jo or Egret Castle because its white-
plastered walls suggests this popular
rice-field bird.

From the tower of the castle there is
an equally grand view of the Inland Sea
and Ejima Islands, as well as the surrounding countryside.

Himeji has a Sister City relationship
with Phoenix, Arizona, USA.

HIROSHIMA (He-roe-she-mah)

Famed in contemporary history because
it was the first city ever to be atom-
bombed--at 8:15 a.m. on August 6, 1945--
Hiroshima dates from 1593, when feudal
lord Terumoto Mori built a castle there
and named it Hiroshima Jo, or Broad
Island Castle. The village that grew up
around the castle gradually came to be
known as Hiroshima.

During the Sino-Japanese War from
1894-1895, Hiroshima Castle was used by
the Emperor Meiji as his headquarters,
while the city itself, facing the Inland
Sea, became a major port. By the beginning of World War II it had a population
of 344,000, and was a major industrial
center.

The single atom bomb that was dropped
on Hiroshima that fateful date in 1945
leveled the city in a flash of light
that was followed by a wind-storm and
great fires. Over 200,000 of the inhabitants of the city were killed out-right,
and in the days and months that followed, thousands more died in agony.

126

Imperial Palace guard post. P. 153

A "Sight fit for the eyes of kings." P. 155

With peace returned and the passing of a law in 1949 called the Law for the Construction of a Hiroshima Peace Commemoration City, the reconstruction of the city picked up pace. Today, it is more than twice as large as it was in 1945.

Once again a major industrial area, Hiroshima is also a popular tourist destination. Each year hundreds of thousands of people go to see the Atomic Bomb Dome, Peace Memorial Park, Peace Memorial Hall, and the Memorial Cenotaph for A-Bomb Victims.

Other places of interest are the famous Shukkei-En Garden, designed by feudal lord Nagaakira Asano in 1620 and now a registered Scenic Place, the restored Hiroshima Castle (the original was totally destroyed by the atom bomb), and the Memorial Cathedral for World Peace (built following an appeal by the Rev. Hugo Lassalle, a German Jesuit priest who was in Hiroshima when the bomb fell.

HISTORY / REKISHI (Rake-shi)

Legend says that Japan's first Emperor, Jimmu Tenno (Jeem-muu Tane-no), ascended the chrysanthemum throne in 660 B.C. (Jimmu means Divine Warrior and Tenno means Heavenly). But written records indicate that in the 1st century A.D., Japan was still a collection of over 100 independent little kingdoms in various parts of the islands.

Some of these tiny fiefdoms had diplomatic contacts, and surely some trade relations, with the Later Han Dynasy in China.

By the 4th century A.D., one of the larger of these kingdoms in the Kansai (Khan-sigh) area, where Osaka, Kobe and Kyoto are now located, had absorbed the smaller groups in the vicinity, and fairly quickly thereafter expanded its rule over the western half of Honshu (Hone-shuu), the northern half of Kyushu (Que-shuu) and all of Shikoku (She-koe-kuu).

The Yamato family that ruled this kingdom during its final stages of consolidation became Japan's Imperial family, whose descendants presently occupy the throne. In some records, this country is referred to as the Kingdom of Yamato (Yah-mah-toe), which figuratively means Great Peace or Great Harmony, but is generally translated as meaning Japan. Yamato is also used when referring to the soul or heart of Japan—Yamato Damashii (Yah-mah-toe Dah-mah-shee).

Two ancient and famous chronicles, the Nihonshoki (Nee-hone-show-kee) and the Kojiki (Koe-jee-kee), both written in the 8th century, say very explicitly that Emperor Jimmu, Japan's first emperor, began his reign on February 11, 660 B.C., and this is the date that is celebrated as Japan's National Foundation Day.

The first inhabitants of Japan are believed to have been a Caucasoid race who call themselves Ainu (Aye-nuu). See AINU.

It is also believed that Japan was still connected to the Asian mainland until some 10,000 or 20,000 years ago. After the separation took place, it was far enough away to be safe from invasion, but close enough for immigration and infusions of culture from Korea and China.

As for the Japanese people, it is generally agreed that they are an Asian Mongoloid race (most Japanese babies are born with a blue mark at the base of the spine, known as the Mongoloid Spot). It is also generally agreed that most of the ancestors of the present-day Japanese came to the islands from different parts of Asia, primarily from Korea, China and Southeast Asia.

The dates of the very first migrations are unknown, but it is known that the Japanese islands were inhabited 10,000 years ago by people very much like modern Japanese.

Before the arrival of the Asian ancestors of the present-day Japanese, the southern part of the islands were inhabited by people who had come up from the South Pacific and Southeast Asia, and the northern third of the islands were populated by a race of people known as Ainu, who were Caucasoid rather than Mongoloid.

The earliest inhabitants of the south were quickly merged in with the new arrivals from Asia, but the Ainu resisted assimilation, and were gradually driven further northward. As the centuries passed, however, the Ainu as well were gradually assimilated into the main body of the population, and today fewer than 20,000 of them remain.

In the Tohoku region of northern Honshu and in Hokkaido, the mixing of the two races is very evident in the Caucasian look of great numbers of the people. These Ainu/Japanese mixtures are responsible in part for the reputation the Tohoku area has for exceptionally beautiful women.

Archeologists have named the time from around 10,000 B.C. to the 3rd or 2nd century B.C. as the Jomon Period, from the type of pottery left by the people. This was followed by the so-called Yayoi Period, which lasted until about the 3rd century A.D., during which time the Japanese mastered the technique of rice cultivation, and gradually established the family or clan system and patterns of social and economic life that were to endure down to the 19th century.

The paramount leader among the various clans was called Okimi or Great Prince. Some time in the 6th century this title was changed to Tenno (Tane-noh) or Emperor.

There is other evidence to support the belief that Japan was a recognized nation prior to the 4th century A.D. A gold seal, unearthed in what is now Fukuoka Prefecture in the 18th century, is mentioned in Chinese records as having been presented by Emperor Kuang Hsu to a ruler in Kyushu in the 1st Century A.D.

Other records show that in the 3rd century the Queen of Yamatai (Yah-mah-tie) sent an envoy to China, and received a Chinese envoy in her Court. The first officially recorded government-level contacts between Japan and Korea were in the 4th century, although unofficial contacts with that country had undoubtedly been frequent for a long period.

With the emergence of one paramount kingdom, trade and cultural relations with Korea and China flourished. The Japanese imported the Chinese writing system, Buddhism, Confucianism and many arts and crafts. The Imperial family and the court nobles also adopted many of the customs and manners of the Imperial Court in China.

From the end of the 6th century to the beginning of the 8th century, the capital of Japan was located in the Asuka region south of present-day Nara. The capital was moved to Nara in 710 and then to Kyoto in 794.

The first major political figure in Japanese history--of which there is record--was Prince Shotoku, who acted as regent for Empress Suiko whose reign extended from the latter part of the 6th century to the early years of the 7th century. He initiated a series of reforms that established a political sys-

tem based on the authority of the emperor, codifying them in a Seventeen Article Constitution. Following the death of Prince Shotoku, the Soga clan gained dominance in Japan, and continued contacts with Korea and China.

In the year 645, Prince Nakano (who later became Emperor Tenchi) joined with clan leader Nakatomi-no Kamatari, founder of the famous Fujiwara dynasty, to crush the Soga clan.

The then dominant Fujiwara clan, along with Emperor Tenchi, embarked on a new series of political reforms, using the Tang government of China as their model. In 702 these reforms were published in the so-called Taiho Code. The codes stipulated the organization of both central and regional governments, divided the country into 62 provinces, and required the central government to assign a governor to each of the provinces.

The Taiho Codes also declared that all agricultural land belonged to the state, that fixed amounts were to be allotted to the people for cultivation, in return for which they were to pay taxes in the form of grain, textiles and labor.

Just before he died, Emperor Tenchi awarded Nakatomi by giving him the highest status in the Court and the new family name of Fujiwara. Thereafter, the Fujiwara family took over the government by providing the Imperial line with consorts and regents, and controlling who became emperor.

This new system of government lasted for about 100 years, then the leading clan families once again began ursuping the state's power, taking possession of both the land and the peasants on it, and creating wealthy and powerful provinces of their own. These estates were known as shoen (show-inn), and were the forerunners of the great feudal fiefs or provinces that were to last until 1868.

These family clans, mostly relatives of the Imperial family, maintained their own armed forces to protect their territories and keep the peasants under control. As time passed, the soldiers formed a distinct hereditary class of professional warriors.

The peak of the Nara Period was the reign of Emperor Shomu (724-749). A firm believer in Buddhism as a way of warding off natural disasters and ensuring the wealth and prosperity of the country, he ordered the construction of branch monasteries and nunneries in the 62 provinces. It was also he who ordered the construction of the Todai Temple in

Nara, the largest wooden building ever built, and had a 16-meter high, seated image of the Buddha cast and installed inside it.

In the intervening centuries, the great Todai was burned and seriously damaged several times, but it was restored each time and still stands today as one of the wonders of early Japan. In a wooden storehouse next to the Todai Temple are preserved many items donated to the temple by the empress on the death of Emperor Shomu.

The power of the Fujiwara family continued to wane during the 9th and 10th centuries, and in the 11th century they began to lose control of the country to the rising warrior clans. They were to maintain their influence at the Imperial Court until 1868, however, and one of their direct lineal descendants, Prince Konoe Fumimaro, served as the Prime Minister of Japan just before and during part of the Second World War.

The introduction of Confucianism and Buddhism from Korean and China resulted in profound changes in Japan. In the 7th century, large numbers of Japanese envoys and scholars went to China. The new knowledge and technology they brought back from the mainland was to further revolutionize the Japanese way of life.

These exchanges continued during the 8th, 9th and 10th centuries, but in the latter part of the 10th century, Japan entered a period of near isolation that lasted for some 200 years. During this long period, the Japanese were literally consumed by the cultural, and political changes taking place in their own country.

By the 9th century, the powerful regional clans, with their own trained armies of professional mounted warriors armed with swords and bows and clad in armor, were already an important political force. Provincial governors as well as court nobles also began retaining their own Samurai, and as time passed the size of these private armies grew, became hereditary and formed a new privileged class.

The leaders of these Samurai families were descendants of the Imperial family or court nobles who had been appointed governors of provinces, but did not return to the capital when their tenure was complete, and made their position hereditary.

The two most powerful of these warrior clans were the Taira and Minamoto, both descended from the Imperial House. As the power of the central government declined and revolts occurred in the provinces, it was these new Samurai lords who put them down.

The power of the Minamoto clan was greatly expanded in the latter half of the 11th century when it put down revolts in the Kanto (Tokyo) region, and thereafter had close connections with the Samurai clans in that area.

In the meantime, the Taira clan was extending its power in the Western end of Japan, and in the latter part of the 12th century seized political power from the Fujiwara family in Kyoto. In the first clashes between the two great Samurai clans, the Taira won and further consolidated their power by marrying into the Imperial family. The head of the Minamoto clan was executed and his oldest son, Yoritomo, was exiled to what is present-day Shizuoka.

A few years later, Yoritomo, with the aid of his younger brother Yoshitsune, enlisted the help of the Samurai of the Kanto plains, and in the famous sea battle in the straits of Danno-ura, totally destroyed the Taira clan.

At the battle of Danno-ura, the first great sea battle in Japan, the Heike (Taira clan) suffered total defeat. The boy Emperor, his mother, grandmother and many court ladies were aboard one of the Heike vessels. When they saw the battle was lost, the Emperor's grandmother took him in her arms and together with many of the other women, jumped into the sea. Only the Emperor's mother was saved.

In 1185 Yoritomo set up a military government, called Bakufu (Bah-kuu-fuu) in Kamakura, a small town just south of Yokohama, in order to avoid the weakning influences of Imperial Kyoto.

In 1192 the reigning emperor officially awarded the title of Shogun to Yoritomo, beginning a government system that was to endure for most of the next 700 years.

The Kamakura Shogunate lasted for 140 years, although Yoritomo's line died out in less than 30 years. Power thereafter was in the hands of the Hojo family, which had served as advisors to the first three Minamoto Shoguns.

The Imperial Court tried to wrest control from the Hojo regents in the Jokyu War, but the Hojo were to remain in power until 1333, when then Emperor Godaigo allied with clan leaders Masashige Kusunoki and Takauji Ashikaga to end the Kamakura Shogunate.

Takauji then turned against Masashige and defeated him, forcing Emperor Godaigo to flee into the mountains of Yoshino. Takauji set up a relative of the Emperor in Kyoto and had himself named Shogun. The two courts and their allies battled for some 60 years, when the Ashikaga clan emerged the victor and began the Ashikaga Shogunate, which was to last for 240 years.

The Ashikaga bakufu was not as powerful as its predecessor, and distant Samurai clan leaders, now called Daimyo (Dime-yoe) or Great Names, began building up their power. The period degenerated into a series of clashes between contending Daimyo, who gained control of all of the provincial estates that were still in the hands of the court nobles.

These powerful Samurai Daimyo built castles and encouraged the construction of temples and shrines, many of which became the nucleus for new villages and towns. See CITIES.

In Kyoto, the Ashikaga Shogunate adopted the manners and practices of the Imperial Court, which was heavily influenced by Zen Buddhism. The 7th Ashikaga Shogun, Yoshimitsu, had the Temple of the Golden Pavilion built. His successor, Yoshimasa, built the Silver Pavilion--both major attractions of modern-day Kyoto.

Relations with China were gradually restored in the 12th century, and were infrequent and relatively minor but continuous during the Sung and Ming dynasties.

Two major events during the 13th century were successive attacks on Japan by the Mongols of China. Kublai Khan demanded that Japan become a vassal state within his empire. The Japanese refused, and in 1274 and 1281, Mongol forces with their Korean allies, invaded northern Kyushu.

In the first attack, the Chinese used massed calvary attacks and catapults that threw gunpowder missiles against the Japanese warriors who were used to single combat. But a typhoon struck, sinking many of the Mongol ships, causing them to abandon the attack.

The second invasion involved a fleet of ships said to be five times as large as the Spanish Armada which attacked England in 1588, making it the largest naval force in history. But once again a typhoon struck, wrecking havoc on the fleet and saving Japan from probable disaster.

This was the last the Japanese were to see of the Mongols, and in gratitude they begin calling the typhoons kamikaze or divine winds, and to believe that Japan had divine protection and could not be invaded or conquered--a feeling that persisted until the 1940s.

Europe first heard of Japan from Marco Polo, that intrepid Italian adventurer who went to China as a boy and became a favorite of Genghis Khan. In the BOOK OF MARCO POLO, published in 1298, Polo referred to Japan as Zipangu.

The first recorded contact between Europeans and Japanese occurred in 1543 when a Portuguese ship ran aground on the island of Tanega, south of Kyushu, during a storm.

Among the things these Portuguese visitors introduced to the Japanese were gunpowder, firearms, tobacco and venereal disease. Soon thereafter, Japan was visited regularly by traders and missionaries from Spain and Portugal, and by traders from Great Britain and Holland.

The 1500s saw the rise to power of Nobunaga Oda, Hideyoshi Toyotomi and Ieyasu Tokugawa. In 1573 Nobunaga came into conflict with the Askikaga Shogun and drove him out of Kyoto. To complete his conquest, he crushed the power of the militant Buddhist monks in the Kyoto area, and was friendly toward the spread of Christianity as a means of diluting the power of the Buddhist temples. He also promoted the abolition of powerful guilds that controlled such commodities as salt, vegetable oils, textiles and paper, and pushed free trade.

Before Nobunaga could consolidate his power, however, he was turned on by a trusted retainer, Mitsuhide Akechi, and forced to commit suicide.

Another of Nobunaga's retainers, Hideyoshi Toyotomi, who had been born a peasant instead of a Samurai but had risen to the rank of a general in Nobunaga's army, attacked and destroyed Mitsuhide's forces, thus becoming heir to political control of the country.

By 1550, Japanese ships of up to 800 tons were plying trade routes to South China, Siam, the Philippines, and other Southeast Asia countries. Among the Japanese entrepreneurs who became involved in this flourishing trade was Hideyoshi Toyotomi, the military ruler of Japan. By 1592 ships bearing his vermillion seal were carrying such things as silver, copper, iron and sulfer, and exchanging them for silk, sugar, leather and lead. Hideyoshi did not become Shogun (he was named Kanpaku or Prime Minister instead). He had the nation surveyed to determine the amount of arable land and its productivity, and then awarded fiefs to his supporters on this basis. He also took all weapons out of the hands of common people, clearly defined the class differences between commoners and the Samurai, and promoted foreign trade. He also built the great Osaka Castle.

Up to this time, the Samurai had engaged in agriculture, but Hideyoshi's program separated them from the land and brought them into castle towns, where they lived on fixed incomes provided by the Daimyo they served.

Fearing that Christianity might become the ideological basis for attempts by the Daimyo of Kyushu to challenge his authority, Hideyoshi outlawed the teaching of Christianity and ordered the deportation of all Christian missionaries. Little was done against the missionaries and their converts for the first 10 years, then the campaign against them was stepped up. Several Japanese converts and a number of foreign priests and monks were crucified in 1597.

With his power of Japan complete, Hideyoshi decided to invaded and conquer China. He ordered Korea to allow his armies to pass through on their way to China. The Koreans refused, and on two occasions Hideyoshi sent large armies to Korea where they fought combined Korean and Chinese forces. The conflict raged on, but in 1598 Hideyoshi died of illness, and the Japanese forces were withdrawn from Korea.

With Hideyoshi dead, Ieyasu Tokugawa, who had been his most powerful ally, defeated several contenders for power, eliminated Hideyoshi's other close allies, including Hideyoshi's young son by his favorite mistress, and in 1603 established the Tokugawa Shogunate, destined to be Japan's last great feudal dynasty.

Ieyasu had begun as a minor Daimyo who allied himself with Nobunaga Oda, and extended his power in south-central Honshu. When Hideyoshi came to power, Ieyasu fought him at first and then joined him, and it was Hideyoshi who ordered Ieyasu to move his domain to the Kanto (Tokyo) region, where he established his headquarters in Edo Castle.

The Tokugawa Shogunate took direct control of more than one-quarter of Japan's land area, including the most important cities, ports and mines. In order to ensure the obediance of the country's other Daimyo--whose numbers ranged between 245 and 295 during the Tokugawa Period--the third Tokugawa Shogun decreed that the Daimyo leave their families in Edo at all times, and themselves spend every other year in Edo, supposedly in attendance on the Shogun.

This system, called Sankin Kotai (Sahn-keen Koe-tie), had profound economic, social and cultural effects on Japan. It cost a great deal for the Daimyo to travel back and forth between their fiefs and Edo and to maintain their families in Edo in impressive circumstances. In order to afford such expenses, the Daimyo had to encourage the progress of agriculture and other industries in their fiefs. This constant coming and going of great numbers of people, who traversed Japan on foot in great processions, resulted in the rapid development of inns and towns along the national roads leading to Edo, and spread the culture of Edo throughout the country.

The Sankin Kotai system and was aimed not only at keeping the fief lords under the Shogun's thumb, but also keeping them from amassing enough wealth to offer a threat to the Shogunate. The system lasted for nearly 250 years. (For more about this amazing phenomenon, see PROCESSIONS OF THE LORDS.)

The Tokugawa system of government was known as baku-han, from baku (the Japanese word for the Shogunate), and han, the word for a feudal domain. The han were ostensibly independent and the baku-han had no authority to collect taxes from them. But in reality the Shogunate levied heavy taxes on them to finance public works, castle-building and so on.

During the early years of the Tokugawa Period, Ieyasu and his grandson successor favored foreign trade. But as trade increased so did the number and influence of Christian missionaries. The preachings of Christianity were incompatible with the philosophy and policies of the Shogunate, and the continued activies and growing power of the missionaries and their converts frightened the government.

In 1635 the Shogunate outlawed the propagation of Christianity, and expelled all foreign missionaries. When the third Tokugawa Shogun, Iemitsu, took over, measures against Christians became more severe. In 1537, all Japanese were forbidden from going abroad, and those already overseas were forbidden from returning home.

Two years later, Christians in Shimabara Peninsula and on the Amakusa Islands south of Kyushu, rebelled against this religious prosecution and heavy taxation. The Shogunate sent an army of 100,000 men to crush the rebellion.

The Shogunate then prohibited Spanish and Portugese ships from coming to Japan to prevent the further spread of Christianity. The English had not been active in missionary work but were losing out to Dutch competition in trade, so they also withdrew from Japan.

The third Tokugawa Shogun in 1639 broke off all foreign relations with foreign countries, prohibited travel from or to Japan, and closed the country off--with one minor recognized exception--for more than 200 years.

Thousands of Japanese had been dispatched abroad to overseas trading posts. In 1639, when the Tokugawa Shogunate closed the country, none of the Japanese traders and their families who were abroad at that time were allowed to return home, and had to live out their lives in exile.

In the city of Hirato in Kyushu, one can today see and read letters written by a girl named Oharu, who was among these unfortunate people, expressing her anguish at not being able to return to her homeland.

During this long period, the Dutch were allowed to keep a small trading post in operation on a tiny island in Nagasaki Bay. The few men who manned this outpost over the generations were not allowed to step foot on the mainland except on very special, guarded occasions. Thus, the isolation of most Japanese from any foreign product, technology or idea was virtually total.

This left only the Chinese and Dutch with official permission to have any intercouse with Japan. An artifical isl'and called De Jima (Day Jee-mah), meaning Exit Island, was constructed in Nagasaki harbor, separated from the mainland by canals, to be used as a base for the Dutch and Chinese traders.

The Dutch were permitted to land one ship a year at Dejima, and were required to present a document to the Shogunate authorities in Nagasaki covering politi-

cal events in the rest of the world. The Soshi clan, on Tsushima, engaged in some trade with Korea and indirectly with China. This system was to prevail for more than 200 years, during which time Japan was left behind by the technological developments of Europe and the Americas.

The power of the Tokugawa Shogunate made this the longest period of peace in Japan's history. During these long and quiet decades, agriculture was the main occupation of most people, but gradually, as cities grew up around the castle headquarters of the Daimyo, manufacturing and commerce became increasingly important.

At first, the Tokugawa Shoguns actually ruled, but as time went by they tended to become figureheads., just as most of their predecessors in the past. Real power shifted to the hands of Shogunate bureaucrats. The same situation developed in the domains of the Daimyo. Having to be in Edo half the time and on the road for up to several months the rest of the time (it took several weeks for the Daimyo from most distant domains to reach Edo), there was no way the Daimyo could directly run their fiefs.

During the long Tokugawa Period, Japan's population remained stable at about 30 million people. The privileged Samurai warrior class made up seven percent of the population. Below them were the townspeople or chonin (choeneen) and the peasant-farmers. Legally, merchants were the lowest class in the country.

Many of the Samurai eventually gave up the way of the warrior for the way of the bureaucrat and the scholar, dedicating themselves to the study and practice of Confucianism and Zen Buddhism.

By the middle of the Tokugawa Era, the rice-based economy had broken down. Economic power was in the hands of the merchant class, many of whom had amassed great fortunes. The Shogunate made three major attempts at economic reform, but the Confucian principles on which the reforms were based were no longer suitable for the times.

Many Samurai married into the merchant classµ others became ronin (masterless Samurai), roaming the country and getting into mischief. Rebellions broke out among peasants who resented the growing burden of taxes needed to support the unproductive Samurai.

The study of Confucianism lost ground to native Japanese scholaship, and what was called kokugaku or native learning. These scholars learned that the Shogunate was not the legitimate holders of power in the country, that the Shoguns had usurped the power of the emperor centuries earlier.

When foreign ships began knocking on Japan's doors in the early 1800s, there were many, especially those in the more distant Daimyo fiefs, who were ready to end Japan's islation.

As the urban populations increased and businessmen prospered, money began to replace rice as the medium of exchange. Since the Samurai families of all the clans, including the Tokugawa, were paid in allotments of rice, their situation grew steadily worse.

By 1800, many Samurai families were in desperate straits. More and more of them were reduced to poverty and had to give up their privileged status or arrange for their sons and daughters to marry into merchant families--something that had been unthinkable in former times.

By this time also, many Western nations were on the move in Asia, seeking new markets and where possible military hegemony over whatever territories they could take by force or guile. Several nations, including Russia, England and the United States, began making overtures to Japan about opening its ports to foreign trade and the establishment of diplomatic relations.

Sheer luck resulted in the U.S.'s Admiral Matthew Perry and his Black Ships, arriving in Japan in 1853, beating the Russians out by a few months.

After a great deal of intense debate and consternation, the feudal government of Japan decided to resume trade and limited relations with the outside world. The position of the Tokugawa Shogunate went from bad to untenable. Powerful Daimyo, especially in Kyushu, the most distant from Edo, began a campaign to topple the Shogunate and restore the Emperor to power.

Long outmoded and unable to contend with the economic and political ferment sweeping the country, Japan's once great and all-powerful bakufu government leaders realized they could no longer run the country.

Finally in 1867 the Bakufu relinquished power to the Emperor, and the following year a new government was formed under Emperor Meiji.

In the following 20 years, the Japanese changed their country from a feudal, cottage industry/agricultural nation of Imperial courtiers, sword-carrying warriors, peasants and plebians to a modern

industrial power--presaging the Japanese miracle that occurred after World War II.

The Japanese achieved this first miracle by importing foreign technology, by inviting foreign technicians and experts in various fields in to guide them, and by an extraordinary demonstration of cooperation between government and industry.

In 1895 Japan went to war against China, and in 1905 hostilities broke out between Japan and Russia. In both wars, the Japanese emerged the winner, gaining a foothold on the Asian mainland, and coming into possession of the island of Taiwan.

The military gained the upper hand in Japan in 1929, subsequently leading the Japanese on a series of territorial conquests that culminated in their attack on Hawaii in 1941, the war with the United States, and finally, rebirth as a democratic nation and one of the world's top industrial powers.

The foreigners who made invaluable contributions to Japan's transformation from a feudal society to a modern power in the late 1800s included Gustave Emile Boissonade, a French specialist in law and legal education. Erwin von Baelz, a German medical educator. William Smith Clark, and American expert in agriculture and education. Edmund Morell, and English railroad engineer. And Gustav Toppe, a German engineer who helped set up Yawata Steel Mill, one of the predecessors of the Nippon Steel Corporation. Altogether 45 Italians, 619 Frenchmen, 913 Germans, 2,764 Americans and 6,177 Britons were retained by the new Japanese government between 1881 and 1898 to virtually remake the country's economic and political system.

All of the supporters of the Shogun did not voluntarily relinquish power. In 1868, the peasant army of the new Imperial government defeated the Samurai supporters of the Shogun in battles at Toba and Fushimi, south of Kyoto. Then the two forces reached a compromise, avoiding a battle for Edo that could have destroyed the city. Edo Castle was turned over to representatives of the Imperial governement in Kyoto, and arrangements were made for the emperor to move into the castle.

France supported the Shogunate, while England supported the Imperial forces. Fortunately, the Japanese refused these offers of help.

With the Restoration complete, the new government appointed a number of the more capable Shogunate officials to high positions in the Imperial government. The last of the Shoguns, Yoshinobu Tokugawa, was designated a prince in a peerage system the new government established.

Most of the new government leaders were from the Samurai clans of Satsuma and Choshu in Kyushu--those that were the furthest away from Edo and had retained most of their independence during the Tokugawa Period. Their goal was to transform Japan into a modern nation in two stages--first establish a unified and centralized government under a strong monarchy, and then to develop a modern industry.

The new Meiji government abolished the system of the feudal han or Daimyo fiefs, and created a new system of prefectures and governors. All feudal classes were also abolished, but all members of the Imperial family and ranking Daimyo became peers in the new system.

Growing pressure of more democratic-minded Japanese finally forced the Meiji government to institute a parlimentary system, and after years of study and compromise, a constitution was adopted on 11 February 1989, and a parliament (called a Diet) was formed, consisting of a House of Representatives and a House of Peers.

Under the new constitution, only adult males who paid a certain amount of taxes could vote, which limited suffurage to about 4.5 percent of the population. Further, for the next several decades, the government continued to be primarily controlled by a small group of elder statesmen, called genro (ganeroe), who had been among the leaders of the Meiji Restoration. In addition, the Cabinet was supervised by the Privy Council, which also had to ratify all laws passed by the Diet.

At this time, Korea was still closed to the outside world, and was known abroad as the Hermit Kingdom. In 1876, Japan coerced Korea into opening its doors to trade by threatening to invade the country. The Japanese immediately begin making economic and political inroads in the country.

China regarded Korea as a vassal state, and opposed the Japanese intrusion. This led to the outbreak of war between Japan and China. The Japanese won an overwhelming victory, and not only continued their inroads into Korea, but were ceded the Liaotung Peninsula, the Pescadores Islands and Taiwan.

After the peace treaty with China, however, Russia, France and Germany forced Japan to return the Liaotung Peninsula to China. Almost immediately thereafter, both Germany and Russia acquired major concessions in China and Manchuria. Russia then took advantage of the Boxer Rebellion in China to occupy Manchuria, and began bringing pressure against Korea.

With both Japan and Russia vying for domination in Korea and Manchuria, war between the two nations broke out in 1904. Japan won quick, decisive victories on both land and sea. With American President Theodore Roosevelt as the mediator, a peace treaty between Russia and Japan was signed in 1905 at Portsmouth in New Jesey.

Japan got the southern half of Sakhalin, its primacy in Korea was recognized, and Russia had to give up its concessions in China. In 1910 Japan annexed Korea, and turned it into a colony.

In 1914, Japan allied itself with the U.S., England and France against Germany, and as a result was awarded all of Germany's concessions in Shangtun and the mandate over Germany's Pacific island colonies. In 1921, Japan forced China to accept 21 demands, of which 11 were later dropped because of American pressure.

In 1918, during the Russian Revolution, Japan sent an army to Siberia in an attempt to bring this huge landmass into its sphere of influence. But the effort failed and the army was withdrawn in 1922.

In the late 1920s, Japan increased its encroachment on China, and in 1931 invaded and occupied Manchuria, setting up a puppet state called Manchukuo. Other attacks against China followed, and undeclared war between the two countries dragged in.

The Great Depression that struck the U.S. in the 1930s also hit Japan, and there were a series of assassinations of moderate government leaders by fanatics who wanted a military dictatorship. The ultra-rightists got what they wanted, and Japan begin to prepare for all out war. Nationalism ran rampant. Civil liberties were suppressed, political parties disbanded, the Diet became completely powerless, and the course of the nation was set by the military, through General Hideki Tojo, who was prime minister when the Pacific War began.

In the grips of expansionist fever, Japan's military-controlled government signed pacts with Germany and Italy in 1940 (the Axis Alliance), and a neutrality pact with Russia in 1941. Taking advantage of the predicament of England, France and the Netherlands in Europe, the Japanese invaded French Indochina.

Negotiations with the U.S. had been going on for some time, but came to a virtual standstill, with the U.S. demanding that Japan withdraw from all the territories it had occupied since the Manchurian Incident. The war in China was also deadlocked.

To break this impasse, the Japanese attacked Pearl Harbor in Honolulu on December 7, 1941. Japan's military leaders believed that following a devastating attack on the naval base at Pearl Harbor and their invasion and occupation of other Western Pacific island outposts, the U.S. would agree to a negotiated settlement of the hostilaties. Even the most rabid Japanese nationalist did not believe that Japan could invade and conquer the U.S.

Before the U.S. could recover from the attack on Hawaii and mount counterattacks, the Japanese seized Hong Kong, Malaysia, Burma, the Philippines, the Dutch East Indies and several other areas in Southeast Asia and the South Pacific.

In 1942 the U.S. began its campaign against Japan, and piece-by-piece began winning back the territories Japan had conquered. From the end of 1944, the U.S. Air Force conducted continuous bombing raids on the home islands of Japan. After a bitter battle in June 1945, American forces captured the island of Okinawa, and began massing for an invasion of the four main islands. In July the terms for Japan's surrender were detailed in the Potsdam Declaration. Japan's leaders ignored the ultimatum.

Knowing the ferocity with which the Japanese fought, and their custom of fighting to the death rather than surrender, the U.S. decided to use the atomic bomb to shock the Japanese into surrendering without the need for an invasion of the main islands.

On 6 August 1945 the U.S. Air Force dropped an atomic bomb on the city of Hiroshima. On August 8 Russia declared war on Japan. On August 9 the U.S. dropped a second atomic bomb on the city of Nagasaki. Both of these two large cities were virtually pulverized.

On August 14 the Japanese government notified the U.S. that it would accept the terms of the Potsdam Declaration. Fearful that the Japanese armed forces and the civilian population might not accept the idea of surrendering, moderate forces in Tokyo prevailed upon Emperor Hirohito, who had played no role in the conduct of the war, to make an unprecedented radio broadcast informing the people that Japan had surrendered and asking the military forces to cease fighting and lay down their arms.

For the first time in their long history, the Japanese had suffered a devastating defeat. Some 2,300,000 servicemen and 800,000 civilians had died in the long drawn-out war, and most of the country's industrial capacity was in total ruins.

American occupation forces began arriving in Japan within the next 10 days, and the documents of surrender were signed on September 2, aboard the battleship U.S.S. Missouri in Tokyo Bay. General Douglas MacArthur took over as Supreme Commander of the Allied Powers (SCAP), setting up his headquarters in the Dai Ichi Insurance Building across from the Imperial Palace.

The Soviets, who had entered the war on virtually the last day, demanded that they be allowed to occupy Hokkaido. The U.S. refused, thus preventing Japan from being partitioned as Germany and Korea were.

The Japanese expected brutal treatment by the Occupation forces. Before the first American servicemen arrived, large numbers of women and children were sent into the countryside. They were shocked to find themselves not only treated kindly but generously by the predominately American occupying forces.

Rather than set up a military government to rule Japan, SCAP, under the inspired leadership of MacArthur, elected to implement the policies of the Occupation through the Japanese government—exercising indirect control. These policies were divided into three major categories: demilitarization, democratization and reconstruction.

In the first two years, Japan was divested of all of its overseas colonies, and over 6,500,000 Japanese living overseas were repatriated. All Japanese military forces were disbanded, and some 180,000 people who had been in senior positions in the political and economic structure of the country were removed from their jobs.

The International Military Tribunal

Garden of the Hall of Poets, Kyoto. P. 119

Hotspring spa bath in winter. P. 145

for the Far East tried 25 of Japan's top leaders who were charged with being responsible for atrocities committed during the war and for the war itself. Five military men, along with former Prime Ministers Hideki Tojo and Koki Hirota, were found guilty and hanged.

The state religion of Shintoism was abolished. The Emperor renounced his claim to divinity on 1 January 1946. A new constitution was drafted under the direction of SCAP and promulgated on 3 November 1946. The new constitution renounced war as a means of settling international disputes, guaranteed the people individual freedom, equality of the sexes, the right of the people to organize and engaged in collective bargaining, and the right to be educated.

The great economic combines (Zaibatsu) were broken up, making room for the development of thousands of new companies. Farm lands were bought from absentee landlords and sold to farmers at low prices, and the educational system was reformed along democratic lines.

By the end of 1947 the fundamental goals of the Occupation had been achieved, and the process of transferring decision-making authority back to the Japanese government was begun. As the so-called cold war between the U.S. and Russia intensified, the American policy in Japan changed dramatically. The U.S. began an all-out campaign to help Japan rebuild its industrial base as rapidly as possible.

The outbreak of the war in Korea in 1950 provided an enormous boost to the Japanese economy. The U.S. military began procuring all kinds of supplies from Japan, and these special procurements made a significant contribution to Japan's miraculous recovery.

Immediately after the outbreak of the Korean War, SCAP ordered the Japanese government to create a self-defense force, originally called the Police Reserve Force.

On 8 September 1951 in San Francisco, the U.S. and 47 other nations signed a peace treaty with Japan. The following year, on 28 April 1952, Japan regained its independence.

Thus ended one of the most extraordinary experiences in the history of any country--an experience that was to totally change the social and political structure of Japan, to alter forever the course of its culture, and to catapult it into a leadership role in the world that went far beyond the wildest dreams of its earlier expansionist military leaders.

The American military occupation of Japan was one of the most dramatic stories of the century, far exceeding in scale any similar event of the past, and it is still to be told. The human drama of the meeting of two such diverse peoples, who were able to work together despite profound differences, is as inspiring as the greatest of plays.

FAMOUS PERIODS IN JAPAN'S HISTORY

NARA PERIOD, 710-784--This was a revolutionary time in Japan's history. The massive imports of Chinese culture, Buddhism, Confucianism, and other powerful social and political ideas from the Asian mainland were being assimilated and adapted to fit the distinctive indigenous Japanese way. The period coincides with the years the Imperial capital was located at Nara, which became a center for the new arts and religions.

A distinctive architecture, sculpture, painting and other cultural forms that had been nurtured during earlier decades began to flower during these years. (The capital was located at Nagaokakyo from 784-794.)

HEIAN PERIOD, 794-1185--In 794 the Imperial capital was moved from Nara to Heiankyo (now Kyoto), and large-scale civil engineering and construction projects were undertaken to build a new metropolis. The city was laid out in grid-fashion (following Chinese patterns), with broad thoroughfares and a system of canals that served as both a water supply system and waterways.

One of the architectual masterpieces of that time is the Phoenix Hall of Byodo Temple, which includes an image of Buddhist paradise. Buddhism as well as other Buddhist-inspired arts flourished during this period.

During these four centuries, Japanese contacts with Korea and China were considerably lessened as they developed their own aristocratic culture based on Chinese concepts but with a decidedly Japanese flavor.

The power of the ancient noble families that had dominated the government and life of the country since its founding, continued to wane and was eventually ursuped completely by the new warrior class that had grown up under the nobles as their military forces.

KAMAKURA PERIOD, 1185-1333--This period marks the beginning of the ascendancy of the Samurai or warrior class, and the establishment of a military government

(Bakufu) at Kamakura, about 50 miles south of present-day Tokyo, by Yoritomo Minamoto, who was officially designated as Shogun by the reigning Emperor in 1192.

Because Zen Buddhism provided much of the philosophical and practical underpinnings for the Samurai and was therefore under their patronage, it flourished. Many of Japan's greatest Zen temples, including Kencho and Enkaku in Kamakura, were built during this period.

It was also during this period that the Great Buddha of Kamakura was cast—a masterpiece of Buddhist sculpture that stands today as a monument to the power and glory of 13th century Buddhism. See GREAT BUDDHA OF KAMAKURA.

It was during this period—in 1274 and 1281—that the Mongols of China mounted two unsuccessful attacks against Japan—and each time were defeated by the divine intervention of a great typhoon.

MUROMACHI PERIOD, 1333-1573—In 1333, with political power now in the hands of the Ashikaga Samurai clan, Japan's administrative capital was moved back to Kyoto, where the rough Samurai came under the influence of the effete cultural that had been developed over the centuries at the Imperial Court.

The third Ashikaga Shogun, Yoshimitsu, built the Kinkaku Ji (Temple of the Golden Pavilion), now one of the great treasures of Kyoto. Landscaping and gardening in general reached its zenith during this period.

The latter half of this period was one of political intrigue and turmoil among the feudal Samurai clans, the larger of which were continuously jousting for power.

It was during the latter decades of this period that Japan had its first recorded contacts with Westerners, and was introduced to cannons, rifles, tobacco, Catholicism and venereal disease.

MOMOYAMA PERIOD (1573-1603)—The Momoyama Period began with the victory of Oda Nobunaga, and his assumption of power over the other clans. Upon his death, the reins of power were seized by Toyotomi Hideyoshi, who had been one of his most successful generals.

Under both Nobunaga and Hideyoshi, trade with Southeast Asia and Europe flourished. Many of the castles built during this period had donjons, patterned after European castles. Merchants engaging in foreign trade amassed great wealth, and were instrumental in spreading culture in Japan to the common people.

The tea ceremony became popular and inspired a new type of architecture called sukiyazukuri, used for the construction of rooms and cottages specifically for the tea ceremony. The manufacture of ceramic teacups and other items used in the ceremony also flourished.

By the end of this period, the government of Japan was already trying to purge the country of the influence of Catholic missionaries, and to keep European powers at arms length.

EDO PERIOD (1603-1868)—In a final series of great battles, Ieyasu Tokugawa defeated the forces of Hideyoshi Toyotomi and in 1603 established what was to become Japan's last feudal Shogunate.

Ieyasu set up his military government in Edo, a small town at the head of what is now Tokyo Bay, and in the next few decades the town grew into one of the world's great cities. One of the primary reasons for Edo's extraordinary growth was the fact that the third Tokugawa Shogun required that the lords of all of Japan's some 270 clans build residences in Edo, keep their families there all year around, and themselves spend every other year in Edo in attendance at his court.

With approximately half of the country's Daimyo lords in Edo at all times, and all of them requiring large numbers of retainers and Samurai soldiers in their retinue, Edo became the site of power and a bustling commercial center almost overnight.

With the power of the Tokugawa Shogunate nearly absolute, and the military strength of the other clans kept strictly limited, Japan entered its longest period of internal peace.

During the 265-year long Edo Period, when most contact with the outside world was cut off, Japan's own unique culture matured. The arts and the theater flourished. Villages became towns, and towns became cities, as the clan headquarters —mostly in castles-required a growing number of services.

The constant traveling between the clan headquarters and Edo, by great processions involving up to 10,000 people, helped spread both economic benefits and culture throughout the country, and thus played a major role in binding the people and the provinces into a national unity. See PROCESSIONS OF THE LORDS.

HISTORICAL TABLE

YEAR   JAPAN/ABROAD

660 B.C. Mythical date of the accension of Japan's first Emperor, Jimmu.

300 A.D.-645 YAMATO PERIOD
476   End of the Roman Empire
538-552   Introduction of Buddhism from Korea
581-618   Sui Dynasty in China
593-622   Regency of Prince Shotoku
607   First envoy sent to China
618-907   Tang Dynasty in China
645   Downfall of the Soga clan, rise of the Fujiwara
702   Promulgation of Japan's first Constitution

710-784   NARA PERIOD
712   Publication of Kojiki (Record of Ancient Matters)
720   Publication of Nihon Shoki (Chronicle of Japan)
752   Dedication of the Great Buddha of Todai Temple in Nara
771-814   Reign of Charlemagne

794-1185 HEIAN PERIOD
894   Sending ofenvoys toChina abolished
995-1027 Heyday of the Fujiwara clan
1002-1019 The great novel, Genji Monogatari, written
1169-1181 Heyday of Kiyomori Taira
1180-1185 War between the Taira and Minamoto clans

1185-1333 KAMAKURA PERIOD
1192   Founding of the Kamakura Shogunate
1215   Magna Charta signed
1260-1368 Yuan Dynasty in China
1274   First Mongol invasion of Japan
1275   Marco Polo leaves Italy for China
1281   Second Mongol attempt to conquer Japan
1333   Kamakura Shogunate falls
1334   Emperor Godaigo temporarily regains power

1338-1573 ASHIGAKA (or MUROMACHI) PERIOD
1338   Founding of the Ashikaga Shogunate
1467-1477 Onin War, between contending clans
1492   Columbus discovers New World
1498   Vasco de Gama reaches India
1543   Portuguese ship lands on Japanese island of Tanega
1549   Catholic, Francis Xavier lands in Kagoshima

1568-1600 AZUCHI-MOMOYAMA PERIOD
1568   Nobunaga Oda seizes Kyoto
1582   Nobunaga assassinated
1585   Hideyoshi Toyotomi appointed civil dictator
1592   Hideyoshi sends army to invade Korea
1600   Ieyasu Tokugawa wins battle of Sekigahara

1600-1868 TOKUGAWA (or EDO) PERIOD
1602   Founding of Dutch East India Company
1603   Founding of the Tokugawa Shogunate
1615   Tokugawa Shogun captures Osaka Castle, eliminates Hideyoshi's heirs
1637-1638 Christians of Shimabara rebell
1639   Japan closed to outside world, except for small Dutch trading post
1789   French Revolution
1853   Commodore Perry arrives at Uraga, Japan
1854   Japan signs Treaty of Kanagawa with U.S.
1858   Treaty of Friendship β Commerce with U.S.
1867   Tokugawa Shogunate gives up power
1868   Emperor Meiji ascends throne, assumes power

1868-1912 MEIJI PERIOD
1868   Feudal clan system abolishedμ industrial transformation started
1877   Rebellion of Satsuma province quelled
1889   First real constitution promulgated
1894-1895 Japan goes to war against China
1902   Japan forms alliance with England
1904-1905 Japan goes to war against Russia
1910   Japan annexes Korea

1912-1926 TAISHO PERIOD
1914   Japan sides with Allies in war against Germany
1915   Japan demands major concessions from China
1918   Japan's first parlimamentary cabinet formed
1923   Great earthquake devastates Tokyo and Yokohama

1926-   SHOWA PERIOD
1931   Japan seizes Manchuria
1933   Japan leaves League of Nations

1933-	War against China continues
1940-1941	Japan expands war into Southeast Asia
1941	Japan bombs Pearl Harbor
1945	Japan surrenders, Pacific War ends
1945-1952	Allied Forces occupy Japan, institute political, social and economic reforms
1952	Japan regains independence, begins rise to position of economic leadership

HOKKAIDO (Hoke-kie-doe)

Japan's northernmost and second largest island, Hokkaido is still regarded by many Japanese as frontier-land. Separated from Honshu by the Tsugaru Straits, from Sakhalin by the Soya Straits, bounded on the east by the Sea of Okhotsk and on the west by the Sea of Japan, Hokkaido is as different from the southern islands of Japan as Alaska is from the lower United States.

Populated by the Ainu, a hairy Caucasoid race, when the Japanese first began arriving in the islands, Hokkaido (then known as Ezo) is first mentioned in Japanese records in 658, when Hirafu Abe went there to meet with the Ainu (also called Ezo) after he had defeated an indigenous tribe called Emishi in the Tohoku (northeastern) region of Honshu.

It is not known when the first Japanese settled in Hokkaido, but is presumed that there were Japanese living along the southern coastline from shortly after the period of Hirafu Abe.

In any event, there were numerous Japanese in Hokkaido by the middle ages --so much so that they had replaced the Ainu as the dominate group. In 1457 an Ainu chieftain named Koshamain led a rebellion against this Japanese encroachment, but the revolt was put down by Nobuhiro Takeda, who went on to subjugate the entire island. See AINU.

The Takeda family was to control Hokkaido for the next several generations, but in 1599 the family changed its name to Matsumae, built a castle at a location by that name, and allied themselves with Ieyasu Tokugawa who was on the verge of establishing the Tokugawa Shogunate.

Hokkaido was to remain in the backwaters of Japanese history during the long Tokugawa period. Under the Treaty of Kanagawa, signed with the U.S. in 1854, Hakodate was made an open port. Two years later the government was moved to the Ainu village of Sapporo, and in 1869 the name of the island was changed from Ezo to Hokkaido (Northern Sea Route). In 1871, Sapporo was laid out-- American-style--as a city, and made the capital of the island.

It was not until 1950 that the Japanese government passed an Hokkaido Development Law and established a Hokkaido Development Agency to spur economic growth on the island.

Hokkaido, which includes the Habomai Islands lying off the eastern tip of the main island and the Kurile Islands to the northeast, has 22 percent of the land area of Japan, but only about five percent of its population.

Like the rest of Japan, Hokkaido is a wonderland of scenic beauty--volcanic mountains, stunning gorges and valleys, thick forests, rolling plains, many lakes and rivers. Several huge areas on the island are so outstanding they have been designated national parks, which are characterized by towering mountains, smouldering volcanoes, deep valleys, primeval forests embracing caldera lakes in their bosom, vast expanses of plains, rare flora and fauna.

There are five such national parks in Hokkaido, along with eight prefectural parks on a smaller scale but of similar beauty.

Hokkaido's climate is similar to that of central Europe--very cold winters, with deep snows, especially in the mountain regions. Spring does not begin until May, and fall is underway by mid September.

The island is now connected with Honshu by an undersea tunnel, making it possible to go from Tokyo to Sapporo by train in less than six hours. Its economy began to boom in the 1960s and 70s.

The leading industries in Hokkaido today include fishing, lumbering, paper and pulp, agriculture, dairy farming, oil refining, cement making, iron and steel, foodstuffs, and brewing various alcoholic drinks.

Sapporo, which looks more foreign than any other Japanese city, and is the 7th largest metropolis in the country, is especially famous for its annual Snow Festival, held from February 1-5, which centers around huge figures carved in snow. It also has a Lilac Festival in May, a Hokkaido Shrine Festival in June, a Summer Festival in August and a Chrysanthemum Festival in the fall.

Sapporo's most famous foreign resident was Dr. William S. Clark, who was invited to Japan by the government to establish the Sapporo Agricultural College in 1876. He lived in Sapporo and taught at the new school for one year, but made a lasting impression on the Japanese. See CLARK, WILLIAM S.

Among Sapporo's other major attractions are the Ainu Museum, dedicated to the Rev. John Batchelor, who lived in the city for 40 years and became an authority on the Ainu, two underground shopping centers (Pole Town and Auroa Town) that are especially popular in the frigid winter months, and the Susukino entertainment district, where there are over 3,000 bars, cabarets, restaurants and overnight inns.

Within 20 to 45 minutes of Sapporo or some of the best ski resorts in Japan. The famous Jozankei Spa on the Toyohira River is just 26 kilometers from the city.

HOMES / IE (E-eh)

Japan has one of the highest rates of home ownership of any country in the world--well over 60 percent and climbing steadily--a situation that is a relatively recent phenomenon.

In the mid-1970s, the Japan Housing Corporation and the Housing Loan Corporation, both government agencies, launched a program to help promote the development of good lowcost housing.

The program was called House 55 Project, in reference to its target completion date in 1980, which would be the 55th year of the Showa Era (the reign of Emperor Hirohito). The goal of the project was to get commercial companies involved in the design and construction of prefabricated houses.

More than 40 companies took part in the program, and three of them--Misawa Homes, Shimizu Construction and a combine of Nippon Steel, Takenaka Komuten (a construction company) and Matsushita Electric Works--came up with winning designs and received government grants to build them

The combine's winning design, called TOPS, which went on sale at the beginning of 1982, is a two-story structure that is fabricated in sections that measure 2.5 meters by 4 meters, and consists of light materials in a honeycomb-type of construction over a steel framework.

A special feature of the Misawa House 55 is a heating system built into the floor, which, claim the makers, has a heat insulation factor 10 times as high as that of a cement floor.

By mid-1982 prefabricated houses accounted for some 10 percent of all the houses being built in Japan, and the percentage was increasing rapidly. By this time several other major Japanese companies had jumped onto the prefabricated house bandwagon, and were beginning to look at overseas markets.

Despite this progress, the average home in Japan is still very small by most standards, and many of them are old and in need of repair.

HOME VISITS

It is not customary for the Japanese to entertain casual friends or business contacts in their homes. There are several reasons for this. Japanese homes have traditionally been small, with enough room for only the immediate members of the family. It has also been, and still is, custom for men to keep their business life and private family life totally separated.

Business entertainment as well as personal entertaining have also traditionally included drinking and eating at public places designed to cater to this type of business. In fact, specific segments of Japan's huge public entertainment business cater primarily to businessmen--the cabarets, lounges, geisha houses and private ryotei restaurant-inns depending almost entirely on the patronage of well-heeled and expense-acgount executives. See individual listings for CABARETS, GEISHA, WATER BUSINESS.

Because of the interest among foreign visitors in the way the Japanese live, however, the Japan Travel Bureau and other travel services in Tokyo and other Japanese cities have made arrangements with some Japanese families to invite tourists into their homes for brief stays.

HONDA MOTOR COMPANY (Hone-dah)

The Honda Motor Company, one of the world's leading automobile and motorcycle manufacturers, epitomizes the special insight, skills and dedication that have characterized Japanese industry since 1945.

In 1946 a young engineer named Soichiro Honda (pronounced Hone-dah, not Hahn-day) began attaching small engines to bicycles. In transportation-starved postwar Japan, the motor-bike was an immediate success.

The limited supply of ready-made

engines was soon used up. Honda decided to build his own, and in 1948 founded the Honda Motor Company with an investment of ∫2,700.

By 1949 Honda had stepped up from motor-bikes to motorcycles. Two years later he and his even younger engineering staff introduced the now historic 146 cc 4-stroke Dream motorcycle.

The engineer who put the motorcycle through its first grueling test was Kiyoshi Kawashima, who was destined to become president of the company. Honda sold nine million of the revolutionary lightweight, easy-to-operate motorcycles.

By the early 1960s, Honda Motor Company was not only the world's largest manufacturer of motorcycles. It made the best motorcyles in the world.

At this time, Soichiro decided to begin making cars--using the same innovative, high-tech, high-quality approach that had made the company so successful with motorcycles.

The company began tooling up to manufacture a line of small, hardy, inexpensive, fuel-efficient cars that would meet the transportation needs of most people around the world. The first Honda car--the Honda Civic--drove off the assembly line in 1972--one year before the great energy crisis began.

In 1975 Honda introduced an almost-pollutioon-free engine called the CVCC, getting another jump on other auto makers who were plagued by rising pollution problems.

Next came larger and more luxurious motorcycles and cars, to meet the continuing market demands for these products. By 1982, Honda had grown into an international enterprise with over 33,000 employees and annual sales in excess of 8 billion dollars.

Honda's extraordinary success is attributed to several factors, includeing timing, correctly perceiving the needs of the market, emphasis on engineering excellence and quality, and a team concept that eventually came to be known as The Honda Way.

The Honda Way refers to management Japanese style, which is more personally oriented and based on a very high level of manager-worker cooperation, quality consciousness, concensus and company loyalty.

HONSHU (Hone-shuu)

This is Japan's largest and main island. Comprising 61.1 percent of the total land area of Japan, it is in the middle of the chain, with the island of Hokkaido just off its northern tip, and Shikoko and Kyushu at its southwestern end.

Honshu curves from east to west and is shaped somewhat like a boomerang. Like all the other islands of Japan, it is extremely mountainous, with well-defined geographical regions.

The mountainous areas are characterized by extinct volcanic peaks, huge craters, lakes, gorges, ravines, narrow valleys and numerous hotsprings.

Honshu is divided into five regions: Tohoku, Kanto, Chubu, Kinki and Chugoku (which see). The bulk of Japan's population and industry are on Honshu. Its major cities include Tokyo, Yokohama, Nagoya, Kyoto, Osaka, Kobe, Hiroshima, Nagasaki, Kawasaki and Sendai.

HORIE, KENICHI (Hoe-ree-eh, Kane-ee-chee)

A world-class adventurer, Kenichi Horie, born in Osaka in 1938, became the first Japanese yachtsman to cross the Pacific alone, in 1962. He then sailed around the world on a non-stop voyage in 1974, and between 1978 and 1982 became the first man to complete a longitudinal solo voyage around the globe.

After returning to Japan in 1962 following his crossing of the Pacific, Horie was immediately arrested and jailed. He was charged with leaving the country without official permission.

The story of Horie's accomplishment made world-wide news, and his being arrested made him even more of a celebrity. Horie was soon released from jail, partly at least because of the favorable publicity he received and the strong criticism the authorities received.

The official reason given for the charges against Horie being dropped was that he apologized and showed regret for having caused so much trouble.

HORSES / UMA (Uu-mah)

Horses were brought into Japan from the Asia mainland some time before recorded history began, but their use was restricted to official government and military pursuits.

In any event, the type of agriculture practiced in Japan did not lend itself to the use of horses as draft animals, and common people were prohibited from using them for riding.

Restrictions governoring the use of horses continued in Japan until the fall of the Tokugawa Shogunate in 1868, but the situation really did not change very much then. Farming methods had not changed, and there was no room or need for horses in most of the country.

The exceptions to this were the Tohoku district of northern Honshu and Hokkaido, where horses had traditionally been raised for the Shogun and lords of feudal Japan. There, in the plains areas, horses became increasingly important, both for work and military use.

Today these areas are noted for their races horses as well as draft animals, and there is a modest but growing use of horses for recreational purposes.

The Tohoku district, in fact, has been compared to the state of Texas in the U.S. because of the popularity of horses, the expansive attitudes of the people, and their habit of claiming that everything in the region is bigger and better than it is anywhere else.

HORS D'OUVRES / TSUMAMI (T-sue-mah-me)

There are several kinds of hors d'ouvres in Japan. Tsumami are the kind that accompany alcoholic drinks and are most likely to be served in bars and cabarets. They generally consist of nuts, small sembi rice crackers wrapped in seaweed and/or dipped in a cayenne pepper-laden soy sauce, or shredded cuttlefish.

In a Japanese inn, hors d'ouvres are likely to be small squares of sweetened bean jam. At a reception or party, hors d'ouvres run the gamut of tidbits of seafood, vegetables, cheeses and meats.

HORYU TEMPLE / HORYU JI (Hoe-ree-you)

The oldest existing temple in Japan and one of the oldest wooden structures in the world, the Horyu, near Nara, was founded in 607 by Prince Shotoku Taishi at the command of Empress Suiko, his aunt.

Considered one of the Seven Great Temples of Nara, the fountainhead of Japanese culture, the Horyu Temple is the headquarters of the Shotoku sect of Buddhism.

The temple is divided into two sections, and altogether includes 45 important buildings, 31 of which are registered as National Treasures and the rest as Important Cultural Properties. There is so much to see in the temple complex, and so much to learn, that a sojourn of a week or more would not be enough to cover it all. The barest description of its treasures would take many pages. Best idea is to go see it.

HOTELS / HOTERU (Hoe-tay-rue)

The first Western-styled hotel in Japan was the Edo, built in 1868, and boasting 102 rooms. It was located in the Tsukiji district of Tokyo, just east of the Ginza shopping and entertainment area. Second was the Club Hotel in Yokohama, which opened in 1869.

The third hotel was the Seiyoken, which opened in Tsukiji in 1871, and was followed rapidly by the Hyogo Hotel in Kobe, the Grand Hotel in Yokohama and the Tokyo Hotel in Tokyo. These were followed by smaller tourist-type hotels in such scenic and historic places as Nikko, Kamakura, Hakone, Karuizawa and Kyoto.

The famous Imperial Hotel, backed by the government which saw the need for a world-class hotel for visiting foreign dignataries, opened on November 3, 1890. The Imperial had 70 rooms, and was to set the standards for Japan's hotel industry until well into the 1960s.

Actually, the luxury hotel with its numerous amenities, was invented in Japan--although it was, of course, Japanese style. In the early 1600s, the Tokugawa Shogunate decreed that all of the country's feudal lords, known as Daimyo (Die-m'yoe) or Great Names, would spend every other year in Edo, the Shogun's headquarters.

This meant the nearly 300 Daimyo thoughout the long island chain had to march, with hundreds to thousands of retainers, from their fiefs to Edo on alternate years. These great processions had to have places to stay over each night, so two special kinds of accommodations were developed along the country's great walking roads, at specified intervals. Those that were developed specifically for the Lords and their closest retainers were beautifully styled and richly decorated, befitting the elite status of their special guests. These luxurious hotels were called Honjin (Hone-jeen).

The second type of hotel/inn that appeared along with the honjin were known as Waki-Honjin (Wah-kee Hone-jeen), or Back-up Honjin, and were designed to accommodate the lesser ranking retainers of these great processions-- and were more like the inns that catered to regular travelers.

Thus when European travelers and travelers in other parts of the world were being put up in basic inns, the elite Samurai and nobles of Japan--with the former spending a major portion of their lives on the road--had the advantage of accommodations that were rich to say the least. See PROCESSIONS OF THE LORDS.

With this long and meticulous tradition of providing travelers with the finest possible accommodations, it is not surprising that Japan's Western-style hotels today are among the finest, if not the finest, in the world.

The larger and best-known of the hotels in Tokyo, for example, have a variety and quality of services and amenities that make leading hotels in New York, London and Paris pale in comparison. It is common for them to have anywhere from half a dozen to two dozen restaurants in a variety of cuisines.

The Imperial Hotel, for example, has a large shopping arcade, a post office, a book store, drug store, a wrapping and forwarding service, a businessman's work lounge and several dozen business offices on its premises. See IMPERIAL HOTEL.

Beginning in the early 1970s, businessmen's hotels began to proliferate in Japan. These hotels are generally smaller than the name luxury hotels, with fewer special amenities. But they are in convenient locations, would mostly rank as first-class, and are significantly less expensive than the huge luxury hotels.

There are well over 500 Western-style hotels in Japan. Tokyo alone has some 400 hotels. All are members of the Japan Hotel Association.

Direct tipping is forbidden in most Japanese hotels. Instead, a service charge of 10 to 15 percent is automatically added to the bill. There is also a 10 percent tax on meals and room charges that are above specified amounts.

Leading hotels in Japan include (TOKYO): the Imperial, Hilton, Okura, New Otani, Akasaka Prince, Takanawa Prince, Keio Plaza, Century Hyatt, New Takanawa Prince, Palace and Grand Palace.

(NAGOYA): Nagoya Castle, International, Meitetsu Grand, Nagoya Kanko, Nagoya Miyako, Nagoya Terminal and Castle Plaza.

(KYOTO): Holiday Inn, Fujita, International, Kyoto Grand, Kyoto, Kyoto Station and Miyako.

(OSAKA): International, New Hankyu, Osaka Airport, Osaka Grand, Plaza, Toyo and Royal.

HOTEL SERVICES

A special feature of leading hotels in Japan is the variety of services they provide visiting foreign businessmen. These services, contracted out, include translation and interpreting, secretarial, photo-copying, research and appointments.

Several hotels have Executive Service Lounges, a service pioneered by the Imperial Hotel in Tokyo. The Imperial's lounge has private work cubicles, typewriters, and telephones, and a library of publications on Japanese industry. It is staffed by bi-lingual members of the Japan External Trade Organization whose sole duty is to aid foreign businessmen who are guests at the hotel.

A special feature of the Okura Hotel's Executive Service Salon are 30-minute English-language tapes on various business topics, from management to robots.

HOTSPRING SPAS / ONSEN (Own-sen)

The volcanic nature of the Japanese islands have blessed them with dozens of thousands of hotsprings, in virtually every region of the country. Several thousand of these springs have been developed into spas. Hundreds of them have been in use and famous for over a thousand years.

Just some of the more popular hotspring spas whose names begin with A include: Akiu, Aone, Arifuku, Arima, Asama, Asamushi, Aso, Asobara, Asozu, Atagawa, Atsumi, Awara, and Awazu.

Other famous ones include Bandai-Atami, Fukiage, Kaminoyama, Noboribetsu, Numa Jiri, Toyako, Unzen, Yoshina and Yunokawa. Kusatsu, some three hours from Tokyo by express train, is one of the oldest and most famous hotspring spas in Japan. In use since ancient times, it was made nationally famous in the 12th century as a result of several visits by Yoritomo Minamoto, who founded Japan's first Shogunate at Kamakura in 1192.

Yoritomo was attracted to the spa because of the reputation its sulphuric, iron, alum and arsenic waters had for relieving such things as rheumatism, gout, skin diseases and other ailments.

The main public bath at Kusatsu, called Netsu-no Yu or Heat Bath, is so hot bathers generally enter the water in unison--200 or so a a time--to shouted commands from a bathmaster. Attendants first stir up the water with long boards to reduce its temperature.

Once the bathers are in the water-- for three or four minutes--they remain absolutely motionless to keep the heat at a minimum. The bathmaster counts off the time, and shouts encouragement to the bathers. At the end of the period, the bathmaster always yells for the bathers to get out of the water slowly--but most of them get out as quickly as they can.

There are more than 130 inns centered around the town square of Kusatsu, which is surrounded by a forest of pine and larch trees. The sulphur content of the water is so high that it is processed, and the collected suphur sold commercially.

Above Kusatsu, on mountain slopes that range from 1,200 to 1,700 meters in altitude, is one of Japan's most famous ski resorts.

There are hotspring spas in or very near virtually every city and town in Japan. In hundreds of cases, the whole town is one huge spa, with dozens to hundreds of inns featuring large and small mineral baths. See individual listings. For a directory of the leading spas in the country, contact the JNTO.

HOUSEHOLDS / KATEI (Kah-tay-e)

Japan has approximately 40 million households, with an average of 3.25 persons per household. In Tokyo, the average household size is only 2.70 persons--the lowest in the country. Nuclear households (couples without children and parents with only their own children) now account for over 60 percent of all households in Japan.

HOUSING

Japan has the world's most advanced home building industry. By the early 1980s, a significant percentage of the industry had been computerized, robotized and automated. Computers draft designs and print out blueprints, keep track of all inventory, order parts as they are needed, and handle marketing.

Builders produce up to 85 percent of their housing units in factories, where cutting, welding, nailing and gluing are done on an assembly line--partly by robots adapted from the auto industry. A typical house is ready for assembly in 40 minutes, and the entire house can be put together on site by a small crew in four hours.

Many of the innovations characterizing Japan's housing industry were pioneered by Sekisui Heim and Misawa Homes, two of its leading home builders.

American home builders have described what Japanese home builders are doing as mind-boggling.

Western-style housing available for foreign businessmen and their families (and for foreigners in other categories) is still premium, however.

Renting a house in Japan may involve several fees or payments besides the monthly rent. Most landlords require the payment of shikikin (she-kee-keen) or so-called key money which may amount to the value of several months rent. Eighty percent of the key money is returned when the renter vacates the premises. Key money may be negotiable, but the lower it is the higher the rent tends to be--primarily because in Japan the law protects the renter, not the owner.

In apartments and condos, there are usually manager's fees to be paid (kyoeki) for cleaning hallways and stairs, etc., as well as parking fees.

In Japan, first-class Western style condominiums and apartment buildings are called mansions (Mahn-shon).

Recommended reading: THE ELEGANT JAPANESE HOUSE--Traditional Sukiya Architecture, by Yukio Futagawa (Weatherhill).

HUMAN FEELINGS / NINJO (Neen-joe)

Japan's strict traditional code of ethics and morality, in which the individual gave up many personal rights for the benefit of the family, the feudal Lord and and often the country, resulted in fundamental clashes between their duty and obligations (giri) and their own personal feelings. See GIRI.

These clashes between giri and human feelings (ninjo) were therefore an integral part of Japanese life, and were uppermost in their minds from a very young age until death. Not only did the words and all their implications play a vital role in the daily lives of the Japanese, they became the central themes in literature and theatrical arts.

The concepts of giri and ninjo are still very important in modernday Japan, although the words themselves appear to be less frequently used in personal and business conversations. The Japanese are especially sensitive about their individual and human rights--most of which they did not have until the end of the feudal family system in 1945.

HUMOR / YUMOA (Yuu-moe-ah)

Those who do not understand the language or culture of another people often seem predisposed to presume that others do not have a sense of humor. This has especially been the case among many Westerners who were not familiar with Japan.

In actuality, the Japanese have a highly developed sense of humor that ranges from the base and bawdy to a level so refined that only the most sophisticated and educated can understand and appreciate it.

Oral and visual humor in Japan have traditions that go back as far as any record, and are no doubt as innate in the Japanese as they are in most homo sapiens. See COMIC STORY TELLERS.

Humor plays a vital role in the lives of most Japanese--perhaps more vital than in the lives of many other people around the globe--because the Japanese have traditionally been more restricted in their behavior than most other people.

With a highly refined and constraining etiquette that prevents the Japanese from being themselves most of the time, humor has been and still is a valuable safety valve that allows them to let off steam.

The Japanese language, with its built-in ambiguities, illusions and double meanings, lends itself to humor to a degree that appears to exceed English-- and probably other languages as well.

See JAPANESE LANGUAGE.

ICE-SCULPTURES

Ice-carving for decorative and festive occasions is a highly advanced art in Japan. Decorative ice-carvings are the specialty of ice chefs in many of Japan's leading hotels, who use them to set off huge banquets.

The most spectacular cold sculptures in Japan are those done in snow for the Sapporo Snow Festival in Hokkaido in winter. See SNOW FESTIVAL.

IKAHO (E-kah-hoe)

This is one of Japan's most celebrated hotspring spas. Located about two train-and-bus hours from Tokyo's Ueno Station, Ikaho is built on a series of terraces on the northeast slope of Mt. Haruna in Niigata Prefecture.

The whole town of Ikaho consists almost entirely of inns built around hotsprings that are approximately 50 degrees centigrade and have an iron and sulphur content (recommended for stomach ailments).

Ikaho is also noted for the beauty of the surrounding hillsides, which are covered with wild flowers from June to September, and with snow in the winter months. The best view of the area is from the grounds of Ikaho Shrine, which overlooks the town.

IKEBANA (Ee-kay-bah-nah)

By the mid-1500s, ikebana or flower arranging was flourishing in Japan as a popular art, with the emphasis on the use of natural materials and the recreation of natural forms. Ikebana literally means living flowers.

As time went by, ikebana became imbued with metaphysical meanings, with the primary goal being to arrange the sprays in such a way as to signify the sky, earth and man, and to serve as a strict aesthetic and moral discipline.

Three basic sprays were developed to portray the harmonious balance of nature. Flower-arranging was primarily seen as a feminine skill. Young girls were expected to study the art as part of their preparation for marriage and adulthood.

While still a national custom, as well as being a profession supported by numerous schools and affiliated exhibitions, ikebana is now divided between the traditionalists and a post-WWII

school that uses lifeless materials (iron, glass, plaster) to give the impression of life through the vitality of form.

The basic techniques of traditional ikebana differ with the particular school, but all include specific ways of cutting, pruning and caring for the flowers. Both traditionalists and avant-garde ikebanists practice the art for interior decoration purposes on a commercial basis as well as for personal aesthetics.

In homes ikebana arrangements are displayed in the tokonoma (toe-koe-no-mah), a special alcove in the living room designed specifically for the exhibit of flowers and hanging scrolls. See FLOWER ARRANGING.

IKEBUKURO (E-kay-buu-kuu-roe)

One of Tokyo's busiest districts, Ikebukuro is in Toshima Ward northwest of downtown. The center of the area is Ikebukuro Station, which is a main stop on the Yamanote Loop Line that encircles the heart of Tokyo. It is also the terminal for four major commutor lines that serve outlying districts, and the Marunouchi Subway Line that begins here, curves through downtown Tokyo and then runs westward to Ogikubo.

Until the 1970s, Ikebukuro was regarded as provincial, and served primarily as a shopping and entertainment center for people who came in from rural areas to the north and west.

Then a building boom began in the area, highlighted by a huge complex called the Sunrise Building, which became a popular office and shop location, and helped attract other businesses. Ikebukuro now draws shoppers and pleasure-seekers from other parts of Tokyo as well as the countryside beyond.

IMMUNIZATION CARDS

At present visitors to Japan are not required to show evidence of immunization unless they are coming from an area known to be infected (usually smallpox or cholera). There may, however, be temporary periods when such cards are needed, so it is best to check with a travel agent or a Japanese embassy or consulate abroad before departure.

IMPERIAL FAMILY / KOSHITSU (Koe-sheet-sue)

Japan's Imperial family is the world's oldest reigning dynasty. According to the Kojiki (Record of Ancient Matters), published in 712, the first emperor of Japan was enthroned in 660

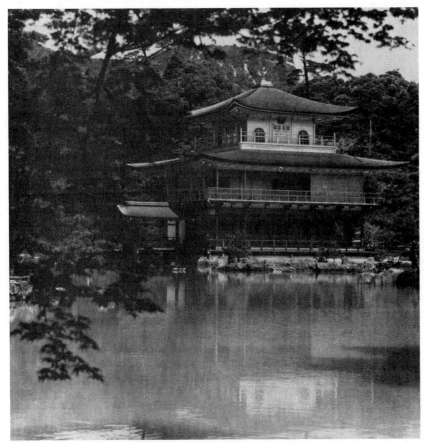

Temple of the Golden Pavilion, Kyoto. P.184

Hanging scroll in a tokonoma. P. 120

Scene from a famous kabuki drama. P. 173

B.C., but this is disputed by some Japanese historians.

Chinese records make references to Japan in later centuries, and there is no doubt that a large area of the country in the Nara-Kyoto-Osaka region was unified under the rule of the Imperial family by 300 A.D.

The head of the Imperial family at this time was named Hatsukunishirasu Sumera Mikoto, who was later referred to as Jimmu Tenno, or Emperor Jimmu.

Following the introduction of the Chinese system of writing into Japan in the 5th and 6th century, records of the reigning emperors and empresses are complete and in detail.

During the earliest centuries, the emperor was both the religious and secular leader of Japan. From around 600 to the death of Emperor Saga in 842, there were many emperors who were outstanding scholars, noted for their wisdom and accomplishments in many fields.

But in the mid-800s, the Fujiwara family, which had intermingled with the Imperial family for some 200 years, gradually took over real political power, first through the office of prime minister and then as regent to the emperor.

From this period until 1868, with only a few brief exceptions, the emperors reigned but did not rule. As more and more of the political and administrative power was usurped by the Fujiwaras, less and less attention was paid to governing the country. The nobles and their families and retainers lived in luxurious splendor, spending their days in aesthetic, artistic and recreational pursuits.

The provincial governors, most of whom were relatives of the Imperial family and the Fujiwaras, began to act on their own and became more and more independent. They began to maintain their own elite armed forces.

Emperor Gosanjo (1034-1073), aware of what was happening, tried to weaken the power of the Fujiwara regents and rule personally. His successor, Emperor Shirakawa (1053-1129), tried a new tact--retiring from the throne and trying to exercise influence over the administration of the contry unofficially.

Subsequent emperors followed suit, but this resulted in weakening the central government further, and a series of civil wars broke out among the powerful provincial clans contending for power.

Kiyomori Taira, the scion of one of the new military families that had grown up in the provinces, fought on behalf of the Imperial Court and emerged the winner in these conflicts. The grateful emperor rewarded him with one promotion after another, until finally he became the prime minister.

Just like the Fujiwaras before him, Kiyomori claimed the power of the emperor for himself, but was careful to see that the Imperial family was not threatened.

The glory of the Taira family was to be short-lived, however, as some 20 years later, in 1185, the clan was totally destroyed by Yoritomo Minamoto.

As the new supreme military power in Japan, Yoritomo obtained permission from the emperor to set up a new administrative system for the provinces--a system made up of shugo (guards) in charge of military and police affairs, and jito (squires), who were in charge of running the economic affairs and collecting the annual rice tax.

Yoritomo appointed his own family members and retainers to these posts, thus eliminating the final vestiges of Imperial power. In 1192, Yoritomo succeeded in having the emperor appoint him Sei-i-Tai-Shogun (Say-e-e-Tie-Sho-goon), or General for the Subjugation of Eastern Barbarians (an old title given to generals sent against the aboriginal Ainu tribesmen of northern Japan centuries earlier).

Yoritomo then set up a military government, called Bakufu (Bah-kuu-fuu) or Camp Office in Kamakura. He then contrived to make the position of Shogun hereditary, and pass it on to his sons, first to Yoriie and then to Sanetomo. But Sanetomo was assassinated by a nephew in 1219 (who hid behind a tree that still stands in Kamakura).

And this ended the days of glory of the Minamoto clan--after only 27 years in power.

The Kamakura Shogunate was to continue, however, in the hands of the Hojo clan, in the guise of regents, who also guaranteed the continuity of the Emperor as the titular head of the country.

Furthermore, the system of shugo guards and jito squires that Yoritomo established was to prevail until 1868--the shugo becoming known as Samurai and the jito becoming feudal lords known as Daimyo. See SAMURAI, HISTORY.

The defense of Japan against the Mongol invasions in 1274 and 1281 (see HISTORY) seriously weakened the Kamakura Shogunate. In Kyoto, Emperor Godaigo (1288-1339) and his nobles plotted to overthrow the Bakufu government and regain real power for the throne.

Spies reported the plotting to the Shogunate, which exiled the Emperor to the island of Oki in the Japan Sea in 1332. He escaped the following year, however, and with the help of four famous Daimyo-generals--Nagatoshi Nawa, Masashige Kusunoki, Yoshisada Nitta and Takauji Ashikaga--defeated the forces of the Shogunate.

Back in power for the first time in centuries, the Imperial Court angered the generals by being more generous in its rewards to the various nobles than to the warriors, and by compelling the provincial Daimyo to pay for the cost of building new palaces in Kyoto.

Takauji Ashikaga led the warriors against Kyoto and captured the city. Emperor Godaigo fled to the mountains of Yoshino and set up his court there. Back in Kyoto, Takauji enthroned a new emperor (a relative of Godaigo's), and established the Ashikaga Shogunate.

For the next 57 years the country had two emperors. In 1392 the Yoshino court merged with the Kyoto court, but real power was still in the hands of the Ashikaga Shogunate.

Takauji's succesors fell victim to the soft life of Kyoto, and became involved in aesthetics and the arts, leaving the running of the country to subordinates. Once again, the provincial lords began to compete for power. Inter-clan warfare broke out between the Hosokawa and Yamana families in 1467, and for the next 130 odd years, the feudal lords kept the country in a state of war as they battled among themselves for supremacy.

In the intervening years, the Imperial Court in Kyoto flourished or waned, depending on the amount of support it got from the Ashikaga Bakufu government. One emperor after another succeeded to the chrysanthemum throne, in a line that remained unbroken--bent sometimes, but not broken.

When the great Ieyasu Tokugawa emerged the winner in this age of civil strife in 1603, and founded Japan's last great Shogun dynasty, he was even more supportive of the Imperial Court than his predecessors had been.

After establishing his Bakufu in Edo (Tokyo), Ieyasu divided the country into four hereditary classes--the kuge or court nobles, the buke or Samurai warriors, farmers, and chonin, or townspeople. While the Emperor and court nobles had the most exalted rank in the land, they had no real administrative power.

The Tokugawa Shogunate was to provide one of the longest periods of peace in Japan's history. As the decades went by, many in the Samurai class became scholars, and learned that in the early history of the country the emperor had actually ruled.

As new economic and social forces began to weaken the Shogunate, these scholars and others began talking and writing about restoring the emperor to his rightful place. During these same decades, the Western powers and Russia began pressuring Japan to open its doors --closed since 1639--to the outside world.

Imperialist sentiment continued to grow in Japan when it became obvious that the Tokugawa Shogunate could not deal with these new forces coming in from the outside. Thus once again it was a revolt against the Bakufu by dissatisfied provincial Daimyo that brought the downfall of the Tokugawas, and returned Emperor Meiji to power in 1868.

Emperor Meiji was to be an enlightened ruler, as emperors go, but the new concepts of democracy and constitutional government that poured into Japan from the 1850s on was to once again set the stage for a drastic change in the position of the Emperor.

Voluntarily reacting to pressure from many sources as well as his own inclinations, the Emperor approved the prolmugation of a constitutional form of government in 1889.

Emperor Meiji was to remain a potent force in Japan's government until his death in 1912, but soon thereafter real power was in the hands of the prime minister and his cabinet--a situation that was to prevail until the end of World War II in 1945, at which time the position of the emperor was constitutionally prescribed to be that of a symbol of the state, with no political or administrative powers--a situation that had been the role of the Imperial family for nearly 1,000 years.

When Emperor Meiji died in July 1912, he was succeeded by his son who became the Emperor Taisho. Never of robust health, Emperor Taisho died in 1926, and was in turned succeeded by his son Prince Hirohito, whose reign was given the name of Showa.

Emperor Hirohito was born April 29, 1901. His Empress, Nagako, born on March 6, 1903, was the daughter of the Kuni family, a branch of the Imperial family. Their first son, Akihito, was born on December 23, 1933, and in April 1959 married Michiko Shoda, the commoner daughter of the president of the Nisshin Flour Milling Company, whom he met on the tennis courts at the Karuizawa summer resort northwest of Tokyo.

This was the first time that a crown prince of Japan had married outside the nobility, and was a popular choice among the people. See HISTORY, SHOGUN.

IMPERIAL HOTEL / TEIKOKU HOTERU (Tay-e-koe-kuu Hoe-tay-rue)

Japan's Imperial Hotel is world-famous for many reasons--not the least of which is its tradition of service fit for royalty. The story of the Imperial Hotel is part of some of the most important and dramatic events in the history of the country.

When the Tokugawa Shogunate was dissolved in 1868, the Emperor moved from the ancient Imperial capital of Kyoto to Edo, which was renamed Tokyo or Eastern Capital. During the next several decades, the country underwent an extraordinary change, transforming itself from a feudal society with an agricultural-cottage industry economy to a modern industrial power.

During these exciting years, the many world statesmen, international businessmen and other foreign notables who came to Tokyo had to be put up in the plush but traditionally styled Japanese inns, where guests sat and slept on floor mats.

Recognizing the need for accommodations more suited to the customs and preferences of the growing number of distinguished foreign visitors, the Imperial Household Authority, Foreign Minister Viscount Inouye and industrial leaders Count Shibusawa and Baron Okura in 1890 sponsored the building of a large Western styled hotel, and named it the Imperial.

For the first several years of its existence, the new Imperial Hotel was anything but a rousing success. By 1906, however, it became necessary to add an annex. Patronage continued to increase, and in 1910 it was decided to replace the building altogether with a larger structure. (This was also the year that the first packaged tour--The Clark World Tour Party, with 500 people--visited Japan, staying at the Imperial Hotel.)

This was a period of great political upheavals around the world, however, and there was a delay in beginning the new Imperial. Eventually the young but already famous Frank Lloyd Wright was engaged to design and supervise the construction of the second Imperial Hotel, which finally got underway in 1917.

The first section of the Mayan-like new Imperial Hotel opened on July 4, 1922. The completed hotel was officially open to the public on August 31, 1923.

The following day, at precisely 11:58 a.m., September 1, 1923, the Tokyo and Yokohama areas were struck by the worst earthquake on record, leaving over 100,000 people dead and vast sections of the two great cities burned-out rubble.

Among the few modern structures that escaped the holocaust with only minor damage was the brand new Imperial Hotel. With a stroke of insight, Wright had floated the pilings of the Imperial Hotel in the spongy subsoil covering the solid strata further down. As a result, his unique creation literally rode out the giant earthquake tremors the way a ship moves with the waves at sea.

As one of the few surviving buildings in central Tokyo with large kitchen facilities, a water supply and at least some food, the Imperial Hotel in a matter of minutes became a combination hospital, field kitchen and general headquarters for relief measures taken to help the thousands left homeless and hungry. It also became the temporary headquarters for dozens of newsmen and diplomatic personnel whose offices and homes had been destroyed.

Order was restored to Tokyo in a few weeks, and with it, the Imperial assumed a major role in Japan's affairs with the outside world--not only as the preeminent hotel in the nation, but often as a national guest house for state visitors, and as a cultural and recreational center for foreign residents.

After World War II ended in August 1945, the first foreign visitor of note to step into the distinctive foyer of the famous Imperial Hotel was Gen. Douglas MacArthur, Supreme Commander of the Allied Powers (SCAP), who was destined to rule Japan for the next four years, very much like the Tokugawa Shoguns had in the centuries before.

The famous general landed in Japan at Atsugi Airbase on August 30, 1945, and went first to Yokohama while quarters were prepared for him in Tokyo. On the morning of September 11, he was driven to the American Embassy in Tokyo, where he was to live for the next four years.

Before leaving Yokohama, MacArthur had someone call the Imperial Hotel and ask that a luncheon be prepared for him and the senior members of his staff. He left the Embassy early and arrived at the Imperial shortly after 11 a.m.

MacArthur asked Tetsuzo Inumaru, who had been general manager of the hotel since it opened, to show him some of the rooms. He then asked Inumaru to take him on a 30-minute tour of the bombed-out city.

MacArthur then requisitioned the hotel as a billet for senior officers and ranking civilians working at his headquarters, which were in the Dai-Ichi Insurance Building just two blocks away.

Rather than be disheartened by the turn of events, Inumaru, who had received his hotel training at the Claridge in London, the Ritz in Paris and the Waldorf-Astoria in New York, called his staff together and told them they were to take advantage of the opportunity to learn all they could, and that they were to provide the same high level of service to the members of the Occupation forces as they had previously done for regular guests.

The Imperial Hotel was returned to its owners in March, 1952, and opened for business on April 1, 1952--exactly four weeks before the Allied Occupation of Japan officially ended.

On December 1, 1954 an East Annex was opened behind the original Imperial. Only two years later a second annex--this time a 9-story tower--was added. By 1967, however, it was obvious that the old Frank Lloyd Wright structure, its floors and walls gradually shifting and sinking as other builders in the area pumped out underground water, had outlive its span of years.

On November 16, 1967, after many a tearful farewell party, the famed Old Imperial closed its doors for the last time. A gleaming new Imperial--the third in its history--made its debut in March, 1970.

As the decade of the 1970s went by, it once again became obvious that the new T-shaped highrise building was not enough. The older East Annexes were demolished and work begun on a new 31-story Imperial Tower.

This new Imperial Tower, which has guest rooms from the 20th to 31st floors, a sauna and swimming pool on the 19th floor, offices on the 5th to 18th floors, with a shopping plaza, meeting rooms and other facilities on the lower floors, opened in March 1983.

With this latest tower, the Imperial is again in the forefront of Japan's most outstanding hotels. It is, in fact, much more than a hotel, being in addition, a major business, recreation and cultural complex.

The Imperial is about 300 meters from the southeast corner of the Outer Moat of the Imperial Palace. It fronts on the city's major thoroughfare, and is across the street from Hibiya Park, formerly the private garden of a Daimyo feudal lord.

The philosophy that has made the Imperial Hotel what it is today was summed up once by an assistant sales manager. He said: We do not work for money alone. We work for the satisfaction, the pleasure and the pride that comes from doing better than just a good job, and being accepted and trusted by our top management.

IMPERIAL PALACE / KYUJO (Que-joe)

Known as both the Chiyoda Castle and Edo Castle during the Tokugawa Period (1603-1868), the Imperial Palace is the center-piece of Tokyo. Located in what is now Chiyoda Ward on the western edge of the downtown district, the Imperial Palace covers an area of 1,150,000 square meters. Its central portion is surrounded by a wide moat, a high pine-clad embankment and stone walls.

The residence of the Tokugawa Shoguns for 265 years., the original Palace was circled by three wide moats. Now only the inner moat remains, and the grounds are secluded behind high stone walls atop the moat ramparts.

During the days of the Shogun, the castle consisted of the main area (Hon Maru) where the residence and staterooms of the Shogun were located, the Western Keep (Nishi-no Maru) where the heir apparent lived, the Second Keep (Ni-no Maru), the Northern Keep (Kita-no Maru) and the Third Keep (San-no Maru).

During the reign of the Tokugawa Shoguns, there were five great gates leading into the castle grounds--Sakura-da Mon, Sakashita Mon, Ote Mon, Hirakawa Mon, and Hanzo Mon. Today, the main gate to the Palace grounds is on the east side, where there are two bridges, one of stone and one of steel, crossing the moat. These bridges are popularly called Niju Bashi (Nee-juu Bah-she) or Double Bridge. The park-like plaza in front of this entrance is called the Imperial Palace Plaza, and is a popular place for office workers from the nearby Marunouchi financial and business district to eat box lunches and wile away the noon hour.

The Palace buildings located in the Western Keep were burned down during World War II, and a new Palace was built for the present Emperor in 1968 in front of the site. While built of ferro-concrete, the new Palace is traditional Japanese in style, and has about 4,000 square meters of floor space.

There are two palaces within the grounds--the Fukiage Palace where the Emperor and Empress live and the New Palace, where public functions are held. The residence of the Crown Prince is also located within the Palace grounds, as is the Imperial Household Agency.

The main entranceway to the Palace is Nijubashi, which is used a few times a year by the Emperor, by ambassadors and ministers and other foreign guests calling on the Emperor. Ordinary citizens are allowed to enter the Imperial grounds only on January 2, to extend New Year's congratulations to the Emperor, and on the Emperor's birthday.

The eastern half of the Imperial Palace grounds is taken up by a garden, the Kokyo Higashi Gyoen or Imperial Palace East Garden, and is open to the public except on Mondays and Fridays. The garden was remodeled from an old garden that was at the center of Chiyoda Castle.

IMPERIAL DETACHED PALACE / OHAMA GOTEN (Oh-hah-mah Go-ten)

Now known as Hama Rikyu, the Imperial Detached Palace began in the early years of the Tokugawa Period as a preserve for falcony, and then became the site for a seaside villa built around 1650 by Tsuneshige Matsudaira, the Lord of Kofu.

In the early 1700s Ienobu Tokugawa had the villa expanded, adding tea houses, a temple, shrine, duck preserve and other attractions.

The first member of foreign royalty to be received by the Emperor of Japan, the Duke of Edinburgh, son of Queen Victoria, was housed in the Detached Palace in 1869. In 1879, ex-President Ullyses S. Grant also stayed at the Ohama Goten, where he had a long meeting with Emperor Meiji.

The Detached Palace was donated to Tokyo in 1945, and has been open to the public as a park since 1946. It is about a 10-minute walk from Shimbashi Station in Tokyo.

INCENSE BURNING / KOH-DO (Koe-doh)

Incense-burning as a religious ritual to calm the mind, expand the senses and achieve spiritual awareness, developed in Japan soon after the introduction of Buddhism in the 6th century. It very quickly became popular at the Imperial Court, and with the country's famous Samurai warrior class after it rose in the 10th and 11th centuries.

Altogether there are some 500 kinds of incense available in Japan, but usually only a few dozen of these are regularly used by koh-do devotees. Most of these are manufactured by Nippon Kodo, the country's leading incense stick-maker.

A full incense-burning ceremony lasts up to 90 minutes, and includes listening to the various scents as well as enjoying their aroma. Sometimes such ceremonies include contests in which the participants try to create literary themes related to the scents of two or more kinds of incense--a practice known as kumi-koh (Kuu-me-koh).

The Oie-Ryu School of Incense Appreciation in Tokyo, currently headed by grand master Sanenori Sanjonishi, a nephew of the Empress, is regarded as the center of the art.

INDUSTRIAL TOURS

One of the most practical and enjoyable ways of getting a good introduction to various aspects of Japan's business world is to take an industrial tour--something the Japanese have been offering to foreign businessmen and regular tourists for decades.

There are regularly scheduled tours in Tokyo, Nagoya, Osaka and other major cities. Several travel agencies, including the huge, national Japan Travel Bureau, handle such tours. In Tokyo, for example, there are two one-day tours each week, on Tuesdays and Fridays. They go to such places as a computer laboratory, a camera factory, and a distillery. The cost is minimal and includes lunch.

The Japanese companies that cooperate with the tours take them seriously, and assign some of their best employees to brief visitors.

Many Japanese companies welcome industrial tours by consumers and other businessmen as part of their overall public and community relations.

Tours of traditional handicraft industries have been popular since shortly after Japan opened its doors to trade in the 1850s. Tours of modern industrial factories date from the 1950s, and have since been an important function of the travel industry in cooperation with business and the government.

Several organizations besides the Japan Travel Bureau, including the Tourist Information Centers of the Japan National Tourist Organization, and the Trade and Tourist Sections of the Tokyo, Nagoya and Osaka governments, conduct regular tours of factories and industrial sites.

Your travel agent can arrange such tours for you.

INLAND SEA / SETO NAIKAI (Say-toe Nie-kie)

The great body of water that separates the islands of Honshu, Shikoku and Kyushu is called Seto Naikai, or the Sea Within Channels. Actually a chain of five small seas linked together, the Inland Sea is, again, so beautiful that it has been described since ancient times as a Sight Fit for the Eyes of a King.

The Inland Sea measures 64 kilometers at its widest point, and 6.4 kilometers at its narrowest. The sea is shallow, seldom reaching more than 40 meters in depth. The Straits of Naruto, between Awaji and Shikoku Islands, are notorious for their giant whirlpools caused by riptides.

The Inland Sea is dotted with jewel-like islands, and its heavily indented coastlines are ringed by pine trees and white-sand beaches. The larger islands in the sea are inhabited and are famous for various products, ranging from oranges, peaches and olives to granite.

The sea is noted for its marine life, and has been a favorite fishing grounds since the arrival of the first inhabitants. In the spring, sea bream, a favorite fish in Japan, enter the sea from the Pacific Ocean to spawn.

From time immemorial, the Inland Sea has played a vital role in the history of Japan, not only as a source of food and as a waterway, but also as a source of spiritual contentment. It was designated a national park in 1934.

The two largest islands in the Seto Naikai are Awaji and Shodo. Awaji has an area of 593 square kilometers, and is densely populated. Bunraku, Japan's traditional puppet theater, originated on this island. Shodo covers only 155.5 square kilometers, and is best-known for its olives, soy sauce and its quarries.

The scenic highlight on Shodo is known as Kankakei or Cold and Misty Gorge, which is a serrated series of rocky peaks, some two kilometers wide and eight kilometers long, in a valley that is filled with azaleas, maple and pine trees, and in the fall is one of the most colorful sights in Japan.

Recommended reading: THE INLAND SEA, by Donald Richie (Weatherhill).

INNS / RYOKAN (Rio-khan)

By 1700 Japan had a network of inns around the country that was unequaled in the world--the result of an edict by the Tokugawa Shogunate requiring all feudal lords to travel to its headquarters in Edo every other year, and bring a prescribed number of retainers with them. See PROCESSIONS OF THE LORDS.

There are still over 100,000 ryokan in Japan, of which over 2,000 are approved by the Ministry of Transportation as Tourist Inns--meaning that their facilities and standards are sufficiently high to meet the needs and expectations of most foreign visitors.

Ryokan are usually one-to-three story wooden structures that look very much like ordinary houses, but there are many ferro-concrete highrise structures in popular tourist resorts that are furnished and operated like inns (and called ryokan).

The distinguishing features of ryokan is that they are Japanese style--that is, they have tatami reed mat floors, only Japanese type furnishings--a low moveable table, cushions for sitting, and ofuton (oh-fuu-tone) floor-mats for sleeping. They also have hot baths that guests share or take turns using, and mostly Japanese style meals served in the guests' rooms.

The atmosphere and service in the typical ryokan is family style--very personal and intimate--and is one of the best possible ways of getting acquainted with traditional Japanese style living. Shoes are exchanged for house slippers at the genkan (gane-khan) entrance. The slippers are worn only in the passages and corridors--not inside the rooms. The dress-of-the-day is the yukata (you-kah-tah), a light kimono-styled robe that is also used as a sleeping garment. One scrubs outside the bathtub and gets in only after a thorough rinsing, to luxuriate in the hot water. All sitting is on the tatami floor (back supports are available in most ryokan).

Since it gets cold in most areas of Japan in the winter, and is hot and humid in the central and southern lowland areas in the summer, the visitor might want to choose a ryokan that has central heating and is air-conditioned in the summer. In any event, they are fun places and are meant to be enjoyed in a way that is not possible in a hotel.

For guests who do choose to stay in unheated ryokan in the winter, thickly padded kimono called tanzen (tahn-zen) and or thick kimono coats called dotera (doe-tay-rah) are provided.

The Japan National Tourist Organization (JNTO) has free directories of the approved tourist ryokan in the country. See JNTO listing for addresses of its offices.

INTERNATIONAL CHRISTIAN UNIVERSITY / ICU

Well-known around the world, Tokyo's International Christian Unverisity was founded in 1953 as a place to educate young people in Christian as well as democratic principles.

Near Mitaka Station on the Chuo Line west of Tokyo, ICU has the largest campus--119 ha.--of any university in Japan.

The school is particularly noted for its Japanese-language course, in which students study only the language for 8-10 hours a day for nine months. A number of well-known foreign scholars and linguists, including Prof. Ray Moore and Leonard Welch, took their language training at ICU.

One prominent student at ICU during the 1960s was Jay Rockefeller.

INTERNATIONAL MARRIAGES / KOKUSAI KEKKON (Koke-sie Keck-kone)

The Japanese refer to marriages between Japanese and foreigners, especially non-Asians, as International Marriages, and generally speaking do not wholly approve of them.

The first marraiges between Japanese and Westerners took place soon after the first Westerners arrived in Japan. The famous ships' pilot Will Adams, who was the role model for Anjin-San in the novel and TV extravaganza SHOGUN, married a Japanese woman in the early 1600s. The famous writer Lafcadio Hearn, who arrived in Japan nearly 200 years later, also married a Japanese woman, and the list goes on.

The phenomenon that led to dozens of thousands of kokusai kekkon was the American and Allied military occupation of Japan from 1945 to 1952. Within two years after the occupation began, the American and other foreign embassies in Tokyo were flooded with applications from members of the occupation forces for marriage certificates.

Many of these romances began in bars and less savory places, and involved young uneducated and unsophisticated GI's who did not speak Japanese and had no affinity or even appreciation of things Japanese, but were strongly attracted to their Japanese girl friends.

At the same time, their prospective brides were also often at the bottom of the social scale, and were primarily seeking a way out of their terrible economic predicament caused by the war. The overall result was that the image of international marriages suffered a great deal.

By the late 1950s, East-West marriages in Japan had slowed down considerably, but the quality of the people involved was much higher and the relationships were more solidly based on mutual understanding and compatibility.

Up to this period, most international marriages had been between Western men and Japanese women. Then the percentage of marriages between Japanese men and Western women began to rise, and in 1975 passed Western men/Japanese women marriages--a trend that has continued.

A high percentage of the East-West marriages that took place in the late 1940s and early 1950s failed for obvious reasons--especially when the groom took his new non-English-speaking still very Japanese bride home with him.

The success rate of such marriages in later years is as good if not better than typical marriages in most Western countries, despite basic cultural differences that are often extreme.

Western women who marry Japanese men generally have the most difficult time adapting to these cultural differences--unless the man has become very Westernized and behaves toward her in the manner to which she is accustomed, in which case it is not really an East-West mar-

THE WHOLE JAPAN BOOK

Formal kimono & cherry blossoms. P. 178

Young students practice kendo. P. 177

157

riage. See ASSOCIATIONS OF FOREIGN WIVES.

The most interesting and promising results of the many East-West marriages are the children of mixed-blood parentage. They are very special. Usually bilingual, often beautiful, they have a remarkable sensitivity to cross-cultural and racial problems that can make them valuable bridges.

INTRODUCTIONS / SHOKAIJO (Sho-kie-joe)

The age-old customs that control relationships between Japanese, whether they are personal or business, make introductions very important. Their importance derives from the fact that Japanese society is based on groupings that are exclusive, and not open to casual entry by outsiders.

It is therefore vital to the Japanese that they know as much as possible about anyone they meet as quickly as possible because they do not automatically accept people on face value. An intro-duction from someone they know helps span this otherwise formidable barrier.

Generally, the only way one can get into a particular group (of whatever kind or nature) is to enter it at the bottom in a formal, institutionalized way. The only acceptable way to deal with a group as an outsider, is through an introduction that not only identifies you but in effect acts as a guarantor of your character and reliability.

Japanese groups as well as individual Japanese are automatically wary of strangers who come to them without credentials or without an introduction from a mutual friend or business contact.

In business, the more important the potential relationship, the more vital it is that one approach a Japanese company with an effective introduction-- meaning one that comes from someone or some other group well-known and respected by the Japanese company concerned.

See JAPANESE MANNERS β ETHICS IN BUSINESS, by Boye De Mente (Phoenix Books/Publishers).

IRON AND STEEL

Beginning almost at zero in 1945, Japan's iron and steel industry produced a total of 119 million tons in 1973, making it one of the top steel manufacturers in the world.

Several factors played a vital role in the growth of Japan's iron and steel industry, including the rapid introduction of the latest technology, huge investments in plants and facilities, and the corresponding expansion of the country's domestic economy and its export industries.

Most of the iron ore Japan uses comes from Australia, Brazil and India. Most of the coal it uses in the industry comes from Australia, the U.S. and Canada.

Japan's top five integrated steel manufacturers are Nippon Steel Corporation (the world's largest steel maker), Nippon Kokan, Kawasaki Steel Corporation, Sumitomo Metal Industries, and Kobe Steel.

ISE-SHIMA NATIONAL PARK (E-say She-mah)

The Ise-Shima National Park, which takes up a large portion of the Ise and Shima districts at the south end of Mie Prefecture, is primarily a sea park with some of the most gorgeous seascapes in the world, but it is most famous for the Ise Jingu Shrines and Pearl Island in Toba Bay. (See PEARL ISLAND and GRAND SHRINES OF ISE.)

The best of the seascapes are in and around the bays of Matoba, Ago, Gokasho and the Kumano Nada Sea, which are bejeweled with dozens of pine-clad islets, and have shores that are thick with a variety of sub-tropical plants.

ISHIKAWA, GOEMON (E-she-kah-wah Go-eh-moan)

A robber chief who lived in the 16th century, and became a folk hero because of his practice of helping common people in their struggle with oppressive Daimyo and ruthless Samurai, Goemon Ishikawa is often referred to as the Robin Hood of Japan.

Goemon's life did not have a happy ending, however. Reputedly hired by Hidetsugu, the nephew of Hideyoshi Toyotomi, to assassinate the latter (who was then the supreme military power in Japan), Goemon was caught and boiled to death in a cauldron of oil, when he was 37 years old.

Even today bathtubs that have iron bottoms and are heated from beneath, are often referred to as Geomon-Buro or Goemon Baths.

ITO (E-toe)

On Izu Peninsula 16.9 kilometers south of the famous hotsprings resort city of Atami, Ito is also a noted seaside spa, with dozens of ryokan featuring hotspring mineral baths. Ito is also a port for ferry boats to and from the volcanic island of Oshima in Tokyo Bay.

IZU PENINSULA (E-zoo)

Extending deep into the Pacific Ocean

from the curved coastline of Honshu south of the Tokyo area, Izu Peninsula (originally called Yu Izu or Hot Water), is like something out of a travel brochure--unbelieveably beautiful coastlines indented by hundreds of tiny coves and ringed by picturesque islets, tree-covered mountains and hills, gorges and ravines traversed by swift-flowing streams, and hundreds of hotsprings.

Among the most famous hotspring resorts on Izu Peninsula are the cities of Atami, Shuzenji, Nagaoka, Ito and Atagawa, along with Inatori Spa, Imai-hama Spa, Yatsu, Mine, Yugano and Rendaiji, to name just a few. The spas are categorized according to their mineral content. One at Yoshina is famous for helping make barren women fertile.

Noted spots on the peninsula are Ito, where Anjin (Pilot) Will Adams built what is believed to have been Japan's first ocean-going vessel for Tokugawa Shogun. Shimoda, where the U.S.'s first envoy to Japan, Townsend Harris, lived for 15 months. Kawana, which boasts one of Japan's most popular golf courses, and the Shuzen Temple, founded by the famous priest, Kobo Daishi between 806 and 810.

Among the famous incidents that took place at the temple was the imprisonment there and subsequent murder of Noriyori Minamoto by his elder brother Yoritomo Minamoto (who founded Japan's first Shogunate at Kamakura), and the assassination of Yoritomo's son, Yoriie, by Tokimasa Hojo in 1215, who then seized power from the Minamoto clan.

There are numerous other historical places on the peninsula, including a memorial to Townsend Harris at Gyokusen Temple where he first lived just outside of the village of Shimoda.

Train and bus lines from the Tokyo and Yokohama area make the hotspring spas, historical sites and picturesque beaches of the Izu Peninsula easily accessible to large numbers of vacationers, and its mild winter climate assures its popularity all year around.

JAPAN / NIPPON (Neep-pone)

The word Japan is believed to have derived from the English pronounciation of the Chinese word Ji-pen, which in Chinese is written with the ideographs meaning Source of the Sun. In Japanese, these characters are pronounced Nippon (Neep-pone) or Nihon (Nee-hone) and have the same meaning as they do in Chinese—thus the use of the sun as the symbol of Japan.

Other sources credit the 7th century's famed Prince Shotoku with using Nippon (Place from where the sun rises) as the name of the country in a letter sent to China. The northern Chinese called Japan Jihpenkuo, and some believe the English word Japan came from Portuguese attempts to pronounce this word. In early Portuguese literature it appears variously as Zipangu and Jipangu. The southern Chinese called Japan Yatpun, and the Dutch pronouciation of this closely resembles Japan.

In addition to the four main islands of Hokkaido, Honshu, Shikoku and Kyushu, Japan has 3,918 smaller islands, with a combined total area of 337,682 square kilometers, which makes it a little larger than Norway, Italy and Malaysia, and a little smaller than Irag, and Morrocco.

Honshu (Hone-shuu), the largest island, is divided into five regions known as: Tohoku (Toe-hoe-kuu), the northern portion of the island. Kanto (Khan-toe), the Tokyo-Yokohama area. Chubu (Chuu-buu), the Nagoya plain and adjoining area. Kinki (Keen-kee), the Kyoto-Osaka-Kobe area. And Chugoku (Chuu-go-kuu), the southwestern area.

Administratively, the country consists of 47 prefectures, of which Hokkaido is one. The Tohoku district includes the seven prefectures of Aomori, Akita, Iwate, Yamagata, Miyagi and Fukushima. The Kanto region consists of Ibaragi, Tochigi, Gunma, Saitama, Chiba, Tokyo and Kanagawa prefectures.

The Chubu region is made up of Shizuoka, Yamanashi, Nagano, Niigata, Toyama, Ishikawa, Fukui, Gifu and Aichi prefectures. Kinki consists of Mie, Shiga, Kyoto, Nara, Osaka, Wakayama and Hyogo prefectures.

Chugoku is made up of Tottori, Okayama, Hiroshima, Shimane and Yamaguchi prefectures. The island of Shikoku is divided into four prefectures: Kagawa, Tokushima, Kochi and Ehime. And Kyushu has seven prefectures: Fukuoka, Saga, Nagasaki, Kumamoto, Oita, Miyazaki, Kagoshima and Okinawa (which is a separate island some 360 miles south of the tip of Kagoshima.

Topographically, 71 percent of Japan is mountainous, with the remainder made up of basins and plains.

The long chain of mountains that traverses Japan from the north to the south divides the country into two distinct regions--one facing the Japan Sea to the West, and the other facing the Pacific Ocean to the east.

The Pacific Ocean side--which has the largest plains and is the most densely populated, has one of the most indented shorelines in the world, with many large bays, thousands of inlets, and numerous offshore islets. There are only a few sandy beaches on the Pacific side of Japan.

The Japan Sea coast side on the west, which has higher and rougher waves, is less indented and has a larger number of sandy beaches. See MOUNTAINS, DISTRICTS OF JAPAN.

JAPAN ACADEMY

The Japan Academy, formerly known as the Imperial Acadamy, is an honorary organization made up of a maximum of 150 members who have been recognized for making distinguished contributions to the arts and sciences. Members are voted into the Academy by organizations of their peers.

JAPAN AIR LINES / NIHON KOKU (Nee-hone Koh-kuu)

The visitor heading for Japan may begin to enjoy some of the pleasures and the ambience of the country while still half way around the world simply by flying Japan Air Lines, the nation's flag carrier.

Each of JAL's planes is a microcosm of the subdued charm and seductiveness that characterizes Japanese culture. This special quality, from the meticulous hospitality extended to guests to the attractive young cabin attendants who epitomize the traditional etiquette for which the Japanese are famous, is in fact the hallmark of Japan Air Lines.

Japan Air Lines was founded in 1951 while the post-World War II military occupation of the country was still in progress. It began with one leased aircraft that was operated by crews from Northwest Airlines.

Later that same year the fledgling company introduced its own planes and Japanese crews. Two years later the company was reoranized under the Japan Air Lines Law, which gave the government 50 percent ownership in the airline.

Over the next 30 years Japan Air Lines grew to be one of the largest airlines in the world, serving over 30 countries around the world, and winning numerous awards for reliability and service.

JAL, as the airline is popularly known, pioneered special services for business travelers in the early 1970s, introducing its Executive Service in 1973.

Among the services offered to businessmen under this program was the printing of bi-lingual business cards and a number of books and booklets designed to help them do business in and enjoy Japan and the Orient.

In 1975 JAL teamed up with JETRO (The Japan External Trade Organization) to open an Executive Service Lounge on the mezzanine floor of the Imperial Hotel. The lounge is staffed with bi-lingual employees of JETRO, and equipped with phones, typewriters, meeting rooms, business and trade publications and other reference material of special interest to visiting businessmen.

For the average businessman in Japan for the first or even tenth time, the lounge can be a godsend, since its staff is there for the express purpose of helping them make appointments and otherwise accomplish their goals.

Other JAL services added in the following years include a special Executive Cabin for businessmen and other individuals. This was followed in 1980 with a three-class fare for business-class travelers.

In 1981 JAL installed the first series of Sky Recliner seats for first-class passengers flying its DC-10-40 aircraft between New York and Tokyo. The padded sleeping chairs were designed exclusively for JAL. In 1982 Sky Recliners were added to all of the first-class sections of JAL's transpacific 747 aircraft.

Another special Executive Service added the same year was advance reservations on Japan's famous Bullet Trains (Shinkansen) through its computerized international reservations system called JALCOM III, along with special hotel check-in facilities at several hotels around the Far East, a 6 p.m. check-out time and the use of a twin-bedded room at the single rate.

In addition to a number of guide and reference books, JAL also has both Japanese and Chinese language casettes available at minimal cost. Another special service JAL offers to regular executive travelers is membership in its Global Club, and the use of private Sakura Lounges in airports around the world.

Among the publications available from the JAL Literature Distribution Center (P.O. Box 10618, Long Island City, New York 11101 USA) are Japan Unescorted, Business in Japan, JAL Guide to the People's Republic of China, Businessman's After Hours Guide to Japan, JAL Executive Business Guide to China, Japanese Language by Sight and Sound, Jet Age Language Tapes/Japanese, and Jet Age Language Tapes/Chinese.

Bi-lingual name-card service is available through JAL for both Japanese and Chinese languages. They must be ordered two weeks prior to departure. Orders can be placed and paid for at any JAL office for pickup in either Japan or Hong Kong.

Finally, there are JAL Hospitality Desks in many major hotels in Japan, where JAL passengers may go for help in arranging traveling, shopping or dining out. The airline also operates a gift-service for passengers departing from the United States.

This service includes specially packaged beef, Alaska King Crab and smoked salmon--gifts that are especially appreciated in Japan. See AIRLINES.

JAPAN ALPS

The name Japan Alps has been given to three lofty mountain ranges that extend north to southwest through the central part of the main island of Honshu. Except for Mt. Fuji, all of Japan's highest mountains are in these three ranges --which are divided into the Southern, Central and Northern Alps.

The name Japan Alps was first used by William Garland in 1881, an English mining engineer, who worked on the Osaka Mint. It was then popularized by a book called MOUNTAINEERING AND EXPLORATION IN THE JAPAN ALPS, written by the Rev. Walter Weston in 1896.

The proper Japanese names for these mountain ranges are, from the north, Hida (He-dah), Kiso (Kee-so) and Akaishi (Ah-kie-she).

The Japan Alps National Park, regarded as the foremost mountain park in the country, encompasses all of the major peaks in the Hida range and extends into the four prefectures of Nagano, Gifu, Toyama and Niigata.

JAPAN ART ACADEMY

The Japan Art Academy, formerly the Imperial Art Academy, is an honorary organization with a maximum of 120 members. Members in the JAA receive annunities in recognition of their work and contributions to art.

JAPAN ASIA AIRWAYS

In 1974 Japan Air Lines began taking steps to establish service to the People's Republic of China, as a result of which Taiwan revoked JAL's right to serve that market. Following negotiations, Taipei agreed to allow another Japanese air line to re-establish service to the island.

Both All Nippon Airways and Toa Domestic Airlines applied to provide the service to Taiwan, but ultimately the franchise was awarded to Japan Asia Airways, a wholly owned subsidiary of Japan Air Lines, set up for that purpose. JAA began its service to Taiwan in September 1975.

JAPAN AUTOMOTIVE NEWS

The trade journal of Japan's automobile industry, the monthly Japan Automotive News covers new product and service news, industry trends and statistics, plus political developments. It is published by Automotive Herald Co., Ltd. See OTHER SOURCES.

JAPAN BRIDGE / NIHON BASHI (Nee-hone Bah-she)

In the center of Tokyo in one of the leading financial districts of the city, the Japan Bridge was built in 1603, the year Ieyasu Tokugawa took over the country as Shogun. When the bridge was built, the river it spans was much wider than it is now, the water was clear, tall pine trees lined both sides, and the third Tokugawa Shogun, Iemitsu, used to go swimming in it when he was a boy.

A year after the bridge was built, the Shogunate officially designated it as the point from which all distances in the country would be measured, and a stone was erected on the spot to mark the center of the country.

The unit of measurement at that time was the ri (ree), the equivalent of about two-and-a-half miles, and immediately there-after, milestones (ichirizuka) were placed at one ri intervals along all of the main roads in the country.

Nihon Bashi quickly developed into the business and public center of Edo. All journeys started from the bridge. All public notices were posted there, and criminals were put on display there as part of their punishment.

In more modern times, an iron post was inserted into the ground near the north end of the bridge to mark the point from which all distances were measured during the Tokugawa Period.

This area, now called Nihonbashi, was once called Muromachi 1-chome, and a nearby area was called Anjin-cho, after the English pilot Will Adams who lived there during the early, exciting days of the Tokugawa Shogunate when he was under the direct patronage of the Shogun.

A monument erected on the spot in 1930, reads: In memory of William Adams, known as Miura Anjin, the first Englishman to settle in Japan, coming as a pilot on board the Charity in 1600, who resided in a mansion built on this spot, who instructed Ieyasu, the first Tokugawa Shogun on gunnery, geography, mathematics, etc., rendering valuable service in foreign affairs, and who married a Japanese lady, Miss Magome, and died on May 16, 1620, at the age of 55 years.

The Japan Bridge, at which so much of the pageantry and drama of the extraordinary Tokugawa era began, now has a expressway running over it. The main thoroughfare that links Shimbashi, the famous Ginza, Kyobashi and Nihonbashi crosses over the bridge, and three of Tokyo's leading department stores (Tokyu, Takashimaya and Maruzen) are nearby.

JAPAN CHAMBER OF COMMERCE β INDUSTRY / NIHON SHOKO KAIGISHO (Nee-hone Show-koe Kie-ghee-show)

The JCCI is one of Japan's most important business organizations. It serves to coordinate the interests of the business community, and also serves as one of several key bridges between industry and government.

The president and other principal officers of the JCCI are always top business leaders in the country, giving it considerable clout.

The Chamber engages in a wide range of ongoing research in trade and industry, sponsors workshops and seminars and maintains a large publishing division. One of its publications that is of special interest to the foreign business community is the English language monthly, Japan Commerce and Industry (JCI).

JCI carries on in-depth studies on Japan's business system, on the various industries and other matters relating to management, manufacturing, labor and trade.

The Japan Chamber of Commerce β Industry is headquartered at 2-2 Marunouchi, 3-chome, Chiyoda-ku, Tokyo 100, Japan (across from the Imperial Palace).

JAPAN ECONOMIC JOURNAL / NIHON KEIZAI SHIMBUN (Nee-hone Kay-e-zie Shim-boon)

The Nihon Keizai Shimbun is Japan's leading business newspaper, similar to New York's Wall Street Journal, but national in scope and with a larger circulation. A weekly edition of the paper is published in English.

JAPAN BOOKS IN ENGLISH

A catalog of some 3,000 English-language books published in Japan, the JAPAN ENGLISH BOOKS IN PRINT is the most comprehensive directory of its type. Each book is listed by title, author, subject and publisher. The catalog also includes a list of some 600 booksellers and subscription agencies outside of Japan that deal in books imported from Asia, along with some 100 Japanese publishing houses that buy Japanese-language rights to books.

The catalog is published by Intercontinental Marketing Corporation, C.P.O. Box 971, Tokyo 100-91 Japan. The same company also publishes a catalog of English-language magazines produced in Japan (Japan English Magazine Directory).

JAPAN FOLKCRAFT MUSEUM / NIHON MINGEI KAN (Nee-hone Meen-gay-e Khan)

A short walk from Komaba Station on the Inokashira Line in Tokyo, the Japan Folkcraft Museum was founded by the famous art critic Muneyoshi Yanagi. Its exhibits include old and new ceramics, dyed and woven fabrics, wood products and various other items gathered from all over Japan and Korea. The exhibit is more of a private collection, and is not presented as being comprehensive.

JAPAN LETTER

One of the oldest, most authoritative and useful newsletters on Japan, The Japan Letter is published twice a month by Asia Letter Ltd., a Hong Kong company with branches in Japan, Los Angeles and Singapore. The letter synthesizes political and economic developments, and predicts future developments in these areas. It also keeps tabs on unusual cultural and social trends, and in each issue features a particular place, thing or event in a Focus Box.

Contact: The Japan Letter, P.O. Box 33477, Sheungwan Post Office, Hong Kong, or P.O. Box 54149, Los Angeles, Ca., 90054, USA.

JAPAN NATIONAL TOURIST ORGANIZATION (JNTO)

Founded in 1959 under the Ministry of Transport, the JNTO is financed by the government and local contributions by the tourist industry, and is Japan's most important tourism organization.

The primary function of the JNTO is to produce and disseminate information about Japan as a tourist destination, including brochures, films and books. To advertise Japan around the world, and to otherwise publicize Japan's tourist attractions.

The JNTO presently maintains three Tourist Information Centers in Japan (in downtown Tokyo, at the Tokyo International Airport and in Kyoto), and operates a number of information offices in the U.S. and other countries. Some of them:

USA: 45 Rockefeller Plaza, New York, New York 10020

333 N. Michigan Ave., Chicago, Illinois 60601

1420 Commerce St., Dallas, Texas 75201

1737 Post St., San Francisco, Calif. 94115

624 S. Grand Ave., Los Angeles, Calif. 90017

2270 Kalakaua Ave., Honolulu, Hawaii 96815

CANADA: 165 University Ave., Toronto, Ont. M5H 3B8

ENGLAND: 167 Regent St., London W.1.

AUSTRALIA: 115 Pitt St., Sydney, N.S.W. 2000

HONG KONG: Peter Bldg., 58 Queen's Road, Central

THAILAND: 56 Suriwong Road, Bangkok

FRANCE: 4-8, Rue Sainte-Anne, 75001, Paris

SWITZERLAND: Rue de Berne 13, Geneve

GERMANY: Biebergasse 6-10, 6000 Frank-
   furt a/M.
MEXICO: Feforma 122, 5th fl., B-2, Mexi-
   co 6, D.F.
BRAZIL: Ave. Paulista, 509-S/405, 01311,
   Sau Paulo

JAPANESE NATIONAL RAILWAYS / NIHON KOKU-TETSU (Nee-hone Koe-kuu-tate-sue)

In 1906 the Japanese government decided to nationalize all the important
railway lines in the country, and 17
lines then being operated privately were
bought by the government. In the following years, other lines were added, and
in 1949 the government-owned railways
were reorganized under a public corporation called Japanese National Railways
(JNR).

Today, the JNR is Japan's largest
enterprise, with some 245 railway lines
and around half a million employees. The
corporation operates approximately 5,300
railway stations, and carries over seven
billion passengers a year.

The 10 busiest stations in the country are Shinjuku (Tokyo), Ikebukuro
(Tokyo), Tokyo Central Station, Shibuya
(Tokyo), Osaka Station, Yokohama Station, Shimbashi (Tokyo), Tennoji (Osaka), Ueno (Tokyo), and Takadanobaba
(Tokyo).

JNR also operates several ferry services between the four main islands and
to islands in the Inland Sea, along with
bus service on some 16,000 kilometers of
routes throughout the country.

In addition to the famous Bullet
Trains (Shinkan Sen) that leave Tokyo
Central Station every few minutes, the
JNR operates some 700 limited express
trains and 1,200 ordinary express trains
on its main lines. To supplement these,
the corporation also operates a network
of inter-city rapid services and over
16,000 local trains.

Trains in the JNR system are classified according to their speed, the number of stops they make and their accommodations, and include rapid express,
limited express, ordinary express and
regular trains.

Long-distance limited express trains
are equipped with dining cars, sleepers,
and coaches with reclining seats. Both
Western and Japanese style meals are
served on the trains, and vendors are
constantly passing up and down the aisles of the coaches, offering various
drinks and snacks.

There are two classes of accommodations on JNR trains, first-class, in
which the coaches are labeled Green
Cars, and second or ordinary class.

First-class cabins on JNR ferries are
called Green Cabins.

All of the famous Bullet Trains and
limited express trains, as well as most
ordinary express trains, are air-conditioned. Trains that are not air-conditioned have overhead fans in the summer
and steam-heat in the winter.

Japan's railway service is world-
famous for its efficiency and punctuality.

JAPAN PETROLEUM β ENERGY WEEKLY

This letter-sized publication carries
news of the activities of Japan's petroleum and energy companies, articles
about the government's energy policies,
plus industry news briefs and statistics
on oil and energy in Japan. It is published by Japan Petroleum Consultants,
Ltd., See OTHER SOURCES.

JAPAN RAIL PASSES

The Japanese National Railway (JNR)
version of the Eurailpass, the Japan
Rail Pass (JRP), inaugurated in 1981,
has become increasingly popular with
foreign visitors. Holders of the JRP are
entitled to travel freely throughout
JNR'S extensive network--including the
famous Bullet Train lines or Shinkansen
(Sheen-khan-sin).

The Rail Pass is also valid for travel on JNR-operated ferry and bus lines
where such service is available. Unlike
its European counterpart, the Japan Rail
Pass offers the travelers the option of
either first class (Green Cars) or regular class. The passes are good for one,
two or three-week periods.

Foreign travelers heading for Japan
can buy Rail Pass vouchers at overseas
offices of the Japan Travel Bureau,
Nippon Travel Agency Pacific offices and
at Japan Air Lines ticket offices in the
U.S. After arrival in Japan, the vouchers are exchanged for Rail Passes.

When used to their fullest extent,
the JRP result in 60 to 70 percent savings on travel in Japan.

JAPAN STATISTICAL YEARBOOK / NIHON TOKEI NENKAN (Nee-hone Toe-kay-e Nane-khan)

The Japan Statistical Yearbook, with
statistics from the Prime Minister's
Office and edited by the Japan Statistical Association and the Mainichi Newspaper Company, is a comprehensive reference book covering the population,
economy, business, finance, living standards and cultural matters.

The yearbook is available through the
Japan Publications Trading Company

(JPTC). See OTHER SOURCES.

JAPAN STEEL JOURNAL

The Japan Steel Journal is a daily (weekdays) newsletter covering the international activities of Japan's steelmakers. It also contains listings of Japanese market prices, and import and export prices of steel. Publisher is the Japan Iron and Steel Journal Co., Ltd. See OTHER SOURCES.

JAPAN TIMES DIRECTORY

The oldest and probably most popular of Japan's English language telephone directories, The Japan Times Directory (Foreign Residents, Business Firms and Organizations) began publication in 1947.

The directory covers Tokyo, Yokohama and Kanagawa Prefectures. Nagoya and Aichi Prefecture. Kyoto, Osaka, Kobe and Hyogo Prefecture, and outlying districts. Its business listings cover airlines, banks, hotels, foreign tourist offices, embassies, consulates, international organizations, government agencies, post offices, area codes and other useful information.

Published annually by The Japan Times Ltd., the director is available from bookstores carrying books on Japan, or by mail-order from The Japan Times Ltd., 5-4 Shibaura, 4-chome, Minato-ku, Tokyo 108 Japan.

JAPAN TRAVEL BUREAU / NIHON KOTSU KOSHA (Nee-hone Koat-sue Koe-shah)

The largest travel agency in Japan (300 domestic offices and 11 offices abroad), JTB was founded in 1893 as the Welcome Society. The founders were young, highly educated and cultured Japanese who wanted to help visiting travelers get to know and understand the country.

A few years later the organization was renamed the Japan Tourist Bureau, and in 1945 became the Japan Travel Bureau. Northwest Orient Airlines began regular flights to Tokyo in 1947, and the same year American President Lines resumed its Far East cruises--all contributing to the rapid postwar growth of JTB.

Other events that contributed to JTB's growth: the return of Haneda International Airport to Japanese control in 1952, the beginning of Japan Air Lines service to San Francisco in 1954, the 1964 Olympics in Tokyo, and the lifting of the government ban on overseas sightseeing the same year.

JTB has a large publishing division, and is noted for its many books on cultural subjects and history, as well as on travel.

The agency's Overseas Travel Division (where I worked in 1953-54) annually sends several hundred thousand tourists abroad.

JAPAN TRAVEL PHONE

Japan's well-organized travel industry has a special telephone number for tourists to call when they need English-language assistance or travel information.

The service is sponsored by the Japan National Tourist Organization (JNTO) through its Travel Information Centers (TIC), and is available from 9 a.m. to 5 p.m. daily throughout the year.

Outside the Kyoto and Tokyo areas, the traveler dials 106 and tells the operator in English: Collect call, T.I.C. (pronounced Tee-Aye-See). Private phones as well as yellow and blue public phones (but NOT red public phones) may be used. When using a public phone it is necessary to insert a 10-yen coin, but the coin is returned.

In Tokyo and Kyoto, the traveler dials the number of the local Tourist Information Center directly. In the Tokyo area that is 502-1461. In Kyoto it is 371-5649. When using public phones to call these two numbers, the charge is 10 yen per three minutes.

Several dozen major Japanese companies provide funds for the operation of the Japan Travel-Phone.

JAPAN YOUTH HOSTELS

There are dozens of youth hostels spotted around Japan in some of the most scenic and desirable travel destinations in the country. The accommodations are basic--usually dormitory style-- but they are often not crowded and you sometimes have them entirely to yourself.

Bathing and laundry facilities, along with substantial, hearty food, are part of the bargain. For more information, contact Japan Youth Hostels, Inc., 1-2 Ichigaya, Sadohara-cho, Shinjuku-ku, Tokyo, Japan. Or in the U.S., American Youth Hostels, 132 Spring St., New York, NY 10012.

JAPANESE FOOD

Japanese cuisine is distinctive in its own right, having been developed within the islands over thousands of years. For close to 2,000 years, it centered around seafood, vegetables, and rice. (Meat was a fairly common staple in the Japanese diet before the introduction of Buddhism in the 5th and 6th centuries, but was then almost totally eliminated on religious grounds.)

It is the preparation, of course, that makes traditional Japanese food unique. The first principle is that the ingredients should retain their natural appearance and taste as far as possible. The second is that they should be compatible with rice and sake.

In traditionally prepared dishes, therefore, most Japanese foods are raw, pickled, boiled or grilled. When seasonings are used, the primary aim is to enhance the natural flavor of the food.

Another important factor in Japanese cuisine was, and still is, in the preparation. Great care is taken to see that the food items harmonize in shapes, sizes and color.

See individual listings for such dishes as SUSHI, SASHIMI, SUKIYAKI, TEMPURA, UDON, and SOBA. Also see RESTAURANTS.

Recommended reading: JAPANESE COOKING: A Simple Art, by Shizuo Tsuji (Kodansha Int'l). THE BOOK OF FOFU and THE BOOK OF MISO, both by William Shurtleff and Akiko Aoyagi (Ten Speed Press).

JAPANESE HOUSES / NIHON NO IE (Nee-hone no E-eh)

The traditional Japanese house is a masterpiece of compromise with nature. They are usually small, built on raised footings so the air will circulate beneath them, and constructed of wood, plaster and paper.

Floors consist of straw mats called tatami (tah-tah-me), that measure 3'x6' and are two and a half inches thick. (These measurements differ somewhat in Western Japan.) Rooms are constructed, and measured, according to this tatami size--a 4-mat room, 6-mat room, 8-mat room, and so on.

Rooms are separated by thick sliding panels called fusuma (fuu-sue-mah), made of paper over wooden frames. Or by shoji (show-jee), very thin squares of rice paper pasted over wooden latticed panels. Nowadays, sliding glass doors provide access to any garden.

For protection against inclement wea-ther, all windows and outside glass doors have sliding wooden doors called amado (ah-mah-doe) that cover them from the outside.

There is a genkan (gain-khan) entryway at the front of each house, where the shoes (and raincoats) are removed before stepping up on a polished wooden landing.

The main room in a Japanese house invariably has a tokonoma (toe-koe-no-mah), a recessed alcove designed for the display of art, flowers or hanging scrolls called kakemono (kah-key-moe-no).

Furnishings are sparse in a traditional Japanese room. During the day, the main room will typically have little more than a low table and sitting cushions or zabuton (zah-buu-tone). Other rooms will usually have chests of drawers and a dresser, along with a few other personal items.

Today, all rooms in Japanese homes tend to be jam-packed with television sets, stereo and numerous other possessions.

Few Japanese homes are equipped with central heating. Houses tend to be very drafty, and except when it is raining or the wind is blowing hard, the windows are usually opened during the day to help prevent mildew from the humidity. Heating is provided by kerosene, propane gas and electric space heaters.

Many homes also have a kotatsu (koe-tot-sue), which is a bathtub-sized pit in the floor in the center of the main room. A table, covered by a heavy cloth or quilt that drapes to the floor on all sides, sets over the kotatsu.

In winter, members of the family and any visitors sit around the table, with their feet dangling into the pit beneath, with the table cover draped over their laps to keep them warm.

In earlier days, charcoal-burning hibachi (he-bah-chee) were usually put in the kotatsu to warm them up. Nowadays specially designed electric heaters are used--making a very cozy and intimate place for people to gather, sip hot tea and read, talk or watch TV.

Japanese who live in houses or apartments with tatami reed-mat floors generally sleep on the floor on layers of thin matresses called futon (fuu-tone). The futon are kept in closets during the day and are spread out at night when needed. This way, rooms are used for various other purposes during the day and can be converted into bedrooms within seconds at night--and when necessary accommodate several people.

JAPANESE LANGUAGE / NIHONGO (Nee-hone-go)

The Japanese language appears to be a mixture of the Altaic languages of northern Asia and the Malasyian-Indonesian-Polynesian languages of Southeast Asia.

In Japanese there is no differentiation between singular and plural. There is no gender. There are no definite or indefiniate articles. Changes in order are expressed by postpositional particles. Adjectives and adverbs are placed in front of nouns and verbs, and the normal grammatical order is subject, object, verb.

Present-day Japanese is based on five vowels (ah, ee, uu, eh, oh) and one additional sound, n. Words are made up of syllables that are always open--they never end in consonants--which is why the Japanese have difficulty pronouncing English. Also in Japanese, two consonants never come together in one syllable, and in order to use such words in English, the Japanese insert a vowel between the consonant letters--for example, trap becomes to-ra-ppu.

There are numerous words in Japanese that have virtually the same pronounciation but different meanings, and these often cause problems. It is sometimes necessary even for the Japanese to write out the kanji character for a particular sound to clarify their meaning.

A survey of 90 publications by the National Language Institute in 1956 revealed that 30,000 words were used, and that of these, Chinese words accounted for 48 percent, Japanese words for 37 percent and foreign words for 10 percent. The rest were mixtures of different languages.

It is now estimated that words adopted from Western languages, primarily English, make up around 20 percent of the words used by the Japanese. The Japanese language is changing so rapidly that some things written less than a 100 years ago cannot be read and understood even by educated people.

The Japanese often say their language is not a tool for transmitting clear, concise thoughts. They say words are containers for transporting feelings which cannot be expressed by words.

There are four ways of writing Japanese--the complicated Chinese ideograms called kanji (kahn-jee), the two kana (kah-nah) syllabaries called hiragana (he-rah-gah-nah) and katakana (kah-tah-kah-nah), and Roman letters or Roma Ji (Roe-mah Jee).

The two kana syllabaries were derived from the kanji Chinese characters--katakana from the radical or the component parts of kanji, and hiragana from the characters themselves. Kibi-no Makibi, an 8th century scholar-statesman is credited with having invented the katakana way of writing Japanese, possibly as a result of having studied Sanskrit.

In addition to being used to transcribe most of the foreign words written in Japanese, the katakana are also always used for sending Japanese-language telegrams.

Recommended study: THE JAPANESE LANGUAGE, by Haruhiko Kindaichi, translated by Umeyo Hirano (Tuttle). JAPANESE MADE EASY, by Tazuko Ajiro Monane (Tuttle). A JAPANESE READER, by Roy Andrew Miller (Tuttle). JAPANESE IN ACTION, by Jack Seward (Weatherhill).

JAPANESE PEOPLE / NIHON-JIN (Nee-hone-Jeen)

The people of Japan do not all look alike, despite this frequent complaint by visitors from abroad. Most Japanese have black or dark auburn hair. Nearly all of them have black or dark brown eyes. Most have the same or similar skin coloring and most are primarily of Mongolian descent.

But within these general guidelines, the facial features of the Japanese are all different, all unique, and all distinguishable. What bothers Western newcomers to Japan is that they have been conditioned to distinguish people on the basis of far wider differences--in hair, eye and skin color, in body size and in extraordinary extremes in individual facial features.

It takes anywhere from a few hours to a few days or weeks for newcomers to learn how to pay attentionn to the finer differences that distinguish the Japanese.

There are, in fact, distinct regional differences in the Japanese--in their height, skin coloring and overall appearance. People from the south tend to be shorter and darker and to show signs of Southeast Asian influence. Those from the north tend to be taller and lighter-skinned. Some of these differences are environmental. Others are racial.

Particularly in northern Honshu and Hokkaido, there is substantial evidence of mixing between the Japanese and the Cacausoid Ainu who inhabited the northern and eastern portions of the island chain when the Mongolian Japanese arrived. See AINU.

But racially speaking, the Japanese are far less mixed than Americans and many other Westerners.

In the cultural area, the Japanese are among the most homogenized people on earth. Living on relatively small islands that were isolated from the rest of the world for most of their history, having a common religious heritage, and having been conditioned by the same economic, social and political systems for many generations, the Japanese--despite many substantial differences--are more alike than the people of any other major nation.

There are strong linguistic differences in various regions of Japan. Some of the regional dialects are close to being separate languages. But all Japanese today also understand and are able to speak what is called standard Japanese.

The Japanese are inscrutable only to those people who don't speak their language or understand their beliefs and customs. Being a thoroughly homogenized people, the Japanese behave in a more institutionalized and predictable way than most Westerners.

Problems arise simply because of lack of knowledge and ability to communicate and because of the inherent differences in the way Japanese and others approach things. The answer to overcoming these problems is equally obvious.

On a personal level, the Japanese are among the world's most likeable people. The are famous for their kindness, politeness and goodwill. There is something special about the Japanese and their culture that attracts many Westerners like a magnet.

This special appeal is a combination of the character and customs of the people, the distinctive food, the traditional dress, the Japanese-style of living, the arts and crafts, and so on. But I have also known dozens of Westerners who did not appreciate any of these latter things and yet stayed on in Japan for many years, unwilling to leave despite their many dislikes.

While it would be easy to dismiss this particular group as being attracted to Japan only because of the cultural emphasis on sex and the sexual permissiveness they are able to participate in, this would not be the whole truth and would be unfair to both my friends and acquaintances as well as the Japanese.

For there is actually a great deal more than sexual pleasures involved in the relationships these people have with Japan, and one way or another they can be traced to the traditional character, personality and manners of the people.

Recommended reading: EXOTIC JAPAN-- The Land, the Climate, the People, the Pleasures, by Boye De Mente (Phoenix Books/Publishers). INTRODUCING JAPAN, by Donald Richie (Kodansha Int'l). THE INLAND SEA, by Donald Richie (Weatherhill). THE JAPANESE, by Jack Seward (Lotus Press). MORE ABOUT THE JAPANESE, by Jack Seward (Lotus Press).

JAPANESE SOCIETY / NIHON SHAKAI (Nee-hone shah-kie)

The key to understanding Japanese society, and undersdtanding and dealing with individual Japanese, lies in understanding the vertical nature of the society, says social anthropologist Dr. Chie Nakane.

By vertical society, Dr. Nakane is referring to the inferior-superior structure of Japanese society--all people fall into a specific lower-higher relationship with everyone else, based on their sex, age, schooling, employment, family, and so on.

And, she continues, it is this relationship that controls or colors the functioning of Japanese society in all areas--in basic behavior, in language use, and in conducting social and business matters.

Superimposed over this vertical structure of Japanese society is an overwhelming tendency to form groups or cliques that are exclusive and take precedence over the individual. These groups encompass virtually every area of Japanese life, but are of particular importance in business and the professions.

Anyone who is not a member of one of these groups is an outsider, and cannot deal with the individual members of the group as if they were individuals. Responsibility within many of these groups, especially in a company setting, is collective.

With the grouping system in Japan, all members are ranked (the higher-lower principle), whether they are people, companies, or things. The privileges, rights and responsibilityies of the individuals within these groupings are determined by their rank in relation to everyone else.

To meet and deal effectively with one of these groups (and individuals within the groups) requires a considerable amount of knowledge of their makeup and psychology, along with experience in the techniques that are acceptable.

While individual competition within groups is taboo, the groups compete fiercely against each other--which is

Lake Hakone, with Mt. Fuji. P. 118

Gion Festival in Kyoto. P. 184

the reason you find little or no contact between different professional groups in Japan that are in the same field.

The overwhelming drive within every group within Japanese society is to be as self-sufficient as possible--not have to depend on outsiders. This syndrome is especially obvious in Japanese companies.

Recommended reading: JAPANESE SOCIETY, by Chie Nakane (University of California Press). JAPANESE MANNERS β ETHICS IN BUSINESS, by Boye De Mente (Phoenix Books/Publishers). THE JAPANESE and MORE ABOUT THE JAPANESE, by Jack Seward (Lotus Press).

JAPANESE TYPEWRITERS

At first-sight Japanese-language typewriters are apt to remind one of a very simple, tiny printing press, which is basically what they are. The first such typewriter was invented in 1915.

The typewriter consists of a tray of some 3,000 metal kanji, hiragana amd katakana characters, a scanner, a hand-lever and a roller or platten. The desired character must first be located in the tray or on a scanning plate, the hand-lever moved into a position over the character, and then the lever pressed, resulting in the character being picked up and slammed against the roller.

Typing on a Japanese style typewriter is thus a laborious and time-consuming chore, and is one of the reasons why typing letters and documents has been the exception rather than the rule in Japan. Generally, only official documents and business papers were typed in this manner.

Nowdays, word processors capable of writing in Japanese are becoming increasingly common, and there are also modern-styled typewriters in use in a growing number of companies.

JETRO (Japan External Trade Organization)

Probably the best-known of Japan's trade organizations, JETRO was founded by the Ministry of International Trade and Industry in 1958 to promote trade. At that time, there were already several government and private sector organizations engaged in trade promotion, but their efforts were not coordinated and were inefficient.

The new organization was charged with seven areas of responsibility: to research foreign trade and publish the resultsµ to publicize Japan's export industries and products abroadµ to provide services to facilitate international tradeµ to publish and distribute printed materials on Japan's exportsµ to sponsor and participate in trade fairsµ to coordinate government efforts to expand tradeµ and to do whatever else it could do to promote Japan's international trade.

By 1980 Japan's success in promoting its foreign trade led to JETRO being given new responsilibities, primarily aimed at heading off growing criticism of Japan and its successes abroad. The role of JETRO was expanded to include the promotion of mutual understanding among trading partners, to encourage and facilitate the export of goods to Japan, to help emerging countries develop their overseas trading capability, and to act as a liaison between small and medium-sized industries in Japan and their counterparts overseas.

JETRO presently has some 30 local and regional offices in Japan, and 78 branch offices in 59 countries around the world. These offices act as information collection centers, and as information dissemination centers for both Japanese and foreign businessmen.

The organization regularly sponsors import and export seminars for both Japanese and foreign businessmen, and carries on an extensive publishing program, along with producing educational films. Its publications include a series on marketing in Japan (Doing Business in Japan, Rights in Japan, Planning for Distribution in Japan, Role of Trading Companies in International Commerce, etc.), FOCUS JAPAN, which features articles on business, trade, labor, employment, overseas investments and other issues of special interest. TRADESCOPE, which is designed to provide developing countries with international trade information, and a NOW IN JAPAN series, which covers problems faced by the Japanese economy (Productivity and QC, The Japanse Experience, The Promotion of Small and Medium Enterprises in Japan).

Other publications include the JETRO China Newsletter, The JETRO Arabic Newsletter, The Japan Industrial and Technological Bulletin, an annual White Paper on International Trade, Keys to Success in the Japanese Market, etc.

Among the films available from JETRO are The Japanese Economy Now, The Door is Open, Kacho--A Section Chief and His Day, and Bridges and Barriers--Americans in Japan,

JETRO maintains large libraries of trade information and materials in its headquarters building in Tokyo, and in its Osaka office. All of its domestic and overseas offices maintain collections of key publications and directories.

In the U.S., JETRO has offices in New York, Chicago, Houston, Los Angeles and San Francisco. JETRO's headquarters in Tokyo are located across the street from the American Embassy, at 2-5 Toranomon, 2-chome, Minato-ku, Tokyo 105, Japan. Tel. 582-5511.

JETRO invites foreign businessmen to view or rent video casettes on Japan's business world at its International Lounge on the 6th floor of its headquarters building in Tokyo. Two new tapes are to be added each month for some time.

Among the casettes now available: Direct Foreign Investment, How a Japanese Company Achieves High Productivity, Point Men for Foreign Business in Japan, Are the Japanese Really Unique?

The Lounge is open weekdays from 9:30 a.m. to noon and 1 p.m. to 4:30 p.m.

JISHU KANRI (Jee-shuu Khan-ree)

This is a phrase that refers to Workers' Volunteer Activity Groups in Japanese management, and is terminology that foreign businessmen should be familiar with.

Jishu Kanri, generally abbreviated as JK, is used in reference to Japan's quality control system, and means simply that small groups of workers, from three to 10, voluntarily form their own group, independent of management, to make sure they maintain the highest possible quality standards with existing technology and continuously strive to improve technology so even higher standards of quality can be achieved.

The JK groups center around the senior employees involved, and are typical of the strong group approach that characterizes Japanese behavior. These groups may also be called ZD circles, or Zero Defect Circles.

JOGGING

Jogging is a popular form of recreation in Japan, and it is common to see both men and women on the streets and in the parks of major cities in all kinds of weather. A favorite place to jog in Tokyo is along the inner moat of the Imperial Palace, which circles the Palace grounds. Foreign businessmen staying in down-town hotels, particularly the Imperial, often jog in Hibiya Park (which was originally the villa garden of a Daimyo feudal lord).

JUDO (Juu-doe)

Modern judo grew out of jujutsu (juu-jute-sute), one of Japan's traditional and deadly martial arts. Educator Jigoro Kano, who founded Tokyo's famous Kodokan (Koe-doe-khan) in 1882, is credited with being the father of this modern form.

Jujutsu, the forerunner of judo, was developed into a formidable martial art by Japan's professional warrior class, the Samurai, from the 12th century on.

Most fighting in early Japan was on a one-on-one basis, in which individual skill with and without weapons was crucial. The Samurai were always concerned about being attacked when they were unarmed and unprepared, and jujutsu was primarily a series of highly developed techniques for unarmed defense--disarming an opponent, and disabling or killing an opponent with the bare hands or feet.

In addition to jabbing and hitting, jujutsu included throwing, holding, strangling and breaking.

With the ascendancy of the Tokugawa Shogunate in 1603, jujutsu became an even more important part of the training of the Samurai because they had no wars to fight. Several rival schools developed, and so fierce was the competition between these schools that tournament matches often ended in serious injury and death.

The two most important of these jujutsu schools were the Tenshin Shin-yo and the Kito.

The father of modernday judo, Dr. Jigoro Kano (1860-1938), first mastered the Tenshin Shin-yo and Kito styles, then modified and refined them into his own system. He eliminated the martial aims of jujutsu, and developed a scientific system of training based on modern athletic principles. He called his new system Kodokan judo (Koe-doe-khan juu-doe).

In Kano's system, judo was divided into three major areas--grappling, throwing and attacking vital points. Following the end of the Pacific war in 1945, judo became popular throughout the world. The World Judo Federation was established in 1952. The first World Judo Championship Tournament was held in Tokyo in May 1956, and it was designated an Olympic sport in 1964.

The practice of judo has three phases --form (kata), free-style exercise (dandori), and competitive matches. In judo matches, only grappling and throwing are allowed.

There are two ranking systems in judo--kyu (que) and dan (dahn). The kyu

171

class is for beginners, with the lowest being 5th kyu and the highest 1st kyu. The dan class of ranking begins with 1st dan and goes to 10th dan, the highest grade attainable.

Japan's Kodokan Judo Hall, at 1-16 Kasuga, Bunkyo-ku, Tokyo, is the mecca of the judo world. Judo is also taught at the Nippon Budokan Hall's Budo Gakuen, 2-3 Kitanomaru Park, Chiyoda-ku, Tokyo.

The primary aim of judo is to discipline and train the mind and body--not to defeat an opponent in battle. Judo was made a part of Japan's educational curriculum in the early 1900s, from middle school onwards, and has played a significant role in shaping the character of the Japanese ever since.

Today, judo is a popular sport in most countries of the world, and is gradually being recognized for its value as a spiritual as well as physical training exercise.

Judo is named after the principle expressed in the saying, Ju yoku go o seisu, or Softness overcomes hardness. Ju means soft or gentle.

An official judo ring is nine meters square (50 tatami mats). Participants wear loose-fitting trousers, jackets and belts, and try to throw each other using various grappling, tripping and flipping techniques.

The various ranks are indicated by the color of the belts the judoists wear. Beginners wear blue belts (and have no ranking). Fifth and 4th kyu grades wear white belts. Third to 1st kyu ranks wear brown belts.

In the senior dan rankings, 1st to 5th dan judoists wear black belts, 6th to 8th dans wear red-and-white belts, 9th and 10th dans wear red belts.

Recommended reading: BEST JUDO, by Isao Inokuma and Nobuyuki Sato (Kodansha Int'l). JUDO FORMAL TECHNIQUES: A Complete Guide to Kodokan Randori no Kata, by Donn Draeger and Tadao Otaki (Tuttle). JUDO FOR THE GENTLEWOMAN, by Ruth B. Gardner (Tuttle).

JUVENILE DELINQUENCY

A democratic form of government and individual freedom have been trade-offs for Japan. A country that had virtually no juvenile delinquency problem prior to 1945, crimes by juveniles have since been on the rise in Japan.

While still less of a problem than in the U.S. and other Western countries, the rate of offenses by juveniles has been climbing rapidly since 1973, and the tendency for delinquency to begin at a younger age has continued.

Offenses by juveniles are divided into five major categories--grave offenses, acts of violence, larceny, intellectual offenses and morals offenses. Larceny is the leading category, followed by acts of violence, intellectual offenses, grave offenses and morals charges.

The total number of juvenile delinquency offenses was still less than 200,000 in 1983.

The number of grave offenses, such as murder and armed robbery, were a little over 2,000 the same year.

KABUKI (Kah-buu-kee)

A maid-servant at the Izumo Taisha Shrine in Kyoto is credited with having originated kabuki in 1603. O-Kuni, as this lady was called, was obviously an extraordinary woman for her time. In a program to raise funds for the repair of the shrine, she got a troupe of performers together and put on a show in the precincts of the famous Kitano Shrine.

Dressed like a man and carrying a sword, O-Kuni pretended to be meeting a sweetheart on the sly, acting out the story with her troupe in a series of comic routines. The act caught on, and soon came to be known as Kabuki Odori, or Kabuki Dance, a corruption of the word kubuku, which referred to unseeming, ill-mannered behavior.

Rivals soon appeared on the scene, with the lead roles being played by professional prostitutes. The shows became so lewd and disrespectful that the Tokugawa Shogunate banned women from appearing in the kabuki plays. Their place was taken by handsome young boys and men.

This change, however, resulted in a sudden spread of the practice of sodomy, which had been common among warriors and the clergy, but encouraged by kabuki became increasingly popular among townsmen. In 1651 the Shogun banned kabuki performances, but two years later granted permission for the kabuki theaters to re-open on condition that all parts in the plays, female as well as male, be performed by adult men.

The kabuki plays became more sophisticated and stylized, and great actors and playwrights arose. Kabuki reached its zenith by 1700, and was thereafter to be one of the most important dramatic arts in Japan. Kabuki actors who became national heroes included Tojuro Sakata (1647-1709), Ayame Yoshizawa (1673-1729), Danjuro Ichikawa (1660-1704) and Shichisaburo Nakamura (1662-1708).

In the decades before the Tokugawa Shogunate fell in 1868, the popularity of kabuki declined. Around the beginning of the Meiji Period (1868), some of the leading kabuki actors of the day initiated a revivalist movement that resulted in the creation of a number of new works that were much more traditional in form--mostly dance-dramas inspired by noh themes.

Some of the plays written during this period have survived the test of time, and are among the most popular fare performed today.

Kabuki continues today as one of the very special arts of Japan, with its stars among the most respected artists in the country. Principal kabuki theaters include the Kabuki Za, Meiji Za, Kokuriku Gekijo and Shimbashi Embujo in Tokyo, the Shin Kabuki Za in Osaka, and the Minami Za in Kyoto.

Stylized and formalized to the nth degree, kabuki features only male actors who play both male and female roles, dressed in very elaborate traditional costumes. There are two categories of kabuki plays: those depicting the lives and fortunes of the noble class and warriors of early Japan, and those based on the lives of common people of an earlier age.

The plays are performed to the accompaniment of traditional Japanese melodies played on the shamisen (shah-me-sane), a 3-stringed lute-like instrument, flutes and other Japanese musical instruments.

The actors perform the dialogue in an established, formalized pattern, making great use of gestures, body movements, and costume changes to further the story. Masks are also commonly used.

Many costume changes take place on stage in full view of the audience, but the actors are aided by assistants dressed totally in black who are so skilful they seem to be almost invisible to the experienced audience caught up in the story.

Kabuki theaters have revolving stages, making set changes possible in just seconds. They also have a long walkway running from the back of the theater to the stage--a device allowing the actors to have close contact with the audience when they enter and leave the stage.

The profession of kabuki actor is generally passed from father to son, and training begins early. Accomplished actors become nationally reknowned, receiving generous sums of money and gifts from well-to-do admirers.

English-language programs are provided for foreign visitors who want to experience the experience of viewing a kabuki play. Schedules of the plays appear regularly in such English-language publications as The Japan Times, Tour Companion and the Tokyo Weekender.

Recommended reading: KABUKI, by Masakatsu Gunji (Kodansha Int'l). THE TRADITIONAL THEATER OF JAPAN, by Yoshinobu

Inoura and Toshio Kawatake (Weatherhill).

KAGOSHIMA (Kah-go-she-mah)

The city of Kagoshima at the southern
tip of Kyushu began as the castle headquarters of the famous Satsuma clan,
which played a leading role in the fall
of the Tokugawa Shogunate in 1868 and
the restoration of power to the Imperial
throne.

The city and its inhabitants have
also played other eventful roles in
Japan's history, particularly during the
years when foreign nations were vying
with each other to force Japan to open
its doors to trade and diplomatic relations with the West.

One of these events involved the
Samurai killing of an Englishman in
1862. On September 14, 1862, C. L Richardson and some companions were out
riding on the Tokaido Road near Nammugi
when they met the Procession of the Lord
of Satsuma. The Samurai escorts of the
Lord of Satsuma cut Richardson down and
wounded two of his companions when they
failed to yield the right of way to the
Daimyo's Procession. Richardson was apparently not aware that everyone was
required to move off the road and bow
down while a feudal lord and his entourage were passing. The survivors of the
outing accused the Satsuma Samurai of
attacking them without justification.

The following year, British naval
forces bombarded Kagoshima, inflicting
heavy damage on the city, in retaliation
for the killing of Richardson.

Other foreigners who ran afoul of
belligerent Samuari during the 1850s and
60s were also cut down when they left
the protection of the enclaves established for foreign residents.

KAISEKI (Kie-say-kee)

The very simple food that is often
served with the tea ceremony, as well as
in temples, is called kaiseki. It is
usually vegetarian.

Recommended reading: KAISEKI--Zen
Taste in Japanese Cookery, by Kaichu
Tsugi (Kodansha Int'1).

KAKEMONO (Kah-kay-moe-no)

Literally a Written Thing, the kakemono is a hanging scroll, made of silk
or heavy paper with a roller at the
bottom, that the Japanese hang on a wall
or in a special alcove called a tokonoma
(toe-koe-no-mah). A kakemono may be a
painting, usually a still-life, or calligraphy, and is customarily chosen to
fit the season. See HANGING SCROLLS.

KAMAKURA (Kah-mah-Kuu-rah)

Now a popular tourist spot and elite
residential community, Kamakura seems an
unlikely place to have played the role
it has in Japan's history. Located at
the neck of the Miura Peninsula in a
narrow valley facing Sagami Bay, about
an hour by train southeast of Tokyo,
Kamakura was no more than an isolated
but picturesque village when feudal lord
Yoritomo Minamoto became the paramount
military leader of Japan and established
his military government there in 1185.

Yoritomo is said to have selected
this remote spot, many days march away
from Kyoto, to avoid the intrigues and
weakening influences of the effete way
life that had developed in the Imperial
Capital.

It was Yoritomo who established Japan's first Shogunate military government (in 1192), after having himself
given the title of Shogun (which means
something like Generalissimo and had not
been used for several centuries) by the
Emperor.

Kamakura was to remain the seat of
the Shogunate government for the next
151 years, during which some of the
country's most important temples and
shrines were built there, and are still
in use today.

Of course, the most famous of its
historic artifacts is the great bronze
image of Buddha (Dai Butsu or Great
Buddha of Kamakura), which was cast in
1252 by Goroemon Ono or Hisatomo Tanji--
both reknowned casters of that time. See
GREAT BUDDHA OF KAMAKURA.

Among the great temples at Kamakura
are the Kencho Ji and the Engaku Ji. Its
shrines include the famous Tsurugaoka
Hachiman Gu. Other points of special
interest include the Kamakura Museum and
the Tomb of Yoritomo. See HISTORY, MINA-
MOTO YORITOMO, SHOGUN, SAMURAI, GREAT
BUDDHA OF KAMAKURA, etc.

KAMIKAZE PILOTS / TOKKOTAI (Toke-koe-tie)

When World War II began to go badly
for the Japanese, the Imperial Army and
Navy established special air attack
forces whose mission was to sink Allied
ships by crashing their bomb-laden
planes into them.

Young pilots, some of them still in
their teens, were recruited and trained
for these one-way suicide flights, which
caused considerable damage to the American fleet before the war ended.

The young airmen were popularly called Kamikaze (Kah-me-kah-zay) or Divine
Wind pilots in reference to the typhoon

winds that saved Japan from great Mongol invasions fleets that attacked the country in 1274 and 1281. See HISTORY, SHOGUN.

KANDA (Khan-dah)

One of the most famous districts in Tokyo, Kanda used to be a ward in itself, but is now part of Chiyoda Ward (which incorporates much of central Tokyo, the Imperial Palace grounds and Government Hill).

Famed in history as one of the centers that bred the true Edokko (Eh-doak-koe) or Edo-ite, Kanda is now noted for being the home of many universities and schools, and for having the largest concentration of new and used bookshops in the country.

The nmost important annual event in Kanda is the Kanda Matsuri (Festival), held from May 12 to 15 by the Kanda Myojin, a Shinto shrine that dates from the 8th century.

KANJI CHARACTERS (Khan-jee)

The ideograms with which the Japanese and Chinese write their languages were developed in China sometime before 1,000 B.C. They grew out of the use of signs and pictograms, and were gradually standardized and institutionalized over many generations of daily practical use.

The Japanese imported the kanji system of writing in the 5/6 centuries A.D., and gradually assimilated it to meet their own needs for a script--but without changing the pronounciation of their own language.

As a result of this, most of the kanji used in Japan still today have two readings: the Chinese reading (the ON reading), and the Japanese or KUN reading. Which reading or pronounciation is used depends upon the particular word and usage over the centuries.

Altogether there are around 50,000 of the Chinese characters, but in Japan only about 3,000 are common, and of this number 1,945 have been designated by the government for daily use, meaning that no more than this number should be used for ordinary purposes.

Besides kanji, there are three other systems for writing Japanese. See JAPANESE LANGUAGE, CALLIGRAPHY.

KANAZAWA (Kah-nah-zah-wah)

On the Japan Sea side of Honshu west of Nagoyo, Kanazawa is the capital of Ishikawa Prefecture, and is noted for having retained much of the look of Old Japan, and for having one of the three most beautiful gardens in Japan (Kenroku-En).

Kanazawa was headquarters for the famous Maeda clan during the Tokugawa Period--one of Japan's largest and most powerful clans. It is said that when the Lord of Maeda made his every-other-year trip to the Shogun's capital of Edo, he took over 10,000 servants, retainers and warriors with him. (See PROCESSIONS OF THE LORDS.)

The Maeda Daimyo's great castle, which once stood in the center of the city, was almost totally destroyed by fire in 1881, but a number of buildings are preserved, and the famous garden that adjoined the castle is intact. It was designed and built by Narihiro Maeda in 1819 while he was the lord of the clan (it is considerably larger than the two other most famous gardens in Japan-- the Kairaku-En in Mito and the Koraku-En in Okayama).

KARA-OKE SINGING (Kah-rah-oh-kay)

For centuries, the Japanese have been raised on lullabies and folksongs, and have learned how to sing as a natural part of growing up. Everybody is expected to join in the singing at festivals, and at parties and other kinds of gatherings it is customary for individuals to take turns singing.

In the 1970s electronic firms began to sell and promote home microphone systems for people to plug into their stereo sets, and entertain themselves by singing on the air. This form of self-entertainment was dubbed Kara-oke, which means Empty pan.

Soon thereafter, many bars and clubs began offering their patrons the opportunity to perform kara-oke in public, and empty pan singing swept the country.

All was not happy, however. Too many kara-oke stars began turning the sound of their stereo sets way up, disturbing their neighbors and bringing on many complaints.

KARATE (Kah-rah-tay)

Karate literally means empty hands, and originally was a form of self-defense developed in China around the 7th century, when ordinary people were not allowed to bear arms. It consisted of highly refined techniques of striking an opponent with the bare hands or feet in especially vulnerable areas, and taking advantage of the added power achieved by delivering blows with extraordinary speed and concentration.

Karate was introduced into Okinawa in the 14th century, but it was to be several more centuries before it made its way to the mainland of Japan--which is surprising, given the extraordinary interest the Samurai class and ninja had in all martial arts.

Today, karate is known and practiced in most countries of the world, especially in Europe and the U.S., primarily as a means of developing physical, spiritual and moral strength.

There are two kinds of karate contests--kumite (kuu-me-tay), and kata (kah-tah). In a kata contest, the contestant performs a series of prescribed, formalized movements--as if defending or attacking--and is judged on the correctness and quality of these drills. The contestant is also judged on the quality of his or her kiai (kee-aye)--the shout that accompanies thrusts or kicks.

In a kumite contest, two opponents spar with each other, going through a variety of movements to demonstrate their skill. The winner is decided on the basis of which had the best form, the best mental attitude and would probably have won if the contest had been for real.

Gichin Funakoshi (1870-1957) was the Okinawan who introduced karate to mainland Japan, and probably had more influence on the sport than any other man.

In Japan the art was substantially improved, with several schools developing, including Shotokan, Goju, Rembukan Shito and Wado.

Karate training includes the basic form (kata) and various punches, jabs and kicks (kumite), which is designed to be practiced by two people, as in real combat.

The concentration of energy, both physical and mental, is such that an experienced karate adept can shatter between 10 and 15 roof slates or five 1.5 cm boards laid on top of each other, with one explosive blow.

Recommended reading: KARATE'S HISTORY β TRADITONS, by Bruce A. Haines (Tuttle). THE KARATE EXPERIENCE--A WAY OF LIFE, by Randall G. Hassell (Tuttle). KARATE: THE ART OF EMPTY-HAND FIGHTING, by Hidetaka Nishiyama and Richard C. Brown (Tuttle). DYNAMIC KARATE, by Masatoshi Nakayama (Kodansha Int'l). KARATE-DO: MY WAY OF LIFE, by Gichin Funakoshi (Kodansha Int'l).

KARUIZAWA (Kah-rue-e-zah-wah)

A picturesque mountain town in the highlands of Niigata some two hours from Ueno Station in Tokyo via limited express, Karuizawa was first made popular as a resort by Archdeacon A. C. Shaw and a Professor Dixon, then of Tokyo University, who began spending their summers there in 1886.

At an altitude of nearly 1,000 meters and surrounded by tall pines, Karuizawa has a permanent population of only about 15,000, but in July and August this swells to over 100,000. There are some 6,000 private summer cottages in the vicinity of the town, and a number of facilities for conventions and other business meetings. The area also has several golf courses.

During the war years in the early 1940s, Karuizawa was used as an internment camp for civilian prisoners of war, many of whom were stateless persons who lived permanently in Japan.

KATO, KIYOMASA (Kah-toe, Kee-yoe-mah-sah)

A celebrated general of the 16th century who served under Hideyoshi Toyotomi, Kiyomasa Kato was in charge of Hideyoshi's war against Korea (1592-1598). When Hideyoshi died in 1598 and the war was called off, Kato allied himself with Hideyoshi's successor, Ieyasu Tokugawa, and became the Daimyo of Higo Province.

It is said that after Ieyasu became Shogun in 1603, he was uneasy about having such a popular, capable and ambitious general on his flank, and contrived to have Kato poisoned during a tea ceremony.

A flamboyant character, Kato wore a helmet that was three feet high, and when on the road or in battle, always carried a banner that was inscribed with the sacred formula of Nichiren Buddhism, Namu myoho renge kyo. There are two Nichiren temples in Kumamoto, Kyushu that are dedicated to Kato.

KATSURA IMPERIAL VILLA (Kot-sue-rah)

One of the showplaces of Kyoto, the Katsura Imperial Villa was commissioned by the Tokugawa Shogunate in 1620 for Prince Toshihito, the brother of Emperor Goyozei, and was completed in 1624.

The villa adjoins the Katsura River and is 4.8 kilomters from Kyoto Station. The buildings and garden of the villa were designed by the famous landscape architect Enshu Kobori and built by his two brothers under the guidance of Prince Toshihito and his son.

A story has it that Kobori would not accept the commission until the Shogun agreed to three things--that there be no limit set on the cost of the villa, that he not have to hurry the work, and that no one was to see the villa and garden until they were completed.

Under the jurisdiction of the Imperial Household since 1883, the villa has been preserved as it was during the Tokugawa period. The villa consists of three apartments in the main building (which includes a veranda especially designed for moon-viewing), a hall for Imperial visits, a tea room, several other apartments in the garden, and another building with 10 rooms.

The garden is a strolling garden, and is designed in such a way that no matter where the viewer stands he appears to be looking at the garden from the front. It contains a pond and several tea houses overlooking it, along with several groves of trees.

The main building and other structures contain paintings by famous masters, and other works of art that are considered national treasures. Permission to enter the villa must be obtained in advance from the Kyoto Office of the Imperial Household Agency.

Recommended reading: EDO ARCHITECTURE--Katsura and Nikko, by Naomi Okawa (Weatherhill).

KAWANA (Kah-wah-nah)

Near the seaside resort of Ito on the Izu Peninsula southwest of Tokyo, Kawana is noted as a golf resort for the rich and famous. Its two golf course are reputedly the best in the Orient. Guests stay at the equally famous Kawana Hotel.

KAWASAKI (Kah-wah-sah-kee)

Japan's eighth largest city, Kawasaki is often literally overlooked because it is sandwiched in between Tokyo and Yokohama along the southern bank of the Tama River.

Originally a Post Station on the famed Tokai-Do Highway that travelers walked between Edo and Kyoto, Kawasaki is now a major industrial complex representing the biggest names in Japan's chemical and heavy industries.

Besides its importance as an industrial center, Kawasaki is noted for: the Heigen Temple, founded in 1128 and dedicated to the great Kobo-Daishi who founded the Shingon doctrine of Buddhism. The Mukoga-oka (Playground) Park, especially designed for children. The Inada-Zutsumi cherry-tree grove. The Ozenji Atomic Power Research Center. Yomiuri Land, a gigantic recreational area (see YOMIURI LAND), and a second famous temple, Ozen, which was once officially designated as the temple for Imperial prayers.

KEGON FALLS / KEGON TAKI (Kay-goan Tah-kee)

Probably the most famous waterfall in Japan, Kegon Taki is in Nikko and is the outlet for Lake Chuzenji, the high volcanic caldera that towers over the town of Nikko, the famous Tokugawa Mausolea and the shrines of Nikko.

A few minutes drive from Nikko town, the falls are some 100 meters high, in a sheer drop-off that turns the water into a lacey white curtain. The whole area is one of the most scenic in all of Japan. See NIKKO, TOKUGAWA.

KEIDANREN (Kay-e-dahn-rane)

The Keidanren, or Federation of Economic Organizations, is regarded as the most important and most powerful business organization in Japan. It is made up of representatives from virtually every major firm and industry in the country.

The Keidanran acts as a liasion between firms and the various industries and as a spokesman for industry in general, particularly in making the views of businessmen known to the government.

The Keidanren maintains a large staff that researches economic areas and problems, and writes position papers that are submitted to government agencies concerned and made available to industry and the public.

The president of Keidanren is always one of the country's most respected and influential businessmen.

KEIO UNIVERSITY / KEIO DAIGAKU (Kay-e-oh Die-gah-kuu)

The oldest university in Japan, Keio is located in the Mita district of Tokyo and is famous for its faculties of law, economics, literature, commerce, medicine, engineering, and its baseball team!

Founded by famed educator Yukichi Fukuzawa in 1858, Keio is always counted among the top five universities in the country and celebrated for its sports rivalry with Waseda, Todai (Tokyo University) and other major schools.

KENDO (Ken-doe)

One of the most popular martial arts of Japan, kendo is sword-fighting or fencing with a kind of stave made of strips of bamboo tightly bound together.

Kendo originated in the 7th or 8th century, but it was around the 16th century that it became a vital part of the training and exercise of the Samurai warrior class. In those days, solid wooden staves were used in training and tournaments, and in the hands of a skilled kendoist could be almost as deadly as a sword.

While used by the Samurai to hone and maintain their sword-fighting skills, kendo stressed the spiritual and moral aspects of the art, as exemplified by Zen Buddhism and Confucianism.

The use of the flexible bamboo staves and protective gear such as face masks, torso guards and gauntlets that are used today date from the 1700s.

Kendo contests today consist of three bouts or rounds, with the winner determined by which one is able to strike his opponent the most times in specifically prescribed places, such as the face, hands, body and throat. Attacks are usually accompanied by loud shouts designed to fluster the opponent.

Recommended reading: MODERN BUJUTSU AND BUDO, by Donn F. Draeger (Weatherhill).

KIKOTSU (Key-kote-sue)

Just as the Samurai class of feudal Japan had their Bushido or Way of the Warrior codes and philosophy, the common people of Japan, particular as the long decades of the Tokugawa Shogunate unfolded, developed a moral code of their own, one that is usually described as incorporating kikotsu—a special kind of spirit.

During the early feudal age, common people were considered chattel by the Samurai—quite literally, property that was owned by them. With such power over ordinary farmers and townspeople, it is not surprising that many Samurai developed an attitude of arrogance that was often translated into callous and brutal behavior.

This situation led to the development of a class of spirited commoners who resented the bullying and depredations of the unprincipled Samurai, and would defend themselves and other common people against them.

These individuals called themselves Men of Men, and were called Kyokaku (K'yoe-kah-kuu) or Hosts of Heroism, by the common people. Their moral code was based on kikotsu or the spirit that gave them the courage to defy and rebel against injustice and oppression.

This spirit gradually imbued the whole population of Japan in varying degrees, and was the foundation for the strong sense of justice and compassion for their fellowmen that has long been characteristic of the common people.

In the Tokugawa Period the leaders of the Kyokaku formed societies called Otokodate (Oh-toe-koe-dot-tay), which basically means If You Are a Man. Similar societies formed by and for the common people were called Machi Yakko (Mah-chee Yack-koe) or Town Men.

Even the lower ranked Samurai, who were at the mercy of their superiors, developed a comparable society in an attempt to protect themselves during the Tokugawa era. Their societies were known as Hatamoto Yakko (Hah-tah-moe-toe Yack-koe) or Banner Men.

These societies became quite powerful after a number of generations, and began to abuse their power. They were finally suppressed by the Shogunate.

KIMONO (Key-moe-no)

The kimono (kee-moe-no), one of the most elaborate and attractive national costumes of any country, was introduced into Japan from China as an undergarment in the the 7th century. Between the 12th and 13th centuries, the Court nobility began making it of highly decorative materials and wearing it as an outer garment.

When the warrior class began replacing the ancient noble families as the rulers of the country in the Muromachi Period (1338-1573), the Samurai also adopted the dress of the nobles, establishing the kimono as everyday wear.

The volumnious trousers that had been part of the original Chinese costume were inconvenient for life outside the court, however, and the Samurai wore them only on ceremonial occasions.

The female versions of the kimono was also transformed over the centuries, especially during the Edo Period of peace and prosperity when the use of expensive, colorful, georgeously decorated silks became common among the well-to-do. This was also the period when the long, wide obi (oh-bee) sash became an integral part of the female kimono.

The Shogunate passed laws prohibiting the common people from wearing luxurious clothing and living in an ostentatious manner, but the feisty Edoites were not to be denied.

The families of well-to-do merchants, geisha and other popular entertainers first began to wear expensive under-garments, and behind walls, to lavishly furnish and decorate their homes. Thus, as the decades passed these laws became more difficult and finally impossible to enforce.

With the coming of industrialization to Japan in the latter 1800s, and a fast-paced life revolving around factories, trains and streetcars, the kimono became very impractical and lost ground to Western style dress. Following the end of the Pacific War in 1945, it seemed that the kimono, traditionally made of silk, would disappear completely.

But with the gradual return of prosperity and the appearance of less expensive silks and other materials, the kimono made a miraculous comeback in the late 1950s and early 1960s, and while primarily worn today for special occasions, it is nevertheless once again very much a part of the traditional beauty and charm of Japan.

In Japan today, kimono are generally worn on two occasions--for special events and as casualwear to relax in around the house or in a ryokan (rio-khan) or inn.

There are several types of kimono for women, in different designs and colors, depending on their age and marital status, and the occasion for which they are to be worn. Women often wear kimono during the New Year holidays, at receptions, graduations, funerals and other special days.

The most common kimono seen in Japan is the informal, cotton yukata (you-kah-tah), which is used as casualwear, a house or bath robe. Yukata are especially popular in hotspring spas and other vacation spots, where they are often worn as the uniform of the day--and night. Recommended reading: THE BOOK OF KIMONO, by Norio Yamanaka (Kodansha Int'l). KIMONO MASTERPIECES--The Nomura Collection, by Tetsuro Kitamura, translated by Junko Pollack (Kodansha Int'l).

KINOKUNIYA DATA BANK SERVICE

In addition to being one of Japan's oldest and largest booksellers, Kinokuniya is also one of the country's largest computer-based information brokers. The company's data bank went on line in Japan in 1971, and linked up with some dozen American information services in 1980.

At present, Kinokuniya has several hundred Japanese clients, including large manufacturing companies, universities and government agencies. More than 90 percent of the information now being accessed from its data bank concerns developments in chemistry and engineering.

Kinokuniya's present project: feed on-line information about Japan to foreign clients abroad.

KISO RAPIDS (Kee-soe)

Rapids-shooting is as popular in Japan as in the American West, and the Kiso River, which begins at the southern end of the Japan Alps in central Honshu and flows through the Nobi Plain near Nagoya, is regarded as the finest river to shoot.

The lower section of the Kiso Rapids is one of the most scenic river areas in Japan, and is known as the Japan Rhine. The boat ride down the rapids--thrilling but not particularly dangerous, lasts about two hours.

Nagoya and Gifu serve as major geteways to the Rapids of Kiso. Public boats operate on the river. But one may also hire private boats--and have the option of stopping along the way.

KITA-KYUSHU (Kee-tah-Que-shuu)

At the northern end of Kyushu, across from Shimonoseki on the tip of Honshu, Kita-Kyushu (North Kyushu) is the 7th largest city in the country, and ranks as one of Japan's four great industrial centers (the others being Keihin in the Tokyo-Yokohama area, Chukyo in the Nagoya area, and Hanshin in the Osaka-Kobe-Kyoto area).

Kita-Kyushu is unique in that it was once five important cities--Kokura, Moji, Tobata, Yahata and Wakamatsu--which were merged in the 1960s to form one giant municipality, with the former cities being reduced to the status of wards. Each of the former independent cities retains many of its old physical characteristics as well its commercial and industrial specialitiesμ but the cities are otherwise well integrated.

The port of Kita-Kyushu is divided into three parts--Moji Port, which handles foreign trade, Kokura Port, which handles both foreign and domestic trade, and Dokai Port, which is an industrial port.

Kita-Kyushu owes much of its early industrial success to vast coal fields in the Chikuho area and trade with Asia. When oil began to replace coal as the primary energy source, the area went into a decline, and did not begin to pull out of it until all of the resources of the area were combined.

Leading industrial products of the Kita-Kyushu area include iron and steel, metalware, machinery, tools, electrical machines, oil and chemical products, items for the publishing and printing industries, and packaged foods.

Traditional industries that are still important include bamboo ware, paper, dolls, cutlery, seaweed and ink-stones.

The area is noted for several festivals, the largest of which are the Mekari Shinji, held by the Mekari Shrine on January 1. Minato Matsuri or Port Festival, in May in the port district of Moji. The Gion Daiko Festival, which includes over 100 floats and a drum-beating contest in front of Kokura Castle, and a folk-dance festival called Numagaku that is held on May 7--an event that has been designated an Intangible Cultural Property.

The line-up of places of special interest in Kita-Kyushu includes the unusual as well as the usual--the Kammon Bridge, which links Kyushu with Honshu and is the longest bridge in the Orient. The Shin Kammon Tunnel, which links the two islands. The Sembutsu Limestone Grotto. Nippon Steel Corporation's Yawata Iron Works, the largest steel producer in the world, and the Hirodai Limestone Bed that is partly under water.

The more usual attractions are the Mekari Shrine, founded by Empress Jingu in the 3rd century, Kokura Castle, which was built in 1602 by Daimyo Tadaoki Hosokawa. In its original glory it had a central tower, 148 secondary towers, 48 gates, and encompassed an area of 12,300 square kilometers that were surrounded by a stone wall 18 meters high.

Most of the castle was destroyed in the fighting that occurred during the time of the Meiji Restoration in the 1860s, but impressive portions of it have been restored.

KITE-FLYING / TAKO-AGE (Tah-koe-ah-gay)

Kite-flying has been a traditional sport in Japan for a long time, and kites come in a number of distinctive shapes and designs. The most popular kite-flying season is New Year's, but they are flown throughout the year.

One category of Japanese kite is very large, and in a stiff breeze has enough pull on the line to support the weight of a man. In earlier years it was common to stage kite competitions, in which the aim was to force competing kites down.

Recommended reading: THE ART OF THE JAPANESE KITE, by Tal Streeter (Weatherhill).

KOBE (Koe-bay)

The capital of Hyogo Prefecture and Western Japan's leading seaport, Kobe has been known as an international city since the early days of Meiji, following the fall of the Tokugawa Shogunate. But it was engaged in foreign commerce as early as the 4th century.

Originally known as Muko-no Minato or the Port of Muko, Kobe was even the administrative capital of Japan for a brief period in the 12th century (six months) when Kiyomori Taira (1118-1181) tried to develop the country through foreign trade.

While the area did not last long as the capital, its port--then called Hyogo --continued to prosper, especially in the 15th and 16th centuries. Kobe was then a suburb of Hyogo.

When Japan was opened to trade with the west, there was strong opposition to making Hyogo a foreign trade port, so in a typically expiditious move, the suburban area of Kobe was designated as the port, and was opened to trade on January 1, 1868.

The newly designated foreign trade port grew rapidly, and in 1889 officially absorbed Hyogo. The port city is now the sixth largest metropolis in Japan, and is famous for its foreign flavor, ranging from its architecture to its selection of international restaurants.

Kobe now handles about 20 percent of Japan's exports, and around 10 percent of its imports. It is also a major industrial area, big in iron and steel, shipbuilding, industrial vehicles and rolling stock, foodstuffs, flour milling, chemicals, rubber, and the distilling of O'sake. Over 10,000 ships call at the port each year.

Kobe is hemmed in by mountains. Its business district is concentrated around the port area, and its residential areas

extend up the slopes of the adjoining mountains--giving it a picturesque atmosphere and a mild climate that has made it popular with foreigners for centuries.

Leading annual events in Kobe include the Opening Ceremony of the Hotspring Bath at Arima Spa on January 2, the Festival to Drive Away Evil Spirits at Nagata Shrine on February 3 or 4, the spring festival of the Ikuta Shrine, the Nanko Festival at Minatogawa Shrine May 24-26, the Kobe Festival on the third weekend in May, and the Hot-Spring Festival at Arima Spa November 2-3.

Unusual places of interest in Kobe (over and above the shrines and temples

Katsura Imperial Villa, Kyoto. P. 176

Moon-viewing on a fall evening. P. 214

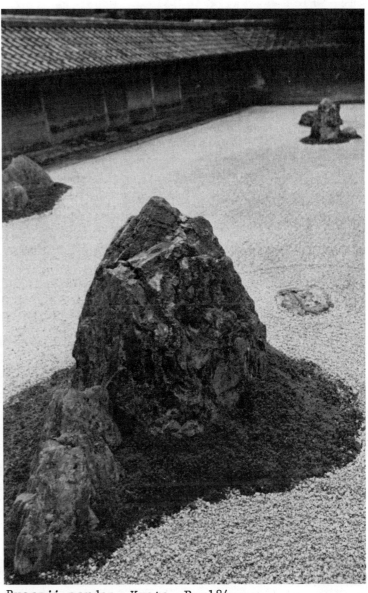

Ryoanji garden, Kyoto. P. 184

and other historical spots), are the port itself, the Port Tower and its adjoining Port Museum, the Rubber Industry Zone, the O'sake breweries in Nada Ward, and the Inland Sea National Park, which includes Mt. Rokko behind Kobe.

KOFU (Koe-fuu)

The capital of Yamanashi Prefecture, about two train-hours west of Shinjuku Station in Tokyo, Kofu was long famous as the headquarters of the Takeda clan during Japan's Daimyo days.

In a basin surrounded by spectacular mountains, including Mt. Fuji, Kofu is now noted for its silk spinning and weaving, and the production of crystalware and wine.

Among the historical attractions of the city is the famous Takeda Shrine, situated on the grounds of Takeda Castle, which was built in 1527 by Nobutora Takeda, father of Shingen, the most famous of the Takeda Daimyo. Another is the Zenko Temple, built by Shingen and patterned after the celebrated temple of the same name in Nagano Prefecture.

The city also has a noted hotspring spa district, in which all of the ryokan (inns) are supplied with hot water bubbling up from the ground.

The famous Shosenkyo Gorge on the Arakawa River is just 30 minutes from Kofu.

KOJIKI (Koe-jee-kee)

The Kojiki is a narrative chronicle of the history of Japan, based on Shinto religious legends that in earlier times was memorized by specially appointed Memory-Historians. The narrative began with the mythological origin of Japan and came down to 628 A.D.

In 712 a man named Yasumaro Ono wrote down in Chinese charcters the entire story as recited by Hiyeda-no Are.

See LITERATURE. Recommended reading: KOJIKI: Record of Ancient Matters (Tuttle).

KOMUSO (Koe-muu-so)

During Japan's feudal age, thousands of Buddhist priests called komuso made a vocation of traveling about the countryside, wearing deep straw hats that covered their faces entirely. Tiny slits in the hats allowed them to see. Some of them were blind and wore the hats to hide their eyes.

Many of the komuso were ronin or masterless Samurai, and were frequently employed by the various Daimyo or the Shogunate to act as spies. See WANDERING PRIESTS.

KORAKU GARDEN / KORAKU EN (Koe-rah-kuu En)

One of Tokyo's most celebrated gardens, Koraku En was designed in 1626 by Yorifusa Tokugawa, the 11th son of the illustrious Ieyasu who founded the Tokugawa Shogunate, and himself the patriarch of the famous Mito branch of the Tokugawa family.

The garden was remodeled by Yorifusa's son Mitsukuni, whom history ranks as one of the greatest of the Mito Tokugawas--who was advised on the remodeling by Chu Shun-shui, a noted Chinese scholar, then a refugee in Japan and under Mitsukuni's patronage.

The third Tokugawa Shogun, Iemitsu, was also to have a hand in the garden. He designed its lake, in which there is an island with a small temple.

The garden is only a few minutes from downtown Tokyo, and a 5-minute walk from Suidobashi Station on the Chuo Line, or Korakuen Station on the Korakuen Subway Line.

KOREANS IN JAPAN / KANKOKU JIN (Khan-koe-kuu Jeen)

Koreans make up the largest community of so-called foreign residents in Japan, numbering nearly 700,000. Most of these are citizens of Japan, and are the descendants of Koreans who came to Japan-- or were brought there--during the period from shortly after the turn of the century to 1945, when Korea was a Japanese possession.

In earlier years, there was considerable discrimination against Koreans in Japan, particularly in the areas of employment and housing, but their situation improved significantly in the 1970s and 80s, and one now seldom hears of overt racial or ethnic incidents.

KOSHI TEMPLE / KOSHI JI (Koe-she Jee)

On the slopes of Asahi Hill in the outskirts of Kyoto, the Koshi Temple was built in 1233 by the famous priest, Dogen, who founded the Soto sect of Buddhism after returning from a trip to China.

Dogen lived at the temple for 11 years as its abbot, before moving to Echizen Province (now Fukui Prefecture), where he built the even more famous Eihei Temple.

During June, July and August, the ancient sport of cormorant fishing is demonstrated in the nearby Uji River.

KOTO (Koe-toe)

The koto is one of the four most popular traditional musical instruments in Japan (the other three being the flute, shamisen and drums), dating from before the beginning of the Nara Period in 710.

A semi-cylindrical zither, the first koto apparently had five strings and was about three feet long. A sixth string was added during the early years of the Nara era, and then in the same period a 13-string koto, modeled after a Chinese instrument, was introduced. This new koto was six feet long and rested on the floor while being played. At first it was used only by court musicians, but from the 15th century on, it became popular among entertainers.

The koto has movable bridges for each string, and players continuously tune it while playing, in order to get more tones out of the instrument.

KOWAKIDANI (Koe-wah-kee-dah-nee)

One of the most famous hotspring spas in the Hakone district, about an hour and a half from Tokyo, Kowakidani (Valley of Lesser Boiling), also known as Ko Jigoku or Little Hell, gets its name from suphur fumes coming out of a cave in the vicinity.

Besides the efficacy of its hot mineral baths (against skin diseases, anemia and nervous disorders), Kowakidani is noted for its scenic veiws of the Hayakawa Valley, the cherry-tree and azalea-covered hills, and a gorgeous waterfall known as Chisuji-no Taki or Falls of 1,000 Threads.

KUMAMOTO (Kuu-mah-moe-toe)

The capital of Kumamoto Prefecture and Kyushu's 3rd largest city, Kumamoto's central position on the island resulted in it being chosen as a southwestern headquarters by the Tokugawa Shogunate (1603-1868).

Today the city is known as an agricultural trading center, and as the home of five colleges and universities, including the national Kumamoto University. Its traditional products include pottery, bamboo ware, rice gluten and things featuring inlay work.

Kumamoto is also the home of one of the three most famous castles in Japan (the other two: Nagoya and Osaka). The castle, on a hill two kilometers northeast of Kumamoto Station, was built in 1601-1607 under the supervision of Kiyomasa Kato (1562-1611), who was lord of the area (then called Higo Province).

The castle was razed during a brief rebellion against the Imperial forces in 1877, but it has since been partially restored (in ferro-concrete). The donjon (main tower) now houses a museum. The whole area is a Place of Special Historical Importance, and the original remnants are Important Cultural Properties. Cherry trees line the ascending approach to the castle.

Other outstanding attractions: several parks (one the former garden of Lord Hosokawa's villa), Buddhist temples and Shinto shrines (including the Fujisaki Hachiman, which dates back to the 3rd century and was dedicated to Emperor Ojin and his mother, the Empress Jingu). There are also a number of spas in the vicinity.

KUSUNOKI, MASASHIGE (Kuu-sue-no-kee, Mah-sah-she-gay)

One of Japan's great feudal-age heroes, Masashige Kusunoki was born in 1294, and lived at the Hino-Zan Monastery in Yamato (near Nara) until he was 15. There he studied military strategy, and became so proficient that his superiors feared for the country and tried to have him murdered.

The clever Kusunoki escaped, and went on to become a reknowned general in the struggle between Emperor Godaigo and the Hojo clan that then controlled the Shogunate through regents.

Takatori Hojo deposed the Emperor and forced him into exile, and then attacked Masashige's forces with an army of 28,000 horsemen. Caught unprepared, Masashige and his army were besieged in a hastily constructed fort.

Masashige had a large funeral prye built and placed the bodies of enemy soldiers on it, set it afire and then escaped under the cover of darkness, spreading the word that he and his men had committed suicide. The Hojo general was deceived by the ruse and withdrew, leaving only a small detachment to hold the fort. A spy sent into the fort by Masashige learned that a convoy of supplies was coming in. He intercepted the convoy, captured it, and secreted his men in the wagons.

Masashige easily regained the fort. The garrison left behind by Hojo switched sides and swore loyalty to him. He and his men then went to the Tenno Temple in Osaka, where he had caused a fake message to be placed among the writings of the great Shotoku Taishi who lived in the 6th century.

Masashige had an oracle read the message, which prediced that he would be victorious against the Emperor's enemies. In 1333 he won a decisive victory over the Hojo forces, ending a Shogunate that had lasted since 1192.

The famous general then besieged and captured Kyoto, but was not able to guarantee the Emperor's safety, and advised him to go to Mt. Hiei. The emperor's courtiers persuaded him to ignore the general's advice, and Masashige withdrew from the city.

A short time later the combined forces of the enemy attacked Masashige at Minatogawa (now in Kobe), and virtually annihilated his army. Masashige, his brother Masasue, and their closest aides retreated to a nearby farmhouse. There, when Masashige took off hisarmor, he found that he had been wounded 11 times.

Knowing they were doomed, Masashige and his brother sat facing each other, and ran each other through with their swords. Before killing themselves, Masashige asked his brother: What shall we do after death?

Masasue replied: I pray that I may be reborn into human life seven times in order to destroy the rebels.

That, echoed Masashige, was exactly his desire.

At that time, Masashige's son, Masatsura, was prevented from joining his father and uncle in death, and in 1348, when he was 23, he raised an army of 1,000 men and captured Chihaya Castle, which was defended by 13,000 men. He then attacked Kyoto, forcing the last Ashikaga Shogun to flee.

Only the next year, Masatsura and his own younger brother were defeated in a battle at Shijo Nawate, and like their father and uncle before them, killed each other rather than submit to capture. Thus ended the attempts of the famous Kusunoki family to help the Emperor regain the power lost by his ancestor some 200 years before.

KYOTO (Ke-yoe-toe)

From ancient times to the year 709, Japan's capital was moved each time a new emperor ascended the throne. That year a permanent capital was built at Nara, but in 784 it was moved to Nagaokakyo, and then in 794 to a new place some distance away called Uda.

The new city was laid out according to Chinese concepts, with nine wide streets running from east to west, and a series of broad north-south avenues intersecting these streets grid-fashion.

Construction of the new city was completed in 805, and it was named Heian Kyo or Capital of Peace. Later this was changed to Miyako (Imperial Capital), and finally this was shortened to Kyoto, which means Capital City.

Kyoto was built on a sloping plain adjoining a river, making it possible to construct a network of canals through the city and divert water into them. As a result, it was one of the best organized and most attractive cities in the world.

Kyoto was to remain the Imperial Capital of Japan for over 1,100 years, becoming the mother-place of arts and crafts and customs that were to distinguish Japanese culture from all others. Nestled among picturesque mountains, it was to become the religious center of Japan as well, with an array of imposing shrines and temples dotting its landscape and the surrounding hills, along with several castles and palaces.

Over the centuries, Kyoto was often ravaged by fires and political strife. When Nobunaga Oda entered the city with his conquering forces in 1569 he found it nearly destroyed. He immediately began a program to rebuilt it--a program that was continued by his successor, Hideyoshi Toyotomi.

During World War II, intercession by a number of Americans who were acquainted with the cultural value of the city resulted in Kyoto being declared an open city, and thus it was saved from bombing.

Today Kyoto still boasts over 1,500 Buddhist temples and over 220 shrines, along with a number of palaces and castles.

Like all of Japan's large cities, Kyoto is divided into wards--nine of them--and covers and area of 610 square kilometers. In addition to being the nation's repository of cultural treasures, it is also a major commercial, industrial and educational center.

It is particularly noted for its Nishijin silk weaving, dyeing, embroidery, porcelain, lacquerware, cloisonne, folding fans, screens, machinery and metal industries, plus sake brewing and the large-scale baking of cookies and pastries.

Kyoto has major annual events every month of the year, including a number that draw visitors from all over the world. See FESTIVALS.

There are so many places of interest in Kyoto that it would take several months time to see them all, resulting in many people going back again and again. Among the most famous of the sights are Kyoto Imperial Park (where princes once lived), Kyoto Imperial Palace, Shokoku Temple, Nishijin (the silk-weaving district), Kitano Shrine, the Temple of the Golden Pavilion, the Daitoku Temple, the Shugakuin Imperial Villa, the Temple of the Silver Pavilion, Nanzen Temple, Nijo Castle, Yasaka Shrine, Gion Corner, Chion Temple, Kiyomizu Temple, Nishi-Hongan Temple, the Katsura Imperial Villa, etc.

There are also dozens of places of special interest in the vicinity of Kyoto, ranging from the Rapids of Hozu and the Byodo Temple (originally the villa of Prime Minister Michinaga Fujiwara (966-1024), to Mt. Hiei, on whose cypress-covered summit is the great and famous Enryaku Temple, founded in 788 by Dengyo Daishi as headquarters for the Tendai Sect of Buddhism.

The temple and monastery buildings grew into a massive complex that housed thousands of priests who became professional warriors in the 15th and 16th centuries. Clad in armor, they made frequent raids on Kyoto. Nobunaga Oda finally destroyed the temple and monastery in the mid-1500s, and dispersed the warrior-monks.

The monastery was restored during the reign of Hideyoshi Toyotomi, Nobunaga's successor, and was greatly enlarged by Tokugawa Shogun Iemitsu, but later generations of monks did not resume the war-like ways of their predecessors.

From the pavilion of Enryaku Temple, one has a magnificent view of Kyoto, Lake Biwa and the surrounding mountains.

There are over 40 annual events of special signififance in Kyoto, some of them lasting for several days. These include:

JANUARY 1: Okera Mairi at Yasaka Shrine, a ceremony to ward off illness during the new year.

JANUARY 8-12: Toka Ebisu, a festival to honor Ebisu, the patron diety of business.

JANUARY 9-16: Ho-onko, memorial services to honor the founder of the Shinshu sect of Buddhism, Priest Shinran.

JANUARY 14: Hadaka Odori, the so-called Nude Dance, held at the Hokai Temple by boys and young men.

JANUARY 15: Toshiya, an archery contest in which archers see who can shoot the most arrows the length of a great hall. The record holder is Daihachiro Wasa, a Samurai of Kii Province who, in one day loosed 13,053 arrows, 8,153 of which went the full length of the range, in 1696.

JANUARY 21: A service at To Temple in honor of Kobo Daishi, founder of the Shingon sect of Buddhism.

FEBRUARY 3 or 4: Setsubun, the bean-throwing good luck ceremony that marks the last day of winter.

FEBRUARY 25: Baikasai or Plum Blossom Festival at Kitano Shrine in honor of the shrine diety.

MARCH 1-3: Hina Matsuri or Doll Festival at Hokyo Temple.

APRIL-May 15: Miyako Odori, also known as the Cherry Dance, at the Kaburenjo Theater in Gion.

APRIL, second Sunday: Yasurai Matsuri, a demon festival to placate the spirits that cause plagues.

APRIL 21-29: Mibu Kyogen, pantomime farcial dances performed since medieval times at the Mibu Temple.

MAY 15: Aoi Matsuri, the reenactment of an Imperial Procession that dates back to the 6th century.

JULY 16-24: Gion Matsuri, one of the three greatest festivals in Japan, consisting of a great parade, floats and other events.

AUGUST 23-24: Matsu-age, in which people toss burning torches onto baskets of wood suspended on high poles.

SEPTEMBER 21-27: Higan-E, services at all Buddhist temples to mark the equinox.

OCTOBER 12: Ushi Matsuri or Bull Festival, a ceremony at the Koryu Temple that began in the 9th century.

OCTOBER 22: Jidai Matsuri, or Festival of the Ages, sponsored by the Heian Shrine, and one of the most spectacular annual events in Japan.

NOVEMBER 2nd Sunday: Momiji Matsuri or Maple Festival, a re-creation of the games and activities of the nobles of 10th century Kyoto.

DECEMBER 1-26: Kao-mise, or All-Star Kabuki performances at the Minami-Za Theater.

DECEMBER 25: Shimai Tenjin, the final celebration of the year in honor of Tenjin, the patron diety of scholars.

There are over 200 listed places of special interest in Kyoto, including shrines, temples, palaces, castles, gardens and other historical and cultural treasures. Large sections of the city are in effect museums of the past, and there is virtually no end to things that attract the historical buff.

Among the dozens of major attractions:

KYOTO IMPERIAL PARK--Formerly the area occupied by residences of Imperial nobles and other high court officials.

The Kyoto office of the Imperial Household Agency is now in the park.

KYOTO IMPERIAL PALACE (Kyoto Gosho) --Originally built in 794 and rebuilt many times since, is a huge complex of gates, gardens, offical greeting rooms, private rooms, sanctuaries, guard houses and offices. It gives an impressive image of the grand life-style of the Emperors and their couriers.

SHOKOKU TEMPLE--Second among the five chief temples of the Rinzai sect of Buddhism, originally erected in 1393 on orders from the emperor. On the grounds are the tombs of Yoshimasa Ashikaga, the 8th Ashikaga Shogun, and Seika Fujiwara (1561-1619), a famous scholar in Chinese classics.

KINKAKU TEMPLE--The famous Gold Pavilion, first designed as the villa of a court noble named Kintsune Saionji, it was later renovated by Yoshimitsu Ashikaga, the 3rd Ashikaga Shogun, who lived there after his retirement.

DAITOKU TEMPLE--One of the chief temples of the Rinzai sect of Buddhism, the Daitoku Temple was founded in 1324. Its main gate was designed and built by the famous tea master, Sen-no Rikyu in 1589. The garden of the temple was designed by the equally famous Enshu Kobori. It is one of the largest temple complexes in Kyoto.

SHUGAKUIN IMPERIAL VILLA--Located at the foot of Mt. Hiei, the first two of these three magnificient villas were built in the 1650s by the Tokugawa Shogunate for ex-Emperor Gomizuno-o. The third villa was added later for his daughter. The villas are separated from each other and have their own gates and gardens, along with summer houses.

GINKAKUJI TEMPLE--Built in 1482 by Yoshimasa Ashikaga as a country villa, this is the famous Silver Pavilion. After Yoshimasa's death it was converted to a temple. Its garden was designed by the great Soami.

HEIAN SHRINE--This shrine commemorates the founding of Heian (Kyoto) in 794 by Emperor Kammu. It sponsors several events each year including the Jidai Matsuri or Festival of the Ages.

NANZEN TEMPLE--There are actually 13 temples on the precincts of the Nanzen Temple, which was founded in 1293. It is the headquarters of the Nanzen school of the Rinzai sect of Buddhism, has several gardens designed by Japan's most reknowned masters, and numerous other cultural treasures.

NIJO CASTLE--Built in 1603 by Ieyasu, the founder of the Tokugawa Shogunate, to serve as his residence when he visited Kyoto, the castle became the temporary seat of government in 1868 when the last Tokugawa Shogun resigned. The large complex has to be one of the most fascinating places in all of Japan. Its great rooms, chambers and halls echo with the color and pageantry of the past. With only a little imagination, one can see the great Tokugawa Shogun holding court in one of the richly decorated halls, or making his way down one of the polished wooden corri-dors.

YASAKA SHRINE--Popularly known as the Gion Shrine, because it is at the east end of the Gionmachi entertainment district, this shrine is dedicated to one of Japan's ranking mythological dieties, Susano-o Mikoto, his consort and their sons, which were transferred to the shrine in 876.

Several parts of the shrine are registered cultural treasures.

CHION TEMPLE--One of the largest and most famous temples in Japan, the Chion-in is the headquarters of the Jodo sect of Bud-dhism, and was erected in 1234 by Priest Genchi, a disciple of Ho-nen who founded the sect. Its gate is regarded as one of the most impressive of all the temple gates in Japan. The great Enshu Kobori designed the garden surrounding the superior's quarters.

KIYOMIZU TEMPLE--On a hill amidst a dense grove of trees, the noted Kiyomizu Temple was founded in 798. The main hall sets on a high cliff overlooking a deep valley. The sprawling complex includes over a dozen buildings and structures, many of which are National Treasures.

HOKO TEMPLE--Built in 1586 by Hideyoshi Toyotomi, who unified the country and set the stage for the foundation of the Tokugawa Shogunate, the Hoko is also called Dai-Butsu-Den or Great Buddha Hall, because it originally housed a huge image of Buddha.

KYOTO NATIONAL MUSEUM--Erected in 1897 by the Imperial Household Agency, the museum has 17 exhibit rooms in which are displayed over 2,000 of the finest and rarest pieces of art, handicrafts and religious objects donated by temples, shrines and individuals in Kyoto.

NISHI HONGAN TEMPLE--School headquarters of the Jodo-Shinshu sect, this great temple complex contains what is regarded as the finest examples of Buddhist architecture in Japan. The temple is dedicated to Kenshin Daishi (1173-1244), who founded the sect. In 1602, the soon-to-be Shogun Ieyasu Tokugawa sponsored the founding of a rival to the Jodo-Shinsu sect by Priest Otani (a former abbot of the Nishi Hongan Temple). The temple of this rival sect was known as the Higashi (East) Hongan Temple.

DAIKAKU TEMPLE--Originally a villa built for Emperor Saga, the Daikaku was converted to a temple in 867 by Emperor Junna, who appointed a favorite prince as its founder and abbot. The temple is famous for its paintings by great masters of the past.

KATSURA IMPERIAL VILLA--Adjacent to the Katsura River, this outstanding example of Japanese architecture and garden design was built in the 1620s for Prince Toshihito, brother of Emperor Goyozei (1571-1617). The complex contains a number of magnificient buildings, including a veranda designed especially for moon-viewing.

See individual listing of many of the above. Recommended reading: INTRODUCING KYOTO, by Herbert Plutschow (Kodansha Int'l).

KYOTO UNIVERSITY / KYOTO DAIGAKU (Die-gah-kuu)

Founded in 1897, and thus the second oldest as well as one of the largest of Japan's state-run universities, Kyoto Daigaku is located just west of Kyoto's world-famous Silver Pavilion or Gin Kaku-Ji.

One of the elite universities of Japan, Kyodai is especially noted for its Faculty of Literature museum, which contains many ancient documents relating to history, archaeology and geography, and for the Yukawa Memorial Institute, built in 1952 and primarily financed by Hideki Yukawa who won the Nobel Prize in physics in 1949.

KYUSHU (Que-shuu)

The southwesternmost of Japan's four main islands, and the closest to the Korean Peninsula and China, Kyushu is considered the heartland of Japanese culture. Tradition says that the first Emperor, Jimmu Tenno, came from Kyushu, and it is well known that the island acted as the conduit for most of the cultural influnces from Korea and China that were to shape and color the civilization of Japan.

The 44,296 square kilometer island of Kyushu is separated from Shikoku on the east by the Bungo Channel, and from Honshu on the north by the Kammon Straits. It is connected to Honshu by two undersea tunnels and a long suspension bridge.

Like all the other major islands of Japan, Kyushu is extremely mountainous, with numerous peaks soaring to over 1,700 meters above sea-level. It is also replete with hundreds of hotsprings--many of which have been developed into famous resort spas for centuries--seascapes that are enchanting in their beauty, and, thousands of off-shore isles and islets that garland the island like jewels.

Kyushu has four of Japan's most beautiful national parks, including Mt. Aso (the world's largest volcano), Unzen-Amakusa, which combines a highland park, a world-reknowned hotspring spa and hundreds of offshore islands, the marine park of Saikai, noted for its seascapes, and Kirishima-Yaku, which encompasses Mt. Takachiho.

In addition to these outstanding areas, Kyushu is also famed for the Hellsprings of Beppu, Yabakei Gorge, the live volcano of Sakurajima in the harbor of Kagoshima, and the Nichinan coast, which is a quasi-national park.

Nagasaki is probably Kyushu's best-known city. After Japan closed its doors to the outside world in 1639, the only crack that was left open was Nagasaki, through which news of the world beyond trickled in ever so slowly over the next 220-odd years.

Nagasaki is also remembered as being the second of Japan's cities to be atom-bombed during World War II (See NAGASAKI).

In earlier times, Kyushu was the landing-place of the Mongol invasion fleets in 1274 and 1281. See HISTORY.

Kyushu's other major cities are Fukuoka, Kita-Kyushu and Kumamoto, which see.

LABOR / RODO (Roe-doe)

Japan's labor force is steadily approaching the 60 million mark, and consists of approximately 63 percent of the population that is age 15 and older. Men still significantly out-number women in the labor force, with a ratio of about 3 to 2.

During the 1950s, 60s and early 70s, when its economy was one of the fastest growing in the world, Japan experienced a labor shortage. But the oil crisis in 1973 slowed economic growth, and it has never recovered its pre-oil-shock pace.

Because of what amounts to life-time employment in government, in public corporations and in larger commercial enterprises, the unemployment rate in Japan has been held very low by worldwide standards—under three percent.

These official figures are misleading, however. In Japan the only people who are officially regarded as unemployed are those who are out of work and have registered as seeking employment. The figures do not count people who have been laid off. They are regarded as being on temporary leave.

People who have lost jobs but are working in family businesses are not counted as unemployed. Neither are housewives who are not actively seeking employment.

If Japan used the American system of counting its jobless, its unemployed figures would be much higher. Furthermore, the system of life-time employment contributes to over-employment in many companies and industries, and thus amounts to a social expense that in other countries is more likely to be pushed off on the government.

Because of the social and economic system that exists in Japan, Japanese workers, generally speaking, are exceptionally diligent and loyal. The Japanese management system is very personal. It is more people-oriented than job-slot oriented.

Young people who go to work for more desirable employers presume that they will be there for life and are therefore very much interested in the success and growth of their employers. They are not about to do anything that would jeopardize their job or their employer.

Japanese workers know they cannot bounce from one job to another, as so many do in the U.S., and are therefore much more concerned about their behavior and productivity.

LABOR UNIONS / RODO KUMIAI (Roe-doe Kuu-me-aye)

Japanese labor unions are organized on a company basis—not on a craft or industry basis as they are in the U.S. In other words, all the members of a particular union belong to the same company, and have nothing to do with other unions around the country.

Individual company unions may belong to a national federation, but they remain independent and handle their own affairs as separate entities. Once a year, individual company unions may cooperate with the national federation in public demonstrations to influence employers to give all workers across-the-board pay increases. See SPRING LABOR OFFENSIVE.

At other times, company unions may stage temporary work-stoppages in their own firms, but these are normally for short, pre-arranged durations, designed to impress the employer with their seriousness but not to seriously harm the company.

The leaders of company labor unions remain employees of the company, and once their term of office is over they resume their work as employees. Negotiations between management and representatives of the company union are ongoing, and are therefore able to prevent most disputes from reaching an impasse.

The percentage of unionized workers in Japan's labor force has been falling steadily since the 1950s, when it was around 40 percent. It is now approximately 30 percent. The percentages vary widely with the type of company.

Some 60 percent of the companies involved in transportation and communications are unionized. While in finance and insurance the percentage is about 55, and in mining about 47. Only around 9 percent of the companies involved in retailing and wholesaling are unionized, and only about 16 percent of the businesses in construction.

Workers in the manufacturing industries, of which some 35 percent are unionized, account for the majority of Japan's union members.

The four leading national union federations are Sohyo (General Council of Trade Unions of Japan), Domei (Japanese Confederation of Labor), Churitsu Roren (Federation of Independent Unions), and

Shinsanbetsu (National Federation of Industrial Organizations).

Recommended reading: LABOR RELATIONS IN JAPAN TODAY, by Tadashi Hanami (Kodansha Int'l).

LACQUERWARE / SHIKKI (Sheek-key)

Lacquerware has been popular in Japan since it was introduced from China in the 7th century. Because of its versatility, durability and beauty, it became a handicraft art as well as a utilitarian product. Numerous pieces of lacquerware dating back to the 7th and 8th centuries are on display in the Horyu (Hoe-ree-you) and other temples in Nara.

Several techniques of lacquering and several ways of producing different designs have traditionally been used in Japan. Colors range from vermilion, green, black and gold, to many combinations. Among the most popular lacquerware products are bowls, trays, and jewelry boxes.

The island of Shikoku is famous for its lacquerware industry, and Wajima lacquerware from the district of Wajima is the most famous of all.

LAKES/ MIZUUMI (Me-zoo-uu-me)

Because of its mountains, rainfall and volcanic nature, there are numerous lakes in Japan. The majority of them are in the mountains, and most are small. The largest and most famous lake in Japan is Lake Biwa (Biwa Ko) near Kyoto in Shiga Prefecture. It is 674 square kilometers or 260 square miles in area.

The deepest lake in the country is Lake Tazawa (Tah-zah-wah), which reaches a depth of 423 meters (1,388 feet), and is near Morioka in northeast Honshu.

Other larger lakes include Kasumigaura in Ibraraki Prefecture, Saroma Ko in Hokkaido (a salt water lake), Inawashiro Ko in Fukushima Prefecture, and Nakaumi in Tottori and Shimane Prefectures (also a salt water lake).

Among the smaller but most beautiful lakes in Japan are Ashino-Ko (popularly known as Lake Hakone), Chuzenji, which is just above Nikko, and Yamanaka and Kawaguchi, two of the five lakes around the waist of Mt. Fuji.

Since early times, Lake Biwa has been noted for its Eight Beautiful Views, called Omi Hakkei (actually, the Eight Beautiful Views of Omi, where the lake is located). These views are: the autumn moon seen from Ishiyama, the evening glow at Seta, dusk and the evening bell at Mii Temple, snow on Mt. Hira at sunset, night rain at Karasaki, boats sailing from Yabase, the sky and the breeze on the lake at Awazu, and wild geese landing on the lake at Katada.

LAND AREA

The Japanese archipelago is made up of over 4,000 islands, all but four of which range from tiny to small. The total land area is approximately 378,000 square kilometers, or 146,000 square miles. This makes Japan only one twenty-fifth the size of the U.S. (about the size of the state of Montana), one twenty-sixth that of China, one twenty-third the size of Brazil, and a little bit larger than Malaysia. Japan is about one and a half times the size of Great Britain, and a little larger than Norway and Italy.

LANGUAGE / KOKUGO (Koe-kuu-go)

The Japanese language is unique in a number of ways. There are theories relating it to the Altaic and Korean family of languages, but these theories have not been substantiated. It has its own peculiar sentence structure, and is very flexible within this structure.

Japanese is based on some 103 syllables made up of only six sounds, and is therefore phonetically very simple. It has five vowels (a, i, u, e, o) and 14 consonants (k, s, t, n, h, m, y, r, w, g, z, d, b and p). Consonants never occur alone--only in combination with vowels. The only other sound in the language is the nasal n.

Japanese is pronounced very much like Spanish, including trilling of the R's. Japanese may be written with Roman letters in a system called Roma-ji, which means Roman letters. Vowels may be pronounced long or short, or may be silent. Consonants are pronounced as they are in English.

Care must be taken to distinguish between single and double consonants, which are stressed as in Italian and French. Doubling a consonant changes the meaning of a word.

Japanese is not a tonal language, like Chinese, but it often requires the accentuation of syllables. Otherwise, the pronunciation is straight-forward.

The following pronunciation charts will give you a good idea of the sound and feel of the language:

A	I	U	E	O
(Ah)	(Ee)	(Uu)	(Eh)	(Oh)
Ka	Ki	Ku	Ke	Ko
(Kah)	(Kee)	(Kuu)	(Kay)	(Koe)
Sa	Shi	Su	Se	So
(Sah)	(She)	(Sue)	(Say)	(Soe)
Ta	Chi	Tsu	Te	To
(Tah)	(Che)	(T'sue)	(Tay)	(Toe)
Na	Ni	Nu	Ne	No
(Nah)	(Nee)	(Nuu)	(Nay)	(No)
Ha	Hi	Hu	He	Ho
(Hah)	(He)	(Who)	(Hay)	(Hoe)
Ma	Mi	Mu	Me	Mo
(Mah)	(Me)	(Muu)	(May)	(Moe)
Ya	I	Yu	E	Yo
(Yah)	(Ee)	(Yuu)	(Eh)	(Yoe)
Ra	Ri	Ru	Re	Ro
(Rah)	Ree)	(Rue)	(Ray)	(Roe)

Trill the R's a bit

Wa	I	U	E	Wo
(Wah)	(Ee)	(Uu)	(Eh)	(Oh)

PRONOUNCIATION CHART #2

Ga	Gi	Gu	Ge	Ge
(Gah)	Ghee)	(Goo)	(Gay)	(Go)
Za	Ji	Zu	Ze	Zo
Zah)	(Jee)	(Zoo)	(Zay)	(Zoe)
Da	Ji	Zu	De	Do
(Dah)	(Jee)	(Zoo)	(Day)	(Doe)
Ba	Bi	Bu	Be	Bo
(Bah)	(Bee)	(Boo)	(Bay)	(Boe)
Pa	Pi	Pu	Pe	Po
(Pah)	(Pee)	(Poo)	(Pay)	(Poe)

PRONOUNCIATION CHART #3

The following 33 syllables are combinations of some of the two sets appearing above.

Rya	Ryu	Ryo
(R'yah)	(R'you)	(Rio)
Mya	Myu	Myo
(M'yah)	(M'you)	(M'yoe)
Nya	Nyu	Nyo
(N⌈yah)	(N'you)	(N'yoe)
Hya	Hyu	Hyo
(H'yah)	(H'you)	(H'yoe)
Cha	Chu	Cho
(Chah)	(Chew)	(Choe)
Sha	Shu	Sho
(Shah)	(Shuu)	(Show)
Kya	Kyu	Kyo
(K'yah)	(Que)	(Q'yoe)
Pya	Pyu	Pyo
(P⌈yah)	(P'you)	(P'yoe)
Bya	Byu	Byo⌈
(B'yah)	(B'you)	(B'yoe)
Ja	Ju	Jo
(Jah)	(Jew)	(Joe)
Gya	Gyu	Gyo
(G'yah)	(G⌈you)	(G'yoe)

The wild card in the Japanese lan-

guage and pronounciation system is the nasal sound N, which is pronounced something like the n in bond. For example, the word for bread is pan, which is made up of two syllables pa and n and is pronounced pahn. Another example: lawyer is bengoshi (be-n-go-shi), pronounced bane-go-she.

There are several good courses in the Japanese language, including a number that are on casette tapes. A key point in studying the language is NOT to study it from the grammatical or vocabulary angle. Learn it by studying dialogues first, and then regular composition.

Also keep in mind that your studying should ALL be outloud in a normal speaking or reading voice. A great part of the challenge of learning a foreign language is not memorizing it, but the mechanical problem of achieving skill with the tongue and mouth in saying the words properly, smoothly and at an appropriate speed. The only way you can achieve this skill is repetition--repeating the dialogues and sentences outloud, over and over, until they become automatic.

In the U.S., several different Japanese language courses and study aids are available from the Kinokuniya bookstore chain, which has shops in Los Angeles, San Francisco and New York.

One of the most useful Japanese language books I have found over the years is the ENGLISH-JAPANESE CONVERSATION-DICTIONARY, by Mr. and Mrs. O. Vaccari, available wherever books on Japan are on sale. See JAPANESE LANGUAGE.

LAWS / HORITSU (Hoe-reet-sue)

During the Tokugawa Shogunate era it was generally believed by the Bakufu government that laws should be kept secret, that it would be dangerous if the public knew the law. When Japan opened its doors to the West it adopted the German system of laws.

The Japanese still prefer arbitration and compromise to recourse to the law, and there is strong pressure from courts for people and corporations to reach out-of-court settlements.

LAWYERS / BENGOSHI (Bane-go-she)

Japan's first regulation concerning lawyers was passed in 1876, and a lawyer law went into effect in 1895, but the bar association was under the direct supervision of chief prosecutors attached to district courts.

The present Lawyer Law was passed in 1949 and Nichibenren (Nee-chee-bane-rane), the Japan Federation of Bar Associations, was founded on the same day. The law guarantees the independence of the association, and sets standards of lawyers.

Persons who pass the national bar examination or have taught law as a university professor for at least five years, as well as foreign lawyers who have been screened by Nichibenren, are eligible to practice law in Japan.

Nichibenren, headquartered in Kasumigaseki, the government center, has 52 local branch offices, including one in each prefecture. All lawyers are required to register with their local branch office and the main office of Nichibenren. Lawyers are required to have offices, and must follow guidelines set by the bar association in charging fees.

Most of Japan's lawyers are in Tokyo and Osaka, and less than 300 of them are women.

Japan has fewer than 15,000 lawyers, as opposed to nearly 450,000 in the U.S. But in Japan a variety of other professionals perform functions that are generally handled by American attorneys.

These other professionals include zeirishi (zay-e-ree-she) or tax attorneys, benrishi (bane-ree-she) or patent attorneys, shiho shoshi (she-hoe show-she), or judicial scriveners, and gyosei shoshi (g'yoe-say-e show-she), or administrative scriveners.

Also, each year hundreds of students who studied law in universities but do not become lawyers enter various companies and government ministeries, and are assigned to departments handling legal affairs.

The traditional laywer in Japan is limited primarily to representing clients in court.

There are no law schools as such in Japan. The universities are divided into semi-independent departments which students enter after completing two years of undergraduate study. The law department is usually the most prestigious of the university departments, and only those with the highest academic credentials (based on the results of their entrance examinations) are accepted into it.

Once in the law department, students study only law, usually concentrating on its theoretical and general aspects.

The national Legal Examination that lawyers, judges and public procurators, must pass before they are licensed to practice is extremely difficult. Each year some 20,000 candidates take it but only about 500 pass.

Under the provisions of Japan's Attorney's Law, passed in 1949 and amended in 1955, foreign attorneys are permitted to practice in Japan as associate members of the bar, which allows them to practice without having passed the Legal Examinationn or knowing the Japanese language.

There are currently some two dozen foreign attorneys in Japan who are registered to handle matters primarily concerning foreign interests. Over the years, only one foreign attorney spoke Japanese well enough to pass the bar examinations in that language.

LIBERAL STAR

This is a monthly tabloid-sized newspaper published by the Liberal Democratic Party of Japan for English readers. It is available overseas by subscription from The Liberal Democratic Party, at 1-11-23 Nagata-cho, Chiyoda-ku, Tokyo 100 Japan. It covers domestic and international affairs, the visits of foreign dignataries and interviews with authorities in various fields.

LITERARY AGENCIES

Japanese literary agents play a leading role in the translation and publication of foreign books in Japan, and to a considerably lesser extent, in the Japanese books that are published abroad in foreign languages.

The top literary agencies in the country are Japan Uni Agency, Nagai Building, 5th floor, 1-1 Jimbo-cho, Kanda, Chiyoda-ku, Tokyo 101 Japan, and the Tuttle-Mori Agency, Fuji Building, 8th floor, 2-15 Jimbo-cho, Kanda, Chiyoda-ku, Tokyo 101 Japan.

Kern Associates, founded by American Lawrence Kern, is also an important agent, with U.S. and European clients. It is at 5-18 Sakae-cho, Sagamihara Shi, Kanagawa Prefecture, Japan.

The Japan Uni Agency works closely with a large pool of professional translators, and is involved in the translation of many of the books it handles.

LITERATURE / BUNGAKU (Boon-gah-kuu)

Only China and Korea have longer, continuous literary histories than Japan. Three of Japan's earliest books were the KOJIKI (Koe-jee-kee), the NIHONSHOKI (Nee-hone-sho-kee) and the MANYOUSHU (Mahn-yoe-shuu).

The Kojiki is an anthology of ancient events as recited by a court official whose task it was to memorize such matters. It was published in book form in the 8th century. The Nihonshoki, also published in the 8th century, is a history of Japan up to that time.

The Manyoshu, a poetry anthology, was also a product of this same century. It contains nearly 4,000 poems, most of which are tanka (tahn-kah), short poems consisting of 31 syllables in lines of 5-7-5-7-7 syllables, and choka (choe-kah), long poems which have any number of pairs of 5-7 syllables and ending with two 7-syllable lines.

The world's first novel of record, the famous GENJI MONOGATARI (Gane-jee Moe-no-gah-tah-ree) or The Tale of Genji, was written in the early part of the 11 century by a woman named Murasaki Shikibu, a member of the Imperial Court in Kyoto. It is a long (54 books), insightful, poetic chronicle of the loves, intrigues, failures and successes of the court nobles of this fascinating period in Japan's history, with the members of the Genji family as the principal set of characters.

The book is available in English in two translations--the first one by Arthur Waley and the second one by Edward Seidensticker.

Another great novel, HEIKE MONOGATARI (Hay-e-kay Moe-no-gah-tah-ree) or Tale of Heike, written in the 13th century, was more of a popular work than the one written by Lady Murasaki. This book tells the story, in epic fashion, of the splendor and decadence of the last ruling family of the ancient era, their defeat and downfall.

Imbued with the Buddhist concept of the transitory nature of all things, and that no matter how high a person or a family may rise, a day of reckoning will come, the story was memorized by story-tellers who traveled around the country, relating it to the accompaniment of the biwa, a stringed instrument.

During these long centuries, the writing of poetry was more than a national custom. Warriors, fatally wounded in combat, would use their last moment to compose a poem.

With the establishment of the Tokugawa Shogunate in 1603, and its strict political and social controls, the nature of Japan's literature underwent a significant change. From the epic narratives of wars and the intrigues of the Imperial Court, writers began turning their attention to both the Samurai and common people in their pursuit of pleasure.

The primary themes in the literature of the 1600s and 1700s was comedy (warai) and amusement (asobi). Numerous books appeared, detailing the pleasures and peccadilloes of the times, particulaly about life in the flourishing gay quarters.

By the late 1700s and early 1800s, the Tokugawa Shogunate had lost its dynamism, and the pleasures of the huge redlight districts, the baths and the baudy theater had become so common-place that writers began looking to the past for themes.

Akinari Ueda (1734-1809), the author of two major collections of short stores, UGETSU MONOGATARI and HARUSAME MONOGATARI, was a leader in this movement. His writing reflected the classical taste of the past.

The historical novel, called yomihon (story book), also came into its own during this period. The two most celebrated authors of this type of book were Kyoden Santo (1761-1816) and Baikin Takizawa (1767-1848). Baikin wrote the long, moralistic novel NANSO SATOMI HAKKENDEN, which covered the period from 1814-1841, and was the longest novel written in Japan during the Tokugawa period.

Novelist Shunsui Tamenaga (1790-1843) is regarded as one of the best of the ninjo-bon (real-life romance books), who flourished during this period. His most representative work was SHUNSHOKU UMEGO-YOMI, which was an insightful story of the amorous relationships between men and women.

Shortly after the beginning of the 1800s, comical books (kok-kei-bon) became vogue. The three most famous examples of this genre were TOKAIDO-CHU HIZAKURIGE or Along the Tokai High Way by Shank's Mare (on foot), by Ikku Jippensha (1765-1831), UKIYO-BURO (The Floating World of the Bath), and UKIYO-DOKO (A Man of the Floating World), by Samba Shiteki (1776-1822).

Hizakurige is the original Road adventure, chronicaling the misadventures of two middle-aged characters from Edo who get away from quarrelsome wives by taking off on a long walking tour of the famous Tokaido, which connected Edo with Kyoto.

Their adventures along the way, especially in the Post Station inns where there were always women of pleasure available, gives a humorous but realistic image of what life was like in Japan at that time.

The floating world is a eupherism for life in the great redlight districts and massage-baths during the long Tokugawa era, and Samba's two novels provide a penetrating look at this fascinating aspect of life in Shogunate Japan.

Ikku's Road novels are available in English: SHANK'S MARE--Being a Translation of the Tokaido Volumes of Hizakurige, Japan's Great Comic Novel of Travel β Ribaldry (Tuttle).

The world of poetry also flourished during the Tokugawa period. The great Buson Yosa (1716-1783), followed Basho as the foremost haiku poet of his day. He was also one of the leading painters of his time. Next came Issa Kobayashi (1763-1827), who was the first to use colloquialisms in his haiku.

Even more dynamic was the development of senryu and kyoka poetry. Senryu, like haiku, has 17 syllables but without the requirement that each one have a seasonal word. Their primary theme was a somewhat cynical or comic view of life. The greatest senryu of this period are in a 24-volume anthology called YANAGI-DARU (1765-1791).

While senryu were especially popular among the masses, the 31-syllable kyoka were more for intellectuals, and were marked by a highly refined wit, with a satircal touch. Shokusanjin Ota (1749-1823) is regarded as the greatest master of the kyoka genre of poetry during the Tokugawa period.

It was during the latter half of the Tokugawa era that kabuki reached its zenith. The two great kabuki dramatists Namboku Tsuruya (1755-1829) and Mokuami Kawatake (1816-1893) were among the most popular writers of their day. And this was the period that gave rise to the noted kabuki actors Danjuro Ichikawa and Kikugoro Onoe, whose successors adopted their names and thus continued the traditions they established down to the present times.

With the fall of the Tokugawa Shogunate, the restoration of the Emperor to power for the first time in many centuries, and the opening of Japan to the outside world for the first time in over 200 years, Japan's literary scene also underwent a series of revolutionary changes.

With both personal and political freedom for the first time in the history of the country, and the influence of many English, French and Russian novels translated into Japanese, Japanese writers began experimenting with new forms of style and expression.

Shoyo Tsubouchi (1859-1935) wrote SHOSETSU SHIZUI (Quintessence of the Novel) advocating the principle of realism in novels, including the use of familiar speech (as opposed to a highly stylized language that had been adapted from Chinese literature). One of the first Japanese writers to take this new approach was Shimei Futabatei (1864-1909), in his novel UKIGUMO, which had a marked influenced on later Japanese novelists.

Other novelists who helped make the transistion from old Japan to new Japan were Koyo Ozaki (1867-1903), Rohan Koda (1867-1947), Roka Tokutomi (1868-1927) and Ichiyo Higuchi (1872-1996).

Tokutomi became known abroad as a result of translations of his work about Japan's feudal family system, which was carried over into the new age, despite its inhuman influence.

The sudden appearance of mass-distributed newspapers and magazines shortly after the turn of the 20th century saw the rise of literary critics (who became more powerful than the poets and novelists they wrote about), and many other commentators on every thing from art to economics.

New-age poets also appeared, expanding on old forms and creating new ones. Shiki Masaoka (1867-1902) was a leader in the haiku field, while Akiko Yosano (1878-1942), one of the first female writers to win fame since the great female novelists of the 11th and 12th centuries, was the brightest of the waka stars.

Kyoshi Takahama (1874-1959) dominated the world of haiku for nearly 50 years. Hakushu Kitahara (1885-1942) and Takuboku Ishikawa (1886-1912) were also noted waka or tanka poets, bringing to this form a more realistic depiction of life.

Several Japanese poets--Toson Shimazaki, Sakutaro Hagiwara, Kyukin Susukida and Ariake Kambara--whose lives spanned the period from 1872 to 1952, became noted for their Western style poetry. Hagiwara was especially known for his realistic poetry in colloquial Japanese.

A naturalistic movement began shortly after the turn of the century, when large numbers of Japan's writers began addressing the social and economic problems of the day. Others, however, turned to the personal, sensual side of life. Among this latter group--who are much better known than the former--were Kafu Nagai (1879-1959), Junichiro Tanizaki

(1886-1965) and Haruo Sato (1892-1964).

The best-known of the traditional-ists, who believed that Japan should go back to the ethics and standards of the Samurai, were Ogai Mori (1862-1922) and Soseki Natsume (1867-1916). Both were important in interpreting various Western philosophies.

The next generation of writers to become famous included Ryunosuke Akutagawa (1892-1927), Kan Kikuchi (1888-1948) and Yuzo Yamamoto (1887-1974). Kikuchi and Yamamoto are known for their realistic plays. Akutagawa is best-known for his attempts to interpret human behavior in his short-stories, as in RASHOMON and KAPPA--A SATIRE, both of which are available in English from the Charles E. Tuttle Company.

From about 1924, a new generation of Japanese writers took up the cause of social reform and modernism. The advocates of social reform were soon suppressed by the government and forbidden to write. They included Takiji Kobayashi (1903-1933), Yuriko Miyamo-to (1899-1951) and Shigeharu Nakano (1902-   ).

The second group, known as neo-sensualists, included Riichi Yokomitsu (1898--1947) and Yasunari Kawabata (1899-1972). Kawabata emphasized sensual beauty through lyricism, while Yokomitsu was more of a stylist. Kawabata thus became famous abroad (winning the Nobel Prize for literature in 1968) while few Westerners ever heard of Yokomitsu.

Other writers in this group, all born around the turn of the century, were Masuji Ibuse, Tatsuo Hori, Fumio Niwa, Osamu Daizu, Kazuo Ozaki, Fumiko Hayashi and Kanoko Okamoto.

All literary freedom was supressed by the government during the war years from 1939 to 1945.

Following the return of Japanese sovereignty in 1952, and the sweeping away of the vestiges of the feudal social and political systems, Japanese writers once again began to flourish in all fields. Historical novels, war novels, detective stories, and very commercial popular novels became the vogue.

The most successful of the historical novelists was Eiji Yoshikawa (1892-1962), while Bunroku Shishi (1893-1969), Jiro Osaragi (1897-1973) and Seicho Matsumoto (1909-) were among the most successful in the popular fields.

Writers who achieved acclaim for their war books included Rinzo Shiina (1911-1973, Shohei O-oka (1909-) and Haruo Umezaki (1915-1965).

One of the most successful and most tragic of Japan's post-1945 writers was Yukio Mishima (1925-1971), whose life reflected so much that was great as well as tragic in the culture of Japan. See MISHIMA, YUKIO.

Other writers who made their mark after 1945: Yasushi Inoue, Shotaro Yasuoka, Junzo Shono, Toshio Shimano, Junnosuke Yoshiyuki, Shusaku Endo, Nobuo Kojima and Kobe Abe.

These were followed by a younger group born in the 1930s, who knew little or nothing about pre-World War II Japan. Most notable among this group were Shintaro Ishihara (1932-) and Kenzaburo Oe (1935-).

Ishihara made an extraordinary splash in the late 1950s with the publication of TAIYO KISETSU or Season of the Sun, which was an intimate portrayal of the sensual, nihilistic life of the post-war affluent young. Ishihara later went on to a succesful career in the movies and as a singer.

Critics described Oe as the most promising writer of this period. His first book appeared in 1957, when he was 22.

The literary world in Japan today is as varied and as dynamic as it is in any other country. Both poetry and the novel continue to flourish. Literary works account for about 20 percent of all the books published in Japan each year, or around 6,000 titles annually.

There are some 100 literary magazines in publication, and nearly all of the newspapers, weeklies and monthlies in the country serialized novels as part of their regular fare.

There are some 30 major literary prizes awarded each year in such fields as poetry, novels, drama, mystery novels, nonfiction, commentary and essays. The Akutagawa Prize and the Naoki Prize, both awarded by the prestigious Bungei Shunju literary magazine since 1935, are the highest of these awards.

Today, with virtually 100 percent literacy, and with formal education and an overpowering thirst for knowledge a primary factor in daily life, the Japanese are among the most avid readers in the world, and support one of the largest and most diverse publishing industries.

See BOOKS and PUBLISHERS. Recommended reading: A HISTORY OF JAPANESE LITERATURE--The first Thousand Years, by Shuichi Kato, translated by David Chibbett (Kodansha Int'l).

LOAN WORDS

Japan probably has more loan words--words adopted from other languages--than any other major tongue, or at least it seems that way. Almost every Japanese conversation is peppered with loan words, as is a great deal of the writing.

The earliest of the borrowings were, of course, from Korean and Chinese, followed by Portuguese, Dutch, English, Italian, French and American.

The primary reason for so much borrowing is that there were no Japanese equivalents for so many of the words concerned. In many cases today, however, the foreign words are used simply because they have a special flavor or ambience that the Japanese like--the same way Americans use certain French words.

In addopting a foreign word, the Japanese simply pronounce it in Japanese--that is convert it into Japanese syllables. For example, blue becomes bu-ru. Merit becomes me-ri-to. Baseball becomes be-su bo-ru, and so on.

Until the foreign student of the Japanese language becomes used to this system, communication can be ragged, because of the number of such words used and because they do not appear in most textbooks on the language.

An interesting aspect of the Japanese propensity to pronouce English words in Japanese is the fact that some people are so familiar with such pronounciation that it is possible to communiate with them entirely in English as long as you pronounce everything as if it were Japanese.

LOCATION / BASHO (Bah-show)

Shaped like a crescent that extends for 3,000 kilometers (1,860 miles) from north to the northwest, Japan lies off the east coast of Asia, parallel to southern Siberia on the north and the southern tip of the Korean Peninsula on the South.

Tokyo is on almost exactly the same latitude as Los Angeles, Athens and Tehran, and five degrees south of New York, Beijing and Ankara.

LOVE AND MARRIAGE

More than 70 percent of young unmarried Japanese women say they prefer to find their own husbands, instead of their parents or a matchmaker arranging a marriage for them. Approximately 80 percent of all single girls in Japan date before they are 20, and between 70 and 80 percent of those who are between 20 and 24 believe premarital sex is all right between those who love each other.

While the overwhelming majority of young Japanese women prefer a love marriage, only about half of them say they would insist on the right to choose their own spouse.

Between 60 and 70 percent of the unmarried young women who are employed say they want to continue working after marriage. About the same proportion of Japanese women feel that sexual equality in Japan has a long way to go. The only areas in which true equality exists, they say, is in cultural and recreational activities.

LUCK / UN (Uun)

Like people everywhere, the Japanese have many lucky and unlucky signs, some of them going back to ancient times--and some of them similar to Western superstitions.

Some of the best-known ones:

If your nose itches, someone you know will have a baby. If you sneeze once, someone is saying nice things about you. If you sneeze twice, someone is talking ill about you. If you sneeze three times, someone loves you. If you sneeze four times, you've caught a cold.

If the first person you meet after leaving home in the morning is a woman, it will be a good day. If it is a Buddhist priest, you're in for trouble. If you are out in the open and bird-droppings fall on you, it is a good omen.

When the cord on your zori or geta breaks, you are in for bad news or some misfortune. If a funeral procession overtakes you on the street, it's a bad luck sign. If a snake crosses the road in front of you, money will come in unexpectedly.

If your ear itches, you will soon hear some good news. If you break a mirror you're in for bad luck, especially if you are a woman. If you stare at someone over your rice bowl (while holding it close to your mouth and eating) you will get uglier as you get older.

MAGAZINES / ZASSHI (Zah-she)

Japan's first magazine, Seiyo Zasshi, was founded in 1867, the year the Tokugawa Shogunate gave up power over the country. This was followed by more than 180 other publications within the next decade, including the well-known Meiroku Zasshi, which appeared in 1874.

These first magazines were take-offs on the journals brought to Japan by Dutch traders during the last years of the Shogunate. Most of them were aimed at educating their readers in Western thought, scholarship and culture.

The next decade saw another boom in the inauguration of new magazines, primarily as a result of the promulgation of the Meiji Constitution. By 1888 there were more than 200 political magazines in the country.

Among the magazine publishers that emerged during this period were Hakubunkan, which quickly developed a large number of low-priced general interest publications, and Jitsugyo-no Nippon Sha, which was founded in 1900. This latter company soon passed Hakubunkan as the country's leading magazine publisher, largely because it developed a system of paying sales commissions to retailers and allowing them to return unsold magazines. By 1907 there were over 400 magazines in Japan.

The present-day giant Kodansha was founded in 1910. Its first magazine, Yuben (Yuu-bane) became a bestseller, as did its Kodan Kurabu (Koe-dahn Kuu-rah-buu), Shonen Kurabu (Show-nane), and several other publications. Kingu (Keen-guu), one of these new magazines, became the first Japanese magazine to achieve a million circulation, in 1927.

By 1931, Kodansha was selling nearly five and a half million magazines a month, or some 80 percent of the market. Increasing governemnt controls and paper shortages devastated the magazine industry during the late 1930s and war years. In 1944 the government forced the closure of all but 996 magazines, and eventually all of these ceased publication.

Freed of wartime controls in 1945, magazine publishers began trying to make a comeback. By getting a special paper allotment from the Allied Occupation authorities, Reader's Digest quickly pushed the circulation of its Japanese edition to 1.4 million copies. Kingu, so

successful before the war, was unable to make a comeback, and its place was taken by Heibon (Hay-e-bone), which emphasized music and films.

There were 4,581 publishers in Japan in 1948, but this fell back to 1,541 by 1953. In 1956, the appearance of Shukan Shincho (Shuu-khan Sheen-choe), the first weekly magazine not published by a newspaper company, heralded the beginning of a weekly magazine boom, which resulted in more than 70 weeklies by 1960.

One of the most popular genre of magazines to appear at this time were the manga (mahn-gah), or comics. Literally hundreds of them appeared, and four of them now have circulations of over one million a week.

There are currently some 2,000 monthly magazines (235 new monthlies were founded in 1980 and 184 new ones in 1981). Not all of the new ones survive, but the overall number continues to climb upward.

The two categories with the largest number of magazines are popular interest (247) and engineering (204). Other categories and their approximate number of magazines are children's (146), women's (27), general interest (77), literary (64), performing arts (30), fine arts (31), music (49), living (105), hobbies (177), sports (78), economics (163), social problems (25), current topics (43), philosophy (26), textbook aids (33), linguistics (33), education (113), geography/history (17), law (28), science (36), medicine (103), and agriculture/fisheries (26).

The total annual print-run of all these monthlies amounts to some 1,846,700,000, of which some 26 percent do not sell (are returned by the retail and wholesale outlets). This means approximately one and one-third trillion monthly magazines are bought in Japan each year.

Among the best-known of the general interest monthly magazines are: Chuo Koron, a serious, high-brow publication that treats political, economic, social and cultural subjects in depth, and is a leader in the field of opionion journalism. Bungei Shunju, the most widely read of Japan's middle-class general interest magazines, which appeals to the modern tastes but traditional sentiments of the Japanese). Gendai, which covers social and economic issues of special interest to the white-collar class. Shosetsu Shincho, a literary publication that runs columns on hobbies and stories by leading writers. And Ohru Yomimono, a

Matsushima, famed beauty spot. P. 202

The "floating shrine" of Miyajima. P. 126

famous fiction publication that awards the prestigious Naoki Literary Prize and the Cartoon Award.

There are 57 well-established weekly magazines in Japan, with an estimated annual printing of one and one-third trillion. The annual rate of returns (unsold) copies of weekly magazines is about 20.5 percent of all printed.

Weekly magazines include seven in the children's field, three women's magazines, 16 popular interest, 14 general interest, 14 specialized and 3 sports magazines.

In addition to their regular issues, some monthly and weekly magazines in Japan also publish one or more supplements each year. This adds some 70 million copies to the overall number of magazines printed.

Top names in the weekly magazine field include several published by the giant newspaper companies. Shukan Asahi, a mix of light and heavy articles, is aimed at students, women and businessmen. Sunday Mainichi (the oldest weekly in Japan), specializes in documentary-type features of general interest. Shukan Yomiuri serializes novels, and runs comments on current events, hobbies and entertainment. And the Shukan Sankei, which runs in-depth stories on events and sidelights skimmed by the daily newspapers.

Other major weeklies are Shukan Gendai (practical information for a predominately male readership), and Asahi Geino (fiction, news and gossip about the entertainment world).

Many Japanese publications are affiliated with foreign publications, and some publish Japanese editions of well-known foreign magazines. There has been a Japanese edition of Playboy, for example, since the 1960s. The Japanese edition of Reader's Digest is one of the most successful publications in the country.

MAINICHI NEWSPAPER / MAINICHI SHIMBUN (My-nee-chee Shim-boon)

Japan's great Mainichi Shimbun originated in Osaka, as did the Asahi Shimbun. They were the first of Japan's major newspapers to take a commercial approach as opposed to a political approach in publishing. By 1912, both the Mainichi and the Asahi had begun to make inroads into the Tokyo area.

It was to be a national disaster--the Great Kanto Earthquake of 1923--that was to bring the two newspapers to Tokyo in force. The earthquake destroyed the printing plants and office facilities of newspapers in both Tokyo and Yokohama, and the Mainichi and Asahi jumped in to fill the vacuum. See NEWSPAPERS.

MAJOR JAPANESE COMPANIES

Nearly one-third of the world's 500 largest companies outside of the U.S. are Japanese. The largest of the Japanese companies--not necessarily in the order of rank--include Toyota Motor Company, Nissan Motor Company, Nippon Steel Corporation, Hitachi, Matsushita, Mitsubishi Heavy Industries, Idemitsu (Oil) Company, Tokyo Shibaura Electric (Toshiba), Nippon Kokan and Toa Nenryo Kogyo.

Also, Maruzen Oil, Honda Motor Company, Sumitomo Metal Industries, Mitsubishi Electric, Kawasaki Steel, Toyo Kogyo, Kobe Steel, Taiyo Fishery Company, Mitsubishi Oil, Mitsubishi Chemical Industries, Sanyo Electric, Nippon Mining Company, Showa Oil, Daikyo Oil, Sony, Nippon Electric, Ishikawajima-Harima Heavy Industries, Sumitomo Chemical, Asahi-Chemical, Bridgestone Tire, Isuzu Motors, and Snow Brand Milk Products.

And, Komatsu, Kawasaki Dockyard, Toyo Rayon, Fujitsu, Mitsui Chemicals, Kubota Iron and Machinery Works, Ube Industries, Nippon Denso, Showa Denko, Furukawa Electric, Asahi Glass, Matsushita Electric Works, Sharp, Sumitomo Electric Industries, Kanegafuchi Spinning, Dai Nippon Printing, Koa Oil and Fuji Photo Film Company. See TRADING COMPANIES.

MANAGEMENT / MANEJIMENTO (Mah-nay-jee-mane-to)

There are several key characteristics pertaining to Japan's world-famous management system. Decision-making is based on a collective consensus. Larger firms practice life-time employment, with promotions and wages based on seniority. Unions are company unions instead of trade unions (with the exception of the seaman's union and a few others). The ratio of borrowed capital is high. There is widespread use of subsidiary and affiliated companies for parts manufacturing, and dependence on the importation of raw materials and the exportation of finished products.

Takashi Ishihara, president of the immensely successful Nissan Motor Company Ltd. in the 1970s and 80s, summed up the secret of Japanese management in two words: corporate vitality, which he said was derived from two sources: (1) The separation of ownership and management, whereby managers are able to make decisions based on long-term company interests, free from the narrow self-interest of owners.

And (2), The fact that Japanese companies tend to be especially well organized, from top to bottom, into highly motivated groups whose primary concern is the long-term growth of the companies.

Ishihara explained that the stock of most major Japanese companies is held by a combination of banks, insurance companies and other businesses, along with a wide variety of public investors, whose primary goals are long-range capital gains.

Managers are therefore free to manage as they see fit, concentrating on long-term growth. This important management feature is reflected in active longterm investments in plants and equipment, he said.

Ishihara added a number of other points that I first began preaching about in 1958--namely, that Japanese companies are social enterprises first and commercial enterprises second. That perpetuation of the company and winning as much of the market as possible take precedence over short-term profits and dividends. That managers work their way up through the ranks, and are part of a human chain that links management with workers.

Also, that the personal nature of the relationships between all employees in a company provides for a high degree of empathy that prevents jobs from be regarded as slots and people from being treated like cogs.

Of course, virtual life-time employment and practically no turnover at all in management personnel is a vital ingredient in the success of Japanese management.

One of the dual concepts that is central to understanding and dealing with the Japanese, in both business and personal matters, is the tatamae (tah-tay-my) / honne (hone-nay) factor.

Tatemae means something like framework or facade, while honne refers to real interests or real intent.

In keeping with their deeply ingrained practice of avoiding conflict, the Japanese first present a general idea of what they are talking about or want--the tatemae. Only later, and gradually, does the honne or real aim emerge.

For a detailed analysis of the unique Japanese management system, and the day-to-day practice of business in Japan, see the author's JAPANESE MANNERS β ETHICS IN BUSINESS (Phoenix Books/Publishers), first brought out in 1960, and HOW TO DO BUSINESS IN JAPAN, first published in 1962. Both have been revised several times.

The Japanese government and Japanese businessmen in general are concerned about the problems that arise from management differences around the world, and have initiated a number of programs to help relieve the situation.

As of July 1983, foreign companies became eligible to join the Japanese Management Association as Associate Members, and may participate in programs and services conducted in English for their benefit.

The aim of the JMA Associate Member system is to provide foreign managers with information about management and productivity in Japan through forums, newsletters, special reports and other publications.

For details about the program, contact the Associate Members' Department, Japan Management Association, 3-1-22 Shiba Park, Minato-Ku, Tokyo 105, Japan.

MANYOSHU (Mahn-yoe-shuu) / COLLECTION OF 10,000 LEAVES

The outstanding literary work of Japan's Nara Period (600-784), was the Manyoshu, an anthology of over 4,500 poems, compiled by the poet Yakamochi Otomo in the 8th century.

The collection contains poems written in many styles, dating from as early as the 4th century, and written by people in all classes, from emperors and members of the nobility to the poorest of common people.

Poems in the anthology are classified as seasonal, love poems, allegorical and occasional. Among the hundreds of poets represented in the work are Akahito and Hitomaro, who are ranked among Japan's Six Great Poets.

The British diplomat F. V. Dickins published an English translation of the Manyoshu in 1906. Translations from the work were also made by another, better known British diplomat/scholar, W. G. Aston.

Altogether, the Manyoshu totals over 120 volumes, with tanka poems (31 syllables) predominating, followed by choka (long poems). One of the best known of the Manyoshu poems is W. G. Aston's translation of one called In Praise of Yamato (Yamato being the early name for Japan). It goes:

> The land of Yamato
> Has mountains in numbers,
> But peerless among them
> Is high Kaguyama.
> I stand on its summit
> My kingdom to view.
> The smoke from the land-plain
> Rises thick in the air,
> The gulls from the sea-plain
> By fits soar aloft.
> O land of Yamato!
> Fair Akitsu-shima!
> Dear art thou to me.

MARRIAGE / KEKKON (Keck-kone)

Prior to 1945, most marriages in Japan were omiai (oh-me-aye), that is, arranged by the parents, a close relative, an employer or a professional go-between. Today, some 70 percent of all marriages in the country are classifed as renai (rain-aye), or love marriages.

In arranged marriages, the couples are brought together to get acquainted only after both families are satisfied that they would make a suitable match from the viewpoint of social, economic and educational standing. Then if the couples approve and like each other, marriage follows.

Most weddings in Japan take place in wedding halls or hotels that have large ballrooms and cater specifically to wedding parties. The better-to-do the families, the more elaborate and splendid the wedding parties. Many parties have 500 or more guests, and may cost well over ∫200 per person.

Weddings may consist of Shinto rites, in which the bride dresses in traditional kimono and the groom in traditional male attire. They exchange O'sake (Oh-sah-kay) wine cups as a symbol of their troth and receive the blessings of a Shinto priest.

Some weddings incorporate Western customs. One that I recently witnessed was held in a famous Chinese restaurant in Harajuku, Tokyo. The bride wore a kimono. The groom wore a tuxedo. They marched into the restaurant to the tune of Here Comes the Bride. After a Shinto ceremony, the couple cut a huge cake with a Samurai sword.

The kimono typically worn by a Japanese bride is the uchikake (Uu-chee-kah-kay), which has a long train, is embroidered with gold and silver threads in bird or flower designs, and is regarded as the most beautiful of all the kimono.

Guests who attend weddings generally bring monetary gifts in special money envelopes. Several members of the party--friends, relatives, employers--make speeches, recounting personal details about the bride and groom, sometimes to their embarrassment. When the wedding is over, the guests are usually presented with a gift from the families of the couple.

At present, the average age of Japanese men at marriage is 27.7. For women it is 25.2.

One lady entreprenuer in the Kansai (Osaka-Kobe-Kyoto) area has built 32 Wedding Palaces where over 45,000 couples a year take advantage of her wedding package--which includes planning, invitations, the ceremony (Buddhist, Shinto or Christian), a banquet of any style, gifts for the guests, and honeymoon arrangements.

On a Taian (Tie-on) lucky day in the fall, several hundred couples tie the knot at these huge halls.

MASSAGERS / AMMA (Ahm-mah)

The practice of massaging was introduced into Japan from China during the 6th and 7th centuries, and the art is mentioned prominently in the Taiho Law of 701. The popularity of the practice waned in the middle ages, but was revived in the 1600s and remains popular in Japan today.

In the Tokugawa period (1603-1868), the profession was reserved exclusively for those who were blind, and the training, by apprenticeship to a master, was long and difficult.

Following the Meiji Restoration in 1868, the profession was opened up to anyone, but it was necessary to pass a government examination to obtain a license. In earlier times, amma announced their presence in neighborhoods by blowing on a flute. In some rural areas they may still be heard, but in the cities, amma are called in by phone.

Amma are especially popular at hot-spring resorts.

MARTIAL ARTS / BUJUTSU (Buu-jute-sue)

The Japanese have apparently always been avid sportsmen, and with the rise of the military class in the 12th century, several martial arts became an important part of the training of the bushi (buu-she) or warriors. These skills included sword-fighting (kenjutsu), sword-drawing (iaijutsu), unarmed combat (jujutsu), archery (kyujutsu), spear handling (sojutsu), horsemanship (bajutsu), and swimming (suijutsu).

From the 15th century on, these martial arts were gradually standardized into schools, and systematized during the long peaceful Tokugawa Shogunate (1603-1868). With the fall of the Shogunate in 1868, interest in the martial arts declined. But with the outbreak of war with China in 1894, this interest was revived and promoted by the government, as militaristic nationalism came to the fore.

In 1895 all martial arts came under the centralized control of the Great Japan Martial Arts Association (Dai Nippon Butoku Kai), and became a part of the national education system in 1911.

In 1926 the term jutsu (arts) was dropped from the names of several of the disciplines, and do (way) was introduced. Thus kenjutsu became kendo, and jujutsu became judo.

Martial arts were banned in Japan by the Allied Occupation Forces in 1945, but the ban was lifted in 1950 and thereafter the arts developed rapidly as

sports instead of martial training.

Judo was added to the Tokyo Olympic Games in 1964, and the first World Kendo Tournament was held at the Japan Martial Arts Hall (Nippon Budokan) in 1970. The World Union of Karate-Do Organizations was also formed and held its first World Championship matches in Tokyo in 1970.

See individual listings for AIKIDO, JUDO, KARATE, KENDO.

Recommended reading: MODERN BUJUTSU AND BUDO, by Donn Draeger (Weatherhill). Also CLASSICAL BUJUTSU, by Donn Draeger, (Weatherhill).

MARU (Mah-rue)

Most people who have anything to do with Japan have asked about or wondered about the meaning of the word maru, which is used as a suffix to the names of passenger liners, merchant ships, fishing boats and yachts (not warships, which use kan/kahn).

Unfortunately, there is no agreement on what the word means or how it came to be applied to ships. One version has that it is a corruption of the word maro, which refers to something valuable or is a term of endearment. Another opinion states that it refers to a person bent over in a circle, taking refuge from the dangers of the sea.

Still another version says that merchants centuries ago used the word to denote a family business, and when they went into the shipping business, maru was attached to indicate it was a family owned ship.

Honmaru refers to the central tower of a castle, and means within the circle, which is the innermost and most protected part of the castle. Since a ship at sea is a man's castle, maru just might have carried over from this usage.

MARUNOUCHI (Mah-rue-no-uu-chee)

The Maruouchi district of Chiyoda Ward in central Tokyo is usually described as the business center of the city, but there are other business centers, such as Otemachi adjoining it on the north, that might dispute the description.

In any event, Marunouchi, which encompasses the area directly in front of the Imperial Palace, has enough of the city's major buildings and companies to hold its own.

These include Tokyo Central Post Office, Tokyo Metropolitan Office, Japanese National Railways Building, Japan Travel Bureau Building, the old and new Marunouchi Buildings, Tokyo Chamber of Commerce and Industry Building, NYK

Building, Kaijo Building, numerous banks, Mitsubishi Shoji, and so on.

Old timers will remember that until the 1960s, much of the area was taken up by three and four-story British style red brick buildings, and was the preserve, so to speak, of the Mitsubishi group of companies. All of the old brick buildings have long since been replaced by beautiful modern buildings, and the area has a totally international, cosmopolitan look.

The story of the Marunouchi district, if I remember it correctly, is typical of the entrepreneurial spirit of leading Japanese businessmen. During the long Tokugawa Shogunate (1603-1868), the district was the site for Daimyo mansions, each of which had a name that ended in maru, and the whole area was referred to as Marunouchi, which can be translated rather generally as The Daimyo Mansions.

When the feudal Daimyo system ended in 1868, the district became government property. The mansions eventually burned down or were razed, and the area was turned into an army drilling grounds and barracks.

In 1890, the budget of the Imperial Diet was cut so drastically by the Opposition, that it resolved to sell the Marunouchi district in order to raise needed funds for various government projects. By this time, the area was a vast weed-covered field.

The government offered the land to the top Zaibatsu families (Mitsui, Mitsubishi, Okura, Shibusawa, etc.) on a bid basis. Finally, Yataro Iwasaki, head of the Mitsubishi family, agreed to buy the area for the then princely sum of 1,500,000 yen--an act that resulted in him being called a fool by less far-sighted individuals. But he was acting on the wise counsel of the banto (manager) of Mitsubishi, Heigoro Soda, who had been in London where he heard how the Lord of Westminister had become immensely wealthy because he owned land in downtown London. Soda urged Iwasaki to buy the land.

Years later, Soda began developing the land, first by putting in a wide, paved boulevard, and then constructing brick and stone buildings along the avenue. It was not until the completion of Tokyo Central Station right in the center of Marunouchi in 1914 that the area began to boom.

By 1921 some of the largest and most important buildings in Japan were situated in the Marunouchi district, but it was the great earthquake of 1923 that turned the area into the business center of Tokyo. Fires following the quake destroyed the majority of the wooden office buildings in central Tokyo, leaving the brick and stone buildings in the Marunouchi district untouched.

Hundreds of companies took up temporary quarters in the area, and many of them were to stay as new buildings were put up to accommodate them.

In the 1960s and 1970s, all of the old English-style brick buildings that had been the hallmark of Marunouchi were replaced by modern highrise office buildings, making it one of the most profitable and valuable pieces of property in the world.

MATSUSHIMA (Mot-sue-she-mah)
On the coast of northeastern Honshu an hour's ride from the city of Sendai, Matsushima is famed as one of the three most scenic spots in Japan. Matsushima means Pine-Clad Island, but refers instead to a bay filled with pine-clad islands--over 260 of them.

Most of the islands of Matsushima Bay are formed of strata of volcanic tuff. Others consist of white sandstone. The range of sizes and shapes of the islands staggers the imagination. Some are mere pinnacles protruding up from the water. Others are large enough to be inhabited.

The winds and water have created archways, caves and tunnels, in the islands, and sculptured the pine trees that cover most of them into countless forms. Viewed from any position, in any kind of weather, the bay presents a picture of nature at the height of its glory.

Some people prefer to view Matsuhima following a snow, others at dawn on a clear day. The island-dotted bay is equally enchanting in rain or on a moonlit night when the light glistens on the water, setting the islands off like jewels.

On shore, on a rocky clif adjoining Matsushima-Kaigan Pier, is a pavilion called Kanrantei (Wave-Viewing Pavilion), built in the 1590s by Hideyoshi Toyotomi and presented to Masamune Date, the Lord of Sendai, as a viewpoint for enjoying the beauty of Matsushima. The sliding door screens in the pavilion were painted by Sanraku Kano, one of the foremost artists of this era.

Next to the Kanrantei is the Matsushima Museum, which contains heirlooms that belonged to the Date family, along with samples of local products.

Besides the Kanrantei pavilion, there are four public viewpoints for enjoying Matsushima Bay that have been celebrated for centuries. These are located at the four corners of Matsushima, and are Tomiyama, Otakamori, Tamonzan and Ogidani. The second of these viewpoints is located on one of the bay islands--Miyato--the largest one in the group, which has some 1,500 residents.

See DATE, MASAMUNE. SENDAI.

MATSUSHITA ELECTRIC INDUSTRIAL COMPANY (Mot-sue-sshtah)

The Matsushita Electric Industrial Company is, of course, one of the largest and most successful companies in the world. The point to be made here is not about the size and success of the company but the philosophy that made the company so successful.

The company was founded in 1918 by Konnosuke Matsushita, who is regarded as the greatest businessman of 20th century Japan. Born into dire poverty, Matsushita had to quit school at the age of nine to go to work as an errand boy. His health was so frail he resigned himself to imminent death several times.

But Matsushita persevered. His philosophy was based on the concept that an enterprise as a whole is as good or as bad as the abilities of the individual employees--not all of the employees as a group. All employees are treated as individuals, and every effort is made to enable them to develope their potential to the fullest. Matsushita holds that a business exists only to contribute to society--not to pursue the goal of profit.

The Matsushita approach to business management epitomizes the Japanese concept of group spirit. It has also been called management by intuition, from Matsushita's lifelong practice of meditating to achieve intellectual and spiritual harmony with the cosmos, and to tap into the universal mind.

Recommended reading: THE MATSUSHITA PHENOMENON, by Rowland Gould (Diamond Sha).

MEDICAL CARE

Some 97 percent of all medical services in Japan are administered through National Health Insurance or Kokumin Kenko Hoken (Koe-kuu-mean Kane-koe Hoe-kane), a government sponsored, tax-supported program which covers from 50 to 70 percent of medical care.

This program is available to foreigners living and working in Japan, but the percentage the patient pays is based on a sliding scale pegged to income, and can be very expensive for someone drawing a high salary. For those who are not

in the program, the fact that medical treatment is going to be expensive is a foregone conclusion.

The primary reason for the high expense of private medical care is that less than three percent of Japan's doctors are in private practice. The overwhelming majority are involved in the national health insurance program.

The doctors who are in private practice operate their own clinics, some of which are as large as modest hospitals, and offer similar services at far higher costs.

Japanese hospitals are spartan by American standards. The families of patients provide them with many of the things they need--sometimes even linen and eating utensils. Families also spend more time visiting patients and helping take care of them.

Most Japanese hospitals are closed to outside (nonstaff) doctors, and with few exceptions, private doctors or consultants are not permitted to treat patients admitted to hospitals. Individuals may admit themselves into hospitals without going through a doctor. A doctor without special connections with a specific hospital cannot refer patients to it.

If a patient is referred to a hospital by a doctor on the staff, the chances of faster and possibly better treatment are vastly improved.

Hospital doctors work on rotating shifts, as do hospitals. Emergency rooms are often not open after 5 p.m. There are often long lines of people waiting in the reception areas of hospitals, and beds are often lacking. Patients may ask for a specific doctor, but this usually entails a much longer waiting period.

The medical profession in Japan centers around the universities from which the doctors graduate, and the affiliated university hospitals. Six years of schooling is usually followed by about five years of internship at at one of the university's hospitals.

Interns often develop unofficial side practices in order to earn enough money to sustain themselves. And doctors employed by hospitals may also operate their own clinics as a means of increasing their income.

In all of Japan's major cities there are doctors in private practice, clinics and hospitals--often affiliated with religions organizations--who cater especially to foreign residents and visitors. They advertise in local English-language media, and are easy to find.

MEIJI (May-e-jee)

Meiji (Great Period) is the name given to the reign of Emperor Mutsuhito who became emperor in 1868 when he was 16 and reigned until his death in 1912, at which time it became his posthumous name. Meiji proved to be an enlightened and able leader and is ranked among the greatest heroes of Japan.

The transfer of power from the Tokugawa Shogunate to the Imperial Court in 1868 is known as the Meiji Restoration. See MEIJI MEMORIAL PICTURE GALLERY, MEIJI PARK, MEIJI SHRINE.

MEIJI MEMORIAL PICTURE GALLERY

Built in memory of Emperor Meiji who died in 1912, the Meiji Memorial Picture Gallery is a large impressive building that is the centerpiece of Meiji Park (which was originally a huge garden estate).

The gallery was built to house 115 great paintings that show memorable scenes during the life and reign of the famous Emperor, beginning with his birth in Kyoto, his death in Tokyo and his internment at the Grand Shrine of Ise.

Half of the paintings, all done by Japanese masters, are in Japanese style. The others are in Western style. The paintings are so arranged in the gallery that visitors may walk through the history of the Meiji period from beginning to end.

In front of each painting is an inscribed plaque that describes the scene depicted, in both Japanese and English. The plaques were redone in 1982, at which time the author of this book at the extraordinary pleasure of writing the English inscriptions.

MEIJI PARK

Officially known as Meiji Shrine Outer Garden and more recently as Meiji Olympic Park, this large landscaped area within central Tokyo was once the private garden and estate of a Daimyo feudal lord.

Beginning in 1912, the grounds were turned into a huge public park and recreational area, and have since been one of the most popular spots in Tokyo. Among the important facilities in the park is the National Stadium, which has a seating capacity of 85,000.

Also in the park are the Jingu Baseball Stadiums (No. 1 and No. 2), the Prince Chichibu Rugby Football Stadium, the Tokyo Gyynasium, the Metrpolitan Indoor Swimming Pool, the Meiji Memorial Picture Gallery, and Meiji Memorial Hall.

MEIJI SHRINE / MEIJI JINJA (May-e-jee Jeen-jah)

Near Harajuku Station in western Tokyo, Meiji Shrine is one of the largest, most beautiful and most popular in Japan. Dedicated to Emperor Meiji who reigned from 1868 to 1912, it was completed in 1920 following a national outpouring of support that was unprecedented.

The grounds of the shrine cover an area of 72.4 ha. and are known as the Inner Garden. There are several entrances to the shrine. The main one, adjoining Jingu Bridge next to Harajuku Station, requires a walk of close to half a mile to reach the principal shrine.

Each of the entrances is marked by a huge torii made of cypress wood that is over 1,700 years old. Behind the main shrine is a Treasure House where many of the things owned and used by the Emperor and Empress are on display.

Set amidst a forest of trees and shrubs donated by people from all over the country, including a large iris garden, and constructed in the traditional Shinto style, the shrine is one of the most impresive structures in Japan.

Many festivals are held each year at the shrine, with the most important being November 1, November 3 and May 3.

On New Year's eve, several hundred thousand people begin converging on Harajuku just before midnight, marching enmasse up the major thoroughfares, to worship at the shrine just after midnight—a traditional pilgrimage known as Hatsu-mairi or the First Visit (to a shrine or temple) of the new year.

MEIJI VILLAGE / MEIJI MIURA (May-e-jee Me-uu-rah)

Adjoining a lake in the foothills about an hour from Nagoya, Miura Village is an open-air museum that contains 65 buildings of the Meiji era (1868-1912) on a 250-acre wooded and landscaped site.

The village, which is visited by more than a million people a year, was created by architect/engineer Yoshiro Taniguchi and Motomo Tsuchikawa, a high school friend who rose to become vice president of the Nagoya Railroad Company.

Concerned that the distinctive architecture of the Meiji period would be totally lost, Taniguchi persuaded Tsuchikawa to raise the money needed to buy the land and buildings and move them to the site.

The village has homes, business,

churches, a railroad, prison, a lighthouse, shops, etc. It also has the front and lobby of the famous old Imperial Hotel, which was designed by Frank Lloyd Wright. (See IMPERIAL HOTEL.) The museum is open to sightseers daily, for a modest fee.

MIKOSHI (Me-koe-she)

This is the portable shrine, some huge in size, that celebrants carry on their shoulders during festivals. The mikoshi symbolizes the shrine sponsoring the festival and is the temporary abode of the shrine God or Goddess during the event. Some of the mikoshi seen throughout Japan each year have not changed in more than a thousand years.

It is customary for the men and women who carry the mikoshi to dress in traditional attire, to swing and sway as they march through the streets to simulate revelry, and to shout Yoisa! Yoisa! to attract the spirit of the shrine.

MINAMOTO, YORITOMO (Me-nah-moe-toe, Yoe-ree-toe-moe)

One of the best-known names in Japanese history, Yoritomo Minamoto was the leader of one of the greatest warrior families, and the man who founded the Shogunate form of government that was to last from 1192 until 1868.

The Minamoto clan, also known as the Genji, were one of many warrior clans that became very powerful in the 11th and 12th centuries, and began to struggle against each other and against the now weakened noble families that had controlled Japan since 660 A.D.

Born in 1147, Yoritomo and his half-brother Yoshitsune waged a 35-year war against the Taira clan (Heike), finally annihilating the clan, the young emperor and several members of the Imperial Court at the sea battle of Danno-Ura in 1185. (The infant Emperor's grandmother took him in her arms and leaped into the sea, followed by his mother and their ladies-in-waiting.)

Following the Battle of Danno-Ura, Yoshitsune married a Taira, earning the wrath of Yoritomo, who set out to destroy him. See MINAMOTO, YOSHITSUNE.

Having achieved military supremacy throughout Japan, and exercising control over the enthronement of a new emperor who became just a figurehead, Yoritomo set up his military headquarters at Kamakura, far away from Kyoto.

In 1192, Yoritomo had himself appointed Shogun by the Emperor--an old title that had been used several hundred years before to designate generals sent a-gainst the Ainu, the Cacausoid race that inhabited central and northern Japan when the Japanese arrived. It translates very well as Generalissimo.

Yoritomo died in 1199, and was succeeded in turn by his two sons, Yoriie and Sanetomo. But Sanetomo was assassinated by his nephew in 1219, bringing an end to the Minamoto House. The Hojo family, the leading advisors to the Shogunate, invited the noble Yoritsune Fujiwara from Kyoto to become Shogun, but the actual power of the government was usurped by Yoshitoko Hojo, whose family was to continue as regents for the military government until 1333.

MINAMOTO, YOSHITSUNE (Me-nah-moe-toe Yoe-sheet-sue-nay)

One of the most romanticized figures in Japan's history, Yoshitsune Minamoto, the younger half-brother of Yoritomo, the man who establshed Japan's first Shogunate, was born in 1159, the 9th son of Yoshitomo Minamoto.

When his father was defeated by Kiyomori Taira, Yoshitsune's life was spared and he was sent to Kuramayama Temple in Kyoto. With the help of a metal dealer named Kichiji, he escaped and fled to northern Japan, where he lived with the family of Hidehira Fujiwara, a branch of the famous noble house that had ruled Japan since 660.

In Mutsu, he spent his early years learning the skills of war and other martial arts, and in 1180, when he was 21, he joined his half-brother Yoritomo who was gathering an army in Izu to go against the Taira clan.

Yoshitsune's skill, daring and courage made him a very successful general-- so much so that his brother became suspicious of his ambitions. After the great Battle of Danno-Ura, at which the Taira were eliminated, Yoshitsune married the daughter of Lord Taira. This made Yoritomo believe Yoshitsune had turned against him.

Yoritomo sent a troop of warriors to kill Yoshitsune, but one of the younger man's faithful friends, Benkei, whom he had met in Mutsu, saved his life. The two of them, along with a small band of trusted retainers, then fled into the mountains of Yoshino.

There the small group was accosted by a band of dangerous yamabushi (yah-mah-buu-she) or itenerant priests, who infested the area and were on Yoritomo's side. This time Yoshitsune was saved by his retainer Tadanobu.

Thereafter, there are conflicting stories about what happened to the popular young warrior, including several more close calls in which his large friend Benkei played a prominent role. But it is known that Yoshitsune was able to reach the castle of Koromogawa where he expected to find his old protector Hidehira Fujiwara.

Hidehira had died, however, and been succeeded by his cowardly son, Yasuhira, who quickly betrayed Yoshitsune, his wife and friends to Yoritomo's agents. The small band of refugees were either killed or committed harakiri.

MINING / KOGYO (Koag-yoe)

Mining is an old and well-established industry in Japan, but the industry is in trouble. Discovering and developing ore deposits is difficult because of convoluted mountainous terrain. The productivity of existing mines is declining, while the age of the miners and the cost of mining is going up. The ores that are found in Japan contain a relatively large percentage of impurities, and pollution problems are becoming increasingly serious.

Among the ores that are mined in Japan: copper, lead, zinc, bauxite, iron, manganese, dolomite and limestone. Except for limestone and sulfide ore, Japan imports most of the minerals it needs, including iron ore, tin, bauxite, copper and coal.

MINSHUKU (Meen-shuu-kuu)

Japan's not-so-well-known minshuku deserved to be better known. They are people's lodges, or inns that are more modest than the popular ryokan and a lot less expensive.

Altogether there are some 24,000 minshuku in Japan, of which approximately 200 have been designated as International Minshuku, meaning their facilities and services are adequate to fit the needs and expectations of most foreign visitors.

Minshuku are run by their family-owners, and are traditional Japanese style, with breakfast, supper and usually a Japanese bath (some have showers). Besides the savings, minshuku offer the foreign visitor to Japan an opportunity to experience Japanese life as it has been lived for centuries.

Guests are expected to bring their own personal articles, and it doesn't hurt to have a towel or two of your own, along with a small supply of toilet paper if you are going into a distant rural area.

Most minshuku are located on farms, in fishing villages, at resorts and near temples.

For detailed information about minshuku, contact the Japan Minshuku Association, Kotsu Kaikan Bldg., 2-10-1 Yurakucho, Chiyoda-ku, Tokyo, Japan, or any of the offices of the Japan National Tourist Organization.

MISHIMA, YUKIO (Yuu-kee-oh, Me-she-mah)

One of Japan's most briliant and controversial 20th century writers, Yukio Mishima was born in 1925 and committed ritual suicide in the way of a Samurai in 1971, at the age of 46.

Mishima wrote novels and plays of extraordinary power and beauty. More of his works have been translated into English than those of any other Asian writer, and during his life-time he was often mentioned as a candidate for the Nobel Prize in literature.

Besides his writing, which he did at night, Mishima was a devotee of the way of Bushido, the ethics of the Samurai of feudal Japan, and was also a champion bodybuilder.

Mishima was a strong nationalist, and trained and equipped his own small elite military force. In 1971, he and his men broke into the Tokyo headquarters of the national self-defense force and attempted to persuade the commanding general to participate in a coup.

Rebuffed by the military and under siege in the office he had seized, Mishima disemboweled himself in the honored tradition of the Samurai, after which his chief aide cut his head off with a sword.

Among Mishima's best-known books are THE TEMPLE OF THE GOLDEN PAVILION, THE SOUND OF WAVES, FIVE MODERN NOH PLAYS, and SUN AND STEEL.

I met Mishima in the 1960s when he was at the height of his fame, and admired him for his dedication to writing, to the development of his body and mind, and for the pursuit of his ideals--but had no thought of where his zeal would lead him.

MISSIONARIES / DENDOSHI (Dane-doe-she)

The very first foreign missionaries in Japan were from Korea and China, probably sometime between 300 and 500 A.D. The first Western missionary of record was Francis Xavier, a Spanish Jesuit who arrived in Kagoshima from Malacca in 1549.

The country was involved in clan warfare at that time, as leading feudal lords (Daimyo) fought to claim power from the weakened and ineffective Ashikaga Shogunate.

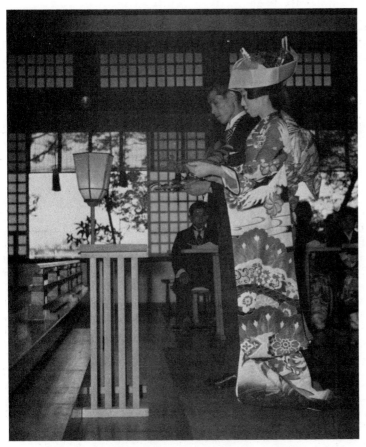

Getting married Shinto style. P. 200

Nagasaki's "Dragon Fesvital." P. 219

The Lord of Satsuma (in Kagoshima) was impressed with Xavier and the gifts he brought, and gave him permission to teach Christianity in the Satsuma fief. Xavier stayed in Japan for 10 months, during which time he made arrangements for other Jesuits to follow him.

Because of the turmoil of the times, several other feudal lords cooperated with the Jesuits (mostly Portuguese) who followed Xavier--primarily because of the guns, ammunition and other Western products the Jesuits used in bartering for religious privileges and converts.

The common Japanese, at the complete mercy of their feudal lords who treated them as chattel, were less cynical in their reaction to Christianity, which talked of individual freedom and human rights. Many thousands of the conversions that followed were as sincere as any religious fevor can be.

These early missionaries were not content to confine themselves to religious work, however. Their political intrigues and the military threat that they posed eventually turned the new Shogunate government against them.

From the late 1500s both Japanese converts and foreign missionaries came under increasing persecution, first from Hideyoshi Toyotomi and then the Tokugawa Shogunate, which began in 1603.

Finally, in the 1630s, the Shogunate decided to totally eliminate the missionary and Christian presence in Japan. All missionaries were deported. In the winter of 1637 the largest group of Japanese converts in the country took refuge in a castle on Shimabara Peninsula.

They were besieged by a Shogunate army and then systematically slaughtered.

Among the very first Westerners to arrive in Japan after the country reopened its doors to the outside world in 1854 were missionaries. But their expectations of soon converting Japan's millions to Christianity were doomed to failure.

With the downfall of the Tokugawa Shogunate in 1868, the lives of the Japanese were revolutionized in a matter of days and weeks. No longer were they owned by feudal lords. For the first time in the history of the country, they had some rights of their own. Western thought and ways began to flood into the islands.

In this new heady atmosphere, taking on a new religion that was intellectually simple-minded, very poorly explained by missionaries who could not speak Japanese, and basically forbade its adherents from doing things that had been traditional for thousands of years, made no sense at all to most Japanese.

Among the first things the missionaries did to the few followers they were able to attract was to forbid them from taking a bath more than once a week. Daily mixed bathing had been the custom in Japan for hundreds of generations and was as innocent as babes in a tub together, but to the sexually obsessed missionaries such behavior was a serious sin.

In subsequent years, Christian missionaries in Japan have continued their efforts to turn Japanese into Christians, but with very limited success. The effort is institutionalized and goes on because it has gone on before, not because there are any real hopes for the situation to change significantly.

Christian missionaries in Japan have, however, made substantial contributions to the country (see HEPBURN, DR. CHARLES), but generally only in an educational sense. Most of them have ended up being little more than English-language teachers.

Japanese who do profess to be Christians also remain Buddhists and Shintoists to some degree, since it is virtually impossible to be Japanese and not be influenced by these two cultural forces.

MISTRESSES / NIGO SAN (Nee-go Sahn)

Until recent times, mistresses were a common and accepted part of Japanese society--just as they were, and still are, in many other parts of the world.

The practice of mistress-keeping in Japan was limited to upper-class men in earlier periods, but eventually became common among the merchant class as well.

Again just as in England, France, Russia and many other nations in earlier ages, there were several reasons why mistress-keeping flourished. There were no religious sanctions against it. There was no element of love in most marriages and it was vitally important to upper-class men that they produce male offspring.

The history of Japan, with its sophisticated Imperial Court and large group of nobles, the long Shogunate dynasties which also maintained a court with numerous retainers, and its 200 plus feudal lords who were like kings in their own domains, is replete with tales of mistresses. Some of them played vital roles in the affairs of the country.

During the long, peaceful and relatively prosperous Tokugawa Shogunate (1603-1868), mistress-keeping came to be a high art, with detailed customs and rules. There were different categories of mistresses and mistress-keepers.

The practice of mistress-keeping in Japan has changed with the times. It is no longer totally sanctioned by society or the law, but exists in the same fashion that one finds in most Catholic countries.

As in the past, most mistress-keeping is closely related to the mizu shobai or water business, i.e. the entertainment trades.

Recommended reading: SOME PREFER GEISHA--The Art of Mistress-Keeping in Japan, by Boye De Mente (Phoenix Books/ Publishers).

MITI (MINISTRY OF INTERNATIONAL TRADE β INDUSTRY / TSUSANSHO (T'sue-sahn-show)

Japan's Ministry of International Trade and Industry, known by its initials, MITI, is one of the most important and best-known of Japan's government agencies.

MITI owes its prominence and power to its role in helping transform Japan from an agricultural/handicraft economy in 1868 to a major industrial economy by 1895, and to helping Japan recover after the disaster of World War II.

Following the downfall of the Tokugawa Shogunate in 1868, the government, primarily through MITI, became directly involved in investing in heavy industries, and in providing support and guidance to industry across the board.

In the decades that followed, the companies financed by the government were turned over to private interests, but MITI and other government agencies have continued to act in the capacity of planner, organizer and coordinator of Japan's industry and trade, and to exercise direct control in the case of energy and power resources.

Unlike in the U.S., where government and industry have traditionally been cast in the role of antagonists, the rleationship between government and industry in Japan has been one of cooperation and support.

The influence that MITI exercises on industry in Japan is generally done through a system known as gyosei shido (g'yoe-say-ee She-doe) or administrative guidance. This guidance is usually accepted voluntarily and in good spirit, because there is both trust and confidence in MITI's methods and goals.

MITO (Me-toe)

In a country filled with places of extraordinary historical interest it is difficult to pick out one that is more outstanding than another, but one of special interest is the city of Mito, capital of Ibaraki Prefecture, 117.5 kilometers northeast of Tokyo.

Mito was the headquarters of the fief Ieyasu Tokugawa gave to his 11th son, Yorifusa, who established one of the three main branches of the Tokugawa family. The Mito Tokugawas were especially noted in Japan for maintaining at the highest level the way of life prescribed for the Samurai by the concepts of Bushido (The Way of the Warrior).

The head of the House of Mito was automatically the Vice-Shogun, but in consideration for this hereditary privilege, was disbarred by law from becoming Shogun. The second head of the Mito branch of the family, Mitsukuni (1628-1700), is regarded as the most outstanding of this line.

Mitsukuni is perhaps best-known for having started compiling the HISTORY OF GREAT JAPAN, which was not completed until 1906, and was comprised of 397 volumes. This work is credited with having had a significance influence on the decision of the last Shogun to step down in favor of the Emperor in 1867/8.

Among the attractions of this picturesque city are the grounds of the Mito lord's castle, and the Kodokan (Koe-doe-khan) a school founded by Nariaki Tokugawa, the 9th lord of Mito, who lived from 1800 to 1860, and Tokiwa Park, also known as Kairaku-En, one of the three most noted landscaped gardens in Japan (the other two are Kenroku-En in Kanazawa City and Koraku-En in Okayama City).

Nariaki designed the garden as a retreat for himself, and it was completed in 1843. It was turned into a public park in 1873, five years after the end of Japan's Shogunate form of government. When first completed the garden contained 10,000 ume (plum) trees--of which some 3,000 remain today and are a major attraction when they begin blooming in late February.

There are literally hundreds of other places in Ibaraki Prefecture that are of special interest (shrines, hotspring spas, etc.), two of which are the Joban Hawaiian Center and Iwaki.

The Joban Hawaiian Center is a seven kilometer-square domed recreational site near Yumoto where hot sulphide spring water is pumped into the center to keep it at summer temperatures all year around. The huge dome contains several swimming pools and water chutes, a number of stages for various kinds of performances, and a garden of tropical plants.

Iwaki is the largest city in Japan in area--almost equal to the total area of Kagawa Prefecture--as the result of combining the towns of Nokoso, Izumi, Yumoto and Taira into one municipal area in 1966. Taira was the castle town of the Ando clan, and Nakoso is celebrated in Japanese history as the site of a huge fortress barrier that was built there in ancient times as protection against raids by Ainu tribesmen. (See AINU).

MITSUI β COMPANY, LTD.

The story of the present-day Mitsui companies is one of the great commercial and personal sagas of Japan, going back to the Fujiwara family, which in the 7th century A.D. usurped the power of the Emperor and through continuous intermarriage with the Imperial family, dominated the government for the next 400 years.

In 1100 A.D. one of the Fujiwara descendants left the Court at Kyoto to seek his fortune in Omi Province near Lake Biwa. There he discovered three wells, in one of which was a treasure of hidden gold.

As was common on momentous occasions, the lucky man changed his name to Mitsui, meaning Three Wells. Despite the fact that those of noble rank and the Samurai class of hereditary warriors that developed during these decades generally did not engage in business, the Mitsui family gradually became merchants, while retaining their Samurai status.

For the next several hundred years, the fortunes of the Mitsui family waxed and wane with the political stability of the country. Finally, in the early 1600s, after the establishment of the Tokugawa Shogunate and the closing of Japan's doors to the outside world (See TOKUGAWA IEYASU, HISTORY, SHOGUNS, etc), Sokubei (or Takatoshi) Mitsui, the head of the family at that time, officially gave up his exalted Samurai rank, and announced that thereafter the family would be commoners and engage in commerce exclusively.

Sokubei opened a sake and shoyu brewing business called Echigo-Ya, after his father who had been the hereditary Lord of Echigo. Later Sokubei's wife opened a pawnshop to help the struggling business survive.

Sokubei died in 1633, but his wife and their eight sons continued operating the business. She sent their oldest son Saburozaemon to Edo (Tokyo), the Shogunate capital, to start up a dry goods store. As the years went by it became apparent that the youngest son, Takatoshi Hachirobei, had the most business talent, and he was sent to Edo to work with Saburozaemon.

Hachirobei was a farsighted man who learned early that dealing with the Daimyo and Samurai was a dangerous business because they could not be forced to pay their bills. He first went into the moneylending business, confining his loans to other merchants and commoners, and in 1673 opened a dry goods store in Kyoto, the Imperial capital.

There, he introduced a startling innovation. Instead of selling his merchandise on long-term credit at inflated prices, as had been done traditionally, he began selling at low fixed prices for cash. He also began selling cloth in any lengths desired, instead of prescribed lengths.

Both innovations were very popular, leading Hachirobei to open a large store in Edo (Tokyo). He became a pioneer in advertising his stores, and soon was the most successful merchant in the country. He became a patron of the most famous woodblock print artists of the time, developed a prototype of double-entry bookkeeping, and the system of settling accounts by money orders.

Hachirobei established exchange houses to provide banking operations for the business. One of these exchanges, set up to handle tax money for the Shogunate government, was the predecessor of Mitsui Bank.

By the time he died in 1694, at the age of 73, Hachirobei had set up his six sons as the heads of collateral families in charge of different phases of the family business--a business that was not only to outlast the Tokugawa Shogunate, but play a leading role in the transformation of fedual Japan to a modern industrial nation in the late 1800s, and in the rebuilding of Japan following the debacle of World War II.

Before the family holdings were broken up by the Allied Occupation forces after the end of WWII, the Mitsui family owned and operated the largest commercial conglomerate the world has ever since, with some 3,000,000 employees. See ZAIBATSU.

The survival and extraordinary growth of the House of Mitsui is attributed to the Family Constitution drawn up by Sochiku Mitsui, the oldest son of Hachirobei, and based on principles laid down in his father's will.

Each male member of the family was required to take the following oath upon coming of age:

In obedience to the precepts of our forefathers and in order to strengthen the everlasting foundation of the families of our House and to expand the enterprise bequeathed by our forefathers, I solemnly vow that I will observe and follow the regulations handed down in the Constitution of our House, and that I will not wantonly seek to alter them. In witness thereof, I take the oath and affix my signature thereto in the presence of the August Spirits of our ancestors.

Today, the Mitsui Group is one of Japan's largest industrial / commercial conglomerates. Each of the companies in the group operates independently, but all cooperate in areas of mutual interest.

Altogether there are several hundred companies and subsidiaries in the group, including four in cement, six in chemicals, six in commerce and trade, six in construction, three in energy, four in engineering, five in finance and insurance, four in food processing, six in machinery, one in mining, six in nonferrous metals, one in paper, two in real estate, one in steel, one in synthetic fibers and plastics, two in transportation, two in warehousing, two in travel and one in the knowledge industry.

Liaison among the group companies is provided by the Nimoku-Kai (Nee-moe-kuu Kie) or Second Thursday Conference, which is made up of the presidents of the 24 leading group companies, and through the Getsuyo Kai (Gates-yoe Kie) or Monday Conference, which is made up of the managing directors of 62 companies in the Mitsui Group.

These two bodies provide a forum for discussions and for the exchange of views. In addition, members of the Group have a number of ongoing committees engaged in public relations and research, and acting as advisors to the Nimoku Kai.

Mitsui β Company, the Group's major trading enterprise, has some 50 offices in Japan and over 130 offices in 77 countries--all linked by privately leased telex and telephone networks.

In fact, the communications system maintained by Mitsui gives an impressive indication of its size and the scope of its operation. It has four large computerized communication centers. One in Tokyo that covers all of Asia. One in New York covering North, Central and South America. One in London covering Europe and Africa, and one in Sydney, Australia, covering Oceania. A sub-center in Bahrain covers the Middle East.

These centers are linked to each other by satellites, and operate 24 hours a day. In addition to these telex and telephone networks, Mitsui operates a mail service equivalent to that of a city with a population in excess of 125,000.

Mitsu's communication centers monitor currencies, political matters, economic activity, social changes--even the weather. They are regarded as being one of the largest and most efficient intelligence systems in the world.

Mitsui's total trading transactions were approximately 63 billion dollars in 1982, and have continued to grow at a healthy rate. Offshore trading by Mitsui, of special importance to the U.S. and several other countries around the world, involves foodstuffs, gas and petroleum, bulk chemical products, metals, textiles, paper, etc.

Recommended reading: THE MITSUI STORY: Three Centuries of Japanese Business (Mitsui β Co., Ltd). THE 100 YEAR HISTORY OF MITSUI β CO., LTD. (Mitsui β Co., Ltd).

In addition to being one of Japan's two largest trading companies, the American branch of Mitsui β Co., Ltd. is the U.S.'s fourth largest trading company.

MIURA PENINSULA (Me-uu-rah)

One of the most beautiful and important geographical features of the island of Honshu, the Miura Peninsula projects into the Pacific Ocean in a southeasternly direction, between Tokyo Bay on the northeast and Sagami Bay on the southwest.

On the Tokyo Bay side of the peninsula, the major city is the great naval port of Yokosuka. Further on down, where a spit reaches out into Tokyo Bay, is Uraga, which is famous in history as the Shogunate check-point for all shipping entering the bay.

On the west or Sagami Bay side of the peninsula are the famous resort/residential cities of Zushi and Hayama, and numerous other smaller cities, towns and villages. Kamakura, the Shogunate capital of Japan from 1192 until 1333, is located at the base of the peninsula, facing Sagami Bay. Just west of Kamakura, at the head of Sagami Bay, is the famous beach and resort area of Enoshima.

The peninsula is a treasure house of historical sites and scenic wonderlands, and is a favorite residential area as well as playground for people from the Tokyo/Kawasaki/Yokohama areas. See KAMAKURA, ENOSHIMA, YOKOSUKA, ADAMS WILLIAM, HISTORY, SHOGUN.

MIYAKO HOTEL (Me-yah-koe)

One of Kyoto's premiere hotels, the Miyako is situated in 16 acres of landscaped gardens on a wooded hillside overlooking the downtown area of the city.

The hotel is distinctive and popular because it combines some of the best of Western comfort with Japanese beauty to achieve one of the most attractive and comfortable hotels in the country. Besides the usual Japanese amenities--which include a steambath and massuers--the hotel has four swimming pools.

MIYAMOTO, MUSASHI (Me-yah-moe-toe, Muu-sah-she)

This is the name of one of Japan's most famous feudal-age Samurai swordsmen. After practicing with the sword for several hours a day for more than 30 years, and taking on dozens of opponents in battles to the death, Miyamoto arrived at the point where he could not be defeated in fair combat.

Miyamoto's skill with the deadly Samurai sword made him a legend in his time, and his immortality was assured when Japanese novelist Eiji Yoshikawa fictionalized his life story in a book by the same name in the mid-1940s.

An English edition of the book, translated by Charles S. Terry, was brought out by the huge Japanese publishing house Kodansha in the early 1980s, and became something of a bestseller in the U.S.

Near the end of his remarkable life, Miyamoto wrote his own biography, explaining his philosophy and telling how he had achieved such mastery with the sword. He called his book the BOOK OF FIVE RINGS. In the early 1980s an American edition of the book was published, and it received some notoriety in the U.S. as a guide to understanding the Japanese business mentality--a phenomenon the Japanese viewed with considerable amusement, if not a little sadness.

MIYANOSHITA (Me-yah-no-shh-tah)

One of the most famous of the hot-spring spas in the Hakone district southwest of Tokyo, Miyanoshita is also a primary gate-way to the resort/recreational area. Roads radiating out from Miyanoshita lead to numerous other resorts and scenic places in and on the great volcanic caldera that makes up Hakone.

The oldest Western-styled hotel in the Hakone district, the world-famous Fujiya which opened in 1878, is also in Miyanoshita. The Miyanoshita hotsprings, with temperatures ranging from 62-78 degrees Centigrade, have been documented as bringing relief to rheumatism, gout, nervous disorders and female ailments.

MOCHI (Moe-chee)

Mochi, often described as rice cake, would better be described as a type of rice bread. It is made of an especially glutinous kind of rice that is thoroughly steamed and pounded with a heavy wooden mall until it is a thick, heavy paste.

This paste, which is cut into small, manageable pieces, hardens. It is used in a thick broth and is also eaten baked and broiled, with soy sauce (or, in recent times, with a sugar coating).

Mochi has been a popular food in Japan since ancient times, and is a traditional New Year's item, when it is eaten in a thick broth called zoni. It is also eated broiled at this time. Most people now buy their mochi ready-made, but until around the 1960s, the majority made it at home in a traditional New Year's ceremony that involved the whole family taking turns with the pounding.

Mochi is also a common ingredient in a number of traditional Japanese dishes, and is a popular gift-item, being regarded as a good luck omen, especially for safe child-birth.

MOHAMMEDAN MOSQUE

Japan has two Islamic mosques, one in Tokyo and the other in Kobe. The mosque in Tokyo is a short distance from Higashi Kitazawa Station on the Odakyu Electric Railway. It is one of the more exotic landmarks in Shibuya Ward.

MONEY / OKANE (Oh-kah-nay)

Until 1868 the wealth of Japan's feudal clans was figured in terms of rice production, but rice was far too cumbersome and complicated to be used as a medium of exchange, so coins and small bars of metal--in units called ryo (rio)-- had been in use as currency for a long time.

The first paper money appeared in Japan in about 1615--in the form of notes issued by merchants in Ise and Yamada. The practice was soon picked up by the larger merchant houses of Osaka and Sakai. See MITSUI β CO.

Then the Daimyo feudal lords began to issue clan notes. The Tokugawa Shogunate realized it should do something to stabilize the situation, but its orders to the clans to stop issuing paper money were ignored. Not being able to control the currency was one of the major problems of the Shogunate, and contributed to its demise in 1868.

The new Meiji Government that took over in 1868 issued four kinds of paper money--all printed on copper plates that could be easily duplicated. Counterfeiting became rife, so the government began having its currency printed in Germany, where printing technology was further advanced.

In 1871 the monetary unit was changed from ryo to yen (pronounced like inn in Japanese). Modern banks appeared in Japan in 1872, and all of them issued their own notes, first printed in the U.S. See BANKS.

Yen presently comes in both coins and bills. There are 10, 50, 100 and 500 yen coins, and 500, 1,000, 5,000 and 10,000 yen bills. The yen floats on the foreign exchange markets.

MONGOL INVASIONS

Twice in the 13th century, Kublai Khan, the first Mongol emperor of China, sent invasion fleets to Japan--the first one in 1274 and the second one in 1281.

Khan first demanded that Japan become a tributory to China in 1268, but the Shogunate authorities in Kamakura ignored the ultimatum. In the next few years several other Chinese envoys arrived, with their demands growing more belligerent. The Shogunate ordered the feudal lords in northern Kyushu to fortify the coastline.

In 1273 the Shogunate rebuffed still another Chinese envoy. In November of the following year, a Chinese armada of some 900 ships and over 30,000 troops, including Mongols, Chinese, Tartars and Koreans, devastated the Japanese islands of Tsushima and Kii in the straits between Kyushu and Korea, and then attacked the port city of Hakata in northern Kyushu.

Used to fighting hand-to-hand combat with swords and spears, the Japanese Samurai were no match for the cavalry tactics and weapons of the Mongols, and were forced to retreat. When night fell, the Mongols withdrew to their ships instead of pressing their advantage-- apparently because of an approaching typhoon.

During the night, the typhoon sank well over half of the Mongol fleet and caused the drowning of close to half of all the troops that were aboard the ships. The surviving ships broke off the attack and returned to China.

Kublai Khan was not to be so easily denied, however. In 1275 he sent another envoy to the court of the Shogun in Kamakura. The envoy was summarily beheaded on Katase Beach near Enoshima. Not content with just this, the Shogunate decided it would take the fight to the enemy, and invade the Khan's vassal state of Korea.

While preparing for the invasion of Korea, the Shogunate ordered the lords of Kyushu to build stone walls along the coast.

In 1279 Khan dispatched another envoy to Japan. He too was executed by the Shogunate, which by this time knew another invasion was imminent.

The second invasion, this time by a fleet said to have been even larger than the Spanish Armada that attacked England, arrived off the coast of northern Kyushu in late 1281. Once again the Japanese defenders were getting the worst of it when, just as before, a typhoon smashed into the Mongol fleet, destroying it--giving rise to the belief that Japan was defended by Kami Kaze (Kah-me Kah-zay) or Divine Winds.

Undaunted, the Mongols planned a third invasion of Japan in 1283 but delayed it because of other affairs. The following year they sent another envoy-- who, being aware of the fate that befell his two predecessors, went only as far as the island of Tsushima.

In 1284, the Mongols invaded Vietnam, giving the Shogunate more time to construct defenses. The Mongols were defeated by the Vietnamese, further delaying their designs against Japan. The

Mongols then turned their attention to Java, which they invaded in 1292--only to withdraw in 1293.

In 1293 the still ambitious Kublai Khan began laying plans for a third invasion of Japan, and ordered Korea to mobilize. He died the following year, however, and the plans for the invasion were cancelled. Five years later, the succesor to Khan sent an envoy to Japan, calling for a trade and friendship treaty between the two countries.

Thus ended the first outside threat the Japanese were to face in their long history. See HISTORY, SHOGUN.

MOON-VIEWING / TSUKI-MI (T'sue-kee-me)

The practice of moon-viewing has been an established aesthetic and artistic custom in Japan since ancient times--now considerably diminished by the fast pace of modern life.

In mid-autumn, when the moon was full, people would gather in parks, on high places, verandas and specially built platforms, to enjoy the beauty of the moon, eat specially prepared foods, drink sake and compose haiku poetry celebrating the moon.

Ages ago, places that were especially outstanding moon-viewing spots came into use, and moon-viewing platforms or pavilions were built on the sites. Some of these platforms and pavilions still exist, and many of the country's noted moon-viewing locations are still used today. See MATSUSHIMA.

MORIOKA (Moe-ree-oh-kah)

In the north-central area of Honshu, Morioka is the capital of Iwate Prefecture and the ironware capital of Japan. During the days of the Shoguns, Morioka was called Nambu and was the castle town of the Nambu clan (the whole provice was called Nambu at that time).

The area has been known for centuries for its Nambu tetsu bin or Nambu iron kettles. It is also known today for its Chagu-Chagu Umakko festival held on June 15 to celebrate horse-raising, and a cherry tree that is listed as a National Monument--the famous Ishiware Zakura or Stone-Breaking Cherry Tree, which has grown up through a fissure in a huge block of granite.

The ruins and grounds of the Nambu clan castle is now a city park. Kei Hara, one of the most famous political leaders of the Taisho era (1912-1926) was born in Morioka. There is a memorial hall in the city dedicated to him.

MOUNTAINS / YAMA (Yah-mah)

Japan is one of the most mountainous island chains in the world. Plains and basis account for only about 29 percent of the total land mass--the remainder is made up of hills and mountains.

The whole archipelago is basically a chain of peaks and ranges with slopes and basins on either side. These high mountain ranges, forming a backbone that traverses the center of the four main islands, have historically divided Japan into two parts--one facing the Pacific and the other facing the Asian mainland. There are 11 peaks that are over 3,000 meters in height and 13 that are over 2,500 meters--all of them on the one main island of Honshu. Of these 24 high peaks, eight are dormant volcanoes, including three of the highest ones in the country.

The top 10 peaks are Mt. Fuji (3,776 meters), Mt. Shirane (3,192), Mt. Hodaka (3,190), Mt. Yariga (3,180), Mt. Arakawa (3,141), Mt. Akaishi (3,120), Mt. On-Take (3,063), Mt. Shiomi (3,047), Mt. Senjoga (3,033), Mt. Norikura (3,026), and Mt. Hijiri (3,011).

There are literally hundreds of other peaks on Honshu and the other islands that range from 1,000 to 2,500 meters. See MT. FUJI, MT. ASO, MT. KOYA. Many peaks in the Japan Alps (see JAPAN ALPS) are over 3,000 meters high, including a number that are also volcanic.

Among them: Shirane-san (She-rah-nay-sahn), 3,192m, in Yamanashi and Shizuoka Prefectures. Hodaka-dake, 3,190m, in Nagano and Gifu Prefectures, and Yariga-take, 3,180m, also in Nagano and Gifu Prefectures.

Mt. Fuji, an extinct volcano cone that rises to a majestic 3,776 meters (12,388 feet), and towers over the islands like a sentinel, is the highest mountain in Japan. See MT. FUJI.

MOVIES / EIGA (A-e-gah)

Japan's first small film studio was established in Tokyo in 1904, but it was not until 1912 when Nikkatsu was founded that the industry really got started. The industry did not come of age internationally until 1950, however, when Akira Kurosawa's masterpiece RASHOMON

(Rah-sho-moan) appeared.

The film industry in Japan today, dominated by the Big Four--Nikkatsu, Toho, Shochiku and Toei--produces several hundred films a year, and is known world-wide for the many innovations it has introduced into the world of films.

Other directors and Japanese-made films that have received international honors are Kenji Mizoguchi and his celebrated UGETSU MONOGATARI, Yasujiro Ozu and THE TALE OF TOKYO, along with Keisuke Kinoshita, Tadashi Imai, Kon Ichikawa, Hiroshi Inagaki, Teinosuke Kinugasa and Kaneto Shindo.

Among the best-known of Japan's actors and actresses from the 1960s into the 1980s were Toshiro Mifune and Machiko Kyo.

For the fascinating story of Japan's film industry, see THE JAPANESE FILM, by Donald Richie (Kodansha Int'l).

MT. ASO (Ah-soe)

Mt. Aso is actually five quite separate volcanic peaks in the Aso National Park in Kumamoto and Oita Prefectures, making up portions of central and northeastern Kyushu. The largest of the peaks --Nakadake--is also the most active. Its crater is about 600 meters across and is 160 meters deep. The highest of the peaks, Takadake, rises 1,592 meters above sea-level.

There are three villages and three towns on the plains adjoining the five peaks--plains which were originally the crater of an even larger volcano, measuring 255 square kilometers in area.

The very least that can be said of the Mt. Aso area is that it is one of the most scenic spots on the face of the earth.

MT. FUJI / FUJI-SAN (Fuu-jee Sahn)

Towering up from the prefectures of Shizuoka and Yamanashi southwest of Tokyo, and visible for hundreds of miles, Mt. Fuji is considered one of the two most beautiful conical volcanoes in the world.

The traditional sysmbol for Japan and the inspiration for poets and artists from time immemorial, Mt. Fuji at 3.776 meters is Japan's highest and best-known mountain. Its name is believed to be derived from an Ainu word meaning Fire Mountain. (The Ainu were the original Caucasoid inhabitants of central and northern Japan).

Mt. Fuji's last eruption was in 1707, when it blanketed Edo (Tokyo), 100 kilometers away, with a thick layer of ash. Prior to that it erupted fairly often--there are 18 eruptions on record--and apparently smoked continuously. Now only wisps of steam, measured at 80 degrees centigrade, waft up from one isolated section of the summit.

Mt. Fuji was considered sacred until the Meiji Restoration in 1868. The practice of climbing the mountain as a sign of religious piety developed very early. Documents written in June 1500 refer to endless streams of people hiking up the graceful peak. Later the mountain became an object of worship, and an organization called Fuji-Ko or Fuji Worshippers, was formed. Women, however, were not allowed to climb the mountain.

Now somewhere around half a million people, including children and elderly people, climb the mountain every summer. The first foreigner to climb Mt. Fuji was Sir Rutherford Alcock, the first British minister, who made the ascent on July 26, 1860. Lady Parkes, the wife of the British minister to the court of Edo, was the first foreign woman to reach the summit--in 1867.

There is a popular saying in Japan that everyone should climb Mt. Fuji once, but anyone who does it twice is a fool. (I have climbed it three times!) The climbing season lasts only from the first of July to the end of August, because of the danger from high winds, and the cold.

The crater of Mt. Fuji, circular in shape, is approximately 300 meters wide, and is relatively level, lying only 220 meters lower than the rim's highest peak. Authorities believe there was once a lake in the crater. Now it is filled with snow about 10 months out of the year--and mountain climbers the rest of the time.

There are six popular climbing routes up the mountain--Yoshida, Kawaguchiko, Shoji, Gotemba, Subashiri and Fujinomiya--each starting from a different point around the base.

Each of the trails is divided into 10 sections called go (go). The distance between the go (or stations as they are called in English) is based on the difficulty of the climb between them.

The beginning of each trail is Ichi Go (1st Station). Next is Ni Go (2nd Station), etc. There are rest-stations at the end of most of the go, with toilet facilities and rough stone-covered shelters. There are sub-stops in between many of the stations--and they can be confusing to tired climbers who are measuring their progress by counting stations.

The tree-line extends to between the

5th and 6th stations, and it is mostly bare from there on to the top.

Many climbers start in the late morning or early afternoon, reach the 7th or 8th station by dark, stay overnight in one of the stone huts, get up to watch the sunrise the next morning, then finish the climb.

The stations serve various Japanese noodle and rice dishes (and beer, which porters tote up the mountain on their backs), but it is always a good idea to take along various kinds of snacks and a canteen of water--along with toilet paper.

Foreigners who do not speak Japanese enjoy the adventure more if they go with Japanese friends.

There is a weather observation radar station on top of Mt. Fuji, able to spot approaching typhoons as much as 800 kilometers away. (Flying into Tokyo from Hawaii, I have seen Mt. Fuji from over 500 miles out--a magnificent sight).

The first portion of the climb up Mt. Fuji is easy, as the ascent is gradual and the footing solid. The last 1,000 or so feet are rather difficult, however, and require both caution and perseverance.

Many climbers buy walking sticks at the beginning of their climb, and get the number of the stations burned onto them as they progress up the mountain. Descending the mountain, many climbers leave the established trails and come down the ash slides, but the practice is dangerous and discouraged.

Most climbers today ride buses partway up the mountain, and begin their hike at Station Three, Four or--most often--Five.

Although the climbing season on Mt. Fuji is limited to July and August, the waist of the mountain, with its five beautiful lakes and extensive forests, is a favorite year-around recreational area.

There are four main gateways to Mt. Fuji and the five Fuji lakes--Gotemba, Fuji-Yoshida, Kawaguchiko and Fujinomiya--and a number of popular tours to the various districts.

The Mt. Fuji lake area is extensively developed as winter and summer resorts. The Lake Yamanaka area is especially popular as a summer resort, with hotels, villas and clubhouses--most of them belonging to colleges and other organizations--lining its shores

On August 26 each year the city of Fuji-Yoshida (the main gateway for people from Tokyo) and the Sengen Shrine stage a Fire Festival that marks the approaching end of the climbing season (August 31).

Dozens of huge bonfires are lighted at different places around the city, and operators of huts on Mt. Fuji's Yoshida Trail follow suit, making a spectacular nighttime display that literally spirals up into the sky. Young men carry a heavy, vermilion-lacquered portable shrine shaped like Mt. Fuji through the streets--a custom that began centuries ago when Mt. Fuji was active, and the festival was intended to keep the god of the mountain quiet.

MT. KOYA / KOYA SAN (Koe-yah Sahn)

An hour and 40 minutes from Osaka, Mt. Koya is famed for the monastery on its summit, founded in 816 by Kobo Daishi, the great exponent of the Shingon sect of Buddhism.

The huge monastery covers over 99 ha., and includes over 120 temple buildings (many others have been lost to fires over the centuries). The precincts of the monastery are surrounded by huge old trees that are as magnificent as the main temple buildings.

In earlier times, women were not allowed to enter the Koyo-san monastery, but today it is visited by more than a million people every year. There are no inns in the little town of Koya, but 51 temples in the vicinity provide lodging and vegetarian food for visitors. The complex is very large and it takes many hours for just a casual introduction to it.

MUSIC / ONGAKU (Own-gah-kuu)

There are several categories and subcategories of traditional Japanese music, classified by period of origin. These include gagaku (gah-gah-kuu), ancient, nogaku (no-gah-kuu), medieval, and the music of the still popular shamisen (shah-me-sen) and koto (koe-toe), recent.

Among the popular subclasses of traditinal Japanese music are sokyoku (soe-k'yoe-kuu), nagauta (nah-gah-uu-tah), kouta (koe-uu-tah), and yokyoku (yoe-k'yoe-kuu).

Sokyoku, developed in the second half

of the 16th century, is music played on the koto, a kind of harp, often in concert with the shamisen and shakuhachi (shah-kuu-hah-chee), a 5-holed bamboo flute.

Nagauta, which means long song, is a kind of epic song that was first identified with the shamisen and later kabuki. It then absorbed elements from regional music (ji-uta), puppet ballads (jouri), and folk songs (minyo), becoming very lively in accompaniment with flutes and hand-drums.

Kouta dates from the early 19th century, but is based on popular songs of the 15th and 16th centuries. Short ditty-like songs sung in quick tempo in a suppressed voice, kouta are accompanied by a shamisen plucked with the bare fingers.

Yokyoku, associated with the noh drama since the 15th and 16th centuries, are rhymes based on 7-5 syllables or 5-7 syllables, with the usual subject being tales from the famous Kojiki and Nihon-shoki historical records, or the great Genji Monogatari and Heike Monogatari epic novels of the 11th and 13th centuries. (See individual listings for these books.) Ordinarily sung to the accompaniment of flutes and drums, Yokyoku is also performed independently of noh.

The history of music in Japan has been closely associated with the importation of musical instruments that have come to be regarded as traditionally Japanese--the koto, the shakuhachi and the shamisen in particular.

The koto, a 13-stringed harp-like instrument, was brought to Japan from China in the 6th century. A primitive form of the shakuhachi or flute arrived from China in the 8th century, and the more modern form was imported from China in the mid-13th century. The popular shamisen came to Japan from China in the mid-16th century via Okinawa.

The koto was throughly Japanized, the shakuhachi disappeared entirely from China, and the shamisen was developed far beyond the early Chinese version. A large plectrum was developed as a pick held in the palm of the hand, and shamisen of different sizes and thicknesses were developed to play different kinds of musics.

An indication of the importance attached to music in early Japan was the creation of an Office of Music in the Imperial Court in 701. Sponsored by this office, the music of court ritual (gagaku) became firmly entrenched and is still practiced today under the auspices of the Imperial Household Agency.

From the 9th century on, the various forms of foreign music imported into Japan were blended with native folk music, resulting in the development of dengaku (dane-gah-kuu), a kind of classical dance that grew out of Shinto rituals connected with planting and harvesting, and sarugaku (sah-rue-gah-kuu), a comic dance that is considered a forerunner of noh.

From the 13th century on, tales from the great epic novel Heike Monogatari (about the rise and fall of the powerful Heike clan in the 12th century) recited to the musical accompaniment of the biwa became popular among the warrior class.

Noh music emerged in the latter part of the 14th century, and the adoption of the shakuhachi by a popular Buddhist sect resulted in a revival for this instrument.

From about 1550, a nationwide renaissance of the performing arts by and for the common people led to a national craze for noh, kabuki and bunraku plays.

The study and performance of koto and shakuhachi music came under the control of iemoto (ee-eh-moe-toe), a school system based on long years of apprenticeship to authorized teachers. Thus both the teaching and playing of these two instruments became the exclusive monopoly of a few people licensed by the masters of these schools. See GRAND MASTERS.

Between 1868 and 1912, Western music spread throughout the Japanese educational system, and thrived alongside of traditional Japanese music.

Western church music first appeared in Japan as far back as 1549--brought in by Christian missionaries. But when Christianity was banned in the early part of the 16th century, Western music totally disappeared.

After the downfall of the Tokugawa Shogunate in 1867/1868, interest in Western music resurfaced, and in 1879 the new government invited musical education experts from the U.S. to come to Japan and help incorporate Western music into the national school system.

By 1910 there were a number of well-known Japanese composers of Western music and songs. This phase ended with the militaristic xenophobia of the 1930s, however, and did not reappear until after the end of World War II in 1945.

Today, both Japanese and Western music flourish in Japan, and constitute a major industry. There are 12 major symphony orchestras in Japan--seven in Tokyo, and one each in Sapporo, Gunma,

Nagoya, Kyoto and Osaka. Their regular concerts and overseas tours draw enthusiastic responses.

The annual Osaka International Festival, originated in 1958, provides Japanese and foreign musicians with the opportunity for cultural exchanges. Individual Japanese artists have won numerous music contests around the world, and several, including Seiji Ozawa and Hiroko Nakamura, became well-known on the international music scene.

NAGASAKI (Nah-gah-sah-kee)

Now the fourth largest city in Kyushu and the capital of Nagasaki Prefecture, Nagasaki is one of the world's most beautiful port cities, and has played a key role in Japan's remarkable history.

The port was known as Fukaenoura or Tamanoura until the latter part of the 12th century when Yoritomo Minamoto, founder of the Kamakura Shogunate, gave it as a fief to Kotaro Nagasaki.

It was not to become important until 1571, however, when it was opened up to foreign trade with China, Southeast Asia and ships from Portugal, Spain and Holland. In 1587 Hideyoshi Toyotomi, the immediate predecessor of Shogun Ieyasu Tokugawa, made it his headquarters in his fight against the Lord of Satsuma, and thereafter it was governed by prefects appointed by the Shogun in Edo.

In 1639 the Tokugawa Shogunate expelled all Spanish and Portugese citizens from the country, and banned all trade with outsiders with the exception of the Chinese and Dutch. One small Dutch trading post was allowed to continue operating on a tiny man-made island called Dejima (Exit Island) in Nagasaki Bay.

For the next 220 some years, this tiny island was Japan's only source of information to the outside world. Foreigners were not allowed into the country, and the thousands of Japanese who happened to be abroad when the exclusion order was give were not allowed to return home. The exclusion policy was total.

During this long period of isolation, some Western learning, particularly medicine, botany and military arts, seeped into Japan through Dutch and Chinese publications--and from the more learned members of the Dutch traders who manned the outpost at Dejima for over two centuries.

When Japan began opening its doors to the West in the 1850s, hundreds of ambitious Japanese flocked to Nagasaki to acquire Western learning. But as other Japanese ports opened, and educational centers were founded in Tokyo and other more accessible areas, Nagasaki faded from the limelight.

Following the fall of the Tokugawa Shogunate in 1868, Nagasaki participated in the rapid modernization program, becoming a major industrial center. It was particularly important in shipbuilding.

This industry was to make Nagasaki the second target for atom bombing at the close of World War II. At exactly 11:02 a.m. on August 9, 1945, the city was to suffer the same fate as Hiroshima had a few days earlier. But in the case of Nagasaki, the destruction was not so utterly complete as it was in Hiroshima because of the hilly terrain of the city.

Today, Nagasaki is a thriving commercial and industrial center, with shipbuilding, electrical machinery and steel the leading products. The Nagasaki Shipyard, managed by Mitsubishi Heavy Industries, is said to be the world's largest.

Nagasaki, with its mild winter climate and sea-breeze tempered summers, superb scenery and uncountable historic sights, is also one of Japan's most important tourist destinations. There are the usual temples, shrines and parks, along with many things from the international community--Catholic churches, Glover Mansion (the old British mansion that was the setting for the opera Madame Butterfly), Dejima (the man-made island where the Dutch were secluded for 213 years), and the Peace Park, which marks the place the atom bomb exploded.

名古屋

NAGOYA (Nah-go-yah)

The capital of Aichi Prefecture and Japan's fourth largest city, Nagoya grew up around a castle first built there in the 1500s by the Imagawa clan, and later replaced by a larger castle built by the Oda clan. The area really began to take off after Ieyasu Tokugawa, the founder of Japan's last Shogunate government, built a magnificient fortified castle there in 1612 for his son Yoshinao.

Situated on Nobi Plain in a commanding position between Tokyo and the Kyoto-Osaka area, Nagoya is sometimes called Chukyo or the Middle Capital, and serves as the central hub for a large portion of the Chubu (Central) District of Honshu, which comprises nine prefectures.

Nagoya is made up of 14 wards (ku), and is famous in Japan for having the widest and straightest major thoroughfares--a legacy of a fast and effective city planning job immediately following the end of the Pacific War in 1945. The city was wisely divided into four districts--the central area for commerce, the east and west districts for residential areas, and the north and south sectors for industry.

Nagoya is two hours from Tokyo via the super-express Hikari (He-kah-ree) Bullet Trains, and two hours and 45-minutes via the slower Kodama trains.

The Nogaya area has been famous for its pottery since ancient times, and is now a center for numerous other industries, including cloisonne, lacquerware, clocks, toys, wooden articles, musical instruments, paper products, sewing and weaving machines, chinaware, along with automobiles, ships and woolen goods.

Nagoya has its share of places of special interest. Among them: Nagoya Castle (visitors may enter the Lord's Room (Hanshu-no Ma) on the top floor) and see dozens of Important Cultural Properties), the Toshogu Shrine (dedicated to Ieyasu Tokugawa, who came from this area), a dozen or more other impressive shrines and temples and several outstanding parks (including one where the great Nobunaga Oda is buried).

There are also dozens of other places of extraordinary interest in the vicinity of Nagoya: the Inuyama Castle on Kiso River, built in 1440 and thus Japan's oldest existing fortified castle, the Kiso Rapids (famous for its boat-runs), and Gifu (where the Nobunaga Oda clan had their family castle).

Within an hour or so of Nagoya are numerous famous shrines, temples, parks and hotspring resort spas (Gamagori being one of the most noted).

NAKAHAMA, MANJIRO (Nah-kah-hah-mah Mahn-jee-roe)

Born in 1826 in the fishing village of Nakanohama on Shikoku, Manjiro Nakahama was to live one of the most extraordinary lives of adventure ever to befall any man, and to play a leading role in the history of his country.

Manjiro's father died when he was very young, forcing him to take up fishing to help earn a livelihood. At the age of 15, he and another youth of 16 and three men set out from the port of Usaura to fish for sea bream in the coastal waters. A violent storm came up, swept them out to sea and finally cast them upon one of the most distant islands in the Izu group.

In late June of 1841 the five castaways were picked up by an American whaling vessel under the command of Captain Whitfield, and taken to Honolulu. The Americans were well aware of Japan's strict policy of not allowing anyone, even Japanese castaways, to enter the country, so Captain Whitfield offered to take Manjiro to sea with him, while his companions were given jobs in Hawaii.

Two years later when Captain Whitfield returned to his home in Fairhaven, Massachusetts, he took Manjiro--now called John Muny--with him. Under the watchful eye of Mrs. Whitfield, Manjiro lived with an American family in Fairhaven and went to school for three years.

In 1846 Manjiro, then 24, returned to Honolulu on the whaler Franklin. One of the three men he had been shipwrecked with had died. The two others had left on a ship headed toward Japan in an attempt to return home. Only his young friend Toraemon, apprenticed as a carpenter, was still in Hawaii.

Just a few days later, however, his two older companions returned to Honolulu, having failed in their efforts to return home, and discouraging Manjiro from making the attempt. Manjiro remained aboard the whaler Franklin, and rose to become second mate before leaving the sea and joining the California Gold Rush.

Still anxious to return to Japan, Manjiro went back to Honolulu and there boarded the vessel Sarah Boyd, whose captain agreed to drop him off in Japan. Going ashore in Kagoshima, one of the more liberal and international-minded feudal fiefs, Manjiro managed to talk the authorities into letting him return to his home village.

The news of Manjiro's return from abroad was reported to the Shogunate in Edo, however, and when Commodore Perry and his Black Ships arrived in Edo Bay in 1853 he was called to Edo to act as a translator. He was kept under close guard and not allowed to meet any members of the American mission.

The Shogunate authorities recognized the value of Manjiro's knowledge, however, and appointed him secretary to the Department of Shipbuilding and Navigation. He subsequently taught English and whaling methods, and served as the captain of a whaler that was wrecked in the Bonin Islands.

Then in 1860 Manjiro was appointed the official interpreter for Japan's first diplomatic mission abroad, during which time he met the president of the

The Great Buddha of Nara. P. 222

Nagoya Castle. P. 219

U.S. and the heads of state of several European countries.

Back in Japan after the long mission, Manjiro was dismissed from his post with the Navy because of his close friendships with many Americans. He was then invited to teach whaling to the Satsuma clan in Kyushu, not returning to Edo until 1867, the year the last Tokugawa Shogun resigned, ending the government of the Shogunate and returning the Emperor to power (the transfer of power actually did not take place until the following year).

Three years later Manjiro was selected to accompany Iwao Oyama (who was later to become Field Marshal Oyama and a major architect of the new Japan), on a mission to the U.S. While there he visited his old friends in Fairhaven, but became ill and returned to Japan.

Recovering his health, Manjiro taught English and navigation during the last years of his life, dying in 1898 at his son's home near Tokyo's famous Ginza district, a poor fisherboy who had grown up to become a legend in his own time.

NAMECARDS / MEISHI (May-e-she)

Business cards or calling cards are a very important part of personal and business etiquette in Japan. Given the nature of interpersonal relationships that have been traditional in Japan for centuries, it is vital that people know the name, rank, position and relative standing of anyone they meet in order to use the right level of language and appropriate behavior toward them.

Normally the younger or lower ranking person offers his or her name card first --turned so the other person can read it immediately. It is impolite to hand out cards that have been written on or damaged.

Foreign visitors going to Japan on business or for pleasure are advised to take an ample supply of meishi. For businessmen, it is also a considerable advantage to have their names, companies and addresses printed in Japanese as well as English, on the reverse side of their cards. (This special service is provided by Japan Air Lines for its passengers.)

The word meishi literally means name-thorn, and apparently derives from the ancient Chinese practice of signing their names with splinters of bamboo or some other wood.

NAMES / NAMAE (Nah-my)

Prior to 1868, common people in Japan generally did not have family names. They were known by their first names and their district, the placed where they worked, their craft or trade--Taro the Tofu Seller, Taro from Owari-cho, and so on.

With the abolishment of the feudal system, people without surnames chose names that referred to their environments and to sentiments that appealed to them. Some adopted the names of their former feudal lords.

Tokugawa, for example, means Virtuous River. Suzuki means Bell Tree. Ogawa means Large River. Hana means Flower.

Feminine given names are generally those of flowers, seasons and esoteric sentiments--Haruko (Spring Child), Yukiko (Snow Child), Natsuko (Summer Child), Yoshiko (Good Child), Kiyoko (Pure Child).

Masculine names often refer to the individual's position in the family--Jiro (Younger Fellow), Saburo (Third Fellow), Goro (Fifth Son). Some consist of numbers: Ichizo (13), Isoroku (56).

At the time that commoners adopted family names, most people also chose family crests for themselves--a privilege that had previously been granted only to the Samurai and nobility. But the use of crests diminished rapidly over the next several decades, so their selection was more of a gesture toward the past than anything else.

NARA (Nah-rah)

The first permanent capital of Japan, from 710 until 784, Nara is the center of an area that is regarded as the cradle of Japanese arts, crafts, literature and industries. Now a major city, with a population of nearly a quarter of a million and the capital of Nara Prefecture, Nara continued to be a major religious and cultural center long after the capital was moved to what is now Kyoto in 794. (It was located in Nagaokakyo from 784 to 794.)

The biggest attraction of the area now is Old Nara, which includes buildings, parks and ponds that date back to the heyday of the city in the 8th century--all in an area of special scenic beauty.

Among the special places of interest in Old Nara are: Nara Park, a 525 ha. tree-covered site that boasts a large herd of tame deer.

Kofuku Temple, founded in 669 by the consort of Kamatari Fujiwara, the founder of one of Japan's first great dynastic families, headquarters of the Hosso sect of Buddhism and one of the Seven Great Temples of Nara.

The much-photographed Five Story Pagoda, the second highest in Japan, and first built in 730.

Also, the Treasure House, built on the premises of Kofuku Temple to store national treasures. The Kasuga Shrine, founded in 768, and the great Todai Temple, grand headquarters of the Kegon sect of Buddhism, built between 745 and 752. It is said to be the largest wooden structure in the world, and houses one of the largest bronze statues in the world.

There are over a dozen other major temples and ancient buildings of importance in Nara, each with its own amazing history. Nara is about an hour's train ride from Kyoto and Osaka.

NARITA (Nah-ree-tah)

Narita, in Chiba Prefecture some 68 kilometers from downtown Tokyo, was famous long before it became the home of the New Tokyo International Airport. The city's major claim to historical fame is the Shinsho Temple, founded there 939 in connection with a rebellion led by Masakado Taira.

The temple belongs to the Shingon Sect of Buddhism, and is dedicated to Fudo, the God of Fire. The grounds today cover nearly 20 ha., and the huge shrine complex includes a great gate, Main Hall, Main Quarters, Three Saints' Hall, Buddha's Hall, a former Main Hall, a belfry and three-storied pagoda, along with a library, museum and school.

The temple attracts more than seven million visitors each year (the largest number on New Year's Day). Another major occasion is the Setsubun or Bean-Throwing Festival on February 3 or 4, along with other events that take place in January, May and September.

In the middle of winter, many men go to the temple to fast and practice asceticism (by pouring icy-cold water over themselves and walking around the Main Hall 100 times while reciting prayers). There is a large, attractive park behind Shinsho Temple.

NASU SPAS (Nah-sue)

Some two train hours northwest of Tokyo along the base of Mt. Nasu, the Seven Spas of Nasu have been famous since ancient times for the beauty of the surrounding area and the efficacy of their mineral baths.

The seven spas include Nasu-Yumoto, Kita, Benten, Omaru, San-dogoya, Takao and Itamuro. Legend has it that the first and largest of the hotsprings, Nasu-Yumoto, was discovered by a warrior who chased a wounded deer into the bushes in the 7th century.

The area is celebrated for its azalea flowers in the spring and golden tree leaves in fall.

NATIONAL ANTHEM

Japan's national anthem, Kimigayo (Key-me-gah-yoe), was taken from a waka poem found in an anthology compiled some time before the 10th century.

The words of the song mean: May the reign of the Emperor continue for a thousand, nay, eight thousand generations and for the eternity it takes for small pebbles to grow into a great rock and become covered with moss.

The melody for the anthem was written by Hiromori Hayashi, an Imperial Court musician in the Meiji period (1868-1912). The song was officially designated as the national anthem in 1893.

NATIONAL BIRD

Japan's national bird is the kiji (kee-jee), or Japanese pheasant. While famed in myths and folklore, the kiji was not designated the national bird until 1947.

Found only in Japan, the kiji is noted for the marked difference in the males and females. The male of the species, much larger than the female, has a red face and dark green neck, breast and stomach. Its back is purplish, and it has a spectacularly long tail with numerous black stripes. The female, light brown with black spots, has a short tail.

The Japanese pheasant appears as a design motif and is often used as an example of beauty unique to Japan.

NATIONAL DIET LIBRARY / KOKURITSU TOSHO-KAN (Koe-kuu-reetsue Toe-sho-khan)

Japan's National Diet Library, adjacent to the National Diet Building on the north side, was completed in 1961. It is a contemporary-styled six-story building with two basement levels, and a total of 26,400 square meters of floor space.

The libarary contains over 2,500,000 books, some 25,000 different periodicals, 37,000 maps, 51,000 phonograph records and over 31,000 reels of microfilm.

The National Diet Library has 30 branches, including one in Ueno Park, the Tokyo Bunko and the Seikado Bunko. The library is open from 9 a.m. to 4:30 p.m. daily except Sundays, national holidays and the last day of the month.

The library has a substantial collection of books in English, and welcomes foreign visitors.

NATIONAL FLAG

Japan's national flag is called Nisshoki (Nees-show-kee), or The flag of the Rising Sun. It consists of a bright red sun in the center of a white banner.

The Rising Sun flag was in use as early as the 16th century to identify ships as being Japanese, and prior to that had been used on banners and shrine flags. It was formally named the national flag in 1870.

NATIONAL FLOWER

While never officially designated as such, the Japanese generally consider the Sakura (Sah-kuu-rah) or cherry as their national flower. The cherry blossom, beautiful, fragile and transitory, has long appealed to the sensibilities of Japanese, and was particularly favored by the Samurai warrior class who saw in it a reflection of their own lives—full of grace and beauty and resigned to an early death.

So taken were the Japanese by the ethereal beauty and fragility of cherry blossoms that well before the turn of the 10th century, cherry-blossom viewing was an organized spring ritual. Every district had its favorite cherry-blossom viewing spots, and the well-to-do had special buildings or grandstands constructed as vantage points from which to view the blossoms while drinking O'sake and, often, writing poetry to celebrate them.

A number of these stands, built nearly a thousand years ago, are still in existence.

Present-day locations that are famous as cherry blossom-viewing spots include Ueno Park in Tokyo and Yoshino near Nara. There are hundreds of other noted places.

The kiku (kee-kuu) or chrysanthemum, traditionally used as the Imperial Crest, has also been used at different times in different ways as symbolic of Japan.

NATIONAL HOLIDAYS

Japan has a large number of national holidays, some of which last for more than one day, and are a vital part of national life.

JANUARY 1-3 - New Years / Oshogatsu (Oh-show-got-sue)--This is Japan's premiere national holiday (it used to last for five days or more), and is marked by visits to families and friends, shrines and temples, special foods and drinks, and numerous other festivities, including the exchanging of gifts.

On New Year's eve millions of people gather at their guardian shrines or famous temples to witness the ringing out of the old year and ringing in the new year.

The first day of work after New Years is usually marked by a party atmosphere, during which people exchange congratulations on the opening of the new year, and express their wishes for a happy and successful new season. The customary greeting on meeting someone for the first time after the turn of the year is: Shin-nen Akemashite Omedeto Gozaima-su or Congratulations on the Opening of the New Year. See FESTIVALS.

JANUARY 15 - Adults' Day / Seijin-no Hi (Say-e-jeen-no He)--This day is dedicated to the young people who have attained their 20th birthday during the year. The new adults are encouraged to persevere in their educational and work goals, and thereafter conduct themselves with all the responsibility expected of adulthood.

FEBRUARY 11 - National Foundation Day / Kenkoku Kinen-no Hi (Kane-koe-kuu Kee-nane-no He)--This is Japan's 4th of July, when the founding of the country is celebrated. The date corresponds to the legendary ascension to the throne of Japan's first Emperor, Jimmu, in 660 B.C.

MARCH 20 or 21 - Vernal Equinox Day / Shumbun-no Hi (Shume-boon-no He)--This day is set aside for the people to commune with nature and reaffirm their relationship with all things in nature.

APRIL 29 - Emperor's Birthday / Tenno Tanjobi (Tane-no Tahn-joe-bee)--On this day the Imperial family appears on the balcony of the Imperial Palace to accept the good wishes of the people and exchange greetings with them. The date will change when Crown Prince Akihito succeeds his father, Hirohito.

MAY 3 - Constitution Memorial Day / Kempo Kinen Bi (Kim-poe Kee-nane Bee)--This day marks the date when Japan's constitution went into effect.

MAY 5 - Children's Day / Kodomo-no Hi (Koe-doe-moe-no He)--May 5 was traditionally celebrated as Boys' Day, but after 1945 it was changed to include all children. Adults are reminded of the need to understand and guide children, and children are reminded of their obligation to respect and obey their parents.

MAY 3 and MAY 5 together are popularly known as Golden Week, and offer many people an opportunity to take off from work for five or more days.

SEPTEMBER 15 - Senior Citizens' Day / Keiro-no Hi (Kay-e-roe-no He)--In Japan respect for the elderly has a long and honorable tradition, and is continued in this special day set aside for them.

SEPTEMBER 23 - Autumn Equinox Day / Shubun-no Hi (Shuu-boon-no He)--This is the day for paying respects and honoring one's ancestors.

OCTOBER 10 - Sports Day / Taiiku-no Hi (Tie-e-kuu-no He)--The mental and physical benefits of sports are celebrated on this day with numerous sports activities around the country.

NOVEMBER 3 - Culture Day / Bunka-no Hi (Boon-kah-no He)--Numerous activities are held to mark the importance of culture, and the love of peace and freedom. This is the day the government makes special awards to people who have made significant contributions to the nation's culture.

See NATIONAL LIVING TREASURES.

NOVEMBER 23 - Labor Thanksgiving Day / Kinro Kansha-no Hi (Keen-roe Khan-shah-no He)--This is the day for honoring workers, and to promote respect for labor and the contributions it makes to the country.

NATIONAL PARKS

Japan is one of the most picturesques countries in the world, with a range and variety of scenic beauty that has deeply influenced the philosophy, religions and daily lives of the Japanese.

The combinations of coastlines, coves, inlets, hills, mountains, rivers, gorges, valleys, volcanoes, trees and other foliage, coupled with four distinct seasons that color the country in a kaleidoscope of hues, has resulted in a land that is blessed with beauty.

Very early in their history as a people, the Japanese recognized the extraordinary beauty of the land, and incorporated a deep appreciation for it in their way of life. Their homes, shrines and temples were built in settings of special beauty so they would be able to enjoy it on a daily basis. The Japanese did not attempt to change nature, but to blend in with it.

In more recent times, great areas of special beauty were set aside as parks, national, quasi-national and prefectural. There are 27 national parks in the country, encompassing nearly five and a half percent of the nation's total land area.

Five of these national parks, including Daisetsuzan, the largest, are in Hokkaido, and are characterized by volcanoes, mountain lakes, hundreds of hotsprings, virgin forests and swamps.

The Towada-Hachimantai National Park in northern Honshu is noted for its superb seascapes. The Nikko National Park is noted for its beautiful forest-covered mountains, Lake Chuzenji, Kegon Falls and Toshogu Shrine, where Shogun Ieyasu Tokugawa is buried. The Fuji-Hakone-Izu National Park encompasses Mt. Fuji, the five lakes around it, the fabulous Hakone hotspring resorts, part of the Izu Peninsula and the Seven Isles of Izu.

The descriptions of mountains, volcanoes, lakes, gorges, waterfalls, and fantastic seacoasts go on and on in an endless litany of beauty.

Besides these huge national parks, there are a total of 47 quasi-national parks that are smaller but no less beautiful in their own way--their size often deliberately limited in the interest of space. Suffice to say that it is impossible to travel very far in any direction in Japan without encountering areas of incredible natural beauty.

Recommended reading: NATIONAL PARKS OF JAPAN, by Mary Sutherland and Dorothy Britton (Kodansha Int'l).

NATIONAL STADIUM

Japan's National Stadium, one of the largest arenas in the world with a seating capacity of 85,000, is located in Tokyo's Meiji Park (Meiji Shrine Outer Garden), midway between Shinanomachi and Sendagaya Stations on the Chuo Line.

The stadium was used during the 1964 Olympics. (That same year a bronze bust relief of Jigoro Kano, the originator of Kodokan judo and a long-time member of the International Olympic Committee, was erected at the main entrance of the stadium.)

NATIONAL THEATER / KOKURITSU GEKIJO (Koe-kuu-reet-sue Gay-kee-joe)

Japan's first state-owned theater, the Kokuritsu Gekijo is one of the most spectacular buildings in the country. Built in traditional-contemporary style (in 1960), it faces the Imperial Palace Grounds, and is a short walk from the National Diet Building.

The building contains two theaters-- one that seats 1,764, and one with 630 seats. The larger hall is used for kabuki and musical performances, including traditional court music and other traditional music and dances. The smaller theater is used for puppet shows (bunraku), traditional comedy shows (kyogen), and Japanese music and dance.

NATIONAL VACATION VILLAGES / KOKUMIN KYUKA MURA (Koe-kuu-meen Que-kah Muu-rah)

Begun in 1961 by the nonprofit National Vacation Village Association, the Kokumin Kyuka Mura are vacation village health resorts located in national parks or quasi-national parks that are noted for their hotsprings and outdoor recreational attractions.

There are some two dozen such villages around the country, and they attract more than a million visitors a year. Accommodations are all Japanese-style,

and inexpensively priced. The villages are open to foreign visitors. For locations and other details, check with the Japan National Tourist Organization. See addresses in this book.)

NETSUKE (Nate-sue-kay)

Traditional Japanese apparel does not have pockets, thus both men and women carry purses or pouches, suspended from their obi or waist bands, when they are dressed in traditional garments. Netsuke are the small, ornamental toggles that are used to attach these accessories.

Netsuke came into common use in the 16th century, but they became a really important part of the costumes of the merchant class during the 17th century, when well-to-do merchants wanted something to compete with the fancy sword-guards of Samurai and Daimyo.

The carving of netsuke thus became a highly paid profession and developed into a special art that flourished throughout the long Tokugawa Shogunate (1603-1868).

Netsuke carved during the Tokugawa period are now collectors' items, and are much in demand in Japan, the U.S. and Europe. Netsuke are carved out of such materials as ivory, shell, coral, wood and precious metals.

Measuring about four centimeters (1.2 inches) across, netsuke are intricately carved in the form of people, animals and other familiar objects.

Dealing in netsuke is a popular profession, and those made by well-known carvers command substantial prices.

Recommended reading: COLLECTORS' NETSUKE, by Raymond Bushell (Weatherhill). MASTERPIECES OF NETSUKE ART, by Bernard Hurtia (Weatherhill).

NEW OTANI HOTEL (Oh-tah-nee)

Tokyo's New Otani, adjoining the famous Akasaka entertainment and restaurant district, is one of the city's more spectacular hotels. It consists of two highrise towers connected by a mall, and has the usual shopping arcade, several restaurants, bars and clubs. But what makes it especially distinctive is its 10-acre 400-year old landscaped garden.

The hotel was built on the site of a Daimyo mansion whose garden was kept and improved on. While not historically famous, the garden now is one of the largest and most beautiful in the city-- an oasis in the heart of teeming, tumultous Tokyo.

NEWSPAPERS / SHIMBUN (Sheem-boon)

During the early decades of the

Bandai Asahi National Park. P. 225

The National Theater, Tokyo. P. 226

Tokugawa Period (1603-1868), the news was brought to the people of Japan via prints made from tile blocks, and were known as Kawara Ban (Kah-wah-rah Bahn) or Roof-Tile Prints. The first kawara ban are believed to have appeared in 1615 to announce the fall of Osaka Castle to the troops of Ieyasu Tokugawa, the retired Shogun. Young boys and men sold the prints in the streets.

The ritual suicide of the 47 ronin of Ako in the early 1700s was reported the same day by kawara ban, whose dealers are said to have made a small fortune because of the number of the prints sold following this celebrated incident. See FORTY-SEVEN RONIN.

The first Japanese language newspaper in Japan, the Batabia Shimbun, was founded in 1862 by the Tokugawa Shogunate, and was made up of translations from a paper published in Batavia. It was printed in magazine format, from woodblocks.

The first English language newspaper in Japan was the biweekly Nagasaki Shipping List and Advertiser, founded in 1861 by A. W. Hansard, an Englishman who lived in Nagasaki.

Japan's first daily newspaper was the Yokohama Mainichi Shimbun, which printed its first issue on 28 January 1871, and survived until 1940. The following year the Tokyo Nichi-Nichi Shimbun, forerunner of today's Mainichi Shimbun, made its debut, along with the Yubin Hochi Shimbun (today's Hochi Shimbun), and the Kochu Shimbun, forerunner of the Yamanashi Nichi-Nichi Shimbun in Kofu City, Yamanashi Prefecture.

For the most part, these first newspapers carried government announcements and proclamations, and were written in classical Chinese kanbun. Readership was primarily limited to the well-educated upper classes.

These newspapers were followed soon thereafter by papers catering to the general public. The great Yomiuri Shimbun began in Tokyo in 1874, and both the Asahi Shimbun and Mainichi Shimbun began in Osaka in the same decade.

Despite a revised version (in 1883) of the Press Law of 1875, which gave the government extraordinary powers over opposition-oriented newspapers, the press continued to expand. In 1882 Yukichi Fukuzawa, regarded as the most enlightened thinker of the time, founded the Jiji Shimbun, which lasted until 1936,

Japan's first true news agency, Jiji Tsushin Sha, was founded in 1888, but lasted for only two years.

The Great Kanto Earthquake of 1923 was responsible for the Mainichi Shimbun and Asahi Shimbun, both founded in Osaka, gaining a foothold in Tokyo and thereafter, along with the Yomiuri, dominating Japan's newspaper world. The quake destroyed the printing plants of the Tokyo newspapers, giving the two Osaka-based papers the opportunity to extend their influence nation-wide.

On 1 January 1924, the Asahi and Mainichi printed a record one million copies each.

With the rise of militarism in Japan in the 1930s, the government consolidated all the news services under the Domei Tsushin Sha (1936), and created an Information Committee to standardize news dissemination. When war broke out with China in 1937, all news became subject to the approval of the army and navy ministers.

By 1944 newsprint shortages had resulted in a drastic reduction in the number of newspapers, and all were limited to no more than two pages. From a high point of 1,200 dailies, the number dwindled down to 55, with only one paper allowed in each prefecture.

Today there are three kinds of newspapers in Japan—national papers, regional papers, and prefectural/local papers. Among the main regional papers are the Hokkaido Shimbun, Tokyo Shimbun, Chunichi Shimbun and the Nishi Nippon Shimbun.

The average number of pages for the national, regional and prefectural dailies is 20-24 for morning editions, and 8-12 for afternoon editions. They produce some 5-6 morning editions and 3-4 evening editions. No evening editions are printed on Sundays. The ratio of news to advertising is about 57 percent news to 43 percent advertising.

Japanese newspapers usually do not give their reporters byline credit for their stories. They also tend to write most of their own stories as opposed to using material from wire services—with the result that they have very large staffs by international standards.

The Asahi, Mainichi and Yomiuri employ well over 1,000 reporters each, and as in other major industries, employment is expected to be for life. It would be unthinkable, for example, for an Asahi man to move to the Mainichi or to any other newspaper.

One of the most controversial characteristics of Japanese journalism is the existence of so-called press clubs, of which there are about 400. Virtually every important news source in the country--government ministries, political parties, key economic organizations, private bodies, local government offices, court houses, police headquarters, etc.--is covered by one specific press or reporter's club.

The individual clubs totally control the dissemination of news from these sources as far as Japanese newspapers are concerned. The only clubs open to foreign correspondents are the club that covers the Prime Minister's office, and the one covering the Foreign Ministry.

Foreign correspondents and other reporters who are not members of these clubs can approach news sources independently, but they are prevented from taking advantage of the official press conferences arranged by sources or by the clubs themselves (and the latter are extemely powerful, since they control access to Japan's leading news media).

There is continuing pressure from the Foreign Correspondents fraternity in Japan for these exclusive clubs to open their doors to non-Japanese press members, but there is little chance of this happening on any broad scale.

Japan's major newspapers maintain large overseas networks (as do news agencies, radio and televisions stations), with some 400 correspondents stationed in 34 different countries. The tendency here again is for Japanese newspapers to depend more on their overseas correspondents than on news agencies.

General interest newspapers in Japan devote an average of 16 percent of their space to international news.

Japanese newspapers are leaders in the use of sophisticated electronic technology in typesetting and printing newspapers. Some have totally automated their production system, including the preparation and loading of bundles going out to delivery agents.

Five of Japan's 177 daily newspapers are national, and have the world's largest daily circulation. These five are the Asahi Shimbun (Ah-sah-he Shim-boon), the Yomiuri Shimbun (Yoe-me-uu-ree Shim-boon), the Mainichi Shimbun (My-nee-chee Shim-boon), the Sankei Shimbun (Sahn-kay-e Shim-boon) and the Nihon Keizai Shimbun (Nee-hone Kay-e-zie Shim-boon). See individual listings.

Yomiuri, the largest, has a morning circulation of approximately nine million. The Asahi has nearly eight million, and the Mainichi nearly five million in circulation. All of these five major dailies are affiliated with one of Tokyo's commercial TV networks--namely, ANB, NTV, TBS, Fuji and Television Tokyo, respectively.

Some 92 percent of Japan's newspaper sales are to regular subscribers through district and neighborhood delivery agents.

NEWSPAPERS IN ENGLISH

There are four daily English-language newspapers in Japan, and a number of weekly specialized tabloids. The dailies are the Asahi Evening News, The Daily Yomiuri, The Japan Times (which also has a daily airmail edition and a weekly edition--The Japan Times Weekly), and the Mainichi Daily News.

The Asahi Evening News, owned by the huge Japanese-language Asahi Shimbun, is Japan's only English-language evening newspaper, and is noted for reflecting the editorial viewpoints of its parent company. William Lederer, who wrote the books THE UGLY AMERICAN and A NATION OF SHEEP and once worked on the Asahi Evening News, described the AEN is the best newspaper in the world.

The Daily Yomiuri, owned by the nationally circulated Yomiuri Shimbun, carries both international and local news, and is particularly known for its coverage of the political scene in Japan.

The Japan Times, the only major English-language daily newspaper in Japan not owned by one of the vernacular papers, has the largest circulation of any of the English-language newspapers and is the oldest (founded in 1897).

The Japan Times is the most internationally oriented of the English-language dailies in Japan, and covers political, social, business, financial, sports and entertainment news. One of the most important of its features is a large Classified Ads section.

Over the decades, many of the foreign writers who have specialized in Japan (including myself) were either contributors or staff members on The Japan Times. Thousands of former foreign residents of Tokyo and other parts of Japan continue to subscribe to The Japan Times after returning to their home countries.

The Mainichi Daily News, a subsidiary of the huge nationally circulated Mainichi Shimbun, has its own personality in that it appears to be less foreignized than the other subsidiary newspapers, with one page devoted entirely to Japanese news.

The weekly Japan Economic Journal is the international edition of the Nihon Kezai Shimbun (Japan Economic Journal), which is the Japanese equivalent of the

Wall Street Journal. It is published in both Tokyo and New York, and covers the economy, trade, finance, the stock market and politics in Japan.

NEWS SERVICES

Japan's first news service, Jiji Tsushin Sha (Jee-jee T'sue-sheen Shah), lasted only from 1888 to 1890, but was follwed by the Teikoku News Agency in 1892, and the Nippon Denpo News Agency (which was to become Dentsu Inc.) in 1901. The first international news agency in Japan appeared in 1914 as a result of an affiliation, arranged by several influential businessmen and diplomats, with the Associated Press of the U.S.

In 1918 government sources sponsored the inauguration of the Toho News Agency to help publicize Japan's side of its activities in regard to China. In 1926 Kokusai and Toho merged to form the Nihon Rengo News Agency.

For the next decade and a half, Rengo, a non-profit company backed by the U.S.'s Associated Press, and Dentsu, a commercial operation backed by United Press of the U.S., competed fiercely against each other.

In 1936 the government ended the competition by forcing the two agencies to merge and become the Domei News Agency. Following the end of World War II in 1945, Domei was declared a monopoly by the U.S. Occupation Forces, and the agency was split into Kyodo News Service and Jiji Press.

Kyodo News Service is a cooperative owned by 63 Japanese newspapers, including the giant Asahi, Yomiuri and Mainichi. Kyodo also supplies news on a contract basis to other newspapers and 60 commercial broadcasting companies. It has working arrangements with AP and UPI of the U.S., Reuters of Britain, Tass of the Soviet Union and Xinhua of China. It also maintains correspondents and stringers in some 40 major cities around the world.

Jiji Press is now a stock company owned by its employees. It distributes to some 150 newspapers and broadcasting stations throughout Japan, by facsimile and leased wire. It has exclusive rights to distribute in Japan stories of Agence France-Press, Reuters Economic Service and Deutsche Press-Agentur. In 1975, Jiji became the first Japanese news agency to inaugurate an overseas facsimile transmission system, which now transmits daily Japanese news to its 13 overseas offices for distribution to Japanse diplomatic missions and Japanese companies.

NEW YEAR'S CALL

It is customary in Japan to pay a courtesy call on customers, superiors and others with whom you have a special relationship, some time after January 3rd to wish them a Happy New Year, and to ask for their continued friendship, goodwill, help or support during the new year.

This is an institutionalized practice that is very meaningful and important in maintaining good relations with clients and others, especially if some or all of your business depends on them. It is also customary to present a gift of some kind on this occasion.

NEW YEAR'S PARTY / SHIN NEN KAI (Sheen nane kie)

In the old days in Japan it was customary to hold New Year's parties sometime from around the 3rd to the 10th, depending on when people went back to their normal routines.

Such parties are still common, but the majority of them are held at the work-place or in restaurants, and involve fellow employees. The parties are actually official New Year greeting occasions, when people congratulate each other on the opening of the new year, and ask for the understanding, goodwill and support of their colleagues and customers for the coming year.

NHK / JAPAN BROADCASTING CORPORATION

NHK, which is short for Nippon Hoso Kyokai (Neep-pone Hoe-so k'yoe-kie), literally the Japan Broadcasting Association, is probably the best-known and most popular radio and television network in the country.

NHK originated radio broadcasting in Japan in 1925, and television broadcasting in 1953, and remains today the only non-commercial public corporation in the broadcasting field--but it is not controlled or operated by the government.

Under the provisions of a Broadcast Law passed in 1950, NHK levies a monthly fee on all households in the country that receive its broadcasts--with those having color TV sets paying a slightly higher fee. The same law prohibits NHK from engaging in commercial advertising.

NHK broadcasts close to 1,000 hours a day over its five domestic networks--two television, two radio and one FM--with virtually 100 percent national coverage.

The various daily programs are divided into news, culture, entertainment and education, with the amount of time devoted to each category varying according to the network.

The First Radio Network devotes 42.7% of its time to news, 31.9% to cultural subjects, 24% to entertainment and 1.4% to education.

The Second Radio Network devotes 81% of its broadcast hours to education, 13.7% to culture and 5.3% to news. The FM Network spends 48.8% of its time on culture, 30.7% on entertainment, 12.6% on news and 7.9% on education.

The General TV Network of NHK devotes 36.4% of its time to culture, 31.8% to news, 22.3% to entertainment and 9.6% to education. The Educational TV Network is devoted solely to education (84.5%) and culture (15.5%).

With this kind of programming, and being strictly non-commercial, NHK commands a high percentage of Japan's television viewers and radio listeners. It is noted for the superior quality and variety of its programs, regularly dispatching teams of directors and crews all over Japan and the world to produce documentaries on every conceivable subject.

NHK also operates a very large Overseas Broadcasting Service, with a daily total of some 38 hours in 23 languages. This service is divided into General and Regional Service.

The General Service division broadcasts for 30 minutes every hour in English and Japanese. The Regional Service is broadcast to specific linguistic areas--in languages ranging from English, French, German, Italian, Arabic, Chinese, Korean, Vietnamese, Malay and Russian to Burmese, Thai, Bengali, Hindi, Urdu and Swahili.

NHK's overseas broadcasts consist of news, entertainment, sports and music.

NICHIREN (Nee-chee-rane)

One of Japan's most famous religious leaders, Nichiren was born in 1222 in the little village of Awa-Kominato in what is now Chiba Prefecture on Boso Peninsula southeast of Tokyo. He became a Buddhist priest at the age of 15, studied for three years at a Buddhist monastery on Mt. Hiei near Kyoto, then returned to his native village.

Nichiren was a firey preacher who began espousing a new doctrine that quickly got him expelled from Kominato. Going to Matsubagayatsu in Kamakura, south of present-day Tokyo in the Miura Peninsula, he built a hermitage and spent the next three years studying, writing and preaching on the streets of Kamakura (which at that time was the Shogunate capital of Japan).

The two most important tracts that Nichiren wrote during these years were THE DEFENSE OF THE STATE, and ON PUBLIC PEACE. The Kamakura Shogunate did not take criticism lightly, and exiled the outspoken priest to Ito, on Izu Peninsula (now a noted hotsprings resort).

On his release from exile, Nichiren returned to Kamakura and began preaching in the streets again--more vehement then ever. He was again arrested and taken to Katase Beach, the official execution grounds, to be beheaded. But the executioner's sword broke when he tested it, and the officials decided to let the priest go.

Nichiren did not choose to stay out of trouble with the Shogunate, and some time later was exiled to the cold island of Sado, off the coast of Niigata in the Japan Sea.

Finally, after a stormy career of over 40 years, Nichiren died in 1282 at the age of 60, in Ikegami, now part of Tokyo. He was buried at Kuon Temple in Minobu, west of Mt. Fuji.

Nichiren's disciples built a temple in Kominato in 1276 to commemorate his birth. The temple, called Tanjo (Birthday) Temple, was destroyed by a tidal wave and fire, and the present building was completed during the Tempo era of the Tokugawa Period (1830-1843).

In February every year, when Nichiren's birthday is celebrated, the temple is filled with visitors. There are several Nichiren sect temples in Kamakura, including the Anokokuron, founded in 1274 by Nichro, one of Nichiren's chief disciples. The primary treasure in the temple is a copy of Nichiren's On Public Peace tract (Ankokuron), transcribed by Nichiro.

NIEMON JIMA (Nee-eh-moan Jee-mah)

If you are ever on the southern tip of Boso Peninsula (Chiba Prefecture)--maybe to see the some 1,500 semi-nude women divers of Shirahama gather seaweed, ear shells and top shells off the pictureesque coast--you are close to a place famous in Japanese history: the tiny islet of Niemon.

Niemon Island is where Yoritomo Minamoto, the founder of Japan's first Shogunate dynasty (in 1192), was hidden from his enemies by the Niemon family prior to becoming the supreme military power in the country.

After becoming Shogun, Yoritomo gave the island to the Niemons as their own private fief.

Today there is a famous Flower Zone adjoining the Niemon pier in the port town of Futomi, where flowers of many kinds are raised in hothouses.

NIGHT CLUBS / NAITO KURABU (Nie-toe Kuu-rah-buu)

Japan has the largest variety of night-time entertainment facilities of any nation in the world, ranging from a dozen or more different kinds of bars, at least as many different types of lounges, plus beer halls, dinner show clubs, geisha inns, cabarets and so on.

Legally speaking, there is no such thing as a night club in Japan, since all entertainment establishments that employ hostesses are classified as cabarets--and all of Japan's so-called night clubs have hostesses.

But there are basic differences between a regular cabaret and a so-called night club. A cabaret that calls itself a night club caters specifically to foreign as well as Japanese clientele. Night club patrons have a choice of whether or not they want the company of a hostess.

Entertainment in a night club is more likely to be Western style or a combination of both Japanese and Western. Night clubs are more likely to have full kitchen facilities and serve full meals.

Night clubs cater to couples as well as single men--and one of the favorite afterhours activities of cabaret hostesses is to get their customers to take them to a night club after their cabaret closes. Cabarets generally close at 11 p.m.--with 30 minutes for everybody to clear out, while night clubs that serve food (and qualify as a restaurant) stay open to the wee hours.

Finally, the clientele of most cabarets are businessmen on expense accounts, and usually charge their bills to their firms. Night clubs, especially where foreign customers are concerned, are morely likely to be on a strict cash basis. Night clubs also have table or cover charges that are separate from any other consideration, while in cabarets the table charge usually comes in the form of a tray or basket of O'tsumami (Oh-t'sue-mah-me), which consists of peanuts, Osembe nuggets, etc.).

There is some crossing over of the distinctions between cabarets and night clubs, depending on the individual place.

NIIGATA (Nee-gah-tah)

The capital city of Niigata Prefecture, Niigata is Japan's chief port on the Japan Sea side of the main island of Honshu. The city sets on an estuary of the Shinano River, and is separated from the sea by a row of low sand hills. It is criss-crossed by many canals which once were important transportation arterials.

Niigata was one of the first ports in Japan to be opened to foreign trade after the fall of the Tokugawa Shogunate in 1868. It is now known for its chemical industry, based on oil and natural gas in the area, and as the gateway to Sado Island. The Niigata Festival, which is held from August 21 to 23 each year, is one of the most popular annual events in the city.

The Bullet Train from Tokyo to Niigata (170 miles/two hours) passes through 23 tunnels, including the 13.8-mile long Shimizu Tunnel.

NIKKO (Neek-koe)

Nikko is both a national park and the mountain town where the spirits of three of Japan's greatest heroes are interred --Yoritomo Minamoto, Hideyoshi Toyotomi and Ieyasu Tokugawa.

Encompassing an area of 140,698 ha., and sprawling over parts of Tochigi, Gunma, Fukushima and Niigata Prefectures northwest of Tokyo, Nikko National Park has two great things going for it--it is one of the most scenic spots on earth, and is the location of the Toshogu (Toe-show-guu), the mausolea of Ieyasu (and his grandson Iemitsu), and the shrine complex that commemorates Ieyasu and the two other heroes named above.

The park is comprised of mountains, rivers, waterfalls, cascades, lakes and huge old trees in a combination that magnificent simply cannot do justice to. Then there are the mausolea and shrines of Nikko, as impressive in their own way as the pyramids of Egypt.

In an attempt to suggest the extraordinary variety and depth of the beauty of Nikko, the Japanese have a saying: Never say kekko (wonderful) until you've seen Nikko! The region has such a variety of geographical diversity, plant life and network of streams that it is often described as one vast natural museum.

Besides the attractions of the Toshogu in Nikko town, the park includes the Kegon Waterfalls and Lake Chuzenji just above Nikko, summer and winter (ski) resorts in Oku-Nikko, and two major spas, Shiobara and Nasu, and numerous lesser ones.

There are three ways of reaching Nikko proper from Tokyo--by the Japanese Natonal Railways (JNR) from either Tokyo or Ueno Stations, Tobu Railway's Nikko Line from Asakusa Station in northeast Tokyo, and by bus or private vehicle via the historically famous Nikko Highway.

The trip from Tokyo to Nikko by train takes a little over two hours.

NIKKO MAUSOLEA

When Shogun Ieyasu Tokugawa, the founder of Japan's last great feudal dyansty and the benefactor of Pilot Will Adams, died in 1616 he was buried temporarily at Kunozan in Shizuoka. But Ieyasu left instructions that he was to buried in the mountain religious center of Nikko, some two train hours north of Tokyo, and this was done the following year.

In 1634, Iemitsu, Ieyasu's grandson and the Shogun at that time, initiated the construction of a mausoleum and shrine to honor his famous grandfather. Thousands of carpenters and artisans were brought from Kyoto and Nara to work on the project. They were organized into teams and set to competing against other, often working around the clock.

The buildings were completed in 1636, and were among the most elaborate and probably the most expensive structures built in Japan up to that time.

Altogether, 15,000 men were employed in the construction of the mausolea and shrine. Over 2,489,000 gold leaf sheets were used in the gilding of the mausolea.

Iemitsu's successor, Ietsuna, granted the memorial a fief to provide for its maintenance, and the Emperor appointed an Imperial Prince to preside over the shrine--a system that was to be continued until 1868, when the last Shogun stepped down.

Some 17 years after the completion of Ieyasu's memorial shrine, a second mausoleum was built for Iemitsu.

During the remainder of the long Tokugawa Shogunate, the buildings were completed renovated ever 20 years. It took 10 years to collect duplicates of the timber and other materials used in the construction of the mausolea and shrine, and another 10 years to complete each renovation, so work of one kind or another was in progress at all times.

All of the feudal lords of Japan were ordered to contribute to the building of the memorial to Ieyasu. Masatsuna Matsudaira could not afford to match the offerings made by some of the richer fiefs, but he came up with a plan that was to make his gift the best of all. He had his men plant Japanese cedars along the roads leading to the shrine--a project that took 20 years. Today, some 13,000 of those trees are still standing.

In 1867 when the last Shogun decided to turn power over to the Emperor, a group of Tokugawa Samurai took possession of the shrine and mausolea and vowed to hold them against the Imperial forces to the death. Fearing that the treasured buildings would be destroyed in any conflict, Count Taisuke Itagaki, a leading statesman of the era, persuaded the Shoguante loyalists to leave the buildings, thus saving them for posterity.

Today the Mausolea of Nikko are one of Japan's most famous sights, attraction hundreds of thousands of Japanese and foreign visitors every year.

The shrine complex, popularly known as the Toshogu (Toe-show-goo) consists of 15 major structures, including a huge granite torii, a five-story pagoda, two huge gates, a main hall, the tomb of Ieyasu, a storehouse, and stables. One of the gates, Yomeimon, is regarded as the most luxurious gate in Japan and itself is a registered National Treasure.

To see all of the wonders of the Toshogu takes several hours at least--it is often said more than in jest that it would take 24 hours just to appreciate all of the features of Yomei Gate.

The big event in Nikko is the Spring Festival of Toshogu Shrine, held each year on May 17 and 18, and featuring a procession of 1,000 people attired in the costumes of Samurai, priests and officials of the Tokugawa era.

On the morning of May 18 the spirits of Yoritomo Minamoto, Hideyoshi Toyotomi and Ieyasu Tokugawa, Japan's greatest military leaders, are transferred to portable shrines (mikoshi), taken in procession to the Sojourning Hall, where sacred music is played, offerings are made and sacred dances performed. Afterward, the spirits are returned to their resting place.

Another event on this day is a demonstration of yabusame, or horseback archery, by horsemen dressed in hunting attire of the feudal age. See YABUSAME.

A smaller Autumn Festival is held on October 17, but it is often attended by a larger number of people than the spring celebration because Nikko is one of the prime beauty spots of Japan during the fall season.

There are other events held in Nikko during different times of the year, and it is one of the nation's major sightseeing destinations throughout the spring, summer and fall.

NIKKO-YUMOTO SPA / NIKKO-YUMOTO ONSEN (Neek-koe Yuu-moe-toe Own-sin)

About 30 kilometers from Nikko Station (and 13 kilometers from Lake Chuzenji above Nikko), the Nikko-Yumoto Spa is famous all year-around for its hot-springs, and in winter for its ski slopes and ice-skating rinks.

The resort is surrounded on three sides by mountains, and is noted for its easy accessibility, the abundance of its hot mineral waters, and other recreational facilities in the area.

NINJA (Neen-jah)

Now a fairly well-known word around the world, a ninja is a practitioner of Ninjutsu (Neen-jute-sue), or The Art of Stealing In, a very special category of secret agent that developed in feudal Japan and played a vital role in the lives and fortunes of the Shogun and the provincial Daimyo lords.

The ninja belonged to specific ninja families, who usually lived in remote mountain areas. They kept their identities secret and trained in secret, beginning virtually as soon as they were able to walk.

They were trained in running (forward, backward and sideways), climbing, jumping, crawling, hiding, hanging from rafters and trees, swimming (especially under water), fighting with an amazing variety of weapons including many that they developed themselves, using poisons, medicines and other chemicals, and so on.

So incredible were their feats of strength, speed and skill, along with their ability to penetrate the most closely guarded areas and never be seen, that common people believed they could make themselves invisible and perform other magical feats.

When at work, the ninja wore especially designed black costumes in which their weapons and other aides were artfully concealed—and they almost always worked at night.

The ninja were hired by the different Daimyo and Samurai families as spies, terrorists and assassins, especially during periods of internal strife, and they were the most feared of all the enemies a person could face.

There are voluminous records of the exploits of ninja, attesting to their total dedication and extraordinary ability to perform feats that would put even 007 of James Bond fame to shame—and their feats were for real.

Just two of the more startling assassination techniques that were successfully used by ninja: a male ninja secreted himself in the excrement of a pit toilet in the home of a victim. When the victim came in and squatted over the pit, the ninja impaled him on a short spear.

A female ninja, assigned to kill a certain man who had an eye for pretty women, secreted a poisoned razor blade in her vagina, and then danced for the man, knowing he would later invite her to his chambers.

Not all of the incredible skills of the ninja have been totally forgotten. There are several ninja devotees in Japan today who are able to duplicate many of the feats of these feudal masters of death.

Recommending reading: NINJUTSU—The Art of Invisibility, by Donn Draeger (Phoenix Books/Publishers). THE NINJA AND THEIR SECRET FIGHTING ART, by Stephen K. Hayes (Tuttle). NINJA: The Invisibile Assassins, by Andrew Adams (Ohara Publications). NINJA: Warrior Path to Togakure, by Stephen K. Hayes (Ohara).

NISHIJIN (Nee-she-jeen)

Nishijin is a district in Kotyo that over the centuries has become famous for its silk brocades and other elaborately woven fabrics. The area got its name during the Onin War (1467-77) when a West Camp (Nishi Jin) was set up on the northwestern outskirts of the city.

Much of Kyoto was destroyed during the war, so most of the weavers in the city moved to Nishi Jin and set up operation there. The area eventually became synonymous with woven fabrics, especially silk brocades.

The district got its biggest boost when the Tokugawa Shogunate ordered that all the nobles and members of the Imperial Court in Kyoto were to wear costumes made of fabrics woven at Nishijin.

Nishijin still makes the finest brocades in Japan, and its fabrics are much in demand by noh and kabuki actors, the tv and film industry, and for making ornamental obi for kimono.

NISSAN MOTOR COMPANY (Neese-sahn)

The manufacturer of Japan's famous Datsun line of cars and trucks, Nissan Motor Company Ltd. was founded in December 1933 as Jidosha Seizo Company, or Car Manufacturing Company, a joint venture between Tobata Imono Company and Nihon Sangyo Company.

The name was soon changed to Nissan, which means Daily Production Company. The name Datsun is the combination of the initials of the three men who developed it (D.A.T.) and son--the son of D, A and T! The spelling of son was changed to sun for the sake of euphony--a common practice in Japan.

Nissan's first fully integrated production plant began operating in 1935, and its first KD units (disassembled cars) were shipped abroad in 1940. The company's facilities were used for the war effort from 1941 to 1945. Peacetime production was resumed at the Yoshiwara plant in 1945.

In 1952, Nissan signed an agreement with England's Austin Motor Company to produce Austins in Japan. The company began to attract international attention in 1958 when its cars took first and fourth places at an Australian rally.

That same year Nissan participated in an Imported Car Show in Los Angeles, and subsequently signed dealer contracts in Los Angeles and New York.

In 1960 Nissan won the 10th Annual Deming Prize for excellence in industrial engineering, and also established Nissan Motor Corporation (USA) in Los Angeles. The following year the company set up a manufacturing plant in Mexico (Nissan Mexicana), which began production in 1966.

Other highlights of 1966 was the opening of Nissan Motor Co. (Australia), and a merger with Prince Motor Company, another Japanese auto maker. That same year, the company produced the Nissan Prince Royal, the first domestically manufactured limousine to be used by the Imperial Family.

In 1970 Nissan established the Japan Automatic Transmission Company as a joint venture with Ford Motor Company and Toyo Kogyo Company, and in the next three years moved into the watercraft, rocket, and weaving machine fields.

Rapid growth continued. New joint ventures were established with German firms, a manufacturing plant was opened in Australia, and in 1977, the company succeeded in developing the world's first industrial robot with multiple arms.

In 1978 Nissan won a technology award from the Japan Society of Mechanical Engineers for the development of a new type of engine that met Japan's strict emission standards--the NAPS-Z engine. That same year the company set up Nissan Trading to facilitate the import of auto parts in Japan.

In 1980 Nissan acquired a 36 percent share (later increased to 54.66 percent) of Motor Iberica of Spain, and set up ARNA, a joint venture with Italy's famous Alfa Romeo. The same year, Nissan announced plans to build a truck manufacturing plant in the U.S.

Nissan's Datsun Sunny passenger car won the U.S.'s top EPA gas mileage rating for the third year in a row in 1980, a joint venture was signed with Volkswagen to produce VW's new Santana line in Japan, and the company opened its new Technical Center in Atsugi, Kanagawa.

The highlight of 1981 was the decision to begin marketing all of its vehicles worldwide under the Nissan name, instead of the Datsun product name.

In December 1983, Nissan celebrated its 50th anniversary, at which time it had over 57,000 employees, annual sales of over three trillion yen (US$12 billion), and was one of the world's top automakers.

By that time, Nissan was producing nearly 20 different passenger car models, including the President, Cedric, Gloria, Fairlady, Laurel, Leopard, Skyline, Bluebird, Silvia, Gazelle, Stanza, Auster, Liberta Villa, Prairie, Sunny, Laurel Spirit, Pulsar, Langley and March. Plus 17 truck and bus models.

Nissan has continued its diversification into other fields, and is presently active in textile machinery, aerospace equipment, forklifts, and marine products.

NITOBE, DR. INAZO (Nee-toe-bay, E-nah-zoe)

Born in 1862 in Morioka on northern Honshu to a well-known Samurai family, Inazo Nitobe attended Sapporo Agricultural College, then served briefly in the Hokkaido Colonial Government before leaving to study economics, history and literature at Johns Hopkins University in the U.S. for three years.

Returning to Japan in 1888, he was appointed an assistant professor at his alma mater, but chose to go to Germany the same year to study at Bonn and Halle Universities.

Back in Japan in 1891, Nitobe again joined Sapporo Agricultural University, became an engineer for the Hokkaido Government, and then engineer to the Government of Taiwan. In 1909 he became a professor at the Tokyo Imperial University, and in 1914 president of Tokyo Women's University.

In 1919 Dr. Nitobe became the Under-Secretary of the League of Nations, a post he held until becoming chairman of the board of directors of the Institute of Pacific Relations in 1926.

Dr. Nitobe was a prolific writer, and published several books, including the bestselling BUSHIDO--The Way of the Warrior, which delved into the moral and philosophical underpinnings of the code of the Samurai. He also achieved an international reputation as an educator and expert in international affairs, and was one of the best-known of Japan's Meiji era figures.

He died in Victoria, British Columbia in 1933, while attending a conference of the Institute of Pacific Relations.

NOBEL PRIZE WINNERS

As of 1983, six Japanese had won Nobel Prizes, primarily in science. The winners were: Hideki Yukawa, who won his prize for showing that the meson provides the nuclear force between the proton and neutron (1949). Shinichiro Tomonaga, for work in the field of quantum electromagnetics (1965). Yasunari Kawabata, for his novels Snow Country, Dancing Girl of Izu, The Thousand Cranes, The Sound of the Mountain, and other works (1968).

Leona Esaki, for research on the tunnel effect in semi-conductors, and development of the Esaki Diode (1973).

Eisaku Sato, for his efforts on behalf of peace (1974), and Kenichi Fukui, for developing the frontier orbital theory in chemical reaction processes (1981).

NOBORIBETSU SPA (No-boe-ree-bate-sue)

In between Muroran and Sapporo on Hokkaido, the Noboribetsu Spa is one of the most extraordinary and famous hot-spring resorts in Japan. Located in a large ravine formed by the Kusurisambetsu River, and walled in by heavily timbered mountains, the spa consists of 11 hotsprings with varying mineral content and temperatures.

The springs have been in use since the 1600s, because it is known that the famous Zen priest Enku visited the hot-springs before the beginning of the Tokugawa Period in 1603. But they really became popular only after 1858 when a man named Kinzo Takimoto went there to get help for a skin disease, and was so impressed with the place he and his wife opened an inn there and began promoting the medicinal value of the hotsprings.

The best-known of the dozens of hot-spring inns in the ravine is still the Daiichi Takimoto. There are 40 baths in its bathing room, with 10 different kinds of mineral water.

Only 400 meters from Noboribetsu is a place called Jigoku Dani or Valley of Hell, which is the source of the hot waters that supply the inns of Noboribetsu. An immense depression (1.6 kilometers in circumference and about 100 meters deep) that is filled with cones and sinter hills, Jigoku Dani is an awesome sight.

A short distance away, up a hill and through the woods, one comes to the rim of an immense chasm that is apparently the remnants of a crater. At the bottom of the crater is a lake of hot mud and boiling water. Sulphurous steam pours out of a peak on the far side of the lake.

There are a number of other hotspring spas in the vicinity, including New Noboribetsu Spa, and Karurusu. The latter is distinctive in that the baths are carved out of bed-rock along the sides of a ravine, instead of being inside the ryokan.

The baths are especially popular, even during the winter months when it is very, very cold. The spa is named after the famous Karlsbad Springs in Czechoslovakia, because its waters are similar in mineral content and are known to be beneficial in relieving the same kind of ailments (nervous disorders, rheumatism, spinal problems, etc.).

There is also an Ainu Museum in the Noboribetsu Spa complex.

NOGI, GENERAL MARESUKE (Mah-ray-sue-kay No-ghee)

One of Japan's most famous post-Shogunate generals, Maresuke Nogi was born in 1849, and took part in the fighting surrounding the fall of the Shogunate in 1868, the war with China in 1995 and the war with Russia in 1905.

As a result of his brilliant performances in the wars against China and Russia, he became a national hero, and was greatly prized by Emperor Meiji to whom he gave total loyalty in the highest Samurai traditions.

When Emperor Meiji died in 1912, General Nogi and his wife committed suicide just as the Emperor's funeral cortege was leaving the palace.

In 1916 a shrine (Nogi Jinja) dedicated to the famous general was built on Momoyama (Peach Hill) on the outskirts of Kyoto near the mausoleum of Emperor and Empress Meiji.

There is also a shrine dedicated to Nogi in Tokyo's Minato Ward, at Nogi-Zaka (Nogi Slope), a stop on the Chiyoda Subway Line.

NOGUCHI, DR. HIDEYO (No-guu-chee, He-day-yoe)

One of the most brilliant scientists of the Meiji and Taisho Eras (1868-1928), Dr. Hideyo Noguchi was born to peasant parents in Fukushima Prefecture in 1876, and took up the study of medicine while still in his teens.

In 1899, Noguchi entered the University of Pennsylvania, where he studied bacteriology. After graduating, he went to work for the Carnegie Science Laboratory, which sent him to Europe to study serum therapy.

Already recognized as a brilliant research scientists by this time, Dr. Noguchi was invited to join the staff of the Rockefeller Institute, and in 1925 went to the African Gold Coast to study the cause of yellow fever.

Noguchi contracted the disease he was studying, and died from it in 1928.

NOH (Noh)

The oldest form of theater in Japan, noh began as a rustic mimetic art form called sarugaku in ancient times, but did not really begin to flourish until the 14th century, when it came under the special patronage of the Samurai or ruling class.

The reknowned Kan'ami and his more famous son Zeami refined the drama form, and gained the official support of Shogun Yoshimitsu Ashikaga (1368-94).

Noh is a highly stylized dance drama performed to the accompaniment of music and singing. Principal noh actors wear masks to enhance the sublimation of reality and symbolic movements, adding to the depth and impact of the form.

Elaborate costumes, along with the masks, are the main elements setting the unique mood and form of noh.

Altogether there are some 250 noh plays, generally grouped into five main classifications according to subject matter. These five categories are Shin (God), nan (man), nyo (woman), kyo (madness) and ki (demons).

The stylized singing that is part of the noh drama is called yokyoku (yoe-k'yoe-kuu), and is also practiced as an independent art.

Early in the Tokugawa Period (1603-1868), the Tokugawa Shogunate licensed five schools of noh for the entertainment of the ruling Samurai class, and it has flourished ever since.

Recommended reading: NOH--The Classical Theater of Japan, by Donald Keene (Kodansha Int'l).

Other traditional drama forms that are popular in Japan:

KYOGEN--Short comic plays that were developed about the same time as noh, and usully on the same bill, kyogen are characterized by their realism and ribald humor.

SHINPA--Developed in the Meiji Era (1868-1912) to depict the manners and customs of contempory Japan, shinpa (sheen-pah) or new school drama, features a more naturalistic style of acting than the traditional kabuki, and includes actresses as well as oyama--male actors who portray female characters.

SHINKOKUGEKI--A form of popular theater that mainly presents realistic period dramas, shinkokugeki (new national theater) dates from the same period as the shinpa.

Japan is also famous for its musical revues, particularly the Takarazuka revues, which feature all female casts. Organized along the lines of French revues, the large-scale Takarazuka musicals attract large audiences, mostly of young women, and their stars are national figures.

Japan's shingeki (sheen-gay-kee) or new theater, grew from the desire to reflect modern social conditions, in contemporary terms. First came translations of Western dramas, then in the 1920s there was the proletarian drama movment. In the late 1960s small avant-garde groups called angura (ahn-guu-rah), short for under-ground, appeared, and won praise for their inovative techniques.

There are some 550 privately owned playhouses and 550 cultural halls in Japan. Most large playhouses are owned by Japan's Big Two entertainment conglomerates, Toho and Shochiku, and present kabuki, shinpa, revues, comedies and other types of stage entertainment. Plays usually run for around a month.

Most shingeki troupes rent theaters as they are needed. Several of the troupes have organized clubs to help them meet their financial needs.

Japan's spectacular Kokuritsu Gekijo (Koe-kuu-reet-sue Gay-kee-joe), or National Theater, constructed in 1960, presents such traditional performing arts as noh and kyogen.

NOREN (No-rane)

Noren are the short, split curtains that one still sees hung in front of many eating and drinking establishments, as well as some shops selling traditional Japanese goods.

Originally designed to help keep out dust and block the sun, noren were already in common use during the Heian era (794-1185). They became even more popular in the Muromachi Period (1333-1568), with the development of larger stores, because they made it easier for large numbers of customers to come and go.

It was during this period that it became customary to dye the noren navy blue and for the name or crest of the shop to appear on them in white. As time went by, the noren/crest of individual shops came to be widely recognized and identified with the image and reputation of the shop.

It also became customary that when a favored apprentice left a shop to set up his own business he would be allowed to use the noren/crest of his master, not only to help him get off to a good start but also has a sign of his obligation to his former master.

Besides their traditional use, noren are now sometimes used for decorative purposes and as room dividers. They are generally made of cotton cloth, but also come in hemp and wood or plastic beads.

NURSERY SONGS

More so perhaps than any other people, Japanese mothers, grandmothers and others sing nursery songs to babies and small children. Many of the songs sung are traditional, having been passed down for generations. Among the most popular

titles: First Star, Bird in the Cage, How Old Are You, Moon?, Through the Bridge, and Zuizuizukkorobashi.

Over a dozen songs of contemporary origin, such as Baby Raven, Dragonfly, Canary, Red Shoes, and Desert in the Moonlight, are also known by virtually every child in Japan.

This age-old custom of singing to babies is one of the reason why most Japanese grow up able to sing fairly well, and are willing to sing at parties and other gatherings without the kind of embarrassment that afflicts the typical Westerner under similar circumstances.

O'BON (Oh-bone)

This is the Buddhist Feast of All Souls, one of Japan's most important festivals. It originated in India as a ceremony to provide some respite for the unhappy souls of the departed who did not enter into Nirvana. They were invited to return to the land of the living during this period when the gates to Hades are temperarily open.

The practice is believed to have started in Japan during the reign of Empress Saimei in the 7th century, although there were Shinto rituals on behalf of the dead prior to that time.

Depending on the area, O'bon is celebrated from July 13-16, or from August 13-16 if the lunar calendar is followed. On the 13th people visit the graves of their ancestors, burn incense and in the evening hang lanterns over the graves. The spirits are then invited to the homes. On the 15th, special foods are prepared and served, with some families setting places for their departed relatives.

In the old days it was customary for people to carry lighted lanterns from the graves to their homes, showing the way for the spirits, and to light bonfires in the front of their homes to help guide the spirirts.

It was also common for the food and other special things prepared for the spirits to be put into small straw boats, lighted with candles, and set adrift in rivers or the ocean to comfort those who died at sea.

Far from being a sad time, O'bon has traditionally been a joyous and welcome occasion, especialllly in the countryside with the rice-planting over, homes cleaned up and special foods prepared, both for the spirits of the dead as well as the return of children and relatives from thecities.

Since ancient times the occasion has been marked all over the country by dancing that was first ritualistic but eventually came to be done for the joy of it--the famous Bon Odori (Bone Oh-doe-ree), or O'bon dances.

These dances usually begin in the early evening around dusk and continue on into the night, either at shrines or temples, or in some places like Tokushima, in the streets. Dancers dress in the light cotton yukata (you-kah-tah) kimono robes and sandals, and dance to the music of flutes, drums and the shamisen, played by musicians on a raised, high platform.

The dances have different names in different regions. The one in Tokushima is the famous Awa Odori (Ah-wah Oh-dore-ree), featured in many movies and television specials, and usually seen each year on TV news during O'bon.

Folk songs are also an integral part of the O'bon festival, one of the most popular being Tanko Bushi (Tahn-koe Buu-shee) or Coal Miners' Song, which is also a popular party song throughout the year.

The traditional Bon Odori song of Mito declares:

> Ha! Bon ga kitano ni
> Odoranu yatsu wa,
> Kibutsu, kanabutsu,
> Are sa, ishi botoke!

> Now O'Bon has come,
> He who does not dance
> Is like a wooden or metal Buddha,
> Or one of stone!

ODA, NOBUNAGA (No-buu-nah-gah Oh-dah)

A descendant of the famous Taira clan and a hereditary Daimyo (provincial lord), Nobunaga Oda was born in 1534. Like his Samurai ancestors, Nobunaga's passion was martial arts and the strategy of war, at which he became an expert.

In fact, Nobunaga spent so much time engaged in military exercises that he neglected his domain until one of his retainers send him a letter, urging him to change his ways before he brought on the downfall of the House of Oda. The retainer then committed suicide for having exceeded his authority in admonishing his own lord.

The letter and his retainer's death sobered Nobunaga, however, and he began to take his reponsibilities seriously. At the age of 20 he married the daughter of Hidetatsu Saito, another well-known Daimyo.

Japan was in turmoil at this time, as the Ashikaga Shoguns had become weak and ineffective, and competing Daimyo fought each other for military supremacy. As a ranking lord and a known military expert, Nobunaga was ordered by the Emperor (Ogimachi) to restore peace to the land.

In 1564, Nobunaga conquered the province of Mino. He then set up his military headquarters at Gifu, southwest of present-day Nagoya, and attacked the powerful Lord of Omi. Nobunaga's forces met especially stiff resistance, however, so he enlisted the aid of several other Daimyo in the area, including Shingen Takeda, Nagamasa Asai and Ieyasu Tokugawa.

With these combined forces, Nobunaga soon defeated the Lord of Omi, making himself the leading power in central Japan. In 1569, Nobunaga went to the rescue of the Ashikaga Shogun Yoshiaki in Kyoto, who came under attack by two local Daimyo.

After defeating the Shogun's attackers, Nobunaga became the patron of both the Emperor and the Shogun. He had new palaces built for both of them, and put the latter under the protection of his most able general, Hideyoshi Toyotomi.

During the previous decades of turmoil, the Buddhist monks of Mt. Hiei, adjoining Kyoto, had taken up the arts of war to protect themselves and their monasteries. But as their skills in the martial arts grew, they became aggressive and demanding, and began demanding tribute and other concessions from the Imperial Court in Kyoto.

Nobunaga resolved in 1570 to end the power of the armed fighting priests, but because they were supported by several Daimyo in the area, he devised the strategem of supporting the growing number of Christian converts and using them as tools to weaken the influence of the Mt. Hiei monks.

He began by having a temple built for the Christians in Kyoto, but this turned his former ally Lord Shingen Takeda against him. Takeda convinced Shogun Yoshiaki that Nobunaga was out to destroy him, and the Shogun agreed to support Takeda in a move against Nobunaga.

Learning of the plan through his spies, Nobunaga attacked the Shogun's palace, captured him and sent him into exile, thus ending the Ashikaga Shogunate that had begun in 1333.

This action precipatated all-out war between the contending clans. With one success after another, and in particular with the help of his peasant-general Hideyoshi Toyotomi, Nobunaga became the de facto ruler of Japan.

Nobunaga used his power to rebuild the portions of Kyoto that had been destroyed in the fighting, and to construct the great castle of Azuchi in Omi near Lake Biwa—a castle that owed some of its styling to pictures he had been shown by Jesuit priests.

But Nobunaga's imperious and arrogant ways made him many enemies, who referred to him as Baka Dono or Lord Fool. In 1582 while resting at the Honno Temple in Kyoto, he was assassinated by one of his own retainers. Thus ended the life of another of Japan's famous warlords. See TOYOTOMI, HIDEYOSHI.

OFUDA (Oh-fuu-dah)

Foreign visitors to temples in Japan are often intrigued by the strips of white paper hanging from the walls, ceilings and pillars. These paper strips are called ofuda, and they bear the names of people who have visited that particular temple.

The practice is said to have originated in the 10th century when Emperor Kazan resigned, became a Buddhist priest and went on a pilgrimage of 33 noted temples in the western part of Honshu.

When he reached the last temple, the Kegon in Mino Province, he inscribed the details of his journey on a board and hung it up at the temple.

The custom grew, and was especially popular during the peaceful days of the Tokugawa era (1603-1868). The ofuda came to be made in elaborate colors and fancy designs, and were much sought after by collectors.

At first, it was only commoners who made such pilgrimages (one of whom vowed to visit 1,000 temples and put his ofuda on all of them), but later many feudal Lords took up the practice--only their ofuda were made of wood instead of paper.

On April 5, 1807 there was a large gathering of ofuda pilgrims in Edo, where ofuda were exchanged. The custom was greatly diminished by World War II and the years immediately thereafter, but by the 1970s it was once again popular.

OGASAWARA ISLANDS (Oh-gah-sah-wah-rah)

This group of 30 islands, lying from 1,000 to 1,200 kilometers southeast of Tokyo in the Pacific, includes Iwojima of World War II fame, when it was the site of a desperate battle between U.S. and Japanese forces.

The islands were settled by the Japanese following their discover in 1593 by Sadayori Ogasawara, the lord of Nagano. The two largest and best-known of the islands are Chichi Jima (Father Island), and Haha Jima (Mother Island).

Residents of the islands are farmers and fishermen, or engage in a thriving tourist business, as the sub-tropical climate and quiet beaches attract many visitors from Tokyo and other areas of the main islands.

The islands are under the administrative jurisdiction of Metropolitan Tokyo.

Japan's National Diet Building. P. 68

Festival in Nikko. P. 232

OKA, TADASUKE (Ohh-kah,Tah-dahs-kay)

More popularly known as Echizen-no Kami, Oka (1677-1751), was the civil governor of Edo during the rule of Shogun Yoshimune, and the most famous judge of his time.

Oka's wise judgements were so popular that a book was written about them. Reading the book, one is struck by the similarity of his wisdom and judgements with those of Solomon. Like Solomon, he depended primarily on common sense and a shrewed knowledge of people.

OKAYAMA (Oh-kah-yah-mah)

Another old castle town founded in the 16th century, Okayama faces the Inland Sea an hour's train ride southwest of Kobe. The capital of Okayama Prefecture, and known for its Bizen-yaki stoneware, cotton textiles, matting, peaches and other products, the city is best-known as the location of one of the three most celebrated gardens in Japan.

The garden in Okayama, now called Korakuen Park, was laid out in 1700 by Tsunamasa Ikeda, Daimyo of the province, as a place for strolling. The garden grounds, landscaped according to the Enshu school, cover 11.5 ha., and include tea houses, several ponds, cascades, mounds and groves of pine, maple, cherry and plum trees.

The garden is across the Asahi River from the ruins of the Okayama Castle, and is accessible via two long foot bridges.

Okayama also has other claims to fame, including the Ikeda Industrial Zoo, established by Takamasa Ikeda who married one of Emperor Hirohito's daughters.

OKAZAKI (Oh-kah-zah-kee)

A city of some quarter of a million people, Okazki is 40.1 kilometers southwest of Nagoya on the famed Tokai-Do train line and is historically famous as the birthplace of Ieyasu Tokugawa, considered by some as the greatest military and political leader Japan has produced.

The grounds of the Tokugawa family castle have been converted to a park (the Okazaki Park), and in 1959 a three-storied castle tower was built on the site of the old castle.

A bridge that spans the Yahagi River near the park is said to be the place where Hideyoshi Toyotomi, later to become the military ruler of Japan and the patron lord of Ieyasu (but then a runaway vagrant) met the famous robber chief Koroku Hachisuka and became a member of his band.

After Hideyoshi became the supreme power in Japan, with the help of Hachisuka, he made the former robber a Daimyo and gave him a fief.

A well on the grounds of the Tokugawa castle provided the water that was used to wash Ieyasu following his birth.

Today Okazaki is also noted for producing over 70 percent of Japan's fireworks and for its 500 spinning and weaving factories.

OKINAWA (Oh-kee-nah-wah)

The prefecture of Okinawa is made up of 60 islands, in four major groups, 685 kilometers south of Kyushu. The largest and best-known of these islands is Okinawa, which has a land area of 1,220 square kilometers.

During World War II, Okinawa was the scene of a great battle between U.S. and Japanese forces, which resulted in the island chain being occupied by American troops and other personnel until 1972. That year the islands were returned to Japan, and became Okinawa Prefecture.

Being closer to Southeast Asia, and the recipient of migrations and cultural influence from that region since long before recorded history--and also being isolated from the mainstream of Japanese life by hundreds of miles of ocean--the Okinawans developed their own distinctive culture that set them apart.

With the coming of the modern era, however, and having the close-knit ties that come with being a a full prefecture, the differences between Okinawa and the rest of Japan are rapidly diminishing.

Agriculture, stock-farming and fishing are still major industries on the islands. But tourism from the main islands of Japan is becoming more and more important, with the development of hotels, entertainment and recreational facilities. At the same time, traditional industries continue to flourish--ceramics, abaca cloth, lacquerware, glassware, leatherware, woven cloth and cotton, plus linen and silk goods dyed in a style known as bingata, which results in bright colors and attractive designs featuring landscapes, plants, animals and geometric patterns.

Okinawa also has its shrines and annual festivals (that are still distinctively Okinawan). The most colorful of these events is called Juriuma, held on January 20, which includes 100 dancing girls in bright folk costumes parading through the streets to the accompaniment of drums, gongs, flutes and the shamisen.

The main island also has its castle and castle ruins, where feudal lords once lived and reigned, along with numerous other historical places and things.

On the southern part of Okinawa is the Okinawa Old Battlefield Quasi-National Park, a 30.8-square-kilometer area where there are 67 monuments to the 244,136 soldiers and civilians who were killed during World War II.

Naha (Nah-Hah) is the largest city, the capital and the political, economic and cultural center of the prefecture. Its population is rapidly approaching half a million.

The second largest city in Okinawa is Okinawa City, located in the central part of the island some 24 kilometers northeast of Naha. The U.S.'s huge Kadena Air Force Base is a short distance west of Okinawa City, which is were most of the GIs go for shopping and recreation.

Besides its semi-tropical climate, beaches, fishing, and growing recreational facilities that are attracting more and more tourists from the main islands of Japan, Okinawa is also famous for its bullfights, which have been taking place since very early times.

The bullfights are staged at Gushikawa, eight kilometers northeast of Okinawa City, every Sunday afternoon. The bulls meet in a 15-meter ring, butt each other, lock horns and try to push each other out of the ring.

Okinawa is most proud of the Okinawa International Ocean Exposition, which was held for six months in 1975, with the theme, The Sea We Would Like to See, and was concerned with both developing and preserving the world's oceans. The Expo included a number of Fish Pavilions, a large Marine Life Zoo, an artificial island city of the future covering 10,000 square meters, a Seaside Bazaar, clusters of pavilions dedicated to science and technology, ethnic studies and history, and a Shore Park planted with subtropical sago palm and adan trees.

The site of the Expo is now a major recreational area and tourist attraction.

OKURA HOTEL (Oh-kuu-rah)

Tokyo's Okura Hotel, consistently recognized as one of the top hotels in the world, is another Japanese hotel with a fascinating story behind it.

When the Tokugawa Shogunate fell in 1868, Baron Kihachiro Okura was one of a handful of extraordinary men who proceeded--with the government's help--to developed several huge commercial and business combines that came to be known as Zaibatsu.

A farsighted man, Baron Okura was one of the founders of the famous Imperial Hotel (see individual listing), which was originally managed by his son Kishichiro (later to inherit his father's extensive business holdings and title).

Between World Wars I and II, Baron Okura, the son, made a special study of the top hotels in Europe, and opened Japan's first resort hotel, the Kawana, in 1928. In 1937 he opened a second resort hotel, the noted Akakura Kanko.

Purged by the Allied Occupation authorities in 1945 (because of his involvement with a major Zaibatsu firm), Baron Okura enlisted the aid of Iwajiro Noda to help him realize a lifelong dream-- the building of a major world-class hotel in Tokyo that would embody the Japanese traditions of art and hospitality with the European tradition of cordiality he had experienced in Europe.

In 1945 Noda, who had been stationed abroad for many years before World War II and married an American wife, was selected by the staff of General Douglas MacArthur, the Supreme Commander of the Allied Powers, and the Japanese government to coordinate the democratization of the Japanese economy.

In the process of breaking up the great Zaibatsu combines, Noda met and impressed Baron Okura. When the Occupation ended the two began making plans for what was to become the Okura Hotel, which opened in May 1962. The hotel, situated on the slope of a low hill overlooking the Imperial Palace and downtown Tokyo, was built on a site that was originally the garden grounds of a museum his father had founded.

The original Okura Hotel is now the flagship of a chain of 10 hotels and resorts in Japan and other countries.

The Okura has an Executive Service Salon designed for visiting businessmen. Its services include data, economic news, secretaries, interpreters, translators, typing, copying, couriers, business-card printing, a library, and pamphlet display space.

The hotel is across the street from the American Embassy and JETRO, and within a block of the American Chamber of Commerce in Japan. The colorful and exciting Akasaka entertainment district is a short walk from the Okura.

ORIENTAL ECONOMIST / TOYO KEIZAI (Toe-yoe Kay-zie)

An authoritative and respected monthly journal aimed at businessmen and financiers, each issue of the Oriental Economist contains a survey of a major industrial sector, along with news and analyses of political and economic issues. Contributors are leading Japanese scholars and businessmen.

The magazine is published by Toyo Keizai Shinposha Ltd. See OTHER SOURCES.

ORI GAMI (Oh-ree Gah-me)

This is the traditional Japanese art of making decorative/ornamental designs out of paper by folding and cutting. It is also referred to as kiri-gami or paper-cutting.

OSAKA (Oh-sah-kah)

Situated on deltas formed by the Yodo and formerly Yamato Rivers, Osaka is Japan's second largest city, a major port, and the primary commercial, industrial and administrative center in the southwestern half of Honshu.

The area had been settled in ancient times, but it was in the 4th century A.D. after the Emperors Ojin and Nintoku both built palaces there (on the hill now occupied by Osaka Castle) that it begin to grow into an important community--and was called Naniwa or Rapid Waves.

It was not until the time of Hideyoshi Toyotomi (1536-1598) that Osaka was to grow into a major commercial city. He built the largest castle in Japan there, and persuaded merchants from the surrounding areas of Sakai and Fushimi to move their businesses there.

All during the long Tokugawa Shogunate from 1603 to 1868, Osaka continued to grow. When it was organized into a municipality in 1889 it had nearly half a million population.

Present-day Osaka, often referred to as the Venice of Japan because of the numerous canals that traverse the city, is divided into 26 wards, and is noted for its commerce and industry, for its huge entertainment and shopping districts, and for its art.

The most popular shopping district in the city is Shinsaibashi (Shee-sie-bah-she), with its long covered-street arcade lined with hundreds of shops and restaurants. The liveliest entertainment area is Dotombori (Doe-tome-boe-ree), with its bars, clubs, cabarets, and restaurants.

The city is especially famous for its wholesale industries, which have their own distinctive areas that date back for centuries--and the merchant class was noted in the old days for greeting people with Are you making money? instead of How are you? Some 40 percent of Japan's exports pass through the city.

Osaka is three hours and 10 minutes from Tokyo via the Hikari Bullet Train, one hour and seven minutes from Nagoya, and 17 minutes from Kyoto.

In a city as old and as large as Osaka, it is not surprising to find that it has dozens of important annual events. Among them: the Ebisu Shrine Festival from January 9-11, during which women in colorful kimono carry palanquins through the streets, and people pray to Ebisu (the patron diety of business and good fortune) for a good year.

The Shiten-no Temple's Doyadoya festival on January 14, during which young men in loin-cloths jostle each other around the temple, is a ritual designed to attract and please the harvest diety.

Other events during the year: the Osaka International Festival, the Osaka Port Festival, a huge boat festival, a summer or palanquin festival, and a Noh festival.

Places of special interest in Osaka would fill a book by themselves. Besides such things as the Umeda Underground (shopping) Center, the Kita (North) and Minami (South) amusement centers, giant-sized cabarets and Turkish baths, there are the Osaka Merchandise Mart, several museums, several major shrines, a number of parks and gardens, and the great Osaka Castle overlooking the city.

The most important of the temples in the city is the Shiten-no, Tenno-Ji for short, founded by Prince Shotoku in 593. The precincts, which cover 9.6 ha., contain some of the oldest buildings and artifacts in Japan, along with other treasures such as the swords of Prince Shotoku.

Within an hour or so of Osaka are literally hundreds of other places of special interest, including the Mausoleum of Emperor Nintoku (one of the founders, you might say, of Osaka) near Mikunigaoka. Called the Daisenryo, it covers 48 ha., is 35 meters high at its highest point, is surrounded by three moats, and is the largest of its kind in the world.

For gourmets who are into Japanese food, Osaka is a mecca. Over the centuries its well-to-do businessmen have been fanciers of specialty dishes developed for their highly discerning palates. Some of these dishes include Osaka-zushi, fugu (globe fish--which is deadly if not prepared right), tako-yaki (tah-koe-yah-kee) or wheat dumplings with bits of octopus.

Osaka's special breed of gourmets are known as kuidoraku (Kuu-e-doe-rah-kuu) or extravagant gourmets.

OSAKA CASTLE / OSAKA JO (Oh-sah-kah Joe)

Built in 1586 by Hideyoshi Toyotomi, then the military ruler of Japan, the Osaka Castle was the largest and most impressive castle in Japan, especially noted for the size of the great granite stones that formed its base. (Hideyoshi requisitioned the stones from his generals.)

In 1615 the castle was attacked by the forces of the Tokugawa Shogunate. Hideyoshi's heirs, including his son, were killed and the castle was almost completely destroyed. It was later rebuilt by the Tokugawa Shoguns as a symbol of their power.

In 1868, when the last Tokugawa Shogun agreed to turn power over to the Emperor, Samurai who did not want the Shogunate to end set fire to the castle and destroyed much of its interior. It was not until 1931 that the castle was once again renovated, this time with the main tower made of ferro-concrete.

The large gardens around the castle are now a park, and encompass the Municipal Museum and the Hokoku Shrine, which is dedicated to the Toyotomi family.

OVERSEAS INVESTMENT

Japanese investment overseas increased sharply in 1972, primarily in response to U.S. President Richard Nixon's Defend-the-Dollar policy. In 1980 alone, the Japanese government approved a total of ∫4.69 billion in investments abroad by private industry. Since 1950, Japan's direct overseas investments have exceeded ∫40 billion.

It is expected that Japan's overseas investment will continue at a brisk pace in order to guarantee its supply of raw materials, to open up new markets, to avoid import quotas and pollution restrictions and to take advantage of the availability of labor.

The bulk of Japan's overseas investments are in North America (approximately one-third), followed by Asia (one-quarter), Latin America, Europe and Oceania.

OZAKI, YUKIO (Oh-zah-kee, Yuu-kee-oh)

Born in Kanagawa Prefecture in 1859 and educated at Keio University and Tokyo Imperial University, Yukio Ozaki was to become one of Japan's leading statesmen and a reknowned orator.

Ozaki began his career as a newspaperman, then joined the government as the Secretary of the Board of Statistics in 1881. The following year he joined Marquis Okuma to form the Progressive Party, one of Japan's first political parties.

But his outspoken attacks against the government of Emperor Meiji resulted in him being exiled. He was ordered to leave Tokyo in 1887 under the provisions of the Peace Preservation Act.

Ozaki chose to travel abroad, and spent the next two years traveling and studying in the U.S. and Europe. He returned home in 1889, was elected to the Diet in 1890, became Councillor to the Foreign Office in 1897 and the Minister of Education in 1898.

In 1900, Ozaki joined the new Seiyukai Party that had just been founded by Prince Hirobumi Ito. He served as the mayor of Tokyo from 1903 to 1912, and then was the Minister of Justice for two years.

After retiring from politics, Ozaki remained a potent behind-the-scenes power for several decades. He wrote several books, including one in English, JAPAN AT THE CROSSROADS, which was published in London in 1932, and widely read in government and diplomatic circles.

Ozaki died in 1954, at the age of 95. His career had spanned the most remarkable period in Japan's extraordinary history. He both saw and helped it change from a feudal kingdom of warlords and warriors to a modern nation.

PACHINKO (Pah-cheen-koe)

This is a pinball game that uses small steel balls in a vertical machine, on which there are numerous holes blocked by obstacles. The object is to get as many balls into the holes as possible. The more difficult the hole, the more it pays off--in more steel balls.

If you have any balls left when you stop playing you can exchange them for such things as candy and cigarettes. Pachinko became very popular shortly after the end of World War II in 1945 as a form of inexpensive entertainment.

The game is still popular and there are pachinko parlors in the entertainment districts of most cities, as well as near many commutor stations. Some players become very skilled at the game, and there are fairly large numbers who do it for profit, selling their prizes back to the parlors or elsewhere for money.

The name pachinko comes from the sound the balls make when they strike the various obstacles in the machine.

PAINTINGS / E (Eh)

As usual, there are two styles of painting in Japan--traditional Japanese style and Western style. Japanese style painting was imported along with Buddhism from China in the 5th and 6th centuries. These early paintings were called suiboku (sooey-boe-kuu), and were black and white drawings of wash and line, stylized and allusive.

As time passed, elaborate paintings on Japanese paper, in sumi (sue-me) or soot-ink, and on silk, using mineral colors, became popular. During the Edo Period (1603-1868), a form of painting called Ukiyoe (Uu-kee-hoe-eh) or Floating World, came into vogue.

Some ukiyoe were painted by hand but it was as prints that they became widely known. The first ukiyoe subjects emphasized the beautiful women of the entertainment districts, but went on to include the theater, sumo wrestlers, historical themes, birds, flowers and landscapes.

In the mid-1800s, Harunobu Suzuki developed a method of multi-color printing, heralding a golden age of color prints. Among the most popular of these prints--especially in the West--was a pornographic genre called shunga (shune-gah).

The arrival of ukiyoe prints in Europe created a stir among artists and collectors, and is said to have had significant influence on French impressionist painters.

Most contemporary Japanese painters paint in the Western style, but there is still an important market for traditional Japanese art in traditional settings.

PAPER DOORS / FUSUMA (Fuu-sue-mah) or SHOJI (Sho-jee)

There are two kinds of sliding paper doors or screens in traditinal Japanese, homes, inns and buildings. One is called fusuma, and consists of thick paper pasted on both sides of a wooden frame and decorated with paintings. The other type is called shoji, and is made up of very thin, white rice paper pasted over wooden laths.

The heavier, totally opaque fusuma are used both as doors and as wall panels. The translucent shoji are usedas partitions between rooms and as substitutes for windows, since they admit a soft, difused light.

The simplicity of the shoji panels as well as the more decorative fusuma are an integral part of the special charm of a Japanese room. The shoji in particular suggest an openness and intimacy that adds to their appeal.

PATENTS / TOKKYO (Toke-yoe)

A very important sign of the technological progress Japan has made since 1971 is the ratio of foreign to Japanese patent applications. In 1971, foreign individuals and companies made 25.9 percent of all the patent applications in Japan. By 1980 this foreign percentage had fallen to 13.2 and it is still dropping.

The U.S. presently accounts for some 40 percent of the foreign patent applications made in Japan each year, followed by West Germany, France, Britain, Switzerland, the Netherlands and others.

The largest number of foreign patent applications are in chemistry. Next is machinery, and third is daily consumer products.

In 1980 a total of 191,020 patent applications were filed in Japan--165,730 of them by Japanese nationals. In the same year, there were 104,329 patent applications filed in the U.S.--of which 12,951 were filed by Japanese citizens.

PEARLS / SHINJU (Sheen-juu)

Until just after the turn of the 20th century, pearls were a relatively rare accident of nature. An irritant of some kind would find its way inside the shell of a oyster or other mollusk, and the mollusk would protect itself from the irritant by covering it with successive layers of nacre, ranging in color from pale white to a lustrous pink.

All of this was to be changed by Kokichi Mikimoto, born in 1858 to a poor noodle-maker in Toba City. While in Yokohama in 1891, he saw tiny, imperfect natural pearls being sold at high prices, and resolved that he would figure out a way to make better pearls faster. He returned to Ago Bay on the south side of Shima Peninsula, and after two years of repeated failures found that a tiny bead of mother-of-pearl inserted into the gonad of an oyster would result in the growth of a pearl that was totally authentic--only the chance factor in its birth was removed.

It was to take 12 more years of heart-breaking endeavor before Mikimoto was to succeed in growing a perfectly spherical pearl, and making his method of pearl culturing commercially feasible.

With this break-through, pearl farming eventually developed into a major industry in Japan. For the first several decades, pearl oysters were collected from natural seabeds for artificial seeding, but now most of them are raised for that purpose.

Young oysters are placed in baskets and suspended into the sea from rafts for two or three years. They are seeded during the summer months (May-October) after they reach six to seven centimeters in size. The mother pearl is wedged open while it is breathing, and a pearl nucleus and tiny piece of mother-of-pearl is inserted into the gonad.

The mother pearl oysters are then suspended from rafts in metal-mesh bags at depths of 0.5 to 1.0 meters. During the growing process, the shells are periodically cleaned, and are moved to warmer areas if the water temperature falls below 15 degrees centigrade (59 degrees F.).

It takes about six months to produce a small pearl (up to seven millimeters) and one-to-two years to produce pearls over seven millimerters in size. November is considered the best time to harvest pearls, but the process goes on all year, and is very popular with tourists who visit the pearl farms.

Japan's best-known pearl farms are in Mie Prefecture near Nagoya, and the most popular tourist spot is Pearl Island, where Mikimoto first succeeded in producing pearls. Pearl culture demonstrat-

ions are held daily on the island, which is attached to the mainland by a 63-meter bridge.

The Mikimoto Pearl Museum in Toba City is also worth a visit.

Kokichi Mikimoto lived to see cultured pearls become accepted world-wide and grow into a multi-million dollar a year industry, dying in 1954 at the age of 96.

PEARL ISLAND

A small island in the harbor of Toba City (just 16 kilometers from the Grand Shrines of Ise), the Mikimoto Pearl Island is where the famous Kokichi Mikimoto, the son of a poor noodle maker, first succeeded in producing a cultured pearl in 1893.

Toba City faces the Bay of Ise on the Pacific Coast side of Shima Peninsula in Mie Prefecture, and is 131.5 kilometers from Nagoya. Besides Pearl Island and its pearl farms, Toba City also boasts a 7-storied air-conditioned Tourist Center, and the Mikimoto Pearl Museum.

PEOPLE'S LODGES / KOKUMIN SHUKUSHA (Koe-kuu-meen Shuu-kuu-shah)

As part of their efforts to encourage outdoor recreation and tourism, many of Japan's prefectures and the central government have helped finance the building of some 500 People's Lodges throughout the country.

The lodges, primarily located in natural parks, are designed to provide basic accommodations for people who cannot afford regular commercial inns and hotels. Several million people use the lodges each year. Foreign visitors may also take advantage of the Kokumin Shukusha by making reservations well in

advance through travel agents or directly with the lodges.

For a list of the lodges, contact the
Japan National Tourist Organization
(which see).

PERMANENT RESIDENCY

It is possible for foreigners who
meet specific requirements to become
permanent residents of Japan. These
requirements include being 20 years of
age or older, with sufficient assets or
income to support one's self and dependents, having good character and good
health, and having lived in Japan for 10
years or more.

This latter requirement is waived in
the case of individuals who have made
significant contributions to Japan, who
are wives of Japanese men or who are
former citizens.

PERRY, COMMODORE MATTHEW C.

Born in 1794 (and the brother of the
famous Oliver Hazard Perry), Commodore
Perry of the U.S. Navy, more by luck
than any thing else, was the first major
power representative to deliver what
amounted to an ultimatum to Japan to
open its ports to Western ships and
trade, in July 1853.

Commodore Perry and his squadron of
12 black warships (later to become
famous in Japan as The Black Ships),
dropped anchor off the barge port of
Uraga on Miura Peninsula at the mouth of
Tokyo Bay (see URAGA), and delivered a
letter--addressed to the Emperor--with
the notice that he would return in six
months for an answer.

The Tokugawa Shogunate had been told
by the Dutch traders on Dejima in Nagasaki Bay (which see), that Perry was
coming, but they had not been informed
that he was bringing a whole fleet of
steam-powered warships, something the
Japanese had not seen before.

The Japanese had expected Perry to
stop at Nagasaki, but when he steamed
into Tokyo Bay, near the Shogun's castle
headquarters in Edo, in large ships that
belched smoke and fire, they were both
impressed and frightened by the implied
threat.

That same year, a Russian envoy named
Poutiantine sailed into the port of
Nagasaki with a similar demand.

The Tokugawa Shogunate, virtually
impotent at this time in Japan's history, had taken the matter up with Emperor
Komei and his Court of advisors in Kyoto. But when Perry and his ships returned in the fall, the Japanese had
still not been able to reach a decision.

This time, Perry anchored his ships
just offshore of what is now the port of
Yokohama, very near the Shogun's capital
in Edo. He informed the officials there
that if they did not soon agree to meet
him at a suitable location there, he
would sail right up to Edo.

Finally, the representives of the
Shogun agreed to meet Perry and his
aides on Yokohama beach, then called
Kanagawa, and began feverish preparations to build a special Treaty House to
receive them. The meeting occurred on
March 8, 1954.

Perry and his chief officers went
ashore with some 300 armed marines. They
were received with great formality and
courtesy. Following several days of
negotiating, the Treaty of Kanagawa was
signed, giving the U.S. access to two
Japanese ports and the right to establish consulates in the country.

Shimoda, at the end of Miura Peninsula, and no more than a tiny fishing
village, was designated as the first
port. Selection of the second port was
port off until some time later.

Thus, America became the first nation
to establish official diplomatic relations with Japan in the history of the
country. The first American Consul in
Japan was to be Townsend Harris. See
HARRIS, TOWNSEND and HISTORY.

PERSONNEL MANAGEMENT

One of the key characteristics of
personnel administration in larger Japanese companies is the custom of regularly and systematically transferring
personnel from one job to another and
from one department to another.

This practice, which shocks the you-
know-what out of American managers, is
regarded by Japanese management as one
of its strongest points.

The positive aspects of this system
are seen as: reducing poor morale, idleness and corruption. Giving all employees the opportunity to learn many jobs
and to learn and appreciate the relationship between departments, and helping
to train managers who will have a well-
rounded view of the company's overall
operation.

In larger Japanese companies, virtually everyone starts at the bottom--
those with technical backgrounds starting out as clerks at the head office,
and those with liberal arts backgrounds
assigned to factories, to give everyone
the widest possible variety of experiences.

This job-rotation system continues as
the employees advance up the escalator

Famous seascape in Iwate. P. 275

Izumo Taisha Shrine. P. 280

of seniority. Individuals with exceptional talent thus become known to the managers of many departments, and are gradually advanced into the more important management positions.

In many companies, job-rotation never ends, unless an individual reaches the very top, and is seen as a process of continuous on-the-job training.

PHP (PEACE, HAPPINESS AND PROSPERITY)

Despite the unusual name, this is one of the most interesting of the English-language magazines on Japan. Established by Konnosuke Matsushita, founder of the great Matsushita Electric Co. and regarded by many as the prototype of the Japanese businessman-philosopher, PHP covers a variety of topics, including business management, conservation, culture, life-styles, etc.

Articles in PHP are written by professionals and expert laymen who have distinguished themselves by innovative thinking and exemplary achievement. It is published by PHP Institute International. See OTHER SOURCES.

POETRY-READING PARTY / UTA KAI HAJIME (Uu-tah Kie Hah-jee-may)

For centuries, one of the most popular New Year's events in Japan has been poetry-reading parties.

There are hundreds of such parties around the country, with the most famous being that held by the Emperor and Empress at the Imperial Palace.

There is also a national poetry contest in which the Imperial family participates.

POLICE / KEISATSU (Kay-e-sot-sue)

Japan's National Police Agency, under the supervision of the National Public Safety Commission, supervises prefectural police departments, which are directly under prefectural public safety commisions and the governors.

The prefectural police organizations and the Tokyo Metropolitan Police Department (which is a separate organization) have precincts under the local jurisdiction of a police station. Each station in turn has a number of the famous koban (koe-bahn) or so-called Police Boxes--street-corner police posts --in its precinct. See POLICE BOXES.

Altogether there are 1,215 police stations in Japan, approximately 6,000 dispatch police boxes, and some 9,600 resident police boxes. The total number of policemen in Japan is approximately 28,500--or about one for every 552 people, as compared to one for every 363 people in the U.S. and one for every 401 persons in Great Britain.

In recent years the number of policewomen in Japan has increased significantly, currently numbering in excess of 7,000--not counting some 11,000 female general employees.

Japan's police agency owns a fairly large fleet of fixed-wing airplanes and helicopters, and has police airfields in 20 of its 47 prefectures.

POLICE BOXES / KOBAN (Koe-bahn)

The system of establishing small police out-posts on important street corners was started in Edo (Tokyo) in 1628 by the Tokugawa Shogunate to help protect the townspeople from being killed by rough-neck Samurai (who no longer had any wars to fight and whose code of Bushido ethics had weakened).

These Samurai would waylay passersby and cut them down to demonstrate their fighting skills and to try out new swords--taking advantage of a law that made it legal for a Samurai to immediately kill a commoner who behaved in an unacceptable manner--a practice that came to be known as Tsuji Giri (T'sue-gee Ghee-ree) or Street-Corner Killing.

These police boxes were under the supervision of the town bugyo (magistrate), and were called Tsuji Ban or Corner Guards. There were eventually three kinds of tsuji ban--one kind operated by the Shogunate, one by the Daimyo and one by Tokugawa retainers. At one time there were 898 koban in Edo (Tokyo).

When modern police methods were adopted in the Meiji period (1868-1912), the old koban system was continued. (When the American Armed Forces took over Japan in 1945, they closed most of the koban in favor of the American system of patrolling.)

Today there are police boxes in every city and town in Japan, and they are a major factor in the world-reknowned safety of Japan's streets.

Besides watching over what is going on in their neighborhoods, the policemen stationed in the koban also serve as sources of information for people looking for addresses in the area. See ADDRESSES.

There are two types of koban--hashutsujo (hah-shute-sue-joe), and chuzaisho (chuu-zie-show). The former dispatch-type are the larger of the two and are located in denser, business sections of towns and cities. The latter, smaller koban are located in residential areas.

POLITICAL PARTIES

Japan's first political party, the Aikoku Koto (Aye-koe-kuu Koe-toe) was formed in 1874 under the leadership of Taisuke Itagaki. One of its first actions was to present a petition to the Emperor requesting the establishment of a parliamentary form of government.

In the years that followed, many parties appeared and disappeared as a result of inter-party struggles or suppression by the government.

The first cabinet to be formed by the leader of a party occurred in 1914, but the famous Genro (Gane-roe), Elder Statesmen who had led Japan during the exciting years of industrialization following the Meiji Restoration, continued to exercise real power. (See GENRO)

It was not until after the end of WWII and the promulgation of the new Constitution in 1946 that true party cabinets were formed.

Japan currently has seven major political parties—the ruling Liberal Democratic Party (LDP), and six opposition parties: the Japan Socialist Party, the Komeito (Clean Government Party), the Democratic Socialist Party, the Japan Communisrt Party, the New Liberal Club, and the United Social Democratic Party.

The Liberal Democratic Party was formed in 1955 through a merger of two conservative parties, and has held power ever since. Despite the name, it is Japan's leading conservative party.

The Japan Socialist Party, formed in 1945 as the result of the merger of several prewar workers' parties, has had one brief stint in power—from May 1947 to March 1948. The JSP opposes the Japan-U.S. security treaty and advocates unarmed neutrality.

The Komeito, formed in 1964 as the political arm of the Soka Gakkai (Soe-kah Gock-kie), a religious organization affiliated with the Nichiren Shoshu sect of Buddhism, advocates a welfare society based on what it calls Humanitarian Socialism. In 1970, the party was split off from the Soka Gakkai, and is now independent.

The Democratic Socialist Party was formed in 1960 by a splinter group that bolted the Japan Socialist Party. It is a middle-of-the-road party dedicated to the creation of a socialist society through democratic processes.

The Japan Communist Party dates from July 1922 when it was founded as an underground political association. The party became legal after the end of the Pacific war in 1945. The JCP works for the communization of Japan.

The New Liberal Club was formed in June 1976 by six Diet members who broke away from the Liberal Democratic Party. Its policies are primarily conservative.

The United Social Democratic Party, founded in March 1978 through a merger of three Socialist Party Diet members and three Socialist Citizens' League members, advocates the creation of a new and liberal socialism.

Generally speaking, Japanese political parties are not based on specifically identifiable constituencies among the voting population. There is no mass registration of members or grassroots organizations that function anywhere near like the Republican and Democratic organizations in the U.S.

The parties—other than the Communist Party and the Komeito—are more in the nature of factions made up of leaders and relatively small groups of supporters.

POLLUTION / KOGAI (Koe-guy)

Japan was a leader in attempts to control automobile exhaust pollution. As a result of laws passed in the early 1970s, the emission of hydrocarbons, nitrogen oxides and carbon monoxide dropped dramatically from 1975.

When compared with the U.S., Japan is a little ahead in the control of hydrocarbons, and substantially ahead in nitrogen oxides and carbon monoxide controls. In permissible automobile noise levels, Japan ranks even with the U.S.

POPULATION / JINKO (Jeen-koe)

In terms of population, Japan is the seventh largest nation in the world, behind China, India, the Soviet Union, the United States, Indonesia and Brazil.

The population is approaching 120 million, most of which—approximately 70 percent—is concentrated along the Pacific seaboard, on the coastal plains between Tokyo and the northern part of Kyushu.

Because some 70 percent of Japan's total land area is mountainous and virtually uninhabitable, the bulk of the population actually lives on less than 10 percent of the land space—or an area about the size of one large county in the U.S.

PORTUGUESE IN JAPAN

The first Westerners of record to set foot in Japan were Portuguese traders who were sailing to Macau when they were blown off course by a typhoon and accidently landed on the tiny island of Tanegashima off the coast of Kyushu in 1543.

Among the things the Portuguese introduced to the islanders were firearms, tobacco and venereal disease. Soon after this, enterprising craftsmen on the island were making muskets and selling them to Daimyo on the main islands (and for many decades, muskets were called Tanegashima).

The Portuguese repaired their ship and continued on to Macau, spreading the news of their discovery of a new land. Within months, Portuguese expeditions set sail for Japan from their settlements in China, India and other areas of Southeast Asia. By 1549 they had established several trading companies in Kyushu and had been followed to Japan by Jesuit priests from the Portuguese colonies of Goa and Macau.

The best-known of these priests was the Spanish missionary Francisco Xavier, who arrived in Kagoshima in 1549, and during a 10-month stay, received permission from the Lord of Satsuma to preach Christianity in Satsuma. He visited Hirado, Yamaguchi, Kyoto and Oita before leaving Japan.

This was a period of almost continuous clan warfare in Japan, and the Daimyo were more interested in the firearms and science of the traders and missionaries than in their new religion. The number of converts the Jesuit missionaries made among the Daimyo and Samurai depended almost entirely on how many guns they were able to deliver.

Lord Nobunaga Oda, who was to become the de facto Shogun of Japan in the 1560s, was impressed with both the learning and the bravery of the Jesuit priests, and acted as their patron during his lifetime.

The religious and financial ambitions of the Portuguese missionaries were to be their undoing, however, as they became more and more involved in trying to keep other traders out of Japan. Hideyoshi Toyotomi, Nobunaga's successor, finally banished Jesuit missionaries from the country, but allowed Portuguese traders to continue their activities.

Finally, in 1639, the third Tokugawa Shogun expelled all foreigners from Japan, except for one small Dutch trading post on an islet called Dejima in Nagasaki Bay.

One of the most remarkable, and important, of the Portuguese Jesuits in Japan during the so-called Christian Century was Joao Rodrigues, one of few early foreigners to become fairly fluent in Japanese. Because of his ability as an interpreter, he was involved in many of the most extraordinary events of his time. His name was used by Robert Clavell in his book SHOGUN.

Recommended reading: THIS ISLAND OF JAPON, by Joao Rodrigues, translated by Michael Cooper, S. J. (Kodansha Int'l).

POSTAL SERVICE / YUBIN (Yuu-bean)

Despite the fact that most streets in Japan are not named and house and building numbers have nothing to do with steets (see ADDRESSES IN JAPAN), the country has one of the world's most efficient postal systems.

Altogether, there are over 23,100 post offices in Japan, and several hundred thousand street mail boxes throughout the country.

Besides handling letters and parcel post, the Japanese postal system offers a variety of financial services, including acting as a repository for savings accounts, paying approximately the same interest rates as banks.

Foreigners may utilize this service, and when they leave Japan may have their savings transferred to an account abroad (this is important because withdrawals from a Japanese post office account--or a Japanese bank account--cannot be made from abroad).

POTTERY / SETOMONO (Say-toe-moe-no)

Pottery was being made in Japan during the Stone Age, and two of its earliest periods are named after the types of pottery pro-duced during those periods--Jomon-type and the later Yayoi-type.

It was not until the 13th century, however, that what is now referred to as ceramic art developed in Japan. Credit for this is given to one Shirozaemon Kato (1169-1249), who established a kiln in a place called Seto in Owari Province (now Aichi Prefecture) after studying the art of ceramic-making in China.

Kato is said to have traveled all over Japan looking for a place that had the best clay, before settling on Seto. From this period on, pottery-making flourished and came to be known as Setomono or Seto Things from the place where it was made.

Other kilns were gradually established in other parts of the country, and many of them were also to become famous. Eventually, virtually all the provinces had their own kilns and particular styles.

One of the most famous of the kilns outside of Seto was one in Arita (Saga Prefecture), founded in 1598 by a Korean potter named Li-San Ping.

During the following Tokugawa period (1603-1868), the art of pottery-making achieved very high levels. A number of the kilns and styles founded during the early Tokugawa years are still flourishing, particularly Kutani of Ishikawa Prefecture and Kyo ware of Kyoto.

Masters of the art of pottery-making have been recognized and honored in Japan since it first began, and their names are an important part of its history. Among contemporary masters were Munemaro Ishiguro (1893-1968), Toyo Kanashige (1896-1967), Hijime Kato (1900-1967), Hazan Itaya (1872-1963), Kenkichi Tomi-moto (1886-1963), and Shoji Hamada (1894-), whom I had the pleasure of watching work on a number of occasions.

In recent decades, many Westerners have gone to Japan to study the art of pottery making.

Recommended reading: THE WORLD OF JAPANESE CERAMICS by Herbert H. Sanders, with Kenkichi Tomimoto (Kodansha Int'l). TAMBA POTTERY: The Timeless Art of a Japanese Village, by Daniel Rhodes (Kodansha Int'l). THE JAPANESE POTTERY HANDBOOK, by Penny Simpson and Kanji Sodeoka (Kodansha Int'l).

PREFECTURES / KEN (Ken)

Japan is divided into 47 prefectures that are grouped into eight regions. From north to southwest, these regions and the prefectures within them are: HOKKAIDO (Hoke-kie-doe)--the only region that is made up entirely of one prefecture, by the same name. TOHOKU (Toe-hoe-kuu)--which includes the prefectures of Aomori, Akita, Iwate, Yamagata, Miyagi and Fukushima. KANTO (Khan-toe)--Ibaraki, Tochigi, Gunma, Saitama, Chiba, Tokyo, Kanagawa.

CHUBU--Shizuoka, Yamanashi, Nagano, Niigata, Toyama, Ishikawa, Fukui, Gifu and Aichi. KINKI (Keen-kee)--Mie, Shiga, Kyoto, Nara, Osaka, Wakayama and Hyogo). CHUGOKU (Chu-go-kuu)--Tottori, Okayama, Hiroshima, Shimane and Yamaguchi.

SHIKOKU (She-koe-kuu)--Kagawa, Tokushima, Kochi and Ehime). KYUSHU (Que-shuu)--Fukuoka, Saga, Nagasaki, Kumamoto, Oita, Miyazaki, Kagoshima and Okinawa).

See JAPAN.

PREPARATORY SCHOOLS / YOBIKO (Yoe-bee-koe)

Talk about prep schools! Japan has more prep schools than any other country by far, and they play a far greater role in the lives of hundreds of thousands of Japanese each year.

Because of the extraordinary competition to get into Japan's most prestigious universities, which is by examination, huge numbers of high school students fail the university entrance exams each year. Large numbers of those who fail these examinations enroll in yobiko in order to cram for retaking the exams the following year.

Students who fail to pass university examinations the first time are popularly referred to as Ronin, meaning Wave Men, in reference to feudal age Samurai who, after loosing their lord for some reason, would roam the country, oftentimes using their sword-fighting ability to cause trouble of some kind.

Over the years, various of the yobiko have developed national reputations for helping large numbers of their students succeed in passing the entrance exams of the most desirable universities, and themselves have become difficult--and costly--to get into because of their success.

PRESS CLUBS / PURESU KURABU (Puu-ray-sue Kuu-rah-buu)

Press clubs in Japan are quite different from press clubs in the U.S. and other countries. In Japan reporters from the major news media belong to specific clubs that are concerned with specific news sources--government ministries and agencies, industries, etc., just as in the U.S. individual correspondents are assigned to the White House, the State Department, and so on.

The key difference is that in Japan the individual clubs have exclusive rights to the specific news conferences. Reporters who are not members of the Steel Industry Press Club, for example, are not allowed to attend steel industry press briefings.

The control of the various important news sources by these press clubs is virtually absolute, and has a lot to do with the way news is reported in Japan. Among other things, these clubs assume the right to be selective in what they report. If they believe that a certain piece of news would be detrimental to

the interests of Japan, it is suppressed.

It was not until the late 1970s that
foreign cprrespondents in Japan won the
right to attend press briefings by the
Prime Minister's Office. See FOREIGN
CORRESPONDENTS.

The press clubs in effect act as a
filter for the news that gets printed
and broadcast by Japan's leading communications media. Reporters from smaller,
less powerful Japanese media are not
allowed to become members of these press
clubs.

Some news sources hold special briefings for reporters not eligible to join
the press clubs. See NEWSPAPERS.

PRISONS / KEIMUSHO (Kay-e-muu-show)

In late 1983 there were 74 major prison facilities in Japan--58 prisons,
nine juvenile reformatories and seven
detention facilities, along with 115
branch facilities made up of nine prisons and 106 detention jails.

A number of these prison facilities
are Open Prisons--that is, the inmates'
activities within the compounds are not
supervised, factories and messhalls remained unlocked, inmates may have private meetings with relatives and other
visitors.

The Justice Ministry has licensed 100
rehabilitation assistance societies to
help parolees, in addition to the publicly employed probation officers and
volunteers who watch over and help parolees.

PROCESSIONS OF THE LORDS / DAIMYO GYORE-TSU (Dime-yoe G'yoe-rate-sue)

In 1635, 32 years after the beginning
of the Tokugawa Shogunate, Japan's last
great Samurai dynasty, the third Tokugawa Shogun Iemitsu established a politi-
cal-control system known as Sankin Kotai
(Sahn-keen Koe-tie) or Alternate Attendance.

Under this system, the Shogunate
government divided the country's some
270 feudal lords, known as Daimyo or
Great Names, into two groups, and made
it the law of the land that all except
the smallest and weakest of them would
build mansions in Edo (Tokyo), keep
their families there at all times, and
themselves spend every other year in Edo
in attendance at the Shogun's Court.

This meant that the Daimyo had to
travel once a year either to or from
their fiefs and Edo. But the law did not
stop there. The Daimyo had to bring a
specific number of retainers with them
on each trip, depending on the size and
wealth of their fiefs. The attire and
equipment of each retainer was prescribed, as was the route the procession was
to follow.

Daimyo of the richer provinces were
required to bring with them 1,000 or
more retainers. The largest of the fief
lords, Maeda, maintained four mansions
in Edo, with a total, permanent staff of
10,000 persons. When he came to Edo for
his turn at Court, he brought several
additional thousand retainers with him.

Since there were over 250 major Daimyo in the country to which the Sankin
Kotai law applied, this meant that at
any one time there were dozens of great,
colorful processions moving along the
national roads in all seasons.

The Daimyo whose fiefs were in distant parts of Japan were thus required
to be on the road for several weeks at a
time, each way.

These great, elaborately costumed
corteges, known as Daimyo Gyoretsu,
moved at a stately pace along the principal roads of Japan, stopping over each
night at Post Stations established for
that purpose. Providing nightly accommodations for such large masses of regular
travelers required a vast network of
inn/hotels, the likes of which existed
in no other country.

But not just any ordinary inn would
suffice for the comfort and convenience
of a powerful Daimyo feudal lord, his
personal attendants, and the other persons of high rank who traveled these
busy thoroughfares.

It thus came about that three categories of Japanese-styled inn/hotels were
established at each of the Post Stations
on all of the national highways leading
to Edo.

First in order of rank and quality
were the Honjin (Hohn-jeen), literally
Headquarters Hotels, which were reserved
for the Daimyo, their highest retainers,
members of the Imperial family, high
government officials and ranking
priests. These Honjin inns were built in
the same style, and with the same dedication to quality, as royal mansions in
Kyoto and Daimyo mansions in Edo.

The second-ranked category of accommodations at these bustling Post Stations were known as Waki Honjin or Annex
Honjin. They were reserved for the exclusive patronage of very important
people who did not rate the Honjin or
couldn't get reservations at the main
Honjin because they were full.

The Honjin hotels were relatively
large and imposing, built of the finest
materials available in Japan, and repre-

THE WHOLE JAPAN BOOK

sentative of classic Japanese architecture. Their standards for service and exclusivity were so exacting that guests were limited to a maximum of 9 or 10 at a time.

The lower-ranking members of these huge feudal lord corteges, along with ordinary travelers, stayed in a third category of lodging known as Hatago (Hah-tah-go).

One can begin to appreciate the number of travelers constantly moving to and fro in Japan from the number of these special inns on just the five most famous of these Processional Roads. On the Tokai-Do, which ran between Kyoto and Edo, there were 111 Honjin, 68 Waki-Honjin and 2,905 Hatago inns.

The Nakasen-Do had 93 Honjin, 102 Waki-Honjin and 1,812 Hatago inns. The Nikko-kai-Do had 23 Honjin, 20 Waki-Honjin and 820 Hatago. The Oshu-kai-Do had 11 Honjin, 11 Waki-Honjin and 267 Hatago. On the Koshu-kai-Do there were 45 Honjin, 44 Waki-Honjin and 505 ordinary inn-hotels.

It is estimated that up to 10 percent of the annual income of the feudal fiefdoms was spent on these annual journeys --which continued for over 200 years and were undoubtedly the most spectacular feature of Japanese life for these many generations.

Not only did these great Daimyo Gyoretsu result in the developed of a highly sophisticated network of inns throughout the country (in which the traditions of service that are still characteristic of Japanese inns and hotels were firmly established), they also contributed to the spread of culture and to the economic well-being of the rural areas through which they passed.

There were, in fact, few areas of Japanese life that were not touched and colored by the Processions of the Lords.

(The inn featured in the novel THE JAPANESE INN, by Oliver Statler, was one of these Post Station inns on the Tokai-Do.)

PROSTITUTION / BAISHUN (By-shune)

Prostitution was legal in Japan until April 1, 1956--on which evening friends and I made farewell visits to Shinjuku 2-Chome and the Yoshiwara in Asakusa, two of Tokyo's most famous red-light districts.

Prostitution had long been an honorable profession in Japan, just as it was and is in many other Eastern as well as Western countries.

The Japanese had some advantages,

however, because sex and Sin were not related. Engaging in premarital or extramarital sex was not a moral issue in Japan. For much of Japan's history, there were strict sanctions against promiscuous sexual behavior by the common people, but among nobles and the privileged Samurai class, such affairs were commonplace.

In later centuries, however, particularly during the long and peaceful Tokugawa Shogunate (1603-1868), gay quarters and other areas of assignation for all classes abounded. Each city had one to a dozen or more licensed redlight districts, and often a similar number of unlicensed or bluelight districts.

In addition, inns within the towns and cities and along the great walking highways commonly served as houses of assignation.

Tokyo's famous Yoshiwara and the gay quarters of Kyoto in particular were colorful, exciting places that inspired many of the arts that flourished during the Tokugawa period.

As in other countries, prostitution in Japan was closely related to economics. In bad times, young girls were regularly sold to prostitution houses, and others chose the trade as the only thing open to them.

The movement to prohibit legal prostitution in Japan was primarily the work of a number of women who were elected to the Diet (Japan's Parliament) just after the end of World War II. Enough male members went along with the women because they were concerned about the bad press Japan was getting around the world.

Naturally enough, prostitution did not disappear from Japan, but there is no doubt that it was considerably diminished by the new law. As in the U.S. and elsewhere, it is now practiced by call-girls, attendants in massage parlors, and by thousands of women involved in the entertainment trades.

PROVERBS / KOTOWAZA (Koe-toe-wah-zah)

Like people everywhere, the Japanese have their favorite proverbs, and because of their very long history, traditions of oral literature and the cultural infusions from China--which is even older--they seem to have more than the average.

Some of their favorites:

Akujo no fuka-nasake
Ugly women are more passionate.

Akusai was hyakunen no fusaku
A bad wife is 100 years of bad harvests.

Atama hagetemo uwaki wa yamanu
Philandering is not stopped by a balding head.

Au wa wakare no hajime
Meeting is the beginning of parting.

Bijin ni toshi nashi
Beautiful women have no age.

Binbonin no ko dakusan
Poor people have many children.

Deru kui wa utareru
A protruding nail is hammered down.

Edo no kataki wo Nagasaki de utsu
Take revenge at an unexpected place.

Go ni irite wa go ni shitagae
When in a village, do as the villagers do.

Hanzai no kage ni onna ari
There is a woman in the shadow of every crime.

Hito wa mikake ni yoranu mono
People are not what they appear to be.

Horeta yokume ni abata mo ekubo
To a lover, pockmarks are dimples.

Hyakubun ikken ni shikazu
Hearing 100 times is not as good as seeing once.

I no naka no kawazu, takai o shirazu
A frog in the well does not know the ocean.

Jigoku no sata mo kane shidai
Even the judgement of hell depends on money.

Ju yoku go o seisu
Win by yielding.

Kane areba baka mo danna
With money a fool can be a lord.

Kanemochi kenka sezu
Rich people do not fight.

Kunshi hyohen
A wise man changes his mind.

Makeru ga kachi
He who is defeated wins.

Musume o miru yori, haha o miyo
Look at the mother instead of the daughter.

Nyobo to tatami wa atarashi ho ga yoi
Wives and tatami are better when new.

Sake wa honshin o arawasu
People reveal their true selves when drunk.

Shojiki mo baka no uchi
Being too honest can be foolish.

Suezen kuwanu wa, otoko no haji
It is shameful for a man to refuse a woman when she offers herself to him.

Tabi no haji wa kakisute
Travelers are shameless.

Wa-kon, Yo-sai
Western knowledge, Japanese spirit.

PUBLIC OPINION

The Japanese government as well as private research organizations regularly take public opionion polls to see what the Japanese think about themselves, about Japan and numerous other subjects.

A recent poll concerning their attitudes about Japan showed that the averge Japanese took special pride in the long history and traditions of the country, the hard-work ethic and talent of the people, the beauty of the land, the high level of culture and arts, the high educational standards, the inherent kindness of the people, economic prosperity, the high level of science and technology, social stability, the people's sense of duty, and national unity—in that order.

Reactions to a survey about prevailing moods was more mixed, but indicative of the times. Asked to list their positive moods, the people named feelings of peacefulness, stability, vigor, comfort, cheerfulness, a sense of responsibility, solidarity, and compassion—in that order.

On the negative side, the things that most bothered people were irresponsibility (of others), egocentrism, changes too rapid, restlessness, unease and irritability, feelings of discontinuity, languor, and gloominess—in that order.

Nearly 45 percent of all Japanese consider themselves in the upper middle-class, and 35 percent consider themselves in the lower middle-class. Over four percent say they are in the lower upper-class, and one percent rank themselves as upper-class. Eight percent say they are in the upper portion of the lower-class and about three percent say they are in the lower portion of the lower-class.

PUBLICATIONS IN ENGLISH ON JAPAN

One of the best sources for information about books, magazines and other informational materials on Japan is International Marketing Corporation, IPO Box 5056, Tokyo 100-31, Japan, or, Pacific Subscription Service, P.O. Box 811, FDR Station, New York, N.Y. 10150.

IMC handles many books and magazines directly as a subscription and export agent, and also publishes two annual catalogs on the books and magazines published in Japan in English by over 1,000 publishers. See OTHER SOURCES.

PUBLISHING / SHUPPAN (Shupe-pahn)

Japan has one of the world's largest and most varied publishing industries. Each year some 30,000 different books and thousands of magazines are published, with the total number of copies well in excess of one billion.

In recent years, books in the social sciences have led the industry, with some 7,000 titles or about 22 percent of the total published. Literature was next with around 6,000 titles or 20 percent of the total, followed by art, technology, natural sciences, juveniles, history, philosophy, industry, language, general and academic reference books.

Altogether, Japan has some 4,300 book publishing companies (and there are approximately 12,200 book stores in the country). There is a Books-On-Japan-In-English Club, which involves 45 leading publishers who produce books in English, along with five printing companies and three book exporting companies.

Japanese book publishers participate in international exhibits around the world each year.

Some 3,000 magazines and other periodicals are published in Japan, with the largest number in engineering (approximately 5,000), followed by economics and statistics (some 250), Medicine and hygiene (170), education (160), literary (185, including 15 on tanka poetry and 30 on haiku), and children's magazines (110).

Other leading categories include foreign affairs, household affairs, agriculture-stock raising-forestry and fisheries, fine arts, sports, general literature, general interest, social sciences, business, and traffic and communications.

The total number of magazine copies printed in Japan each year is well over three billion.

The four biggest women's magazines in the country are Fujin Kurabu (Ladies' Club), Shufu no Tomo (Housewives' Friend), Fujin Seikatsu (Ladies and Living), and Shufu to Seikatsu (Housewives and Living).

The leading general readership monthly magazines include Bungei Shunju (literally Literary-Art-Spring-Fall), Chuo Koron (Central Review), and Sekai (World).

There are some 50 magazines published in English in Japan, ranging from professional journals and business publications to cultural and religious.

See OTHER ENGLISH-LANGUAGE SOURCES, MAGAZINES, etc.

QUALITY / HINSHITSU (Heen-sheet-sue)

Japan's reputation for the quality of its products has swung from one extreme to the other. In the 16th century, most Japanese exports were folk-crafts and handicrafts of such high quality they often qualified as masterpieces.

When Japan began industrializing in the 1870s, all of the Western-type products it made were imitations, and usually cheap imitations at that. Western importers who flocked to Japan from this period until the beginning of World War II, and again soon after the war ended, had one primary interest in mind--price.

Import houses and especially major American retail chains like Sears and Wards bought huge quantities of consumer merchandise from Japan strictly on the basis of price. Their buyers controlled the quality of the goods they bought by setting the price they would pay.

As the first editor of a pioneer English-language trade journal covering Japanese-made consumer merchandise for export, first called ORIENTAL AMERICA and then THE IMPORTER, I was to witness this interplay between Japanese manufacturers and Western importers thousands of times from the mid-1950s until 1962.

To the Japanese, who had been imbued with traditions of quality for generations, much of the merchandise they turned out for American and European markets --at the behest of foreign buyers--was not fit for sale in Japan.

By the late 1950s the Japanese had begun to turn this situation around. They began upgrading the quality of their products despite pressure from foreign importers to keep both the quality and price down.

Within a decade, Japan was world-famous for the quality of almost everything it exported, and was recognized as the leader in a number of product categories. One of the reasons Japanese manufacturers were able to achieve this remarkable position so rapidly was that they began doing their own selling a-broad, by-passing importers who were mostly interested in making big money fast.

QUALITY CONTROL (QC)

Much to their surprise, the Japanese suddenly became famous for their quality control in the 1970s--surprised because they imported the concept of quality control from the U.S. between 1945 and 1950.

During the early years of the U.S. military occupation of Japan, the U.S. Army introduced the principles of statistical quality control to Japanese industry. Dr. W. E. Deming, an American quality control authority who had written extensively about the subject, was invited to Japan to help spread the idea.

In 1949, the Union of Japanese Scientists and Engineers (JUSE) established a Quality Control Research Group, and began holding seminars on the subject. That same year an Industrial Standardization Law was passed and the use of the Japan Industrial Standards (JIS) mark on certain products became law.

The Japanese Standards Association (JSA) was founded and began research in QC methods. In 1950, JUSE began publishing a magazine called Standard Quality Control, and JSA began publishing Standardization and Quality Control.

In 1951 the Deming Prize for Application was established, followed in 1953 by the Ministry of International Trade and Industry Prize and the QC Literature Prize in 1954.

But there were problems, including a tendency for excessive statistical methods and formality in standardization, and the fact that QC primarily involved only top management.

In 1954, Dr. J. M. Juran, another American QC expert was invited to Japan to help rationalize the Japanese approach. He emphasized that quality control had to be applied on all levels of management to be successful.

For the next five years Japanese industry adapted the Deming and Juran approaches to fit their own environment, involving top managers as well as foreman and workers. In 1960, National Quality Month was started, and the Q Flag and Q Mark were established.

In 1962, the first QC Circles were organized, and publication of a magazine called GENBATO-QC (QC for the Foreman) was inaugurated. Next came CWQC, or Company-Wide Quality Control, and the Japanese were on their way to creating a revolution in both the concept and practice of quality control that would impact on the rest of the world in the 1970s and 80s.

A Quality Circle is a group of 5 to 10 people made up of a leader, who may be a manager, foreman or worker, that acts independently of management to improve product quality, productivity, human relations and the talents and skills of the individuals involved. There are presently over one million QC in Japan, and numerous annual activities to promote their growth and effectiveness.

OC Circle Conferences are held over 100 times a year throughout the country. October and November are quality control promotion months. A QC Control Headquarters with eight regional branches, established by JUSE, coordinates quality control activities throughout the country.

One of the secrets of the success of quality control in Japan is the fundamental Japanese business philosophy that learning and training is an unending process that continues from the first day an employee enters the company to the day of retirement. Some companies re-train their top management every three years, and their middle management every five years.

RACE / JINSHU (Jeen-shuu)

Since most Japanese babies are born with a blue mark known as the Mongolian Spot at the base of the spine, it is apparent that the Japanese are primarily an Asian Mongoloid race.

Paleolithic stone implements and human bones found in Japan show that the islands have been inhabited for over 10,000 years—probably for a much longer period—by a Mongolian people as well as by a Caucasoid people known as Ainu (See AINU).

Recent research indicates that these early Mongolian people were the true ancestors of the present Japanese, and that later migrations of Koreans, Chinese and people from Southeast Asia were absorbed by these first settlers.

Except for mixtures between Japanese and the Ainu (who originally inhabited Hokkaido and the main island of Honshu if not the other islands as well), along with inter-marriages with other non Asian races, all Japanese have Mongoloid features, from the color of the hair and the epicanthic fold of the eye to skin coloration.

Within these boundaries, the Japanese vary widely in appearance. See JAPANESE.

RACE RELATIONS / JINSHU KANKEI (Jeen-shuu Khan-kay-e)

Japan is an island nation that has been isolated from the rest of the world for most of its history. With the exception of the Ainu, the Caucasoid aboriginal race that apparently first settled in the islands, the Japanese are also one of the most homogenous of any national groups.

The Japanese, over their centuries of virtual isolation, also developed a singular culture and ethnic viewpoint that traditionally and still today results in them automatically distinguishing between things and people that are not visibly Japanese.

These factors conditioned the Japanese to be even more racial conscious than most Westerners. This consciousness, along with cultural traditions that proclaimed their superiority, has resulted in numerous incidents of racial discrimination in the past.

At the same time, a very limited exposure to other races and a philosophy of tolerance and acceptance serves to reduce the impact of racial bias in Japan. However, the non-Japanese in Japan, including Chinese and Koreans, are always made to feel foreign, to feel out of place—even when the reception is positive.

This attitude persists among the Japanese even when the foreigner is totally bi-lingual, was born and raised in Japan and is familiar with the Japanese way of doing things. Fortunately, most of this attitude is benign.

RADIO BROADCASTING / HOSO (Hoe-so)

A public demonstration of radio broadcasting was staged in Nagoya in 1919 by the Shin Aichi Shimbun, but the first officially founded broadcasting company was the Tokyo Broadcasting Station, which began operating on 22 March 1925, as a semi-government corporation. This is the date now celebrated as Broadcasting Day.

This was followed in 1926 by the Osaka Broadcasting Station and the Nagoya Broadcasting Station, all three of which were to merge into Nippon Hoso Kyokai, the predecessor of today's NHK.

Japan began overseas shortwave broadcasting in 1935, and thereafter, radio was to play a key role in the country's history.

New postwar laws opened the way for the rapid growth of Japan's broadcasting industry from 1951 on.

Today broadcasting is a major industry in Japan. There are 1,018 radio broadcasting stations, including 504 medium-wave stations, 491 FM stations and 23 short-wave stations. Among the medium-wave stations, 315 are owned by the Japan Broadcasting Corporation (NHK), a public broadcasting network financed by the government and monthly fees paid by TV owners directly to NHK.

There are 48 commercial broadcasting companies in the country, with a total of 189 stations. NHK also owns 484 of the country's FM stations. The other seven are owned by commercial companies. And finally, NHK's Radio Japan arm owns 21 of the 23 short-wave radio broadcasting stations.

NHK's major broadcast facilities are in Tokyo, Nagoya and Osaka, with local stations spread throughout the country. Most of its programs are planned and produced in Tokyo at the corporate headquarters, but some are done by local stations.

NHK is known world-wide for the quan-

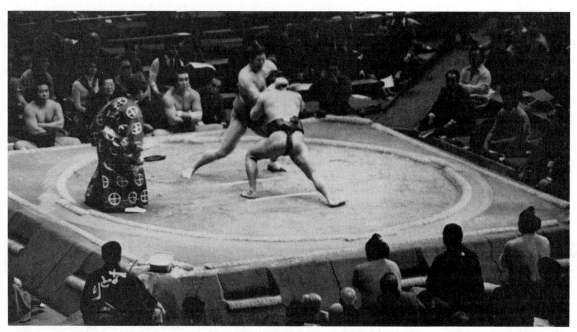

Sumo, Japan's national sport. P. 293

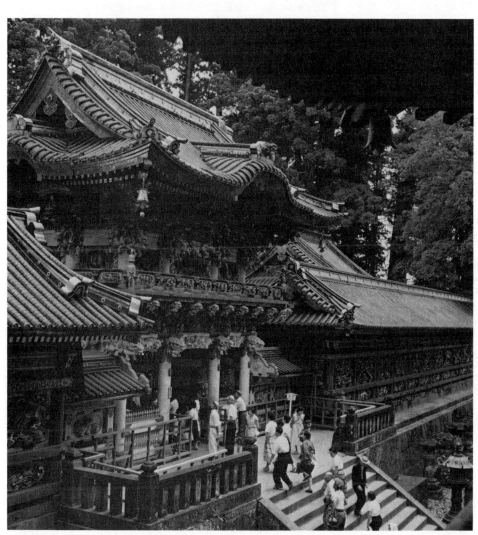

Nikko's famed Toshogu Shrine. P. 232

tity and quality of its documentary programs. It hires top directors, writers and photographers and sends them all over the world to do films on every imaginable topic. Its short-wave broadcasts in foreign languages, covering cultural, economic and social subjects, are also highly regarded.

NHK devotes approximately 39 percent of its broadcast time to news, 25 percent to cultural topics, 25 percent to entertainment, and some two percent to education.

The corporation is able to get virtually all of Japan's top entertainers to appear at least once and often several times a year on special shows, without charge or for just token fees.

RAILROADS / TETSUDO (Tate-sue-doe)

The first railway in Japan was opened in 1872 between Shimbashi (Tokyo) and Yokohama, under the supervision of British engineers. Today there are some 30,000 kilometers (18,000 miles) of railways.

There are both government-owned and privately owned railways in Japan, with the government-owned Japanese National Railways (JNR) operating all long-distance lines and many of the short-distance commutor lines.

Japan is famous for its so-called Bullet Trains, which were first inaugurated in 1964, and were the fastest (127 mph) and most efficient trains in the world. Some of the newer Bullet Trains cruise at 136 mph. In Japanese the Bullet Trains are referred to as the Shinkansen (Sheen-khan-sen) or New Trunk Lines.

For statistic buffs, the JNR has nearly 5,300 stations throughout the country, carries around seven billion passengers a year, has well over 400,000 employees, and loses money every year.

All of Japan's railways are often crowded well beyond their rated capacity. Some coaches carry more than twice the number of passengers they are designed for, during morning and evening rush hours. In winter, when people wear heavy overcoats, the crowding on local commutor trains especially is so intense that station platform attendants are employed to push protruding passengers far enough inside to get the doors closed. On frequent occasions, the pressure of densed-packed commutors pushes windows out.

Despite the overcrowding, Japan's railroads are probably the most efficiently run in the world, and are famous for their incredible punctuality. They normally leave from and arrive at stations within one to 10 seconds of their schedule.

RAIN / AME (Ah-may)

All areas of Japan except for Hokkaido, the northernmost island, have a hot, humid rainy season, called baiu (by-uu) or tsuyu (t'sue-yuu), which begins in early June and ends around mid-July.

There is a well-defined typhoon season from August through October during which the southwestern half of the islands--including the Tokyo area--are regularly hit by storms that include a considerable amount of rain.

It rains frequently in between the rainy season and typhoons, but most of these periods are brief, and in the summer, fall and winter there are frequent dry spells that last for several weeks.

Generally speaking, winters on the Pacific side of Japan are relatively dry, with many clear (but often windy) days. In the central mountainous areas and on the Japan Sea side, winters are marked by heavy snowfalls.

The average rainfall in Tokyo is 1,503 millimeters. The wettest month, October, has an avegage of 320 mm. The driest month, December, averages 43 mm of rain.

Rainfall in Tokyo during the June-July rainy season is regular but relatively light.

Experienced visitors to Japan often taken a raincoat regardless of the season, but they will normally buy umbrellas there only if they need them (they are plentiful and readily available around transportation terminals).

RANKING

Japan has been described as having a vertical society, meaning that people--and things--are ranked according to seniority (which may be determined by a number of factors).

Generally speaking, most ranking in Japan today is based on length of time in school, in a company or organization, and on position. Age is also an important factor, both personally and professionally.

Also generally speaking, all promotions in Japan, business and professional, are based on a time factor rather than ability or performance until one reaches the higher echelons of management. Then, and only then in most cases, are individuals selected out on the basis of personal ability and accomplishments.

This fundamental attitude and policy permeates the Japanese system, and contributes enormously to the cooperative spirit of Japanese employees and the low turn-over rate in companies. To advance their economic and social level, they must generally stay with the same employer.

The promotion system in most Japanese companies is very much like that in the military. Everybody enters the company on the lowest level, and must spend a specific number of years in grade before being advanced to the next position up.

It is also customary in Japan to rank companies according to their annual sales, paid in capital and/or market share, and number of employees. This ranking tendency carries over into other areas of Japan's economic and social life, including the height of buildings, towers, and so on.

When the Tokugawa Shogunate fell in 1868, the new government set up a system of noble ranks for the various members of the Imperial family and hereditary Court nobles and Daimyo. There were 16 grades or ranks in the court peerage, originally based on the step of the staircase at the Imperial Palace on which the noblemen took positions on formal occasions.

The peerage system was abolished at the end of World War II in 1945.

RAW FISH / NAMA ZAKANA (Nah-mah Zah-kah-nah)

Certain types of raw fish are considered a delicacy among the majority of Japanese, and have long been an important part of the national diet.

Raw fish is generally eaten as sashimi (sah-she-me)--sliced fish--or as sushi (sue-she)--slices of raw fish on vinegered buns of rice--after it is dipped in shoyu, a soy sauce.

People who literally turn up their noses at sashimi or sushi do so because they presume it will both smell and taste bad. Many of those who have the courage to try raw fish Japanese style find that it does not have a dead-fish smell and does not taste yucky. Both the smell and taste are new, but once many people get beyond their hangups about

raw fish they become aficionados.

If you want to extend the pleasures of your palate with sushi or sashimi, try maguro (mah-guu-roe) or tuna first. It has a mild, almost sweet taste that is refreshing.

RECEPTIONISTS / UKETSUKE (Uu-kate-sue-kay)

Many large office buildings in Japan, as well as department stores, have receptionists or information clerks stationed in the main lobby or near their main entrances.

This is especially important because almost no Japanese company office has an in-office receptionist. When you walk into the door of a company you are more often than not right in the middle of a bunch of desks, and no one in the office is specifically responsible for taking care of visitors.

In smaller buildings that do not have lobby receptionists, you have no choice but to go right into the middle of things, and once in, signal your presence (by bowing) to who ever looks up and notices you). See HOW TO DO BUSINESS IN JAPAN, by Boye De Mente (Phoenix Books /Publishers).

Where there are uketsuke, proper etiquette requires you to identify yourself, and give the name of the person or department that you have business with to the receptionist. He or she will call the individual concerned and announce your presence.

REISCHAUER, EDWIN O.

The only American Ambassador to Japan who spoke Japanese, internationally known educator and author Edwin O. Reischauer was born in Tokyo on October 15, 1910 to American missionary parents. He was graduated from the American School in Japan in 1927, and then went on to take degrees from Oberlin College and Harvard University. He then spent a year each at Tokyo University, Kyoto University and in Peking, China.

Reischauer then taught Japanese history at Harvard. When World War II broke out he joined the State Department and later the U.S. Army. He was discharged from the army in 1945 as a Lt. Colonel, and rejoined the faculty of Harvard.

In 1961 Reischauer was appointed American Ambassador to Japan, a post he was to hold until August 1966. Reischauer and his Japanese-American wife were one of the most popular American diplomatic couples ever to serve in Japan.

Reischauer's many books include: Japan

Past and Present. The United States and Japan. Translations from Early Japanese Literature. Wanted: An Asian Policy. East Asia: The Great Tradition. Japan: The Story of a Nation, and The Japanese.

RELIGIONS / SHUKYO (Shuu-k'yoe)

The Japanese are frequently referred to as being Shintoists, Buddhists, Christians, and so on, but they are also often described as being non-religious. The truth of the matter is the Japanese are poly-religious. They practice some tenants of several religions as part of their everyday lives, without thinking of the practices as being religious or belonging to any particular religion.

The reason for this polytheistic approach to religion appears to derive from the influence of Shintoism, the native religion, which grew out of a naturalistic reverence for all things, with cleanliness, fertility and paying proper respect to the spirits of all things as its foundation.

Shintoism was not an exclusive or predatory religion. There was no written liturgy, and it did not seek converts. It was simply a way of life....one that included the concept of self-less love for everybody and everthing. See SHINTOISM, BUDDHISM, CHRISTIANITY, CONFUCIANISM.

Japan's shrines, temples and churches are listed according to classifications set by the Religious Judicial Persons Law, which gives religious organizations legal standing.

Shinto shrines, Buddhist temples, Christian churches, monasteries and similar organizations that have facilities for worship fall under a category called Tan'i Hojin or Unit Corporations. While sects, denominations, churches, orders, dioceses and similar organizations that have jurisdiction over the units listed in category one are called Hokatsu Hojin, or Comprehensive Corporations.

There are presently some 85,000 Shinto shrines and organizations in the country, approximately 77,000 Buddhist temples and related organizations, over 3,000 Christian churches and their affiliates, and some 15,500 others.

Some 98 million Japanese are listed as followers of Shinto, 88 million are counted as Buddhists, about one million are described as Christian, and nearly 14 million as Other. This adds up to more than the population of Japan because many people are listed in more than one category.

The history of Buddhism in Japan is so intimately integrated with the culture, politics and society in general that they cannot be separated. Shintoist rites constituted the nucleus of government functions until the 8th century, when it was supplemented by Buddhist rites, and again from 1868 until 1945, when it was the state religion of Japan.

Between 710 and 794 six different Buddhist schools of thought were introduced into Japan. During the Heian Period from 794-1185 two famous Japanese monks, Dengyo Daishi and Kobo Daishi, laid the foundations for what was to become True Japanese Buddhism.

Dengyo Daishi established the Tendai Sect at the Enryaku Temple on Mt. Hiei north of Kyoto, and Kobo Daishi established the Shingon Sect on Mt. Koya south of Nara. These two places are now regarded as the birthplaces of Japanese Buddhism.

There were to be numerous other sects of Buddhism formed in subsequent centuries, including Jodo, Rinzai, Soto, and Nichiren in historical times, and Reiyukai, Rissho Kose-kai, Tenrikyo, Seicho no Ie, Sekai Kyuseikyo, and PL Kyodan in more recent years. Among the most important of these earlier sects was Zen Buddhism introduced from China by the noted monks, Eisai and Dogen. Eisai founded the Rinzai sect, Dogen the Soto sect).

Zen was to have a profound, seminal effect on Japan's history from the 13th century on, helping shape the core of Samurai ethics and philosophy, and influencing both the nature and quality of the feudal government along with the total culture of the country.

RETAIL CHAIN STORES

Retail chain stores are one of the mainstays of Japan's mass consumer market. The top 10 chains, which together have nearly 900 branches, do a significant amount of Japan's total retail business.

The top 10 chains are Daiei (Die-eh), a supermarket chain that is by far the largest retail operation in the country (well over one billion yen in annual sales). Ito Yokado (E-toe Yoe-kah-doe), another supermarket chain, Seiyu (Say-e-yuu), also a supermarket chain. Jusco, a supermarket chain. And Mitsukoshi (Meet-sue-koe-shie), Japan's leading department store chain.

Plus Nichii (Nee-cheee), a supermarket chain. Daimaru (Die-mah-rue), a department store chain. Takashimaya (Tah-kah-she-mah-yah) and Seibu (Say-e-buu), both department store chains, and Yuni (Yuu-nee), the smallest of the supermarket chains.

RETIREMENT / INTAI (Een-inn-tie)

Soon after 1945, the retirment age in Japan was more or less officially set at the age of 55. At that time the average lifespan of the Japanese was in the early 60s.

As the standard of living went up and the lifespan increased, pressure to extend the age of retirement beyond 55 also grew. By the early 1980s, some 40 percent of Japan's larger firms had advanced their retirement age to 60. Others have set their retirement age at 58, and the overall tendency is for other comanies to push theirs upward.

Since the wages Japanese companies pay rise, almost automatically, with seniority, the aging of the workforce beyond 55 is a serious problem. Retirement benefits also increase dramatically with seniority, so the longer an employee has been with a company the heavier the financial burden the company must bear.

In a company that is capitalized at 500 million yen or above and has 1,000 or more employees, a retiring employee may receive a lump sum payment amounting to 40 times the monthly salary at the time of retirement--or nearly three and a half years of pay. Of course, the smaller the company, the smaller the retirement allowance is likely to be.

Most Japanese companies that have more than 30 employees have mandatory retirement systems. In the large, major firms, 99.5 to 99.9 percent of the companies have mandatory retirement. In medium-sized companies (100-999 employees), from 93.7 to 98.3 percent require their employees to retire at specific ages.

The smaller the company, however, the higher the mandatory retiremnt age is likely to be. Some 40 percent of companies with 30-99 employees have 60 as their retirement age. Over 30 percent of those with 100-299 employees also keep employees until they are 60. Only 25 percent of those with 300-999 employes, 23 percent of those with 1,000-4,999 employees and 28 percent of those with 5,000 employees and more have 60 as

their retirement age.

In order to relieve the cost of retirement, some companies require employees to retire at 55, and then hire them back as temporary employees at reduced salaries. Other companies, especially larger ones, also make arrangements for retired employees on the managerial level to go to work for subsidiary firms at lower wages.

Another effect of older retirement age is that it blocks the promotion of younger people, who have to wait longer for positions to open up.

The combination of the seniority and retirement system in Japan is of course another factor that discourages job-changing, and works to perpetuate the life-time employment system.

There is another form of retirement in Japan that is unusual if not unique, called Inkyo (Een-k'yoe), which originated in old Japan when retirement was sometimes preferred to the responsibilities of life or office.

In this type of retirement, the head of a family (or company or country) abdicated to a successor in order to be free to take up other pursuits or just enjoy life. In the case of a number of Emperors, Shoguns, Daimyo and even common people, the aim was to continue to exercise control from the background without any of the day-to-day responsibilities.

This form of retirement from public life is still common in Japan, especially among politicians and successful businessmen.

RESTAURANTS / SHOKUDO (Show-kuu-doe)

There are nearly 700,000 places in Japan where one may eat out, making Japan one of the restaurant capitals of the world, and providing a special ambience that is a major part of the attraction of visiting and living in the country.

These eating establishments include restaurants, noodle shops, sushi shops, ryotei (Japanese style restaurants), cabarets, night clubs, bars, beer halls, coffee shops and other places that are not easily classified.

There are over 228,000 places classified as restaurants, including over 26,000 noodle shops, some 47,000 sushi shops, approximately 13,000 ryotei, 121,000 coffee shops and over 30,000 others.

These places range in size from tiny closet-like shops offering one specialty, to department-store sized buildings with dozens of specialties and styles offered on the different floors.

Japan has some of the best Chinese restaurants, some of the best steak houses and some of the best French restaurants to be found anywhere. Within the range of traditional Japanese food restaurants are hundreds that have a nationwide reputation for the quality of their food.

See DINING OUT and FOOD.

There are some eight or night categories of Japanese restaurants, depending on your definitions, and at least a dozen other specialty type restaurants. The main restaurant categories include: osoba-ya (ya means shops), koryori-ya, shokuji dokoro, sushi-ya, chuka ryori-ya, shokudo, kissaten (coffee shops), nomi-ya (drinking places), and the specialty restaurants.

Osoba shops are usually modest in size and price and are one of the most common type of restaurants in Japan. They usually feature several Japanese noodle dishes and several Chinese noodle dishes. There are five types of Japanese noodles.

Soba noodles, which were originated in Japan, are long, brownish-gray noodles made of buckwheat flour, and are square-shaped instead of round. They are served in a hot soup stock granished with bits of meat and vegetables--or cold, with a soy sauce.

Udon noodles are long and white and made from flour, and are fat and round. Hiya mugi noodles are long, thin white noodles made from wheat flour, and served chilled in the summer. Somen are also long, thin white wheat flour noodles, generally served in a bowl of chilled water in summer. In the Osaka area, somen is called kishimen.

Chinese noodles, long, thin and light yellow, are made of flour, eggs and a mineral water called kansui. They are served boiled or fried in many different dishes, each with its own distinctive appearance and additional ingredients.

The more popular dishes include chashu men (noodles in pork bouillon, with slices of pork and a few pieces of spinach or other green vegetable). And gomoku soba (noodles in a pork broth with a few pieces of meat, fish cake, bits of vegetables, half of a boiled egg and a few other odds and ends.

Sushi shops are regarded as the most distinctively Japanese of all the different types of restaurants in the country. They serve the now famous (mostly) raw fish and other types of seafood on top of buns of rice that have been delicately flavored with vinegar, sugar and salt. See SUSHI.

Koryori-ya restaurants are usually small and often have a folk-craft decor, along with private or semi-private tatami-mat rooms for individual parties. They serve a variety of fish and vegetable dishes prepared in the traditional way. Some of these restaurants are exclusive and expensive.

Shokuji Dokoro are small, less expensive versions of the Koryori-ya, and are sometimes called meshi-ya (places to eat). They usually have a counter and a few tables, with a limited menu of more popular dishes.

The Chuka Ryori-ya are modestly decorated, inexpensive neighborhood Japanized Chinese-style restaurants that mostly serve rice and noodle dishes (not Peking Duck and all the other specialties). They are found in virtually every commutor station and neighborhood shopping street district.

The popular shokudo restaurants are sometimes described as cafes or mixed restaurants because they offer a variety of Japanese, Chinese and Western dishes in an inexpensive setting. Like most non-exclusive restaurants in Japan, they have wax models of their dishes on display.

Japan's speciality restaurants come in all sizes and price ranges, and are named after the food they serve. The smaller, less expensive ones include oden-ya, okonomiyaki-ya, onigiri-ya, and yakitori-ya.

Restaurants specializing in kamameshi (rice mixed with meats and vegetables cooked in a pot), tempura, tonkatsu (pork cutlets), and unagi (eel) are likely to be larger in size and higher priced.

Next come sukiyaki, kani (crab), teppan yaki (beef and vegetables cooked on an open grill), and kyodo ryori, or restaurants that specialize in regional dishes.

Both nomi-ya (drinking places) and kissaten (coffee shops) offer a variety of snack-type foods, with the latter generally being Western style.

The most elaborate and generally most expensive traditional Japanese meals are served in the exclusive ryotei (rio-tay-e) restaurants, which look more like inns than restaurants. All meals are served by appointment in private Japanese-styled rooms. It is necessary to have an introduction to make a reservation at some of these places.

This just begins to touch on the variety of restaurants and foods in Japan. In addition to traditional and contemporary Japanese style restaurants, Japan also boasts some of the best Western style restaurants in the world, including French, Greek, Chinese, Indian, German, and American styles.

Tokyo, Yokohama, Kobe and Osaka are world-reknowned for their steak houses, which serve the famous Kobe or Matsutaka beef.

For a fine introduction to traditional Japanese foods, see EATING CHEAP IN JAPAN--The Gaijin Gourmet's Guide to Ordering in Non-Tourist Restaurants, by Kimiko Nagasawa and Camy Condon (Shufunotomo Co. Ltd.)

RICE / KOME (Koe-may)

Wet rice farming was introduced into Japan from Korea and China some time during the first centuries A.D. Thereafter it was to become the primary occupation of the bulk of the population, and play a seminal role in the development of Japan's economic, social and political systems.

The cooperative approach to farming required by the massive irrigation of rice fields is credited with being a primary factor in molding the distinctive character of the Japanese.

Until 1868, rice was the basic economic unit in Japan, very much like the role that gold played in Europe in earlier days. The size (tax obligations, political clout and social standing) of Japan's feudal fiefs were expressed in terms of how many koku (Koe-kuu) of rice the land produced. (One koku = approximate five bushels.)

Rice, historically the center-piece of Japan's economy, is still the staple food and of vital importance to the well-being of the country. As technology has advanced, however, the number of Japanese farm families engaged in the production of rice has dropped dramatically since 1945.

At present, some five percent of the population is engaged in farming, which is characterized by the small size of individual farms. Japan's rice-producing potential is given as around 13.6 million tons, but annual production is some 10 million--over two million tons more than the market will absorb each year.

The Japanese governement buys all rice produced in the country at a fixed price (which is well above the market price), and then sells it back to dealers. Thus each year the government is faced with a growing surplus of rice and higher subsidies. The price of rice in Japan today is approximately five times the world price, so none of this surplus can be exported.

RIKUGIEN GARDEN (Ree-kuu-ghee-in)

One of the most famous landscaped gardens in Tokyo, the Rikugien was designed by feudal lord Yoshiyasu Yanagisawa (1658-1714) in the early 1700s. The garden includes a large pond with an island and a hill covered with a dense grove of trees.

A teahouse on the hill is said to have been a favorite resting place of the fifth Tokugawa Shogun, Tsunayoshi, as well as other high officials of the early 18th century.

The garden was given to the city of Tokyo by Baron Kyuya Iwasaki, the head of the great House of Mitsui, in 1934. It is located a short distance from Komagome Station on the Yamanote Line.

Only a short walk from Rikugien is the Oriental Library (Toyo Bunka), a branch of the National Diet Library, which has nearly half a million titles primarily dealing with Asia.

RIVERS / KAWA (Kah-wah)

Rivers in Japan, of which there are many, are mostly short and fast-flowing because of the mountainous terrain and limited size of the country's plains. The longest river in the country, the Shinano (She-nah-no), is only 367 kilometers (228 miles) long. It begins in the mountains northwest of Tokyo, and flows into the Japan Sea at Niigata on the west side of Honshu.

The four other longer rivers in Japan are the Tone Gawa which flows through Gunma and Chiba Prefectures and is 322 km long, the Ishikari Gawa in Hokkaido which is 268 km, the Kitakami Gawa in Iwate and Miyagi Prefectures, 249 km. And the Kiso Gawa in Nagano and Aichi Prefectures, 227 km.

Because the majority of Japan's rivers drop from great heights very quickly, they provide considerable hydroelectrical power, and have carved out canyons and gorges that are unsurpassed anywhere in the world for their senic beauty. But only a few of Japan's rivers can be used, for short distances, as waterways.

There are a number of other rivers in

Japan that are far more famous than the above, in particular the ones that flow through major cities, such as the Sumida (Sue-me-dah) in Tokyo, and the ones flowing between the Tokyo area and the Kyoto area that travelers had to cross in order to reach these cities and all those in between.

During the long Tokugawa Period (1603-1868) the Shogunate prohibited the construction of bridges as a means of military control, thus making it necessary to cross rivers by boat or on foot.

Because of heavy rainfall during the annual rainy season and also during the typhoon season, all these rivers were subject to frequent flooding, making passage dangerous or impossible. Ferry boat and palanquin stations developed on the banks of all of the larger of these rivers, offering their services to travelers who chose not to ford the streams on foot—or try to swim them during flooding.

Among the most famous of these rivers was the Shinagawa and Tamagawa, which separated Edo (Tokyo) from all the main cities of the southwest.

ROADS / DORO (Doe-roe).

Japan has a total of some 1,105,000 kilometers of roadways, of which only about 45 percent are paved. Over 95 percent of the country's national highways are paved, however, as are some 83 percent of the prefectual roads.

Japan's first expressway (freeway), the Meishin Expressway, was completed in 1965. This was quickly followed by the Tomei Expressway, the Chuo Expressway and others. The country's expresways currently total over 3,000 kilometers, and are steadily being expanded.

The story of Japan's roads is the story of the country to a degree far beyond the usual expectations.

In the 7th century, Japan was divided into eight administrative regions—one in the vicinity of Kyoto, the capital, called Kinai (kee-nie) or Within the District, and seven in the country at large, called Do (Doe) or Circuits, each of which was made up of six to 15 provinces.

Main highways were built radiating out from the capital to the regional headquarters of each of these eight regions, to facilitate travel and the transportation of rice and other produce. Government officials in charge of transportation were stationed on each of these roads.

The roads to the seven Circuits were given names based on the areas they passed through—names that were to become famous in Japanese history thereafter.

They were the Tokai Do (Toe-kie Doe) or Eastern Seaboard Highway. The San-in Do (Sahn-inn Doe) or Japan Seaboard Highway. The Sanyo Do (Sahn-yoe Doe) or the Inland Sea Highway. The Saikai Do (Sie-kie Doe) in Kyushu. The Nankai Do (Nahn-kie Doe) in Shikoku. The Hokuriku Do (Hoe-kuu-ree-kuu Doe) on the Japan Seacoast side of central Honshu and the Tosan Do (Toe-sahn Doe) in northern Honshu.

By the 900s, these roads were divided into three classifications—Great Roads, Medium Roads and Minor Roads. One of the Great Roads was called Sanyo Do, which went from Kyoto to Kyushu and was the most important road in the country at that time. There were post-stations along these roads, with a post-station master and staff, every 30 ri (about 72 miles), which maintained horses for use by officials (common people were not allowed to ride horses as transportation). Stations on the Great Roads kept 20 horses, those on Medium Roads, 10, and those on Minor Roads, five.

As early as 710 the government ordered local lords to plant trees along the roads in their domains, and Buddhist priests made a practice of building rest-houses along the roads.

When Kamakura became the military capital of Japan in 1192, the Tokai Do or Eastern Sea Road from Kamakura to Kyoto replaced the Sanyo Do as the most important highway in the country.

In 1557 Nobunaga Oda set up national standards for the roads, requiring that main roads be three ken two shaku (five and a half meters) wide. Secondary roads were to be two ken two shaku wide, and minor roads, one ken wide. Oda also ordered local Daimyo to plant pine or willor trees along the roads, and instituted a system of distance markers along the highways.

When Ieyasu Tokugawa became Shogun in 1603 and made Edo (Tokyo) the new seat of government, he ordered that all distances in the country were to be measured from Nihon Bashi (Nee-hone Bah-she) or Japan Bridge in the center of the city, and the Tokai Do, Nakasen Do, Oshukai Do, Koshuikai Do and Nikkokai Do quickly became the most important highways in the country.

The Tokugawa Shogunate then ordered that major roads be widened to 10.8 meters, secondary roads to 5.4 meters, and that lanes and horse paths be 3.6 meters, walk-ways 1.8 meters and field-paths 0.9 meters. He had milestones placed every ri (about three miles) along the roads.

Tokugawa also ordered the planting of more trees, and on the heavily traveled Tokai-Do, he stipulated that 100 horses and 100 men be maintained at post-stations. The Nakasen-Do stations were to have 50 horses and 50 men, the Nikko-Do and other roads 25 horses and 25 men.

Because of the importance of these great roads to the provincial lords who had to travel to Yedo every other year by law (See PROCESSIONS OF THE LORDS), the Shogunate assigned a special magistrate to administer the affairs of each one. There were toll barriers at different places along the roads, and the fees charged to travel them were high. To avoid these tolls, common people and merchants often used the unofficial minor roads which ran through the mountains.

There were 53 posting stations on the Tokai-Do, the most traveled of all the highways. These stations were immortalized by the famous Ukiyoe artist Hiroshige Ando, after he made a trip in 1832 from Edo to Kyoto as a member of an official party to present a horse to the Emperor. Hiroshige called his series of prints Gojusan Tsugi or Fifty-three Posting Stations.

Most of these famous stations are now cities or towns. Among those that are still prominent: Shinagawa, Kawasaki, Kanagawa, Hodogaya, Totsuka, Fujisawa, Hiratsuka, Oiso, Odawara, Hakone, Mishima, Numazu, Yoshiwara, Okitsu, Kuwana, Yokkaichi, Seki, Sakanoshita, Ishibe, Kusatsu and Otsu.

Japan entered the era of modern high-speed toll express-ways in 1959 with the formation of the Tokyo Expressway Corporation, and by 1973 had 10 major freeways in operation. Many more have since been added.

ROBOTS / ROBATO (Roe-bah-toe)

Japan's robot population in 1983 was over 70,000--the largest in the world. It has been growing by robotic leaps and bounds since. The first industrial robot in Japan was not made there, however, it was imported from AMF of the U.S. in 1967.

The progress of Japan's robots and their impact on industry is covered by a company called Survey Japan, which publishes The Japan Robot News, a quarterly newsletter. Survey Japan is located at 61 No. 6 Building, 4-5 Kojimachi, Chiyoda-ku, Tokyo, 102, Japan.

There is also a growing volume of robot literature by Japanese authorities, available from Survey Japan and from other publishers. Some of the titles: Robot Revolution (Nihon Keizai Shimbun), Robots in the Japanese Economy (Survey Japan), Industrial Robot (Nihon Keizai Shimbun), The Practical Manual of Industrial Robots (Shin Gijutsu Kaihatsu Center).

In early 1983, scientists at Nippon Telegraph and Telephone Public Corporation announced that they had developed a robot that could read the news with 99.5 percent accuracy.

Described as half computer-half humanoid, the scientists said the robot was able to deliver sentences with the proper inflections.

Major robot manufacturers in Japan include Matsushita Electric Industry Co., Kawasaki Heavy Industries Co., Yasakawa Electric Manufacturing Co., Dainichi Kiko Co. and Star Seiki Co. Others that are rapidly expanding their production include Hitachi Ltd., Mitsubishi Electric, Nippon Electric and Fanuc Ltd.

Altogether, there are over 120 companies in Japan producing robots.

RONIN (Roe-neen)

Literally Wave Men, Ronin refers to Samurai who became masterless during Japan's feudal age, and to high school graduates in present-day Japan who fail to pass entrance examinations to universities and are out in the cold.

In feudal Japan when Samurai lost their masters because of war or politics or because they were discharged for some offense, they were in a serious predicament. They could not go into commercial business, and other Daimyo in the country were unlikly to take them on because their loyalty would always be questionable.

Many of these men roamed the country, looking for odd jobs--hiring their deadly swords out to unscrupulous lords, merchants and others--or becoming highway robbers.

The more turbulent the times, the larger the number of ronin there were likely to be and the more mischief they were likely to get into.

There are many stories of ronin whose high values prevented them from resorting to unethical or illegal ways of making a living. For such men, suicide was often the only way out. There were also some who practiced a kind of extortion on the more kind-hearted Daimyo.

These ronin would present themselves at the mansions of these lords, and ask permission to use a corner of their garden in which to commit harakiri. The ronin expected the lords to take pity on them and give them a sum of money.

A favorite theme of chambara movies is the good-hearted but desperate Samurai who unknowingly goes to the villa of a mean-hearted lord. The lord readily gives the ronin permission to kill himself, and then orders his retainers to make sure he does--even though he has pawned his real sword and must use one made of wood to saw open his stomach.

The most famous historical event involving ronin is one of the great dramas of Japan. See FORTY SEVEN RONIN.

Applying the word ronin to high school graduates who fail to get into the university of their choice is both poetic--in a sad way--and satirical. Some students are lucky and remain ronin for only a year. Others fail the university examinations year-after-year, and remain in limbo like the less fortunate ronin of an earlier age.

ROPPONGI (Rope-pong-ghee)

The Roppongi area of Minato Ward in Tokyo, on a low hill a short distance from downtown, is one of the city's several dozen famous entertainment areas. What makes this one different is that it is especially popular among foreign residents, and is a hang-out for well-known Japanese movie and television stars.

Roppongi has more restaurants, bars, night clubs, cabarets, teahouses, snack shops and discos than many countries. At night it literally throbs with the sound of people enjoying themselves, and with other people who go there to watch people enjoying themselves.

There are several dozen foreign-style restaurants in Roppongi, including a number owned and operated by foreigners.

SADO ISLAND (Sah-doe)

The fifth largest of Japan's major islands, Sado lies in the Japan Sea off the coast of Niigata, and is part of Niigata Prefecture. Only 857 square kilometers in land area, Sado has a population of around 100,000. It has two parallel mountain chains that divide it, but provide a fertile plain in between where rice is grown.

Isolated in the cold waters of the northern Japan Sea until recent times, Sado is famous in Japanese history because it was used as a place of exile for political figures, including one Emperor, Juntoku (1197-1242), whose forces were defeated by the Regent Yoshitoki Hojo when the Emperor tried to overthrow the Kamakura Shogunate and gain real power for the throne.

The island is also noted for its okesa (oh-kay-sah) ballad songs, the Japanese crested ibis (found only on Sado), and its gold mines--which have been worked since the discovery of gold there in 1601. During the Edo (Tokugawa) Period, the mines were worked by prison labor. They became Imperial property when the Shogunate ended in 1868.

Sado is now a popular tourist destination in the summer.

SAGA (Sah-gah)

Saga is the capital of the prefecture by the same name, and now known as a distribution center for rice and other agriculural products. Historically it is noted as the castle town of the famous Nabeshima clan, and for the man who was Daimyo of the clan when the Tokugawa Shogunate fell in 1868 and the daimyo/clan system was abolished.

This memorable figure was Naomasa Nabeshima (1814-1871), better known as Kanso, who played a leading role in the movement to restore Imperial authority to Japan, primarily by selecting and championing exceptionally able young men for the new government.

The two best-known of Nabeshima's proteges were Count Taneomi Soejima (1828-1905) and Marquis Shigenobu Okuma (1838-1922), who became leading statesmen of their time.

Saga is also known for its annual mid-October Menfuryu festival, which has been sponsored by the Saga and Matsubara shrines since around 1475. Youths wear goblin masks and dance in the streets to the music of gongs and drums.

SAIGO, TAKAMORI (Sie-go, Tah-kah-moe-ree)

One of the most important leaders in the movement that brought about the downfall of the Tokugawa Shogunate and the restoration of Imperial power in Japan in the 1860s, Takamori Saigo, from the powerful Satsuma clan in Kyushu, was made a Marshal of the Imperial army in 1872.

But Saigo soon broke with the government over its policy of intervention in the affairs of Korea, and retired to Kagoshima.

There he founded a school to train young men in political and military science. The Meiji government was sure Saigo was preparing for a rebellion, and tried unsuccessfully to lure him to Tokyo.

Finally in February, 1877, Saigo took command of Kagoshima and then marched toward Kumamoto. He and his army of 15,000 men were met on the road by an army sent out from Kumamoto. His forces were victorious, and laid seige to the city. But after several battles, reinforcements sent in by the Meiji government from all over Japan, forced him to retreat to Kagoshima.

Imperial forces surrounded Kagoshima, and the final battle took place on September 24, 1877 at Shiroyama. Saigo was wounded and his army was routed. He had one of his retainers, Shinsuke Beppu, behead him.

Despite the fact that he had revolted against the Imperial governement, Saigo was regarded as a hero for his role in ending the Tokugawa Shogunate, and was much admired for his courage and loyalty to his ideals. A huge statue was erected in his honor in Ueno Park in Tokyo, and in 1922 his son received the title of Marquis.

SAKE (Sah-kay)

Sake or rice wine has been brewed in Japan since the beginning of Japanese civilization, and was the only alcoholic drink known in the country until the introduction of wines and whiskeys by foreign traders in the 16th century.

In early Japan, brewing and drinking of sake was closely related to Shintoism. Every community shrine had its own rice paddies, and it was the rice from these fields that was made into sake--which in its earliest days was a gruel that was eaten.

After sake had been further refined into a clear liquid, it was still considered a special offering to the gods, but as time passed it became common to drink it at parties and banquets not associated with shrine rituals.

To make sake, the rice is washed, soaked and then steamed until well-done. Then yeast and fresh spring water is added to induce fermentation. After fermentation, the wine is separated from the rice residue by running though a press. The wine is then filtered and then placed in large vats, where it settles and becomes clear.

The alcoholic content of sake taken from the upper portion of the vat is from 12 to 14 percent. That take from lower turbid portion has up to 17 or 18 percent alcohol, while that distilled from the dregs, called shochu (sho-chuu) ranges from 50 to 60 percent alcohol.

A sweetened variety of sake, called mirin (me-reen), has from 9 to 21 percent alcohol.

Sake is graded on the basis of taste, color and aroma and comes in three grades--tokkyu (1st grade), ikkyu (2nd grade), and nikkyu (3rd grade).

There are several standard sizes for sake bottles, but one of the most popular holds 1.8 liters or almost half a gallon of the potent brew. It is normally served in small rounded pitchers called tokkuri, and drank from tiny thimble-sized cups called sakazuki.

In sake-drinking etiquette the individual who pours his own or allows his drinking companions to pour their own is considered unlettered or impolite. You fill the other persons's cup, and they fill yours. Your cup should always be picked up and held in your hand when the other person is pouring.

If someone offers you more sake and your sakazuki is still full, etiquette requires you to at least take a sip from it and then hold it out for refilling. (The same goes for beer drinking).

It is common practice for women to place an honorific O in front of sake, i.e., O'sake. More polite men may do the same. Several districts in Japan have been noted for the quality of their sake since ancient times. These include Nada (in Kobe), Akita, Nagano and Hiroshima.

During the fermentation process, the mixture seems to be almost alive, bubbling and making sounds. A visit to a sake brewery is quite an experience (the aroma permeates the area for many blocks in all directions).

Popular sake brands include Hakutsuru (White Crane), Ozeki and Gekkeikan.

The Gekkeikan brand of sake, brewed by Okura Shuzo Company of Kyoto, was originated in 1637 under the auspices of a Samurai family. During the long reign of the Tokugawa Shogunate, it became a favorite of the Samurai class, and still today is one of the most prestigious brands in the country.

SAMURAI (Sah-muu-rie)

From the latter part of the Heian Era (794-1192), warriors were called Bushi (Buu-she), a term that had been introduced from China. In earlier times, court officials who waited upon the Emperor were known as Saburo-bito from the word saburo which means to serve or wait upon. Bushi assigned to guard the Emperor came to be known as Saburai. By the 13th century, hereditary warriors as well as officials serving princes, court ministers and other persons of high rank were called Saburai.

Originally this word referred only to higher class warriors and court officials, and eventually was changed to Samurai just to make it easier to pronounce.

Japan's famous class of Samurai warriors was further strengthened by an institution established in 1185 by Yoritomo Minamoto, a few years before he set up the country's first Shogunate government.

Achieving military success in the country, Yoritomo obtained permission from the emperor to establish a system of shugo (shuu-go) or guards for all of the districts and provinces as a means of keeping order.

The position of shugo gradually became hereditary and consolidated the development of an elite class of professional warriors. As the generations passed, these warrior families became clans and grew to be more powerful than the hereditary lords they served (most of whom were descendants of noble familes from Kyoto).

These shugo gradually came to be known as Samurai (which is another reading for guards). They developed a code, based on Confucian and Zen Buddhist principles, that came to be known as Bushido or The Way of the Warrior. This code was to dictate virtually every aspect of their lives, and influence the total culture of the country down until modern times.

The essence of the Samurai code was total loyalty to their feudal lord, a willingness to give their lives in the defense of their lord, his honor and their own, a strict regime of martial

Ceremony by a sumo grand champion. P. 293

Tokyo's famous Yasukuni Shrine. P. 283

The Kotohira Shrine in Kagawa. P. 278

training and a sternly refined etiquette that governed their actions and behavior in all things.

Part of the code of the Samurai was to commit suicide rather than be captured in war or be dishonored by failure. The code of the Samurai applied to the women as well as the men in this elite class.

One special category of Samurai were the hatamoto (hah-tah-moe-toe), the higher ranking warriors who were the Shogun's personal guard. During the Tokugawa Shogunate (1603-1868), the hatamoto were direct vassals of the Shogun, and their annual revenue was fixed at a minmum of 10,000 bales of rice.

After the privileged class of Samurai was abolished in 1868, the word Shizoku, which is the Chinese pronounciation of the same word, was substituted and extensively used until 1945, so that former Samurai families were still distinguished from the common people.

Recommended reading: HAGAKURE: The Book of the Samurai, by Tsunetomo Yamamoto, translated by William Scott Wilson (Kodansha Int'l).

SAN BONAVENTURA

The San Bonaventura was apparently the first Japanese ship to cross the Pacific Ocean. Reportedly built under the supervision of Will Adams, the English pilot who had become an advisor to Shogun Ieyasu Tokugawa, the ship was dispatched in 1613 by Masamune Date, the Lord of Sendai, under the command of one Rokuemon Hasekura (with a Franciscan priest aboard as interpreter and guide).

Lord Date's purpose in sending the ship eastward is not known but it is presumed that he was interested in the wealth and power that had come into the hands of the lords on the southern island of Kyushu, and wanted his own foreign contacts.

The ship, with a crew of 68 Japanese and Portuguese, left Tsukinoura in what is now Miyagi Prefecture on 15 September 1613, took the Great Circle route along the Aleutian Islands (where they must have frozen), skirted the California coast and four months later arrived in Acapulco.

From Acapulco the ship made its way to Seville, Spain, arriving in November 1614, where Hasekura and his mission was given an audience by the King of Spain and he was later baptized as a Catholic. After three months in Seville, the San Bonaventura called on numerous ports in the Mediterranean, arriving at Naples, Italy in November 1915.

In Italy the Japanese were greeted by Pope Paul V., and Hasekura's portrait was painted for the Vatican archives. What happened from this point on is unknown, until Hasekura arrived back in Sendai near the end of 1920, presumably having circumvented the globe.

Japan had changed a great deal while Hasekura was gone, and despite the rich gifts and books he back to his master, he was ordered to renounce the Christian faith. He refused and was forced to retire and was under house arrest until he died of natural causes two years later. Twenty years later, his son Tsuneyori, who had also become a Christian, was put to death by Tadamune Date, the son of Hasekura's master, Masamune. See DATE MASAMUNE, PORTUGUESE IN JAPAN, ADAMS.

SAN MON (Sahn Moan)

Entrances to the grounds of Buddhist temples are marked by gates (san mon), some of which are very large and elaborate--so large and elaborate that visitors to Japan sometimes think the gate is the temple. The gates to Buddhist temples are quite different from Shinto shrine gates. See TORII.

SCENIC TRIO

Japan has three areas that are so beautiful they have been known and celebrated since ancient times--Amanohashidate on the Japan Sea side of Honshu west of Kyoto, Matsushima near Sendai in northeastern Honshu, and Miyajima near Hiroshima. See individual listings.

SCIENCE CITY

Until the 1960s, Tsukuba was a cluster of small rural towns set amidst farms and pine groves 37 miles from Tokyo. It has since been transformed into a bustling Science City, with a population of thousands of scientists, engineers, technicians and their families.

Tsukuba is now the home for 43 governmental and four private research institutes, along with two universities, representing some 40 percent of Japan's research effort.

Research projects at Tsukuba include such fields as lasers, robotics, bionics and sophisticated electronics.

Several hundred foreign scholars and technicians are conducting research at Tsukuba, and the city is visited each year by thousands of scientists, government officials and the curious from around the world.

Manufacturing plants are banned in

the Tsukuba area, as are such distract-ions as pachinko parlors, but the city has 94 parks and plazas and numerous pools and pedestrain walkways for the benefit of its residents.

SEASCAPES / KAIHIN (Kie-heen)

Mention has already been made of Japan's long coastline and its scenic beauty. Altogher, Japan has 16,120 miles of sea coast that alternates between white-sand beaches bordered by groves of gnarled pines, precipitous cliffs also clad in pines, lagoon-like bays dotted with emerald islets, secluded coves and inlets bounded by jagged walls of stone, caves, natural bridges and gates sculpt-ured from fantastic rock formations.

Offshore, Japan is ringed by a neck-lace of islands setting in blue water, adding to seemingly unending stretches of coastline so beautiful that many who are more finely attuned find themselves intoxicated by the sight.

SEASONS / KISETSU (Kee-sate-sue)

The spring, summer, fall and winter seasons are very pronounced in Japan, particularly as you go northward. In the Kanto and Kinki districts of central Honshu, where the bulk of the population lives, the spring months are March, April and May--sometimes lapping over into June. Summer begins in June when the rainy season ends, and officially goes through August. As far as tempe-ratures are concerned, it is still sum-mer until the latter part of September, especially in the lowland areas.

Fall really begins in late September and usually ends in mid-November. Natur-ally, the further north you are the earlier winter begins and the longer it lasts. In Hokkaido, it generally begins snowing in October, while southern Kyu-shu is still enjoying warm days.

SEATING ETIQUETTE

There is a specific place of honor in a Japanese-style room that determines the order of seating of guests. The primary seat of honor is the one in front of and nearest to the tokonoma (toe-koe-no-mah) beauty alcove.

The chief guest sits with his or her back to the tokonoma, with the second ranking guest on his or her left and the third ranking guest on the other side of the room, facing the first guest. The host sits at the lower end of the room--usually near-est the door.

In any situation where two people are sitting side-by-side, the ranking person is on the left. The wife is always ex-pected to sit on her husband's right.

SEKIGAHARA (Say-kee-gah-hah-rah)

This is the site of the Battle of Sekigahara in Mino Province (now Gifu Prefecture), where on October 21, 1600, Ieyasu Tokugawa's army of 80,000 men met and defeated Hideyori Toyotomi's army of 130,000 men, thus setting the stage for Ieyasu to become Shogun three years later.

Hideyori, the son and heir of Hideyo-shi Toyotomi, with whom Ieyasu had been allied until Hideyoshi died in 1598, was only seven years old at that time, and the army that fought at Sekigahara was commanded by Mitsunari Ishida, the lead-ing general of the Toyotomi clan.

SELF-DEFENSE FORCES

Japan's military organization, known as Self-Defense Forces (SDF), were form-ally established in 1954, and consist of a Ground Self-Defense Force (army), Ma-ritime Self-Defense Force (navy) and Air Self-Defense Force (air force).

There are approximately 250,000 uni-formed personnel in the three branches of the military (over 60 percent of whom are in the Ground SDF or army), and all of whom are volunteers. Japan has no conscription system.

Japan's constitution forbids the use of its military forces for any purpose other than self-defense against an at-tack by an outside enemy, and to preser-ve public order. So far, the SDF has never been mobilized for either purpose.

Besides defense patrols and training maneuvers, the SDF has primarily been used to aid disaster-stricken areas caused by typhoons and so on, and in construction projects. It is also occa-sionally used to help in crowd-control during athletic events.

SENDAI (Sen-die)

Three train hours north of Tokyo, Sendai is the capital of Miyagi Prefect-ure and the economic, political and cultural center of the Tohoku District of northeastern Honshu--an area that was once referred to as Michinoku or The Black Country, because of its severe winters, mountainous terrain and the difficulties involved in developing it.

These same snowy winters and pictur-esque mountains, along with distinctive life-styles and characteristics that set its inhabitants apart, now make the Sendai area a popular tourist destinat-ion.

THE WHOLE JAPAN BOOK

During the long Tokugawa Period, Sendai was the headquarters of the famous Date clan. In 1602, Lord Masamune Date built his castle on a hill overlooking the town from the west, following which the town gradually grew into a city.

Masamune was the most powerful Daimyo in northeastern Honshu prior to and during the Tokugawa era. He was a close ally of Hideyoshi Toyotomi, Ieyasu Tokugawa's predecessor, and when Ieyasu became Shogun in 1603 he continued this key role with the Shogunate.

Masamune was interested in Christianity, and when Ieyasu's successor began to jail Christians in Edo, he obtained the release of the Franciscan priest F. Luis Sotelo and brought him to Sendai. He also sent his own emmisary to Spain and Rome, with Sotelo going along as interpreter and guide.

When he died in 1636, Masamune had the largest fief north of Edo, and Sendai was the leading city in northern Japan.

Although primarily known for its handicraft industries, Sendai was nearly destroyed by bombing raids during World War II. When the war ended, the city took advantage of the opportunity to plan its streets and roads, and it is now one of the most rational cities in the country.

Sendai is surrounded by heavily forested hills, and there are so many wooded areas within the city limits it is known as The Metropolis of Woods. Its primary industries today are metal, iron and steel products, electrical appliances, rubber, woodenware, foodstuffs, lacquerware, beer and Osake. Products made of a dark brown or black ignite rock called umoregi, found in the nearby hills, is a specialty of the city.

Places of special interest in Sendai include the ruins of the Date castle, called Aobajo or Green-leaf Castle, the Osaki Hachiman Shrine, and a wild-flower botanical garden. Within a short distance of the city are several noted hot-spring spas (Akiu, Jogi, Sakunami), the Zuigan Temple, and a pavilion especially designed on a rocky cliff near the Matsushima-Kaigan Pier to view the beauty of the bay (Kanrantei).

The centerpiece of scenic Tohoku is Matsushima, known since ancient times as one of the three most beautiful places in Japan. Matsushima means Pine-Clad Island, but this is a whole bay of islands--260 of them--dotting Matsushima Bay. See MATSUSHIMA.

Before the coming of the Japanese, the Tohoku district was inhabited by a Cacausoid race known as Ainu. White of skin, with very large, round eyes, and heavy body-hair, the Ainu were gradually driven northward by the Japanese, but intermingling over the centuries produced a mixed race of Ainu-Japanese that is much in evidence in the Sendai area, especially in small towns and villages on the way to Sendai. See AINU.

SEN-NO RIKYU (Sin-no Ree-que)

Probably the best-known of Japan's tea masters, Sen-no Rikyu was born in 1521 and lived until 1591, at which time he was forced to commit suicide by Hideyoshi Toyotomi who had previously been his patron.

Also a noted poet and master of the art of flower arranging, Rikyu was appointed offical tea master by Nobunaga Oda, the most powerful Daimyo of his day and the de facto ruler of Japan, in the 1560s.

When Nobunaga died in 1582, Hideyoshi became his successor and made Rikyu his chief tea master. The roving eye of the Taiko (Great Person), as Hideyoshi was called, also fell upon Rikyu's beautiful daughter. But Rikyu refused to send her to his master, thus incurring his wrath.

Apparently reluctant to attack the famous tea master directly, Hideyoshi bidded his time. Sometime later Rikyu was accused of putting a statue of himself in the temple of Murasakino. Hideyoshi accused him of gross arrogance unbefitting the grand master of tea, and invited him to commit harakiri.

A request from the Taiko was a command. Rikyu, then in his 70th year, asked to be allowed to conduct one more tea ceremony before taking his own life. His request was granted--and the ceremony is said to have been one of the best the old master ever conducted.

The essence of the tea ceremony promoted by Rikyu was simplicity and rusticity within very strict standards of beauty and naturalness--a style that is city within very strict standards of beauty and naturalness--a style that is referred to as wabi-cha or rustic tea.

The particular style of tea ceremony originated by Rikyu was split into three schools by his grandsons--and were called the Three Houses of Sen. These three schools--Omote Senke, Ura Senke and Mushanokoji Senke--are still among the most popular tea ceremony schools in Japan today.

The terms Omote (Front) and Ura (Rear) came into use because the older and younger brothers of one of Rikyu's great grandsons, were teaching the tea ceremony on the same premises in Kyoto, the older brother in the front of the house and the younger brother in the rear. As time went by, the separate locations diverged into separate schools.

In addition to having helped establish the tea ceremony as an important cultural activity, Sen-no Rikyu was also a celebrated master of the art of landscape gardening. See GARDENS.

SETO (Seto)

Forty-five minutes from Nagoya by the Seto train line, Seto City is one of Japan's main porcelain centers. The first kiln was established there by Toshiro Kato around 1200--after which he reportedly traveled to China to study the art of porcelain-making and then went all over Japan seeking a place that had better clay than Seto.

Failing to find anything better, Kato returned to Seto and gave birth to an industry that now includes nearly 1,000 factories and well over a 1,000 kilns. Visitors to Seto are welcomed in many of the kilns.

SETSUBUN (Sate-sue-bune)

This is the popular Throwing of the Beans ceremony to mark the end of the coldest period of the year on February 4th. Going back to ancient times when it was a ritual to ward off evil and ensure good luck, Setsubun is now practiced at homes as well as at shrines and temples, which often invite famous movie stars or other personalities to participate in ceremonies that are frequently televised.

Large crowds gather at these places to watch the Mame-maki (Mah-may-mah-kee), or Throwing of the Beans, and hopefully catch a few for good luck. When throwing the beans the thrower calls out loudly: Fuku wa uchi! Fuku wa uchi! Oni wa soto!--Good fortune come in! Good fortune come in! Devils get out!

SEVEN GODS OF GOOD LUCK

In Japanese religious mythology, there are seven gods of good luck who have played an important role in the cultural history of the country. These seven gods are:

Benten (Bane-tane), a female diety, usually shown seated on a dragon or serpeant and playing a lute, who is the goddess of eloquence and the arts.

Bishamon (Be-shah-moan), the god of war, a wild looking fellow in armor, holding a spear in one hand and a pagoda in the other, who does in evil-doers.

Daikoku (Die-koe-kuu), the god of wealth, is a smiling old man wearing a hood, sitting on bales of rice, carrying a bag full of treasures over his shoulder, and holding a small mallet.

Ebisu, the god of fishermen (and merchants), a smiling, portly figure in court robes, holding a large red snapper in one hand, with a fishing rod over his shoulder.

Fukurokuju (Fuu-kuu-roe-kuu-juu), the god of wealth and longevity, who has a short body but long head and beard, and is usually depicted holding a stick with a sutra scroll tied to it. He is usually attended by a crane or tortoise, both symbols of longevity.

Hotei (Hoe-tay-e), the god of contentment and happiness, is a fat fellow with a large, protruding stomach and a happy face. He carries a bag on his back, and holds a fan.

Jurojin (Juu-roe-jeen), the god of longevity, is an old man with a long white beard. He carries a holy staff bearing a sacred scroll, and holds a fan. He is usually accompanied by a stag or crane.

SEVEN ISLES OF IZU / IZU SHICHI TO (E-zoo She-chee Toe)

These seven islands lie off the coast of Izu Peninsula and extend in a chain from the lower reaches of Tokyo Bay southward for some 290 kilometers. The most famous of the islands, all of which are volcanic and are an extension of the chain that includes Mt. Fuji, are Oshima and Hachiojijima. The others are Toshima, Niijima, Kozushima, Miyakejima and Mikurajima.

Oshima, the largest of the seven islands, boasts a live volcano, a picturesque way of life that goes back for centuries, a mild climate, huge fields of camellia flowers and a thriving dairy industry.

Passenger ferries leave Tokyo for Oshima daily, and are almost always crowded with tourists and locals returning home after a visit to the big city.

In ancient times, all the of Isles of Izu were used as places of exile for out-of-favor notables. Two of the most famous of these exiles were Tametomo Minamoto (1139-1170), a famous archer who was banished to Oshima when he was 17, and Hideie Ukita, a feudal lord (Daimyo) under Hideyoshi Toyotomi, whom Ieyasu Tokugawa defeated at Sekigahara in 1600 and sent to Hachiojima in 1611, where he survived for another 44 years.

SEVERANCE PAYMENTS

It is an established practice for Japanese companies to make severance payments to workers who are let go for whatever reason (other than some serious criminal offense). These payments are based on the length of time the employee worked, the basic monthly wage and the employee's reason for leaving.

Such payments are made when an employee is fired, when a company goes out of business and when the employee retires. See RETIREMENT.

SEX / SEI (Say-e)

Unlike Christianized countries, sexual morality in Japan has never been associated with religion or any sense of sin. It has always been recognized as a physical action necessary for both procreation and mental and physical well-being--at least for men.

There was traditionally a double-sex standard. Premarital and extra-marital sex for men was regarded as a natural part of life, but their partners in such liaisons were generally public women who worked in the entertainment trades.

At the same time, romantic liaisons were also common among the upper classes, particularly the nobles. The Shoguns, Daimyo and upperclass Samurai typically had one or more mistresses.

Until 1956 legal redlight districts flourished in Japan, and most of the thousands of inns around the country functioned as houses of assignation. Today, there are thousands of so-called love-tels in major cities catering to couples by the hour or by the night.

The Japan Sexual Education Association reports that young Japanese women are becoming more sexually liberated--decline of family traditions.

The JSEA said a recent survey showed that 13.4 percent of the females from age 13 to 21 had engaged in sex, while 18.7 of the males in the same age group reported having had sex.

Girls now think and act more freely in sexual matters, the report said.

Sex is one business in Japan that seems to be immune to economic ups and downs. A recent review by Kyodo News Agency of sex-related businesses in Tokyo showed that love-hotels, Turkish bathhouses and similar establishments were doing better than ever.

Kyodo said there were about 35,000 of the so-called love-hotels in Tokyo, and that they have an average of 20 rooms each, which are used by an average of

2.3 couples per day. The total earnings of the Tokyo love-hotels was estimated at three trillion yen the previous year.

SHIKOKU (She-koe-kuu)

The smallest of Japan's four main islands, Shikoku has a total land area of 18,787 square kilometers, and is divided into four prefectures--Tokushima, Kagawa, Ehime and Kochi. The island is traversed by several mountain ranges and has a number of rivers, including the Yoshino (194 km) and the Shimanto (145 km).

While not in the mainstream of Japanese life, Shikoku has been populated since the earliest times. The famous Buddhist priest Kukai, known posthumously as Kobo Daishi, was born on the island in 774. He was the founder of or is related to 88 Buddhist temples scattered around the island and famous since the early 1600s as a sacred pilgrimage.

Still today over 100,000 people a year complete the circuit of the temples --many of them on foot, as it was always done in the olden days.

Suffice to say, Shikoku abounds in historic and scenic places that make it a popular destination for travelers. The island is especially noted for the beautiful Awa Odori folk dance, Ritsuin Park in Takamatsu, dog-fighting in Kochi, bullfighting in Uwajima, and the hot-springs in Matsuyama.

Shikoku is also known for its agriculture, lacquerware and pottery. See JAPAN.

Recommended reading: JAPANESE PILGRIMAGE, by Oliver Statler (Morrow).

SHIMABARA (She-mah-bah-rah)

On a gourd-shaped peninsula east of Nagasaki, Shimabara is famous as the place where some 38,000 Christian converts took refuge from a Tokugawa Shogunate army of 120,000 in the early 1600s, and after a siege that lasted for three months, were annihilated.

The peninsula, part of the Unzen Amakusa National Park, is one of the most scenic spots in Japan.

SHIMODA (She-moe-dah)

Near the tip-end of Izu Peninsula on the southeast side, Shimoda is now an important port and fishing base, as well as a gate-way for sightseeing and recreational facilities in the area. It is best-known in history, however, as the place where Townsend Harris, America's first diplomatic envoy to Japan, lived for more than a year, beginning on September 3, 1856.

Shimoda was also the first port opened to trade with the U.S. by the Tokugawa Shogunate, following the Treaty of Kanagawa, which was signed in 1854.

As it happened, however, designating Shimoda as a trading port was a subterfuge by the Shogunate to delay the opening of the country as long as possible. The port was far removed from the population centers and principal roads.

Harris soon found out that Shimoda was useless as a foreign trade port. After he received permission to move the consulate to Edo (Tokyo), in November 1857, Shimoda was out of the limelight until 1934, when Japanese and American diplomats helped launch an annual festival called Kuro Fune Matsuri or Black Ship Festival to mark the arrival of Commodore Perry and his fleet of black warships in 1853.

The festival, held in mid-May each year, is one of the major events on the Izu Peninsula, and attracts members of the diploma-tic corp in Tokyo as well as tourists and Japanese.

See HARRIS, TOWNSEND. PERRY, COMMODORE MATTHEW C.

SHIMONOSEKI (She-moe-no-say-kee)

On the southernmost tip of Honshu across from Kyushu's port city of Moji, Shimonoseki has been a gateway to Honshu, the largest island, since Japan's earliest days, but it owes its fame to two major historical events.

The first of these events was the Battle of Danno-ura offshore and on the beach of the city in 1185, when the Taira (Heike) clan was wiped out by the Minamoto (Genji) clan--a great battle recounted in GENJI MONOGATARI, regarded as the world's first novel.

In 1863 the Choshu clan, joining those who wanted to expell the barbarians and keep Japan closed to the outside, fired on ships passing through the straits, and sealed it off. The following year a fleet of American, French, British and Dutch ships retaliated by bombarding Shimonoseki for three days, inflicting heavy damage.

This demonstration of naval power convinced the Choshu leaders that the Shogunate should go and that Japan should modernize. They joined the Satsuma clan of Kyushu in opposing the Shogun and demanding that the Emperor be returned to power.

SHINAGAWA (She-nah-gah-wah)

Now an important residential and hotel area as well as a major commuter train terminal, Shinagawa was known in Tokugawa times as one of the Post Stations on the great Tokai-Do walk-way, just outside of Edo (Tokyo). It was the first stop for travelers leaving Edo, and the last stop before travelers entered Edo--and was therefore of special importance.

The Kaian Temple in the area was founded by Tokiyori Hojo, the fifth regent of the Kamakura Shogunate, in the 13th century. Two of Japan's most famous statesmen, Prince Tomomi Iwakura (1825-1883) and Lord Yoshinaga Matsudaira (1828-1890) are buried on the grounds of the Temple.

A short distance away, near Oimachi Station on the Yamanote Line that encircles central Tokyo, is the tomb of Hirobumi Ito, who played a key role in the drafting of Japan's first constitution (which went into effect in 1889), and was the country's first prime minister. See ITO, HIROBUMI. GEISHA.

The Pacific Hotel, the Takanawa Prince Hotel and the New Takanawa Prince Hotel are located within walking distance of Shinagawa Station.

SHINJUKU (Sheen-juu-kuu)

Adjoining Chiyoda Ward, which encompasses the Imperial Palace and much of Tokyo's financial and government districts, Shinjuku was originally the site for several huge feudal lord estates, and then developed into a popular residential area because of its higher elevation and proximity to downtown Tokyo.

It is still a popular residential district, but the area around Shinjuku Station, which is one of the largest and busiest commutor terminals in the country, has become a major business, hotel and entertainment center and is a city within its own right.

Four of Japan's leading department stores--Isetan, Mitsukoshi, Odakyu and Keio--have stores there, and there are hundreds of restaurants, bars and cabarets, along with half a dozen movie theaters and other entertainment establishments.

In the 1970s several huge highrise buildings were erected on the west side of the station area, including the 225-meter high Mitsui Building, the highest building in Japan.

Leading hotels in the area include the Keio Plaza, the Century Hyatt and the Tokyo Hilton.

Shinjuku Station by itself is like a small city, with dozens of shops, restaurants and other facilities within its premises. Well over a million people pass through the 8-story 3-basement station each day.

SHINJUKU NATIONAL GARDEN / SHINJUKU GYO-EN (Sheen-juu-kuu G'yoe-inn)

Formerly the villa grounds of the Naito Daimyo family, the Shinjuku National Garden is near Sendagaya Station on Tokyo's Chuo Line, close to the city's famous Meiji Shrine Outer Garden.

When the system of feudal Daimyo lords was abolished in 1868, the grounds became the property of the Imperial Household. After World War II they were transferred to the state, which opened the garden portion up to the public.

The garden is filled with cherry trees and a huge greenhouse that contains orchids and other kinds of subtropical and tropical plants.

In November of each year chrysanthemum shows are held in the garden, and are traditionally attended by the Emperor and Empress.

SHIN KAMMON TUNNEL (Sheen Kahm-moan Toe-nay-rue)

Completed in 1974, this undersea train tunnel passes beneath the Kammon Straits, connecting the islands of Honshu and Kyushu. The tunnel is 18,675 meters long, making it the world's longest undersea tunnel, but only 880 meters of this distance is under the sea floor.

It is used exclusively by the famous Shinkansen Bullet Trains, and is 9.6 meters wide and 8.1 meters high.

SHINTO / THE WAY OF THE GODS (Sheen-toe)

The indigenous religion of Japan, Shinto is basically a worship of or paying reverence to all things in nature, eventually including one's ancestors. Shinto teaches that all things, animate and inanimate, have their own kami (kah-me), spirits or gods.

The greater of these kami are to be worshipped at jinja (jeen-jah) or shrines. Since there were many gods in the Shinto pantheon, shrines abound in Japan. If one included all the tiny roadside and hillside jinja, the number, in earlier years, would probably have been in the millions. Today, there are well over 100,000 shrines of all sizes, and 100s of major ones.

From earliest times, Shinto emphasized bodily cleanliness and fertility. One result of this was the Japanese were among the first if not the first to invent the hot bath and make it a daily ritual. Another result was the development of religious festivals that were both to celebrate and increase human fertility.

Early Shintoism inferred to the Japanese that they were descendants of divine beings and were therefore very special. In the latter part of the 19th century, Shintoism was made the national religion of Japan and its teaching and activities came under the control of the government. The Emperor was deified, and people were taught that he was a living god.

At the end of WWII in 1945, the state religion was abolished, and Shinto observances became a matter of personal choice. Today the Japanese do not necessarily practice Shintoism as a religion, but many typical and traditional customs are Shintoist--taking newborn children to shrines, wedding ceremonies, dedicating buildings, etc.

It is also a popular custom for people to visit famous shrines around the country, especially during the New Year period. All local shrines have their own festivals that are well-attended by people living in the neighborhood--and if the shrines are famous, by people from all over the country.

One of the dance and music forms that accompanies Shinto ceremonies is called kagura (kah-guu-rah), and is performed by young shrine maidens praying for a good harvest.

The best way to tell a Shinto shrine from a Buddhist temple is the torii (toe-reee) gate--two upright pillars with a cross-piece on top.

Thus while few Japanese (only around two million) list themselves as being Shintoists, all Japanese are influenced by and at one time or another follow Shinto precepts.

Some 90 percent of the Shinto shrines in the country belong to the Jinja Honcho or Association of Shinto Shrines. The association recognizes the Grand Shrines of Ise as the chief shrine in the country. Amaterasu Omikami, the ancestral diety of the Imperial family, is enshrined at Ise. Each prefecture has a shrine board that administers matters concerning the members.

Shinto has no specific founder and has never had an explicit dogma. Because different shrines have different kami (gods) and somewhat different teachings, the Association of Shinto Shrines has drawn up and published a set of principles to define Shinto (The way of the Gods).

The manifesto, called General Principles of a Pious Life, states:

Shinto is the great way of eternal heaven and earth. It fosters a noble spirit and lays the foundation of great peace. Its mission is achieved through revering the merciful consideration of the kami, transmitting our ancestors' teachings, manifesting the essence of the way of the kami, and promoting the welfare of humanity. Here are set forth the general principles of the Correct Way, which we will endeavor to practice. We hereby pledge our efforts to enhance the way of the kami:

1. By being grateful for the blessings of kami and the favor of ancestors, and by devoting ourselves to ritual activities with a pure and sincere heart.

2. By serving the world and other people, and by building and reinforcing the world in the service of kami.

3. By embracing the merciful mind of kami, by leading a harmonious life, and by praying for the prosperity of the nation as well as the peaceful coexistence and prosperity of the entire world.

Japan has always been a fertile land for the propagation of religous thought, with the exception of Christianity. Despite an enormous amount of effort since the late 1850s, Christian missionaries in Japan have not down well. The humane precepts of Christianity are nothing new to the Japanese, and now that they are free to believe and practice whatever they wish, the other aspects of Christianity appear to hold very little appeal for them.

Total acceptance of Christian dogma virtually requires that one be raised in the religion from young childhood. By the time the missionaries get to most Japanese, it is too late.

Recommended reading: SHINTO: Japan's Spiritual Roots, by Stuart Picken (Kodansha Int'l). THE LOOKING GLASS GOD, by M. Nahum Stiskin (Weatherhill). Stiskin's book delves into the deepest meanings of Shintoism by analyzing the root kanji originally used to describe it, showing that it is a far more profound and comprensive body of thought than believed by most Western scholars.

SHIOBARA SPAS (She-oh-bah-rah)

The famed Shiobara spas--there are 11 of them--are located in a V-shaped valley formed by two immense mountains, Mt.

Takahara and Mt. Nasu, approximately two-and-a-half hours northwest of Tokyo in the grand Nikko National Park.

The swift-flowing Hoki River rushes down the valley in a series of cascades that rival those on the Hayakawa River of Hakone. Numerous tributary streams from the two mountain peaks career down deep ravines to join the Hoki River, adding to the indescribable beauty of the area.

These spas were discovered in the 9th century, and have been in use ever since, but it was not until the 1870s, after the noted Viscount Michitsune Mishima, then governor of Tochigi Prefecture, had roads built to them, that they began to attract visitors from outside of the district.

Among the best-known of the Shiobara spas are Oami, Fukuwata, Shinoyu, Shiogama, Monzen, Furumachi, and Oku-Shibara. The inns of Shionoyu Spa are situated along a ridge above the springs, so guests must descend some 100 steps to enter the outdoor baths, many of which are hewn out of natural rocks.

Each of the Shiobara spas is noted for the natural beauty of its setting, and several have their own unique attractions. Among the sights near Oami is a pool of boiling water so deep the bottom has not been found.

SHIPS / FUNE (Fuu-nay)

The Japanese were not known as shipbuilders during the early history of the country, but by the first centuries A.D. they were regularly sailing to Korea and China, and in later centuries to Southeast Asia.

Encouraged by the shipbuilding knowledge of the pilot Will Adams, Shogun Ieyasu Tokugawa had a number of seagoing vessels built in the early 1600s, and carried on a thriving trade with the Asian mainland and the islands of Southeast Asia. During the heyday of this trade, from 1604-1635, Japanese ships swarmed all over Southeast Asia, going as far as Thailand and Borneo, and carrying such goods as rice, pottery, lacquerware, silver and copper, and returning with silk, sugar, sandal wood, leather products and other items.

Japanese pirate ships also flourished during this period, and were feared throughout Southeast Asia.

One of the Japanese sailors who went to Taiwan in 1615--formerly a palanquin bearer for the Lord of Numazu--wound up in Thailand, where he became the leader of the large Japanese community, a trusted advisor and general for the King and married a Thai princess--only later to be poisoned by a jealous opponent.

The life story of this remarkable merchant-adventurer-soldier was made into a movie by Daiei Motion Picture Co. in 1959.

Even after the country closed its doors to the outside world in 1639, coastal shipping was an important part of the Japanese economy throughout the 200-plus years of the Tokugawa era.

Some of the ships plying the coasts of Japan were especially designed to carry specific cargoes--sake, rice and other products.

SHIZUOKA (She-zoo-oh-kah)

On the famous Bullet Train line midway between Tokyo and Nagoya, Shizuoka City is now noted as the tea trading center of Japan and the capital of Shizuoka Prefecture, which is also first or second in the production of mandarin oranges in Japan.

In the olden days Shizuoka was famous not only for its tea and mandarin oranges, but because it was the 20th Post Station on the fabulous Tokai Do Highway that connected Edo (Tokyo), with Kyoto (See PROCESSIONS OF THE LORDS), and was also the home for 25 years of the great Ieyasu Tokugawa, who founded the Tokugawa Shogunate (and befriended Will Adams, the English ship's anjin (ahn-jeen) pilot.

During his many years in Shizuoka, Ieyasu lived in the Castle of the Floating Isle, the ruins of which can still be seen. The castle site, surrounded by moats and a stone wall, is now part of a park in the northern part of the city.

Contemplating the scene today, one is able to imagine the splendor and glory of the place when Japan's most powerful man lived there--a place he chose in part because of its outstanding scenic beauty and the healthy climate.

During the days of the Tokugawa Shogunate, Shizuoka was called Sumpu (Sumepuu), and was strategically important because it served as a western outpost of Edo.

SHOCHU (Show-chuu)

Shochu, the White Lightening of Japan, is distilled from the dregs of sake, Japan's national drink. It is the fourth most consumed alcoholic beverage in that country--following beer, sake and various whiskeys and brandies.

Considerably stronger than sake, shochu is consumed almost entirely by the laboring class, and is a special favorite of construction workers.

Another drink popular with some laborers is one called awamori (ah-wah-moe-ree), which is now distilled from rice but was originally made from millet (awa). It is even stronger than shochu.

SHOGUN (Show-goon)

The title Shogun is a derivative of Sei-i-Tai-Shogun, which translates, more or less, as Great Barbarian Subduing General, and was first used around the 6th century to designate generals sent to subdue Caucasoid Ainu tribesmen inhabiting the eastern and northern portions of Honshu.

In 1192, when Minamoto clan leader Yoritomo established himself as the supreme military power in the country, he was given the title Sei-i-Tai-Shogun by the Emperor, apparently because it was the highest military title in the land.

The closest English approximation would probably be Generalissimo, but in effect in meant that Yoritomo was the military dictator of Japan.

Yoritomo thus became Japan's first Shogun. Rather then remain in Kyoto, which he saw as an effete society of weaklings, Yoritomo chose Kamakura in distant eastern Honshu for the site of his administrative government, which was called Bakufu or Camp Office. He retired in 1199 in favor of his son, Yoriie, in order to ensure that the position would be passed on to his descendants. Yoriie was succeeded by his younger brother Senetomo, but the latter was assassinated in 1219.

Sanetomo was the last of Yoritomo's family, so the Hojo's, the most powerful members of the Bakufu government in Kamakura, invited Yoritsune Fujiwara, whose family had virtually ruled Japan for the previous 300-plus years, to fill the post of Shogun.

Yoritsune accepted the invitation, but actual power was in the hands of Yoshitoki Hojo. His descendants were to continue acting as regents for the Shogun until 1333 when the Kamakura Shogunate fell.

The fifth Kamakura Shogun was also a Fujiwara (Yoritsugu), but from 1252 on, the Hojo's invited Imperial princes to assume the role, while they maintained power. The Imperial prince-Shoguns were Munetaka (1252-1266), Koreyasu (1266-1289), Hisaakira (1289-1308) and Morikuni (1308-1333).

In 1333, Takauji Ashikaga rose in rebellion and defeated the Kamakura Shogunate, which had been weakened by its defense against the Mongol invasions of 1274 and 1281. He was appointed Shogun in 1338. His descendants were to rule as Shogun for the next 235 years-- or until 1573.

By the 1500s the Ashikaga Shoguns, who had set up their government in Kyoto, had lost control of the country, bringing on an age of wars between clan leaders fighting for supremacy.

First there was Nobunaga Oda (1534-1582), a descendant of the famous Taira clan. In a series of battles, he emerged as the paramount leader but was assassinated by one of his own retainers when he was 49 years old.

Nobunaga was succeeded by Hideyoshi Toyotomi, his ablest general, who went on to consolidate his power over all of Japan. Hideyoshi chose not to assume the title of Shogun, and when he died in 1598 his son Hideyori was still a young boy.

In the battles that followed Hideyoshi's death, one of his chief allies, Ieyasu Tokugawa, emerged the victor and in 1603 established the Tokugawa Shogunate in Edo (Tokyo).

Fourteen of Ieyasu's direct descendants were to reign as Shogun--until the year 1868, when the last one, Yoshinobu, abdicated in favor of restoring the Emperor to power.

Western contact with Japan began in earnest in the last half of the 1500s, but was to end abruptly in the 1630s when Tokugawa Iemitsu, Ieyasu's grandson, closed the country to outsiders.

Finally, it was the inability of the last four Tokugawa Shoguns to deal with internal problems and the Western powers that brought the downfall of Japan's last great feudal dynasty.

See HISTORY. ODA, NOBUNAGA. TOYOTOMI, HIDEYOSHI. TOKUGAWA, IEYASU. ADAMS, WILL.

SHOTOKU TAISHI (Show-toe-kuu Tie-she)

Revered in Japan as one of its great scholars and most influential cultural figures, Shotoku Taishi was the son of Emperor Yomei who reigned in the 6th century. Taishi persuaded his father that Buddhism did not conflict with Shintoism, and thereafter did all he could to propagate the faith, including having the famous Shitenno Temple built in Osaka.

Prince Shotoku became the regent to his aunt, Empress Suiko, during which time he composed the country's first written laws. The Prince died in 621. In his later years he was known as The Prince With Many Wise Ears, because he could reputedly give wise answers to as many as 10 people talking to him at the same time.

Prince Shotoku encouraged the spread of literature and painting, and was responsible for the construction of so many temples he is still honored as the patron saint of carpenters.

SHRINES / JINJA (Jeen-jah)

Shinto edifices are called shrines (while Buddhist buildings are called temples). In earliest times, the only Shinto shrine in Japan was the Imperial Palace, where the Emperor, a direct descendant of the Shinto gods who created the islands, lived and where the Three Sacred Treasures (Imperial Regalia), a Mirror, Sword and Jewel, were kept.

According to Japanese mythology, the Mirror was given by the Sun Goddess, Amaterasu Omikami, to her grandson, Ninigi-no Mikoto, when he came down to earth to reign, with instructions to keep it in the Imperial Palace.

At this time, the Emperor himself was the chief high priest, and there was little if any distinction between his secular and religious duties.

In 92 B.C. it was decided that the Mirror might become desecrated by being so close to so many people in the Palace, and it was moved outside of the Palace. Then around the 3rd century A.D., it was decided to move it still further away, and a shrine was built for it at Kasanui, near Nara (which was to become the Imperial Capital in 710).

Eighty-eight years later, the decision was made to build a new, much more elaborate shrine for the Sacred Mirror at a place called Ise on the southeastern tip of the Kii Peninsula--a place that was isolated at that time, and known for its extraordinary beauty.

Thus the shrine built at Ise, called Jingu, which may be translated as Abode of the Gods, became the national shrine of Shinto, where the spirits of emperors went to dwell upon death.

See GRAND SHRINES OF ISE.

Then as the population grew and the Imperial kingdom expanded, it became customary to build branch shrines in other areas. Finally, there was hardly a community in the country that did not have its local Shinto shrine, and there were hundreds of others in distant, often isolated mountain regions--places deliberately sought out for their beauty and isolation, both of which were deemed pleasing to the Shinto gods.

It also became the practice to erect miniature Shinto shrines along roads, at crossroads, where auspicious events occurred, and simply on any hilltop or rise in the vicinity, since it was believed that the spirits of things were to be found in high places.

Still today is is customary for the Emperor and other high officials to visit the Grand Shrines of Ise, and for events of national importance to be reported to the shrines.

Shinto shrines generally face toward the south, and sometimes to the east-- never to the west or north, which are considered unlucky. Shrines are almost always accompanied by groves of sakaki trees, which are considered sacred, and are built of lumber from hinoki or Japanese cypress, a tree with an especially beautiful grain that is easy to work with but very durable.

There are now several architectual types of Shinto shrines, but they are always simple and austere when compared to Buddhist temples.

The entrance way to Shinto shrines is marked by a distinctive gateway called torii (toe-reee), which consists of two upright posts and two horizontal cross-pieces at the top. The materials of the torii vary from wood to stone, but the design is always the same--four inter-secting lines, three of which are always straight, with the top one sometimes curved in a graceful arc.

In some cases, the torii are quite some distance from the shrines themselves--reputedly to give adherents time to compose themselves before they arrive on the sacred precincts of the shrine.

The torii were originally bird perches on which live cocks, brought as offerings to the Sun Goddess, Amatersu Omikami, were placed by worshippers. In the beginning, the torii were placed on all sides of the shrines. Eventually, the perches came to be symbolic of shrines, and were made large and placed only in the front.

At first, the torii were only of unpainted wood, but later many of them were painted. Now some of them are made of metal or concrete, and there are some half a dozen different designs.

Another interesting note: drums have traditionally been associated with Shinto shrines, as part of their ceremonies and festivals (while bells are associated with Buddhist temples).

SHURI-KEN JUTSU (Shuu-ree-ken Jute-sue)

During the inter-clan intrigues and fighting in the 16th century, a new weapon that came into use was a small star-shaped metal disk with very sharp points, called shuri-ken, which was used for throwing.

Prior to this, the two most important throwing weapons were small swords or daggers. The advantage of the shuri-ken was that it required far less skill to throw it effectively, since there were deadly points all around the disc.

The shuri-ken became one of the favorite weapons of the ninja--the professional agent/assassin families that flourished in feudal Japan. It could be easily concealed and dozens of them could be carried at one time.

Special schools were established to teach the art of throwing shuri-ken (called shuri-ken jutsu). Among the most famous of these were the Yagyu, Negishi and Shrai schools.

Many of the ninja, Samurai and others of this era developed incredible skill with the shuri-ken. They were able to throw them from any position or angle with devastating accuracy. They are often seen in presentday Samurai movies.

SIGNS / KAMBAN (Kham-bahn)

I believe there are more signs in Japan, of one kind or another, than in any other country. At least they are numerous, and most of them are in Japanese kana or kanji characters so if you do not read the language they are a formidable barrier. Another of my own books, READING YOUR WAY AROUND JAPAN--A Sign for Every Occasion (Phoenix Books /Publishers), is designed to help overcome this problem.

Highrise buildings in Shinjuku. P. 279

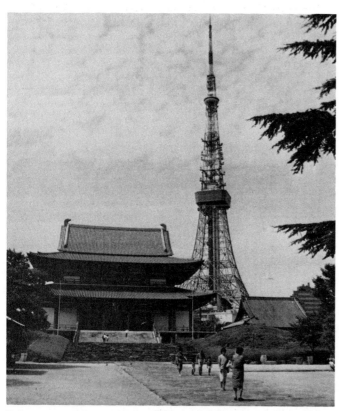

Tokyo Tower, a famed tourist spot. P. 309

Nara's noted deer & pagoda. P. 222

There are, however, many visual signs that are international in nature and can be readily understood by most people. The following commonly see signs are courtesy of the Japan National Tourist Organization:

At Airport

Rest Room

Men's Room

Ladies' Room

Information

Temporary Luggage Storage

Shopping

Restaurant

Bus

Taxi

Hand Rail

End Moving Walkway, 10m

Money Exchange

Arrival

Departure

Meeting Service

Hand Baggage

At Station

Ticket Window

Temporary Parcel Storage

Coin Locker

Public Telephone

Stairway (Down)

Stairway (Up)

No Smoking

Super Express Train Platform

In the Street

Subways (Eidan)

Subways (Toei)

Taxi Stand

Post Office

SILK / KINU (Kee-nuu)

Silk has been produced in Japan since the 2nd century, B.C., and for a long time, the Japanese were the world's largest producers of raw silk.

The two major centers of silk production in Japan today are Nagano and Aichi Prefectures, and there is a Silk Center and a Silk Museum in Yokohama.

Until modern times (which began in Japan in 1868), the kimono of the Samu-rai and nobility of Japan were made of silk. Today most of the silk produced in Japan is exported.

SISTER CITIES

Some 150 of Japan's cities have Sister City ties with cities abroad. Usually these ties involve cities that have a number of things in common--size, principle economic activity, etc., and one city may have several such relationships.

Yokohama, for example, has Sister City ties with Bombay, Lyon, Manila, Odessa, San Diego, Shanghai and Vancouver. Hiroshima's Sister Cities are Honolulu and Volgograd. Nikko's Sister City is Palm Springs. Himeji's Sister City is Phoenix, Arizona.

Others: Okayama-San Jose. Osaka-San Francisco-Sao Paulo-Shanghai. Sapporo-Munchen-Portland. Sesebo-Albuquerque. Sendai-Acapulco-Minsk-Rennes-Riverside. Shimoda-New Port (R.I.). Takamatsu-St. Petersburg. Takayama-Denver. Tokyo-New York. Toyota-Detroit, and Wakayama-Bakersfield.

Sister Cities sponsor cultural and educational exchange programs, and otherwise work to develop close, cooperative and beneficial relations.

SIZE (HEIGHT) SEI (Say-e)

One of the more remarkable changes in Japan since 1945 has been in the average height of the people. In the two decades between 1961 and 1981, the average height of boys at the age of six went from 112 centimeters to 115.9cm. Twelve year-olds went from 142.3cm to 149.8cm. Fifteen year-olds went from 161.8cm to 167.3cm, and 17-year olds went from 165.2cm to 169.7cm.

Girls have undergone a similar spurt in the average height, with corresponding increases in the average weight of both sexes.

The dramatic change is attributed to better diets, including the consumption of grains other than rice, along with more meat and dairy products. It is predicted by some that the average height of the Japanese will continue to increase until it is comparable to that of other people who eat similar diets.

SKIING / SUKIINGU (Suu-kee-ing-guu)

With its great mountain ranges and wintertime snowfalls, plus the ubiquitous hotsprings, Japan is a skiers paradise. There are, in fact, 47 noted ski resorts in the country--three of them in Hokkaido, six in northeastern Honshu, 34 in east-central Honshu and four in west-central Honshu.

In Hokkaido the ski season starts as early as October at the Mt. Daisetsu ski resort, in November at the Teine Olympia Ski Resort near Sapporo, and in December at the Niseko resort near Kutchan.

On the main island of Honshu, the starting of the ski season depends on the altitude and location of the resort, some of them opening in November, but most of them in December.

Among the best-known resorts on Honshu are Akakura, Bandai, Iwappara, Kusatsu, Nikko, Nozawa, Shiga Heights, Yuzawa, Tateyama, Zao and Mt. Daisen.

Many of the ski resorts are combination hotspring spas, providing patrons with the opportunity to enjoy the best of both worlds. During the ski season, Ueno Station in Tokyo becomes a forest of skis and poles, with as many as 100,000 skiers passing through the station in a 24 hour period.

A complete list of the ski resorts in Japan is available from the Japan National Tourist Organization. See JNTO listing.

SLEEPING MATS / FUTON (Fuu-tone)

Traditional Japanese bedding consists of floor mattresses and quilts called futon, sized for the individual, that are placed on the floor at night and stowed in closets during the day.

The futon are placed directly on the clean, aromatic reed-mat (tatami) floors when needed, and folded up each morning --or hung outside in the sun to air out.

Futon are not only comfortable, they are imminently practical, since it is possible to provide sleeping space for additional people just by spreading other futon, and to make other use of the same room during the day. They are also less expensive than Western style beds.

Futon are sold in children and adult lengths.

The word futon comes from the Japanese pronounciation of the Sung Dynasty in China (10th and 11th centuries), and was brought to Japan by Japanese priests who went there to study Buddhism. When the word first came into use in Japan it referred to the cushions Zen priests sat on.

Until that time, Japanese bedding appears to have been straw mats, with coverings made of the same material. The oldest Japanese word for bedding is yobusuma (yoe-buu-suu-mah), which means night dress. As these straw mattresses and quilts were improved, they gradually came to be called futon, from the more attractive and comfortable floor cushions imported from China.

SMOKING / TOBAKO WO SUIMASU (Toe-bah-koe oh sooey-mahs)

The pattern of smoking tobacco in Japan is similar to that of the U.S.-- the percentage of men smoking has begun to decline, while more and more women are taking up the habit.

At present, some 28 million Japanese males smoke, and some seven and a half million females. Among adult males, this is one of the highest percentages in the world (over 70 percent).

There is a movement in Japan to encourage smokers to give up the habit, and prevent young people from taking up the habit. But the movement is far behind that of similar programs in other countries.

The three most popular Japanese cigarette brands are Mild Seven, Seven Star and Hi-Lite. Each year well over 300 billion cigarettes are consumed in Japan. The industry is operated and controlled by the Japan Tobacco and Salt Public Corporation, a government monopoly.

Tobacco smoking was introduced into Japan by Portuguese traders who were shipwrecked on the island of Tanegashima south of Kyushu in the early 1540s. See PORTUGUESE IN JAPAN.

SNOW FESTIVAL / YUKI MATSURI (Yuu-kee Mot-sue-ree)

One of the biggest and most spectacular winter events in Japan is the Snow year from February 1 through 5 in O-dori Park and at Makomanai.

Hundreds of people spend days carving huge and elaborate snow sculptures, depicting mythological creatures, castles and so on, out of tons of snow. Participants compete for prizes and awards, and the festival attracts visitors from all over the country as well as from overseas.

SOCIAL SECURITY / SHAKAI FUKUSHI (Shah-kie Fuu-kuu-she)

In Japan Social Security--for those in need who have not reached retirement age or do not receive adequate pensions --is referred to as Livelihood Assistance. At present, some one and a half million people are receiving varying amounts of financial support from the government. Reasons for receiving such support include injury or illness, a drastic fall in earned income, mother-child households, and age.

There are several pensions systems in Japan, all coming under government regulations. They include the plans of private corporations, a national plan covering employees of firms with less than five employees (most of which are unincorporated) and self-employed individuals, along with mutual aid societies.

Foreigners resident in Japan can participate in national pension plans.

A study that has been underway for sometime would integrate all the present public pension programs into one. This new program would cover everyone, and those over the age of 65 would received fixed amounts.

Japanese law stipulates that every citizen must have some kind of health insurance, and all come under a national medical care program. Individuals making use of this program pay only a nominal amount when they go to doctors, clinics and hospitals that cooperate in the program.

SOGORO'S SACRIFICE (Soe-go-roe)

In the mid-1600s, the Daimyo of the province that is now Chiba Prefecture, Masanobu Hotta, was inexperienced and incapable, and his retainers took advantage of the situation to impose heavier and heavier taxes on the 4,000 or so farmers in the Kozu district.

Sogoro Kiuchi, head man of the village of Kozu, agreed to act as spokesman for the farmers, and presented a petition to the Daimyo, asking that the taxes be reduced. The request was denied. Finally, Sogoro decided that the only way out of the dilemma was to present a petition to the Shogun himself--an act that was punishable by death.

Saying goodby to his family, Sogoro went to Edo, and waited for an opportunity. In the winter of 1650, the Shogun went to Ueno to visit the temples there. Sogoro evaded the Shogun's Samurai guards, rushed up to his palanquin and thrust the petition into the hands of the surprised Shogun.

After reading the petition, the Shogun ordered Daimyo Hotta to investigate the charges and remedy the situation if they were justified. This was done, but Hotta was so angered by the incident that he had Sogoro, his wife and their two sons, one three and the other 11, beheaded.

Sogo and his family were buried in the garden of the Tosho Temple in the village by that name, and a sanctuary called the Sogo Reido was built in their memory. In 1753, on the 100th anniversary of their execution, the descendants of the Daimyo who had brought about their deaths, erected tombstones over their graves. The old sanctuary was replaced in 1921.

The story of Sogoro has been told many times, and is the subject of a famous Kabuki play.

SOKAIYA (So-kie-yah)

The Sokaiya are minority stockholders in major companies, closely linked with organized crime, who for decades made a profitable business of controlling stockholders meetings by intimadating other stockholders and preventing them from raising questions about the company or its board of directors. They would then charge the companies substantial sums of money for this so-called service.

To avoid problems with the sokaiya, the victimized companies paid off, officially charging the money off to consulting fees.

A revision of the country's commercial codes in 1982--the first since 1950--went a long way toward eliminating the power of the sokaiya, but they are not expected to give up so easily and predictions are they will find some other way to stay in business.

SONY

One of the most impressive of Japan's post-war industrial miracles, the company that is now known world-wide as Sony was founded in 1946 by two young ex-Japanese Navy men, Masaru Ibuka and Akio Morita.

The fledgling Sony empire began in a bombed-out store in a suburb of Tokyo, with 500 dollars Morita borrowed from his sake-brewing father. The new company was named Tokyo Tsushin Kogyo Kabushiki Kaisha, or Tokyo Communications Industrial Co. Ltd.

In 1956 the company was still struggling, but it was on the verge of a major break-through. Using new American-invented transistors, the company had produced a tiny radio that was given the brand name Sony.

TTKK begin looking for foreign agents for their new product. Among other things, the company placed a one-sixth of a page advertisement in a brand new trade publication called ORIENTAL AMERICA, which had been founded in Tokyo a few months earlier by American Ray Woodside, and was being mailed to selected importers in the U.S., Canada and Europe.

Shortly thereafter, TTKK made contact with General Distributors in Canada and

Delmonico in the U.S. These two firms immediately saw the potential of the new Sony radio, and became agents for the innovative new product.

The following year, TTKK changed its name to Sony. On the fifth anniversary of the name-change, Sony celebrated by placing ads in many publications. A full page ad was sent to ORIENTAL AMERICA (where I was the editor)--the first ad the magazine had received from Sony since its original 3-month contract in 1956. The camera-ready ad had been made up by Sony's own inhouse advertising department, and contained some bad English.

Woodside called Sony and ask permission to correct the English. The advertising manager refused to allow any changes in the ad. Woodside refused to carry the ad. Both companies went on to become very successful without any help from each other.

There are so many reasons why Sony became such a huge success so quickly-- many of them factors that also applied to other Japanese companies that grew up during this period. But Sony had something special as well. Its two founders were extraordinary men, even in a country filled with extraordinary men.

One of the early policies of TTKK had been to employee only engineers, and if memory serves me correctly, there was one year in the late 1950s when every employee (400, I believe) was in fact an engineer.

Perhaps more important, however, was Akio Morita, the senior partner in the firm, and the company's front man. Exceptionally intelligent, quick-witted, filled with ambition and energy, Morita was similar in many ways to the young Samurai of the 1860s, 70s and 80s who helped transform a feudal, agricultural society into a major industrial power in under three decades.

In typical Japanese fashion, the more successful Sony became, the more of a philosopher Morita became. With his ability to speak English (an ability he worked prodigiously to develop), and his outgoing personality, Morita also became a leading spokesman for Japan on the international scene.

SOPHIA UNIVERSITY / JOCHI DAIGAKU (Joe-chee Die-gah-kuu)

Sophia University has long been well-known in Japan and abroad because of the large number of foreign students who attend its International Department, and the quality of the English-language ability of its Japanese graduates.

In the 1960s and 70s, Sophia also became known for its economic research activities headed by Father Robert Ballon, who authored several books on Japanese business, labor and management.

Operated by a Jesuit order of the Catholic Church, Jochi is located in the Yotsuya district of Tokyo's Chiyoda Ward, just west of the Imperial Palace grounds. The university has grown enormously in both size and repute since 1953-1955 when I was a student there.

SPACE EXPLORATION

Japan's space industry made its first launching--of a pencil-type rocket--in 1960. Ten years later, Japan became the fourth nation in the world to orbit an artificial satellite. This was followed by a series of launchings of weather satellites and small stations designed for experiments in communications, broadcasting and X-ray astronomy.

The industry is steadily advancing the use of interplanetary space probes and broadcasting service satellites. Japan's space ports are located at Uchinoura, and on Tanega Shima. See TANEGA SHIMA for the role this tiny island played in Japan's first encounter with Westerners.

SPLIT-LEVEL ECONOMY

People around the world have heard about the giants of Japanese industry-- Toyota, Nissan, Sony, Matsushita, Mitsui, Mitsubishi, and so on, giving the impression that all or most Japanese companies are very large and powerful.

In fact, only 0.6 percent of all Japanese enterprises are large-scale. The overwhelming majority--99.4 percent --are very small (three employees or less) to medium-sized (300-999 employees).

Small enterprises in Japan account for some 53 percent of manufacturing, 61 percent of all wholesaling, 79 percent of the retail business, and 15 percent of all exports of industrial products.

It is characteristic of the Japanese economy that the relatively small number of very large companies subcontract a significant percentage of their production and assembly work to smaller wholly owned subsidiaries or affiliated companies.

For a detailed discussion of this aspect of the Japanese economy, see HOW TO DO BUSINESS IN JAPAN (Phoenix Books /Publishers), by Boye De Mente.

SPRING LABOR OFFENSIVE / SHUNTO (Shune-toe)

Japanese labor union federations, and individual unions as well, have developed the custom of negotiating for wage increases once a year, from April through May, in a process that is known by the abbreviation Shunto or Spring Labor Offensive.

During this period, the federations meet with their counterparts in management in ongoing negotiations, and also hold large labor rallies in the streets, marching along prescribed routes.

The marchers carry colorful banners and flags and wear headbands to signify their unity. See HACHIMAKI. Since many of the labor banners are red or have red lettering on white, foreign visitors in Japan sometimes mistakenly believe the marches are Communist inspired.

The indepedent unions of some companies may hold strikes during these negotiations, but they are mostly symbolic, and care is generally take to ensure that work stoppages are minor, and do not harm the company. The unions of public service companies, however, are more militant and have caused work delays of several days in past years.

STAGECOACHES / BASHA (Bah-shah)

Before the ending of the Tokugawa Shogunate in 1868, Japan had no wheeled passenger transportation of any kind. Only the elite Samurai upper class and members of the nobility were allowed to ride horses or be carried in palanquins. Everybody else walked.

But in the 1870s two enterprising New Zealand brothers named Hoyt established a stagecoach line between Tokyo and Yokohama, and another company operated between Odawara and Oiso. Japanese entrepreneurs got into the business, and in some remote areas of Japan stagecoaches were in use until the introduction of buses.

Two of the Hoyt brothers' stagecoach drivers, Tom Sayers and Frank Rutherford, were Americans. Rutherford died of smallpox in 1871 and was buried in the now famous foreign cemetery in Yokohama.

STANDARDS INFORMATION CENTER (SIC)

The Standards Information Center, founded in Tokyo by the Ministry of International Trade and Industry in 1983, is designed to provide foreign exporters information about Japan's test standards drafting procedures.

Specifically, the SIC is charged with collecting and publicizing MITI's production standards, responding to queries about these procedures, helping manufacturers and exporters abroad get information about new standards to be introduced, and serving as a go-between for foreign companies seeking information about standards set by private organizations in Japan.

Contact: Officer in Charge, Standards Information Center, Export and Design Division, Trade Administration Bureau, MITI, 1-3 Kasumigaseki, Chiyoda-Ku, Tokyo, Japan.

STATION BOX-LUNCHES / EKI-BEN (Eh-kee-bane)

One of the special pleasures of long-distance train riding in Japan is taking advantage of the special box-lunches that are sold in and near stations and on the boarding platforms. At many stations, eki-ben sellers go up and down the platforms during stops, and passengers buy through their coach windows. Some long-distance trains have eki-ben vendors on board, going to an fro through the aisles, pushing small carts or carrying trays.

The first eki-ben dealer is said to have appeared at Utsunomiya Station around 1887, selling rice balls and pickles wrapped in bamboo leaves. Today dozens of stations around the country are noted for certain kinds of eki-ben. The specialty of Yokohama, for example, is shumai, a flour bun filled with bits of meat and vegetables, a favorite Chinese snack.

At Tokyo Station one can buy several different varities of eki-ben, including chicken, sushi, rice and an assortment of vegetables and seafood, and sandwiches on white bread. Station vendors also sell tea, beer and sake, so it is possible to have a full meal on trains without dining facilities.

Some station vendors sell their tea in attractive pots made locally--so the traveler ends up with a very practical souvenir.

STONE LANTERNS / ISHI DORO (Ee-she Doe-roe)

Seen in yards, gardens, and temple and shrine grounds all over Japan, ishi doro developed from torches and bonfires lit at shrines and temples in ancient times to provide light for services and rituals. Gradually, they came to be placed around homes and on roadsides to guide people at night.

The Toma Temple in Yamato, near Nara, has a stone lantern that dates from 682.

As the centuries passed, the lanterns became more varied and artistic in their shapes and sizes. Tea masters in the 16th and 17th centuries adapted small versions of the lanterns for use in private gardens and the gardens of tea houses.

Most stone lanterns are made of granite, but there are many made of metal as well. Temples and shrines often have ishi doro made of bronze. Tokyo's popular Oriental Bazaar in the Harajuku district sells stone lanterns to many foreign visitors.

One famous stone lantern maker in Tokyo has been in business for several hundred years.

STORY TELLING / RAKUGO (Rah-kuu-go)

One of the most popular forms of traditional Japanese entertaiment is the telling of long humorous stories, mainly in the form of monologues, called rakugo (rah-kuu-go).

Dating from the early years of the 16th century, rakugo was well-entrenched by the middle of the 17th century, and by this time included the use of gestures and facial expressions, along with a punch-line at the end of the story.

Rakugo entertainers are ranked according to skill and experience, with beginners known as zenza (zen-zah), or curtain raisers, referring to the fact that they go on first or while the audience is being seated, to warm up the crowd.

One who has earned the reputation of being a master of rakugo is called a shin'uchi (sheen uuchee)--one who strikes the heart, or one of true value, because of his or her ability to attract large audiences. The shin'uchi, like all stars, is the last to perform.

There are three other kinds of storytelling in Japan: manzai (mahn-zie), naniwabushi (nah-nee-wah-buu-she), and kodan (koe-dahn).

Manzai features two performers who specialize in slapstick, wisecracks and comic skits, and is a modernized version of a dramatic form that originated in the 13th century (and had to do with driving away demons and bringing in good luck). Manzai performers usually write their own material. In recent year, 3-

member manzai teams have appeared on the scene, and some have introduced musical instruments as part of their act.

Naniwabushi, favored by older people, consists of a solo recitation that is partly sung in a very stylized, sober voice, and partly narrated as dialogue. The most popular naniwabushi theme is love versus duty or good versus evil.

Less popular than the other forms, kodan storytelling is the recitation of a famous historical event that is of special human interest. The stories are told in a flat, monotonous chant. Kodan dates from the 17th century.

The most famous kodan-shi (kodan story teller) of the Tokugawa era was a man named Shidoken, who arrived in Edo in 1692 at the age of 20, after having run away from a temple. Without any money to feed himself, he happened upon a storyteller nicknamed Ginnan Osho (Ginko Tree Priest) who sat under a ginko tree at the Kannon Temple in Asakusa and told stories, after which people would toss him money.

Shidoken thought this was an ideal way to make a living, so he picked out a nearby spot for himself, sat down and also began telling stories, adding a special touch that quickly attracted the crowds. He became so popular that Ginnan Osho had to leave and find a new place.

Shidoken's audiences became so large he had to build a platform to sit on so his audiences could see and hear him him. He was soon a famous figure in Edo, and continued the profession of kodan for the next 63 years, dying at the age of 83 in 1765.

STUDENTS / GAKUSEI (Gock-say-e)

Japan often seems to be a land of students, and with nearly 30 million attending school in a small country where the population is concentrated in a tiny percentage of the land-mass, this impression is valid.

The attendance rate for those of compulsory school age in Japan was 99.98 percent until 1980, when it went up a little as a result of a law passed in April 1979 making it mandatory that all mentally and physically handicapped children, as well as children who are chronically ill, be educated.

Approximately 95 percent of all students in Japan go to upper secondary schools after completing the nine compulsory grades (six years of elementary and three years of lower secondary school).

Some 65 percent of Japan's children attend kindergarten, and another 26 percent attend child-care centers. Around 38 percent of Japan's high school graduates go on to colleges and universities.

On the average, Japanese youth are more studious than their Western counterparts, at least until they are through high school. A primary reason for this is that entry into the more desirable schools is by examination, and graduating from an IN school is a vital factor in later employment opportunities.

Parents bring extraordinary pressure on their children to do well in school, knowing that their success in school will determine the quality of the rest of their lives.

During the late 1950s and 60s, hundreds of thousands of university students in Japan were very active politically. A number of student organizations, especially the Zengakuren (All-Japan Students Federation), achieved considerable prominence and power.

These students played a vital role in the downfall of the Kishi government in the early 1960s and later delayed the opening of the New Tokyo International Airport in Narita for several years.

SUBWAYS / CHIKATETSU (Chee-kah-tate-sue)

Japan's subways, particularly those in Tokyo, are world-famous for their efficiency and for being crowded during morning and evening rush hours. There are presently subway lines in Tokyo, Osaka, Kyoto, Nagoya, Kobe, Yokohama and Sapporo, with plans to open one in Fukuoka.

There are 11 subway lines in Tokyo alone, most of them intersecting at various points around the city, making it possible to transfer from one line to another. Seven of the lines come together or within walking distance of each other in the Hibiya/Tsukiyabashi/Ginza areas of downtown Tokyo.

Station names in the Japanese subway systems appear in Roman letters (Romaji), in hiragana and in kanji, so that children who have not yet learned kanji, as well as foreign visitors, can read the names.

SUICIDE (Ritual) / HARAKIRI (Hah-rah-kee-ree)

Ritual suicide, harakiri in common language and seppuku (sape-puu-kuu) in formal language, was an important aspect of feudal Japan (1192-1868). It developed as an integral part of the code and discipline of the Samurai warrior class.

Harakiri which literally means stomach-cutting, is a particularly painful method of self-destruction, and prior to the emergence of the Samurai as a professional warrior class, it was totally alien to the Japanese.

The early history of Japan reveals quite clearly that the Japanese were far more interested in living the good life than in dying a painful death. It was not until well after the introduction of Buddhism, with its theme of the transitory nature of life and the glory of death, that such a development became possible.

To the Samurai, seppuku, whether meted out as punishement or chosen as preferable to a dishonorable death at the hands of an enemy, was an unquestionable demonstration of their honor, their courage and their moral character.

When on the battlefield, acts of harakiri were often carried out rapildy and with very little formal preparation. But when done on other occasions and when ordered by a feudal lord or the Shogun, they were very formal ceremonies, requiring witnesses and considerable preparation.

In 1868, Lord Redesdale, a British diplomat stationed in Japan, along with six other foreigners, was asked to serve as witnesses at the seppuku of a Samurai of the Bizen clan who had ordered Japanese soldiers to fire on the foreign settlement in Kobe (then called Hyogo).

The detailed description of the ceremony which Lord Redesdale published in his book, TALES OF OLD JAPAN, was the first account by a foreigner of this remarkable custom. In this, the victim was a handsome 32-year old man who carried out the ceremony to perfection, both fascinating and shocking the Englishman.

Not all Japanese Samurai or lords believed in harakiri, even though many of them followed the custom. The great Ieyasu Tokugawa who founded Japan's last Shogunate dynasty in 1603, eventually issued an edict forbidding harakiri to both secondary and primary retainers.

The custom was so deeply entrenched, however, that it continued, and in 1663, at the urging of Lord Nobutsuna Matsudaira of Izu, the Shogunate government issued another stronger edict, prohibiting ritual suicide. This was followed up by very stern punishments for any lord who allowed any of his followers to commit harakiri.

Still the practice continued throughout the long Tokugawa reign, but was considerably diminished as time went by.

There were many forms of harakiri, including a form to show contempt or hatred of an enemy, one as a protest against injustice, and as a self-sacrifice to save others.

The location of an officially ordered seppuku ceremony was important, and included temples (but not Shinto shrines), the gardens of villas, and sometimes, inside homes. The size of the area available was important, and was prescribed precisely for people of high rank.

All other matters relating to the act were as carefully prescribed and carried out in the most meticulous manner. The most conspicuous participant in seppuku, other than the victim, was the kaishaku (kie-shah-kuu) or assistant, who was responsible for cutting off the victim's head after he had sliced his abdomen open.

The kaishaku was generally a close friend or associate of the condemned.

Recommended reading: HARAKIRI--Japanese Ritual Suicide, by Jack Seward (Tuttle).

Ordinary suicide, called jisatsu (jee-sot-sue), is common in Japan today but the Japanese do not lead the world in suicides. Japan's suicide rate is only slightly higher than the official number in the U.S., and well below that of Switzerland and other North European and East Bloc countries.

The reputation that Japan has for suicides is a hold-over from the days of the Samurai, and more recent war years when Japanese soldiers committed suicide rather than be captured, and Kami-Kaze (Divine Wind) pilots were used in suicidal missions against the U.S. armed forces advancing on Japan.

In present-day Japan, people kill themselves for reasons that are familiar --failed businesses, too much business pressure, and involvement in scandals. Other somewhat less common reasons are the failure of young children to pass competitive school examinations, love triangles, and lovers who cannot be together.

While suicide is deplored in Japan, it does not have the sinful overtones that are common in the West.

SUICIDE FOREST

The United States has its Golden Gate Bridge and other favorite suicide spots. Japan has the Forest of Aokigahara, at the foot of famed Mt. Fuji.

For apparently the same reason that the Golden Gate Bridge acts as a magnet on people contemplating suicide, the dense forest of Aokigahara attracts suicidal people from all over Japan.

Police estimate that from 20 to 50 people kill themselves each year in the dense woods, which is known in Japanese as Jukai or Sea of Trees. The number of people who die in the forest each year is uncertain because it is presumed that all of the bodies are not found.

The television dramatization in the early 1970s of a popular book, NAMI NO TO (Tower of Waves), by Seicho Matsumoto, turned Aokigaha into a mecca of suicides. In the book, a woman vanishes into the forest, leaving the implication that she went there to die.

SUMO (Sue-moe)

Dating back to mythical times, when it is said that it was popular among the gods, sumo is a unique form of wrestling that was widely practiced before the 6th century as a sport as well as a form of divination to predict the outcome of harvests and invoke the goodwill of the gods.

Sometime around the 6th century, sumo wrestling left the precincts of Shinto shrines and became an immensely popular spectator sport, patronized by both emperors and shoguns as the centuries went by.

The practices and traditions of sumo have continued down to the present time, and sumo remains one of the most distinctive and popular sports in the country.

Sumo is distinctive in many ways. The wrestlers begin training when they are in their early teens. They eat a special food called chanko-nabe (chan-koe-nah-bay), engage in strenuous exercises and practice sessions several hours a day, and grow to huge sizes--usually between six and seven feet in height, and weighing from 250 to 375 pounds.

The sport is controlled by the Japan Sumo Wrestling Association, which sponsors six 15-day tournaments a year-- three in Tokyo (in January, May and September), and one each in Osaka (March), Nagoya (July) and Fukuoka (November).

There are four grades of first-class or senior class wrestlers. The highest is Grand Champion or Yokozuna (Yoe-koe-zuu-nah) of which there may be several. Next are the Champions, or Ozeki (Oh-zay-kee). There are usually from two to four Ozeki. Then comes the Sekiwake (Say-kee-wah-kay) and Komusubi (Koe-muu-sue-bee) grades, with several wrestlers in each grade.

In the junior class there are five grades: Juryo (Juu-rio), Makushita (Mah-kuussh-tah), Sandame (Sahn-dah-may), Jo-ni-dan (Joe-nee-dahn), and Jo-no-kuchi (Joe-no-kuu-chee). Altogether, there are several dozen junior grade wrestlers.

The wrestlers belong to beya (bay-yah) or stables that are usually owned and presided over by retired champions or grand champions. Altogether, there are 28 beya. The beya are divided into East and West camps for tournament purposes.

The bouts take place in large halls that have a raised 14.9 square feet ring in the center. The aim of sumo is for one wrestler to eject the other from the ring or to cause the other wrestler to touch the ground anywhere with anything other than his feet--by shoving, tripping, throwing, slapping, etc., in a prescribed and named move that all sumo fans know by heart. The action may be over in seconds, or may last for several minutes and is often dangerous, since wrestlers regularly get tossed completely out of the high ring.

To win promotion to a higher grade, wrestlers must win eight or more of their 15 bouts each tournament, and all except the grand champions are usually demoted if they do not consistently win the majority of their fights. The more bouts a sumo wins, the faster the promotions.

Wrestlers who win a tournament--by having no losses or the least number of losses--receive the Emperor's Cup and numerous other trophies and prizes, including money. Beginning in the late 1950s, David Jones, an American employee of Pan American Airways stationed in Tokyo, began presenting every tournament winner with a huge trophy, and reading the winner's citation in the Japanese dialect where the tournament is being held.

This extraordinary event, always shown on national television with the rest of the proceedings, became a traditional feature of sumo tournaments--and, of course, made Jones and Pan Am famous in Japan.

When an Ozeki class wrestler wins two or three tournaments--especially in a row--he is usually promoted to grand champion. When lower ranked sumo win

tournaments they are generally jumped several grades in rank--only to be demoted, however, if they fall below eight wins in subsequent tournaments.

A sumo tournament is filled with pageantry and color. The huge wrestlers, wearing only stylized loin-cloths, go through a prescribed ceremony, including the throwing of salt, before each bout. There is also a traditional ceremony at the beginning and end of each tournament.

Sumo wrestlers, especially champions and grand champions, become national heroes, and in recent decades also usually become wealthy. Some have gone on to successful careers in the movies, but most of the champions continue in the sport following retirement.

One of the greatest sumo wrestlers of all time was a young man named Taiho (Tie-hoe) from Hokkaido, whose heyday was in the late 1950s and 1960s. He still holds the record for the number of tournament wins--16. Other great champions of recent decades have been Wakanohana, Kagamisato and Futabayama, who once won 69 bouts in a row, the most that anyone has won in some 2,000 years.

SUPERMARKETS / SUPA (Sue-pah)

In Japan, supermarkets are called superstores. There are 10 major superstore chains in the country. The largest is Daiei, followed by Ito-Yokado, Seiyu, Jusco, Nichii, Uny, Nagaskiya, Izumiya, Kotobukiya and Chujitsu.

The primary merchandise lines in superstores are foodstuffs, clothing, sundries, household utensils, and miscellaneous.

SUPERSTITIONS / MEISHIN (May-e-sheen)

The Japanese, like most people, have their supersititons--perhaps more than most until recent times. Most Japanese superstitons concern numbers or dates and directions.

Unlucky days include the 4th and 14th. The luckiest days of the month are the 15th and 28th, and these are good days for starting new things, and trips.

Unlucky ages are 19, 33 and 42. In the Zodiac, the Year of the Horse and Monkey are considered unlucky. With directions, the best are east and south. The unluckiest are north and northeast. Many people today are still concerned about which way their houses face, and where the doors are.

Many Japanese give credence to divination, and to such arts as palm-reading and tea-leaf reading--but today probably no more so than Americans or Europeans.

SUPREME COURT / SAIKO SAIBAN SHO (Sie-koe Sie-bahn Sho)

There are 15 justices, including the chief justice, on Japan's Supreme Court. There are also some 20 judicial research officers assigned to the court. These officials, all qualified judges, help clarify disputed points on the basis of judicial theory and precedents (both Japanese and foreign). They are sometimes asked to state their opinions during trials, and therefore play an important role in the court's work.

Japan's Court Organization Law requires that all Supreme Court justices be at least 40 years old, and that at least 10 of them be judges, public prosecutors, lawyers, or professors of law. The remaining five are required to be persons of great insight with a knowledge of the law.

Most justices are around 60 years old when appointed, so the average age of the members of the court tends to be high.

SUSHI (Sue-she)

One of the most popular of all Japanese foods, sushi consists of slices or pieces of fish, shellfish, egg and (in one variety) a vegetable placed on top (or inside) a bun or roll of rice that has been flavored with vinegar, salt, sugar and mirin, a sweet rice wine.

The individual pieces are generally dipped into soy sauce, in which a dab of grated horse-radish has been mixed, just before eating.

There are some two dozen popular varities of sushi, based on the species of fish, shellfish or other delicacy that makes up the topping for the rice bun. Tuna and eel are two of the most popular.

Shops that serve only sushi--and there are thousands of them in Japan-- are called sushi-ya (sushi shops). They are usually small, and often have only a counter, at which the customer sits and points to samples of whatever he or she wants.

A set lunch or dinner of sushi includes several varieties, including one or two that are generally eaten last to sharpen the palate. One of these, nori-maki, is a roll of rice wrapped in seaweed, with pieces of pickled radish on the inside.

Traditionally sushi fans drank sake with their mealsμ but many now opt for beer.

Recommended reading: THE BOOK OF SUSHI, by Kinjiro Omae and Yuzuru Tachibana (Kodansha Int'l).

SWORDS / KATANA (Kah-tah-nah)

Like so many other things, the art of sword-making was introduced into Japan from China and Korea in the early centuries. But, typically, the Japanese modified and improved upon the imported technology.

Swords were to play an extraordinary role in the country's history, beginning with the mythology of its creation. The Sun Goddess Amaterasu Omikami is said to have given her grandson Ninigi-no Mikoto a sword when he was sent down to reign on earth. Swords made in the 6th and 7th centuries B.C. have been found in burial mounds.

The sword was the primary weapon of the Japanese from earliest times, and was to be developed to a higher degree of technical perfection, than in any other country, before or since.

With the rise of the Samurai warrior class in the 10th, 11th and 12th centuries, and the development of the code of Bushido, swords became a virtual extension of the warriors' bodies, and became objects of reverence--even worship.

The sword was regarded as more than a physical weapon. It was imbued with a moral spirit of its own, that was a means of achieving self-mastery, as a symbol of justice and good versus evil. The most binding oath a Japanese Samurai or noble could take was to swear on his sword.

Between the 9th and 12th centuries, Japan's swords became wider across the base than the tip, and curved abruptly near the base. The art of sword-making was hereditary by this time, and master makers began stamping their names onto their handiwork.

Other changes occurred in the 13th century with the ascendancy of the Samurai warriors, each of whom carried one long sword and one short one. The blade became broader, the breadth between the tip and base was reduced, the tip was shortened and given a sharper angle.

This was the beginning of a golden age of Japanese swords. Special heating, forging and hardening techniques made the swords incredibly tough and gave them a cutting edge that has never been equaled. The heyday of the art of sword-making was the Kamakura Period (1192-1333), and the greatest swordsmith of all was Masamune Nyudo. The art was passed on from father to son, and the process of forging was surrounded by Shinto rituals that were meticulously followed.

It was believed that only the purest of heart, with the highest moral standards, could become a master swordsmith. Thus those who mastered the art were honored and highly prized by their fief lords.

Practicing swordsmanship was one of the prime responsibilities of the Samurai, since the development of skill was equated with the development of moral character and honor. As a class, the Samurai thus became the most skilful swordsmen the world had ever seen.

Their greatest swordsmen developed an instinct and a 6th sense that made them virtually unbeatable in even combat. There are records of single masters fighting several other swordsmen at the same time, and killing them all.

The second, short sword that became a part of the Samurai uniform around the end of the 14th century, was mainly for personal protection as opposed to regular battle.

Stories of great swordsmen abound in the chronicles covering the 13th to 18th centuries. Some are known to have confronted a dozen or more enemies at the same time, and emerged the victor after battles that lasted for an hour or more.

This honing of extraordinay skill with the sword continued until 1868, when the last Shogunate government fell. There are a few masters of the art in Japan today, and kendo, which is the practice of swordsmanship using a bamboo stave, is a widely practiced martial art in Japan.

The prowess of Japanese swordsmen of these early years is an important factor in the on-going popularity of a genre of movie films known as chanbara, which depict stories about Japan's feudal Samurai days.

Today Japanese swords made before the end of the 16th century are referred to as Old Swords, while those made since then are regarded as New Swords.

Recommended reading: THE SAMURAI SWORD, by John M Yumoto (Tuttle).

The best-known sword maker in Japan today is the Japan Sword Company in Tokyo. The ancient techniques and Shinto rituals of the early masters have been preserved by the swordsmiths at this company--and visitors are welcomed by appointment to view the key steps in forging a new sword.

TACHIKAWA (Tah-chee-kah-wah)

A city of some 140,000 about 30 minutes west of Tokyo's Shinjuku Station on the Chuo Line, Tachikawa is known to many foreigners, especially Americans, as the site of a major U.S. air force base following the end of World War II.

The original airfield was constructed there in 1922 by the Japanese Army.

Besides the airfield, which is still in operation, the city today is a thriving industrial and business center as well as being a residential area for people who work in Tokyo.

TAIKUN (Tie-koon)

This is the title used by the Tokugawa Shoguns during their dealings with Americans and other foreigners from about 1854 to 1867. It means something like Great Leader. During the first years of their contact with Japan, Westerners believed that the Shogun was the Emperor, and were shocked when they discovered the truth.

The English word tycoon comes from Taikun.

TAIRA, KIYOMORI (Tie-rah, Kee-yoe-moe-ree)

The glory of the Taira (Heike) clan lasted for only about 20 years, but it was one of the most extraordinary 20 years in Japan's history. By the middle of the 12th century, the power of the famous Fujiwara clan, which had virtually controlled the country for over 300 years, had ebbed.

The provincial lords, mostly descended from noble rank, had begun to keep their own private armies as protection and to further their own ambitions at the expense of their neighbors and the central government.

Following the usual pattern, the profession of warrior had become hereditary, giving rise to a new class that were to eventually be called Samurai, which literally means to be on guard.

In the middle of the 12th century, one of the most powerful and ambitious of these lords was Kiyomori Taira, head of the Taira clan, who became the governor of the province of Aki. The Tairas were descendants of the Emperor Kwammu (786-853), and were the blood enemies of the Minamoto clan, who were also from royal descent. During the Hogen war (1156-1160), which came about when Em-peror Shirakawa tried to wrest power from the Fujiwara family whose regents had controlled the throne for several centuries, Kiyomori supported him, and was victorious in the war.

As a result of this victory, Kiyomori became very powerful at court. He sent Yoritomo Minamoto, his arch rival, into exile and took Yoshitomo Minamoto's favorite concubine as his mistress.

In 1167 Kiyomori got himself appointed Prime Minister (Dajo Daijin), and immediately parceled out every important post in the country to his relatives. The following year, he came down with a strange burning disease that was incurable--and is believed to have been responsible for some of his cruelty and arbitrary ways.

One of the stories about him is that he once assembled thousands of craftsmen in an attempt to build a temple in just one day in order to win a lady as his mistress.

Kiyomori died in 1181, one of the most disliked men in the realm. Kiyomori's son, Shigemori, on the other hand, was reknowned for his loyalty to the emperor and for his prowess as a warrior. He tried to get support to build a canal from Lake Biwa to the sea, but died prematurely in 1179. See HISTORY, MINAMOTO, SAMURAI.

TAKARAZUKA (Tah-kah-rah-zoo-kah)

Takarazuka refers to a famous resort spa, to an even more famous opera house and to a form of theater that is one of the most popular attractions in the country--among young Japanese girls.

The resort spa of Takarazuka is located on the banks of the Muko River in the foothills 24.8 kilometers from Osaka's Hankyu Station, and is the most popular resort in the Osaka-Kobe area.

In addition to its dozens of ryokan inns along the banks of the Muko Gawa, the city has a large entertainment district known as Takarazuka Family Land.

The Family Land includes theaters, a health center, zoological and botanical gardens, a science amusement park and an opera house that will seat 4,000 people.

It is this huge Takarazuka opera house, and its affiliated music school, that has made the spa nationally famous. The school accepts only female students. The operas presented in the theater--all musical renditions of Japanese and Western stories--feature only women performers, who play both male and female roles.

The female performers are divided into four troupes that take turns presenting the operas--at the theater in Takarazuka and at a branch Takarazuka Theater in the Hibiya district of Tokyo, across the street from the Imperial Hotel.

The Takarazuka operas are spectacular shows, and the stars attract huge numbers of young female fans.

TAKAYAMA (Tah-kah-yah-mah)

People who want to see and experience what much of old Japan used to look like are advised to go to the small city of Takayama, secluded in the moutains of Hida in the Japan Alps National Park, about two hours from Gifu on the Takayama Line.

Often called Little Kyoto, the streets of Takayama are built in the cross-bar pattern of Kyoto, and many of its houses and buildings are in the style of the Edo or Tokugawa period (1603-1868).

Besides its nostalgia for historical buffs, Takayama is also noted for the Hie Shrine and its annual Sanno Festival, held on April 14 and 15.

The festival is one of the largest and grandest in all of Japan, with 23 high-wheeled wagon floats (yatai), gorgeously decorated with gold and elaborate carvings, being pulled through the streets by sake-fired, shouting young men.

Other cultural treasures in the city are the Kokubun Temple, founded in 1588, the Minzoku Kan or Folklore Museum, and the Shoren Temple, dating from 1504. Nearby are the famed Takahara Gorge and Hirayu hotsprings spa.

TANEGASHIMA (Tah-nay-gah-she-mah)

This is a tiny island in the Satsunan group, lying between Kyushu and Taiwan, that traditionally came under the influence and control of the lords of Kyushu. It is the place where several storm-tossed Portuguese, enroute to Macau, became the first Westerners of record to set foot on Japanese soil, in 1543.

Among the things these Portuguese drifters introduced into Japan were firearms, tobacco and venereal disease. They were to be followed within a few years by a steady stream of traders, priests and others who would alter the course of Japan's history and set the stage for one of the most dramatic and important periods in the lives of any people.

Tanegashima is 3-4 hours from Kagoshima by boat, and some 30 minutes by air. The Misaki Shrine on the southern end of the island, where the Portuguese landed, includes a memorial marking the event.

TANKA POETRY (Tahn-kah)

The tanka form of Japanese poetry has been popular since ancient times. Consisting of five lines of 5-7-5-7-7 syllables, it is a lyrical poetry primarily used to express emotion, especially stressing the beauty of life and nature.

The aim of the tanka poet is to express this yearning for beauty with such vivid power that all the most powerful emotions are intermingled in an allusive feeling referred to as yojo (yoe-joe).

Purists say that to be tanka, a poem must include the element of yojo.

TATAMI (Tah-tah-me)

The floors of traditionally style Japanese rooms are covered with thick, rectangular straw mats called tatami. These mats measure approximately two inches thick, three feet in width and six feet in length--and are the standard unit of measure in speaking of a Japanese room--4-mat room, 6-mat room, etc

Tatami are made from tightly woven rice straw that is then covered with woven rush grass. The edges are bound with a band of sturdy cotton cloth, usually black or dark blue. The mats are firm but resilient, and when fresh, give off a delightful aroma that is part of their special attraction.

In earlier times, those who could afford it changed the tatami in their homes every spring.

Tatami floors are still the norm in older Japanese homes and in inns, and contemporary-built Western-styled homes will generally have one or more tatami rooms. Some meeting and athletic halls have tatami floors, and are often the size of huge auditoriums.

TAXES / ZEIKIN (Zay-e-keen)

There are two kinds of taxes in Japan, local and national. Local taxes include village, town, city and prefectural taxes, and account for about 30 percent of the revenue of local governments.

National taxes include income taxes, corporate taxes and inheritance taxes--which are direct--along with gasoline taxes, liquor taxes, commodity taxes, stamp revenues and taxes collected by the Japan Tobacco β Salt Corporation (a government monopoly), which are all indirect.

Taxes in Japan currently amount to about 23 percent of the per capita income.

The tea ceremony teaches harmony. P. 300

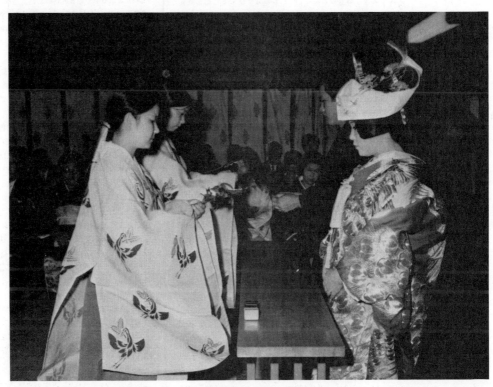

A traditional wedding ceremony. P. 322

お茶

TEA / CHA (Chah)

The custom of drinking tea was imported into Japan from China--where it originated, according to legend, some 5,000 years ago when a Chinese emperor was sitting under a camellia tree, with a pot of boiling water in front of him. Leaves falling from the tea landed in the pot, sending out a fragrant aroma.

The emperor taste-tested the new brew and immediately named it Heavenly Dew.

Emperor Shomu (701-756) is credited with introducing tea-drinking into Japan when Ganjin, a famous Chinese priest, brought him some medicines, among which was tea. This tea was called tan-cha (tahn-chah), and came in the form of steamed tea leaves pressed into bricks and dried, for either chewing or steeping in hot water.

During the Heian Period (794-1192), matcha (mot-chah), a tea made of steamed and dried green tea leaves ground into powder and stirred into hot water, became popular--and is the kind of tea used in the tea ceremony, still practiced today.

In the early decades, tea-drinking was wide-spread only among priests, who used it to help fight off fatigue while they were studying. Because priests were the primary source of learning, the custom gradually spread among the general population.

Tea-drinking was raised to an art form by Sen-no Rikyu (1521-1591), a famous Sakai (Osaka) merchant, who developed the tea ceremony as a way of countering the snobbery and pretention that existed among his rich fellow merchants. He stressed simplicity and spiritual tranquility, and communion with nature in the sado (sah-doe) or tea ceremony (which see).

There are several types of tea that are popular in Japan, along with a number of tea-like drinks that are made with something other than tea leaves.

These include ban-cha, which is the cheapest and one of the most common. Sen-cha, which is a medium-priced tea that one usually serves to guests. Gyokuro, the highest and most expensive grade, reserved for special occasions.

Other popular kinds of tea are hoji-cha, which is ban-cha tea leaves that have been roasted (giving them a smoky flavor), and genmai-cha, which consists of tea leaves mixed with roasted and popped rice.

The non-tea tea drinks are mugi-cha, made from roasted barley and usually served cool or chilled, kobu-cha, made from powdered seaweed (and tasting very much like salt-soup), habu-cha, made from stinkweed seed, and sakura yu, which is made from salt-pickled cherry blossoms (and is for special ceremonial occasions).

The tea that is used in the famous tea ceremony is called hiki-cha or mat-cha, and is made from young tender leaves picked from aged tea plants, dried and then ground in stone mortars.

Tea leaves are graded according to the way they are grown and picked. The best are the ones that are grown in shaded areas and picked when very young. They are kept green by steaming and heating to prevent oxidation.

The only Japanese tea that is sweetened is a summer drink made from powdered tea leaves.

TEA CEREMONY / CHA-NO-YU (Chah-no-yuu)

The tea ceremony, a ritualized way of preparing and drinking tea, was perfected in the latter part of the 16th century by the famous Rikyu Sen. The chan-no-yu is an exercise in aestheticism, in the highest level of mental control and refined manners, and results in a state of serenity and right feeling.

The tea ceremony is Zen in spirit, and was strongly influenced by the discipline and ideals of the Samurai class. The main thing is the selfless spirit in which the tea is made and served, although the ritual manner of the ceremony is a vital part.

When the tea plant was first imported from Japan, it was primarily seen as a medicine which, according to early historians, was highly prized for its power to relieve fatigue, repair the eyesight, strengthen the will and delight the soul. The Taoists in China used it in their immortality elixier, and the Buddhists used it to help them stay awake during their long hours of meditation.

It was the Buddhists of the Zen sect of southern China, who had adopted many Taoist concepts, who developed tea drinking into a formalized ritual. These priests would gather in front of an image of Buddha and take turns drinking tea from a common bowl.

Tea-drinking was a popular custom in Japan by the end of the 7th century. Emperor Shomu (who reigned from 724-749) once invited 100 Buddhist monks to the Imperial Palace for a tea party. But it was not until the 15th century that the tea ceremony, under the patronage of Shogun Yoshimasa Ashikaga, became a full-fledged independent aesthetic, spiritual and philosophical ritual.

The teahouse or sukiya that developed along with the ceremony consists of a tearoom proper designed to accommodate a maximum of five guests, a service or wash room (mizu-ya) where the utensils are washed and readied, and a separate waiting room (yoritsuki), where guests wait until they are summoned to the tearoom.

The tearoom measures about 2.7 meters square and has two entrances--one for the host and another one for guests. The doorway for the guests is very low, requiring that they enter the room on their hands and knees (and thus humble themselves in preparation for the ceremony).

There are are several tea ceremony schools, each of which has its own style. Some are very formal, others are rather casual and may include food. But in all cases, the purpose is the same-- to exercise and sharpen the aesthetic sense, to still the spirit and develop harmony with the universe.

In the more formal schools there is a main guest (shokyaku), and the ceremony takes up to three hours. The three most popular chanoyu schools today are the Ura-Senke, Omote-Senke and Mushakoji.

There are several teahouses in Japan that are over 300 years old, some of which are registered as National Treasures. These include the Ginkaku or Silver Pavilion in Kyoto (designed by the Father of the Tea Ceremony, Shuko, in the 15th century), the Shokintei in the Katsura Imperial Villa in Kyoto (designed by Enshu Kobori who lived from 1579-1647), the Kohoan and Shinjuan in Kyoto's Daitoku Temple, the Myokian in Kyoto (the residence of Sen-no Rikyu (1521-1591), one of the greatest of the tea masters), and the Rokusoan in the National Museum in Tokyo.

Basically, a ceremony begins by a host inviting guests and then beginning the preparations well before their arrival. The location may be inside or outside, but is preferably a quiet room where disruptions are unlikely. Devotees prefer a Japanese-style room or separate cottage (in some exceptionally beautiful place) made especially for the ceremony.

The host takes great care to clean and prepare the room and utensils to be used, as well as the outside garden or area, along with special dishes that may be served.

Any conversation before the ceremony begins is light and calm and designed to enhance a contemplative, serene mood. Once the guests have all arrived, and the time is right, the host laddles powdered green tea into each guest's cup in turn, pours hot water over it and then uses a whisk to stir it to a foam.

The taste of the tea is astringent, and meant to stimulate the taste buds and help the person feel alive and at one with nature and the universe.

Once the tea is drunk, the guests take turns commenting on the beauty of the tea cups, and expressing their appreciation to the host for the hospitality.

An essential part of the tea ceremony is scrutinizing and appreciating the utensils used--known as dogu-haiken or inspection of the utensils. The various items are passed one at a time to each guest, who is expected to demonstrate both aesthetic ability and refinement in commenting on and appreciating the beauty and artistry of the implements.

Genuine teaists look forward especially to the first tea ceremony of each new year, called hatsu gama or first ceremony.

Today the tea ceremony is most popular with women--as a way of developing good manners and a calm, harmonious attitude when they are young, and as a way to sustain their spririt, get along with friends and commune with nature as they grow older.

Recommended reading: CHA-NO YU: The Japanese Tea Ceremony, by A. L. Sadler (Tuttle). THE BOOK OF TEA, by Kakuzo Okakura (Tuttle).

TELEPHONES / DENWA (Dane-wa)

Japan ranks second in the world, behind the U.S., in the number of telephones in use--well over 50 million--all of which are on automatic exchanges. Japan also has direct-dial telephone links with 83 countries and island groups around the world.

Telephone service in Japan dates from 1890 when a line was opened between Tokyo and Yokohama. It was 1899 before Tokyo was linked with Osaka and Kobe. In 1925 battery-operated phones were introduced into the country's six largest cities. Japan appears to have more outside public telephones than any other country--and they come in different colors and sizes. Public phones that are of regular size and are blue, pink or red are for local calls. Calls are limited to three minutes per coin. A chime sounds 30 seconds before the three minutes are up and you must insert another coin to maintain the connection.

Large-sized red phones will accept up to six coins at one time, and return any that are unused. Yellow phones may be used for either local or long-distance calls--but unused coins or amounts are not returned.

Japanese cities and the surrounding environs have their own area codes. See AREA CODES.

TELEVISION / TERUBI (Tay-rue-bee)

There are 1,502 VHF television broadcasting stations and 9,453 UHF stations in Japan. Of the former, 1,113 are owned by NHK--507 of them general and 506 of them educational. Forty-eight commercial companies own the other 489 VHF stations.

NHK is also the primary owner of UHF stations--altogether 5,338, of which 2,699 are general and 2,639 are educational. Forty-six commercial companies own the remaining 4,115 commercial stations.

As for programming, Japanese TV devotes approximately 14 percent of its time to news, 25 percent to culture, 45 percent to entertainment, 12 percent to education 2.5 percent to sports and the balance to advertising and other things.

Japanese television is similar to American television, with the same type of programs. Japanese programmers have more leeway, however, in the nature of the content, particularly where language and sex are concerned--or at least they did have during the 1960s, 70s and early 80s. American television has followed suit and is now into very mature (read sexual) things.

The Yomiuri Newspaper's famous Matsutaro Shoriki was instrumental in introducing television to Japan. Research into TV had been carried on by NHK in the 1930s, and in 1939 and 1940, experimental broadcasting was open to the public. But all such activity ended with the beginning of the Pacific war. NHK opened its first TV station February 1, 1953, followed by Shoriki's NTV on August 28, 1953. Radio Tokyo TV, now TBS, began operating on April 1, 1955.

Color television broadcasting began in Japan in September of 1960 by NHK and commercial broadcasters in Tokyo and Osaka. At that time, there were only 1,200 color TV sets in the whole country. The switch from B/W to color television in Japan was greatly accelerated by the Tokyo Olympics in 1964.

TEMPLE LODGINGS / SHUKUBO (Shuu-kuu-boe)

Inns for travelers have existed in Japan for hundreds of years, but long before they came along travelers were able to put up at night at many of the temples that dotted the countryside and urban areas.

These temples lodged travelers out of religious conviction as well as a means of earning income for the upkeep of their temples.

This tradition continues in Japan today, although on a smaller scale. The accommodations are simple and rustic in most temples, and the food is usually vegetarian, but it is inexpensive and comes with an experience that in itself is valuable.

Many of those who take advantage of temple shukubo today are on temple pilgrimages, visiting a large number of noted temples during a single trip.

TEMPLE SCHOOLS / TERA KOYA (Tay-rah Koya)

Shortly after the end of the Kamakura Period in 1333, a system of temple schools was developed throughout Japan, where the children of Samurai were taught religion, the Chinese kanji characters and other subjects by Buddhist priests.

In later centuries, some of these temple schools were open to the children of common people, but they were not required to attend school and most did not. The tera koya continued in operation until 1868, when a modern school system was established.

TEMPURA (Tim-puu-rah)

One of the few Japanese dishes that Westerns like immediately, tempura is a variety of seafoods and vegetables, dipped in a batter made of wheat flour mixed with egg, and deep-fried in vegetable oil.

Tempura are best when hot, dipped in a sauce made of fish broth, sweet rice wine and soy sauce, along with some grated ginger or radish.

A favorite variation is tempura placed on top of a bowl of noodles (tempura soba or tempura udon)--with soba being small brownish noodles and udon being large white noodles.

TENGU (Tane-goo)

The tengu are mythical man-like creatures that are a popular part of Japanese folklore. The tengu are usually depicted as having very long noses or a beak, with long beards, and wings. They are said to live in groups in the mountains, and to take special pleasure in kidnapping people, especially children, and carrying them off.

When Westerners, with their long noses and beards, first began appearing in Japan, they were often compared to the tengu. It would, in fact, be interesting to make a case out of the possibility that foreigners cast upon the shores of Japan in ancient times might have been responsible for the myth.

Japanese folklore attributes the tengu to priests gone bad who were transformed by the powers of evil.

THUNDER GOD / RAIDEN (Rie-dane)

Visitors to Japan are often attracted to the statue of a large, red-faced demon that has two claws on each foot, carries several drums fasted to a rope, and reputedly loves to dine on human navels.

This is Raiden, the God of Thunder, and he is enshrined as a protection against lightening. Besides his eating habits, he is a nice fellow to have around during thunder storms.

TIPPING / CHIPU (Cheep-pu)

One of the special pleasures of living and traveling in Japan is the general absence of tipping taxi drivers, bartenders, waiters and other service employees. The Japanese travel industry goes to great lengths to prevent the Western custom of direct tipping from spreading.

About the only time one is expected to tip directly in Japan is to interpreters, guides, redcaps at airports and train stations, and when a taxi driver goes out of his way to find an obscure location--including getting out of the cab one or more times (often in the rain) to inquire at police boxes, etc.--or is especially helpful with a carload of luggage.

Employees of hotels and the Japanese National Railways are instructed to refuse tips if offered, and this policy is strictly enforced.

Virtually no one tips at an ordinary restaurant. Tipping at special, exclusive restaurants is generally done in connection with entertaining special guests--and traditionally such tips were given before the meal, not afterward.

The rationale here is that you are much more apt to get good service if you tip in advance.

TOBACCO MONOPOLY

Tobacco was first introduced into Japan in 1543 when a Portuguese ship ran aground on Tanega Island, south of Kyushu during a storm. The smoking habit spread slowly at first. It was denounced by the Shogunate authorities as an unhealthy and dangerous habit--particularly since Japanese homes and other wood and paper buildings were so susceptible to fire, but to no avail.

The Japanese developed a long-stemmed, tiny bowled pipe called kiseru (kee-say-rue), adding to the popularity of the smoking habit. Today, the consumption of tobacco in Japan on a per capita basis is the second highest in the world, following the U.S.

In Japan the sale of tobacco and cigarettes is exclusively controlled by a government monopoly, the Japan Tobacco and Salt Corporation. About 60 percent of the revenue produced by tobacco sales goes to the national and regional governments.

TOFU (Toe-fuu)

A favorite Japanese food that is rapidly becoming popular world-wide, tofu is a curd made of soybean paste. Soy beans are boiled and then made into a smooth pudding by adding bittern (what remains after sodium chloride is crystalized out of sea water).

Tofu is used as an ingredient in soups, sukiyaki and in numerous other dishes. It is eaten raw, boiled and or fried, with or without soy sauce. The protein content of tofu is very high (higher than meats), and it is easy to digest.

Recommended: THE BOOK OF TOFU, by William Shurtleff β Akiko Aoyagi (Ten Speed Press).

TOGO, ADMIRAL HEIHACHIRO (Hay-e-hah-chee-roe Toe-go)

One of Japan's greatest naval heroes, Admiral Heihachiro Togo (1847-1934), was in charge of the naval forces that defeated the Russian fleet in the Russo-Japanese war of 1904-05. His flagship, the battleship Mikasa, is now a memorial in Yokosuka.

The large Togo Shrine in Tokyo's Harajuku district is dedicated to the admiral.

TOGU PALACE (Toe-guu)

The Togu Palace, located in the Aoyama district of Tokyo, a short distance southwest of the Imperial Palace grounds, is where the Crown Prince and Princess live. Built in a combination of Japanese and Western style, the palace has over 40 ha. of floor space.

TOILETS / BENJO (Bane-joe)

The traditional Japanese-style toilet --a pit beneath the house, enclosed in a small room--is still common in Japan. At present only about 35 percent of all households in the country are connected to sewage lines, but approximately half of all toilets are the flush-type.

The toilet pits are emptied periodically by sewage trucks equipped with suction pumps.

Extreme cleanliness has been a very important part of Japanese life since their history began. Rigorous sanitary conditions are applied in all areas, particularly kitchens and toilets. The Japanese traditionally equated cleanliness with one's cultural and spiritual standards.

TOKAI DO (Toe-kie Doe)

The Tokai Do, which means Eastern Seaway Road, was the most famous and most traveled of the seven great Do roads of feudal Japan, from the end of the 12th century on. It began in Kyoto and traversed 15 old provinces to Edo (Tokyo). See ROADS.

The Tokai Do was immortalized by woodblock-print master Hiroshige, who traveled the road in the early 1800s and then produced a print on each of the 53 stages of the famous highway. (Reproductions of the prints are available in gift-shops in Tokyo, Kyoto and other major cities.)

The Tokai Do covered a distance of 323 miles from the Bridge of Japan (Nihon Bashi) in Edo to the center of Kyoto, through rice fields, along picturesque coastlines, over scenic mountains and through dozens of rural towns and villages. It was traveled by peddlers, merchants, priests, entertainers, religious pilgrims, Shogunate messengers, Imperial envoys and clan lords and their retainers as they made their bi-annual trips to and from Edo to attend the Shogun's court. See PROCESSIONS OF THE LORDS.

Most traffic on the Tokai Do and Japan's other great highways was pedestrian, as only the nobility, ranking Samurai and official envoys or messengers were allowed to travel by palanquin or horseback. Thus there was a constant, colorful steam of people walking the highways, stopping over at roadside inns and fast-food restaurants at frequent intervals.

For nearly 250 years of the Tokugawa Shogunate, the Tokai Do and other national highways of Japan were not only the political and economic life-lines of the country, they were also a central theme in the social life of the country.

See PROCESSIONS OF THE LORDS. TOKUGAWA.

TOKONOMA (Toe-koe-no-mah)

The tokonoma is a recessed alcove in the main room of Japanese homes, and in the rooms of inns and other traditional Japanese buildings, for the express purpose of displaying flower arrangements, hanging scrolls or other art forms meant to be appreciated for their beauty and philosophical sentiments.

The Japanese are apparently the only people ever to make the deliberate, institutionalized appreciation of beauty an integral part of their life-style, and the universal tokonoma is one of the most important parts of this traditional custom.

The tokonoma itself is typically a work of art, with very special care taken in the selection of the materials used in its construction, and in the craftsmanship with which it is installed.

This special alcove originated as a Buddhist altar, where an incense burner, flowers and a Buddhist scroll were placed.

TOKUGAWA, IEYASU (Toe-kuu-gah-wah, E-eh-yah-sue)

Ieyasu Tokugawa, the founder of Japan's last great feudal house, the Tokugawa Shogunate, was born in 1543 to Hirotada Matsudaira, a warrior who was later to change his last name to Tokugawa.

The Matsudaira family was a minor clan that first appeared in history around 1400, when it was located in the foothills of what is now Aichi Prefecture near Nagoya. The clan was then headed by Chikauji Matsudaira. The family gradually extended its control over the surrounding territory, and by the mid-1500s ruled most of the province.

In 1535, Kiyoyasu Matsudaira, then only 24, was killed and succeeded by his young son Hirotada as head of the clan. Hirotada allied himself with Yoshitomo Imagawa, a powerful neighboring lord (Daimyo). Twelve years later, the two had a falling out, and Hirotada was compelled to send his young son Takechiyo (later changed to Ieyasu) to Imagawa as a hostage.

Enroute to the Imagawa castle, the young boy was captured by another powerful warlord, Nobuhide Oda, who held him until his father was killed two years later and then sent him on to Imagawa. In 1560 Imagawa was killed in battle, and the 17-year old Ieyasu was allowed to return home.

The following year, as the head of his family, Ieyasu allied himself with Nobunaga Oda, Nobuhide's son. In 1567 he changed his name from Takechiyo Matsudaira to Ieyasu Tokugawa (an old ancestral name that had disappeared), to avoid conflicts with other members of the Matsudaira clan who coveted his role as head of the family.

Nobunaga Oda became the paramount power in Japan, and Ieyasu's fortunes rose with him. When Oda was killed and succeeded by his ablest general, Hideyoshi Toyotomi, Ieyasu became one of Hideyoshi's leading supporters.

Finally, when Hideyoshi died of natural causes in 1598, Ieyasu took up the fight against his enemies. His victory at the Battle of Sekigahara in 1600 made him the military master of Japan. In 1603 Emperor Yozei conferred the title of Shogun on Ieyasu, thus formally recognizing his supremacy. Two years later, Ieyasu abdicated in favor of his 26-year old son, Hidetada, as a way of assuring that the position of Shogun would remain in his family.

Ieyasu then retired to Shizuoka, midway between Edo and Nagoya, and while he continued to direct the affairs of the country from behind the scenes, he also spent a lot of time studying literature and writing poetry.

In 1611, Ieyasu went to Kyoto in an attempt to heal the break between himself and the Toyotomi family by arranging a marriage between his grand-daughter and Hideyori Toyotomi.

The family merger did not come off, however, and finally, in May 1615, Ieyasu's Samurai troops stormed the Toyotomi's castle in Osaka and killed Hideyori and the rest of his family.

In 1615 Ieyasu further consolidated his Shogunate by decreeing 13 articles (called Buke-Shohatto) that the feudal lords were required to obey. These articles controlled such things as castle repairs, road repairs, and marriage.

The first two articles ordered the Samurai to devote themselves to literature and arms, and to refrain from debauchery. Articles 3-5 covered how the Daimyo were to govern their fiefs. Articles 6-8 prohibited conspiracies or other activities by the Daimyo against the Shogunate. Articles 9-11 prescribed the clothing that each class was to wear, the vehicles that each could use and the manners appropriate to each class. The last two articles called for Samurai to live in a frugal manner, and for the Daimyo to promote their retainers on the basis of merit.

Thus the Daimyo were privileged to exercise absolute power in some areas within their domains--particularly the lives and fortunes of their subjects--but they were controlled in all areas of national interest by the laws of the Shogun, and could be removed or executed by the Shogunate government.

The Daimyo were divided into two groups--those who had supported Ieyasu before the Battle of Sekigahara which assured his becoming Shogun, and those who had not. Those who had allied themselves with him were known as fudai (fuu-die) or hereditary daimyo.

With the Tokugawa position secure, Ieyasu once again retired to Shizuoka, where he died in 1616 at the age of 74. See ADAMS, WILLIAM. TOYOTOMI, HIDEYOSHI. HISTORY, etc.

There were to be 15 Tokugawa Shoguns over the next 264 years, and the Tokugawa family was to grow into 20 different branches, including the main lineage that held the Shogunate. This main lineage was known as honke (hone-kay) or the main family, while the others were called bunke (boon-kay) or branch families.

The primary branch families were the three established by the younger sons of Ieyasu, in Mito, Nagoya and Wakayama. Later Tokugawa Shoguns were to establish other primary branch families in the 17th century.

The Tokugawa Shoguns and the dates of their rule were: Iemitsu (1623-1651), Ietsuna (1651-1680), Tsunayoshi (1680-1709), Ienobu (1709-1712), Ietsugu (1713-1716), Yoshimune (1716-1745), Ieshige (1745-1760), Ieharu (1760-1786), Ienari (1787-1837), Ieyoshi (1837-1853),

Iesada (1853-1858), Iemochi (1858-Yoshi-nobu (1867-1867).

During the Tokugawa Shogunate, day-to-day government of cities and areas was in the hands of bugyo (boog-yoe) or magistrates, appointed directly by the Shogun. The most important of these bugyo were those who were in charge of financial matters and supervising local governors and the people (kanjo bugyo), along with those who were responsible for legal affairs and running the cities (machi bugyo), and the ones who administered the affairs of temples, shrines and priests (jisha bugyo).

The machi bugyo generally had a police sergeant and constable as assistants. The magistrates were rotated from one city to another on a monthly basis (to keep them from establishing power bases, no doubt), and were therefore frequent travelers on Japan's great walking roads.

One of the most popular TV programs in Japan during the 1970s and 80s was a serial that recounted the road adventures of one of the most famous of the Tokugawa Shogunate magistrates and his assistants. They were always coming to the rescue of the oppressed, and bringing the bad ones (usually Samurai gone bad) to justice.

Ieyasu is revered in Japan as one of its greatest warriors and most skilful administrators. The system of government he devised, and that was elaborated upon by his descendants, was to give Japan one of its longest periods of peace and prosperity.

Of his 15 descendants who were to hold the position of Shogun, only a few were of outstanding character or ability. Iemitsu (1603-1651), the third Tokugawa Shogun, was the one who shut Japan's doors to the outside world, expelled the Christian missionaries, and originated the policy of having the Daimyo leave their families in Edo as hostages and themselves spend every other year there. See PROSSESSIONS OF THE LORDS.

The eighth Tokugawa Shogun, Yoshimune (1677-1751), is ranked as the wisest, most humane and ablest of Ieyasu's descendants. He was a patron of the arts, removed the ban on translating and reading European books, promoted trade between the provinces, and was active in improving medical treatment for the poor. He also is credited with having introduced the sweet potato to Japan.

Generally listed among the greatest families in Japanese history (the others being the Fujiwara, Minamoto and Hojo), the Tokugawas are believed to have been descended from Yoshishige Nitta, the grandson of Yoshiie Minamoto (1041-1108).

TOKUSHIMA (Toe-kuu-she-mah)

The capital of Shikoku Island's Tokushima Prefecture, the city of Tokushima is noted today for its Awa Odori folk dances, puppet shows, cotton crepe fabrics and wood furniture.

Situated on one of the channels of the Yoshino River, Tokushima began as the castle town of Daimyo Iemasa Hachisuka in 1586, and is now one of the largest and most important cities on Shikoku.

Besides its nationally famous folk dances (which are performed in the streets each year from August 15 to 18) and its puppet dramas (staged between farming seasons by farmers traditionally skilled in the art), Tokushima is also known as the home of Wenceslao de Moraes, a Portuguese naval officer who came to Japan in 1893 in the consular service.

After retiring from the service, Moraes moved to Tokushima, the home of his Japanese wife, and devoted the rest of his life to studying and writing about things Japanese. He published 16 books--all in Portuguese--and today is often regarded as a Portuguese Lafcadio Hearn. See HEARN, LAFCADIO.

Special attractions in Tokushima include Tokushima Park, formerly the castle grounds of Lord Hachisuka and considered to be one of the finest examples of Momoyama period landscape gardening in the country, the ancient Nyorin Temple, headquarters of the Hoju-Shingon sect of Buddhism, and the cherry blossom re-sort of Bizan Park on the slopes of Otaki Hill, with its Peace Memorial Pagoda.

The house where Moraes lived is at the foot of Otaki Hill.

TOKYO

The only TO (Toe) or Metropolitan District in Japan, Tokyo consists of 23 semi-autonomous wards (ku), 26 cities, seven towns, eight villages, the seven islands of Izu, and the Ogasawara Islands.

The site that is now Tokyo was first mentioned near the end of the 12th century, when Taro Shigenaga Edo, the son of Shiro Shigetsu Edo of the Taira clan, was appointed political agent of the province of Musashi for Shogun Yoritomo Minamoto, and gave his name (Edo) to a tiny fishing-farming village on an estuary at the head of a great bay (which came to be known as Edo Gulf).

Or it may have been the other way around. Since edo means estuary, which is what the area was, Taro may have adopted it as his last name!

In 1457 Dokan Ota, a member of the Ogigayatsu Uesugi family, chose the site for a castle-fortress. Ota (1432–1486), also known as a poet, described the area around Edo in a famous poem:

Musahino wa	The wide plain
Tsuki no irubeki	of Musashi
Yama mo nashi	Has no hills at all
Kusa yori idete	Where the moon sets
Kusa ni koso ire	Over a sea of grass.

The area was not to change very much until 1590, when Ieyasu Tokugawa, the man who was to establish the Tokugawa Shogunate, Japan's last great feudal dynasty, was given the region as his fief, and established his headquarters in the castle Dokan had built over 130 years earlier.

Edo grew quickly with the arrival of Ieyasu and his 70,000 retainers, but it was to expand even more rapidly a short time later when the Tokugawa Shogunate, as part of its military control of the land, required the more than 200 larger feudal lords throughout the country to build mansions in Yedo, leave their families there at all times, and themselves spend every other year in attendance at the Shogun's court.

This policy resulted in a tremendous influx of people into Edo from all over the country--not only the lords and their families, but their retainers and servants, along with thousands of artisans, shopkeepers, merchants, priests, entertainers and others to serve their needs. Within less than a decade, Edo was one of the most populous and sophisticated cities in the world.

With the downfall of the Tokugawa dynasty in 1868 and restoration of power to the Emperor, Japan's Imperial capital was moved from Kyoto to Edo, and the name was changed to Tokyo, meaning Eastern Capital. Edo Castle became the Imperial Palace.

But the city never really became an integrated community. The Edo mansions of each of the clan lords tended to become the center of a separate community made up of the retainers of the lord and the various tradespeople from their fief who set up business there to serve them.

Thus Edo was made up of a huge cluster of dozens of communities whose outlines are still recognizable in present-day Tokyo, and some of whose names have been handed down in the form of the Cho and Machi that make up Tokyo area names. This is also one of the reasons why Tokyo's streets form such a maze.

By 1731, the population of Edo was nearly 600,000. Only 56 years later, it had passed 1,386,000, making it one of the largest cities in the world.

In 1657, following a disasterous fire that destroyed much of the city, a serious attempt was made to widen and improve the main streets, but the effort was only marginally successful because people rebuilt their homes and shops as rapidly as possible in the same location.

Tokyo's 23 wards make up the main metropolitan area of the city. These wards are Chiyoda, Chuo, Minato, Taito, Shinjuku, Bunkyo, Sumida, Koto, Shinagawa, Meguro, Ota, Setagya, Shibuya, Nakano, Suginami, Toshima, Kita, Arakawa, Itabashi, Nerima, Adachi, Katsushika, and Edogawa.

Most of the 26 cities that are within the jurisdiction of Tokyo-To are in the so-called Tama District to the west of the city. These include Musashino, Mitaka, Koganei, Kokubunji, Kunitachi, Tachikawa, Hino, Hachioji, Fuchu, Chofu, Komae, Inagi, Tama, Machida, Hoya, Tanashi, Higashi Kurume, Kiyose, Higashi Murayama, Kodaira, Higashi Yamato, Musashi Murayama, Akishima, Fussa, Akigawa and Ome.

Downtown Tokyo is primarily located in the two wards of Chuo and Chiyoda, with portions of it extending over into Minato. Some of the more famous districts in Tokyo--each one virtually a city within itself--are the Ginza, Shimbashi, Kanda, Aoyama, Roppongi, Harajuku, Shibuya and Shinjuku.

Tokyo-To is administered by a governor elected by the residents, and a Metropolitan Council of 125 members. Several satellite cities adjoin the metropolis, including Urawa, Omiya, Funabashi and Chiba.

Central Tokyo, in which the Imperial Palace (formerly Edo Castle) is the hub, is divided into districts--one known as Uptown (Yamanote) and primarily residential, and the other known as Downtown (Shitamachi), and primarily commercial and industrial.

Metropolitan Tokyo now has a population in excess of 12 million, and is one of the most cosmopolitan and colorful cities in the world, famous for its great department stores, dozens of huge shopping areas and entertainment districts, numerous theaters, and as many resturants as are found in many well-known countries.

Practically speaking, the central area of Tokyo is made up of over a dozen centers, usually clustered around major commutor terminals, that are like cities within themselves. These include Yurakucho and the Ginza, Shimbashi, Shinagawa, Gotanda, Shibuya, Harajuku, Shinjuku, Ikebukuro, Ueno, Kanda, Nihonbashi, Akasaka, Roppongi and Asakusa.

Although unbelievably crowded, Tokyo has one of the best transportation systems in the world, including loop-line trains, suburban railways, 11 subway lines, numerous bus lines and several expressways. It also has several large taxi fleets that have to be the most efficiently and courteously run taxi service in the world. See SUBWAYS,

The numerous transportaion terminals that result from this system make up another primary characteristic of Tokyo--nearly 100 train and or subway stations, sometimes combined, that form population, commercial and industrial centers. Among the largest of these centers are Shibuya and Shinjuku.

The Tokyo Metropolitan Government publishes a quarterly journal in English called Tokyo Municipal News, which covers the various problems, policies and plans of the city, and is available to interested foreigners.

TOKYO CLIMATE

The weather in Tokyo is similar to that in Washington, D.C.--hot, humid summers, warm to cool falls, cool to cold winters, and cool to warm springs. During the spring rainy season it is cloudy and rainy in Tokyo about three-fourths of the time. Throughout the rest of the year it is cloudy and rainy about one-third of the time.

October is the wettest month in Tokyo because of fall typhoons, and December is the driest month. There are usually two or three light snowfalls in Tokyo every winter. A fairly heavy snowfall comes along only about once every 10 years.

In August, the hottest month, temperatures range from 91 to 93 degrees F. Winter lows are 23-25 degress F., but on the average it is above freezing.

Annual rainfall averages 1,503mm or some 63 inches. The weather is most likely to run to extremes in the winter --from sunny and dry to wet, windy and cold.

TOKYO DISNEYLAND

Japan's Disneyland, usually referred to as the Tokyo Disneyland, but officially named the Magic Kingdom, opened May 15, 1983. Located six miles from downtown Tokyo on land reclaimed from Tokyo Bay, the 115-acre amusement park cost 650 million dollars to build.

The Tokyo Disneyland is owned by the Oriental Land Company, which is owned in turn by the Keisei Railway Company and Mitsui Real Estate Development Company. Oriental Land Company bought the rights to use the Disneyland name and knowhow from Walt Disney Enterprises in the U.S., and pays the American company a royalty of 10 percent of all admission fees and 5 percent of the revenue from restaurants and shops.

Among the attractions of the Magic Kingdom are a World Bazaar which is the re-creation of a Victorian Era shopping center about the size of a baseball stadium, and completely covered by a transparent roof, and Cinderella's Castle, which is as high a 13-story building.

Altogether, the park has 28 facilities for staging various shows, 25 restaurants, 34 boutiques and hundreds of other shops and entertainment facilities. On the average, visitors are able to cover only about one-third of what the Magic Kingdom has to offer during a one-day period. See DISNEYLAND.

TOKYO JOURNAL

A monthly tabloid-sized magazine, Tokyo Journal is published with the cooperation of the Foundation of International Education and People to People organization of Japan. The publication covers entertainment, social and other events in the Tokyo areaμ carries book reviews, essays and columns. It is well-done, informative and useful. Subscriptions are available through Intercontinental Marketing Corp. See OTHER SOURCES in back.

TOKYO STATION / TOKYO EKI (Eh-kee)

The picturesque Tokyo Station Building, designed by Kingo Tatsuno and completed in 1914, was virtually destroyed during World War II, but was soon restored and in subsequent years greatly enlarged. The original three-story red brick building now constitutes the main west entrance to the station.

Tokyo Station is the main terminal of Japanese National Railways, where the famous Bullet Trains (Shinkan Sen) begin and end their journeys. It is also the home station for Tokyo's popular Yamanote Loop Line that circles the heart of the city, the Chuo Line as well as several others.

The station complex includes numerous offices and facilities, and adjoins a number of important buildings, including the Japanese National Railways Building, the Japan Travel Bureau Building, the Tokyo Central Post Office, the Daimarui Department Store and the Kokusai Kanko Kaikan (International Travel Building).

A shopping center under the station extends over an immense area and has more than 400 stores and restaurants that cater to train travelers.

Although nearly two million passengers pass through Tokyo Station every day, it is still only the second busiest one in the city. That distinction goes to Shinjuku Station, on the west side of town.

TOKYO TOWER

Completed in December 1958 by the Nippon Television City Corporation, the 333-meter high, independent steel Tokyo Tower has been a conspicuous feature of Tokyo's skyline ever since.

Located near the southwest corner of Shiba Park, the tower has two observation platforms—one at the 150-meter level and the other 250 meters high—both providing a spectacular view of the surrounding city.

The tower is a major tourist attraction, drawing hundreds of thousands of people a year. It also houses the telecasting center of Tokyo's Channel 12.

TOKYO UNIVERSITY / TOKYO DAIGAKU (Tok'yoe Die-gah-kuu)

The ranking university in Japan, Tokyo University, or Todai as it is often called, was founded in 1869 as a state university that grew out of a number of schools established during the last years of the Tokugawa Shogunate.

The campus area was formerly the estate of the Maeda family, one of Japan's largest and most powerful feudal clans. The only thing remaining on campus from the days of the feudal lords is the Aka Mon or Red Gate which stands near the main gate of the campus, facing the thoroughfare that is now called Hongo Avenue, from the name of the district.

The university is particularly noted for its medical, science, economics, literature and law departments. It is also noted for having what is almost a monopoly on placing graduates in the top government ministries and bureaus.

As the most prestigious university in Japan, Todai's annual entrance examinations attracts dozens of thousands of students competing for the limited number of openings. See RONIN, EXAMINATION HELL, STUDENTS.

TOKYO WEEKENDER

A weekly English-language newspaper that is subtitled A Forum for Foreigners in Japan, the TOKYO WEEKENDER was founded in 1969 by American journalist and jack-of-all-trades Millard (Corky) Alexander.

The Weekender covers entertainment, dining out, sports, travel information and foreign-resident social news, in a spritely, sometimes clever and often humorous approach that puts it several rungs above the average journalistic fare.

Several of Tokyo's most talented and far-out foreign residents are regular contributors to the Weekender, and have helped make it must reading for the foreign community and large numbers of bilingual Japanese.

Many foreigners who leave Japan after several years residence choose to subscribe to the Tokyo Weekender to keep up with the news. Address: Oriental Building, 1-55-11 Yayoi-cho, Nakano-ku, Tokyo 164, Japan.

TOUR COMPANION

A weekly tourist publication that covers events, shopping, dining and night-time entertainment in Tokyo, TOUR COMPANION is a valuable aid for visitors in the city. It includes maps of the city and major shopping areas and the subway system, along with all kinds of other information useful to tourists-- from how to use the public telephones, postal rates, currency exchange rates, train time-tables, television programs in English, to tips on taxis, tipping and otherwise staying out of trouble.

Tour Companion is available free in hotels, airline offices, and tourist shops.

TOURISM / KANKO (Kahn-koe)

Tourism is one of the best organized, most efficiently run industries in Japan. With one of the most scenic island countries in the world, historical sites that are almost endless, an equally endless curiosity about things, and travel traditions that go back centuries, it is not surprising to learn that sightseeing and other forms of travel are so much a part of Japanese life.

The industry is organized on the highest level, with the Prime Minister's Office, the Ministry of Transport, the Ministry of Foreign Affairs, of Finance and of Health and Welfare all involved in coordinating and promoting international tourism. On the domestic side there are even more government agencies and bureaus that play major roles in tourism.

In 1963 the Japanese government enacted a Basic Tourism Law that was designed to promote international friendship, the development of the national economy, and the adjustment of regional differences in social and economic conditions.

An Inter-Ministerial Liaison Council on Tourism was established in the Prime Minister's Office to coordinate policies on tourism, and a Department of Tourism was set up within the Ministry of Transport to supervise the tourism industry. This department has three divisions-- Planning, Tourist Promotion and Facilities.

The Department of Tourism supervises the activities of the Japan National Tourist Organization, conducts national examinations of tourist guides under the Guide-Interpreter Business Law, provides assistance to guides, and registers and supervises travel agents under the Travel Agency Business Law.

The Department is also responsible for the registration and supervision of inns and hotels, for tourism statistics, and for maintaining liaison and cooperation with all other domestic and international tourist bodies.

On the local level, each of Japan's 47 prefectures has its own tourist office that helps promote local tourism as well as coordinating the industry with national and international bodies.

There are also some two dozen other bureaus under the Ministry of Transport that has tourist offices in key cities, and works closely with local tourism interests in a supervisory as well as a liaison and support capacity. See the JAPAN NATIONAL TOURIST ORGANIZATION.

TOURISTS IN JAPAN

The first full-fledged tourist group arrived in Japan in 1860 aboard a passenger ship called the Aden, less than seven years after the arrival of Commodore Perry and his Black Ships, and seven years before the fall of the Tokugawa Shogunate and the restoration of Imperial power. An American, Silas K. Burrows, is recorded as claiming to have been the first tourist in Japan in 1854, the same year Japan signed its first treaty with the outside world and ended its long centuries of isolation.

TOYAMA (Toe-yah-mah)

Some 225 kilometers north of Gifu on the Japan Sea side of Honshu, the large port city of Toyama has a rather unusual claim to fame. In the 17th century a physician from the province of Okayama visited Toyama and presented the ruling Daimyo, Masatoshi Maeda, with some medicines prepared from old family recipes.

The Daimyo was so impressed with the medicines he ordered his retainers to set up a factory to manufacture the medicines on a commerical scale, and to market them as widely as possible.

The new enterprise established a network of peddler-salesmen who traveled to every corner of the country. Eventually, the medicines were sold in Korea, China and Southeast Asia, helping to make the fief one of the richest in the country.

As one of the largest and richest of the Daimyo during the To-kugawa period, Maeda took some 10,000 retainers with him when he made his bi-annual trip to Edo (Tokyo). See PROCESSIONS OF THE LORDS.

Still today Toyama is a center for the manufacture of traditional as well as modern medicines, with its production valued well in excess of 85 billion yen a year.

TOYOTOMI, HIDEYOSHI (Toe-yoe-toe-me, He-day-yoe-she)

Given the nature of society in feudal Japan, in which class more than anything else was the determining factor in the fortunes of men and women, it is an unending wonder that one of the country's greatest men was born a peasant and yet rose to become a leader of leaders.

The man history knows as Hideyoshi Toyotomi was born to a poor farmer named Yaemon in the village of Nakamura, in Owari Province in the year 1536. Being peasants, the family did not have a last name, and the boy was called Hiyoshimaru. The little boy looked so much like a monkey that he was nicknamed Ko Zaru or Little Monkey--and was to be called Saru-men Kwanpaku or Monkey Face Prime Minister (behind his back) even after he had attained the highest office in the land.

Hiyoshimaru apparently behaved like a rowdy young monkey, and caused so much trouble his parents couldn't control him. In desperation, they sent him to a temple where they thought the stern priests might be able to teach him gentler ways.

The priests also found Hiyoshimaru uncontrollable and unteachable, but because of the entreaties of his parents, they kept him until he was 12 years old. In the meantime, his father had died and his mother had married a retainer of Lord Nobunaga Oda, Daimyo of the Omi Province.

His mother and step-father apprenticed him several times, but each time he quit or was dismissed. Finally, after running away from the shop of a porcelain dealer, he set out for Okazaki to seek his fortune in the city.

While asleep alongside the road, a gang of robbers came by. One of them kicked the young boy just to have some

fun with him. Hiyoshimaru jumped up hopping mad, ready to fight the entire gang. A loud argument ensured, with Hiyoshimaru holding his own against the robber who had disturbed him.

The leader of the gang, Koroku Hachisuka, who was notorious in the area, was so impressed with Hiyoshimaru's courage and spirit--and the fact that he came from their own district--that he decided to take the boy along with the gang.

The gang leader later apprenticed Hiyoshimaru to a blacksmith and then a carpenter. While virtually uneducated, Hiyoshimaru had a natural intelligence, and an incredibly quick mind that set him apart from other men. He also had an overwhelming ambition to achieve great things, and when he was in his 20s managed to become the sandal-keeper to Lord Nobunaga Oda.

Although a nameless peasant so far below the lordly Samurai that to address one in the wrong manner could mean instant death, Hiyoshimaru so impressed the great Nobunaga that he was put in charge of repairing Kiyosu Castle.

Completing the work in a far shorter time than expected, Hiyoshimaru was again promoted. Soon thereafter, he took advantage of his connections with the notorious robber Koroku Hachisuka, rounded up a gang of outlaws and attacked one of Nobunaga's strongest enemies.

The attack was successful, and Hiyoshimaru was both promoted and given a new name, Hideyoshi Kinoshita, which was the equivalent of being elevated to the Samurai class--something very rare in Japan's history.

In 1570, Hideyoshi, by then the commander of an army of Samurai, fought several successful battles against Yoshikage Asakura, another of Nobunaga's rivals. This time he was rewarded with an annual income of 30,000 koku (approximately 150,000 bushels) of rice, putting him on the level of a smaller Daimyo.

Three years later, Hideyoshi attacked and captured the powerful Nagamasa Asai and his castle at Odani. Asai's fief, valued at 180,000 koku of rice a year, became Hideyoshi's property. Just one year later he captured Nagahama Castle, on the shores of Lake Biwa, and kept it for himself. He also adopted a new family name, Hashiba.

Within five years, Hideyoshi had subjugated the five western provinces of central Honshu. By 1482 he was the leader of an army of 60,000 men. He then attacked the famous Takamatsu Castle, which was regarded as virtually impregnable. He engineered a way to flood the castle, and captured it easily.

While still in Takamatsu, Hideyoshi received the news that his benefactor, Nobunaga Oda, who was then the military ruler of the country, had been assassinated by Mitsuhide Akechi, one of his own generals.

Hideyoshi immediately set out to avenge Nobunaga's death and prevent Akechi from usurping his power. He caught up with Akechi's army at Amagasaki, near Osaka, and destroyed it. Rather than face capture and execution, Akechi committed suicide.

This made Hideyoshi the supreme power in the country. In recognition of this, the Imperial Court gave him the title of Lieutenant General. Later in the same year, he accepted the formal position of a Privy Councillor. He then had the magnificent Osaka Castle built, and went there to live.

Hideyoshi had not yet achieved the success he craved. He still did not have an official surname, which identified him as being low-born. He asked the last Ashikaga Shogun to adopt him so he would have a proper name, but the Shogun refused. He finally petition the Emperor to allow him to officially take the name Toyotomi, which he made up, and his petition was granted.

In 1586, Hideyoshi was appointed Kwampaku (Prime Minister), a position that had previously been held only by ranking Imperial nobles. This aroused more ire among the great Daimyo who resented Hideyoshi, and one of them, the Lord of Satsuma in Kyushu, challenged Hideyoshi. In 1587, Hideyoshi led a force of 150,000 men against the Satsuma clan, and won a decisive victory.

The following year, in a further move to consolidate his power, Hideyoshi ordered that all swords in the country not in the hands of approved Samurai, be turned over to his military forces.

But two other leading clan lords, Ujimasa Hojo and Masamune Date, also refused to accept the supremacy of Hideyoshi, and in 1590 he attacked and defeated them. This left him in total control of the country.

In 1591 Hideyoshi issued an edict establishing four distinct classes of people--Samurai, farmers, artisans and merchants (in that order), thus freezing social mobility in the country, essentially for the next 277--and making it impossible for anyone else to rise from peasant to prime minister, as he had done.

He then turned the position of prime minister over to his adopted son, Hidetsugu, and was given the title of Taiko or Retired Prime Minister. Not content with having become the master of Japan, Hideyoshi began making preparations to invade and conquer Korea and China.

When ready, he dispatched an expedition of 150,000 men to Korea. Fierce fighters, and well-experienced in combat from their years of campaigning in Japan, Hideyoshi's armies began a successful march through Korea, killing huge numbers of Korean defenders (and collecting mountains of severed ears to prove it).

With victory in sight, Hideyoshi fell ill. When it became apparent that he was not going to survive, he ordered his generals to break off the attack and return to Osaka. He died, in 1598, before they returned.

Thus ended the life and career of one of the most remarkable men in Japan's long and colorful history--a man who is often compared to Napoleon in his skill as a general and as a great leader.

Recommended reading: TOYOTOMI HIDEYOSHI, by Walter Denning.

TRADE / BOEKI (Boe-aa-kee)

Despite its small size and lack of most vital raw materials, Japan is responsible for over seven percent of the world's exports and approximately seven and a half percent of its imports.

Raw material supplies account for around 66 percent of Japan's imports, while its exports consist almost entirely of manufactured industrial products.

Japan's imports and exports are about evenly divided among developing and undeveloped nations. Major imports include fossil fuels, raw materials (textile raw materials, metallic raw materials, timber and lumber), foodstuffs, machinery and equipment, and chemical products. Major exports are machinery and equipment (autos, electrical machinery, general machinery), nonmetallic miners, textiles and foods.

The United States remains Japan's primary export market, taking well over 20 percent of its total exports, and resulting in a substantial imbalance of payments with the U.S. Some 12 percent of Japan's exports go to European countries, and approximately five percent goes to Oceania.

TRADING COMPANIES / BOEKI GAISHA (Boe-a-kee Guy-shah)

Japan's huge general trading companies have been world-famous since shortly after the turn of the century. Developed soon after industrialization began in 1868, the trading companies were closely tied in with the country's largest banks and with the top companies in each of the major industrial areas.

With access to capital and ties with the ranking manufacturing corporations, the trading companies enjoyed something of a national monopoly in all the key industries. The result of this was very rapid growth and tremendous power in the national economy.

When World War II ended, the huge Zaibatsu combines, each of which had its own trading arm, were broken up. But soon after the end of the occupation of Japan by the Allied Powers in 1952, the groups came back together again in relatively loose federations. The break-up temporarily weakened the large trading companies, and allowed several of the pre-war medium-sized companies to gain a substantial foothold in the country's import and export industries.

Despite the fact that several thousand small to medium-sized Japanese manufacturers, particularly in consumer product fields, began to export directly in the 1950s, both the pre-war and post-war trading giants were able to capture a significant percentage of the country's import-export trade.

Today Japan's nine largest trading companies account for over 50 percent of the nation's total import and export trade. They were able to achieve this because of their ability to arrange financing for both imports and exports, because of the expertize they developed in buying from and selling to foreign markets, and because they were able to arrange for product distribution, new manufacturing ventures and reliable supplies of raw materials on a massive scale.

The Big Nine of Japan's general trading companies are Mitsubishi Shoji, Mitsui Bussan, Marubeni, Ito-Chu, Sumitomo Shoji, Nissho-Iwai, Toyo Menka, Kanematsu-Gosho and Nichimen.

All of these companies have their own network of offices and related companies overseas, but the two largest, Mitsubishi and Mitsui, are especially noted for the size and efficiency of their foreign networks. With offices in almost every country in the free world, they are able to supply a continuous stream of trade information to their headquarters that gives them a special advantage in this highly competitive world.

These huge, diversified trading companies are called Sogo Sho Sha (Soe-go Show Shah), or General Trading Companies.

One of the most important and significant functions of Japan's big GTC is their offshore trading activities--trading within and between other countries that does not involve Japan. In this category, the American branch of Mitsui β Company is the U.S.'s fourth largest trader. See MITSUI β COMPANY.

TRADEPIA INTERNATIONAL

A well-written and edited 32-page quarterly magazine published by Nissho Iwai Corporation, Tradepia International covers trade issues, along with Japan's international political and economic relations, management and marketing in Japan, new technology, social issues, the economic outlook, and so on. See OTHER SOURCES.

TRAINS / KISHA (Kee-shah)

Japan is world-famous for its trains --not only their punctuality, efficiency and speed, but also for the incredible number of passengers they carry every day.

There are two train systems in Japan --one operated by the government-owned Japanese National Railways (JNR) and the other operated by private owners.

JNR operates national, regional and local lines, while the private lines are limited to regional and local service. The private lines account for about 15 percent of Japan's passenger service and less than one percent of the freight transport.

The most famous of the JNR trains are the so-called Bullet Trains of the Shin Kan Sen or New Trunk Line, which began its first service on October 1, 1964. These trains leave Tokyo Central Station every few minutes--on the second. See JAPANESE NATIONAL RAILWAYS.

TRAPPISTS IN JAPAN

Two of the most unexpected attractions in Hokkaido are a Trappist Convent about 20 minutes outside of Hakodate, near the famous Yunokawa hotspring spa, and a Trappist Monastery, also a short distance from Hakodate, and just outside the town of Oshima-Tobetsu.

The monastery was founded in 1898 by eight French monks, and is now operated by some 80 Trappistines divided into two groups--those who spend their time meditating and praying (and dress in white robes), and those who work at stock and dairy farming, and make butter and candy. The working Trappistines wear brown robes.

Women are not allowed to enter the monastery buildings. Butter made at the monastery is available in some Tokyo shops.

TRAVEL / RYOKO (Rio-koe)

The Japanese are inveterate travelers, and have been for generations. Perhaps because traveling within Japan--with some exceptions--was either prohibited or discouraged during most of the country's long history, and was in fact not feasible for most Japanese until the mid 1960s, they developed an insatiable appetite for sightseeing and experiencing far away places.

Another factor that encouraged traveling within Japan was the fact that the islands are incredibly scenic. The volcanic and mountainous nature of the terrain, the exceptionally long and varied coastlines and the thousands of islets and islands ringing the main islands like so many jewels, has blessed the country with a variety and quality of scenery that is unsurpassed.

During the long, peaceful Tokugawa Period (1603-18687), Japan's great walking roads were crowded with people--with gamblers, salesmen, priests, messengers, tradesmen, religious pilgrims visiting distant shrines and temples, wandering Samurai who had lost their hereditary positions (the famous ronin), and entertainers. See ROADS.

With the tight security established by the Tokugawa Shogunate in the early 1600s, travel in Japan became much safer than what it had been in earlier ages. Two special types of traveling became vogue during the middle and latter years of the Tokugawa Period--monomode (Moe-no-moe-day) or pilgrimages to famous shrines and temples around the country (of which there were thousands), and yusan-tabi (yuu-sahn-tah-bee) or sightseeing trips to scenic areas of the country, which are virtually endless.

Japan's most famous travel book series dates from the 1802-1822 period. Written by Ikku Jippensha and called TOKAI DOCHU HIZAKURIGE or Traveling the Tokai Do by Shank's Mare (on foot), the series chronicled the adventures of two men, Yajirobei and Hananosuke (later called Kitahachi), who preferred the perils and pleasures of the road over the carping of their wives.

The two typical Edo types get into just about every comic situation imaginable, and in the process of telling their stories, Jippensha provides a vivid account of life, manners and traveling in Japan during that era.

Recommended: SHANKS MARE (Tuttle).

Soon after the Meiji Restoration in 1868, when the last Tokugawa Shogun relinquished power to the Emperor, school trips to different parts of the country were made a part of the educational system. This system continues, and beginning in the 1950s, various village and rural organizations annually sponsor trips to major cities and scenic locations.

In addition, it has been traditional for decades for Japanese companies to once a year take all of their employees on company trips to beach or mountain resorts. Altogether the Japanese average over 130 million trips a year within Japan--or slightly more than one trip per person for the whole population.

Each year, some four million Japanese travel abroad. Favorite destinations include Korea, Taiwan, Hong Kong, Thailand, Singapore, Guam, Hawaii, mainland U.S. and all the major countries of Europe.

TSUKIJI HONGAN TEMPLE / TSUKIJI HONGAN JI (Ski-kee-jee Hohn-ghan Jee)

Founded in 1630, this is the Tokyo branch of the Nishi Hongan Temple of Kyoto, headquarters of the Jodo-Shinshu sect of Buddhism. A landmark in Tokyo since its founding, the temple has been destroyed by fire several times.

The present structure, built in ancient Hindu style in 1935, is both earthquake and fire-proof. It will seat over 1,000 worshipers, and includes a number of modern-day facilities not found in other temples in Japan.

It is frequently used for funeral services.

TSUKIJI WHOLESALE MARKET (Ski-jee)

One of 11 markets under the Central Wholesale Market of Tokyo, the Tsukiji Wholesale Market is one of the the largest fish markets in the world, and has become a national attraction.

The market was originally located in Nihonbashi in the center of the city, and was one of the primary features of Edo and then Tokyo for nearly 300 years.

In its present location just 10 minutes from central Tokyo, the market handles some 90 percent of the fish haul that arrives in the city daily, along with meat, eggs, vegetables and fruits.

There are several sashimi (raw fish) restaurants in the immediate vicinity of the market that attract customers from all over the country. Real sashimi lovers like to arrive at the restaurants before dawn in order to enjoy fish that was unloaded from ships that same night.

TSU ISLANDS / TSUSHIMA (T'sue-she-mah)

Some 76 kilometers northwest of the northern tip of Kyushu, about half way between Japan and Korea, Tsushima consists of two islands that acted as a link between the Asian mainland and the Japanese archipelago from earliest times.

The two islands--Kami (247 square kilometers) and Shimo (435 square kilometers)--are too mountainous to support much agriculture, and fishing is the main industry. The So clan ruled the islands from 1168 to 1860, and the ruins of their castle can be seen on the outskirts of the town of Izuhara. The islands are in Nagasaki Prefecture.

TUNNELS / TONERU (Toe-nay-rue)

Being exceptionally mountainous, Japan's well-developed railroad and highway system led to the boring of many tunnels. One of the newest and most awe-inspiring of these tunnels is the Seikan (Say-e-khan) undersea railway tunnel that connects the island of Honshu with Hokkaido, beneath Tsugaru Straits.

Began in 1964 and completed in 1983, the Seikan tunnel is 33.49 miles long--making it the longest undersea tunnel in the world--and is 787 feet below the sea.

The tunnel, built by the Japanese Railway Construction Corporation, was designed for Japan's famous high-speed Shinkansen Bullet Trains.

Other major tunnels in Japan include the one between the southern tip of Honshu and the island of Kyushu.

TURKISH BATHHOUSES / TORUKO BURO (Toe-rue-koe Buu-roe)

Bathhouses offering massage services have been popular in Japan from early times. When the great gay quarters of Edo fell into disfavor with the Shogunate during the early years of the Tokugawa period (1603-1868), this kind of bathhouse quickly developed into a special category of its own.

The massage baths grew both in size and number, and became Sex Palaces patronized by all the classes that could afford them.

Massage baths, now called Turkish baths, still abound in Japan. They are no longer the open fun houses of Edo, but some of them are larger and quite luxurious by present-day standards, and scantily-clad girls are still the featured attraction.

Most of the Turkish baths (there are over 200 in Tokyo), are in or near well-known entertainment districts. Most of them cater to men, but there are several that welcome both men and women.

In all of them, the routine is similar. The patron is given a steambath, a hot water bath and then a lengthy massage by a girl dressed in halter-bra and shorts.

Most Turkish baths have beer and soft drinks available. Some adjoin restaurants, and offer their patrons hotel-type room-service. Many of them also launder the patron's underwear while he or she is being administered to.

One of Osaka's largest Turkish baths consists of eight stories above ground and two below, and includes one floor reserved for women, a huge public bath on the fifth floor and a garden bath on the seventh floor.

Some of the Turkish baths cater to Western clientele, and stock their waiting lounges with English language business publications, such as Wall Street Journal and Fortune.

Many of Japan's leading hotels have in-house Turkish baths for the convenience of their guests--although these are more likely to be conservative in the special services they offer.

UENO (Way-no)

In Taito Ward just north of central Tokyo, Ueno has long been one of the most popular districts in Tokyo. The site of a major Daimyo estate at the beginning of the Tokugawa Shogunate in 1603, Ueno is now one of the city's primary shopping and entertainment districts, and is especially noted for Ueno Park, in which are a number of the country's most important cultural facilities. See UENO PARK.

Ueno Station is the gateway for Japanese National Railway trains leaving for northern Honshu. It is crowded all the time, but especially so in winter when hundreds of thousands of Tokyoites flock to the ski resorts of north-central Honshu.

The station area and park are only about 15 train minutes from downtown Tokyo.

UENO PARK / UENO KOEN (Way-no Koe-en)

Formerly the estate of a Daimyo, this 84 ha. (201.6 acres) site was taken over by the Tokugawa Shogun in the early 1600s. He had a huge temple built on the grounds for the exclusive use of the Tokugawa family.

This temple was destroyed during the fighting that accompanied the Meiji Restoration in 1867. In 1878, the new Meiji government turned the grounds into a public park--now one of the largest and most popular in Tokyo, and a major cultural center.

Among the facilities and attractions in the park are the Tokyo National Museum, the Horyu Temple Treasure House, the Gallery of Eastern Antiquities, Tokyo Metropolitan Fine Art Gallery, National Science Museum, National Museum of Western Art, the Ueno Zoological Garden, the Japan Art Academy, Tokyo Metropolitan Festival Hall, several temples, the Ueno Library, the Toshogu Shrine, and an immense statue of Takamori Saigo, a hero of the Meiji Restoration. There is also a large pond and numerous walkways.

The main entrance to Ueno Park is a short walk from Ueno Station, the third busiest railway terminal in the city, and the nucleus of a major shopping and entertainment district.

UENO ZOO / UENO DOBUTSU-EN (Way-no Doe-boot-sue-inn)

Regarded as one of the best zoos in the world, the Ueno Zoo was founded in 1882 by the Ministry of Agriculture. It was later transferred to the Imperial Household, and finally turned over to the city of Tokyo in 1924.

Located on a 13 ha. (31.2 acres) site in Ueno Park (which altogether covers 84 ha. and was formerly the garden estate of a Daimyo feudal lord), the zoo has over 813 species of animals and birds, and sponsors numerous special events during the year.

It is open daily from 9 a.m. to 4:30 p.m. except from December 29 to 31.

UJI SHRINE / UJI JINJA (Uu-jee Jeen-jah)

Founded in 313 on the site of the residence of Prince Wakiiratsuko Uji, this is one of Kyoto's oldest shrines. It is dedicated to Emperor Nintoku, the Prince's older stepbrother, and to his father, Emperor Ojin--both famous in Japanese history.

There are two shrines on the grounds, one of which was constructed in the 10th century and is said to be the oldest shrine building extant in Japan. Both shrines are registered as National Treasures.

A short distance from the Uji Shrine, on the slopes of Asahi Hill, stands the Koshi Temple, the first Buddhist temple of the Soto sect of Buddhism built in Japan (in 1233).

See KOSHI TEMPLE.

UKIYO-E (Ou-Key-yoe-eh)

One of the most famous of Japan's traditional schools of painting (at least among Westerners), Ukiyo-e or Paintings of the Floating World, first appeared in the early 17th century, and primarily depicted the social life of the lower classes.

The first ukiyo-e were illustrations for story-books, but they soon began to appear as independent prints. Iwasa Matabei (1578-1650) is sometimes named as the father of ukiyo-e, but his art was not aimed at the lower classes. The first great ukiyo-e master was Moronobu Hishikawa who flourished from 1688-1704. He was followed by Harunobu Suzuki (1725-1770), Utamaro Kitagawa (1753-1806), Sharaku Saito (Toshusai), Toyokuni Utagawa (1769-1825), Hokusai Katsushika (1760-1849), and Hiroshige Ando (1797-1858).

Wood-block prints or hanga (hahn-gah) had been produced in Japan since the Nara Period in the 8th century, but it was the genius of these ukiyo-e painters that brought them to the forefront of Japanese art. At first, the prints were largely ignored by artistic circles and the well-to-do, who considered them too plebian, but when Western connoiseurs began to collect the hanga as masterpieces, their reputation soared.

The best-known hanga masters became famous for certain types of subject matter. Shunsho, Sharaku and Toyokuni for portraits of actors. Harunobu, Kiyonaga, Eishi, Utamaro and Toyokuni for pictures of beautiful women. Hokusai and Hiroshige for landscapes.

Dutch traders stationed on the man-made island of Dejima in Nagasaki Bay from the early days of the Tokugawa Shogunate (1603-1867), sent the first hanga to Europe--sometimes as wrapping paper. It was not until the 1850s, however, when they were put on sale at a popular shop in Paris that they really caught on in the West.

Several artists tried to introduce Western techniques into hanga during the late 1800s and early 1900s, but with little success. In 1931 the traditionalist theme was reaffirmed with the formation of the Nippon Hanga Kyokai (Neeppone Hahn-gah K'yoe-kie) or Japan Woodblock-Print Association.

The art has evolved with the times, however, and the work of a number of contemporary hanga artists is now very popular.

The ukiyo style of painting and woodblock prints were associated with a style of literature that flourished during the Edo Period--a style that came to be known as Ukiyo Zoshi, or Novels of the Floating World.

These novels were realistic depictions of Japanese society during this period, ranging from the highly formal and rigid life-style of the Samurai to the loose, sensual and often frivolous lives of the townspeople.

One of the best-known of the writers who made this genre famous was Saikaku Ihara. See LITERATURE.

UMEDA β UMEDA UNDERGROUND CENTER (Uu-may-dah)

The area around Osaka Station is officially named Umeda, but popularly called Kita, or North. It is the city's primary transportation terminal for numerous train and bus lines, and includes a huge complex of office buildings, department stores, shops, restaurants, theaters and night spots.

Beneath much of the area is the immense Umeda Underground Center, which is like a small city within itself, with hundreds of stores and restaurants lining its passageways. The underground center links Osaka Station with many of the larger buildings in the district, as well as the Umeda Subway Station.

UNIONS / RODO KUMIAI (Roe-doe Kuu-me-aye)

In Japan unions are not organized on a craft, occupation or job basis as they are in the U.S. Instead, they are organized on a company basis--a difference that is of extraordinary importance to both management and labor.

While federated into national bodies by industry, each union remains independent. All employees of a unionized company are automatically members of the union when they are hired. This means all who advance to supervisory and management positions have had union experience, and often served as union leaders.

The relationship between Japan's company union members and management is, therefore, quite different not only because of the nature of the union itself, but also because employees know they will most likely work for the company until they retire. They also know they will not find comparable work elsewhere if they quit or if the company fails, and in the case of many, because they expect to be promoted to management or to return to the folds of management when their term as union leaders end.

Approximately 30 percent of Japan's labor force is unionized, and there are some 72,200 individual unions, most of which belong to one or the other of several national federations.

There are three major national union federations in Japan. SOHYO (The General Council of Japanese Trade Unions), is the largest, with nearly five million members. It is also the most influential of the labor federations.

Next is DOMEI (Confederation of Japan Labor Unions), which has some two and a third million members. CHURITSU ROREN (Liaison Council of Neutral Labor Unions of Japan), has around three and a third million members.

SOHYO generally supports the Japan Socialist Party, and is the strongest in public sector unions (teachers, employees of Japanese National Railways, and other government operated enterprises).

In addition to these Big Three, there is the IMFJC (International Metalworkers Federation--Japan Council), some of whose members belong to the three largest federations. The IMFJC opposes the socialist tendencies of SOHYO, and advocates trade unionism and federation of all private enterprise unions.

Approximately 75 percent of Japan's labor force works a 5-day week.

In 1982 a new union federation, the All-Japan Council of Private Unions, or Zenminrokyo (Zen-meen-roe-k'yoe), was formed out of the amalgamation of 41 industrial unions with a combined membership of 4.25 million. The new federation's goals are to achieve unification of the labor front by bringing the majority of the private sector unions together.

To the Japanese way of thinking, the underlying philosophy of American unions is not only incompatible with the social nature of an enterprise, it is basically destructive. They say American unions do not care if a company fails and goes out of business because of union demands. American unionism, they say, is based on the idea that a company's primary obligation is to provide the level of working conditions and wages proposed by the union—and any company that cannot or will not do this does not deserve to survive.

UNIVERSITIES / DAIGAKU (Die-gah-kuu)

There are 93 national universities in Japan, 34 prefectural and municipal universities, and 319 private universities. In addition, there are 520 junior colleges in the country, plus a United Nations University which was established in Tokyo by the UN in the 1970s.

Tokyo University (Tokyo Daigaku) is one of the oldest and most famous university in Japan. Its predecessors, the Kaiseisho (Kie-say-e-sho) amd Igakusho (Ee-gah-kuu-sho), were founded by the Tokugawa Shogunate. Todai, as the university is popularly known, dates from 1877 when these two Bakufu schools were merged.

Other famous national universities include Kyoto University, Tohoku University, Kyushu University, Hokkaido University, Osaka University and Nagoya University.

Among the most famous private universities are Keio and Waseda. Top-ranked Christian universities in Japan include Doshisha, Rikkyo, Sophia, Kwansei Gakuin, Kobe College and Aoyama Gakuin. See individual listings and EXAMINATION HELL.

UNLUCKY NUMBERS

The two unluckiest numbers in Japan are four and nine—four because the term for this, shi (she), is the same sound for the word that means death, and nine because ku (kuu), the word for nine, suggests suffering. Thirteen is also an unlucky number (and seems to have been borrowed from the West.

As a result of these supersititions, many hotels in Japan do not have rooms numbered four, nine or thirteen.

UNZEN-AMAKUSA NATIONAL PARK

In a land blessed with scenery that often surpasses description, the Unzen-Amakusa National Park is a stand-out. The park covers some 256 square kilometers, which includes a big portion of the Shimabara Peninsula near Nagasaki, the Ariake Sea on the east side of the peninsula, Chijiwa Bay on the west and the Amakusa Islands to the south and east.

The park contains Mt. Unzen, which actually consists of three major mountain peaks and several lesser ones—all volcanic. Plus Unzen Spa which also consists of three different hotspring resorts, all at an altitude of over 700 meters in totally gorgeous surroundings. Along with swimming and surfing beaches at Chijiwa, Obama, Kuzusa and Shimabara, plus many other hotsprings, geysers, solfataras and fumaroles.

There are also mountain passes, Lake Shirakumo, waterfalls, campsites, the Tsukumo Isles off of Shimabara Port (formed in 1792 when Mt. Maruyama west of the city erupted), the Shimabara Castle, at which nearly all of the Christian converts in Japan were slaughtered in 1637 and the beautiful Amakusa Islands.

Lying south of Shimabara Peninsula, the Amakusa Islands (there are 70 in the group), are all mountainous, and abound in one scenic spot after another—most of them with fantastic views of the surrounding seas.

The two largest of the islands—Amakusa Upper and Amakusa Lower—are connected by a draw-bridge. Several of the other islands are also connected by bridges (completed in 1966), which are all high enough to allow the passage of large ships beneath them.

Besides attracting vacationers and tourists, the islands are noted for their Amakusa dolls, camelia oil, pottery and processed seafood.

URAGA (Uu-rah-gah)

Now a part of the port city of Yokosuka on Miura Peninsula (where Shogun Ieyasu Tokugawa gave the English pilot Will Adams a fief), and known as the dockyard of the Uraga Heavy Industry Company, one of Japan's major shipbuilders, Uraga played a vital role in the history of Japan during the Tokugawa period.

After establishing his Shogunate headquarters in Edo (Tokyo) in 1603, Ieyasu made Uraga port the holding place for barges waiting for inspection before they could enter Tokyo Bay.

This is also the place where, in 1846, the American Commodore James Biddle and his two warships dropped anchor and gave the local Shogunate officials a letter addressed to the Emperor.

The officials took the letter but didn't deliver it. Seven years later, Commodore Matthew C. Perry and his squadron of Black Ships showed up on the same mission--to get Japan to open its doors to the outside world. By that time, the situation in Japan had changed. Perry's letter was officially accepted at Kurihama, near Uraga, and delivered not to the Emperor but to the Shogun, who was the real power in the country (a fact that the Western powers did not learn for several more years).

UTSUNOMIYA (Uut-sue-no-me-yah)

The prefectual capital of Tochigi, Utsunomiya is a large city some 70 train minutes north of Tokyo on the way to Nikko. The castle town of the feudal lord of the province, Utsunomiya was also one of Japan's famous Post Stations, where the Daimyo Processions and other travelers of the Edo period put up at night.

In addition to being a thriving industrial and commercial center, Utsunomiya is also known for the Oya Temple, believed to have been founded by Kobo Daishi (774-835), who introduced the Shingon doctrines of Buddhism into the country. Part of the temple is inside a huge cave, the walls of which are decorated with the images of 10 Buddhas carved in relief.

This is the area where Frank Lloyd Wright got the soft brown stone (Oya stone) he used in building the famous (former) Imperial Hotel in Tokyo.

VACCARI, MR. β MRS. ORESTE

Oreste and Elisa Vaccari are well-known names to almost every person who has studied the Japanese language since the end of World War II in 1945--if not before.

An Italian who first went to Japan in the 1930s, Vaccari soon realized the need for a different kind of learning tool in the study of Japanese, and in 1939 published the first edition of his ENGLISH-JAPANESE CONVERSATION DICTIONARY.

Over the next several decades, Vacarri and his wife turned out a steady stream of learning aides for both English and Italian students of the Japanese language.

Eventually, Vaccari and his wife established Vaccari's Language Institute in the Jingumae district of Tokyo's Shibuya Ward, to publish their works.

VIEWING FACILITIES

Cultural and recreational viewing facilities in Japan include 72 aquariums, 312 art museums, 93 botanical gardens, 2,085 movie theaters, 1,135 museums, 741 stage theaters, and 88 zoos (including safari parks).

VISAS / RYOKEN (Rio-ken)

There are over a dozen different types of visas for entering Japan, depending on the purpose. A transient visa (4-1-3) is good for 15 days, a tourist visa (4-1-4) is good for 90 days.

Other categories and periods of stay include: businessmen (4-1-5) three years, journalists (4-1-11) three years, students (4-1-6) one year, entertainers (4-1-9) 60 days, teachers (4-1-7) three years.

The visas of government officials and those assigned to embassies and consular offices are good for the duration of their assignment, however long it might be. In most cases, term visas may be extended one or more times.

Visas to enter Japan are available from the nearest Japanese Embassy or Consulate. Tourist visas are usually issued immediately on request. Commercial and other special category visas requiring documentation are generally sent to Tokyo for approval, and take from several days to a few weeks.

Foreigners who are in Japan for whatever reason must have a new visa or a re-entry permit if they leave the country and intend to return. Some visas, such as tourist, are multiple-entry visas, meaning the bearer can enter Japan any number of times during the valid period of the visa (which in the case of a tourist visa is four years as long as the passport remains valid).

The citizens of more than 45 countries do not need visas to visit Japan because the nations involved have visa exemption agreements with Japan. The countries include Austria, Federal Republic of Germany, Ireland, Liechtenstein, Mexico, Switzerland, the United Kingdom, Argentina, Belgium, Canada, Denmark, France, Greece, Holland, Norway, Pakistan, Sweden, Turkey and New Zealand.

VOLCANOES / KAZAN (Kah-zahn)

Japan has about one-tenth of the active volcanoes in the world, and hundreds of inactive ones. The highest mountain in Japan--Mt. Fuji--is a dormant volcano that last erupted in the 1700s. See MT. FUJI, MT. ASO, MOUNTAINS.

WAKAYAMA (Wah-kah-yah-mah)

Less than an hour by train from Osaka, the city of Wakayama, on Kii Peninsula, has long been celebrated for its mild climate, scenic beauty and its own special ambience that has made it a favorite with the Japanese as well as foreign residents.

Another castle town that developed into a major city, Wakayama owes its early prominence to one of the most extraordinary figures in Japan's history, Hideyoshi Toyotomi, who ordered a castle built there in 1585.

During the long Edo era, Wakayama was of special importance because the Daimyo of the province was a relative of the Tokugawa Shogun. Besides being the capital of Wakayama Prefecture, the city today is an industrial and commercial center, best-known for its cotton flannel factories.

WAKKANAI (Wok-kah-nie)

Japan's northernmost city, Wakkanai is on the west shore of Soya Bay, near the tip of the Soya district of Hokkaido, which faces Sakhalin (Russia) just across the Soya Straits.

The warming Tsushima Current, which comes up through the Japan Sea from the South Pacific, keeps Wakkanai's port from freezing over in winter, and it is Hokkaido's top fishing port.

In earlier centuries, Wakkanai was the jumping off point for Japanese explorers and travelers going to Sakhalin and the Kurile Islands. In the spring of 1957, it was the jumping off point for myself and Australian adventurer Ben Carlin, with whom I crossed the North Pacific and Bering Sea in an amphibious jeep called Half-Safe.

Recommended reading: ONCE A FOOL--From Japan to Alaska by Amphibious Jeep, by Boye De Mente (Phoenix Books/Publishers).

WANDERING PRIESTS / KOMUSO (Koe-muu-soe)

One of the obligations of priests belonging to the Fuke sect of Zen Buddhism is to go on pilgrimages to collect alms. Soon after Zen Buddhism was introduced into Japan in the middle ages such wandering priests became a common sight throughout the country.

Dressed in kimono robes and wearing a large braided hat that covered the head and hid their faces, the priests played long, 5-hole bamboo flutes as they walked solemnly through villages and towns, and along the great walking roads of the day.

Because of the dangers from road bandits, rogue Samurai and other unsavory types, the komuso also carried swords to protect themselves--and they knew how to use them. Some komuso were, in fact, former Samuari who had given up the way of the warrior for the way of the cloth, and were expert at various martial arts.

During the turbulent periods in Japan's middle ages, it was also common for Samurai and others to disguise themselves as komuso in order to travel about the country without arousing suspicion. Many movies and television shows about this period make use of this theme.

It was common during periods of turmoil for some komuso, especially ex-Samurai, to be hired as spies by contending forces. See KOMUSO.

WARRIOR MONKS

In 788 Emperor Kammu ordered the famous priest Saicho (767-822), later known as Dengyo Daishi, to establish a temple on the summit of Mt. Hiei to protect the new capital of Kyoto from evil spirits. The temple was named Enryaku, and still today is one of the most important temples in Japan.

Situated in a thick grove of cypress trees, the temple grew over the centuries into a great monastery, with thousands of priests. To protect themselves and the treasures of the massive temple complex, the priests took up the practice of military arts. Their favorite weapon was the halberd--a sword at the end of a long handle--which had developed in the early 1200s and was commonly used by the poorest of the Samurai.

By the 1400s the monks of Mt. Hiei had become fierce warriors, and often raided sections of Kyoto in pursuit of enemies, and threatened the Emperor. Finally, in the mid-1500s, Nobunaga Oda, then the supreme military power in Japan, declared war against the maurading monks and in a number of battles, destroyed them.

See ENRYAKU TEMPLE.

WASEDA UNIVERSITY / WASEDA DAIGAKU (Wah-say-dah Die-gah-kuu)

One of Japan's premiere universities, Waseda was founded by Marquis Shigenobu Okuma in 1882, on grounds that were part of his estate, in what is now Shinjuku Ward.

Waseda is famous for a number of things besides its academic standing, including its baseball team, its rivalry with Keio University and its success in placing graduates in leading newspaper companies.

It is also popular with foreign students.

WATER / MIZU (Me-zoo)

First-time visitors to Japan are often concerned about the quality of the drinking water--needlessly so. Tap water in Japan is perfectly safe to drink, and on the average is better than that in most advanced countries.

At this time, approximately 95 percent of the households in Japan are provided with potable tap water.

WATER BUSINESS / MIZU SHOBAI (Me-zoo Show-bye)

Mizu Shobai, literally Water Busines, refers to Japan's night-time entertainment trades, in particular bars, cabarets, night clubs, Geisha houses, Turkish bathhouses, hotspring spas and theaters--which employ a significant percentage of the working population.

Use of the term Water Business to describe this area of entertainment and recreation is typically Japanese--the connotation being that the various pleasures dispensed by these businesses is an ephemeral thing that evaporates like mist rising from a bath, or dew on the morning flowers. And, of course, hotbaths have traditionally played a central role in Japan's Floating World of pleasure.

The use of the term Mizu Shobai has diminished in recent decades, but it is still very much a part of life in Japan.

Recommended reading: BACHELOR'S JAPAN, by Boye De Mente (Tuttle).

WAX FOOD-MODELS

Several categories of Japanese restaurants use a very unusual and very effective method of promoting their food--they display wax models of the various dishes in windows or display cases.

The wax food models are incredibly life-like, so much so that when I first saw them I thought they were real.

Signs giving the name of the dish, and usually the price, go along with the displays, so in effect you are able to see the menu before going inside, or just inside the entrance in the foyer or cashier's area.

WEDDING CEREMONIES / KEKKON SHIKI (Keck-kone She-kee)

In earlier Japan, weddings were relatively simple affairs, many of them taking place in the bridegroom's home, or at shrines or temples. When held at larger shrines or temples, they were more elaborate. Some of those held at Shinto shrines by the well-to-do were especially impressive.

Both the bride and the groom dressed in traditional clothing, the kimono and headdress of the bride being particularly elaborate. The highlight of these ceremonies was when the coupled exchanged tiny cups of sake nine times in a ritual that is called San San Ku Do (sahn sahn kuu doe).

Weddings in Japan today are very big business. Those who can afford it, utilize specialized commercial wedding halls, the banquet rooms of leading hotels, or the banquet rooms of large restaurants.

Ordinary working families go to considerable expense to stage impressive weddings that include full meals, drinks and gifts for all the guests. The more affluent may have from 100 to 500 or more guests, all of whom are wined and dined in a very impressive manner--and given gifts.

The cost of such weddings range from several thousand dollars for a relatively modest affair to five or ten times that amount.

In today's weddings, the bride still wears the traditional wedding kimono, but the groom may opt for formal Western wear. Most ceremonies include the san san ku do exchange of sake cups, but some also have prayers by a Shinto or Buddhist priest.

While dining recently at a large Chinese restaurant in Tokyo's Harajuku area, my host and I were treated to a very modern Japanese wedding. The couple marched in to the tune of Here Comes the Bride. The bride was in the traditional kimono, the groom in a coat with tails.

A Shinto priest performed a sacred ritual and chanted prayers. The two exchanged sake cups. Then, together they cut a huge Western wedding cake with a Samurai sword.

WEIGHTS and MEASURES

Japan has been on the metric system since 1904 (although the old, traditional Japanese system of weights and measures was commonly used in personal and cottage industry areas until well after 1945).

Even when just visiting, it helps to

Nikko's spectacular Kegon Waterfall. P. 232

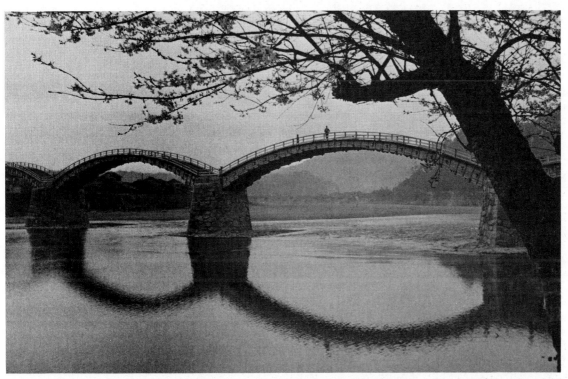

Kintaisha Bridge in Yamaguchi. P. 237

know a few of the most common weights and measures in the metric system. So if you are going to be visiting Japan, you might want to bone up a bit.

WINDS / KAZE (Kah-zay)

The Japanese-and-English monthly in-flight magazine of Japan Air Lines, Winds covers travel destinations, food, life-styles and other aspects of Japanese culture calculated to be of special interest to visitors. Its color features and insightful articles by well-known writers on Japan make it a popular subscription publication. See OTHER SOURCES.

WINE / BUDOSHU (Buu-doe-shuu)

Western style wine is now consumed by many Japanese, and wine-making is a growing industry. Sake is generally described as a rice wine, since it is fermented from rice. A sweetened version of sake, called mirin, also apparently qualifies as a wine.

One of the more popular Japanese wine brands is Akadama (Ah-kah-dah-mah), a sweet red wine.

WOMEN DIVERS / AMA (Ah-mah)

Japan has long been noted for its ama--women who dive, semi-nude, for shellfish, agar-agar and various other seafood. A traditional custom that goes back for uncounted centuries, the practice is still seen in several places around the islands, such as Hekura, Onjuku, Shirahama and Wagu.

While the women do the diving, their husbands or menfolk handle the boats. There are a number of reasons given to explain why the women instead of the men do the diving--one being that women are better able to stand the chilly ocean waters.

The ama of Hekura are of special interest. Hekura is a small island 48 kilometers off the northern tip of Noto Peninsula which juts out into the Japan Sea from Ishikawa Prefecture on Western Honshu.

Each summer about 700 families leave the port city of Wajima on Noto Peninsula and go to the island of Hejima, where the spend the entire summer season, the women diving and the men taking care of their catch.

The annual migration is very systematically done, with the families accompanied by their children, teachers, doctors, and one or more police officers.

One of the largest community of women divers is in Shirahama on Boso Peninsula, southeast of Tokyo. There some 1,500

women spend the summer months gathering top-shells, ear shells and sea weed from the waters off the picturesque coast.

In the small fishing village of Onjuku, also on Boso Peninsula, are some 400 ama who practice this ancient form of harvesting the ocean.

Wagu is the center of the ama divers on Shima Peninsula near the famous Pearl Island and Toba, south of Nagoya. Here, much of the coastline is made up of picturesque cliffs and sheer rock islets just off-shore, making this one of the most scenic areas noted for ama.

WOMEN'S ORGANIZATIONS

Given the tendency of the Japanese to form groups, it is not surprising to find that there are numerous national women's organizations in Japan--some of them quite powerful. A number of times in the 1950s and 60s, concerted action by some of these organizations resulted in new legislation concerning food standards, and changes in consumer prices.

Among the leading general organizations are The League of Women Voters, Japanese Women's Democratic Club, Japan Housewives Association, National Women's Association of Agricultural Cooperation, the National Federation of Regional Women's Organizations, Japan Liaison Council for the National Congress of Mothers, Consumer Science Association and the Lib Shinjuku Center.

There are several important vocational organizations, including the Medical Association of Japanese Women, Japan Midwives Association, Japanese Nursing Association, Women's Dentist Assocaiton, the National Federation of Women Teachers, and the Federation of Japanese Women's Organizations.

WOMEN'S RIGHTS

Article 14 of Japan's Constitution, prolmugated in 1947, states: All of the people are equal under the law and there shall be no discrimination in political, economic or social relations because of race, creed, sex, social status or family origin.

Laws have also been passed guaranteeing equal educational opportunities for the sexes, equal payment for the same work, and equal treatment in matters of inheritance (increasing the wife's share of an inheritance from one-third to one-half).

Changing economic and social circumstances have also drastically altered the options now open to Japanese women and the treatment they receive. On a practical basis, however, there is still considerable discrimination against women, but in more subtle ways than in the past (and similar to that found in the U.S.).

Some 53 percent of all office workers in Japan are women. Some 43 percent of all technicians and specialists are female, and approximately 40 percent of the country's sales workers are women. On the managerial side, however, only about seven percent are women.

Labor regulations in Japan provide paid maternity leaves for female employees, prohibit their being employed to work between 10 p.nm. and 5 a.m. except for those who work in the entertainment trades and other special areasas), ban their employment for jobs requiring heavy lifting or involving physical danger, and guaranteeing them menstrual leave if they have painful monthly periods.

WOODBLOCK PRINTS / HANGA (Hahn-gha)

The first record of woodblock printing (moku han) in Japan occurred in 764 when Empress Koken ordered some sutras printed in this manner. The printing of the sutras, destined for distribution to temples around the country, was completed in 770.

For the next several hundred years, woodblock printing was used primarily for printing sutras and Buddhist pictures. The first book printed on moku han in Japan came out in 1346 (there is a copy preserved at the National Museum in Tokyo).

Thereafter moku han books became fairly popular, but it was in the late 1600s before woodblock prints began to catch on. These first woodblock prints were in one color. The first multi-colored print was produced in 1765 by Harunobu Suzuki.

Woodblock prints became increasingly popular following the appearance of full-color prints, and were one of the first Japanese arts to attract interest in the West. Most of this popularity was due to the appearance of the great hanga artists Hokusai Katsushika and Hiroshige Ando, whose depictions of the everyday life of Japan, of actors and beautiful women in the entertainment trades and the scenic beauty of the country, heralded a golden age for woodblock prints.

The particular style developed by these famous hanga artists came to be known as Ukiyo-e (Uu-kee-yoe-eh), or Pictures of the Floating World.

Hokusai is especially noted for a series he painted depicting sights along the great Tokai Do walkway that connected Edo with Kyoto.

The names of woodblock print artists that end in sai, ken or an, originally referred to their studio, rather than to the artists themselves. Besides their real names, which are seldom if ever used, they also generally had professional names.

It is said that Europeans first became acquainted with Japanese woodblock prints because they were often used as wrapping paper on other items being shipped abroad. It wasn't too long thereafter that prints by the masters were much in demand, and commanded high prices.

Among the best-known woodblock print dealers in Tokyo are Kaigado, Uchida Art Company, Yokoyama and Yoseido.

Recommended reading: THE JAPANESE PRINT--Its Evolution and Essence, by Muneshige Narazaki, adapted by C. H. Mitchell (Kodansha Int'l). UTAMARO by Tadashi Kobayashi, translated by Mark A. Harbison (Kodansha Int'l). WHO'S WHO IN MODERN JAPANESE PRINTS by Frances Blakemore (Weatherhill). THE JAPANESE PRINT: A Historical Guide, by Hugo Munsterberg (Weatherhill).

WOODEN CLOGS / GETA (Gay-tah)

One of two types of traditional Japanese footwear (the other being zori), geta are elevated wooden platform clogs that are traditionally worn on more formal occasions when one is dressed up.

The geta are cut out of single blocks of wood, with a front and back ridge left on the bottom to act as the sole. These ridges are of varying heights, depending on the purpose of the geta. The standard height is about two inches, but geta made to be worn in the rain (amageta) have sole-ridges that are between three and four inches high.

Geta for men are made of plain wood, and the v-shaped thongs that hold the geta on the feet are usually black. Geta for women are often lacquered black or vermilion or some other color, and have colorful thongs of velvet or silk.

WRAPPING CLOTH / FUROSHIKI (Fuu-roe-she-kee)

Furoshiki literally means bath cloth, because it was originally used to wrap one's clothes at a public bath, or to sit on, but over the centuries it gradually became a general wrapping/carrying cloth for anything and everything.

Now usually made of cotton, silk or synthetic cloth, furoshiki are often decorated with artistic renditions of plants or flowers, crests, and so on. While considerably less in evidence today because of the wide-spread availability of shopping bags and other kinds of bags, furoshiki are nevertheless still popular in Japan, and are a favorite gift item.

WRITING JAPANESE

Writing Japanese is a special challenge, because there are three sets of characters to learn--the well-known kanji (khan-jee), and the less well-known hiragana (he-rah-gah-nah) and katakana (kah-tah-kah-nah). The language can also be written with Roman letters, but this system is still not common and cannot be read fluently by most Japanese.

Most nouns, root verbs and adjectives are written in the more complicated kanji characters which were borrowed from China in the 6th and 7th centuries. Because the characters were not totally adaptable to the Japanese languages, Japanese scholars developed a series of phonetic characters, called manyokana (mahn-yoe-kah-nah), that were used to express the verb and adjective endings, and the tenses.

In the 9th century, this phonetic system was further rationalized, and divided into two sets of characters-- hiragana and katakana--each with 46 symbols. Adverbs can be written in either kanji or kana characters.

By the beginning of modern times, the hiragana characters, which are soft and flowing, were widely favored over the katakana symbols, which are hard and static. It thereafter gradually became customary to use the katakana characters to write foreign words that were adopted into the Japanese langauge.

Japanese children learn the hiragana symbols first, often before they start to school.

In earlier years, Japanese was almost always written in vertical lines. Now there is a growing tendency for it to be written in a horizontal format.

See CALLIGRAPHY.

YABUIRI (Yah-buu-ee-ree)

This word literally means Going Back to the Bush, and refers to the traditional practice of giving servants and apprentices holidays to return to their rural homes on January 16. In earlier times it referred to wives visiting the homes of their parents, along with their husbands, after Obon in the summer to help cut wood and clear land.

Until well into this century it was common for young boys to be apprenticed to tradesmen when they were as young as eight or nine, and to live in the shops where they worked. Until they were 15, their masters would give them two days off a year at their convenience, but after they came of age, they were allowed to take their holidays during yabuiri.

The custom of yabuiri, called by different names in different parts of the country, is still practiced in Japan, but its old meanings have been virtually forgotten.

YAKI-TORI (Yah-kee-Toe-ree)

This is chicken barbecued Japanese-style--cut up in tiny chunks and broiled over an open charcoal fire, along with pieces of such vegetables as onions and pimento.

The various pieces are impaled on metal or bamboo skewers, dipped in a sweetened barbecue soy sauce or sprinkled with salt (as the diner chooses), and then broiled.

Yaki-tori ya, or yaki tori shops, abound all over Japan, especially in entertainment districts, as they are a popular evening and late-night snack. Many such shops have only a counter. Others are standup-and-take-out places. Most are marked by a distinctive paper lantern called chochin (choe-cheen).

This is another typical Japanese dish that is immediately pleasing to the palates of most foreigners.

YAKUZA (Yah-kuu-zah)

The yakuza are Japan's professional criminal class, and are sometimes compared to the mafia. The yakuza have a long and somewhat honorable history in Japan.

The yakuza began as low-class gamblers and gangsters in Japan's early feudal days. Having to learn how to protect themselves from disgruntled victims as well as from raids by the authorities, the yakuza eventually began to use their skills to protect helpless citizens from marauders and ronin (masterless) Samurai.

While continuing to function outside the law, the yakuza adopted their own codes similar to the ethics of the Samurai, and in the case of a number of individuals became folk heroes in their own time.

Today there are some half a dozen major yukuza gangs in Japan--referred to as kumi (kuu-me) or gumi (guu-me), usually translated as group--Yoshida Gumi, Tanaka Gumi, etc.--with a total of some 100,000 members.

Present-day yakuza gangs are involved in sports activities, in the entertainment business, in running Turkish bathhouses, pachinko parlors, clandestine gambling dens and other enterprises, including bars and night clubs.

While known to the police, the yakuza usually managed to avoid arrest. When they make the news, it is usually the result of a squabble over territory.

YAMAGUCHI CITY (Yah-mah-guu-chee)

The capital of Yamaguchi Prefecture, which is on the southwestern tip of Honshu across from the southernmost main island of Kyushu, Yamaguchi City is old as a community, but it did not come into the limelight until the 14th century when it was taken over by the Ouchi clan.

The Ouchi's greatly expanded the economic activity of the city, and built a large number of magnificent temples in imitation of those in Kyoto. In the 16th century when Francis Xavier, the Spanish missionary, visited there, Yamaguchi was at the height of its glory. It was often called the Kyoto of the West at this time.

The province then came into the hands of the Mori clan, which fought on the losing side against Ieyasu Tokugawa in the Battle of Sekigahara in 1603. The Mori Daimyo was exiled to Hagi on the cold Japan Sea coast, and the fortunes of Yamaguchi declined.

When the movement against the Tokugawa Shogunate became intense in 1863, Yamaguchi became the base of its operations and again rose to prominence.

Today Yamaguchi is noted for its Yasaka Shrine, built in 1370, for Kameyama Park where the Ouchi Villa stood, and Yuda Spa.

YAMANASHI PREFECTURAL VISITOR CENTER (Yah-mah-nah-she)

Formerly the Fuji National Park Museum, the Yamanashi Visitor Center, is near the shores of Lake Kawaguchi, one of the five lakes that ring the waist of Mt. Fuji, and one that is popular both as a winter and a summer resort.

The Visitor Center, near the toll-gate of the 29.5 kilometer Fuji Subarui Line that leads up to the 5th Station on one of the climbing trails of Mt. Fuji, contains numerous exhibits about the natural history of Mt. Fuji.

The Lake Kawaguchi areas is a little over two train hours from Shinjuku Station in Tokyo. The north shore of the lake has been famous since ancient times for its fantastic view of Mt. Fuji, towering over the lake as well as reflected in its waters.

YAMATO (Yah-mah-toe)

Yamato was a province in what is now Nara Prefecture, east of Kyoto, and was the location of the Court of Japan's first fully documented ruler, Hatsukuni-shirasu Sumera-Mikoto, who later came to be known as Jimmu Tenno or Emperor Jimmu.

At that time, the kingdom over which Hatsukunishirasu ruled was also known as Yamato, and for a long time thereafter is what the Japanese called their country. See JAPAN.

The son of Emperor Keiko (71-130 A.D.) was named Prince Takeru Yamato, which indicates this may have been the name of the Imperial family.

YASUKUNI SHRINE / YASUKUNI JINJA (Yah-sue-kuu-nee Jeen-jah)

This great shrine, on Kudan Hill on the northwest side of the Imperial Palace Grounds in Tokyo, is dedicated to Japan's national heroes, in partiuclar those who gave their lives in war.

When Shintoism was the state religion, from shortly after the Meiji Restoration in 1868 until 1945, Yasukuni Jinja was one of the most important shrines in the country, and played a key role in the military-oriented affairs of government.

Today, Yasukuni Jinja is more like a national war memorial, and is visited by large numbers of people throughout the year. Its entryway is marked by the largest granite torii in Japan, and by a second colossal torii of bronze that is 22 meters high.

The shrine sponsors two major festivals every year, in the spring from April 21-23, and in the fall from October 17-19.

YELLOW PAGES

One of the most useful publications for foreign residents and business visitors in Tokyo, the YELLOW PAGES is just what it sounds like--a large telephone directory, primarily covering the Tokyo area, that lists in its Index Section emergency and public phones, other detailed information about using the phone system in Japan, the postal system, zip codes, public holidays and festivals, trade fairs and exhibitions, international conferences--and museums.

In Section 1, airlines and travel businesses, hotels, night clubs and cabarets, and restaurants are listed. Section 2 includes government agenices, followed by regular Yellow Page-type listings under the approrpiate product or service category.

Yellow Pages is published twice a year by Japan Yellow Pages Ltd., ST Building, 4-6-9 Iidabashi, Chiyoda-ku, Tokyo 102, Japan.

YEN / EN (Inn)

Japanese currency, the yen, is pronounced something like inn in Japanese. It was established as the legal currency of the land in 1871. It comes in 10, 50, 100 and 500 yen coins, and in 500, 1,000, 5,000 and 10,000 yen bills. See MONEY.

横浜

YOKOHAMA

One of the world's great port cities and the third largest city in Japan, Yokohama is on the west side of Tokyo Bay in Kanagawa Prefecture, some 20 miles southwest of Tokyo.

Associated with trade and foreign residents since the last years of the Tokugawa Shogunate, Yokohama was a small fishing village in 1859 when it was designated as a foreign trade port city and open to residency by foreigners.

At that time, the town was divided into two sections--Kan Nai (Inside the Barrier) and Kan Gai (Outside the Barrier). Foreigners could live only Inside the Barrier, which faced the harbor and was walled off from the rest of the town. Foreign residents could leave their enclave only with permission on special occasions.

The foreign residents of Yokohama, with their strange clothing and even stranger habits, were subjects of intense curiosity among the Japanese, and people traveled from distant areas in the hopes of getting a glimpse of the exotic-looking Gaijin (Outside People).

By 1889, when Yokohama was organized into a city, the population had exploded to 121,000. It was to continue to grow rapidly as the harbor and harbor facilities were improved, and the volume of foreign trade handled by the port increased at a remarkable rate. Much of the city was destroyed by the great earthquake of 1923, however, and again by fire-bomb raids during World War II, but it was quickly rebuilt each time.

Yokohama today is not only a great port but also is a major industrial center (automobiles, ships, chemicals, foodstuffs). The city is divided into 14 wards, and has its popular and distinctive entertainment, shopping and residential districts--several of them with a foreign overlay that gives the area an attractive cosmopolitan appearance.

There are also numerous shrines, temples and other places of special interest in the city, including the Silk Center, Children's Country (Kodomo-no Kuni), China Town (which boasts some 70 Chinese restaurants and two dozen shops selling Chinese foodstuffs and spices), Motomachi Shopping Street, and the Sankei En (Sankei Garden) which features a number of cultural properties moved there from various parts of Japan-- including the villa of the Tokugawa family in Kii Province, which is the only remaining example of feudal lord villa architecture. Also a tea ceremony house built by the third Tokugawa Shogun in the 1640s, a large farmhouse built in Gifu in the early 1700s without the use of nails or cramps, and a temple built by Hideyoshi Toyotomi for his mother in 1592 and originally in the courtyard of the Daitoku Temple in Kyoto.

YOKOSUKA (Yoe-kose-kah)

The largest city on the Miura Peninsula, a little over an hour southwest of Tokyo, Yokosuka has been famous as a naval base since World War I. It was the leading Japanese naval facility in eastern Japan until the end of World War II, when it was taken over by the U.S.'s 7th Fleet and Japan's Maritime Self-Defense Force.

Since 1945, Yokosuka has developed into a major fishing and trade port, and a gateway for sightseeing around the picturesque peninsula.

Besides being noted for its entertainment districts catering to naval personnel, Yokosuka is also famous as the final resting place of the Japanese battleship Mikasa, which was the flagship of Admiral Heihachiro Togo during the Russo-Japanese War in 1904-05.

Embedded in concrete in 1961, the Mikasa is now a memorial that attracts large numbers of people annually. Also of special interest in the area are Tuskayama Park, where the English pilot Will Adams and his Japanese wife are buried (see ADAMS, WILLIAM), and Kinugasa Park south of the city, which incorporates the grounds and ruins of Kinugasa Castle, headquarters of the lord of Miura that was destroyed in 1180.

YOMIURI LAND (Yoe-me-uu-ree)

A large recreational area on the banks of the Tama River between Tokyo and Yokohama, Yomiuri Land was built by the giant Yomiuri Newspaper Company in the 1960s. It includes a fishing center, swimming pool, public golf courses, a roller skating rink, ski-jump platforms and slopes, an oberservation platform and parachute tower.

Other attractions include a marine aquarium, jungle zoo and a TV studio. A two-and-a-half kilometer long monorail connects the various facilities.

YOMIURI NEWSPAPER / YOMIURI SHIMBUN (Yoe-me-uu-ree Shim-boon)

The Yomiuri, with nearly 14 million daily circulation, is the world's largest newspaper. It has 436 bureaus in Japan, 28 overseas, and an editorial staff of over 3,000. See NEWSPAPERS.

YOUTH HOSTELS

In 1958 the Japanese government instituted a policy of providing funds for the construction of modern, well-equipped Western-style youth hostels around the country, in locations noted for their beauty and or recreational facilities.

There are presently some 600 of the hostels, most of which are managed by Japan Youth Hostels, Inc. (JYH). The hostels have bedrooms, dining rooms, showers and central heating. Public kitchens are equipped with utensils that are for rent.

Japanese youth hostels are operated in accordance with international rules governing hostels. They offer simple but adequate accommodations that are neat, clean and inexpensive. Their purpose is to promote wholesome travel by young people as a way of furthering good mental and physical health, and strengthening international friendship.

Length of stay at individual hostels is three days unless there are vacancies, in which case one may extend for one or more nights. Directories of Japan's youth hostels are available from the Japan National Tourist Organization. See listing.

YOUTH TRAVEL VILLAGES / SEISHONEN RYOKO SON (Say-e-sho-nane Rio-koe Sone)

Another government-backed program, the Youth Travel Villages are located in popular resort areas and are aimed at providing young people with the opportunity to enjoy wholesome recreation at low cost.

Each Youth Travel Village is equipped with a clubhouse, campsites, lodging facilities (including some private accommodations), ball parks and other outdoor sports facilities.

There are presently some three dozen of the villages across the country--mostly used by Japanese groups.

YOSHINO (Yoe-she-no)

A small town on the crest of a ridge in the Yoshino Mountains, about a hour from Osaka, Yoshino is famous for its cherry trees, and for two weeks out of the year is one of the most popular sightseeing destinations in Japan.

The area has four large groves containing some 100,000 cherry trees, first planted in the 7th century by Enno Ozuna, a Buddhist priest, who made nearby Mt. Sajogadake his headquarters.

The groves, gradually ascending the slopes of the mountain, blossom at different times, beginning in early April on the lowest level, and going on through late April. An annual cherry blossom festival is held on April 11 and 12.

There are several ancient temples and shrines in the Yoshino area, and a number of places noted as being good spots from which to view the cherry tree groves. The famous priest-poet-sage Saigyo (1118-1190) had a hermitage adjoining one of the groves--a spot now marked by the Kokeshimizu Shrine.

YOYOGI SPORTS CENTER (Yoe-yoe-ghee)

Adjoining the famous Meiji Shrine and just a short walk from Harajuku Station in Tokyo's Shibuya Ward, the Yoyogi Sports Center was built as the Olympic Village for the 1964 Tokyo Olympic Games.

Hundreds of thousands of Americans who spent time in Japan during the Occupation following World World War II would remember the location as Washington Heights, a major residential area for American dependents during that era.

Prior to being taken over by the U.S Occupation forces, the site was the Yoyogi Parade Grounds of the Imperial Japanese Army.

The primary structure in the sports center is the Kishi Memorial Gymnasium, which can accommodate 15,000 spectators for indoor events. An annex, housing a basketball gym, will seat 4,000.

A historical note: Yoshitoshi Tokugawa (1884-1963), a descendent of the Tokugawa Shoguns (who voluntarily gave up power in 1868), made the first airplane flight in Japan on December 19, 1910 on this site. He flew for four minutes and gained an altitude of 70 meters.

The plane Captain Tokugawa flew is on display at the Transportation Museum in Sudacho, Kanda, Chiyoda Ward, Tokyo.

YUKATA (Yuu-kah-tah)

A thin, unlined cotton kimono that is worn as casual wear and often as a sleeping gown--especially in resort spas--the yukata is another distinctive feature of Japanese culture. Nearly all hotels and inns in Japan provide their guests with the handy, comfortable gown.

Yukata come with numerous design patterns, ranging from very conservative geometric motifs to elaborate scenes from nature. Those made for women tend to have more elaborate designs, as do those provided by resort inns for their guests.

The yukata provided by hotels are often so popular with guests they sometimes take them home--unofficially. To help prevent this kind of loss, the management in some hotels have room-signs advising their guests that the yukata may be bought in one of the hotel's arcade shops.

YUNOKAWA SPA (Yuu-no-kah-wah)

On Matsukawa River seven kilometers southeast of the Hokkaido port of Hakodate, Yunokawa is one of the largest and reportedly the best-equipped hotsprings spa in southern Hokkaido.

There are over 100 ryokan (inns) with hotspring baths clustered in the area of Yunokawa. The average temperature of the springs is 66 degrees centigrade. The spa has been popular since the mid-1600s.

YUSHIMA SEIDO (Yuu-she-mah Say-e-doe)

Situated on a small rise facing Tokyo's Ochonomizu Station on the north side of the Kanda River, the Yushima Seido or Yushima Hall is a shrine dedicated to Confucius, first erected in 1690 by Tsunayoshi Tokugawa, the fifth Tokugawa Shogun.

Later, the hall became the center for the teaching of Confucianism under the patronage of the Shogunate, and the head of a government school called Shoheiko, where many of the famous scholars and statesmen of the last Shogunate received their Confucian education. (The Shoheiko was one of the forerunners of Tokyo University.)

During the Tokugawa era the shrine burned down several times. The present buildings were constructed in 1935.

ZAIBATSU (Zie-bot-sue)

Following the Meiji Restoration, when the last of the Tokugawa Shoguns relinquished power to Emperor Meiji in 1868, the new Japanese government took the lead in a crash program to industrialize the country.

Realizing that small, under-fiananced companies would not be able to effect such a revolutionary change, the government provided financing and other help to a number of well-to-do families that allowed them to establish industrial and financial conglomerates (Zaibatsu) in all the key areas of business.

There were three types of Zaibatsu established: one that combined financial and industrial enterprises (Mitsui, Mitsubishi and Sumitomo). Those that were primarily in banking but utilized their resources to participate in industry (Yasuda, Nomura, etc.), and the industrial Zaibatsu, such as Asano, Okura and Furukawa.

Each of these great conglomerates was controlled by a single holding company which owned all of the shares in all affiliated companies, with all power concentrated in the hands of the family head who was the sole owner of the holding company.

Each of the family-controlled Zaibatsu maintained strong ties with the leading political parties. Each group worked independently to increase its market share and competitive power, and to consolidate and strengthen its overall role in the nation's economy. Before the outbreak of World War II, Mitsui was the largest commercial organization ever seen, with over three million employees.

The Zaibatsu were operated like independent feudal kingdoms, with their own house laws, and their owners were among the most powerful and wealthy men in the world.

Following WWII and the subsequent military occupation of Japan by the U.S., the Zabatsu were ordered to disband. Ostensibly this was done, but in actuality the management simply went underground.

When the Occupation of Japan ended and soverign power was returned to the people and government, the Zaibatsu reemerged in the form of industrial groups, but with some very important differences--the individual families that had once controlled them absolutely were no longer in power, and the various members of the groups operated semi-independently.

These newly reborn Zaibatsu-like conglomerates, played a seminal role in Japan's postwar economic miracle. The postwar years also saw the rapid development of several other major industrial groupings patterned after the new Zaibatsu, including the Fuyo group centered around the Fuji Bank, the Sanwa group linked with the Sanwa Bank, and such manufacturing and processing groups as those headed by Nippon Steel, Toyota, Hitachi and Matsushita.

There are over a dozen zaibatsu-type groups in Japan today. The six largest and best-known are the Mitsubishi Group, the Mitsui Group, the Sumitomo Group, the Fuji Group, the Sanwa Group and the Dai-Ichi Kangyo Group.

All of these groups are centered around a major bank, and include companies that are among the leaders in their fields. The Mitsubishi Group, the largest and most powerful, is made up of 28 ranking companies centered around Mitsubishi Bank. Its coordinating body is called the Kinyobi Kai or Friday Club--because that is the day on which the presidents of the various companies meet to discuss problems, policies and mutual interests.

The Mitsui Group includes such giant corporations as Toyota Motor Company, Toshiba Machine and Toray Industries, along with all the Mitsui companies as well as several other firms, with a total of 23 in the main group.

The Sumitomo Group is regarded as the most cohesive of all the Zaibatsu groupings. The principal organ of collaboration and coordination is the Hakusui Kai or White Wednesday Club. Besides all the Sumitomo companies, this group includes Nippon Electric, Asahi Chemical Industry, Nippon Sheet Glass and the automobile manufacturer Toyo Kogyo (Mazda), with a total of 16 (and not counting subsidiaries and affiliated companies).

The Fuji Group, not as closely coordinated as the others, generally counts 29 major companies that are within its sphere of influence. The Sanwa Group lists 36 companies on its roster. The Dai-Ichi Kangyo Group has 44 members, making it the largest in number of affiliated companies.

The importance of these groups should not be ignored or downplayed by any foreign company wanting to do business in or with Japan. While independent in most ways, the various companies are obligated to coordinate many of their activities with the group--which means, for example, that the trading company member may not take on a foreign product line for sale in Japan because one of its group members is involved in that line.

ZAIKAI (Zie-kie)

Zaikai translates more or less as Financial Group or Circle and refers to a specific number of high-level, powerful businessmen who influence both economic and political policies in Japan by virtue of their financial clout.

The Zaikai are not organized as such and do not present a common front. They make their influence felt through such business organizations as Keidanren (which see) and through their financial support of various politicians, the ruling party and specific programs.

There is also a business publication called ZAIKAI, aimed at top-level businessmen and government officials.

ZAO SKI RESORT (Zah-oh)

The largest ski resort in northeastern Japan, the Zao Spa and ski ground is in the Zao Quasi-National Park and is part of the Mt. Zao range of dormant volcanic peaks.

Accessible from Sendai by three scenic toll roads, the area is noted for its magnificient scenery in both summer and winter. It is a land of peaks, gorges, slopes, plateaus and hotspring spas.

ZEAMI (ZAY-AH-ME)

Zeami Kanze (1363-1443), the son of Kanami Kanze, the man credited with establishing the foundations of modern noh, carried on his father's work and raised noh (which had previously been mostly juggling and acrobatics) to a classic fine art of music, dancing and story-telling.

Under Zeami's tutleage, the essence of noh was subtlety (yugen) as exemplified in the highly stylized beauty and grace of court nobles and their ladies. See NOH.

ZEMPUKU TEMPLE / ZEMPUKU JI (Zim-puu-kuu Jee)

On one of Tokyo's main thoroughfares near Shiba Park and the Tokyo Tower, the Zempuku Temple was founded by the famed priest Kobo Daishi, who also founded the Shingon sect of Buddhism, in the 9th century.

In 1859 the temple became the headquarters for the first American Minister in Japan, and served as both the Consulate and the residence of Minister Townsend Harris.

The Zempuku, now the property of the Honganji school of the Jodo Shinshu sect of Buddhism, is a nostalgic landmark in the heart of modern-day Tokyo. See HARRIS, TOWNSEND.

ZEN (Zen)

Zen Buddhism was founded in the 6th century in India by a monk named Bodhidharma, who shortly thereafter left for China--apparently because he was unhappy with the dwindling of Buddhist adherents in his own country.

There is some conflict about the year of his arrival in China, but it appears to have been in 520. In China he ran afoul of a local Lord and was told to leave town. He traveled northward to a Shaolin Temple, where he sat facing a wall for nine years, meditating until he achievement enlightenment. At that time, he is said to have been so in tune with nature that he could hear the conversation of ants.

The word Zen comes from the Chinese ch'an, a corruption of the Sanskrit word Dhyana and the Pali word Jhana.

Introduced into Japan from China by the Buddhist priests Eisai (1141-1215) and Dogen (1200-1253), Zen taught salvation, self-control and the development of one's inner powers through meditation and a regime of strict mental and physical discipline. A Zen adept is one whose thoughts are free of intellectual questioning, and are totally natural, spontaneous and in tune with nature.

This new discipline was quickly adopted by the leaders of the Shogunate government in Kamakura and the professional military families that were to become known as Samurai.

Zen was both the inspiration and vehicle of much that came to be known as Bushido or the Way of the Warrior. Since the Samurai were to become Japan's ruling class for the next 600 years, following the principles of Zen themselves as well as establishing Zen-based standards for the common people to follow, the philosophy was to have an especially profound influence on the lives of all Japanese.

As the centuries passed, the Zen concept of life and truth also became the spiritual guidelines of Japan's equally famous tea ceremony, flower arranging and other aesthetic pursuits.

In Japan today the philosophy of Zen has three main branches--Renzai, Soto and Obaku. The main temple of the Rinzai sect is the Myoshin in Kyoto. The Mampuku Temple at Uji south of Kyoto is the headquarters of the Obaku sect of Zen. Soto Zen has two major temples, the Eihei near Fukui and the Soji in the Tsurumi district of Yokohama.

The great Daitoku Temple in Kyoto is regarded as the true birthplace of Zen in Japan. It was founded in 1324 and has since been closely associated with some of the greatest figures in Japanese history. See DAITOKU TEMPLE.

Advocates of the Soto Zen sect believe in prolonged meditation to achieve enlightment. The Rinzai sect believes in instant enlightment, brought on by presenting the mind with a riddle (koan) that, if pursed persistently, results in breaking the mind free of its physical and intellectual restraints.

The goal of Soto practitioners is to perceive the truth in all things through direct personal experience, which they believe can be achieved by the rigorous and prolonged practice of zazen (zah-sen), or sitting in meditation.

Recommended reading: ZEN FLESH-ZEN BONES, by Paul Reps (Tuttle), ZEN TELE-GRAMS, by Paul Reps (Tuttle), ZEN DICT-IONARY, by Ernest Wood (Tuttle). THE ZEN LIFE, by Koji Sato (Weatherhill). ZEN MIND, BEGINNER'S MIND, by Shunyu Suzuki (Weatherhill). ZEN MASTER DOGEN, by Yuho Yokoi (Weatherhill). ZEN INKLINGS, by Donald Richie (Weatherhill). ZEN AT DAITOKU-JI, by Jon Covell and Sobin Yamada (Kodansha International).

Today, many people practice zazen as a way to help them cope with the stress of modern life, as well as to clear the mind and strengthen the mind for the pursuit of excellence in the arts, in sports, in business and other endeavors. Many of Japan's thousands of temples were founded by Zen priests, and are still practicing centers for Zen Buddhism.

Zen advocates do not study scriptures or just listen to lectures. They spend hours to years in silent meditation (with a fellow standing behind them with a stout stick in his hands to whack them on the shoulders if they nod off).

In feudal days, the Samurai turned to Zen to concentrate their thoughts and strength and to enhance their courage. The principles of Zen thought--austerity, simplicity, and the direct expression of oneness with nature--became the guiding principles of the tea cermony, flower arranging and landscape garden designing.

The state of spiritual enlightenment sought by Zen devotees is known as sato-ri (sah-toe-ree). Once emancipated from worldly passions and one with the universe, the Zen master's life is illuminated. He or she is able to discern the difference between reality and illusion. between the truth and falsehood.

There are dozens of famous Zen Buddhist temples in Japan, where one may go to practice zazen under the watchful eyes of Zen masters. See ZEN TEMPLES.

In practicing zazen, one sits cross-legged, with the right foot resting on the left thigh and the left foot on the right thigh--a position that stops some would-be meditators right there! The neck and back should be perfectly straight. The hands should be cupped with the right hand under the left hand, the thumbs just touching, and the hands resting in the lap.

During the practice of zazen, the eyes are slightly open--not closed, as one would ordinarily expect. Reason for this is to help one concentrate on a single thing or thought, and avoid the jumble of thoughts that normally assails the mind when the outside world is closed off entirely.

The discipline in Zen temples is very strict, and is certainly not for the wishy-washy or faint-hearted. Just being able to successfully complete several months of such training is a considerable accomplishment, and enough to turn many people around.

The famous riddles that Zen masters pose for their pupils--in an attempt to help them concentrate on one thing for several seconds, thereby strengthening their powers of concentration and understanding--are called koan (koe-ahn). The koan are described as intuitive dialogues between masters and disciples.

Zen Buddhist temples are called Zen-Dera, and are divided into three structures--the place where the chief priest lives (hojo), the place where the master teaches (hatto), and the place where disciples practice zazen (sodo).

Other interesting books on Zen: ZEN TRAINING METHODS AND PHILOSOPHY, by Katsuki Sekida (Weatherhill). A ZEN WAVE: Basho's Haiku and Zen, by Robert Aitken (Weatherhill). ZEN AND JAPANESE BUDDHISM by Daisetsu Suzuki (Japan Travel Bureau).

Suzuki, who was over 90 when he died, was one of contemporary Japan's greatest Zen masters, ranking with many of the noted names of the past. He lived and taught in Kamakura, about an hour south-

Neighborhood lane in Yamaguchi City. P. 237

Zen meditators at Eihei Temple. P. 333

west of Tokyo, when I was working for JTB, his publisher.

ZEN FOOD

More and more people are being turned on to the vegetarian dishes--shojin ryori--that have been standard fare in Zen temples since the 15th century. This popularity is likely to grow in the future as the result of the enterprise of two nuns at the Sanko Temple in the outskirts of Tokyo.

Soei Yoneda, abbess of the temple, who studied Zen cooking at another temple, and nun Koei Hoshino, have published a book called GOOD FOOD FROM A JAPANESE TEMPLE (Kodansha), which gives recipes of 230 Zen dishes.

Said the abbess: We are Zen nuns, but there is no reason why we should keep the secrets of Zen cooking to ourselves.

She added that the secret of good cooking was to retain and enhance the natural flavors of food, and to prepare it with tender loving care.

ZENI-ARAI BENTEN (Zay-nee-Ah-rie Bane-tane)

At Sasuke, a few minutes walk northwest of Kamakura Station, the Zen-Arai Benten is a shrine dedicated to doubling your money. Benten is the god of wealth, and Zen-Arai means Money-Cleansing. The idea being that money washed in the water of a spring from a cave on the grounds, on a Zodical day of the Snake, will later double or even triple.

ZENIYA, GOHEI (Go-hay-e Zay-nee-yah)

An important but tragic figure in the history of the Kaga clan, Gohei Zeniya (1773-1852) was a member of a wealthy shipping family who lived in Kanaiwa, near Kanazawa.

A terrible famine occurred in the early 1800s, bringing much suffering to the fief of the Kaga's. Gohei was asked to advise the Kaga Daimyo on relief measures that could be taken. He suggested that the province begin trading with Korea and China, just across the Japan Sea--knowing that all trade except through the Dejima Dutch enclave in the port of Nagasaki was strictly forbidden by the Tokugawa Shogunate. See DEJIMA.

The Kaga Daimyo accepted Gohei's advice. Soon the trade was thriving, enriching both the Daimyo and Gohei.

Eventually, the Shogunate in Edo learned about the forbidden enterprise. To avoid retribution by the Shogun, the Daimyo and his chief retainers accused Gohei of poisoning the fish in Kahoku

Lagoon and causing a plague. They imprisoned him and confiscated all of his property.

With Gohei in prison and pennyless, the Shogunate dropped its investigation. Gohei died in prison in 1852, just one year before Commodore Matthew Perry and his Black Ships arrived to open Japan to trade and diplomatic relations with the rest of the world.

ZENKO TEMPLE / ZENKO JI (Zen-koe Jee)

One of the most popular temples in Japan, the Zenko Temple occupies an area of 59,000 square meters on the northern edge of the city of Nagano. Founded in 642, the main hall was reconstructed in 1707, and is now registered as a National Treasure.

Bronze Buddhist statues in the temple are believed to have been presented to Japanese religious leaders by the king of the Paikche Dynasty of Korea in 552. Opponents of Buddhism tried to burn the images and then threw them into a canal in Naniwa (Osaka). They were recovered by a man named Yoshimitsu Honda in 602, who took them to his home village in Shinano Province and later built a small temple to house them.

Following numerous other adventures, the statues were restored to the Zenko Temple in 1598. The name of the temple comes from Yoshimitsu, which can also be read Zenko.

Administered by two groups, one made up of priests and the other of priestesses, the Zenko Temple attracts worshippers from all over Japan for its morning services. Many of them go in the hopes of touching the main statue while passing through the darkened tunnel in which it is kept.

Services at the temple begin about half an hour after dawn, with the abbot and abbess waiting on the walkway to greet arrivals.

Nagano itself is one of the most spectacular prefectures in Japan and is often called The Roof of Japan because of its location in the Japan Alps, the highest mountain range in the country, with 11 peaks that are over 3,000 meters high.

The city of Nagano is approximately three hours from Tokyo's Ueno Station by limited express on the Shin-etsu Main Line.

ZENKOKU KINRO SEISHONEN KAIKAN (Zen-koe-kuu Keen-roe Say-e-show-nane Kie-khan)

Known in English as the All-Japan Working Youths Hall, and generally referred to as the Sun Plaza, this is a 21-story building near Nakano Station in Tokyo that is devoted to providing working youths with a place to study, exercise and play.

The program is operated by the Employment Promotion Project Corporation, under the Ministry of Labor. The building includes study rooms, a theater, libraries, convention and ceremonial halls, hotel rooms, restaurants, a bowling alley, and gymnasium.

ZENTSU TEMPLE / ZENTSU JI (Zen-t'sue Jee)

Located at Zentsuji, some 38 kilometers from Takamatsu on the island of Shikoku, the famous Zentsu Temple is the birthplace of Kobo Daishi and headquarters of the Shingon sect of Buddhism, which he founded.

The temple dates from 813 and is on ground owned by Zentsu Saeki, Kobo Daishi's father. The temple complex consists of several buildings--the Main Hall, a pagoda, and a treasure house.

Two camphor trees on the grounds are said to have been growing since the temple was founded.

Zentsu is the 75th temple among Shikoku's Eighty-Eight Sacred Places--temples commemorating Kobo Daishi.

Recommended reading: JAPANESE PILGRIMAGE, by Oliver Statler (Morrow)--a chronicle of Statler's own pilgrimage on foot to the 88 Shikoku temples dedicated to Kobo Daishi. Statler will be remembered as the author of JAPANESE INN, which told much of the history of the fabulous Tokugawa Shogunate from the viewpoint of an inn along the great Tokai Do walkway.

In Japanese Pilgrimage, Statler uses the same technique to tell much of the early history of Shikoku and Japan, along with present-day travel impressions.

ZODIAC / JUNI-SHI (Juu-nee-she)

Popular in Japan since ancient times, the junishi (12 animals, one bird and a reptile) were imported into Japan from China along with the Chinese lunar calendar. The signs cover a 12 year period, but the complete zodiac embraces 60 years--believed by the Chinese to be the end of man's ordinary life-cycle.

According to Chinese--and later Japanese--beliefs, people born in different year-cycles had different characters and personalities, and that some were compatible while others were not.

The junishi are Ne (Rat), Ushi (Ox), Tora (Tiger), U (Hare), Tatsu (Dragon), Mi (Snake), Uma (Horse), Hitsuji (Sheep), Saru (Monkey), Tori (Cock), Inu (Dog), and I (Wild Boar).

One of the bestselling calendars in Japan is the Takashima Ekidan, an almanac based on the Chinese Book of Changes (I Ching). Besides giving all the signs of the zodiac and their various readings, the calendar covers lucky and unlucky dates for traveling and getting married, breaking ground for a new building, launching a ship, burying the dead, and so on.

The story behind these Zodiac animals is of special interest. They are the only ones, it is said, that hurried to the bedside of Buddha to express their sorrow when he died. The cat is not included in the group because it did not believe in the teachings of Buddha. The rat is first in the line-up because it played a trick on the cow, which was really the first to hurry to the Buddha's bedside.

The rat jumped on the cow's back and stayed there until it arrived at the Buddha's hut. It then jumped off of the cow, and ran into the hut first.

ZOJO TEMPLE / ZOJO JI (Zoe-joe Jee)

On Hibiya Dori, the main avenue that runs through central Tokyo between the Imperial Palace Plaza and the Marunouchi financial and business district (and near the Shiba Koen Subway Station), the Zojo Temple was founded in 1393. During the Tokugawa Shogunate (1603-1868) it was the family temple of the Tokugawas.

Today the Zojo Ji is the Kanto District headquarters of the Jodo sect of Buddhism, and is also a treasure trove of culturally important objects preserved from the past.

The huge red gate (Sam mon) that faces Hibiya Avenue was built in 1605, and is listed as an Important Cultural Property. The Hondo or Main Hall of the temple was destroyed during World War II. The present ferro-concrete structure was completed in 1974.

ZORI (Zoe-ree)

Zori are one of the traditional styles of Japanese footwear (the other being geta or wooden clogs and setta, leather-soled sandals). Zori sandals were first made of straw. In more recent times, rubber zori were introduced. Now they are also made of plastic and other materials.

I happened to be one of the first to import rubber zori into the U.S., in 1952, but was unable to persuade the zori-makers of the Asakusa district in

Tokyo to give me a realistic export price, and soon gave up. Four years later, zori sales in the U.S. amounted to several million dollars a year.

ZUIGAN TEMPLE / ZUIGAN JI (Zuu-e-ghan Jee)

On a small island in the famous Matsushima Bay (one of the Three Scenic Wonders of Japan), Zuigan Temple was founded in 828 and the present buildings were constructed in 1609 by order of Masamune Date, the leading Daimyo of northeastern Japan.

The buildings are all registered as National Treasures, and contain many important cultural properties, including sliding screens in the main hall that were painted by the Kano School masters of the day.

In the beautiful Peacock Room is a seated one-eyed statue of Masamune Date in full armor. He lost the eye in one of his many battles.

Japanese cedars and many caves line the approach to the temple. The caves were used by traveling priests for shelter as well as places to meditate in early times. The temple is about an hour from Sendai.

ZUIRYU HILL (Zuu-e-ree-yuu)

A short distance from Mito, headquarters of the famous Mito clan during the Tokugawa period, Zuiryu Hill is the cemetery for the House of Mito, and contains the tombs of 13 lords of Mito.

It is situated on a slope densely forested with pines and cedars. See MITO.

ZUISEN TEMPLE / ZUISEN JI (Zuu-e-sen Jee)

In Kamakura, about one kilometer east of the Kamakura Shrine, in a secluded vale, the Zuisen Temple was founded in 1327 by Muso Kokushi, one of the era's most celebrated Zen priests.

The temple was renovated by Motouji Ashikaga (1340-1367), brother of the second Ashikaga Shogun, while he was governor of the Kanto District, and a few decades later was designated as the second most important of the 10 Rinzai temples in the Kanto area by Emperor Gokameyama.

The Founder's Hall, listed as an Important Cultural Property, includes a wooden statue of Kokushi.

The garden of the temple is regarded as one of the most beautiful Zen-inspired gardens in Japan. It is especially popular for its plum blossoms in Februa-ry and its golden maple leaves in November.

ZUSHI (Zuu-she)

On the Sagami Bay side of the Miura Peninsula, south of Yokohama, Zushi is a popular seaside resort and residential area for affluent commutors who work in Yokohama and Tokyo. It is situated between Kamakura (which was the Shogunate capital of Japan from 1192 until 1333), and Hayama to the south. The latter is the location of the Imperial Villa, where Emperor Hirohito spent so much time studying sea-life in the area.

神社

OTHER ENGLISH-LANGUAGE SOURCES

AMERICAN CHAMBER OF COMMERCE IN JAPAN
(Zainichi Beikoku Shoko Kaigi Sho)
Fukide Building #2
4-1-21 Toranomon, Minato-ku, Tokyo 105 Japan
Publications: The Journal of the American Chamber of Commerce
in Japan
Living in Japan, etc.

ASAHI EVENING NEWS
7-8-5 Tsukiji, Chuo-ku, Tokyo 104 Japan
Publications: The Asahi Evening News

ASAHI SHIMBUN
5-3-2 Tsukiji, Chuo-ku, Tokyo 104 Japan
Publications: The Japan Quarterly

ASSN FOR INT'L COOPERATION OF AGRICULTURE β FORESTRY
(Kokusai Noringyo Kyoryoku Kyokai)
19 Ichinban-cho, Chiyoda-ku, Tokyo 100 Japan
Publications: Japan's Agricultural Review

ASSN FOR RESEARCH OF ECONOMIC β FOREIGN AFFAIRS
(Keizai Gaiko Kenkyu Kai)
Seno Building
3-14-9 Roppongi, Minato-ku, Tokyo 106 Japan
Publications: Statistical Survey of Japan's Economy

ASSN OF AGRICULTURE β FORESTRY STATISTICS
(Norin Tokei Kyokai)
Publications: Abstract of Statistics on Agriculture, Forestry
and Fisheries
Monthly Statistics of Agriculture, Forestry and
Fisheries
Statistical Yearbook of the Ministry of
Agriculture, Forestry and Fisheries

AUTOMOTIVE HERALD CO. LTD.
Shinto Building #3
5-21-5 Shinbashi, Minato-ku, Tokyo 105 Japan
Publications: Japan Automotive News

BANK OF JAPAN
Nihon Ginko
2-2-1 Hongoku-cho, Nihonbashi, Chuo-ku, Tokyo 103 Japan
Publications: Balance of Payments Monthly
Economic Statistics Annual
Economic Statistics Monthly
Monthly Economic Review
Price Indexes Annual
Price Indexes Monthly
Sales Agent: Japan Publications Trading Co., Ltd.

BUSINESS INTERCOMMUNICATIONS, INC. (BII)
C.P.O. Box 587, Tokyo 100-91 Japan
Publications: Directory of Foreign Capital Affiliated Enterprises
in Japan
A Wage Survey of Foreign Capital Affiliated

Enterprises in Japan
White Paper on the Japanese Economy

CENTER FOR JAPANESE SOCIAL AND POLITICAL STUDIES
(Nihon Shakai Shiso Kyenkyu Sho)
9-29-12 Seijo, Setagaya-ku, Tokyo 157 Japan
Publications: The Japan Interpreter

CHARLES E. TUTTLE CO., INC.
1-2-6 Suido, Bunkyo-Ku, Tokyo 112 Japan
U.S. address: 28 S. Main St., Rutland, Vt. 05701
Publications: Numerous books on Japan

CHEMICAL ECONOMY RESEARCH INSTITUTE
(Kagaku Keizai Kenkyu Sho)
1-13-7 Uchikanda, Chiyoda-ku, Tokyo 101 Japan
Publications: Chemical Economic and Engineering Review

DAIWA SECURITIES CO., LTD.
Research Department
2-6-4 Otemachi, Chiyoda-ku, Tokyo 100 Japan
Publications: Analysts' Guide

DEFENSE AGENCY OF JAPAN
Public Information Division
9-7-45 Akasaka, Minato-ku, Tokyo 107 Japan
Publications: Defense Bulletin

DEMPA PUBLICATIONS, INC.
(Dempa Shimbun Sha)
1-11-15 Higashi Gotanda, Shinagawa-ku, Tokyo 141 Japan
Publications: Japan Electronics Almanac
             Japan Electronics Buyers Guide
             Journal of Asia Electronics Union
             Journal of Electronic Engineering
             Journal of Electronics Industry

DENTSU, INC.
Publications Department
1-11 Tsukiji, Chuo-ku, Tokyo 104 Japan
Publications: Dentsu Japan Marketing/Advertising

DIAMOND LEAD CO., LTD.
1-4-2 Kasumigaseki, Chiyoda-ku, Tokyo 100 Japan
Publications: Diamond's Economic Journal INDUSTRIA
             Diamond's Japan Business Directory

EAST PUBLICATIONS, INC.
3-19-7-101 Minami-Azabu, Minato-ku, Tokyo 106 Japan
Publications: The East

ECONOMIC PLANNING AGENCY
3-1-1 Kasumigaseki, Chiyoda-ku, Tokyo 100 Japan
Publications: Annual Report on National Life
             Economic Outlook Japan
             Monthly Economic Report
             Outlook and Basic Policy for the National Economy
Sales Agent: Government Publications Service Center

FAR EAST REPORTERS, INC.
1-4-28 Moto-Azabu, Minato-Ku, Tokyo 106 Japan
Publications: Far East Traveler Magazine

FARMING JAPAN CO., LTD.
1-11-13 Uchikanda, Chiyoda-ku, Tokyo 101 Japan
Publications: Farming Japan

FEDERATION OF BANKERS ASSOCIATIONS OF JAPAN
(Zenkoku Ginko Kyokai Rengo-Kai)
1-3-1 Marunouchi, Chiyoda-ku, Tokyo 100 Japan
Publications: Banking System in Japan

FOREIGN PRESS CENTER OF JAPAN
Nippon Press Center Building
2-2-1 Uchisaiwaicho, Chiyoda-ku, Tokyo 100 Japan
Publications: About Japan Series
              Diplomatic Bluebook
Sales Agent: Government Publications Service Center

GOVERNMENT PUBLICATIONS SERVICE CENTER (GPSC)
(Seifu Kankobutsu Service Center)
1-2 Kasumigaseki. Chiyoda-ku, Tokyo 100 Japan
Sales agent for numerous government publications

HITACHI, LTD.
Advertising Department
Nippon Building
2-6-2 Otemachi, Chiyoda-ku, Tokyo 100 Japan
Publications: Hitachi Review

HONDA MOTOR CO., LTD.
Overseas Public Relations Dept.
6-27-8 Jingumae, Shibuya-ku, Tokyo 150 Japan
Publications: News from Honda

INDUSTRIAL BANK OF JAPAN LTD.
(Nihon Kogyo Ginko)
1-3-3 Marunouchi, Chiyoda-ku, Tokyo 100 Japan
Publications: IBJ Monthly Report
              Japanese Finance β Industry: Quarterly Survey

INDUSTRIAL NEWS AGENCY
(Kogyo Jiji Tsushin Sha)
3-10 Kanda Ogawa-cho, Chiyoda-ku, Tokyo 101 Japan
Publications: Industrial News Weekly

INSTITUTE FOR FINANCIAL AFFAIRS, INC.
(Kinyu Zaisei Jijo Kenkyu Kai)
19 Minami Moto-machi, Shinjuku-ku, Tokyo 160 Japan
Publications: Handbook of the Japanese Bond Market

INSTITUTE OF ADMINISTRATIVE MANAGEMENT
(Gyosei Kanri Kenkyu Center)
3-1-1 Higashi Ikebukuro, Toshima-Ku, Tokyo 170 Japan
Publications: Organization of the Government of Japan

INSTITUTE OF ENERGY ECONOMICS
(Nihon Enerugi Keizai Kenkyu Sho)
Mori Building #10
1-18-1 Toranomon, Minato-Ku, Tokyo 105 Japan
Publications: Energy in Japan

INSTITUTE OF LABOR ADMINISTRATION

(Romu Gyosei Kenkyu Sho)
1-4-2 Higashi-Azabu, Minato-Ku, Tokyo 106 Japan
Publications: Labor Laws of Japan

INTERCONTINENTAL MARKETING CORP.
C.P.O. Box 971, Tokyo 100-91
Publications: Japan English Books in Print
              Japan English Magazine Directory, etc.
Sales agent for many books, publications on Japan

INT'L MANAGEMENT ASSN OF JAPAN, INC.
(Sekai Keiei Kyogi Kai)
Mori Building #10
1-18-1 Toranomon, Minato-Ku, Tokyo 105 Japan
Publications: Management Japan

INT'L SOCIETY FOR EDUCATIONAL INFORMATION, INC.
(Kokusai Kyoiku Joho Center)
2-7-8 Shintomi, Chuo-Ku, Tokyo 104 Japan
Publications: Understanding Japan

INT'L TRADE β INDUSTRY STATISTICS ASSN
(Tsusan Tokei Kyo Kai)
6-15-2 Ginza, Chuo-Ku, Tokyo 104 Japan
Publications: Statistics on Japanese Industries

JAPAN AIR LINES CO., LTD. (JAL)
2-7-3 Marunouchi, Chiyoda-ku, Tokyo 100 Japan
Publications: Winds
              Japan Unescorted
              JAL Shopping β Dining Guide to Tokyo

JAPAN ATOMIC INDUSTRIAL FORUM, INC.
(Nihon Genshi-ryoku Sangyo Kaigi)
Yasudakasai Otemachi Building
1-5-4 Otemachi, Chiyoda-ku, Tokyo 100 Japan
Publications: Atoms in Japan

JAPAN AUTOMOBILE MANUFACTURERS ASSN INC.
(Nihon Jidosha Kogyo Kai)
1-6-6 Otemachi, Chiyoda-Ku, Tokyo 100 Japan
Publications: Motor Vehicle Statistics of Japan

JAPAN CHAMBER OF COMMERCE β INDUSTRY
(Nihon Shoko Kaigi Sho)
Overseas Publishing Department
World Trade Center Building
2-4-1 Hamamatsu-cho, Minato-ku, Tokyo 105 Japan
Publications: Japan Commerce β Industry
              JCCI Business Guide
              New Products β Marketable Commodities
              Standard Trade Index of Japan

JAPAN COMMERCE, LTD.
(Kaiun Boeki Tsushin Sha)
Tanaka-Yaesu Building
1-5-15 Yaesu, Chuo-Ku, Tokyo 103 Japan
Publications: The Japan Commerce--Iron β Steel (Daily)

JAPAN ECHO, INC.
2-10-2 Nagato-cho, Chiyoda-Ku, Tokyo 100 Japan
Publications: Japan Echo

JAPAN ECONOMIC JOURNAL
(Nihon Keizai Shimbun Sha)
1-9-5 Otemachi, Chiyoda-Ku, Tokyo 100 Japan
Publications: Industrial Review of Japan
              The Japan Economic Journal

JAPAN ECONOMIC RESEARCH CENTER
(Nihon Keizai Kenkyu Center)
Nikkei Building
1-9-5 Otemachi, Chiyoda-Ku, Tokyo 100 Japan
Publications: A Five-Year Economic Forecast
              Long-Term Economic Forecast Series
              Quarterly Forecast of Japan's Economy

JAPAN ECONOMIC REVIEW, LTD.
1-5-8 Nishi-Shinbashi, Minato-Ku, Tokyo 105 Japan
Publications: Japan Economic Review

JAPAN EXTERNAL TRADE ORGANIZATION (JETRO)
(Nihon Boeki Shinko Kai)
JETRO Building
2-2-5 Toranomon, Minato-Ku, Tokyo 105 Japan
Publications: Access to Japan's Import Market
              China Newsletter
              Exporting to Japan
              Facts and Finds Series
              Focus Japan
              Japan Industrial β Technological Bulletin
              JETRO Marketing SEries
              Update
              White Paper on International Trade
              Your Market in Japan
Available from JETRO's overseas offices

JAPAN FOREIGN TRADE COUNCIL, INC.
(Nihon Boeki Kai)
World Trade Center Building. 6th Floor
2-4-1 Hamamatsu-cho, Minato-Ku, Tokyo 105 Japan
Publications: JFTC News

JAPAN INSTITUTE OF INTERNATIONAL AFFAIRS
(Nihon Kokusai Mondai Kenkyu Sho)
Mori Building #19
1-2-20 Toranomon, Minato-Ku, Tokyo 105 Japan
Publications: Project 80s: Foreign Policy Guidelines of Japan
              White Papers of Japan

JAPAN INSTITUTE OF LABOR
(Nihon Rodo Kyokai)
1-7-6 Shiba Koen, Minato-Ku, Tokyo 105 Japan
Publications: Japan Labor Bulletin
              Japanese Industrial Relations Series
Sales agent: Overseas Courier Service Co. (OCS)

JAPAN INT'L SOCIAL SECURITY ASSN
(Nihon Kokusai Shakai Hosho Kyokai)
1-2-2 Kasumigaseki, Chiyoda-Ku, Tokyo 100 Japan
Publications: Outline of Social Insurance in Japan

JAPAN IRON β STEEL FEDERATION
(Nihon Tekko Renmei)

Keidanren Kaikan
1-9-4 Otemachi, Chiyoda-Ku, Tokyo 100 Japan
Publications: Japan Steel Bulletin
              The Steel Industry of Japan
              Monthly Iron β Steel Statistics

JAPAN IRON β STEEL JOURNAL CO., LTD.
Ohki-Sudacho Building, 6th Floor
1-23 Kanda, Sudacho, Chiyoda-Ku, Tokyo 101 Japan
Publications: Japan Steel Journal

JAPAN JOURNAL, INC.
C.P.O. Box 702, Tokyo 100-91 Japan
Publications: The Japan Stock Journal

JAPAN NEWSPAPER PUBLISHERS AND EDITORS ASSN
(Nihon Shimbun Kyokai)
Nippon Press Center Bldg.
2-2-1 Uchisaiwaicho, Chiyoda-Ku, Tokyo 100 Japan
Publications: The Japanese Press

JAPAN PETROLEUM CONSULTANTS, LTD.
Sanwa Building #3
4-5-4 Iidabashi, Chiyoda-Ku, Tokyo 102 Japan
Publications: Japan Petroleum β Energy Weekly
              Japan Petroleum β Energy Yearbook

JAPAN PETROLEUM INSTITUTE
(Nihon Sekiyu Gakkai)
3-27-12 Nishi-Ikebukuro, Tomshima-Ku, Tokyo 171 Japan
Publications: Journal of the Japan Petroleum Institute

JAPAN PUBLICATIONS TRADING CO., LTD.
(Nihon Shuppan Boeki)
1-2-1 Sarugaku-cho, Chiyoda-Ku, Tokyo 101 Japan
I.P.O. Box 5030, Tokyo 100-31 Japan
Exporters and sales agents for numerous publications

JAPAN SOCIETY, INC.
Japan Society Library
333 E. 47th St.
New York, New York 10017
Tel. 212-832-1155
The Japan Society Library acts as a book ordering service for
members of the Society, each year sending them an updated catalog
of recommended titles. Orders are sent to the librarian, who
consolidates them and forwards them to the appropriate publishers
for fulfillment. Titles in the JSL catalog are classified by category: The Arts. Literature, Religion and Philosophy. Politics,
Economics and Business. History and Culture.

JAPAN STATISTICAL ASSOCIATION
(Nihon Tekei Kyokai)
95 Wakamatsu-cho, Shinjuku-Ku, Tokyo 162 Japan
Publications: Annual Report on the Consumer Price Index
              Annual Report on Family Income and Expenditure sur-
              vey
              Annual Report on Labor Force Survey
              Annual Report on Retail Price Survey
              Annual Report on Unincorporated Enterprise survey
              Employment Status Survey
              Establishment Census of Japan

              Family Saving Survey
              Housing Survey of Japan
              Japan Statistical Yearbook, etc.

JAPAN TARIFF ASSOCIATION
(Nihon Kanzei Kyokai)
Jibiki Building #2
4-7-8 Kojimachi, Chiyoda-Ku, Tokyo 102 Japan
Publications: Customs Tariff Schedules of Japan
             Export Statistical Schedule
             Import Statistical Schedule
             Japan Exports and Imports (commodity by country)
             Japan Exports and Imports (country by commodity)
             Japan Laws and Regulations Concerning Customs dut-
             ies and Customs Procedures
             Summary Report: Trade of Japan

JAPAN TIMES, LTD.
4-5-4 Shibaura, Minato-Ku, Tokyo 108 Japan
Publications: The Japan Times (daily newspaper)
             The Japan Times Weekly
             The Japan Times Directory (of foreign residents
             and enterprises in Japan)
             Defense of Japan
             Economic Survey of Japan
And various popular books

JAPAN TRADE β INDUSTRY PUBLICITY, INC.
(Tsusan Seisaku Koho Sha)
Toranomon Kotohira Kaikan
1-2-8 Toranomon, Minato-Ku, Tokyo 105 Japan
Publications: Digest of Japanese Industry β Technology
             MITI Handbook

JAPAN YELLOW PAGES, LTD.
ST Building
4-6-9 Iidabashi, Chiyoda-Ku, Tokyo 102 Japan
Publications: Yellow Pages--Japan Telephone Book

JAPANESE NATIONAL COMMISSION FOR UNESCO
C/O Ministry of Education
3-2-2 Kasumigaseki, Chiyoda-Ku, Tokyo 100 Japan
Publications: Crosscurrents

JAPANESE NAT'L COMMITTEE OF THE WORLD PETROLEUM CONGRESSES
Kasahara Building
1-6-10 Uchikanda, Chiyoda-Ku, Tokyo 101 Japan
Publications: The Petroleum Industry in Japan

JOHN WEATHERHILL, INC.
7-6-13 Roppongi, Minato-Ku, Tokyo, Japan
U.S. address: 6 E. 39th St., New York, NY 10016
Publications: Numerous books on Japan

KEIDANREN (FEDERATION OF ECONOMIC ORGANIZATIONS)
(Keizai Dantai Rengo Kai)
Keidanren Kaikan
1-9-4 Otemachi, Chiyoda-Ku, Tokyo 100 Japan
Publications: Keidanren Review on Japanese Economy

KEIZAI KOHO CENTER
(Japan Institute for Social and Economic Affairs)

Otemachi Building
1-6-1 Otemachi, Chiyoda-Ku, Tokyo 100 Japan
Publications: Economic Eye
                 Japan 1981: An International Comparison
                 Speaking of Japan

KODANSHA INTERNATIONAL
2-12-21 Otowa, Bunkyo-Ku, Tokyo, Japan
U.S. address: Harper β Row Bldg.
10 E. 53rd St., New York, NY 10022
Publications: Numerous books on Japan

LOCAL GOVERNMENT RESEARCH β DATA CENTER
(Chiho Jichi Kenkyu Shiryo Center)
4-6-2 Minami-Azabu, Minato-Ku, Tokyo 106 Japan
Publications: Local Government Review in Japan

LOOK JAPAN LTD
Kawate Building
2-2 Kanda, Ogawa-cho, Chiyoda-Ku, Tokyo 101 Japan
Publications: Look Japan
                 Report on the Present State of Communications
                 in Japan

LOTUS PRESS, LTD
Chofu P.O. Box 15, Chofu Shi, Tokyo 182-91 Japan
Publications: Shopping Your Way Around Japan
                 Pioneer American Merchants in Japan
                 The Emperor's Islands
                 American and Japan--The Twain Meet
                 The Japanese
                 More About the Japanese
                 Inside Japan, Inc.
                 Japan: The Coming Social Crisis
                 Japan: The Coming Economic Crisis
                 And other titles

MAINICHI NEWSPAPERS
(Mainichi Shimbun Sha)
1-1-1 Hitotsubashi, Chiyoda-Ku, Tokyo 100 Japan
Publications: Mainichi Daily News
                 Japan Statistical Yearbook

MINISTRY OF FINANCE
(Okura Sho)
Printing Bureau
2-4-2 Toranomon, Minato-Ku, Tokyo 105 Japan
Publications: Annual Report on Business Cycle Indicators
                 Indicators of Science and Technology
                 Japanese Economic Indicators
                 An Outline of Japanese Taxes
                 Polls on Preferences in National Life
                 Quality of the Environment in Japan
Sales agent: Government Publications Service Center

MINISTRY OF FOREIGN AFFAIRS
(Gaimusho)
Public Information and Cultural Affairs Bureau
2-1-2 Kasumigaseki, Chiyoda-Ku, Tokyo 100 Japan
Publications: Information Bulletin
Sales agent: GPSC

MINISTRY OF INTERNATIONAL TRADE β INDUSTRY (MITI)
(Tsusansho)
Information Office
1-3-1 Kasumigaseki, Chiyoda-Ku, Tokyo 100 Japan
Publications: Background Information
            Japan Reporting
            News from MITI

MITSUBISHI CORPORATION
Corporate Communications Office
2-6-3 Marunouchi, Chyoda-Ku, Tokyo 100 Japan
Publication: Tokyo Newsletter

MITSUI β CO., LTD.
Corporate Planning Division
Public Relations Department
1-2-1 Otemachi, Chiyoda-Ku, Tokyo 100 Japan
Publications: Mitsui Trade News

NATIONAL DIET LIBRARY
(Kokuritsu Kokkai Toshokan)
1-10-1 Nagata-cho, Chiyoda-Ku, Tokyo 100 Japan
Publications: National Diet Library Newsletter

NIHON BOEKI SHIMBUN SHA
(Japan Foreign Trade Newspaper Co.)
1-7-2 Otemachi, Chiyoda-Ku, Tokyo 100 Japan
Publications: Japan Foreign Trade Journal

NIHON KOGYO SHIMBUN
(Japan Industrial Newspaper)
1-7-2 Otemachi, Chyoda-Ku, Tokyo 100 Japan
Publications: Business Japan

NIKKEIREN (JAPAN FEDERATION OF EMPLOYERS' ASSNS)
(Nihon Keiei Sha Dantai Renmei)
1-4-6 Marunouchi, Chiyoda-Ku, Tokyo 100 Japan
Publications: Report of the Committee for the Study of Labor
            Questions

NIPPON STEEL CORPORATION
(Shin Nippon Seitetsu)
Secretary's Office, Public Relations Section
2-6-3 Otemachi, Chiyoda-Ku, Tokyo 100 Japan
Publications: Nippon Steel News
            Japan--The Land and its People

NISSHO IWAI CORPORATION
Public Relations Center, Editorial Office
2-4-5 Akasaka, Minato-Ku, Tokyo 107 Japan
Publications: Tradepia International

NOMURA RESEARCH INSTITUTE
(Nomura Sogo Kenkyu Sho)
1-11-1 Nihonbashi, Chuo-Ku, Tokyo 103 Japan
Publications: NRI Quarterly Economic Review

OHARA PUBLICATIONS, INC.
1813 Victory Place
Burbank, CA. 91504 USA
Pubblishers of numerous books on Japan's martial arts.

OVERSEAS COURIER SERVICE CO., LTD. (OCS)
(Kaigai Shimbun Fukyu)
2-9 Shiba-ura, Minato-Ku, Tokyo 108 Japan
Overseas distributor for numerous publications
See local offices

OVERSEAS ELECTRICAL INDUSTRY SURVEY INSTITUTE, INC.
(Kaigai Denryoku Chosa Kai)
1-4-2 Uchisaiwaicho, Chiyoda-Ku, Tokyo 100 Japan
Publications: Electric Power Industry in Japan

PHP INSTITUTE INTERNATIONAL, INC.
(Kokusai PHP Kenkyu Sho)
Mori Building #32, 6th Floor
3-4-30 Shiba Koen, Minato-Ku, Tokyo 105 Japan
Publications: PHP

PRIME MINISTER'S OFFICE
Statistics Bureau
95 Wakamatsu-cho, Shinjuku-Ku, Tokyo 162 Japan
Publications: Statistical Handbook of Japan
              White Papers on Japan
              Etc.
Sales agent: Japan Publications Trading Co., Ltd.

PUBLISHERS ASSOCIATION FOR CULTURAL EXCHANGE
(Shuppan Bunka Kokusai Koryu Kai)
1-2-1 Sarugaku-cho, Chiyoda-Ku, Tokyo 101 Japan
Publications: Guide to Publishers β Related Businesses in Japan

RESEARCH β TRAINING INSTITUTE OF THE MINISTRY OF JUSTICE
(Homu Sogo Kenkyu Sho)
1-1-1 Kasumigaseki, Chiyoda-Ku, Tokyo 100 Japan
Publications: Summary of the White Paper on Crime

RESEARCH INSTITUTE FOR PEACE AND SECURITY
(Heiwa Anzen Hosho Kenkyu Sho)
Roppongi Denki Building
6-1-20 Roppongi, Minato-Ku, Tokyo 106 Japan
Publications: Asian Security

RESEARCH INSTITUTE OF INTERNATIONAL TRADE β INDUSTRY
(Tsuho Sangyo Chosa Kai)
6-15-2 Ginza, Chuo-Ku, Tokyo 104 Japan
Publications: Industrial Statistics Monthly

SANGYO HOREI CENTER, INC.
Sakata Building
3-4-3 Iidabashi, Chiyoda-Ku, Tokyo 102 Japan
Publications: The Japan Business Law Journal

SANGYO PRESS, LTD.
Toei Building, 8th Floor
4-2 Nihonbashi Muromachi, Chuo-Ku, Tokyo 103 Japan
Publications: Japan Metal Bulletin

SANWA BANK, LTD.
International Department
1-1-1 Otemachi, Chiyoda-Ku, Tokyo 100 Japan
Publications: Sanwa Bank Economic Letter

SHUFU NO TOMO SHA
1-6 Kanda Surugadai, Chiyoda-Ku, Tokyo 101 Japan
Publications: Eating Cheap in Japan
              P's β Ques for Travelers in Japan
              Other books on Japan

SOCIAL INSURANCE AGENCY
(Shakai Hoken Cho)
1-2-1 Kasumigaseki, Chiyoda-Ku, Tokyo 100 Japan
Publications: Guide to Social Insurance Systems in Japan

SUMITOMO CORPORATION
Public Relations Department
C.P.O. Box 1524, Tokyo 100-91 Japan
Publications: Sumitomo Corporation News

TELECOMMUNICATIONS ASSOCIATION
(Denki Tsushin Kyokai)
New Yurakucho Building, 11th Floor
1-12-1 Yuraku-cho, Chiyoda-Ku, Tokyo 100 Japan
Publications: Japan Telecommunications Review

THREE (I) PUBLICATIONS, LTD.
Kamakura-cho Parking Building
1-5-16 Uchikanda, Chiyoda-Ku, Tokyo 101 Japan
Publications: Cement Technology and Plant Engineering
              Oil Substituting Energy and Energy-Saving Tech-
              nology
              Solar Heating, Cooling and Hot Water Supply
              Systems

TOKYO METROPOLITAN GOVERNMENT
Int'l Communications Division, Bureau of Citizens and Cultural
Affairs
3-5-1 Marunouchi, Chiyoda-Ku, Tokyo 100 Japan
Publications: Tokyo Municipal News

TOKYO NEWS SERVICE, LTD.
5-3-3 Tsukiji, Chuo-Ku, Tokyo 104 Japan
Publications: Shipping β Trade News

TOYO KEIZAI SHIMPO SHA
(The Oriental Economist)
1-4 Hongoku-cho, Nihonbashi, Chuo-Ku, Tokyo 103 Japan
Publications: Japan Company Yearbook
              Japan Economic Yearbook
              The Oriental Economist (monthly)

TOYOTA FOUNDATION
Shinjuku Mitsui Building, 37th Floor
2-1-1 Nishi Shinjuku, Shinjuku_ku, Tokyo 160 Japan
Publications: The Toyota Foundation Annual Report
              The Toyota Foundation Occasional Report

TOYOTA MOTOR SALES CO., LTD.
2-3-18 Kudan-Minami, Chiyoda-Ku, Tokyo 102 Japan
Publications: The Motor Industry of Japan
              The Wheel Extended

TRUST COMPANY ASSOCIATION OF JAPAN
(Shintaku Kyokai)
Nippon Building

2-6-2 Otemachi, Chiyoda-Ku, Tokyo 100 Japan
Publications: Trust Banks of Japan

UNION OF JAPENESE SCIENTISTS AND ENGINEERS (JUSE)
 Nihon Kagaku Gijutsu Renmei)
5-10-11 Sendagaya, Shibuya-Ku, Tokyo 151 Japan
Publications: Reports of Statistical Applicate Research

UNIQUE PUBLICATIONS
7011 Sunset Blvd.
Hollywood, CA. 90028-7597
Tel. 213-467-1300
Publishers of books on martial arts.

UNIVERSAL MEDIA CORPORATION
C.P.O. Box 46, Tokyo 100-91 Japan
Publications: Bulletin of the Japanese Market (BOJAM)

UNIVERSITY OF TOKYO PRESS
7-3-1 Hongo, Bunkyo-Ku, Tokyo 113 Japan
Publications: Various titles on Japan

WORLD TRADE CENTER OF JAPAN
2-4-1 Hamamatsu-cho, Minato-Ku, Tokyo 105 Japan
Publications: World Traders

YOMIURI NEWSPAPER
(Yomiuri Shimbun)
1-7-1 Otemachi, Chiyoda-Ku, Tokyo 100 Japan
Publications: The Daily Yomirui

ZAIKEI SHOHO SHA
1-2-14 Higashi-Shinbashi, Minato-Ku, Tokyo 105 Japan
Publications: Guide to Japanese Taxes

ABOUT THE AUTHOR

Boye De Mente first went to Japan in 1949 as a member of the Army Security Agency, assigned to an intelligence processing unit in Tokyo. He left the service in 1952, took a one-year course at the American Graduate School of International Management in Glendale, Arizona, and returned to Tokyo in 1953.

There he went to work for the Japan Travel Bureau—the first full-time foreign staff member hired by the Bureau following World War II—and enrolled in night classes at Jochi University, where he studied Japanese and economics.

In 1954 De Mente became editor of PREVIEW, a general interest English-language magazine published in Tokyo and distributed by Reader's Digest. A year later he joined George Pokrovsky in co-founding the FAR EAST REPORTER magazine (now the FAR EAST TRAVE-LER) and served as its first editor.

In 1956, De Mente joined THE JAPAN TIMES and also helped found TODAY'S JAPAN, a monthly cultural magazine, published by Marvin Meyer.

In the spring of 1957, De Mente joined Australian adventurer Ben Carlin on a 4-month crossing of the Pacific Ocean aboard a 14.7-feet-long amphibious jeep called HALF-SAFE—a remarkable journey he later chronicled in a book entitled ONCE A FOOL—From Japan to Alaska by Amphibious Jeep.

Following a period of recuperation in Phoenix, Arizona, De Mente returned to Tokyo in 1958 as editor of THE IMPORTER magazine (briefly known as Oriental America), founded 18 months earlier by Ray A. Woodside, another alumnus of the American Graduate School of International Management.

During the next four years, the Importer became the leading English-language journal covering Japanese consumer products aimed at world markets, and played a seminal role in the development of Japan's export industry.

In January 1960, De Mente published his first book, JAPANESE MANNERS & ETHICS IN BUSINESS, the pioneer work on Japan's unique management philosphy. This was followed in rapid succession by THE TOURIST & THE REAL JAPAN; BACHELOR'S JAPAN and HOW TO DO BUS-INESS IN JAPAN—A Guide for International Businessmen.

The latter title was to become the bible of foreign importers dealing with Japan—"but was virtually ignored by the American business community in general, which was very slow in picking up on the Japanese challenge."

De Mente resigned from salaried employment in 1962, and began writing, consulting and lecturing on Japan full-time. In 1967 he co-authored, with Fred Perry, THE JAPENSE AS CONSUMERS—Asia's First Great Mass Market; another pioneer work.

His other titles on Japan include EXOTIC JAPAN—The Land, the People, the Places and Pleasures; JAPANESE SECRETS OF GRACEFUL LIVING; SOME PREFER GEISHA; BUSINESSMAN'S LANGUAGE GUIDE TO JAPAN; and READING YOUR WAY AROUND JAPAN.

In the early 1970s De Mente taught a course on doing business in Japan at the American Graduate School of International Management, and was adjunct professor of Asian studies at Arizona State University.

In 1978 De Mente founded the Arizona Author's Association--which had over 300 members by the end of the first year, making it the largest and most successful writers' group in the Southwest.

De Mente is married to Margaret Warren. They have two daughters, Dawn and Demetra, and make their home in Paradise Valley, Arizona.

In addition to writing and consulting on Japan, De Mente is senior editor of Far East Traveler magazine in Tokyo, where he spends several months each year.